SOCIAL PSYCHOLOGY BASIC AND APPLIED

Herbert Harari
Robert M. Kaplan
San Diego State University

Brooks/Cole Publishing Company • Monterey, California

Consulting Editor: *Lawrence S. Wrightsman, University of Kansas*

Brooks/Cole Publishing Company
A Division of Wadsworth, Inc.

© 1982 by Wadsworth, Inc., Belmont, California 94002.
All rights reserved. No part of this book may be reproduced,
stored in a retrieval system, or transcribed, in any form or by any means—
electronic, mechanical, photocopying, recording, or otherwise—
without the prior written permission of the publisher,
Brooks/Cole Publishing Company, Monterey, California 93940,
a division of Wadsworth, Inc.

Printed in the United States of America
10 9 8 7 6 5 4 3 2 1

Library of Congress Cataloging in Publication Data

Harari, Herbert.
   Social psychology.

   Bibliography: p.
   Includes index.
   1. Social psychology. I. Kaplan, Robert M.
II. Title.
HM251.H226   302   81-15468
ISBN 0-8185-0481-1   AACR2

Acknowledgements

We would like to thank the following for their contributions to this book: Cathie Atkins, Linda Berg-Cross, John C. Brigham, Vernon P. Estes, Suzanne Ewing, Michael Feiler, Donald Kaesser, Victoria Nelson, Robert Rowe, Barbara Stetson, Connie Toevs, Claire Verduin, and Lawrence S. Wrightsman.

Subject Editor: *Claire L. Verduin*
Manuscript Editor: *Victoria Nelson*
Production Editor: *Suzanne Ewing*
Production Assistant: *Louise Rixey*
Interior Design: *Angela Lee*
Cover Design: *Lori Hughes*
Photo Researchers: *Diana Boudrez & Roberta Spieckerman*
Typesetting: *Instant Type, Monterey, California*

CREDITS

CHAPTER 1
3, Photograph © Glenn R. Steiner. **5,** Photographs © Glenn R. Steiner. **6,** Photographs © Glenn R. Steiner. **15,** Photographs © Glenn R. Steiner. **18,** Photograph by Nancy Roger, All rights reserved. **25,** Box 1-2 adapted from "Attribution Theory and Research," by H. H. Kelley and J. L. Michela. Reproduced, with permission, from the *Annual Review of Psychology, Vol. 31.* © 1980 by Annual Reviews Inc.

CHAPTER 2
34, Table 2-1 from "Self-Monitoring of Expressive Behavior," by M. Snyder. In *Journal of Personality and Social Psychology*, 1974, *30*, 526–537. Copyright 1974 by the American Psychological Association. Reprinted by permission. **37,** Photograph © Glenn R. Steiner. **38,** Table 2-2 from "Generalized Expectancies for Internal Versus External Control of Reinforcement," by J. B. Rotter. In *Psychological Monographs*, 1966, *80*, 1–28. Copyright 1966 by the American Psychological Association. Reprinted by permission. **40,** Photograph © Glenn R. Steiner. **43,** Upper photograph © Glenn R. Steiner. Lower photograph © Eric Kroll. Courtesy of Taurus Photos, New York. **47,** Photograph © Glenn R. Steiner. **48,** Photograph © Glenn R. Steiner.

CHAPTER 3
57, Figure 3-2 from "Effect of Initial Selling Price on Subsequent Sales," by A. N. Doob, J. M. Carlsmith, J. L. Freedman, T. K. Landauer, and S. Tom. In *Journal of Personality and Social Psychology*, 1969, *4*, 345–350. Copyright 1969 by the American Psychological Association. Reprinted by permission. **59,** Photograph courtesy of the U.S. Treasury Department and the Ad Council. **60,** Photograph courtesy of the U.S. Treasury Department and the Ad Council. **68,** Photograph courtesy Wide World Photos.

CHAPTER 4
83, Photograph © Glenn R. Steiner. **85,** Photograph © Richard Wood. Courtesy of Taurus Photos, New York. **86,** Photograph © Glenn R. Steiner. **90,** Photograph © Glenn R. Steiner. **93,** Table 4-2 from "Faculty Helpfulness to Students: A Comparison of Compliance Techniques," by H. Harari, D. Mohr, and K. Hosey. In *Personality and Social Psychology Bulletin,* © 1980, by Sage Publication, Inc. Reprinted by permission. **94,** Table 4-3 adapted from *Introduction to Psychology, 6th Edition*, by E. R. Hilgard, R. C. Atkinson, and R. L. Atkinson. © 1979 by Harcourt Brace Jovanovich, Inc. Reprinted by permission. **96–98,** CBS Interview with Mike Wallace and a participant in the My Lai incident during the Vietnam War. © 1974 by The New York Times Company. Reprinted by permission. **101,** Table 4-4 is specified data from *Obedience to Authority* by Stanley Milgram. Copyright © 1974 by Stanley Milgram. Reprinted by permission of Harper & Row, Publishers, Inc. and Tavistock Publications Ltd., London. **104,** Photograph © Glenn R. Steiner. **114,** Cartoon by Ryan Cooper.

CHAPTER 5
125, Table 5-1 from "Power Strategies in Intimate Relationships," by T. Falbo and L. A. Peplau. In *Journal of Personality and Social Psychology*, 1980, *38*, 618–628. Copyright 1980 by the American Psychological Association. Reprinted by permission. **127,** Table 5-2 from "Gain and Loss of Esteem as Determinants of Interpersonal Attractiveness," by E. Aronson and D. Linder. In *Journal of Experimental Social Psychology*, 1965, *1*, 156–171. © 1965 by Academic Press. Reprinted by permission. **126,** Photographs © Glenn R. STeiner. **131,** Photograph © Robert W. Kelley, *Life* Magazine. **131,** Figure 5-2 reprinted from *Social Pressures in Informal Groups* by Leon Festinger, Stanley Schachter, and Kurt Back, with permission of the publisher, Stanford University Press. © 1978, 1950 by Leon Festinger, Stanley Schachter, and Kurt Back. **134,** Table 5-3 from "Comparison of Two Dimensions of Attitude Similarity on Heterosexual Attraction, by J. C. Touhey. In *Journal of Personality and Social Psychology*, 1972, 23, 8–10. Copyright 1972 by the American Psychological Association. Reprinted by permission. **137,** Table 5-4 from "Similarity in Real-Life Adolescent Friendship Pairs," by D. B. Kandel. In *Journal of Personality and Social Psychology*, 1978, *36*, 306–312. Copyright 1978 by the American Psychological Association. Reprinted by permission. **141,** Photograph © Glenn R. Steiner. **145,** Table 5-6 from *Liking and Loving: An Invitation to Social Psychology*, by Z. Rubin. © 1973 by Holt, Rinehart & Winston, Inc. Reprinted by permission. **149,** Table 5-7 from "Situational Determinants of Expression of Jealousy," by J. B. Bryson. Paper presented at the meeting of the American Psychology Association, San Francisco, 1977. Reprinted by permission of the author. **151,** Photograph © Glenn R. Steiner. **156,** Photograph © Popper Foto, Courtesy of Pictorial Parade, New York.

CHAPTER 6
158, Table 6-2 from "Who Buys Bloodshed and Why," by R. Kahn. Reprinted from *Psychology Today* Magazine, 1972, *6*, 47–48, 82–84. Copyright © 1972, Ziff-Davis Publishing Company. **159,** Photograph © Wide World Photos. **159–160,** Quotations from *Aggression in Man and Animals*, by R. N. Johnson. Copyright © 1972 by W. B. Saunders Company. Reprinted by permission of Holt, Rinehart, and Winston. **163,** Photographs courtesy of Dr. Philip G. Zimbardo and reprinted from 1969 Nebraska Symposium on Motivation edited by William J. Arnold and David Levine. Copyright © 1970 by the University of Nebraska Press. **167,** Figure 6-2 adapted from "A Longitudinal Content Analysis of Sexual Violence in the Best-Selling Erotica Magazines," by N. M. Malamuth and B. Spinner. In *Journal of Sex Research*, 1980. Reprinted by permission. **170,** Photograph from "Transmission of Aggression Through Imitation and Aggressive Models," by A. Bandura, D. Ross, and S. A. Ross. In *Journal of Abnormal and Social Psychology*, 1961, *63*, 575–592. Copyright 1961 by the American Psychological Association. Reprinted by permission. **175,** Photographs © Jim Engle. **179,** Photograph courtesy of Wide World Photos. **180,** Photograph © Paul Seder, Ph.D., courtesy of Taurus Photos, New York.

CHAPTER 7
185, Photograph © Glenn R. Steiner. **200,** Photographs © Glenn R. Steiner. **202,** Figure 7-1 from "Sex and Helping: Regional Differences," by B. Latané. In Proceedings of the 80th Annual Convention of the American Psychological Association, 1972, 904. Reprinted by permission of the author.

CREDITS

CHAPTER 8
209, Photograph © Glenn R. Steiner. **216**, Photographs all from Stanford Prison Experiment, August, 1971. Courtesy of Dr. Philip G. Zimbardo. **218**, Photograph © Glenn R. Steiner. **220**, Table 8-1 from "Identifying Victims of Groupthink from Public Statements," by P. E. Tetlock. In *Journal of Personality and Social Psychology*, 1979, *37*, 1314–1324. Copyright 1979 by the American Psychological Association. Reprinted by permission. **221**, Photograph © Glenn R. Steiner. **223**, Table 8-2 from "Effects of Group Size, Problem Difficulty, and Sex on Group Performance and Member Reactions," by R. M. Bray, N. L. Kerr, and R. S. Atkin. In *Journal of Personality and Social Psychology*, 1978, *36*, 1224–1240. Copyright 1978 by the American Psychological Association. Reprinted by permission. Photograph © Glenn R. Steiner.

CHAPTER 9
237, 238, Photographs © A.F.P., courtesy of Pictorial Parade, Inc., New York. **246**, Photograph © Glenn R. Steiner. **249**, Photograph courtesy of Jim Pinckney. **252**, Table 9-3 adapted from *Studies in Machiavellianism*, by R. Christie and F. L. Geis. Copyright © 1970 by Academic Press. Reprinted by permission. **256**, Table 9-4 from portions of Table 7, pp. 255–257 in *The Authoritarian Personality* by T. W. Adorno et al. Copyright 1950 by the American Jewish Committee. Reprinted by permission of Harper & Row, Publishers, Inc. **261**, Photographs courtesy of Wide World Photo.

CHAPTER 10
270, Photographs from "The Affectional Systems," by H. F. Harlow and M. K. Harlow. In A. M. Schrier, H. F. Harlow, and F. Stollmitz (Eds.), *Behavior of Non-Human Primates, Vol. II*. Copyright © 1965 by Academic Press. Reprinted by permission of the publisher and Harry F. Harlow. **273**, Figure 10-3 from "Correlates of Heterosexual Somatic Preference," by J. S. Wiggins, N. Wiggins, and J. C. Conger. In *Journal of Personality and Social Psychology*, 1968, *10*, 82–89. Copyright 1968 by the American Psychological Association. Reprinted by permission. **280–281**, Quotations from "Homogenizing the American Woman: The Power of an Unconscious Ideology," by S. L. Bem and D. J. Bem. © 1973 by Sandra and Daryl Bem. Reprinted by permission. **283**, Photograph by Laimute Druskis, courtesy of Taurus Photos, New York. **285**, Photograph © Glenn R. Steiner. **286**, Table 10-3 from "Sex-Role Stereotypes and Clinical Judgments of Mental Health," by I. K. Broverman, D. M. Broverman, F. E. Clarkson, P. S. Rosenkrantz, and S. R. Vogel. In *Journal of Consulting and Clinical Psychology*, 1970, *34*, 1–7. Copyright 1970 by the Consulting Psychologists Press, Inc. Reprinted by permission. **289**, Photograph © Eric Kroll, 1979, courtesy of Taurus Photos, New York. **290**, Table 10-4 from "The Measurement of Psychological Androgyny," by S. L. Bem. In *Journal of Consulting and Clinical Psychology*, 1974, *42*, 155–162. Copyright 1974 by the Consulting Psychologists Press, Inc. Reprinted by permission. **291**, Photograph © Rose Wulff.

CHAPTER 11
296, Photograph © Christopher Morrow and Stock, Boston, Inc., 1976. **302**, Photograph © Glenn R. Steiner. **305**, Table 11-2 from "Subjects' Recent Life Changes and Their Near-Future Illness Reports," by R. H. Rahe. In *Annals of Clinical Research*, 1972, *4*, 250–265. Reprinted by permission. **309**, Figure 11-3 from "Physiological, Motivational, and Cognitive Effects of Aircraft Noise on Children: Moving from Laboratory to the Field," by S. Cohen, G. W. Evans, D. S. Krantz, and D. Stokols. In *American Psychologist*, 1980, *35*, 321–343. Copyright 1980 by the American Psychological Association. Reprinted by permission. **310**, Figure 11-4 from "Ambient Temperature and the Occurrence of Collective Violence: A New Analysis," by J. M. Carlsmith and C. A. Anderson. In *Journal of Personality and Social Psychology*, 1979, *37*, 337–344. Copyright 1979 by the American Psychological Association. Reprinted by permission. **312**, Photograph © Eric Kroll, 1979, courtesy of Taurus Photos, New York. **313**, Figure 11-5 from "Reducing Stress of High Density Living: An Architectural Intervention," by A. Baum and G. E. Davis. In *Journal of Personality and Social Psychology*, 1980, *38*, 471–481. Copyright 1980 by the American Psychological Association. Reprinted by permission. **314**, Photograph © Stan Rice. **315**, Figure 11-6 from "Invasion of Personal Space," by N. J. Russo and R. Sommer. In *Social Problems*, 1966, *14*, 206–214, by permission of the Society for the Study of Social Problems. **320**, Photograph © Glenn R. Steiner.

CHAPTER 12
344, Table 12-2 from *Social Psychology: Individuals, Groups, Societies*, by J. W. McDavid and H. Harari. © 1968 by permission of Harper & Row Publishers, Inc., New York. **347**, Figure 12-1 reprinted from *Interaction Process Analysis: A Method for the Study of Small Groups*, by F. F. Bales by permission of The University of Chicago Press, copyright 1950.

A NOTE TO THE READER

ABOUT THIS BOOK...

This book is one of many textbooks in social psychology for college students. Is it bigger? Definitely not. Is it better? Not necessarily. Like most other contemporary textbooks in the field, it too attempts to combine psychology as a scientific discipline with applied problems of modern times. Where it differs, we believe, is in its personalized coverage of topics and its manner of presentation.

Most modern textbooks in social psychology want to be "relevant." To that end—once the basic aspects of the discipline of social psychology are covered—attempts are made to apply research findings to diverse areas such as law and order problems, mass media effects, women's issues, racial tensions, political controversies, environmental pollution, consumer advocacy, and the like.

We have also followed this course (see under Social Issues, the chapters on prejudice and morality, sex roles and sexism, and social ecology), but go one step further by making you, the reader, the center of our attention. We try our best to talk *to* you, rather than down at you. In a direct and informal way we try to describe to you how people perceive themselves and one another (see, under Social Perception, the chapters on person perception, the self and others); how they relate to each other (see, under Social Interaction, the chapters on attraction and intimacy, anger and aggression, altruism and helping, and groups and leadership); and, to be sure, despite the negative connotation, how they manipulate one another (see, under Social Influence, the chapters on changing attitudes and influencing behavior). You, the reader, can place yourself in the role of perceiver or perceived. You may find yourself the initiator of a social interaction or its terminator. You may take the role of the manipulator and sometimes (unfortunately, perhaps) the role of the manipulated. At the same time, you will be exposed to the work of many psychologists whose findings can be extended to your daily activities on the job, at home, at study, and at play. Ultimately, we hope, such information can be useful when experiencing the rewards of effective living.

...AND ITS STYLE

What we say here is based on empirical evidence gathered from over 900 carefully selected, up-to-date studies published in the most respectable professional journals and books, which are cross-referenced throughout the text. *How* we say it is, in fact, the way we lecture in class. Both of us have written textbooks and articles using the traditional pedantic writing style. We tried to avoid that style in this book because it is not the way we talk to people or describe psychology in class. As you will see, however, the casual style employed in this book does not mean that we have taken its content casually.

Herbert Harari
Robert M. Kaplan

CONTENTS

CHAPTER 1 PERSON PERCEPTION 3

Perceptual Content: What One Perceives 4
Physical effects: From short shrift to fancy clothes 4
Nonverbal effects: From the body to not much else 9
Role effects: From name to race 12
Order effects: From first to last impressions 14

Perceptual Processes: How One Perceives 16
Adaptation: Everything is relative 16
Balance: Peace of mind—or else 17
Attribution: Theories of pinning labels 22
Misattribution: Just or capricious? 25

Summary Highlights 29

CHAPTER 2 THE SELF AND OTHERS 30

Self-Presentation 30
The "me" self and the "not me" self 30
Self-disclosure: Telling all 32
Self-monitoring: Showing yourself 33

Self-Perception 35
Stability: How we see ourselves and others 35
Internality/externality: Control and helplessness 37
Self-schemata: Your personal script 41

Self-Prediction 43
Personality prediction: A low score for tradition 43
Template matching: Fitting your mold 45
Self-efficacy: Knowing you can 46

Summary Highlights 48

CHAPTER 3 CHANGING ATTITUDES 52

Attitudes and Propaganda 52
Persuasion, American style 52

Changing Attitudes 54
The first step: Arousal and attention 54
The second step: Presentation of arguments 58
The third step: Knowing your audience 64

**PART ONE
SOCIAL
PERCEPTION**

**PART TWO
SOCIAL
INFLUENCE**

The fourth step: Gaining and maintaining credibility   65
The final step: Immunization against counterpropaganda   69

Summary Highlights   73

CHAPTER 4 INFLUENCING BEHAVIOR   75

Power   75

Practicing and preaching   75
Six power plays   76
Does power corrupt?   77

Compliance   80

Fear: It does strange things to you   80
Guilt: Do it for mother!   82
Sympathy: Have a heart!   83
Force: The stick and the carrot   84
Guile: A foot in the door and low-balling   89
Concession: A door in the face   91
Impugnment: The art of name calling   92
Hypnosis: A matter of concentration   94

Obedience   96

Following orders: The road to atrocity   96
Breeding grounds for blind obedience   99

Conformity   102

Can you be your own person?   102
Breeding grounds for conformity   106
Profiles in conformity   108

Behavior Modification   108

Some principles of learning   108
Classical conditioning: Learning the passive way   110
Operant conditioning: Behaviors that pay off   112
The power of social reinforcement   113

Summary Highlights   117

PART THREE SOCIAL INTERACTION

CHAPTER 5 ATTRACTION AND INTIMACY   122

Popularity and Liking   122

Popularity: Moving in (the right) circles   122
Exchange: The interpersonal marketplace   123
Exposure: Familiarity makes the heart grow fonder   127
Propinquity: The folks next door   130
Similarity: Birds of a feather flock together   133
Self-perception: If the adrenalin flows, it must be love   137
Climate: Cool temperatures and hot passions   139

Dating and Mating   139

The winners: Beautiful and adored   139
The losers: Homely and ignored   140
The trophy: Lots of love but few data   142
The game plan: The girl next door who plays hard to get   145
The penalties: No points for jealousy   148

Marriage Problems   150
Traditional: The law of infidelity   150
Divorce: The end of the road   152

Summary Highlights   153

CHAPTER 6 ANGER AND AGGRESSION   155

Aggression Defined   156
Outcome, intent, means to an end, and plain meanness   157

Aggression Determinants   158
Organic: Bad brains, mean genes, instincts, and evolution   158
Psychological: Anger, arousal, and provocation   162
Learning: Conditioning and imitation   168

Aggression Prediction   171
From birth to maturity   171

Aggression Reduction   173
Catharsis: Drain it off!   173
Cognition: Think cool!   174
Empathy: How would you like it?   176
Humor: The right jokes   178

Aggression Effects   179
Television and aggression: A complicated picture   179

Summary Highlights   181

CHAPTER 7 ALTRUISM AND HELPING   183

Help: A Matter of Definition   183
The prosocial altruist   183

When Help Is Needed   183
People in distress   183
Ripped-off institutions   185

When Help Is Given Or Withheld   186
Clarity: Social comparison   187
Responsibility: Diffusing it   189
Reciprocity: Mutual backscratching   190
Imitation: Following the leader   191
Reinforcement: Cost and reward   193
Location: Urban and rural   195

Help-Givers and Receivers   199
Race: To each his own?   199
Sex: Is chivalry dead?   201
Physical handicap: Is there a credibility gap?   202
Lifestyle: Is hipness kindness?   203
Request style: Accentuate the positive   204

Summary Highlights   205

CHAPTER 8 GROUPS AND LEADERSHIP 207

Group Formation 207

Diads, triads, and small groups in general 207
The joiners: Anxious, curious, or just shopping around 209
Role, position, and status 211
Group communication: Circles, chains, wheels, and Ys 217

Group Output 219

Quality: Groupthink failures 219
Size: How many cooks spoil the broth? 221
Activity: A case of social loafing 222
Composition: To mix or not to mix? 224
Climate: Autocratic, democratic, or doing your thing 225
Style: Cautious or risky? 226

Leadership 227

Leadership and personality: Are leaders born or made? 227
Effective leadership: The contingency model 228
Leaders and followers: Banking idiosyncracy credit 229

Summary Highlights 230

PART FOUR SOCIAL ISSUES

CHAPTER 9 PREJUDICE AND MORALITY 234

Misperceptions and Prejudice 234

In search of "true" perception 234
Halo wearers, stereotypers, and bigots 237

Morality: Individual Development 245

Moving through stages 245
Machiavellianism: Any means to an end 250

Morality: Social Development 253

Law and order versus personal conscience 253
Morality, politics, and religion 254
Alienation: Getting away from it all 258

Summary Highlights 262

CHAPTER 10 SEX ROLES AND SEXISM 264

Sex Typing 264

The battle of the sexes 264
What men think women think—and vice versa 266

Sexist Studies 267

Monkeymen and women 267
The body watchers 271

Women's Liberation 274

Women's lib begins in the crib 275
Is anatomy destiny? 277

Sexist Games 280

Will Anne succeed in medical school? 280

Who was that doctor? 282
Who does the housework? 284

Adjustment Problems and Solutions 285

Healthy for women—sick for men 285
The solution: Psychological androgyny? 288

Summary Highlights 294

CHAPTER 11 SOCIAL ECOLOGY 295

Stress and Environments 295

Classifying environments 296
The nature of stress: Frustration, conflict, and pressure 297
Stressful environments can kill! 299

Environmental Sources of Stress 304

Future shock: Too many changes 304
Noise: Quiet, you're disturbing my blood pressure! 306
Heat: Hot tempers and big tips 308
Crowds: Are they maddening? 311
Proxemics: Getting too close 314
The moon: It doesn't cause lunacy 316
The economy: Recession inflates problems 316

Coping With Environments 317

Ecological psychology: The study of behavioral settings 317
The medical environment: Coping with pain 318
General adaptation: Nature's own way 321

Modifying Environments 322

Therapeutic environments and sick societies 322
Disarming the population bomb 324
Cash for trash 325
Nutritional balance acts 325
Modifying the energy crisis 326

Summary Highlights 326

CHAPTER 12 RESEARCH METHODS IN SOCIAL PSYCHOLOGY 328

Research Basis of Social Psychology 328

Rational and empirical approaches 328

Research Considerations 331

Methodological, economical, and ethical issues 331

Research Designs 334

Experimental and control groups 334
Validity and reliability 335
Evaluating experimental designs 336
Problem experiments 336
True experiments 338

Quasi-experiments   338
Confounding factors   339

Research Settings   339

Field studies   339
Natural experiments   340
Field experiments   340
Laboratory experiments   341
Simulation experiments   342

Research Techniques   343

Interviews and surveys   343
Attitude studies   344
Interaction analyses   345
Content analyses   346

Research Statistics   348

Types of data   349
Correlational methods   349
Parametric and nonparametric statistics   351
Univariate and multivariate statistics   352
Some examples of specific procedures   352

Glossary   355
References   362
Name Index   402
Subject Index   409

SOCIAL PSYCHOLOGY BASIC AND APPLIED

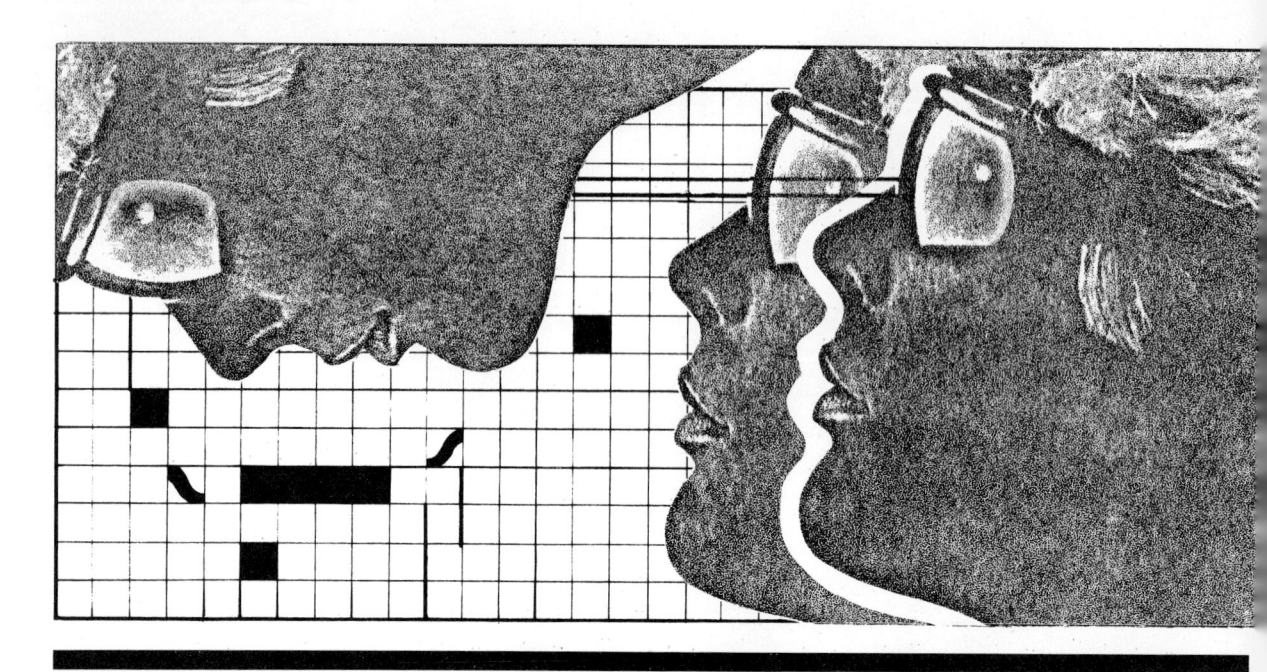

PART

SOCIAL

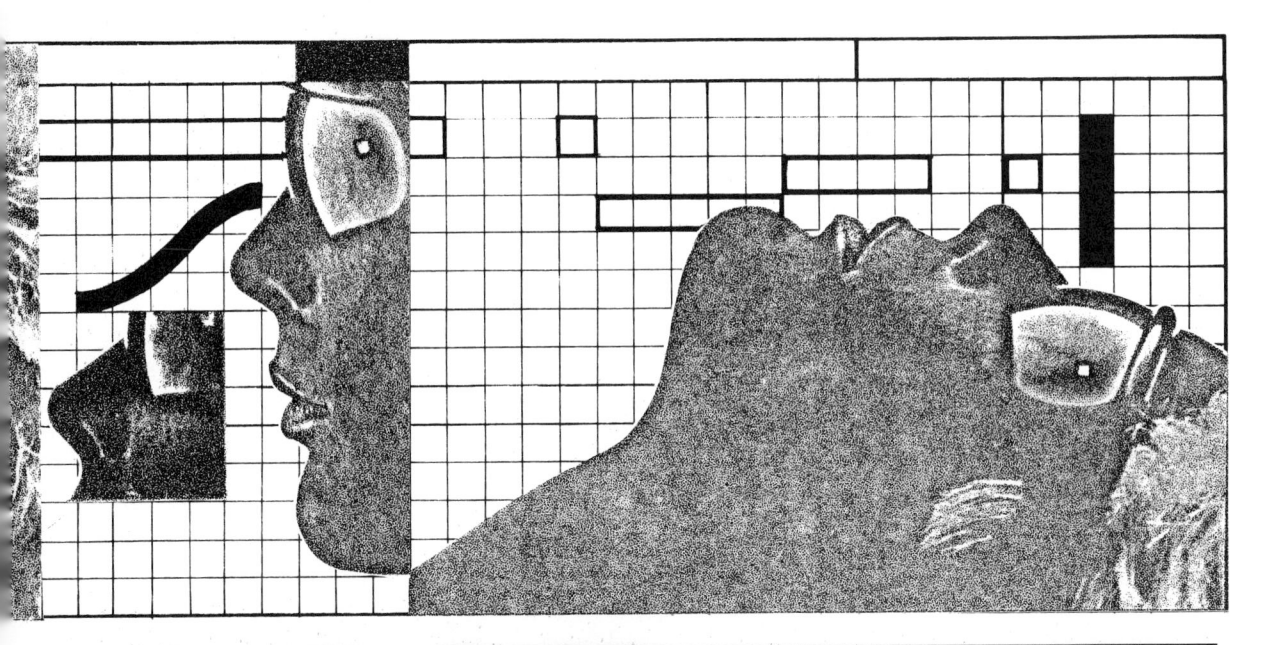

ONE

PERCEPTION

CHAPTER 1 PERSON PERCEPTION

PERCEPTUAL CONTENT: WHAT ONE PERCEIVES
    Physical effects: From short shrift to fancy clothes
    Nonverbal effects: From the body to not much else
    Role effects: From name to race
    Order effects: From first to last impressions

PERCEPTUAL PROCESSES: HOW ONE PERCEIVES
    Adaptation: Everything is relative
    Balance: Peace of mind—or else
    Attribution: Theories of pinning labels
    Misattribution: Just or capricious?

SUMMARY HIGHLIGHTS

Before you turn the page, look carefully at the person in Figure 1-1. Then estimate her IQ. Write down your estimate.

Figure 1-1. Estimate this person's IQ.

Now look at the picture in Figure 10 (p. 15). If you were asked to rate that person first, do you think you would have assigned a lower IQ rating to her than to the person in Figure 1-1? Probably so, even though the persons in both pictures are one and the same. If you have any doubts, ask some of your friends to do the same task. Let some of them rate the first picture, and others the second picture. Take the average rating for each picture and compare.

What made the difference? The glasses, of course. Why? Because it is assumed that people with glasses are more bookish, studious, and intelligent.[1] But are they really? Is there evidence to show that people who wear glasses are more studious than those who do not? Even if it were so, does it necessarily follow that because such people are studious, they are also more intelligent? To answer these questions, let us turn to the "what" and "how" of social perception.

PERCEPTUAL CONTENT: WHAT ONE PERCEIVES

We shall first consider some of the factors that govern the content of people's perception. For illustrative purposes, here are several 10-point scales:

FRIENDLY	1	2	3	4	5	6	7	8	9	10	UNFRIENDLY
RELIABLE	1	2	3	4	5	6	7	8	9	10	UNRELIABLE
INTELLIGENT	1	2	3	4	5	6	7	8	9	10	UNINTELLIGENT
POPULAR	1	2	3	4	5	6	7	8	9	10	UNPOPULAR
FORMAL	1	2	3	4	5	6	7	8	9	10	INFORMAL
AMBITIOUS	1	2	3	4	5	6	7	8	9	10	UNAMBITIOUS
MODEST	1	2	3	4	5	6	7	8	9	10	CONCEITED
SOCIABLE	1	2	3	4	5	6	7	8	9	10	UNSOCIABLE
HONEST	1	2	3	4	5	6	7	8	9	10	DISHONEST
ATHLETIC	1	2	3	4	5	6	7	8	9	10	UNATHLETIC

Ask some of your friends to use these scales in rating the people pictured in Figures 1-2 through 1-5. For example, if they consider the person to be very friendly, they circle either 1 or 2. The numbers continue in the direction of unfriendliness. Considerable unfriendliness means circling 9 or 10; a somewhat neutral perception is reflected in circling 4, 5, or 6; and so on.

After your friends have completed their ratings, average their scores for each scale. Now ask *another* group of friends to do the same thing for the people pictured in Figures 1-6 through 1-9. Compare the scores on each scale. If some of them differ considerably, it is probably due to variations in the pictures of the same people. Among such variables are size (Figure 1-6), eye contact (Figure 1-7), posture (Figure 1-8), and occupation (Figure 1-9). You can readily see that some of these variables are related to physical effects while others exercise an effect because they are social labels or roles.

Physical effects: From short shrift to fancy clothes

Size
The size of a perceived person can have a marked effect on the perceiver. In one experimental study 160 college men were divided into two groups

---
[1]THORNTON, 1944; MANZ & LUECK, 1968.

PERSON PERCEPTION 5

Figure 1-2.

Figure 1-3.

Figure 1-4.

Figure 1-5.

Figures 1-2 through 1-5. Rate these people on the 10-point scales (see text).

6 CHAPTER 1

Figure 1-6.

Figure 1-7.

Figure 1-8.

Figure 1-9.

Figures 1-6 through 1-9. Rate these people on the 10-point scales (see text).

according to their height: tall (6 feet and over), and short (5 feet 8 and less). The subjects' task consisted of guessing one another's height. It was found that both groups of subjects were inaccurate in their perceptions of one another. These results are not surprising. Small persons facing a tall person will generally overestimate the size of what appears to them to be a giant. Tall persons will generally underestimate the size of what appears to them to be a "shrimp." The interesting finding, however, was that the short subjects were significantly more inaccurate than the tall subjects.[2] The most plausible explanation for these findings is that it is somehow more desirable to be tall than small, and that what we see is distorted by our likes and dislikes.

That short men in our society are given short shrift has been shown in a UPI dispatch from Case Western Reserve University in Cleveland. In the somewhat tongue-in-cheek report, Saul D. Feldman, an indignant 5-feet-4 professor of sociology, discussed the prevalence of discrimination on the basis of height. "Heightism," according to Feldman, suggests that the ideal man is viewed as tall, dark, and handsome. Impractical people are short-sighted; dishonest cashiers shortchange customers; electrical failures are known as short circuits; and individuals with little money, no matter their height, will explain their financial troubles by stating, "I'm short." In political affairs, with one exception (Jimmy Carter), the taller of the two presidential candidates since 1900 has always won. In business, tall men (6 feet 2 and taller) receive an average starting salary 12.4% higher than those men who are under 6 feet. In sports such as basketball, baseball, and football, America's obsession with height is most evident. The only exception is horse racing, but according to Feldman, "in this sport the short jockey is given second place to the horse."

If you do not take Professor Feldman's lament seriously, consider the combined effect of status and size on people's perception. In a study designed to assess the effects of status on perception accuracy, the same individual was introduced to college students at various times as a student, an assistant, a lecturer, or a professor at Cambridge University. After the individual's departure, the students were asked to estimate his height. As the status of that person increased, there was a corresponding increase in overestimation of height![3]

Weight

Short people are not the only ones who are given short shrift in our society. Fat people are stigmatized too. David Krantz, a psychologist at the University of Southern California, has examined the bulk of social-psychological research findings on obesity and concluded that overweight people are perceived as obnoxious and lacking self-control. As a result, the social pressures generated by the norm of "slim is beautiful" are of such magnitude that they lead to heightened self-consciousness and exaggerated concern with appearances among overweight people who behave like, and define themselves as, social deviants.[4]

[2]HINCKLEY & ROETHLINGSHAFER, 1951. [3]WILSON, 1968. [4]KRANTZ, 1978.

Smell

Are unpleasant smelling people perceived unpleasantly? Up to a point, according to an extensive study conducted by psychologist Donald McBurney and his colleagues. In a complex arrangement involving instructions to subjects not to wash, bathe, or use a deodorant while engaging in a protracted series of strenuous physical exercise, it was found that subjects producing unpleasant odors were also perceived as unsociable, unfriendly, unintelligent, nervous, unpopular, unhealthy, ugly, and fat! On the other hand, these very same subjects were also attributed with some socially desirable traits, such as being active, strong, industrious and athletic.[5]

Hair

Neither is Professor Feldman off base in claiming the good fortunes of the tall, dark, and handsome. Dark-haired men do fare better than their blond or red-headed counterparts. They are perceived as more intelligent, rugged, and masculine.[6] Also, at least in line with current fashions, abundance of hair is quite an asset for males. Men with body hair are perceived as more active and potent than their counterparts, just as bearded men are perceived as more virile than clean-shaven men.[7]

Looks

Good looks is another perceptual asset. Good-looking people are perceived as being more sensitive and stronger than their unattractive counterparts. They are also perceived as leading a more interesting life than others. And that's not all. Essays purportedly written by college women shown in attached photographs were rated higher when the picture showed an attractive woman than a less attractive one.[8] Even teachers get in on the act. When asked to judge students on the basis of report cards that had the purported students' pictures attached to them, attractive children were amply rewarded with favorable predictions by their teachers. Compared to the less attractive children, they were attributed with higher IQs, better peer relations, and better futures in general.[9] If they are lucky enough to turn into attractive adults, they will have better job prospects,[10] greater political success,[11] and even when before a jury as defendants, receive better breaks than their less attractive counterparts.[12] (There is more to say on the topic of physical attractiveness, as you will see in Chapter 10.)

Physical Handicap

There is little doubt that physical handicaps generate perceptions that lead to tension and inhibition in both perceivers and perceived (the handicapped). Nonhandicapped individuals, upon interacting with handicapped ones, often experience discomfort and uncertainty, display rigid behavior patterns, express socially desirable opinions that are not truly representative of their actual beliefs, and even end the interaction sooner than they do when

---

[5]McBurney, Levine, & Cavanaugh, 1977. [6]Lawson, 1971. [7]Verinis & Roll, 1970; Roll & Verinis, 1971. [8]Dion, Berscheid, & Walster, 1972; Landy & Sigall, 1974. [9]Clifford & Walster, 1973. [10]Dipboye, Fromkin, & Wiback, 1975. [11]Berscheid & Walster, 1972. [12]Efran, 1974; Sigall & Ostrove, 1975.

interacting with other nonhandicapped individuals.[13] Unfortunately, the same tension and discomfort is experienced by handicapped persons in their perception of nonhandicapped individuals. According to psychologist Albert Hastorf and his colleagues, the proven best tactic for tension reduction in such cases is one of acknowledgment: if the handicapped person freely acknowledges his or her handicap, however obvious, in a conversation at the onset of the interaction with the nonhandicapped person, the interaction will eventually manifest the same mood and tempo as that between nonhandicapped persons.[14]

Clothes

Finally, we come to the issue of clothing. The evidence suggests that people do judge a book by its cover. Put in another way, there seems to be truth to the old adage that clothes make the man—and especially the woman. In judging photographs of fashion outfits, females found little difficulty in attributing such qualities as snobbishness, rebelliousness, liveliness, and shyness to potential wearers of such outfits.[15] As a rule, however, variations in clothing as such do not have a significant effect. When they do, it is more likely because such variations are indicative of a person's age or socioeconomic class.

Nonverbal effects: From the body to not much else

People's smile, posture, voice, and eye contact are all forms of **nonverbal communication** that can often convey important messages to the perceiver even if nothing much else is said (see Box 1-1). Research findings indicate the following:

Smile

Despite the fact that smiling is one of the most common nonverbal signals used in interpersonal communication, there is really very little known about what causes it, and even its social functions are not always clear. In general, it is assumed that smiling reflects either happiness and contentment or a social intention to establish friendly relations with others (regardless of the state of one's own emotions). The former is known as the *emotional*, and the latter as the *social hypothesis* of smiling. In an extensive study of the smiling behavior of hundreds of bowlers and hockey fans, the results tended to favor the social hypothesis. That is, there was less smiling when subjects hit spares and strikes, or when the fan's team was ahead in the game (in both cases, causes for happiness) than when the bowlers and the hockey fans interacted with others in the vicinity (even when bowling poorly, or when the team was behind.)[16] In short, smiling may be a social message of sorts, but it is by no means a reliable indicator of the smiler's true emotional state.

Posture

Posture is another important factor in what people perceive. You may be surprised at what people can infer about you from your body posture. As a

[13]KLECK, ONO, & HASTORF, 1966; KLECK, 1968.   [14]HASTORF, WILDFOGEL, & CASSMAN, 1979.   [15]GIBBINS, 1969.
[16]KRAUT & JOHNSTON, 1979.

rule, a forward posture communicates an attentive and positive image, while a backward-leaning posture communicates a rejecting and negative image. If you display an expanded chest, an erect or backward-leaning trunk, an erect head, and raised shoulders, you are likely to be judged as conceited and arrogant. If your trunk is forward leaning, your head is bowed, and your shoulders are drooping, your image is one of depression and dejection. Variations in hand and arm positions yield additional categories of perception. For example, openness of arms indicates warmth, whereas arms akimbo while standing indicates unfriendliness. A relaxed, rather than tense, posture is also an indication of friendliness.[17] Of course, it can also be an indication of bad manners. To a large extent, posture depends on the status of the interacting people. Observations of staff conferences in clinical settings, for example, have shown that the most relaxed and casual postures (putting feet on table, for example) were displayed by the high-status psychiatrists; lower-status participants, such as interns, tended to assume a more rigid body posture.[18]

Voice

People's voices are another important factor in the impression they generate. You may be familiar with the story of the Jewish immigrant who came to America from the old country (Europe) at the turn of the century. Despite his illiteracy and lack of social graces, this immigrant worked hard at many jobs and was beginning to prosper. One day a telegram arrived from his family, whom he had left behind. Not being able to read, he asked a friend to read the telegram to him. The latter, a rough and uneducated individual, read in a loud and commanding voice: "Things are rough here. Send money immediately!" "Who do they think they are, commanding me to send money immediately!" exclaimed the indignant immigrant. He sent no money, of course. Two months later another telegram arrived. This time he took it to a gentle rabbi, who read in a pleading voice: "Things are rough here. Send money immediately." "*Now* they're making sense. They must have learned a lesson," exclaimed the mollified immigrant, and promptly wired the money.

Accent, inflection, pitch, and tempo—all these are critical factors in how a voice generates an image. High-pitched voices evoke perceptions of nervousness, lack of empathy, and lack of sincerity. A slow tempo is equally detrimental, since slow talkers are perceived as passive, unpersuasive, and lacking in sincerity[19], perhaps because it appears that the speaker carefully weighs each word.[20] A person employing a rapid speech rate is usually perceived as more competent and is attributed with greater credibility,[21] provided the delivery reflects spontaneity. An overall unpolished message, even if delivered haltingly, creates an image of credibility, because it is perceived as spontaneous.[22]

Several studies have used taped messages to assess listeners' perceptions. In one such study, the same speaker either spoke English flawlessly or displayed a slight Jewish accent. The listeners, non-Jewish and Jewish college students, rated the speaker with the Jewish accent lower in attractiveness of appearance, height, and leadership qualities.[23] Similarly, French and English

---

[17]JAMES, 1932. [18]GOFFMAN, 1961. [19]APPLE, STREETER, & KRAUSS, 1979. [20]BUGENTHAL, 1974. [21]BUGENTHAL, 1974; SMITH, BROWN, STRONG, & RENCHER, 1975. [22]MILLER, MARUYAMA, BEABER, & VALONE, 1976. [23]ANISFELD, BOGO, & LAMBERT, 1962.

Canadians attributed more positive personality traits to English Canadians.[24] In another study, it was found that loud voices are attributed to assertive individuals.[25] All this may be extended to the way you rate your college professors' performances. One study demonstrated that a lecturer who presented a topic in an active, joke-studded style received very favorable evaluations even though the content of his lecture was meaningless. In fact, observers of this lecturer thought they had learned something even though the logic in the lecture rendered it senseless. Thus, a flashy presentation may create an illusion of learning.[26]

Box 1-1. The scientific art of medicine: The case for nonverbal perception

Recent years have seen major advances in the science of medical care. Ultrasonic methods of diagnosis, surgery under electron microscopes, and the development of wonder drugs like interferon all represent technological advances that have made medical care one of America's largest and most prosperous industries. Yet at the same time that the science of medicine has been making great strides forward, growing disenchantment with medical doctors has emerged in the public sector. In fact, there seems to be an increasing interest in holistic healing and a nostalgic longing for the nontechnical doctors of yesteryear who may not have known about radical surgeries or wonder drugs but did care about their patients.[27]

Besides a technology of medical care, there is also an art of care. Until recently, compassion and an effective bedside manner were about all a physician had to offer to a patient. These aspects of the "art of medical care" have recently received the attention of social psychologists. Not all doctors are equally good at expressing their empathy and concern for patients. Studies by psychologist Robin DiMatteo have demonstrated that, in addition to being able to read X rays, doctors also need to read nonverbal cues. For example, studies in an urban community teaching hospital showed that doctors who were able to read emotion accurately by attending to body posture were rated more favorably by their patients. Being able to perceive nonverbal cues of others accurately on the basis of posture, facial expression, or voice inflection is a necessary skill for those who need to gather information about a patient.[28]

Besides learning to read the nonverbal expressions of others, doctors need to be able to express their own concern through nonverbal channels. Patients often form an impression from the doctor's facial expressions[29] and empathic quality of voice. When patients feel that the doctor is concerned, they are more likely to continue the therapeutic relationship and to comply with the doctor's instructions.[30]

Careful studies in the science of the art of medicine have helped DiMatteo identify some important aspects of nonverbal communication that make for better communication between doctors and their patients.[31] Now she is in the process of developing methods for training doctors to become more empathic and to be better senders and receivers of nonverbal information.

---

[24]Lambert, Hodgson, Gardner, & Fillenbaum, 1960. [25]Scherer, 1971. [26]Naftulin, Ware, & Donnelly, 1973. [27]Eisenberg, 1977. [28]DiMatteo, Friedman, & Taranta, 1979. [29]Friedman, 1981. [30]Milmoe, Rosenthal, Blane, Chafetz, & Wolf, 1967. [31]DiMatteo, Prince, & Taranta, 1979; DiMatteo & Hall, 1979; DiMatteo, 1981.

Eye Contact

We see with our eyes, but we are also seen and judged *by* our eyes. There is much evidence to show that how people use their eyes has an effect on how they are perceived. As small a difference as two glances or none can yield considerable influence on the formation of an impression, as demonstrated in one study. Subjects rated a person reading aloud a page of experimental directions without glancing up even once as formal and tense. The same person, looking up twice, was perceived as relatively informal and relaxed.[32] Indeed, according to psychologist Albert Mehrabian, if you want to be perceived as friendly, your best bet is to try to increase your eye contact with others.[33] This is good advice—up to a point. Prolonged staring can make people uncomfortable and is more likely to be perceived as hostile.[34] Moreover, you should be aware of the context in which your eye contact occurs. If the situation is distressing or threatening to the other person, the *less* you gaze at that person, the more tact and understanding will be attributed to you.[35] Eye contact studies have also been useful in validating some popular beliefs. The old notion of the woman who "modestly averts her glance" evidently does not fit today's modern woman. Systematic observations have shown that women engage in more visual contact than males, regardless of the sex of the person with whom they interact.[36] On the other hand, the notion of the "sensitive-intuitive" woman may have some validity. Compared to men, women tend to read more into social relationships on the basis of eye contact alone.[37]

Role effects: From name to race

A person's hair, posture, and voice are attributes. In a sense, so are his or her name, age, occupation, sex, and race. But the latter are also labels that indicate a person's position among others. Those positions, in turn, generate roles that set up certain expectations. If you are 17 years old, you are expected to (and probably do) display behavior different from that of a 48-year-old. The same applies whether you are a physician or a plumber, a man or a woman, your name is Goldberg or O'Brien, or you are white or black. As we shall see later, some of these expectations are unrealistic, unfair, and based on distorted prejudgments. But it is equally unrealistic to assume that such labels do not generate generalized expectations, thereby affecting a person's perception.

Names

Let us begin with names. College students were asked to rank photographs of 30 women on beauty, intelligence, character, ambition, and general likeability. At the end of two months the procedure was repeated, but this time the photographs showed purported surnames: Jewish (Rabinowitz, Finkelstein),

[32]LE COMPTE & ROSENFELD, 1971. [33]MEHRABIAN, 1968. [34]ELLSWORTH, CARLSMITH, & HENSON, 1972. [35]ELLSWORTH & CARLSMITH, 1968. [36]EXLINE, GRAY, SCHUETTE, 1965. [37]THAYER & SCHIFF, 1974.

Italian (Scarano, Grisolia), and "old American" Anglo-Saxon (Adams, Clark). The addition of Jewish and Italian surnames to the photographs that they had judged earlier caused a considerable drop in ratings of likeability. To a lesser degree, there was also a drop of ratings in character and . . . beauty! (This is especially noteworthy. One can understand, if not condone, that a certain kind of perceiver likes a woman less because she is Jewish or Italian; it is more difficult to understand why this perceiver also considers the same women less beautiful than before.) In the examples with Jewish surnames, there was also an increase in the attributed characteristic of ambition.[38]

An argument could be made that we are dealing here with prejudice and bigotry, and that the perception of people who are not bigoted will be immune to the effect of names. Assuming that *you* are one of those people who are immune to prejudice, consider the following three names:

HERMAN
JIM
ADRIAN

Now ask yourself who of the three is athletic, who is stupid, and who is artistic? Unless your own name is on the list and you do not think that you fit the expected category, or unless you know someone by one of the names, who does not fit that category, your answers are predictable. To make sure, ask several of your friends. Given that particular choice, they will say that Jim is athletic, Herman is stupid, and Adrian is artistic. Yet you and your friends can hardly be accused of being bigoted in this case. (More on names in Chapter 9.)

Age

Age is more than simply a physical attribute because it often denotes status, which in turn calls for certain role behavior. Moreover, age, as we all know, is a relative concept. People are constantly comparing themselves and others in terms of what behavior is "appropriate" for a given age range. It is a very important comparison dimension, even more so than gender. That is, people are more likely to compare behaviors within their own age range than to compare them with same-sex persons who are older or younger.[39] When it comes to the very old, however, there is less flexibility in perception. The elderly of America have been stereotyped and cast into roles that are far from flattering. Research has suggested that between one-fifth and one-third of all adults in this society perceive the elderly in negative terms.[40]

Psychologist Karen Hosey conducted a study in which two college students interacted with a third student with the instructions to treat the latter (who was unaware of the manipulation) as if he were an old man. Subsequent observations by independent judges (who were also unaware of the experimental manipulation) showed that the third student was perceived as despondent, unappealing, weak, and submissive.[41] Hosey suggested that a self-fulfilling prophecy may have been at work: the third student, being treated negatively as the "old" person—even though he did not know that he

---

[38]RAZRAN, 1950. [39]SULS, GASTORF, & LAWHON, 1978. [40]GORDON & HALLAUER, 1976. [41]HOSEY, 1978.

was so designated—actually *became* the way he was expected to behave! Hosey's conclusions are certainly food for thought:

> The overall findings of the present research suggest that negative attitudes toward the elderly still exist among college students, that being treated as if old causes subjects to experience more anxiety, and the self-fulfilling prophecies seem to work in personality attributions to the aged. Perhaps the best way (to combat "ageism") is to reverse the process of the self-fulfilling prophecy: If people really do become as we treat them, we could capitalize on this effect by treating them the way we want them to become [p. 51].

Occupation

A person's occupation generates expectancies and impressions that can overshadow other personality attributes. In our society, physicians enjoy high status and are perceived as intelligent, calm, and confident. So are lawyers, but they are also attributed with a degree of selfishness and manipulativeness. College professors are perceived as sensitive and intelligent, but also as radical and not particularly flexible. Schoolteachers are perceived as intelligent, unselfish, and sensitive, but lacking in confidence. Business executives are perceived as powerful, conservative, assertive, and selfish. Accountants are perceived as conformist, cautious, conservative, and generally cold individuals. Artists are perceived as highly sensitive but moody, impulsive, and attention-demanding individuals.[42]

Race, Religion, and Sex

Last, but by no means least, people's race, religion, and sex have a profound effect on how they perceive and are perceived by others. Such perceptions are also frequently associated with prejudice, bigotry, and discriminatory practices. The social issues involved are of such significance that we have dedicated two chapters (9 and 10) to cover them in greater depth.

Order effects: From first to last impressions

Do you judge others on the basis of first impressions? If you do, you adhere to what is known as the **primacy effect** in interpersonal perception. Consider the following description of a young man named Jim:

> Jim left the house to get some stationery. He walked out in the sun-filled street with two of his friends, basking in the sun as he walked. Jim entered the stationery store, which was full of people. Jim talked with an acquaintance while he waited for the clerk to catch his eye. On his way out, he stopped to chat with a school friend who was just coming into the store. Leaving the store, he walked toward school. On his way out he met the girl to whom he had been introduced the night before. They talked for a short while, and then Jim left for school.

On the basis of this description, do you perceive Jim as an outgoing, extroverted person? Or do you consider him to be more of a withdrawn, introverted person? When psychologist Abraham Luchins presented this

[42]BEARDSLEE & O'DOWD, 1962.

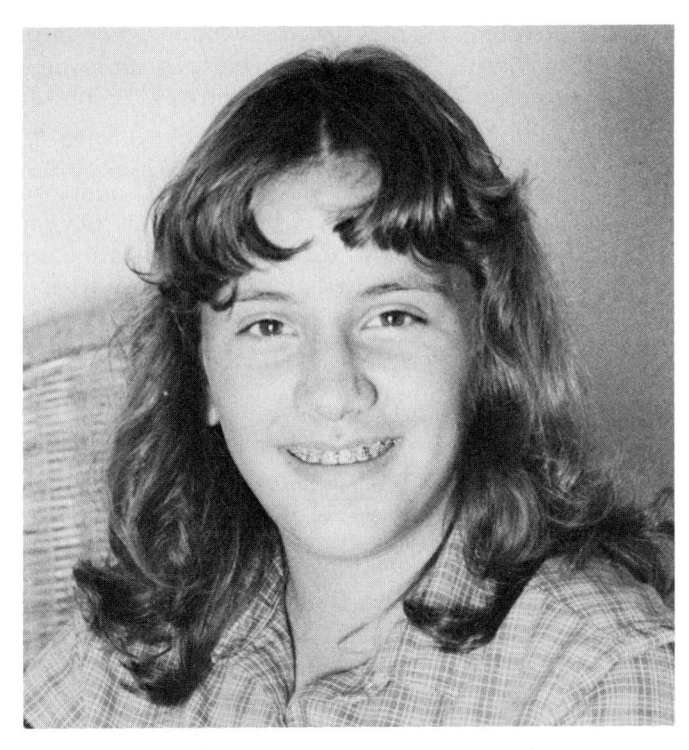

Figure 1-10.
Estimate this person's IQ.

description to a group of students, a majority (79%) judged Jim to be extroverted (sociable, friendly, outgoing, popular, and happy), while a minority (14%) judged him to be introverted (shy, quiet, reserved, lonely, unpopular, and unfriendly). These findings show that most people agree in their perception of a given situation, but that there are some who differ radically from the majority and still others (7%, in this case) who either cannot make up their minds or who come up with no clear-cut judgments.

Now consider this description of Jim, given to the second group of subjects:

After school Jim left the classroom alone. Leaving the school, he started on his long walk home. The street was brilliantly filled with sunshine. Jim walked down the street on the shady side. Coming down the street toward him, he saw the pretty girl whom he had met on the previous evening. Jim crossed the street and entered the candy store. The store was crowded with students, and he noticed a few familiar faces. Jim waited quietly until the counterman caught his eye and then gave his order. Taking a drink, he sat down at a side table. When he had finished his drink, he went home.

A great majority (73%) agreed that Jim was introverted, even though some (16%) thought he was extroverted and others (11%) fell in the undecided category.

Two remaining groups were presented with descriptions of Jim that combined introversion and extroversion, but in reversed order: the third group was presented with the extroverted character description first, followed by the introverted description; the fourth group was presented with the introverted description first and then the extroverted description. When the first description indicated extroversion, Jim was subsequently perceived more often as extroverted (52%) than introverted (36%). On the other hand, when the first description indicated introversion, he was perceived more often as introverted (56%) than extroverted (34%).[43]

First impressions evidently do last. Bear in mind, however, that with a sizable minority the process is reversed. This phenomenon (where last impressions are significant in one's perception) is known as the **recency effect**. The recency effect increases considerably when perceivers are forewarned of the fallacies of first impressions or when contradictory descriptions of the person are separated by unrelated activities.[44]

PERCEPTUAL PROCESSES: HOW ONE PERCEIVES

Adaptation: Everything is relative

Historically speaking, the study of interpersonal perception is relatively new. As late as the turn of the century, psychologists concerned themselves primarily with *sensory psychology*. They focused their interest on such issues as the functions of rods and cones in the human eye or the structure of auditory pathways. Individual differences were minimized, and so was any reference to the meaning that individuals attach to their sensory input. Eventually, however, interest shifted to individual differences in the perception of objects. To the extent that such differences were culturally induced, they fell under the label of *social perception*. In a sense, this was a misnomer, because the perception of objects is not the same as the perception of people. Interpersonal perception is a more complex phenomenon than object perception, since it involves additional dimensions such as judgments, decisions, attitudes, and beliefs.

Most of the earlier studies dealt with issues such as: Do we perceive what we like faster than what we dislike? Do we fail to perceive (at least temporarily) what we dislike? Do we perceive what we like as being larger than what we do not like?[45] Some of these studies were quite interesting. Even though they did not deal with the perception of people, they told us something about the perceiver. For example, 35 years ago Harry Helson and other psychologists developed the notion of **adaptation level** in perception and judgment.[46] They postulated that perceivers respond to three types of stimuli: focal, background, and residual. The focal stimulus is what faces the perceiver directly; the background stimulus serves as such for the focal stimulus; and the residual stimulus is a function of the perceiver's past experience with the other two stimuli.

Consider the following numbers as background stimuli:

    12   115   1218   10,986   118,340   1,104,812

Now consider the concept *few* as a *focal stimulus*. Without hesitation, do the following: blurt out a number which you consider as being a *few* relative to each background number. What is a *few* for 12? What is a *few* for 115? What is a *few* for 1218? And so on. Write the numbers down. If your answers are similar

---

[43]LUCHINS, 1957a. [44]LUCHINS, 1957b; MILLER & CAMPBELL, 1959. [45]POSTMAN & SCHNEIDER, 1951; MCGINNIES, 1949; LAMBERT, SOLOMON, & WATSON, 1949. [46]HELSON, 1948; HELSON, DWORKIN, & MICHELS, 1956.

to Perceiver A's in Table 1-1, they are in line with most people's responses. That is, in terms of absolute numbers there is an increase of what is perceived as a few, but in terms of percentages to the background numbers there is a steady decline. Perceiver B pays strict attention to the focal stimulus while largely ignoring the background stimulus. This somewhat rigid perception is sometimes an indication of certain personality problems. Perceiver C is most interesting because his or her perceptions of the focal and background stimuli covary almost perfectly. Perhaps this person is a mathematician, a statistician, or someone familiar with numbers, and thus brings an appropriate residual stimulus into the process. In any event, Perceiver C's fastidiousness and precision tell us quite a lot about him or her.

TABLE 1-1 Variations in adaptation level

Focal/background	A's perception	%[a]	B's perception	%	C's perception	%
"Few" out of 12 is	3	(25)	3	(25)	3	(25)
"Few" out of 115 is	26	(22)	6	(5)	29	(25)
"Few" out of 1218 is	100	(8)	6	(5)	315	(26)
"Few" out of 10,986 is	550	(5)	5	(.05)	2750	(25)
"Few" out of 118,342 is	1200	(1)	6	(.005)	30,750	(26)
"Few" out of 1,104,812 is	3250	(.3)	5	(.0005)	300,000	(25)

[a]The focal/background relationship is expressed in approximate percentage scores. For example, if the perceiver says that "few" out of 12 is 3, the percentage score is 25 (3/12 × 100). Variations in the relationship may be indicative of residual stimuli effects rooted in the perceiver's personality and past experience. Perceiver B's rigid perception is almost totally oblivious of the background stimuli (rapid decline of percentage scores). Perceiver C's mathematical precision indicates the importance of background stimuli in his or her perception (percentage scores kept constant). Perceiver A's response is a common one. Initially, background stimuli are involved (slow decline of percentage scores); as background numbers become so large that they cannot be clearly conceptualized, however, the effect of background stimuli begins to evaporate (rapid decline in percentage scores).

Another set of earlier studies dealt with the effects of past experience on perception in a different manner. A group of psychologists at Princeton University under the direction of Warren Wittreich had set up a specially constructed room. The room was trapezoidal in shape but provided the same image on the viewer's retina as would a rectangular room. Expecting the context of the familiar rectangular room, the confused viewer experienced considerable perceptual distortions (see Figure 1-11). But when the viewer perceived familiar target persons such as spouses or friends, their sizes remained relatively stable. Familiarity with a perceived person caused the room to distort around the person, rather than vice versa.[47]

Balance: Peace of mind—or else

One of the most fascinating theories of person perception has been advanced by Fritz Heider, a psychologist at the University of Kansas. In its simplest form, his theory deals with the smallest interacting unit (a *diad*, or two-person group), but it can be extended to larger units as well. Our main interest is in the interaction between two people: the perceiver and the perceived person.[48]

[47]WITTREICH, 1952. [48]HEIDER, 1958.

Figure 1-11.
A distorted room demonstration. To unfamiliar perceivers, the children appear as tall as the adults.

Heider's theory is based on what he calls "common sense" psychology and is one of a group of **balance theories**. He assumes that what perceivers want most is logical consistency. If what perceivers see makes sense to them, all is well. As far as the perceivers are concerned, the perceptual situation is *balanced*. If what they perceived does not make sense to them, they experience *imbalance*. Imbalanced situations are unpleasant. They are confusing, disturbing, and tension producing. If they can, perceivers will do their best to avoid imbalanced situations. But what can they do if they are already in a state of imbalance? Heider suggests that a perceiver will change perceptions until they fit a balanced situation. In short, peace of mind (that is, balance) must be regained even though imbalance is initially unavoidable.

Heider's theory is also known as the **p-o-x model** of interpersonal perception because of its three components: p, the perceiver; o, the other (perceived) person; and x, an object, act, or event. The interaction among p, o, and x is governed by *sentiments* and *cognitions*. Sentiments reflect p's regard and affection for the other person, object, act, or event. They are expressed primarily in terms of liking or disliking. In Heider's terminology, liking is represented by the symbol L, and disliking by the symbol $-L$. Cognitions are the logical associations among persons, objects, acts, or events. They occur through similarity, proximity, and especially through the attribution of causation. The symbol C stands for "causes" (to happen), and $-C$ represents "does not cause" (to happen). If all this is confusing to you, consider the following in Heider's abbreviated terminology:

SUSAN LIKES JIM. If Susan is the perceiver and Jim the perceived person, we can say that

pLo: The perceiver likes the other person.

SUSAN LIKES STIMULATING CONVERSATION. If x is stimulating conversation, we can say that

pLx: The perceiver likes stimulating conversation.

JIM PROVIDES STIMULATING CONVERSATION. As perceived by Susan, we can say that

oCx: Jim (the other person) causes stimulating conversation (the event) to happen.

As far as Susan is concerned, the given situation is definitely balanced. Would *you* be upset if the person you like causes what you like to occur? Obviously not. But now consider this situation:

SUSAN LIKES JIM. Once again, Susan is the perceiver and Jim is the other (perceived) person, and therefore

$$pLo$$

SUSAN DISLIKES TEETH PICKING. If x is the act of picking one's teeth, we have

$$p\text{-}Lx$$

JIM IS PICKING HIS TEETH. As perceived by Susan, Jim causes x (teeth picking) to occur. We can say that

$$oCx$$

Susan has an imbalanced situation on hand. There is something disturbing about Jim, whom she likes, standing around picking his teeth. It is a logically inconsistent situation. According to Heider, interactions between two people can be condensed into eight basic situations, as shown in Table 1-2.

TABLE 1-2 Heider's p-o-x interpersonal situations

Situation	p-o-x pattern	Description
Type I balanced	pLo, oCx, pLx	Perceiver (p) likes other person (o) who causes what perceiver likes (x).
Type II balanced	$pLo, o\text{-}Cx, p\text{-}Lx$	Perceiver (p) likes other person (o) who does not cause what perceiver dislikes (x).
Type III balanced	$p\text{-}Lo, oCx, p\text{-}Lx$	Perceiver (p) dislikes other person (o) who causes what perceiver dislikes (x).
Type IV balanced	$p\text{-}Lo, o\text{-}Cx, pLx$	Perceiver (p) dislikes other person (o) who does not cause what perceiver likes (x).
Type V imbalanced	$pLo, oCx, p\text{-}Lx$	Perceiver (p) likes other person (o) who causes what perceiver dislikes (x).
Type VI imbalanced	$pLo, o\text{-}Cx, pLx$	Perceiver (p) likes other person (o) who does not cause what perceiver likes (x).
Type VII imbalanced	$p\text{-}Lo, oCx, pLx$	Perceiver (p) dislikes other person (o) who causes what perceiver likes (x).
Type VIII imbalanced	$p\text{-}Lo, o\text{-}Cx, p\text{-}Lx$	Perceiver (p) dislikes other person (o) who does not cause what perceiver dislikes (x).

p = perceiver
o = perceived other
x = any object or event
C = causes
L = likes

Let us now examine how people react to imbalanced situations. Imagine Susan being faced with the following situation:

SUSAN HATES JIM, THINKS HE IS A CREEP. SUSAN ALSO WANTS TO BE ELECTED PRESIDENT OF THE CLUB TO WHICH BOTH SHE AND JIM BELONG. SHE FINDS OUT THAT JIM IS CONDUCTING A MAJOR CAMPAIGN IN HER BEHALF IN A VERY EFFECTIVE MANNER. EVENTUALLY SUSAN IS ELECTED PRESIDENT.

Common sense dictates that the situation is imbalanced for Susan. She wanted the presidency, but look who has been instrumental in getting it for her—of all people, Jim, whom she detests. In Heider's terminology, Susan is facing a Type VII situation,

$$p\text{-}Lo,\ oCx,\ pLx$$

with p denoting Susan, o denoting Jim, and x denoting the desire to be president.

What can Susan say to herself when faced with this unpleasant situation? Put yourself in her shoes and consider how *you* would react under the circumstances. You will be surprised to learn that your reaction is fairly predictable. To get out of your predicament, you will come up with one of the following possible solutions:

Solution #1. JIM IS NOT A BAD GUY AFTER ALL! If Susan (or you, for that matter) chooses this way of thinking, she has changed her *sentiment* toward Jim. She likes him now. In other words, *p-Lo* becomes *pLo*. The situation has turned into a Type I situation: Susan likes Jim who helped her get the presidency that she wanted. Susan has regained balance.

Solution #2. I REALLY DON'T WANT TO BE PRESIDENT! Choosing this solution entails a change in *attitude* toward the event. Now Susan no longer wants the presidency. Instead of *pLx*, it is *p-Lx*. The situation has turned into a Type III situation: Susan continues to dislike Jim, who helped her get elected. But since she does not want the presidency any more, she has no obligation to Jim. Susan has regained balance.

Solution #3. JIM REALLY DID NOT HELP AT ALL. I DID IT ON MY OWN! Choosing this solution entails a change of *perception* in causality. Susan maintains that Jim did not help her get elected. Instead of *oCx*, it is *o-Cx*. Susan now faces a Type IV situation: since Jim did not help her get elected to the coveted presidency, she can continue to dislike him with impunity. Susan has regained balance.

Solution #4. SO WHAT? Choosing this solution does not alter the original imbalanced situation. Heider would say that Susan has not really solved anything. She *says* that the situation does not bother her, but she will continue to experience imbalance (and discomfort and tension) until the situation is perceived otherwise. However, it is also possible that this type of reaction implies tolerance of imbalance or that the situation was never perceived as imbalanced from the beginning.

Heider's theory has generated a considerable amount of research, some of it highly significant. As a theoretical framework for interpersonal perception, it lacks the quantitative aspects that are necessary for meaningful interpretations. For example, if Jim *(p)* is invited by his friend Susan *(o)* for dinner and she serves spinach *(x)*, which he detests, the ensuing *pLo, oCx, p-Lx* situation is only meaningfully imbalanced as long as Jim's liking for Susan is of equal magnitude to his dislike of spinach. In real life, of course, expectancies and likings are rarely of equal magnitude. Recent research has addressed itself increasingly to quantitative extensions of Heider's theory.[49]

[49] INSKO & ADEWOLE, 1979; CROCKETT, 1974.

From a more practical perspective, some studies involving Heider's theory have shown that the personality of an individual has an effect on the way he or she chooses to react to imbalanced situations.[50] To illustrate the point, let us once more take up Susan's situation after she won the presidency with the help of Jim, whom she dislikes. Suppose you knew something about Susan's personality: for example, that she is support seeking, or recognition seeking, or independent, or benevolent. What could you predict about her reaction to the situation facing her?

Support-seeking individuals, facing Susan's situation, tend to change sentiments. You can predict that Susan will begin to like Jim and thus solve her imbalance.

Recognition-seeking individuals in the same situation will change their perception of causality. Susan will deny that Jim helped her. She will attribute her success to her own endeavors and thus solve her imbalance.

Independent individuals in the same situation will change their attitude. Susan will relinquish her presidency just so she does not have to be obligated to someone she intends to continue to dislike.

What about individuals who can be characterized as displaying leadership behavior, or those who are characterized by benevolence? Strangely enough, they will display identical reactions, even though their reasoning may differ. Both individuals will take a "so what" attitude. In other words, they either tolerate the situation or do not find it disturbing in the first place. The leader may reason something like this: "I won the presidency because I am the best person and everyone (including Jim) has to acknowledge this fact." The benevolent individual's reasons may be based on the assumption that everyone (Jim included) ought to help people who are running for office.

Findings such as these, have considerable implications for interpersonal situations in which one person is troubled and seeks out the advice of another. We shall limit our discussion to counseling situations, because counselors are supposed to do more than just give advice. A skillful counselor has the ability to ferret out the root of the problem before making suggestions. More often than not, a counselor can trace a client's problem to interpersonal difficulties (with parents, spouse, friends, and so on). The counselor also has at hand various testing instruments to measure the skills and personality traits of clients.

How, then, can a counselor apply the principles of balance theory to help clients? If you were the client and your counselor was aware that certain people show a tendency to solve imbalanced situations in a given way, your chances of getting effective advice would increase considerably. For example, if the tests show that you are a support-seeking individual, your counselor will focus on changing your sentiments. He or she might give you the traditional love-thy-neighbor advice by showing you the benefits of getting to know your adversary better, by pointing out that the person you dislike really has good qualities, by appealing to your altruistic nature, and so on.

But what if the counselor has ascertained that you are a highly independent individual or a highly recognition-seeking individual? Under those circumstances, the traditional love-thy-neighbor advice will be a waste of time. In

[50]HARARI, 1967.

both cases, you are neither ready nor willing to like the other person. If you are a recognition-seeking person, your counselor will be most effective if he or she reassures you that it is perfectly all right to dislike the other person, particularly since the latter does nothing for you anyway (you are making it on your own). For an independent individual in the same situation, the best advice that your counselor can give is not to accept any help from others if it does not allow you to continue to dislike them. Such advice is unconventional—but since it will help you regain your balance, it is effective advice.

We must remember that people who are habitually placed in the position of advice givers—be they friends, counselors, or psychotherapists—inevitably must ask themselves: How effective is my advice? Am I doing better than chance? Fortunately, Heider and other psychologists have provided us with basic tools for making certain predictions about people's cognitive processes and emotions. For example, studies have shown that normal and delinquent adolescents respond differently to conflict situations. Normal youngsters tend to judge others on the basis of their own moral obligation to act, while delinquents in the same situation make their judgments on the basis of the power of others to act. As a result, psychotherapists' messages to their patients can be varied systematically: with some patients a psychotherapist can play a forceful and directive role; with other patients, the same psychotherapist can assume a minimal role and shift the burden of problem solving to them. In either case, a lot of guesswork is taken out of who, when, and what to advise.[51]

Attribution: Theories of pinning labels

Imagine the following situation. Two groups are performing calisthenics. One group consists of classmates you like, the other group consists of classmates you dislike. On different occasions, both perform their tasks. Scoring by outside observers indicates that the disliked group performed perfectly. The liked group did not perform well. Unknown to you, they made intentional mistakes in their performance.

Some time later, you are asked to comment about the quality of the performances you witnessed earlier. Which group, if any, will you remember as having given a better performance? Even though you may take pride in your sense of fair play and objectivity, the chances are that you will remember the liked group as having performed well and the disliked group as having performed poorly. As with the case in an actual study, "bad" acts are simply attributed to "bad" people.[52]

Suppose now that you see another person stooping to pat a stray dog. You are asked to judge that person. Among other things, you label him or her as a dog lover. What are the chances that you will maintain this judgment, which, after all, is based on a single episode?

According to Harold Kelley, a psychologist at UCLA, three factors operate in people's perception: distinctiveness, consistency, and consensus.[53] In the case at hand, Kelley would suggest that you would be most likely to stick to

[51]Harari, 1971, 1972. [52]Zillig, 1928. [53]Kelley, 1972.

your judgment if the following occurs. You know that the other person is limiting fondness to dogs and does not extend it to other pets (distinctiveness); you know that he or she extends this feeling toward all types of dogs over periods of time (consistency); and it is generally assumed that people who display fondness toward dogs are dog lovers (consensus).

What happens to a person's perception when the situation is reversed? That is, when you know that the other person is kind not only to dogs but to animals in general, but that this kindness depends on the person's mood and the situation; and that, in general, he or she seems to be no more interested in dogs than any other people around. Under these conditions, according to Kelley, you will have a different perception for the identical act of that person's patting the dog. You will attribute causality to the dog (for example, "This dog is hungry and wants a handout") (see also Chapter 2, "Self-Perception").

In contemporary psychology, most studies on person perception deal with the attributes of *causal* ability. It is assumed that how people perceive others is governed by their inferences about the other person's intent, ability, power, or moral obligation to act. To this end, numerous theoretical frameworks have been suggested and tested by psychologists. Heider's balance theory and Kelley's formulations about distinctiveness, consistency, and consensus are part of this framework, which falls under the loosely formed general label of **attribution theory**. Within the context of this book, a comprehensive discussion of two such theories should therefore suffice.

Bernard Weiner and his colleagues[54] have analyzed four factors to which people attribute achievement outcomes: ability, effort, task difficulty, and luck. The four factors also differ along the dimensions of stability and internality. (For more detailed discussion, see Chapter 2, "Self-Perception.") As Figure 1-12 indicates, a student's success or failure on a test can be attributed to various causes. There are, of course, situational variations across causal attributions. A recent developmental study of grade school children showed that a child does not use the same type of causal explanations across situations. For example, success in academic testing was attributed (in order of importance) to effort and ability, and failure to lack of effort; finishing an art project successfully to ability and effort, and failure to lack of same; and catching frogs successfully to effort and task ease, and failure to task difficulty and lack of ability.[55]

Psychologists Edward Jones and Robert Nisbett have developed an attributional framework that is geared more closely to person perception. In much-documented research, they argue that the type of attribution made depends on whether the observer or the actor (the observed person) does the explaining: "Actors attribute cause to situations, while observers attribute cause to dispositions." For example, what would happen in the following situations? A failing student (actor) explaining her academic problem to a faculty advisor (observer); or a nonhelping bystander (actor) to a criminal assault explaining his lack of help to a newscaster (observer). In all cases, claim Jones and Nisbett,

[54]Weiner, Frieze, Kukla, Reed, Rest, & Rosenbaum, 1971. [55]Frieze & Snyder, 1980.

Example: *Susan received an A in the course (success)*
Susan received an F in the course (failure)

LOCUS OF CONTROL

	Internal	External
Stable	Ability *Because she is so smart* *Because she is not too bright*	Task difficulty *Because the test was too easy, anyone could pass* *Because the test was unfair and difficult*
Unstable	Effort *Because she studied day and night* *Because she was too lazy and did not bother to study*	Luck *Because she was lucky; the test's major items were on the few topics she managed to study* *Because she was unlucky; the test's major items were on topics she did not study*

STABILITY

Figure 1-12. Weiner's two-dimensional analysis of attribution of responsibility for success and failure.

the observer will be more likely to make causal attributions about the actors' behavior on the basis of some trait or disposition that resides within the actors, whereas the actors' own attributions will be made on the basis of explanations that are rooted in the environment.[56]

To illustrate this point further, imagine that you are given a list of adjectives describing personality traits, including one option, "It depends on the situation," and are asked to apply them in describing yourself, your father, your best friend, an admired acquaintance, and a public figure (Walter Cronkite, for example). According to Jones and Nisbett,[57] you will use the situational option most often for yourself (average +8 out of 20 times) and least often for the person you know the least, Walter Cronkite (average +5 out of 20 times). These findings point to a certain paradox: the less we know someone, the more we are likely to pin a "permanent" personality on him or her. Another "situational bias" exists when you are compared to liked or disliked others. A recent study that employed 2800 adjectives to be chosen by 400 college students who served as subjects was in line with the conclusion that "the situational

[56] JONES & NISBETT, 1972. [57] JONES & NISBETT, 1972; NISBETT, CAPUTTO, LEGANT, & MARECEK, 1973.

response is used most often when describing oneself, somewhat less often when describing a neutral other, and least often when describing either a well-liked or disliked other."[58]

Box 1-2. The practical side of attribution theory

Despite its abstract and sometimes complex aspects, attribution theory has generated considerable applied research. Psychologists Harold Kelley and John Michela have presented a summary of many studies. Some notable findings:

Advertising. Most people pride themselves on being perfectly aware that it is possible, perhaps even probable, that there is a discrepancy between the message ("commercial") and the advertised product in it. This is because we understand the persuaders' intention, namely, that they are motivated to induce people to buy things. Children's awareness of the persuasive intent and the biases of television commercials, however, follows a different pattern.

While 90% of the third graders and 100% of the fifth graders observed attributed persuasive intent to television commercials, only 50% of the first graders did so. Recent hearings of the Federal Trade Commission have raised the issue of whether the first graders' vulnerability deserves protection.

Psychotherapy. The treatment of hyperactivity in children by means of drugs is common medical practice. It also promotes external attribution, that is, the notion that the problem is "organic." While such attributions often make both parents and children feel comfortable, they strongly interfere with treatment programs that rely on teaching and self-control strategies.

Education. Students who persistently fail develop low self-esteem. They also understandably lose interest and persistence in the task. Providing feedback that encourages attributions of lack of effort as the major cause of failure has been found to increase both students' persistence and their self-esteem.

Sports. To reach maximum effectiveness, high ability *and* effort attributions should be encouraged whenever athletes evaluate themselves and their teams. This is particularly important in the case of failure, because in those situations athletes limit these two attributions to themselves but reduce them for the team.

Ecology. People often become aroused whenever their personal space is violated (see Chapter 11, "Proxemics"). They also attribute the *cause* of this arousal, sometimes erroneously, to "crowding." As a result of such attributions, people in high-density living conditions (such as elderly people living in inner cities) may feel that anxiety and loss of control over the environment and interactions with others is inevitable. This can often be corrected by systematically encouraging a change of attributions to factors other than "crowding."

Source: Kelley & Michela, 1980.

Misattribution: Just or capricious?

In the course of people's lifetimes, many things over which they have no real control can happen: They may be bitten by mosquitoes while working in their backyards. They may slip on a banana peel and break an ankle. They may step on a rusty nail and develop blood poisoning. Their house may be razed by a

[58]GOLDBERG, 1978.

hurricane. They may develop a debilitating disease. They may become the crippled survivors of an airplane crash.

What can these unfortunate people expect from you? Not much, really. They all had misfortunes. They are the helpless victims of fate. Surely, though, they can expect to get your sympathy. This is what our moral code dictates. After all, nobody likes to see innocent people suffer.

Not quite. You are likely to sympathize with the person who got bitten by the mosquito or the one who slipped on a banana peel, or the one who experienced some familiar *small* misfortunes. But as you ponder about the more serious cases, you begin to have a vague feeling that perhaps the misfortune was not beyond control. Perhaps the victim's house could have been saved if the weather warning service would have been more efficient. Perhaps the patient's doctor was a quack. Perhaps the pilot of the crashed plane faked his way through a qualifying health examination.

Why this urgent concern to pin the responsibility for the accident on *someone?* Why not accept it as unavoidable fate? The reason, according to psychologist Elaine Walster, is that your acceptance that this is the kind of thing that could happen to anyone comes dangerously close to an admission that a catastrophe of such magnitude could happen to *you*. Pinning the responsibility on someone for a serious accident makes you feel more comfortable because it supplies cues for future action on your part. It prepares you to watch for certain danger signals. When Walster presented her subjects with a hypothetical car accident, the more serious the consequences were for the victims, the less the accident was attributed to fate.[59]

From this point on, things move on with a relentless logic. Suppose that *no one* can be held responsible for the victim's plight. Suppose the weather warning service had been issuing the proper bulletins, the patient's doctor has a fine reputation, or the airline pilot had passed the health examination with flying colors. What then? At that point, according to Walster, you begin to take a closer look at the victims. If, in some way, you can pin the responsibility on *them*, it is reassuring. You can then reassure yourself that you are a different kind of person from the victims, or that you would behave differently under similar circumstances. Thus, if one victim would not have been walking so carelessly, he would not have stepped on a rusty nail. If another would have had the sense to buy a sturdier house, it would have withstood the hurricane. If she would have been smart enough to undergo an annual checkup, or eat her vitamins, she would not have this terrible disease. If instead of flying in such bad weather he would have taken the train, he would not be a cripple today. With such reasoning you feel protected from catastrophe. In her experiment Walster found that the driver of the car was judged as more responsible for the accident when consequences were severe than when consequences were trivial.

Now that the responsibility is pinned on the victims, the next step is inevitable. You begin to put distance between yourself and the victims. You consider them somewhat clumsy, perhaps stupid, perhaps even deserving of their fate. This, too, can be reassuring. Oddly enough, all this is done without

[59]WALSTER, 1966.

violating any moral principle. In fact, it is based on moral principles of the highest order: your belief in a *just world*. The process, according to psychologist Melvin Lerner, works as follows:

> We do not want to believe that . . . [disasters] . . . can happen, but they do. At least we do not want to believe they can happen to people like ourselves—good, decent people. If these things can happen, what is the use of struggling, planning, and working to build a secure future for one's self and family? . . .
>
> What I am postulating here is that for their own security, if for no other reason, people want to believe they live in a just world where people get what they deserve.[60]

To sum it all up, anything that jeopardizes our belief in a just world where people get what they deserve produces dissonance. To resolve this dissonance we must attribute responsibility to someone, even if it is a hapless victim of circumstances. This moral concept employs a circular logic of sorts: *People get what they deserve—and deserve what they get!*

Paradoxically, the widespread belief in a just world can put a severe strain on equity and justice. Psychologists Cathaleene Jones and Elliot Aronson point out the startling fact that the more respectable a victim of disaster is, the more fault is attributed to him or her.[61] For example, what does a bystander say when a person known to be a heroin pusher, child molester, or spouse beater walks across the street, steps in an open manhole, and fractures both legs? Probably, "Aha, the bastard got what he deserved." But what if the same thing happened to a gentle, caring, underpaid welfare worker? To maintain their belief in a just world, the bystanders must invent some justification for the tragedy that can be attributed to the victim. For example, "He should not have walked without a flashlight . . . he was distracted . . . he was preoccupied with the troubles of others . . . he had one martini too many before dinner," and so on. The point is that more responsibility (fault) is attributed to the more respectable victim.

Jones and Aronson then proceeded to describe to their subjects a victim in a rape case. Depending on the experimental condition, she was described as being either married, a virgin, or a divorcee. The case itself was described (again, depending on the experimental condition) as either an attempted rape or an actual rape by a "muscular man, 5 feet 10, 175 pounds, 26 years old . . . working as an auto mechanic at a local service station." Following a detailed description of the incident, the subjects were asked to act as judges and determine the number of years of imprisonment the defendant rapist should receive (ranging from less than 1 to more than 40, with 5-year intervals marked). As a corollary activity, the subjects were also asked to rate, on a 21-point scale, how much of the crime was the victim's fault.

What does common sense—and justice, for that matter—dictate in this case? First, a somewhat more lenient judgment for the defendant who attempted the crime than for the defendant who perpetrated the crime. Second, in either case the fact that the victim was a virgin, married, or divorced should be of no consequence. Rape is rape, and as such should be judged on the circumstances.

[60]LERNER, 1970. [61]JONES & ARONSON, 1973.

Unfortunately, old-fashioned sexist norms combine with the exalted belief in a just world to produce an uneven distribution of justice. As expected, the average punishment for the defendant in the actual rape case (16 years) was more severe than in the attempted rape case (10 years). But in both cases the status of the victim played an important part in the subjects' decision. The more respectable the victim was, the harder was the assigned punishment for the criminal. Since in our society married women are assumed to enjoy the highest status, closely followed by virgins, with the divorcee at the bottom of the pole, the rapist of the married woman received 18 years, the rapist of the virgin received 15 years, and the rapist of the divorcee received 14 years. In the attempted rape case, the criminal received 11 years for attacking the married woman or the virgin, but only 8 years for attacking the divorcee. As if this twisted morality is not enough, it was in direct contrast to the amount of fault attributed to the victim. The pious belief in a just world dictates that the more respectable the victim, the greater the need to attribute fault to her actions since it is difficult to attribute fault to her character. Accordingly, the married women were faulted more than the virgins, and almost twice as much as the divorcees, for their part in the crime. This was bad enough. The fact that subsequent punishment of the criminal was most severe in the case of the married woman defies both common sense and justice.

While the belief in a just world can lead to distorted judgments, the opposite holds true as well. Several studies have shown that *less* fault is attributed to the victim of a serious misfortune than of a small misfortune.[62] The judges in those cases, however, were not necessarily more accurate and equitable in their perception. Rather, they displayed what is known as **defensive attribution**. The defensive attribution hypothesis suggests that people's self-perceptions are governed by self-serving biases.[63] In the case of the aforementioned accident studies, instead of believing in a just world, people sometimes find it advantageous to believe in a *capricious* world. The desire not to attribute a severe accident to chance is overridden by the desire to avoid being blamed for an accident. The thinking in such cases may go as follows: "*I* may cause a similar accident in the future; if I do, I will want people to think chance is responsible, and not I." The apparent sympathy for the victim (who is blamed less than chance) is really not sympathy at all. It stems from the desire to avoid potential trouble should one find himself or herself in a predicament similar to that of the victim.

It is possible to continue almost endlessly with the strange logic of believers in a just or capricious world. For example, what could be expected of young men's reactions to the military draft lottery numbers allocated to their peers during the height of the unpopular war in Vietnam? When 19-year-old males listened to a live broadcast of the 1971 national draft lottery, the overall reaction was one of sympathy for those who drew bad lots (high-priority numbers) as opposed to good lots (low-priority numbers). Still, a considerable number of subjects showed little sympathy for those who drew high-priority numbers. Not too surprisingly, these were the same people who on previous

[62]SHAVER, 1970; CHAIKIN & DARLEY, 1973. [63]BRADLEY, 1978.

test measures had made it clear that they believe that the world is a just place where good people are rewarded and bad people are punished.[64]

There is even evidence that the victims themselves engage in self-derogation as a result of their beliefs in a just world. In the previously cited study on the draft lottery, it was found that individuals who received low priority numbers experienced an increase in self-esteem immediately after the lottery, and those with high priority numbers (draft imminent) experienced decrease in self-esteem, even though their fate was clearly determined by chance! Similarly, many depressed people or seriously ill people have been found to advance "reasons" for their problems which, while totally unrealistic, put the blame squarely on themselves.[65]

SUMMARY HIGHLIGHTS

1. Many factors influence how judgments about other people are made. Some of the factors are physical, such as the assumption that people wearing glasses are more intelligent, that physically attractive children are better behaved, that overweight people are obnoxious, and that men with facial hair are more masculine than men without beards or moustaches.
2. Communication with others is carried out both in speech and in *nonverbal communication*. Smiling may not be an accurate reflection of the smiler's emotional state; leaning forward during conversation is usually taken as a sign of attentiveness; soothing voice, or good eye contact, may be interpreted as sincerity.
3. Age, gender, occupation, race, religion, and even names are believed to be associated with particular *social roles*, which elicit impressions of others based on role-appropriate appraisals.
4. People tend to make social judgments relative to a frame of reference (for example, a 5-foot adult male is tall relative to second-grade boys but not to other adult males).
5. Perceivers also attempt to keep their judgments *balanced*, in line with what they perceive as common sense persistence.
6. Attributions are based on such factors as consistency, distinctiveness, consensus, ability, luck, effort, and task difficulty.
7. There is a tendency to explain one's own behavior in terms of situations, and the behavior of others in terms of their personality traits.
8. Although people may be unaware of it, they have a tendency to believe that we live in a *just world*. This belief can often lead to instances in which victims are blamed for their own misfortunes.

[64]RUBIN & PEPLAU, 1973. [65]LERNER & MILLER, 1978.

CHAPTER 2 THE SELF AND OTHERS

SELF-PRESENTATION
    The "me" self and the "not me" self
    Self-disclosure: Telling all
    Self-monitoring: Showing yourself

SELF-PERCEPTION
    Stability: How we see ourselves and others
    Internality/externality: Control and helplessness

    Self-schemata: Your personal script

SELF-PREDICTION
    Personality prediction: A low score for tradition
    Template matching: Fitting your mold
    Self-efficacy: Knowing you can

SUMMARY HIGHLIGHTS

SELF-PRESENTATION

The "me" self and the "not me" self

The camera pans in on a quiet actor in the background of the scene. A voice is heard asking "Who are you?" Now the screen is filled with the man's face as the figure slowly replies "I don't really know."

    Corny? Of course it is. Yet scenes like this are among the most common themes in soap operas, fiction, and live drama. Their popularity derives in part from the widespread feeling that each one of us can be many different people. This is an irony because most people can easily find a group of labels, such as "ambitious," "aggressive," or "friendly," to attach to other people. Yet when we think about ourselves, we know that we can be friendly in some situations and cold in others. We might be shy sometimes and on other occasions be highly assertive. Thus, learning the way we perceive ourselves in relation to other people has become an important area of social psychology.

    The term *self* is widely used in psychology. It is frequently combined into composite terms such as self-concept, self-insight, self-esteem, self-acceptance, self-image, and so on. We believe that, to achieve clarity in the usage of these terms, it is best to present you with two basic approaches to the notion of self.

    The first approach to the self is rooted in the history of personality theory. Its primary aim is to account for the unique organization of behavior within each individual. Sigmund Freud used the term *ego* to refer to this organized aspect of personality. Regardless of terminology, this conceptualization of the self minimizes the role of others in the process of what the individual considers as "me." Each individual is presented as an active agent who selectively guides admission of new experiences into conceptual categories. Individual adjustment is perceived as a function of acting flexibly. If, for example, you have filtered into your cognitive system sufficient information to perceive yourself as a straight-A honor student, you should be able to take the information that you have just earned a C grade in stride. But if your filtering system is rigid, you will probably engage in various defensive maneuvers to deny the occurrence of what you consider a formidable blow to your self-image; or you may accept it and become depressed. Either way, you will have a problem. All this does not mean that flexibility in filtering information is a cure-all. If every time you earn an A you perceive yourself as a genius and every time you fail a test you consider yourself hopelessly stupid, you obviously lack a stable and serviceable estimate of yourself. You are, in fact, displaying what Freud would call "low ego strength," which is detrimental to coping with effective long-range planning and decision making.

As described so far, the term *self* emphasizes the role of the perceiver. There is, however, another approach which suggests that the perceiver is not only concerned with what is "me" but also with what is "not me." The notion of a social self implies that what each of us perceives as "me" is simply the sum total of what *others* think of us. Notice that each individual continues to be an active agent and evaluator, but whatever information is filtered is primarily dependent on the action of others. The more important and significant these others are to the perceiver, the greater their impact on his or her perception of self.

The idea that the self is a product of the perception of others was developed at the turn of the century by sociologist Charles Cooley[1] and expanded some time later by sociologist George Mead.[2] It was largely ignored by clinical psychologists, who at the time were fascinated with Freud's notion of "ego function." Social psychologists, on the other hand, eagerly accepted the idea of the social self. Moreover, they transferred many of Cooley's and Mead's ideas into workable research hypotheses. In a now-classic study, psychologist Melvin Manis arranged to assess the self-concepts of a number of young men before, during, and after a series of social interactions. The subjects were 101 male freshmen between the ages of 17 and 19 who were strangers to one another before they came to the University of Illinois. They were divided into 8-man groups and housed in adjacent dormitory rooms for about 11 weeks. By comparing each subject's description of himself to others' descriptions of him, Manis was able to demonstrate the existence of the social self. He showed that as time went on, each subject's self-concept and the average concept held of him by others tended to converge. More important, Manis found that this "meeting of the minds" or compromise between what people think of themselves and what others think of them was largely a one-sided affair. The subjects' descriptions of themselves changed more often in the direction of the descriptions that others had made of them than vice versa. This strong influence of others on individual self-perception was particularly evident when the subjects initially viewed themselves less favorably than the group viewed them. The reasons for this phenomenon are obvious. It is relatively easy for people to revise their self-concepts in line with others' conception of them if it involves a change for the better. The same people would understandably be reluctant to accept changes for the worse in order to meet whatever expectations others may have of them.[3]

Consider the implications of the Manis study for clinical practice. "Acting-out" patients, especially those engaged in antisocial activities, are generally

[1] COOLEY, 1902. [2] MEAD, 1934. [3] MANIS, 1955.

perceived as more suitable candidates for group psychotherapy than patients who are shy, withdrawn, and socially isolated.[4] One possible reason for this preference is that groups composed of "acting-out" patients tend to resemble what psychotherapy groups *should* look like. In such groups tempers fly, tears are shed, and psyches are bared. In groups composed of social isolates, nothing much seems to happen. Whatever social interaction occurs is interrupted by prolonged periods of silence. As the Manis study implies, it is precisely this type of patient who will benefit most from group psychotherapy, clinical tradition notwithstanding. The "acting-out" patient often displays an unreasonably high self-concept bolstered by bragging, boasting, and lying. As Manis has shown, it is very difficult to bring this self-concept down to realistic levels because of the patient's reluctance to change for the worse. The self-concept of "withdrawn" candidates for the group is so low that even minimal support from the others will create a change for the better in them.

The **social self** is part of the vicious circle that stereotyping generates. Any time a person is treated on the basis of class membership, discriminatory action is inevitable, since the perceiver ignores individual differences. If the discriminatory practices are painful to the target person, the ensuing adjustment problem is obvious. If you are an aging and physically unattractive used-car salesman called Harvey Glook, you will be the recipient of rather harsh treatment. Whether such treatment is justified is beside the point. Like so many self-fulfilling prophecies that operate in members of oppressed minorities, your self-concept will be low. What about the flip side of the coin? If you are a young and physically attractive physician called Michael West, your self-concept is more likely to be high because others evaluate you more positively—sometimes too high, as a matter of fact. Since all young Dr. Wests are *not* alike, you may find it difficult to live up to undeserved judgments. This, too, can create adjustment problems.

Self-disclosure: Telling all

What can people do to avoid problems resulting from faulty interpersonal perception? Not much, really. Just as stereotyping is going to be with us forever, so are some of the problems caused by misperceptions. One possible remedy is to educate perceivers to refrain as much as possible from making judgments of others on the basis of categorized classes. Another solution is to urge people to disclose more about themselves. One could argue that those who engage in frank and open behavior are less likely to be judged inaccurately, since those who perceive them will have to rely less on stereotyping.

The problem is that the term *self-disclosure* is rather complex. As originally coined by psychologist Sydney Jourard, it refers to any information about himself or herself that person A communicates verbally to person B. For purposes of measurement, person B is often presented as person A's mother, father, best opposite-sex friend, and same-sex friend. Information items to be measured deal with person A's attitudes and opinions, tastes and interests, work or studies, money, personality, and body. Items are scored as 0 (no disclosure to person B), 1 (disclosure in general terms only), and 2 (full and

[4]Harari, 1972.

complete disclosure).[5] With increasing interest in the topic among psychologists, several other measures of self-disclosure have been developed.[6]

The major problem in the measurement of self-disclosure is that it is not enough to find out how much people are willing to disclose about themselves. Of equal, and possibly greater, importance is the kind of information they are willing to disclose. For example, the evidence is generally inconclusive whether there is a difference between how much men and women disclose about themselves, but women disclose more intimate information about themselves than men do (especially to same-sex friends).[7] Along similar lines, cross-cultural studies have shown that compared to Germans, Americans disclose a lot about themselves, but the friendships the Americans form are rather superficial in nature; Germans do not disclose a lot about themselves, but they form intimate relationships with others, nevertheless.[8]

One of the nice things about self-disclosure is that it begets self-disclosure. The more you tell about yourself, the more others will tell about themselves.[9] As an extra bonus, you will also be perceived as more trustworthy and likeable in general.[10] The entire encounter group movement is, in fact, based on the premise that all of us will benefit from being maximally open with another. This may be so, but a word of caution is due nevertheless. Have you ever been part of an encounter group? Many participants in such groups have been turned off by excessive demands to "tell all." If they refuse to go all the way in disclosing information about themselves, they come under heavy fire. A prominent advocate of the encounter movement has labeled these withholders of information as "hermits, prudes, paranoids, or rascals."[11] If such views prevail, we may very well have on our hands what some psychologists call the "tyranny of openness."[12] Under such conditions individuals will have very little freedom to harbor private thoughts that they may cherish. Psychologist Paul Cozby suggests the following hypothesis on the basis of recent research:

> Persons with positive mental health (given that they can be identified) are characterized by high disclosure to a few significant others and medium disclosure to others in the social environment. Individuals who are poorly adjusted . . . are characterized by either high or low self-disclosure to virtually everyone in the social environment. (p. 73).[13]

Like so many other acts that affect our lives, self-disclosure is most beneficial when practiced in moderation.

Self-monitoring: Showing yourself

Regardless of how you practice self-disclosure, there is little doubt that social interaction involves self-management. Sociologist Ervin Goffman likens the participants in social interaction to actors trying to maintain behavior appropriate to the situation at hand. It is a form of constant **self-monitoring** aimed at presenting yourself in the best possible light. People do this because of their need to be approved and liked, even if they practice very little

---

[5]Jourard Lasakow, 1958; Jourard, 1964. [6]West & Zingle, 1969; Vondracek & Vondracek, 1971. [7]Pederson & Breglio, 1968. [8]Lewin, 1940. [9]Chittick & Himmelstein, 1967; Ehrlich & Graeven, 1971. [10]Drag, 1969; Jourard & Friedman, 1970. [11]Bennett, 1967. [12]Altman & Taylor, 1973. [13]Cozby, 1973.

self-disclosure. For example, if you want to be perceived as the strong-and-silent type of person, you probably have in your repertoire many facial expressions and body postures to present yourself successfully.[14] Psychologist Mark Snyder has developed an interesting measuring device for social presentation.[15] His scale, which has been used for self-presentation in social situations, is shown in Table 2-1.

TABLE 2-1 Three factors of self-monitoring

Extroversion
  I feel a bit awkward in company and do not show up quite as well as I should. (R)
  At a party I let others keep the jokes and stories going. (R)
  In a group of people I am rarely the center of attention. (R)
  I am not particularly good at making other people like me. (R)
  I have never been good at games like charades or improvisational acting. (R)
  I have trouble changing my behavior to suit different people and different situations. (R)

Other-Directedness
  In different situations and with different people, I often act like very different persons.
  In order to get along and be liked, I tend to be what people expect me to be rather than anything else.
  I'm not always the person I appear to be.
  I guess I put on a show to impress or entertain people.
  Even if I am not enjoying myself, I often pretend to be having a good time.
  I may deceive people by being friendly when I really dislike them.
  I would not change my opinions (or the way I do things) in order to please someone else or win their favor. (R)
  I feel a bit awkward in company and do not show up quite as well as I should. (R)
  When I am uncertain how to act in social situations, I look to the behavior of others for cues.
  My behavior is usually an expression of my true inner feelings, attitudes and beliefs. (R)
  At parties and social gatherings, I do not attempt to do or say things that others will like. (R)

Acting
  I would probably make a good actor.
  I have considered being an entertainer.
  I have never been good at games like charades or improvisational acting. (R)
  I can make impromptu speeches on topics about which I have almost no information.
  I can look anyone in the eye and tell a lie with a straight face (if for a right end).

Scoring: Answer each item as either true or false for you. If the item has an (R) by it, give yourself 1 point for a false answer. For all other items, give yourself 1 point for each true answer. The higher your score, the higher your social sensitivity and ability to look good to others.

Source: Snyder, 1974; Briggs, Cheek, & Buss, 1980.

In studying self-monitoring, psychologists have used a method known as factor analysis to divide the Self-Monitoring Scale into different dimensions.[16] Using these methods, they have found that people monitor themselves in at least three different ways. One type of self-monitoring is *acting,* such as liking to speak and entertain. Another is *extroversion,* such as enjoying parties and being with others. The final type is *other-directedness,* a willingness to change behavior in order to suit others. The different dimensions of self-monitoring have been shown to relate to important social behaviors among college students. For example, those who scored high on extroversion also tended to score high on measures of sociability and low on measures of

[14]GOFFMAN, 1967. [15]SNYDER, 1974. [16]GABRENYA & ARKIN, 1980.

shyness. Scoring high on other-directedness was associated with shyness and low self-esteem.[17]

Stability: How we see ourselves and others

Did you ever have plans to meet others for the first time and know that you would have to spend a lot of time with them? When you have a blind date, or when a distant relative whom you have never seen announces that he or she will be visiting for a few days, you might be eager to learn what the person is like. Are they kind, honest, trustworthy, interesting, amusing? Personality traits provide us with convenient ways of organizing information about others, for describing how they have behaved in the past, and for making predictions about how they will act in the future.[18]

Much of the history of the study of personality has been devoted to creating categories of traits, developing methods for measuring them, and finding out how groups of traits cluster together. Indeed, the very concept of personality assumes that there are characteristics of persons which are stable over time. If Martha is an aggressive person, we expect her to be aggressive in many different situations. Although we commonly use trait names to describe other people, the evidence that personality characteristics are stable is itself a little shaky. For example, psychologist Walter Mischel has shown that personality traits are simply not good predictors of how people will behave in particular situations.[19] In a well-argued attack on trait theorists, Mischel demonstrated that knowing how someone scores on measures of psychological traits rarely gives better than chance insight about how the person will act in any situation. Thus, trait theorists were forced to retreat and rethink their trade.

Another problem for traditional trait theories is research on a relatively new approach to personality and social psychology known as attribution theory. If you recall, we dealt with this theory in Chapter 1. Thus, some of what follows may be slightly repetitious. There is, however, a different emphasis in this chapter. Originally, attribution theory only considered how people make judgments about others. However, there has been an enormous expansion of interest in attribution. Research in this area now covers all aspects of how people attempt to understand the causes of events in their lives including their "selfs."

The ideas behind attribution theory were first presented by Fritz Heider[20] in the mid-nineteen forties but were not made popular until the late sixties.[21] Psychologist Harold Kelley suggested that possible causes of events in a person's environment could be caused by one of three potential sources: persons, entities (things of some aspect of the environment), and times (situations).

To determine which (or which combination) of these sources has caused the event, an observer uses three criteria: distinctiveness, consensus, and consistency (see also Chapter 1, "Attribution"). For example, if we were looking for an explanation of why John gobbled down the food at the Chinese restaurant, we would need to ask whether it had something to do with the

SELF-PERCEPTION

[17]BRIGGS, CHEEK, & BUSS, 1980. [18]KELLEY, 1967; JONES & NISBETT, 1971. [19]MISCHEL, 1968, 1979. [20]HEIDER, 1944; 1958. [21]JONES & DAVIS, 1965; KELLEY, 1967.

situation that one evening (distinctiveness), whether others in the same situation also enjoyed the food (consensus), or whether John would respond the same way if exposed repeatedly to the same situation (consistency).

Attribution theory is less concerned with predicting behavior in particular situations than it is with studying how individuals make judgments about the causes of behavior. Some researchers have suggested that the selection of a trait or a situational explanation for behavior will depend on the role played by the person offering the judgment. When we are *observers* and are making judgments about other people, we tend to use dispositional or trait explanations. We do not use trait explanations to explain our own behavior, however. When we are the *actors* in a situation, we see our own behavior in terms of the situation. In other words, we describe others in terms of traits, but we explain our own behavior in terms of situations.

Why would there be a difference between the attributions of actors and observers? Psychologists Edward Jones and Robert Nisbett suggest that we know more about ourselves than we know about others. By searching our memory, we can remember behaving in many different situations. When we make judgments about others, however, we do not have as much information about how situations caused them to act differently.[22]

Another potential explanation is that our eyes, ears, and other sensory apparatus are focused on the environment rather than on the self. We observe the environment, while the observers observe us. Psychologist Michael Storms used videotapes to demonstrate that, when the actor is shown a situation from the vantage point of the observer (or when we are shown videotapes of ourselves), she/he will describe behavior in terms of traits. Similarly, when the observer is shown the situation from the vantage point of the actor, situational attributions are more likely.[23]

Attribution theorists are not concerned with the inadequacy of traditional trait tests for predicting behavior. For them, traits are only important because people use them to describe behavior of others. Attribution research attempts to answer the question "Why do people believe that personality is stable?" Extensive studies have demonstrated that laypeople as well as experienced clinical psychologists tend to favor explaining behavior in terms of enduring dispositions (traits) instead of in terms of the situation.[24] Psychologist Lee Ross has labeled the persistent tendency to overestimate the importance of traits and underestimate the importance of situations the **fundamental attribution error**.[25] For example, the logic of the intuitive psychologist is somewhat backward. Instead of inferring the specific (how someone will behave in a particular situation) from the general (trait), the common response is to do the opposite: general characteristics (traits) are inferred from specific fragmented bits of information obtained in a limited sample of situations.[26]

Some studies suggest that the manner in which we make judgments about others may not be that strongly associated with past experiences. For example, psychologist Warren Norman studied peer ratings given by different groups of men. One group had lived together in the same fraternity for three

[22]JONES & NISBETT, 1971. [23]STORMS, 1973. [24]TVERKSY & KAHNEMAN, 1980; HARARI & HOSEY, 1979. [25]ROSS, 1977. [26]NISBETT & BORGIDA, 1975; BORGIDA & NISBETT, 1977.

years, while another group was less closely associated. Although the two groups had very different amounts of intimate contact, they used highly similar dimensions to make judgments about one another.[27]

Interestingly, these same dimensions of judgment emerged in another study in which subjects rated complete strangers.[28] These studies demonstrate that we use the same dimensions to rate others—whether or not we know the people we are evaluating. Thus, trait ratings may tell us more about the raters than about the people they are rating. We do not know whether traits help us understand behavior. We are certain, however, that observers will continue to perceive information in a way that will support trait interpretations. Repeated experiments have consistently demonstrated that people put too much faith in the value of personality traits, at the expense of situational factors.[29]

Internality/externality: Control and helplessness

When would you feel more relaxed, driving a motorcycle or riding as a passenger in the back? Most people report that they would rather be the driver because they have more control over the situation. In fact, personal control is among the most important influences on social behavior.

Individuals differ in the degree to which they believe they have control over important events in their lives. Table 2-2 shows a locus of control scale similar to one commonly used to separate those who believe they have control from those who believe important events in their lives are beyond their personal control. Those who think there is a strong connection between what they do and what happens to them are usually labeled *internals*, whereas those who believe that what happens to them is primarily the result of luck or chance are called *externals*.[30] Many studies have shown that those who believe that they

Driving a motorcycle is less fear-arousing than being a passenger for most people. The driver has a greater feeling of personal control than the passenger.

[27]NORMAN, 1963. [28]PASSINI & NORMAN, 1966. [29]JONES, 1979. [30]ROTTER, 1966.

have no control over what happens to them experience depression, frequent illness, and anger.

TABLE 2-2 Locus of control scale
To find out whether you are inclined toward internal or external control, simply add your choices on each side (left = internal, right = external).

I more strongly believe that:	or
Promotions are earned through hard work and persistence.	Making a lot of money is largely a matter of getting the right breaks.
In my experience I have noticed that there is usually a direct connection between how hard I study and the grades I get.	Many times the reactions of teachers seem haphazard to me.
The number of divorces indicates that more and more people are not trying to make their marriages work.	Marriage is largely a gamble.
When I am right I can convince others.	It is silly to think that one can really change another person's basic attitudes.
In our society a man's future earning power is dependent upon his ability.	Getting promoted is really a matter of being a little luckier than the next guy.
If one knows how to deal with people they are really quite easily led.	I have little influence over the way other people behave.
In my case the grades I make are the results of my own efforts; luck has little or nothing to do with it.	Sometimes I feel that I have little to do with the grades I get.
People like me can change the course of world affairs if we make ourselves heard.	It is only wishful thinking to believe that one can really influence what happens in society at large.
I am the master of my fate.	A great deal that happens to me is probably a matter of chance.
Getting along with people is a skill that must be practiced.	It is almost impossible to figure out how to please some people.

Source: Rotter, 1971. Reprinted with permission of the author. These items were taken from an earlier, discarded form of the test and are not included in currently used measures.

Many experimental studies actually take control away from subjects in order to determine how lack of personal control affects behavior. Some of the most dramatic experiments have been done by psychologist Martin Seligman. In these experiments, healthy dogs were placed in a box and forced to wait on an electrified floor while they received electric shocks on a random schedule. Later, the situation was changed and the dogs were allowed to escape the shock by jumping over a small hurdle. Normally, dogs can easily learn how to make this escape in a very short time. Dogs that were exposed to random shock over which they had no personal control, however, seemed unable to learn how to get away. Instead, they just lay on the shock grid and took the punishment.[32]

Many experiments with humans have produced similar results. Subjects who have been put in situations over which they have no control seem unable to learn new responses. For example, suppose that you are in an experiment

[31]TAYLOR, 1979. [32]SELIGMAN, 1975.

in which you are attempting to solve a series of hard problems. The only information you have about whether or not you are doing the task correctly comes from feedback you get from the experimenter. The experimenter, however, does not really pay attention to what you are doing. Instead, he or she randomly tells you that you are solving the problem correctly or incorrectly. Experiments have shown that this sort of treatment results in (1) inability to perform well on new problems, (2) lack of motivation to continue responding, and (3) depression. This syndrome has come to be known as **learned helplessness.**

Through a variety of experiences in which our behavior does not give us control over the environment, we may actually learn to be helpless. In other words, we have learned not to attempt to solve problems. In many cases, this can lead to disinterest in life and depression.[33]

Once people come to think of themselves as ineffective, what can be done to get them going again? Some experiments suggest that helping people gain a feeling of control over their environment can give them a great boost. For example, psychologists Judith Rodin and Ellen Langer found that elderly patients in nursing homes often felt depressed and had lost interest in living. To combat this effect, the two psychologists intervened by attempting to give the patients more control over their lives. This was done by giving the patients more say in decisions about their activities and by making each patient responsible for the care of a plant. A year later, there were fewer deaths among the patients who had gained some control over their environments in comparison to a control group of patients who lived in the same home but on a different floor.[34]

The way people assign responsibility for their own successes and failures also has important influences on their future successes and failures. In Chapter 1 we discussed psychologist Bernard Weiner's work on attributions of responsibility for success and failure. Weiner and his associates have discovered that children and adults will attribute their successes and failures to one of four causes: ability, effort, task difficulty, and luck. Ability and effort are internal causes while task difficulty and luck are external causes. The four causes of success and failure can also be thought of as either stable (ability and task difficulty) or unstable/changeable (effort, luck).[35] If you need to refresh your memory about these causes of success and failure, you might check back to Figure 1-12 in Chapter 1.

Weiner and his associates have also found that children who succeed in school tend to attribute their successes to ability and their failures to effort. This tendency ensures continued motivation because ability is internal and stable and effort is internal but unstable. When children like these fail, they might think "I am smart, but I failed because I didn't try hard enough." On the next occasion, they might try harder. On the other hand, children who tend to fail in school attribute their successes to external unstable sources, such as luck. If luck is the only reason you succeed, why try? Perhaps the most damning perception of low-achievement children is that they attribute their failures to an *internal* stable source—ability. They usually report that they

[33]Seligman, 1975; Koller & Kaplan, 1978. [34]Rodin & Langer, 1977. [35]Weiner, Frieze, Kukla, Reed, Rest, & Rosenbaum, 1971.

Control extends life span. Making patients in nursing homes responsible for simple tasks such as caring for a plant, may provide a great morale boost, even prolong their lives.

failed because they are "dumb." Since ability is part of you and unchangeable, why try in the future?

One way of helping children achieve more is to rearrange their attribution patterns. For example, people will feel more pride and satisfaction when they attribute their successes to an internal rather than an external cause.[36] When teachers believe some children are very bright, they teach them the attribution patterns of more successful children. For example, when these children succeed, their teachers may communicate "Of course you did well, because you're smart" (internal stable). When they fail, the teacher might communicate "I know you're smart; you failed because you didn't try" (internal unstable). Thus, it was no surprise to Weiner and his associates when a study in the San Francisco school district demonstrated that simply telling teachers that some children were "late bloomers" served to increase the test scores of these children. Labeling the children stimulated the teachers to communicate the attribution pattern of the more successful children.[37]

Problems begin, however, if you *consistently* attribute success or failure to any of the just-named factors or a combination thereof. For example, psychologist John Nicholls has shown that in their perception some people consistently use the process of "self-defense," whereas others use the process "self-denigration."[38] If you are self-defensive, you consistently attribute your success to ability and/or effort and your failure to lack of effort and/or bad

[36]Weiner, 1979. [37]Rosenthal & Jacobson, 1968. [38]Nicholls, 1975.

luck. If you are self-denigratory, you consistently attribute success to good luck and/or ease of task and failure to lack of ability. The net result of such perceptions is that you lock yourself into a position that leaves you with little, if any, maneuverability. Since your inflexible perception of the situation may have been off-base to begin with, you are obviously headed for trouble. For example, if you are self-defensive, how would you feel if it begins to dawn on you that your success so far has been due merely to good luck but your failure has been primarily due to lack of ability?

Self-schemata: Your personal script

Every day, you are bombarded with a massive amount of information. There is so much coming at you that you may be unable to deal with it all. As a way of coping with all this information, you must be selective in what you notice, learn, or remember about any particular situation. Thus, a whole new area known as *cognitive science* has been developed to study the way people organize and encode information. The structures people use to encode information are called *frames*,[39] *scripts*,[40] or *schemata*.[41]

One important type of information is information about yourself. In fact, much of what you derive from your interactions with others is information you use to form impressions of yourself. For example, if someone is nasty to you, or if you get a good grade on an exam, you might come to examine your own view of yourself.[42] The abundant information about self can be organized using **self-schemata.** Psychologist Hazel Markus defined self-schemata as "cognitive generalizations about the self, derived from past experience, that organize and guide the procession of self-related information contained in the individual's social experiences."[43]

A self-schema might be based on specific events. For example, you might think to yourself "I hesitated before speaking in yesterday's discussion because I wasn't sure I was right, only to hear someone else make the same point."

In other cases, the self-schema might be more general and derived from your repeated exposure to other people (for example, "I am very talkative in groups of three or four but shy in large gatherings"). Experiments have shown that such self-schemata help us organize, summarize, and explain our own behavior. For example, if you think of yourself as "independent," you will use a variety of adjectives associated with independence to describe yourself. These same adjectives will not be chosen as self-descriptive by people who do not see themselves as independent.

Some experiments have shown that self-schemata determine what we remember. For example, psychologist Deborah Kendzierski had subjects rate 47 adjectives that were divided into four groups. The task for the subjects differed for the various groups of adjectives. For one group, the subjects were only required to rate a structural characteristic of the word, such as whether or not it was printed in big letters. For other groups, the task was to rate whether the word fit correctly into a sentence or whether it was a synonym for

---

[39]MINSKY, 1975. [40]ABELSON, 1975. [41]BOBROW & NORMAN, 1975. [42]BEM, 1972. [43]MARKUS, 1977. THE FOLLOWING EXAMPLES ARE ALSO FROM MARKUS, 1977.

another adjective. For the critical group, the subjects had to say whether or not adjectives described a quality of themselves. When later asked to recall the adjectives, the subjects remembered more words from the list from which they were asked to make self-referent judgments.[44] In another experiment, subjects were asked to decide whether a group of trait names described either themselves or other people. Traits that had been chosen as self-referent were better remembered than those used to describe other people.[45]

Although most studies on self-schemata are concerned with our perception of personal traits, this framework has also been useful in showing how we develop and defend social attitudes. Psychologists Charles Judd and James Kulik had college students rate the degree to which they agreed or disagreed with 54 attitude statements on the Equal Rights Amendment, capital punishment, and majority rule in South Africa. The next day the students were asked to recall the items they had rated the day before. Recall was better for items the students either strongly agreed with or strongly disagreed with. Careful analysis demonstrated that these results were not due to unique characteristics of either the subjects or the items.[46] These findings imply that what you already think will determine what you remember about the questions you have been asked.

A major problem with research on self-schemata is that the concept of "self" is hard to define and measure. One way of getting at how people perceive themselves is to study how long it takes them to decide whether or not some trait is characteristic of themselves. Psychologists Hazel Markus, Ruth Hamill, and Jeanne Smith employed a computer to help them time these judgments, using standard psychological measures to identify self-schemata central in the way a person views himself or herself. In one experiment, for instance, two groups of subjects were identified. For one group, masculinity was a very important personal characteristic. For the other group, being masculine or feminine was not particularly important. Both groups were placed at a computer terminal as a series of adjectives flashed on the screen. The subjects were asked to hit a button on the computer terminal saying either "me" or "not me" each time an adjective was presented. Subjects with "masculine" schemata hit the "me" key significantly faster to words reflecting concepts such as "aggressive" or "athletic" and significantly slower to words traditionally associated with femininity. The quick response may reflect the amount of time the person has already spent thinking about that trait. If you think of yourself as athletic, you may have already spent much time sifting through information about what it is like to be athletic, and you have stored this information in an often-consulted part of your mind.

One of the most important implications of self-schemata is that people do not attend to, or remember, what is inconsistent with their self-schemata. Thus, they can become extremely resistant to attempts to change the way they think of themselves. According to Markus and her University of Michigan colleagues, "An obese person who finds it difficult to slim down must work on shedding his 'fat schema' as well as pounds and inches." Included in this fat schema may be such notions as "exercise is damaging," "big meals are important to health," and the like.[47]

[44]KENDZIERSKI, 1980. [45]LORD, 1980. [46]JUDD & KULIK, 1980. [47]MARKUS, HAMILL, & SMITH, 1980.

In experiments on self-schemata, adjectives flash on the screen of a computer terminal. Response time for subjects hitting keys for *me* and *not me* are automatically recorded.

SELF-PREDICTION

Personality prediction: A low score for tradition

Do you need to watch what you say in front of psychologists because they will know too well what you are going to do next? One of the pervasive myths in the field of psychology is that someone else can predict your behavior on the basis of clues you are unaware of yourself. Over the course of many years, studies have shown that clinical psychologists, with or without the benefit of psychological tests, possess no special magic for predicting your future behavior.[48]

Losing weight may require shedding the fat schema as well as pounds and inches.

[48]WIGGINS, 1973.

Some studies even show that training in clinical psychology may result in *less* accurate prediction of future behavior. According to psychologist Walter Mischel,

> Clinicians, like other scientists and indeed like the ordinary lay person, easily tend to infer, generalize, and predict too much while observing too little. Moreover, the judgments of clinicians—like everyone else's judgments—are subject to certain systematic biases that can produce serious distortions and oversimplifications in inferences and predictions. [p. 740].[49]

One of the major reasons why clinicians are so poor at predicting behavior is that they tend to make their predictions on the basis of personality characteristics. Psychological tests, for example, usually attempt to determine which "traits" characterize people. These trait explanations ignore what we all know too well—namely, that we do not always behave the same. If you are characterized by the trait "shy," it would be assumed that you are shy in all situations. Yet you may be shy in some situations and not shy at all in others.

As we mentioned earlier in the chapter, psychologist Lee Ross has labeled this tendency to underestimate the importance on situations in predicting behavior the fundamental attribution error.[50] Some psychologists have recommended that, instead of attempting to predict behavior on the basis of traits, we instead attempt to predict all behavior on the basis of situations.[51] When considering the question "Will John work hard in school?" trait-oriented psychologists would want to know about John's own characteristics. How high does he score on scales that measure need for achievement, on motivation, or on other traits related to his schoolwork? In contrast, situation-oriented psychologists would want to measure characteristics of John's school environment: What is the psychosocial climate? Is John's studying reinforced? and similar questions.

To a growing number of psychologists, whether traits or situations are more important in determining behavior is a "pseudo" question.[52] It is meaningless to ask whether trait or situation is more important in explaining behavior when it is clear that personal characteristics and the situation are both important. This position, a compromise between trait and situational approaches to personality assessment, acknowledges the importance of personality characteristics as well as the role of situations.[53] The "interactionists" support their position by reporting the degree to which behavior is explained by person, by situation, and by the **interaction** between person and situation.

You might think of this by drawing a pie and dividing it to represent all the different influences upon human behavior. Figure 2-1 shows the pie. One slice represents the proportion of the variation that is attributable to personality traits. Another slice represents the proportion of the variation caused by situational influences. A third slice is for the interaction between situational influences and dispositional or trait influences. The interaction is due to unique combinations of traits and situations. For example, an interaction might describe how Bill reacts to stress. This is different from characteristics of Bill (in all situations) or the effects of stress upon other people.

[49]Mischel, 1979. [50]Ross, 1977. [51]Moos, 1973. [52]Endler, 1973. [53]Endler & Hunt, 1968; Endler, 1973; Endler & Magnussen, 1976; Magnussen & Endler, 1977.

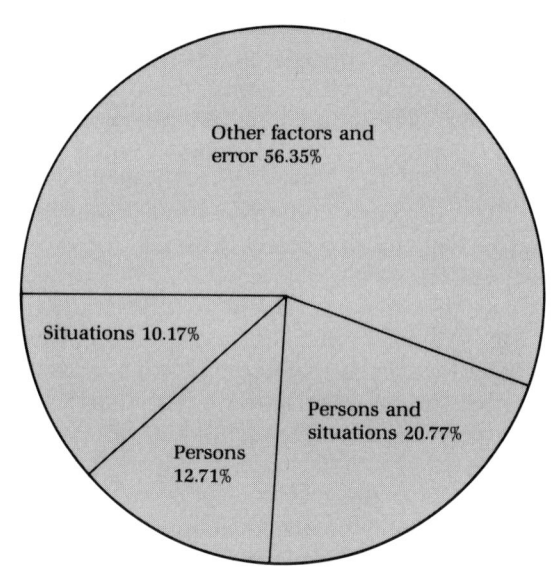

Figure 2-1.
Factors influencing behavior. This "pie" is divided according to the proportion of variation in behavior accounted for by trait, situation, and the interaction between trait and situation. The interaction is first among the three sources of influence. Unexplained, or error, variance is much larger than any other factor, however. *Source:* Bowers, 1973.

After reviewing many studies on the influences of person and situation, psychologists, Irwin Sarason, Ron Smith, and Ed Diener concluded that none of the three sources accounted for an impressive share of the variation when compared to the amount of variation left unexplained. Although the interaction is a slightly better predictor than either trait or situation, it is only slightly better.[54] Thus, the need was still present for measurement methods that could be used to predict more of the people more of the time.

Template matching: Fitting your mold

By 1979, many psychologists were convinced that the interaction between person and situation best predicts behavior.[55] Finding exact person times situation interactions was difficult, however. One important study demonstrated that some individuals may be highly consistent in some personality characteristics yet highly inconsistent in others. This is a radical departure from traditional trait approaches to personality, which assume that all traits characterize all people. Instead, investigators proposed that some traits characterize some people and other traits characterize other people. Some people may not be characterized by any traits at all.

Psychologists Daryl Bem and Andrea Allen demonstrated this effect by asking college students to rate whether their behavior would be consistent or inconsistent across different situations. These ratings were made for different

[54]SARASON, SMITH, & DIENER, 1975. [55]BEM & ALLEN, 1974; ENDLER & MAGNUSSEN, 1976; MAGNUSSEN & ENDLER, 1977.

traits, such as friendliness and conscientiousness. They found that students who identified themselves as consistently friendly did indeed appear to be friendly in a variety of situations. In contrast, those who rated themselves as inconsistently friendly were found to be friendly in some situations but unfriendly in others. Thus, the trait "friendliness" does not characterize all people. Some people are consistent on another trait, such as conscientiousness. An even more exciting aspect of this finding is that the students could predict their own consistencies and inconsistencies very well—fancy testing devices were not needed!

This insight called for new measurement methods that would lead to more accurate predictions of behavior. Recently, Daryl Bem and David Funder have introduced a descriptive system that can be used to take advantage of people's ability to predict their own behavior in particular situations. They call their approach the **template-matching technique**, proposing that "situations be characterized as sets of template-behavior pairs, each template being a personality description of an idealized type of person expected to behave in a specified way in that setting." The system attempts to match personality to a specific template of behavior. To employ the technique, you must specify how a person would behave in a certain situation without any information about the person. For example, consider how to answer the question "Should Cathie watch the Super Bowl?" With the template-matching technique, you would first be asked to make this judgment as though you knew nothing at all about Cathie. Perhaps the best way to guide Cathie would be to describe the Super Bowl in terms of how several hypothetical people might react to it. People who are squeamish may enjoy the game but may be disturbed by the violence. Or people who have a favorite football team may not like it because their team is not playing. Now Cathie can predict her own reaction to the game by matching her characteristics with the set of "templates" that describe how others react to the situation. The probability that a given person will behave in a given way in a situation, according to Bem and Funder, is a function of the match between his or her characteristics and a template. For example, if Cathie's personality and attitudinal characteristics matched the template for those who hate football games, she might be best advised to avoid watching the Super Bowl.[56]

The difficulty with a technology of person/situation interactions is that there are so many potential combinations of persons and situations. Bem and Funder were able to demonstrate that they could predict behavior very well in three given situations, yet the number of potential person/situation combinations literally staggers the mind.[57] Nevertheless, the template-matching approach represents a rebirth in trust for self-reports. People are actually very good at predicting their own behavior if they are asked the right questions.

Self-efficacy: Knowing you can

Suppose your doctor tells you that you can expect to be in better health if you exercise more. Will this mean that you will be able to exercise more? For many people, just knowing that something is good for them is not enough to bring

[56]BEM & FUNDER, 1978. [57]CRONBACH, 1975.

about a change in behavior. Beyond knowing that you should do something, you need to know that you *can* do it. This is what psychologist Albert Bandura calls **self-efficacy**.[58]

According to self-efficacy theory, knowing that you *should* exercise is not as helpful in maintaining an exercise program as knowing that you *can.*

According to Bandura, people learn that they can do something from four main sources. The most effective way to learn that they can do something is through personal accomplishment. You will be less afraid to give a speech in front of others if you have already done it successfully. The best way to know you can do something is to have done it already. Another way people can learn is by watching others. This is not quite as effective, however. Similarly, they can be persuaded by others that they can do something, or they can be tricked into mislabeling their arousal so that they believe that they can do it. Nothing, however, substitutes for having done it yourself.

Bandura and some of his associates have shown that when people succeed at something they were formerly afraid to do, the fear goes away. For example, among four groups of people who were afraid of snakes, those who were guided though an experience in which they successfully interacted with the reptile eventually became least afraid. Among all four groups of subjects, the very best predictor of how close a person would come to the snake was that person's own prediction.[59]

The results of these and other studies suggest that you can be very good at predicting your own behavior. You can increase your accuracy by limiting your predictions to highly specific situations (such as "Would I like taking a course that involves a lot of math?"). Finally, you will be most accurate in predicting how you will do at things you have done before. Doing new things and succeeding at them (even under controlled conditions) will help you gain confidence that you can perform similar activities.

[58]Bandura, 1977a. [59]Bandura, Adams & Beyer, 1977.

Self-efficacy and fear of snakes. Knowing that you should not be afraid is not enough to bring about behavior change. Once convinced through experience that you *can* touch the snake, your fear may be considerably reduced.

SUMMARY HIGHLIGHTS

1. *Self* is among the most widely used terms in psychology. How you view your "self" might derive from information gained from your own experiences or might reflect the sum total of what others think of you.
2. *Self-disclosure* is information about yourself communicated to others. People differ in the amount of information they disclose. Women tend to disclose more personal information about themselves than men do, especially when they are talking to other women. Social adjustment seems related to being selective in sharing the details of your personal life with others.
3. People also differ in the way they present themselves to others, known as *self-monitoring:* by acting, by extroversion, or by other-directedness.
4. Personality psychologists have traditionally studied *traits*, or characteristics, of individuals that are stable over time. Social psychologists are more likely to focus on the effects of social *situations* upon behavior. Research on *attribution theory* suggests that people explain the behavior of others in terms of stable personality traits but their own behavior in terms of the situations that they encounter.
5. Some people believe that they have control over important events in their lives, while others believe these events are beyond personal control. These people differ in their perceived *locus of control*. Experimental studies often take personal control away from subjects by punishing and rewarding them on a random schedule. The result is *learned helplessness*—a state associated with inability to learn the solution to problems, low motivation, and depression.
6. Information about the self is organized according to a *self schema*. These

schemata are mental generalizations about the self gained from past experiences. Schemata are needed because most people are bombarded with so much self-relevant information that they cannot process it. The self-schema helps to organize responses to new information in a way consistent with past experiences.
7. Evidence from *template-matching* studies (in which subjects compare themselves to templates, that is, how others react to situations) suggests that people are very good at predicting their own behavior in highly specific situations.
8. The belief that you can perform required behavior is known as *self-efficacy*. Past successes in given situations are the best predictors for future performance of the behavior.

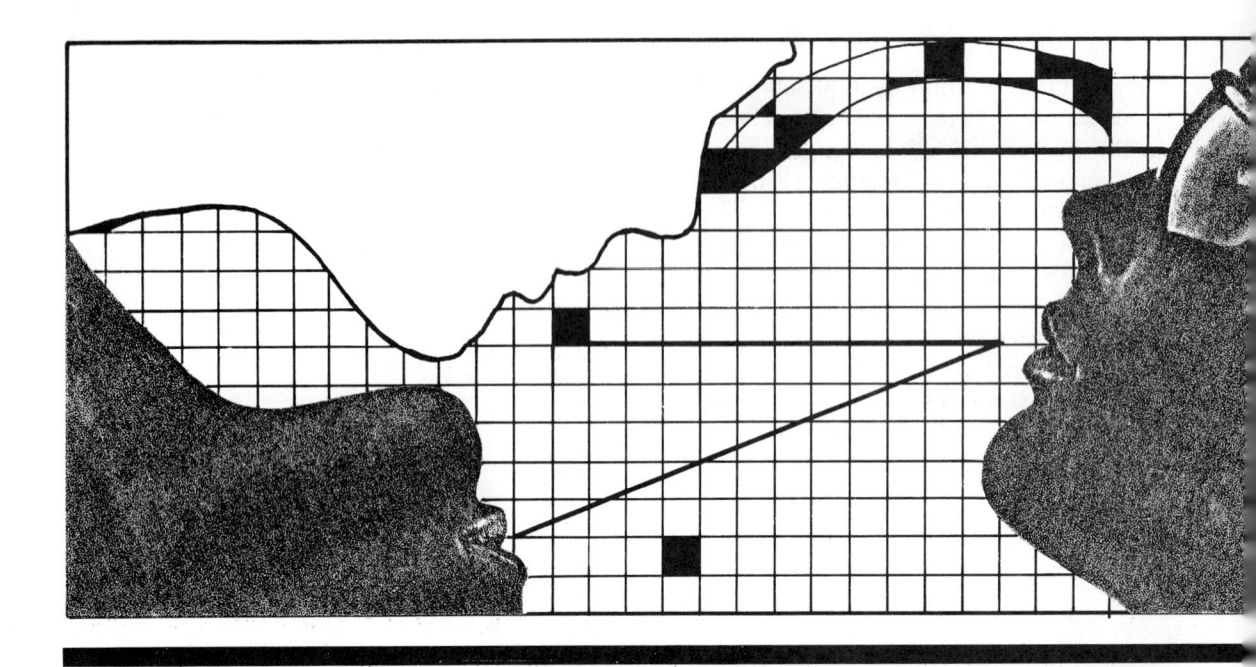

PART

SOCIAL

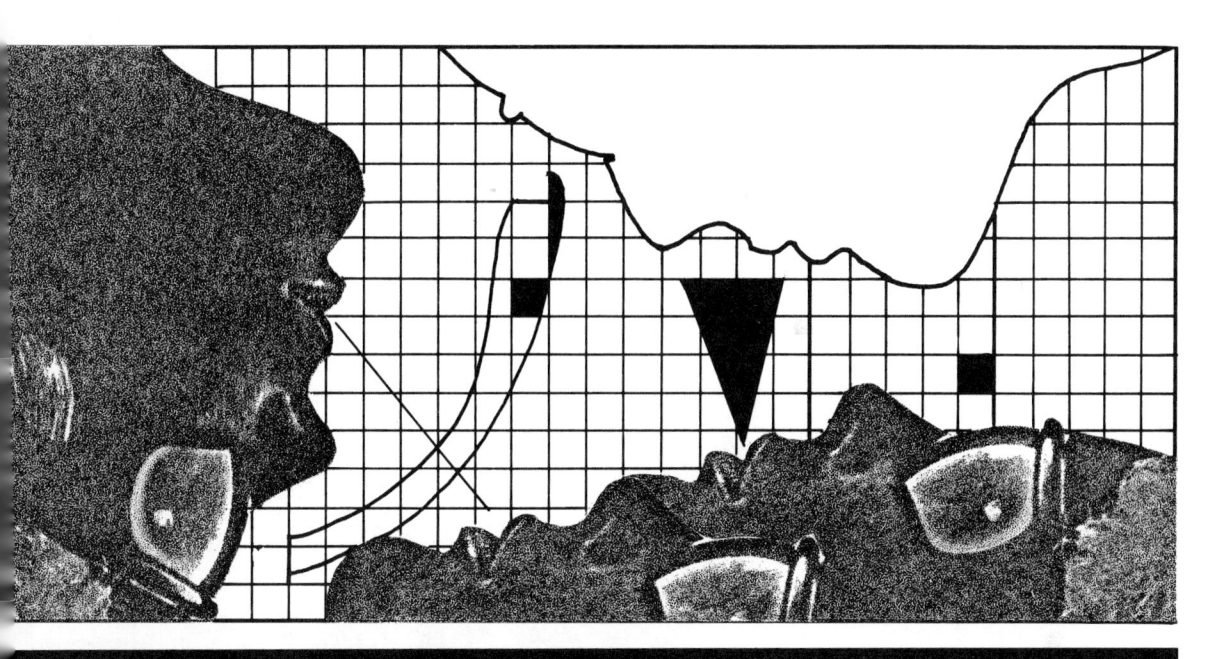

TWO

INFLUENCE

CHAPTER 3   CHANGING ATTITUDES

ATTITUDES AND PROPAGANDA
   Persuasion, American style

CHANGING ATTITUDES
   The first step: Arousal and attention
   The second step: Presentation of arguments

The third step: Knowing your audience
The fourth step: Gaining and maintaining credibility
The final step: Immunization against counterpropaganda

SUMMARY HIGHLIGHTS

ATTITUDES AND PROPAGANDA

Persuasion, American style

This chapter is a hybrid creation. At one time we doubted whether it was necessary to write it at all. When we finally decided that it should be written, it was hard to decide where it belonged. Even though the term **attitude** is frequently mentioned by psychologists, it is also an extremely ill-defined term. Some psychologists ignore the term altogether; other psychologists include in it just about every aspect of human behavior. Moreover, the idea of changing attitudes evokes the notion of *manipulation,* a term that has some very unpleasant connotations. To be labeled as a manipulator is not exactly a compliment. If you are perceived as manipulative, you are likely to encounter scorn and contempt (of course, if you are perceived as influential or persuasive, you earn mostly respect and admiration). In any event, we shall do our best to explain to you why we finally decided to combine the ambiguous (attitudes) with the obnoxious (manipulation) in one brief chapter.

We can make short shrift of the argument that manipulation is bad. At the risk of burdening you with what might seem to be a well-worn cliché, we shall flatly state that life is a continual process of manipulation. Parents do it. Children do it. Spouses do it. Friends do it. Bosses do it. Employees do it. In every type of human interaction—at work, at home, or at play—there is at least someone who (wittingly or unwittingly) manipulates someone else. In turn, the manipulated party can easily become the manipulator when the proper circumstances arise. To make you feel better, you can gild the lily by referring to the process as influencing, persuading, begging, cajoling, flattering, requesting, asking, demonstrating, or probing. In the final analysis, it all boils down to manipulation. Even if you honestly believe that you would never stoop so low as to manipulate others, the next two chapters should still be of value to you—the knowledge of how *others* manipulate can put you on guard.

The concept of attitude presents greater difficulty. The dictionary defines attitude as "a state of mind or conduct of a person regarding some matter."

This is precisely the rub. Is an attitude a state of mind, such as a cognitive structure in our heads? Or is it some conduct or behavior, or at least a predisposition to act in a given way? If it is both a state of mind and a form of conduct, as the dictionary suggests, then the assessment of attitudes would be an efficient and inexpensive way of predicting behavior. But if the two are not necessarily one and the same, what good does the study of attitude do to the process of understanding human behavior? Why study what a person *says* or *thinks* (attitude) if it has little or no relation to what that person *does* (behavior)?

Psychologists have addressed themselves at length to the problem of possible discrepancies between attitudes and behavior.[1] We shall accordingly examine this issue in the next chapter, since changing attitudes and/or behavior invariably involve some aspects of manipulation and power play. In the meantime, we proceed from the reasonable assumption that people who express strong attitudes are likely to act accordingly. There is, in fact, some (but by no means conclusive) evidence to support our assumption.[2] But, regardless of their predictive value, attitudes and opinions are existing phenomena and therefore deserve to be studied. Like the chapter that follows it, this chapter will describe an aspect of human manipulation by exploring attitudes in familiar contexts: propaganda, advertising, and public opinion.

The term **propaganda** is derived from the seventeenth-century Christian College of Propaganda, which trained priests in missionary work for the propagation of the Christian faith. Despite its illustrious origin, the term generally evokes visions of manipulation, conniving, and half-truths. Propagandists are aware of the negative connotations of the term, and even the most callous of them refer to their product as education. Once again, semantics seem to exercise undue control in this matter. *Any* attempt to influence the development of attitudes or to change them may properly be called propaganda. Education, though it sounds infinitely better, is regarded as just another form of propaganda in some quarters.

The basic function of propaganda is the activation of dormant attitudes in a certain direction, with the hope that these attitudes will ultimately convert into manifest behavior such as buying, voting, or choosing.[3] Advertising is probably the most blatant case in point. It is essentially an exercise in persuasion and attitude change, since the assessment and manipulation of attitudes toward certain products and services is the basis of every advertising campaign. Following the assessment of consumer attitudes and habits, these research findings are translated into policy decisions concerning the naming of products, their packaging and presentation in stores, and their advertising through mass media such as newspapers, magazines, radio, and television. In effect, without several decades of research in the social psychology of attitudes, there would be no contemporary legend of "Madison Avenue." At the same time, the very relationship between propaganda (a term infused with negative connotations) and advertising has frequently been cited by critics as evidence of unethical and manipulative aspects in current American advertising practices. The proponents of such practices, on the other hand, are

[1]Wicker, 1969, 1971; Ajzen & Fishbein, 1970; Fishbein, 1972. [2]Fendrich, 1967; Green, 1969. [3]Lazarsfeld, Berelson, & Gaudet, 1944.

generally quite willing to concede that the aim of advertising is to persuade the consumer. But they also see advertising as the American way, ultimately benefitting the consumer in better products.

CHANGING ATTITUDES

From here to the end of the chapter we will focus on five broad approaches for the effective achievement of attitude change in others: arousal and attention; presentation of arguments; knowing the audience; gaining and maintaining credibility; and immunization against counterpropaganda. The ordering of these approaches is quite arbitrary: You do not have to follow the listed sequence to achieve effective attitude change. You can employ these approaches in any order or manner you wish and still be an effective propagandist. Moreover, these five approaches by no means exhaust all the possibilities for achieving attitude change. Chapter 4, in slightly different contexts, will acquaint you with many additional ways and means to achieve changes in attitudes and behavior.

The first step: Arousal and attention

Do you know what Figure 3-1 means? It spells out a message: EAT JOE'S BEEFBURGER! You could not tell at first glance because it is printed backwards, as seen in a mirror. Even if you knew that, it would still be difficult to get the message because the letters are bunched together in an uncharacteristic fashion. If this is Joe's message to you, he certainly chose an awkward way to induce you to buy his product. But he did capture one essential ingredient in his attempt to persuade you—your attention.

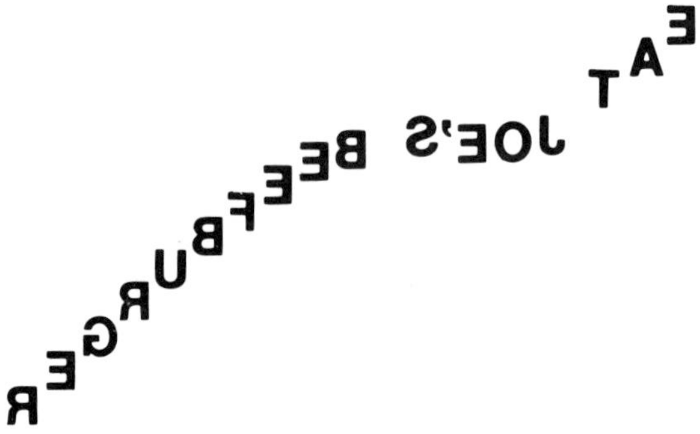

Figure 3-1. What does it say? Put the book to a mirror and see. It is an awkward way to get a message across—but it arouses curiosity and attention.

Shocking messages, large splashes of color, elaborate and unusual lettering, loud jingles, and catchy tunes are all part of the hard-sell approach aimed at capturing your attention. What worries the persuader, however, is that in the process of capturing your attention, you might inadvertently be distracted from the message itself. You may be paying too much attention to the format of the message rather than to its content.

To the delight of the hard-sell persuaders, evidence from earlier studies showed that distraction actually *increased* the persuasive impact of a message.[4] A possible explanation for this effect was audience sensitization, which

---

[4]McGuire & Papageorgis, 1962; Festinger & Maccoby, 1964.

assumed that arousal and distraction prevent the recipients of a persuasive message from forming counterarguments to its content. According to this logic, if you were hungry and faced with a straight message from Joe to buy his beefburger, you could eventually come up with several reasons for not buying: there are cheaper places nearby, eating now will spoil your appetite for later, beef has too much cholesterol, and so on. On the other hand, if Joe presented you with an arousing message that captured your attention, you would be so busy enjoying the catchy tune or unscrambling the shocking message (with hunger gnawing at you all the while) that you simply would have no time to formulate reasons for not buying.

Subsequent studies somewhat dampened the enthusiasm of the proponents of arousal and distraction. In one of these studies, subjects were presented with a persuasive message while being positively distracted (watching sexually provoking slides). Another group of subjects was neutrally distracted (watching slides of ordinary scenery). Still another group was negatively distracted (watching slides showing gory details of dismembered limbs). The positively and neutrally distracted subjects changed their attitudes in the direction of the persuasive message more often than did the negatively distracted subjects.[5] The implications for the persuader are clear: don't overdo! Some of your arousal techniques can be so unpleasantly distracting as to decrease the effect of your message.

Some persuaders discount the effect of attention altogether. Since attention is related to awareness and consciousness, these persuaders emphasize arousal and communication at a subconscious level instead. Probably the most controversial and frequently criticized method of manipulating buying behavior is the one commonly known as **motivational research** (MR). The basic assumption of psychologist Ernst Dichter, president of the Institute for Motivational Research, Inc., and his associates is that a person's buying behavior is based on deeply ingrained needs of which he or she may not even be aware. To find out the true nature of such needs, MR employs a variety of clinical tools, such as depth interviews, which involve intensive probing for hidden motives and attitudes of respondents and may take up to three hours. According to Dichter, "depth psychology teaches us that unconscious reasons are usually more basic and powerful than the conscious ones. Obviously, a direct question runs no chance of success in uncovering unconscious motivations."[6] One depth interview, for example, revealed that eating candy was associated with mastering disagreeable jobs; the advertising theme was accordingly changed from "smooth, rich, creamy-coated chocolate—everybody likes 'em" to "make the tough job easier—you deserve M & M candy," and sales promptly soared.[7] Another MR study solved the mystery of why a rationally designed advertising campaign to increase airplane ticket sales was failing miserably. The typical business executive who used that airline somehow did not respond positively to the information that its new jets would get him speedily to his destination. The reason for this became clear after MR stepped in to investigate. It seems that deep down these

[5]ZIMBARDO, EBBESEN, & FRASER, 1968. [6]DICHTER, 1943. [7]SMITH, 1953.

travelers felt guilty for leaving their homes and families for business (and perhaps for some fun, too). The advertising copy was subsequently changed so that it extolled the new jets which allowed the customers to make a quick *return* to their points of departure. Sales rose promptly.[8]

MR has been subjected to repeated criticisms on moral grounds. Its methods raise the frightening specter of intrusion into people's privacy by means of depth interviews that go too far in probing into minds.[9] In *The Feminine Mystique*, Betty Friedan painted an alarming picture of MR as the frontrunner of a gigantic plot by businessmen to keep the frustrated housewife (euphemistically referred to as "homemaker") imprisoned in her kitchen. For example, washing machines and electric ranges function best when operated with one or two control switches. Such simple operations are very frustrating to the college-educated woman, especially when she compares them to the complexity of her husband's work. The answer, according to MR, is to equip washers and ranges with complicated control panels not unlike those on airplanes. They may be useless, but they certainly give the frustrated housewife a sense of achievement in overcoming a "complicated" set of operations![10]

The furor and interest generated by MR has somewhat abated during recent years, particularly because of the popularity of experimental methods that involve observations in real-life situations (field experiments). For example, it is commonly believed that the introductory low-price offer by marketers is related to the human need for acquisition. From the marketer's point of view, the low-price offer works like this: the new product is offered for a low price for a short time; once the price is raised, profits will increase accordingly; the low price, however, will not only attract marginal buyers who will purchase other goods, but, it is hoped, many of them will learn to like the product enough so they will continue to purchase it even at the higher price. Unfortunately for the marketer, this may be a vain hope. In a series of field experiments matched pairs of discount houses arranged to sell the same product (mouthwash, toothpaste, aluminum foil, light bulbs, and cookies) at either a discounted price or at the regular price for a short period of time. The prices were then made the same for all stores. Without exception, subsequent sales were higher for products which had initially cost more! As can be seen in the case of aluminum foil sales (see Figure 3-2), during the first three weeks consumers bought more low-priced aluminum foils than high-priced ones, although the latter were steadily gaining in volume of sales. Once the price change was instituted, the expected drop in sales of the initially low-priced materialized.[11]

How can one explain the continuing increase in sales of the initially high-priced aluminum foil? According to the authors of the study, the most plausible explanation for this paradox can be derived from the theory of **cognitive dissonance**. According to this theory (which will be discussed in greater detail in Chapter 4), the more effort a person exerts to attain a goal, the more dissonance and discomfort is aroused if the goal turns out to be less valuable than expected. One way of eliminating such discomfort is to attach

[8]ZIMBARDO, EBBESEN, & MASLACH, 1977.   [9]PACKARD, 1957.   [10]FRIEDAN, 1963.   [11]DOOB, CARLSMITH, FREEDMAN, LANDAUER, & TOM, 1969.

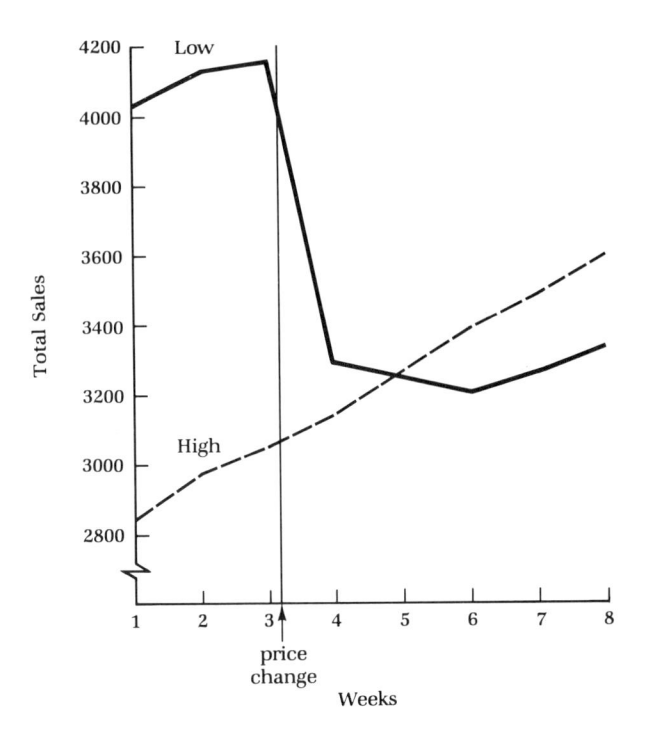

Figure 3-2.
The sale of low- and high-priced aluminum foil. After five weeks, customers are hooked into brand loyalty to the high-priced product (see text). *Source:* Doob et al., 1969.

greater value to the product, and to like it more. Thus, the consumer who initially bought the high-priced aluminum foil (thereby putting in more effort) reacted to the lower-priced aluminum foil (which caused the first brand to appear less valuable) by increasing his or her liking for the high-priced aluminum foil. This liking then developed into brand loyalty in the form of repeat purchases. The most interesting fact, of course, is that at no time were the consumers aware of the underlying reasons for their paradoxical behavior.

The same principle of cognitive dissonance also operates in the political arena. Each candidate for office undoubtedly would like to believe that he or she starts the election process by presenting exciting, new, and unique ideas to the voters, who then decide upon the candidate who offered the ideas most appealing to them. In reality, studies have shown that the process is reversed. People intend to vote for somebody to begin with; then, to justify this choice and avoid possible dissonance, they see that candidate as advocating positions more similar to theirs (and view the rejected candidate's view as more dissimilar to theirs), than is in fact the case.[12] This powerful assimilation effect of the views of the liked candidate continues to exist on all the important issues expounded by that candidate. Interestingly enough, the contrasted (to their own) views of the rejected, and increasingly disliked, candidate are justified and maintained by virtue of even just one single negative attribute, such as the candidate's manner of dressing, posture, or some other trivial excuse. All this goes on as people maintain their earnest belief that they are making wise and rational choices.

[12] KINDER, 1978.

While we are on the topic of awareness and attention, it might be worthwhile to mention **subliminal advertising**. This somewhat faddish concept emerged about 25 years ago and has not ceased to fascinate people, despite the fact that its effectiveness has never been fully demonstrated.[13] Briefly, subliminal (that is, below the threshold of conscious perceptual awareness) advertising attempts to induce attitude and behavior change by communicating with the consumer at a subconscious level. Subliminal advertising came to public attention in 1957 through reports showing that when the phrases "eat popcorn" and "drink Coca-Cola" were flashed at the speed of 1/3000 of a second on a movie screen before an unsuspecting audience, sales of the two products promptly increased. Although such findings may bring joy to the heart of many a manufacturer, subliminal advertising can produce marketing problems (in addition to legal problems brought up by people who resent the questionable ethics of the technique). For example, a group of college students serving as a control group was shown a 16-minute movie on the psychology of learning. A similar group of students, serving as the experimental group, saw the same movie with the word "beef" superimposed every 7 seconds at the speed of 1/200 per second. At the conclusion of the movie, both groups filled out questionnaires and checklists concerning their food preferences in sandwiches (tuna, hamburger, cheese, steak, or roast beef), and their hunger state (on a 5-point scale ranging from not at all hungry to very hungry). There was no difference between the groups in their expressed preference for a particular type of sandwich, but the students in the experimental group rated themselves higher on hunger than those in the control group.[14] These results are not too impressive. Moreover, for the purposes of national advertising, they are practically useless. A subliminal advertising campaign urging the consumer to "drink Coca-Cola" would perhaps increase your thirst, but would have no impact on whether you chose to drink Pepsi Cola, 7-Up, beer, juice, or plain water.

The second step: Presentation of arguments

What you say in your persuasive message and how you say it are critical elements in any study on attitude development and change. Broadly speaking, your arguments can take the form of either rational or emotional propaganda, or both. *Rational propaganda* attempts to persuade the audience that the advocated attitude is rational and logically sound. For example, certain toothpastes have been directly endorsed by dentists as successfully combatting tooth decay, providing an advantageous rational appeal for the advertising of those toothpaste manufacturers. Too often, however, these rational approaches assume questionable characteristics (see Figure 3-3). You are undoubtedly familiar with television commercial messages in which an imposing individual holding a leatherbound "scientific report" extolls the merits of his fortified product. The animated cartoons in which the advertised pill chases the competitor's pill through a maze of pipes purported to represent a stomach are just as pseudorational as the subsequent graphic representation that it arrived there first for quick relief.

[13]DeFleur & Petranoff, 1959; Goldiamond, 1966. [14]Byrne, 1959.

Retirement is not another word for nothing left to do.

That's why you need Direct Deposit. Because there's plenty you can do if you don't have to wait for your Social Security check—to receive it or deposit it.

When you sign up, payments go directly into your account so you're free to go directly to your favorite vacation spot. Retirement is a time to look forward to, especially when you have the convenience of Direct Deposit.

Ask for it where you have a checking or savings account.

DIRECT DEPOSIT
You'll never have to wait for your money.

Figure 3-3.
The rational propaganda approach in advertising. This ad appeals to reason.

Emotional propaganda tends to capitalize on evoked or existing feelings such as anxiety, shame, guilt, greed, and pride. Such feelings are powerful motivators. Because of their potency, they can be effectively employed to change both attitudes and behavior. We shall take a closer look at these forces in the next chapter. In advertising, of course, emotional themes are all too familiar (see Figure 3-4). Threats that failure to use a certain toothpaste will result in bad breath or that the use of a wrong brand of coffee will wreck marriages are often substituted for convincing, rational information.

Messages catering to prestige identifications with highly regarded reference groups or individuals ("for those who think young," or "Tracy Austin eats Knudsen's yogurt") are also loaded with emotional overtones. One note-

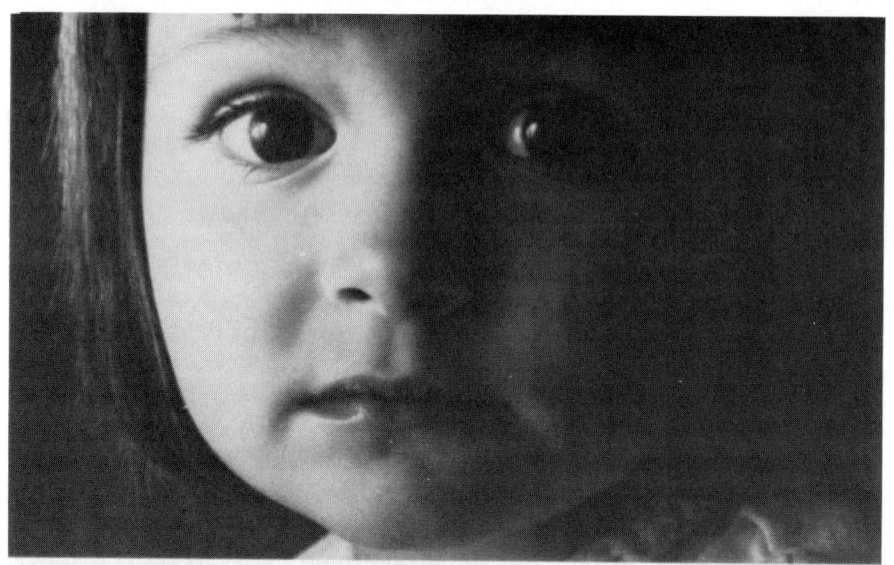

No one wakes up thinking, "Today I'm going to abuse my child."

Abuse is not something we think about. It's something we do. It runs against our nature, yet it comes naturally. It's a major epidemic and a contagious one. Abused children often become abusive parents. Abuse perpetuates abuse.

Child abuse is a major cause of death for children under two. Last year in America, an estimated one million children suffered physical, sexual or emotional abuse and neglect (many cases go unreported). At least 2,000 died needless, painful deaths. And if you think child abuse is confined to any particular race, religion, income group or social stratum, you're wrong. It's everybody's problem.

What's being done about prevention? Not enough. Preventive facilities are simply inadequate. Most social agencies deal with abusers and their victims after the damage has been done.

Child abuse doesn't have to happen. With your help, most abusers could be helped. Your community needs your aid in forming crisis centers, self-help programs for abusers, and other grass roots organizations. Please write for more information on child abuse and how you can help.

What will you do today that's more important?

Abused children are helpless. Unless you help.

Write: National Committee for Prevention of Child Abuse, Box 2866, Chicago, Ill. 60690

A Public Service of This Magazine & The Advertising Council

Figure 3-4. Compassion—a feeling that emotional propaganda can evoke.

worthy study in prestige identification described the personality stereotypes associated with five well-known automobiles. During 1956, and then again in 1957, college students were given a list of adjectives and asked to check those descriptions they thought were typical of Cadillac owners, Buick owners, and so forth. The students were obviously not representative of the total consumer population, but it was thought that even in such a limited population any variation in the image of the owner of a particular make of car (from 1956 to 1957) may have some bearing on the type of advertising that had been used in promoting that car. As expected, the Cadillac-Buick-Chevrolet comparison was strictly along class lines. In both 1956 and 1957, the Cadillac owner was perceived as rich, high-class, famous, important, fancy, proud, superior, and successful. The Buick owner was perceived as middle-class, brave, masculine, strong, modern, and pleasant. The Chevrolet owner was perceived as poor, low-class, ordinary, plain, simple, practical, common, average, and friendly. There was, however, a significant difference between the two years in the way the Plymouth owner was perceived. In 1956, the Plymouth owner had a stodgy image: quiet, careful, slow, silent, moral, fat, gentle, calm, sad, patient, honest, understanding, and content. To dispel this image, the Chrysler Corporation started a 1957 campaign which described the new Plymouth as "Three full years ahead—the only car that dares to break the time barrier! ... The fabulous new Fury '301' V-8 engine ... exhilarating sportscar handling ... dramatic Flight-Sweep Styling. The car you might have expected in 1960 is at your dealer's *now!*" The effect of such high-powered advertising was to completely shatter the old Plymouth image. The new image of the Plymouth owner consisted of six words: high-class, feminine, important, rich, different, and particular. The image of the 1957 Chevrolet, on the other hand, remained as nondescript as it had been in 1956, presumably because its advertising described it as "sweet, smooth, and sassy," without the additional description of a dramatically changed automobile.[15]

The argument between those who think that advertising is a form of education aimed at promoting a better lifestyle or a fraudulent process promulgated by greedy promoters will probably go on for many years to come. But even the most dyed-in-the-wool opponents of advertising would have to admit that appeals to public opinion are a legitimate avenue for educating the public. In fact, they will have to resort to such appeals if they ever hope to get across the message that advertising is corrupt. Surely, then, they could benefit from the knowledge of how to present their arguments in the most efficient and convincing manner.

Psychologists have devoted considerable time and effort to studying the process of public opinion and attitude change. More than 25 years ago, Carl Hovland and his students at Yale University pioneered such efforts.[16] Literally hundreds of studies have been published since then. It would be impossible, within the confines of this book, to describe the full scope of these studies. Instead, we are going to briefly list some advocated techniques for presenting

---

[15]WELLS, GOI, & SEADER, 1958. [16]HOVLAND, LUMSDAINE, & SHEFFIELD, 1949; HOVLAND & WEISS, 1951; HOVLAND & MANDELL, 1952; HOVLAND & SHERIF, 1952; HOVLAND, HARVEY, & SHERIF, 1957; HOVLAND, CAMPBELL, & BROCK, 1957; HOVLAND & PRITZKER, 1957.

effective, persuasive messages (without necessarily citing in detail the studies that led up to them). In most cases from here on, you may also find it useful to put yourself in the place of a persuader addressing a somewhat hostile audience (if the audience is extremely hostile, you will probably never get a chance to reach it, and thus no attitude change will occur; if the audience is extremely friendly, little if any persuasion is needed to effect attitude change). Also, when we talk of attitude change as a result of persuasive efforts, you should not expect total conversion to your point of view. To the best of our knowledge, none of the hundreds of studies on attitude change have ever reported such unqualified success. At best, they report a shift in the direction of the advocating message after it was presented. In our model, for example, you might wish to picture yourself as advocating a message to a high school audience. The gist of the message is that the minimum age for obtaining a driver's license should be raised to 18. You can expect the audience to be somewhat hostile to the idea, to say the least. If your presentation makes so much as a dent in the students' attitudes, consider yourself a successful persuader. The techniques listed here are aimed at making dents in attitudes, and the bigger the dent, the better. Most research studies suggest the following:

1. *Do not let facts speak for themselves.* Many persuaders are tempted to be so factual in their presentation as to exclude even a hint of what they are advocating. They assume that because the facts in their possession are so clear and unequivocal, there is no need to tell people what to think. Letting the facts speak for themselves also has the appearance of greater objectivity. The procedure is, nevertheless, ill advised. There is evidence that "objectivity" in persuasive communications does not lead to rationality and enlightenment, but to the hardening of existing attitudes.[17] Moreover, just because the facts speak clearly to you does not necessarily mean that they speak as clearly to your audience. Even if they do, there is always the risk that the conclusions drawn by your listeners will be different from those you advocate. State your conclusions explicitly and use the facts to buttress your arguments.
2. *Forewarn your listeners that you are attempting to change their attitude.* There is no need, for the sake of apparent objectivity, to hide the fact that you are embarking on a course of attitude change. Your listeners will find it out anyway. If you forewarn them explicitly,[18] there is evidence of subtle psychological forces at work. Your listeners want to avoid the possibility of appearing gullible (both to others and to themselves) should they be convinced by your persuasive message. By forewarning them, you allow them time for anticipatory adjustment to avoid a possible loss of self-esteem.[19] The only exception to this rule is if the issue at hand is clearly one of direct and immediate involvement for the listener. In such cases, the initial listener's antagonism may be so high that forewarning will immediately lead to the formation of counterarguments that will distract from the persuasive power of your message.[20]

[17]LORD, ROSS, & LEPPER, 1979. [18]MANN, PALEG, & HAWKINS, 1978. [19]COOPER & JONES, 1970. [20]PETTY & CACIOPPO, 1979.

3. *Use humor and satire in your major arguments, but sparingly and judiciously.* Do not let your dread of sounding dull tempt you to use humor and satire as a steady diet. For one thing, what is funny to you may not be funny to others. You may emerge with an even duller image than you feared. Opening jokes, however, or occasional forays into humor are not only permissible but advisable. Several studies in educational settings have clearly indicated that fast-paced and relevant humor facilitates the retention of information and is an important factor in persuasibility.[21] Remember, however, that humor and satire are no substitute for substantive arguments. Satire in particular can be an ineffective tool.[22] Cutting down people and issues rarely earns dividends.
4. *Gauge the timing of your major argument to audience interest.* Your major argument is the most precious weapon in your arsenal. Do not waste it. If initial audience interest does not seem to be high, present your major argument early. If initial audience interest seems to be high, save your major argument for the end. Initially disinterested listeners need something to arouse and maintain their interest. Initially interested listeners, upon hearing your major argument early in the presentation, will expect even more important arguments as you proceed. Since you will not be able to present them with any, they may become disappointed and lose interest. In any event, do not present your major arguments in the middle of a communication. Used this way, they are least remembered and have the least impact.[23]
5. *Begin by endorsing some audience view.* This technique, also known as flogging a dead horse, calls for the endorsement of some audience views not related to the issue being advocated. For example, in addressing high school students about increased age requirements for getting a driver's license (to which they are hostile), you may begin by coming out in favor of greater freedom in course selection (knowing that they are almost unanimously in favor of it). Many persuaders shy away from this approach, either because they think it is irrelevant to the topic at hand or because they are afraid that they will be perceived as trying to ingratiate themselves with their audience. But it works![24]
6. *Advocate extreme changes.* This statement needs to be qualified. If you advocate something totally distasteful to your audience, they may not even let you communicate with them in the first place. In fact, you may create a boomerang effect that will backfire into the direction opposite to that intended in your message.[25] If, however, the changes that you advocate are within reason, you are better off advocating extreme changes than moderate changes. The larger the change advocated, the greater the change produced.[26]
7. *Present two sides of the argument.* This does not necessarily mean that you should treat the two sides evenly. You are expected to allocate more weight, time, and effort to the side advocated by you. But to ignore totally the opposite side of the issue provides you at best with temporary attitude change, primarily in friendly audiences.[27] With more hostile

[21]KAPLAN & PASCOE, 1977; ZILLMAN, WILLIAMS, BRYANT, BOYNTON, & WOLF, 1980. [22]GRUNER, 1965, 1967. [23]HOVLAND, JANIS, & KELLEY, 1953; SHAW, 1961. [24]WEISS, 1957. [25]WHITTAKER, 1965. [26]HOVLAND & PRITZKER, 1957. [27]HOVLAND, LUMSDAINE, & SHEFFIELD, 1949.

audiences, one-sided presentations are rejected as arrogant and narrow minded.
8. *Use repetition in moderation.* Contrary to some popular views in advertising circles that extol the merits of repetitiveness, recent research on persuasibility shows that the benefits of repetition are modest and temporary. With increased repetitiveness, there is decreasing agreement with the speaker, increasing counterargumentation, and increasing thinking about subjects other than the topic.[28]

The third step: Knowing your audience

Some people are easier to persuade than others. If you are one of these people, you may not necessarily be aware of it. Psychologists Janis and Field found that self-ratings of subjects on susceptibility to influence had little bearing on their actual attitude changes during an experiment.[29] If some people are more persuasible than others, what are the characteristics of persuasible audiences? Psychological research on personality and persuasibility is extensive, but, as we have pointed out several times already, it is also quite contradictory. Nevertheless, it is possible to extract several broad principles that may provide some help in how to persuade audiences with different characteristics:

1. *Try to establish patterns of similarity between yourself and the audience.* If you are out to persuade a group of people, the chances are that they differ from you on various dimensions. You can, however, demonstrate certain attitudes and behaviors that would lead to greater communality between you and your listeners (such as interests, hobbies, mannerisms, and the like). Whether such similarities are based on reality is beside the point. As long as your listeners perceive themselves as somewhat similar to you, a multitude of halo effects (see Chapter 9) will emerge. Since you are perceived as similar, you will also be perceived as more attractive, more sincere, and more of an expert.[30] Your chances as a successful persuader increase accordingly.
2. *Gear your level of presentation to the listeners' self-esteem.* As a rule, people with low self-esteem are easier to manipulate than people with high self-esteem.[31] Make sure, however, to present your arguments clearly to listeners whom you suspect of being low in self-esteem. By "clearly," we mean that your arguments must be presented in an easy-to-follow manner, even at the risk of resorting to very rudimentary forms of communication. Your listeners must understand your message, because if there is one thing people with low self-esteem dread, it is failure. However plausible your message might be, if it is difficult to understand it raises the possibility of failure to the audience. When this occurs, people with low self-esteem will be the hardest audience to persuade.[32]
3. *Let the intelligence level of your audience dictate your use of appeals.*

[28]CACIOPPO & PETTY, 1979.   [29]JANIS & FIELD, 1967.   [30]BERSCHEID, 1966; JELLISON & MILLS, 1967; MILLS & JELLISON, 1968.   [31]ASCH, 1968; BERKOWITZ & LUNDY, 1957; JANIS, 1954, 1955; HOVLAND & JANIS, 1959; COX & BAUER, 1964.   [32]NISBETT & GORDON, 1967.

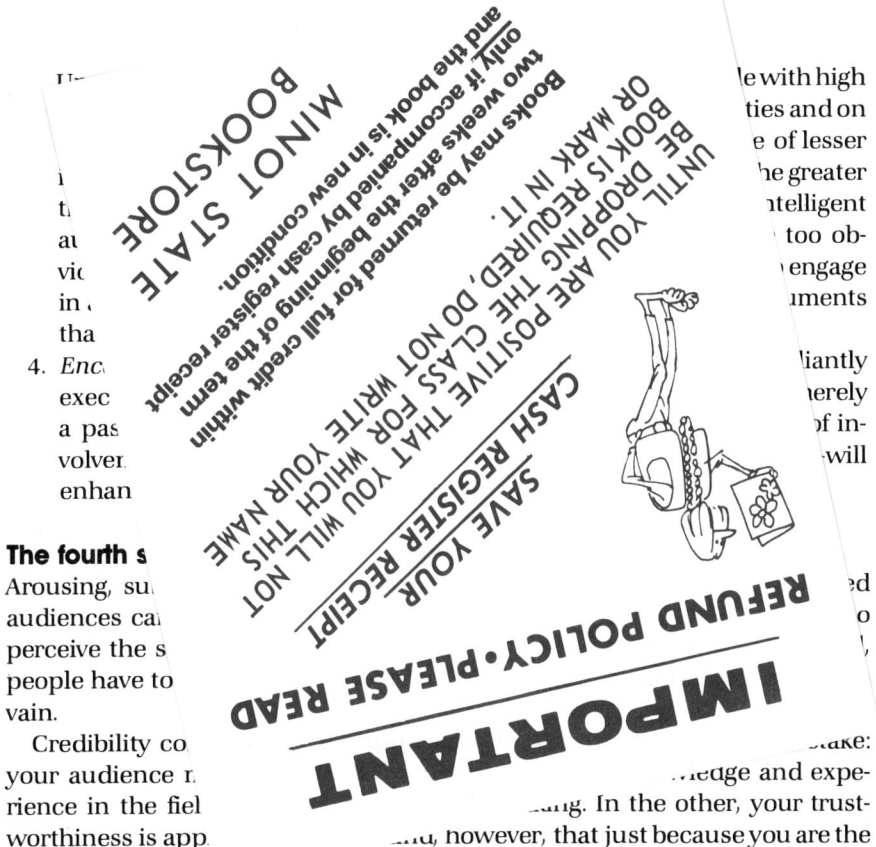

worthiness is app_____, however, that just because you are the expert does not ne_____rily mean that your audience is confident that you are going to present your message honestly and objectively.[36] Moreover, the moment you stray from your specific area of expertise, your prestige tends to drop sharply and your credibility may suffer.[37]

As a persuader, what can you do upon encountering lack of faith in your credibility from your audience? Not much, really. For one thing, you are probably deserving of it: you either showed that you did not know what you were talking about or you did not attempt to communicate the assertions you considered most valid. In such cases, there seems little you can do, short of resorting to deliberate misrepresentation. For example, flashy presentations of messages with meaningless content have been shown to be effective as long as the persuader faked his credentials as an expert.[38] Then there is the *sleeper effect*. For many years, psychologists took it for granted that a communication works while the audience "sleeps on it." As a result, it was suggested that with the passage of time, people tend to forget *who* presented the argument (the source) more rapidly than *what* the argument (the content) was all about. If this were true, the implications would be clear: nonsubstantive but flashy presentations by a low-credibility persuader have a better chance to be remembered than dull presentations by a high-credibility persuader. This apparent advantage of style over substance opens the specter of the "big lie"

---

[33]Hovland, Janis, & Kelley, 1953. [34]Carmet, Miles, & Cervin, 1965. [35]Hereford, 1963; Zimbardo, 1965; Janis & Mann, 1965. [36]Hovland, Janis, & Kelley, 1966. [37]Rhine & Kaplan, 1972. [38]Naftulin, Ware, & Donnelly, 1973.

technique, as used by Nazi Germany propagandists: malign a person long enough with catchy, demagogic phrases and people will eventually believe you, regardless of your credibility. Most psychologists today believe in the sleeper effect, even though it has been shown to be more complex than previously believed.[39] At least one study, however, has clearly and unequivocally demonstrated that the sleeper effect does not exist. Seven replications of the original sleeper effect study (a flimsy study to begin with) failed to show that there is such a phenomenon.[40]

Conflicting results are the rule rather than the exception in studies of attitude change. This holds particularly true for the area of persuader credibility and attractiveness. The problem with focusing on the persuader is that it may involve personality variables that are difficult to pin down. Obviously, the more attractive you are as a persuader, the more effective you become in influencing your listeners. Some situational factors, however, seem to operate across the board. This means that you may be recognized as a high-prestige expert, or even be perceived as personally honest and objective, and still lack credibility. It all depends on what and whom you represent. For example, although given identical communications about the effects of smoking on health, subjects' attitudes changed more in the advocated position when the alleged message was cited from the "Surgeon General's Report on Smoking and Health" than from a popular magazine article, and even more so than when cited from an advertisement by the American Tobacco Company.[41] Similarly, a purported prosecuting attorney and a purported criminal, "Joe the Shoulder," who presented messages advocating more or less power to prosecutors and police, gained equal credibility as long as they were advocating positions opposed to their own interest.[42] Perhaps there is less suspicion about the motives of communicators about to embark on an unpopular course; or they may be admired merely for their courage. In either case, their credibility and effectiveness as persuaders increase considerably.

Most of the research done by psychologists has focused on persuaders' attempts to gain and maintain credibility. One interesting study dealt with attempts to *restore* credibility. Psychologist Marriana Torrano presented her subjects with a tape-recorded session of a purported faculty/student campus committee. The committee was part of a progressive campus and enjoyed the credibility of the students. In the first part of the experiment, subjects were told of a decision by the committee regarding two students who had been engaged in a demonstration involving some turbulence and slight damage to dormitory buildings. The decision was to give the students an official reprimand on their transcript and to dismiss them irrevocably from the college. The seemingly harsh and unjust decision led to a considerable drop in credibility ratings that subjects gave to the committee. In the second part of the experiment, the coordinator of the committee tried to restore credibility by taking one of the following steps (each step corresponds to an experimental condition):

  1. Denial of wrongdoing. The coordinator simply reaffirmed the commit-

[39]GRUDER, COOK, HENNIGAN, FLAY, ALESSIS, & HALAMAJ, 1978. [40]GILLIG & GREENWALD, 1974. [41]ZAGORA & HARTER, 1966. [42]WALSTER, ARONSON, & ABRAHAMS, 1966.

tee's original decision. He pointed out that he and his colleagues were elected to the committee because of their expertise and personal integrity, and on that basis their decision should be accepted unquestioningly.

2. *Denial of wrongdoing, with information withheld.* The coordinator reaffirmed the committee's original decision but pointed out that the decision was made on the basis of additional information that could not be divulged without hurting people needlessly.

3. *Denial of wrongdoing, with information divulged.* The coordinator reaffirmed the committee's original decision but presented further facts which, for ethical reasons, could not have been divulged previously. The two accused students were now reported as having been engaged in far more serious activities than a protest march. They had been paid by an off-campus group that intended to foster dissension on campus to disrupt the faculty/student cooperation program; furthermore, the students had previously been involved in embezzlement of campus funds and had been well aware of the consequences of their activities.

4. *Admission of wrongdoing.* The coordinator stated that the committee was reversing its original decision. The students were found to be innocent. The coordinator announced that the committee was willing to assume responsibility for a decision that it sincerely regretted as unfortunate.

5. *Admission of wrongdoing, with information withheld.* The coordinator announced that the committee had reversed its unfortunate original decision on the basis of additional information. He explained that this information could not be disclosed for fear of hurting people needlessly.

6. *Admission of wrongdoing, with information divulged.* The coordinator announced that the committee was reversing its unfortunate original decision because additional information showed that the students' involvement, though real, had been an effort to stem the riot rather than to aggravate it.

Before we get to Torrano's results, let us present an analogy from a political leader who has lost credibility and wants to restore it. Former President Nixon's declarations after the Watergate incident and late President Johnson's Vietnam policy are cases in point. To paraphrase Torrano's six experimental conditions, here is what these leaders could have said in their attempts to restore credibility:

"I am right. Trust me." (1)
"I am right and have additional information to prove it, but for certain good reasons (national security) I cannot divulge it." (2)
"I am right, and here are the facts to prove it." (3)
"I was wrong. It was a mistake." (4)
"I was wrong, and there was a reason for it, but in the interest of your welfare I cannot reveal why." (5)
"I was wrong, but this information I'm giving you will explain why." (6)

As a good citizen, what would you want your leader to do? Presumably, you would prefer full information (3) if he claims he was right; and full information

(6), or at least repentance (4), if he admits that he was wrong. According to Torrano, however, complete denial of wrongdoing with barely any justification (1) is the most effective way to restore credibility.

The fate of former President Nixon seems to justify Torrano's findings (her study, incidentally, was conducted before the Watergate incident). In the early phases of the Watergate incident, even with the common knowledge that potentially condemning tapes did exist, Nixon flatly denied any wrongdoing (1) and stated that the tapes "have been under my sole personal control and will remain so." He may have been better off maintaining this stance, even with the potential risk of having to destroy the tapes. Instead, he subsequently shifted to evoking national security reasons (2). He finally released what he labeled supporting evidence (3), which sealed his fate. Nixon's only possible consolation could lie in the fact that he refused to listen to those who recommended that he should admit wrongdoing. According to Torrano, admissions of wrongdoing are ineffective in restoring credibility. Total repentance (4), in particular, was found to be ineffective (as the repentant late President Kennedy found out when he lost some credibility on the failure of the Cuban Bay of Pigs invasion).

Richard Nixon never admitted wrongdoing in the Watergate affair. Under the circumstances, it was the most effective strategy, according to Torrano's research.

The sad but true fact is that consistency (even when in the form of flat denials of wrongdoings) is often perceived as truthfulness. Fortunately, as Torrano pointed out, flat denials of wrongdoings are only relatively effective in attempts to restore credibility. They are a more effective technique than others, but the gains are exceedingly small. It seems that once credibility is lost, very little can be done to restore it.[43]

[43]TORRANO, 1972.

The final step: Immunization against counterpropaganda

When you catch the flu, contract measles, or come down with a viral infection, it is often because at a given time your resistance happened to be low. It is, therefore, sound practice to take early preventive steps to minimize your chances for contracting the disease. Supportive therapy would suggest that you engage in daily exercise, maintain a proper diet, and get plenty of rest. But you could also be immunized by being inoculated with a weak virus of the very disease you may contract, because it helps to mobilize your body's defenses. When both types of therapy are available and appropriate, inoculation is superior to supportive therapy.

Psychologists William McGuire and Demetrios Papageorgis used this analogy from medicine to demonstrate that the effects of one-sided persuasive arguments are generally short-lived, whereas two-sided arguments inoculate listeners against future counterpropaganda. As an example, they cited the furor in the United States after the Korean War, when it became public knowledge that some American soldiers had been successfully brainwashed by their Chinese captors (see Chapter 4). To many a Congressman, both the diagnosis and remedy were simple. Those who were brainwashed, it was suggested, succumbed because they were not patriotic enough or lacked convincing evidence for the superiority of the American way of life. The remedy, therefore, should be in the form of supportive therapy: subject the soldiers to massive doses of what is commonly referred to as "Americanism" and thus avoid future incidents of successful brainwashing (counterpropaganda). Contrary to this advocated one-sided approach, McGuire and Papageorgis argued that the soldiers would be more resistant to counterpropaganda if they were properly inoculated. In practice, this would mean that the best way to combat brainwashing and other forms of counterpropaganda (the disease) is to use two-sided arguments. The major and stronger argument should be supportive (in this case, pro-American), while the minor and weaker argument (pro-Communist) would act like a virus in helping the soldiers to mobilize their defenses against future attacks. McGuire and Papageorgis supported these contentions in a series of interesting psychological laboratory studies.[44]

We have done our best in this chapter to present you with some (by no means all) of the more important findings in the area of attitude development and change. They are also important because of their applications to other areas, such as clinical psychology and mental health (see Box 3-1), despite the wealth of conflicting evidence. As we pointed out earlier, even if the evidence were more conclusive, attitude studies would still be plagued by the nagging question: is what a person says or thinks (attitude) predictive of his or her actions (behavior)? Because of this problem, we found it best, in the next chapter, to gradually move away from the study of attitudes to the study of behavior.

Perhaps the best way to conclude this chapter is to cite an experience of

[44]McGuire & Papageorgis, 1961.

ours that demonstrates both the usefulness and futility of studying attitude change. Despite the wealth of conflicting evidence, some psychologists succeed from time to time in gathering enough information to establish unique but effective techniques for changing attitudes. One such psychologist, Jacobo Varela from Montevideo, Uruguay, put together an amalgamation of findings from attitude research studies and used them effectively to overcome sales resistance by retailers to wholesalers.[45] The most intriguing part of Varela's technique consisted of choosing attitudes which the persuader knew the listeners favored anyway, and denouncing these attitudes. When that occurred, the listeners, as expected, disagreed with the persuader. Without being aware that they were led, the listeners gradually began to negate *everything* the persuader said, including statements that incorporated the very attitude that the persuader wanted to change in the first place. It is a truly fiendish technique, because it makes you appear fair and objective while you are playing devil's advocate.

Box 3-1. Social influence in clinical practice: A controversial issue

The problem of manipulation and what it connotes becomes more obvious within the context of personal and social adjustment. Problems are created when significant people in our lives try to exercise control. Too often a parent, a spouse, or a boss will try to get you to do something you do not want to do. Control is a form of manipulation, and there are a lot of people around us who thirst for this type of control.

Even friends get into the act. One way friends or family may attempt to control your behavior is through the advice that they give you. The essence of the manipulation—to get you to accept the advice—will not vary in intent (after all, it was given for *your* benefit!). What may vary is its format. Your friend may use rational arguments, plead with you, call you a fool, or express disappointment in some way (for example, an exasperated shrug of the shoulder that implies "It's *your* life, after all").

If you go to a professional counselor or psychotherapist, there are additional operating factors: **position, role,** and **status.** The moment you enter a so-called therapeutic relationship, the role boundaries are very well defined. The expectations of whose problem is dealt with, at what time, for how long, and at what cost are clearly spelled out.

Whether or not the degree of manipulation is spelled out clearly is open to debate. Nobody denies that both parties want something from each other. Many clinicians, however, will vehemently deny that they are manipulative (or directive, or persuasive, or trying to impose their will). Ironically, the same clinicians will frequently not hesitate to attribute manipulativeness to their patients or clients.

We have no quarrel with those clinicians. We are convinced that in their own minds they are indeed nonmanipulative. Considering that many therapists are directive and even manipulative in the worst sense of the word, anyone who is, or wants to be, *less* manipulative is at least going in the right direction. We do

(continued)

---

[45]ZIMBARDO, EEBBESEN, & MASLACH, 1977.

(Box 3-1 continued)

wonder, however, if anyone in the business of solving adjustment problems can truly be nonmanipulative. For this reason, we would like to introduce you to the controversial concept of **social influence therapy**.

Psychologist John S. Gillis, the chief proponent of social influence therapy, is a controversial person. His views have been endorsed as fantastic, intriguing, and revealing, or dismissed as deceptive and dishonest[46]—all because he embraces the concept of manipulation in therapy.

We, too, have some reservation about the type of therapy advocated by Gillis, yet we do not think that a blanket indictment of him is justified. It is possible to accept many of Gillis' basic premises without necessarily arriving at the same conclusion that he did.

In an article called "The Therapist as Manipulator," Gillis stated his case as follows:

> All modern psychotherapists, whether they know it or not, engage in maneuvers and manipulations that add to their power over the patient (p. 91).

This seems to be a factual statement. He then continues:

> The social influence position not only recognizes this very human fact, but embraces it (p. 91).

What does this mean for the therapist/patient relationship? According to Gillis, it is up to the therapist to change the patient's attitudes and beliefs by effective means, be they directive or even devious.[47]

Can the manipulation techniques described in this chapter (and the one following it) be considered appropriate for social influence therapy? Not necessarily. It is one thing for the therapist to be *aware* of the manipulative power inherent in the therapist role, but quite another to deliberately decide to *apply* manipulative techniques. On the contrary, awareness of the role and knowledge of the techniques may help nondirective therapists in their efforts to *reduce* manipulation.

Awareness and knowledge of what constitutes manipulation can help both patient and therapist, regardless of their orientation or expectations. You may not agree with the therapeutic techniques Gillis advocates, yet still find little fault with his basic premise:

> Psychotherapy . . . is not the unique relationship that many therapists think it is. Instead, it resembles various ordinary social interactions, particularly those that involve authority, power, and influence. When the therapist manages . . . to give peace of mind to the anxious and the fearful . . . he's doing things that happen every day outside their offices. *He's using techniques that have developed over thousands of years in law, politics, religion, education, commerce, and advertising (p. 92). [emphasis is ours]*.

The techniques presented in this chapter are of the same variety as those to which Gillis is referring.

When we described Varela's technique to our students, many of them became intrigued and wanted to try it. At that time the war in Vietnam, with all

[46]*Psychology Today*, 1975. [47]Gillis, 1974.

its ramifications, was at its peak. One student, initially skeptical of the method, eventually agreed to try it to change the attitude of his uncle. That gentleman was a crusty retired Army general who seemed to differ with his nephew on practically every dimension that a generation gap could produce. In particular, the nephew was irritated by the continuing discrimination that the uncle, now the head of a prospering business, seemed to practice against young people (not hiring long-haired or informally dressed job applicants, for example). At that time, too, General Hershey headed the Selective Service System. This was particularly galling to war resisters, who regarded Hershey as an inflexible ancient relic who was sending young men to die.

With the help and advice of his classmates, the nephew decided to change his uncle's attitude about the Army draft system. Following Varela's procedure, he noted several of his uncle's attitudes and arranged them on a favorable/unfavorable continuum as follows:

Modern army is blessed with fantastically high morale. (Uncle expected to disagree most vehemently with this statement.)
Modern army stresses physical fitness. (Uncle expected to disagree with this statement, but somewhat less vehemently than with the preceding one.)
Modern army stresses patriotism. (Uncle expected to disagree mildly with this statement.)
Modern army is effective primarily due to its draft board. (Uncle expected to agree mildly with this statement.)
Modern army should have only men over 40 on its draft board. (Uncle expected to agree strongly with this statement.)
Modern army has the best draft system. (Uncle expected to agree vehemently with this statement, reflecting the attitude which the nephew wanted to change.)

The next step was to choose carefully an appropriate setting. It was finally decided that an impending dinner party would serve best, since if changes in attitudes are pronounced publicly they are more likely to persist.[48] As reported by the nephew to his classmates, the conversation with his uncle went something like this:

Nephew: Maybe there are at least *some* views on the military both of us agree with. The morale of the modern army is fantastically high, don't you think so?
Uncle *(as expected):* You call this morale? What do these young soldiers know about the American way, about the privilege of being a member of the armed forces? There is *no* morale, period!
Nephew *(goadingly, pretending surprise):* You may be right, but at least admit that there is considerable emphasis on physical fitness now.
Uncle *(increasingly angry):* You call that program physical fitness? These soft punks who only sleep and drink? Now, when *we* were

[48]SULLIVAN & PALLAK, 1976.

young soldiers we ran ten miles daily, come rain or shine. We were hard as nails!

Nephew: Really? At least we agree on this: the modern army stresses patriotism.

Uncle *(still angry):* Never! The modern army has newfangled useless ideas about everything, including patriotism.

Nephew: You can kick the modern army as much as you like, but I know it is great. Why? Because of its current draft board.

Uncle *(mockingly):* Since when do *you* know what makes an Army tick? There are *other* things besides draft boards, you know.

Nephew: Is that so? Well, even you will have to admit that it is good to have only men over 40 on the draft board!

Uncle *(sneeringly):* Why 40? Why not 20, or 30, or 50, or 60? What's so magical about 40? It's the men, not the age, that counts.

Nephew: I guess you're right on that point. But I am surprised. Next thing you're going to tell me is that the modern army's draft system is not the best!

Uncle *(with finality):* Well, I will. It is a poor system. It needs overhauling. As it is now, the draft system is for the birds!

Well, finally, there it was! The impossible achieved, as the exultant nephew told his classmates, the first step in his uncle's "rehabilitation." At the end of the semester, the crestfallen nephew reported to the class that nothing had really changed. The uncle was as hawkish as ever on the war and his discriminatory practices continued as before. The only change was that on that specific point, the draft system, the uncle was relatively mute. Which is precisely the point we have been raising all along. It is possible, perhaps even probable in some cases, that changes in attitude will lead to corresponding changes in behavior. Certainly the avenue of changing attitudes should not be closed in attempts to change behavior. But, as we shall see from here on, such changes require additional study.

SUMMARY HIGHLIGHTS

1. Methods designed to change attitudes make use of *propaganda.* Although the term has negative connotations, it includes any attempt to influence the development of attitudes or to change them.
2. The attitude change process can be broken down into five steps. The first step requires getting the attention of the audience. Methods for accomplishing this include appealing to hidden motives, using emotionally arousing material, or introducing a product to the market at either a high or a low price. Data show that a high price introduction may lead eventually to higher sales, and that overly arousing messages may be ineffective. The value of *subliminal advertising* (appealing to subconscious motivations) has generally not been supported in experimental studies.
3. The second step is the presentation of arguments. When attempting to persuade others, the persuader should: not let the facts speak for themselves, forewarn listeners about forthcoming attempts to change their

attitudes, use humor judiciously in major arguments, gauge the timing of the major argument to the time of maximum audience interest, begin by endorsing some audience view, advocate extreme changes, present two sides of the argument, and avoid too much repetition in the presentation.

4. It is also important to know the audience. To be truly effective, the persuader must try to establish patterns of similarity with the audience and gear the level of presentation to listeners' self-esteem and the average level of their intelligence.

5. Communications are more persuasive when the communicator is credible. *Credibility* consists of two components: expertise and trustworthiness. In some cases where the communicator is not credible, he or she may actually gain credibility by arguing against his or her own self-interest.

6. Once persuaded, the audience must be *immunized* against *counterpropaganda*. This can be accomplished by exposure to arguments that advocate opposing views. When presenting such arguments, however, instructions for rebuttal should also be provided.

CHAPTER 4 INFLUENCING BEHAVIOR

POWER
    Practicing and preaching
    Six power plays
    Does power corrupt?

COMPLIANCE
    Fear: It does strange things to you
    Guilt: Do it for mother!
    Sympathy: Have a heart!
    Force: The stick and the carrot
    Guile: A foot in the door and low-balling
    Concession: A door in the face
    Impugnment: The art of name calling
    Hypnosis: A matter of concentration

OBEDIENCE
    Following orders: The road to atrocity
    Breeding grounds for blind obedience

CONFORMITY
    Can you be your own person?
    Breeding grounds for conformity
    Profiles in conformity

BEHAVIOR MODIFICATION
    Some principles of learning
    Classical conditioning: Learning the passive way
    Operant conditioning: Behaviors that pay off
    The power of social reinforcement

SUMMARY HIGHLIGHTS

POWER

Practicing and preaching

When discussing attitudes, we often assume that the sentiments we express are directly related to actions we may take. Positive feelings are related to getting involved in an action that expresses these attitudes. If you favor one political candidate, you are more likely to go to work for him or her than you are to go to work for the opponent. Similarly, negative feelings toward somebody may get you involved in action. If you dislike a political candidate, you may go out and campaign against him or her.

    Psychologists have shown that even though we say that we will behave in certain ways, our stated attitudes are not always predictive of how we actually behave. Preaching is not necessarily practicing. No matter how many times you can make other people say, "I prefer Coca-Cola," the ultimate test is whether they will drink Coca-Cola if given the opportunity. You can make many men speak glowingly of their preference for egalitarian relationships. But when these men live with their wives or girlfriends, the real question is, who does the dishes? Sharing in household duties usually assigned to women would be a behavioral manifestation of the men's expressed attitude.

    Whether attitudes cause behavior or vice versa is in certain ways an insoluble "which comes first, chicken or egg?" problem. Nevertheless, psychologists have certain sophisticated statistical techniques that can yield something more than an educated guess in that matter. Using one such technique, the cross-lagged panel analysis, psychologists Lynn Kahle and John Berman tackled four issues: Jimmy Carter's candidacy, Gerald Ford's candidacy, drinking, and religion. Each issue involved the assessment of attitudes (for example, "I like to drink") on a scale ranging from strongly agree (1) to strongly disagree (9), and behavior ("How many times in the past 14 days have you had at least one drink?"). The authors found not only a strong relation between attitudes and behavior, but also a strong "causal predominance" of the former over the latter. Practically speaking, this would indicate that people do what they preach, and the implications, according to the authors, are important "for the politicians, theologians, and therapists who may be interested in knowing whether their efforts to change attitudes will help them to achieve their ultimate goals of changing behavior" (p. 320).[1]

It thus seems safe in most cases to make predictions from attitudes to behavior. Still, we all know that there are at least some instances in which, perhaps because of special circumstances, differences between practicing and preaching cannot be ignored. One innovative study involving the nurse/physician relationship is a good case in point. Boxes containing pills (actually placebos, which are harmless pills) were labeled "Astrogen, 5 mg" and placed in 22 wards in a public and a private hospital. A man who curtly identified himself as Dr. Smith telephoned each ward and ordered the attending nurse to give a certain patient 20 milligrams of Astrogen. This was to be done at once, the doctor explained, since he was in a hurry and could not do it himself. Standard rules dictate that nurses do not take orders over the phone, especially from physicians they do not know. Moreover, clearly marked on the pill box was the notice that the maximum daily dose of the drug was *10* milligrams. Observers stationed near each medicine cabinet recorded that 21 out of 22 nurses promptly complied with the unfamiliar doctor's order. It was obvious that the *behavior* of nurses was in compliance with the telephoned orders of an unknown physician.[2]

Would the conclusions have been the same if the investigators had simply asked nurses what they would do in such a situation? When graduate nurses were presented with the same hypothetical situation (or given the exact details of the situation created for the experiment), 21 out of 22 claimed they would have refused to carry out the order without written instructions. The lesson from this experiment is obvious. There may be a considerable discrepancy between the attitudes people express and the behavior in which they engage. Psychological and sociological literature abounds with other examples of this phenomenon. In this chapter, we will gradually turn our attention away from attitudes and focus on actual behavior.

Six power plays

If we want to exert influence over somebody, we usually try to use some form of manipulation. Psychologist Bert Raven and his associates have identified six types of social **power**. Let us take a brief look at their formulations.

[1] KAHLE & BERMAN, 1979. [2] HOFLING, BROTZMAN, DALRYMPLE, GRAVES, & PIERCE, 1966.

Informational power occurs when you are manipulated by what a message says. It has nothing to do with the person who presents the message or with the style in which the message is delivered. The content of the message as such carries the power.

Coercive power occurs when the manipulator is able to control punishments. You yield to coercive power because you do not want the power agent to hurt you.

Reward power occurs when the manipulator is able to give you rewards for going along with him or her.

Legitimate power stems from an internalization of values advocated by an authoritative source. You yield to the manipulator by virtue of his or her recognized authority.

Referent power occurs when you yield because you recognize and respect the prestige of the manipulator.

Expert power does not depend on the content of a communication. You yield to the manipulator because of his or her credentials as an expert.[3]

Table 4-1 shows how the six forms of social power might be used by parents in an attempt to influence their children not to smoke marijuana. Figure 4-1 illustrates how the six forms of power are reflected in the relationship between officers and enlistees, and between college professors and students.

The six forms of social power have been studied extensively by social and industrial psychologists. One study that incorporated both social and industrial approaches showed that among workers, information power yielded by the supervisor ("We have just finished a study that shows this method is superior. Why don't you use it instead?") was most effective in inducing private acceptance of the advocated change; reward power ("If you use this instead, you will get promoted soon") and referent power ("We seem to have a lot in common. I've always used this method; why don't you use it too?") were most conducive to mutual evaluation and liking; and coercive power ("You'd better use it instead; otherwise, you'll never get promoted") and legitimate power ("As your supervisor, I'd prefer that you use this method instead") were least effective on all counts.[4]

Does power corrupt?

A British statesman, Lord Acton, once made the well-known observation that "power tends to corrupt and absolute power corrupts absolutely." Philosophers, clergymen, economists, and many great thinkers throughout the ages have pondered the same issue. Psychologists have begun to grapple with this problem only recently. The results of all these deliberations are markedly similar: a majority believes that power corrupts; a minority believes that power can produce beneficial changes.

The course of history, as well as of documented research, does little to substantiate the minority view that power is ennobling. You may, of course, accept Rousseau's idea that a person is a noble savage at birth and whatever corruption there is can be found in society. You may even accept recent suggestions that the burden of power produces compassion and understand-

[3]Collins & Raven, 1969; French & Raven, 1959; Raven, 1965. [4]Litman-Adizes, Fontaine, & Raven, 1978.

POWER!
in the military

POWER!
in the classroom

This officer/enlistee relationship may involve the following:

INFORMATION POWER
Rank seniority gives officer more information than enlistee about military practices.

LEGITIMATE POWER
Rank seniority empowers officer to control enlistee in certain areas.

REWARD POWER
Rank seniority allows officer to reward enlistee with assignments and promotion.

COERCIVE POWER
Rank seniority allows officer to punish enlistee with assignments and promotion.

REFERENT POWER
Rank seniority may induce personal respect.

EXPERT POWER
Rank seniority may indicate differences in ability and expertise.

This professor/student relationship may involve the following:

INFORMATION POWER
Professorial role gives teacher more information than student about campus policies.

LEGITIMATE POWER
Professorial role empowers teacher to control range and topic of course.

REWARD POWER
Professorial role allows teacher to reward student with grades and attention.

COERCIVE POWER
Professorial role allows teacher to punish student with grades and inattention.

REFERENT POWER
Professorial role and status may induce admiration and respect in student.

EXPERT POWER
Professorial role may cause teacher to be perceived as more knowledgeable than student.

Figure 4-1. Examples of social power.

ing.[5] Then there is the jaundiced view that at least some powerholders act in a benevolent way because they were deprived of affection as children.[6] One study even showed that college students choose not to exercise power unwisely when given the opportunity to do so. In that study, one of the experimenters posed as a professor. Previous ratings by students had established her as an exceptionally good or an exceptionally bad professor (depending on the experimental condition). The students were subsequently given the opportunity to decide on the professor's future. The results indi-

[5]BERLE, 1967; CARTWRIGHT & ZANDER, 1968. [6]ROGOW & LASWELL, 1963.

TABLE 4-1 Six power plays: How parents may use power to influence their teenage children not to smoke marijuana

Type of power	How it would be stated
Information	"Smoking marijuana is not good for you."
Coercion	"If you smoke marijuana, I can have you arrested and sent to jail."
Reward	"If you don't smoke marijuana, I will increase your allowance."
Legitimate	"As your parent, I have the right to make you stop smoking marijuana."
Referent	"Bruce Jenner is down on people who smoke marijuana."
Expert	"Scientific research shows that smoking marijuana causes a decreased white blood cell count and poor health."

cated that there was a significant gap between the rhetorical demand for, and the exercise of, student power. As expected, when the professor was rated "good," everyone agreed to hire or maintain her. When she was rated "bad," a curious thing happened. When the professor had given her "bad" lecture, the students were unanimous in their harshness. They decided that this kind of professor has no place in a university. But when they thought that the "bad" lecture came from a real-life faculty member (or applicant for the position), they suddenly turned lenient and were willing to give that professor a chance to continue teaching. Considering that the teaching to which they had been subjected consisted of monotonous mumbling and pointed references to those who dared to ask questions, to go to the library, the students' compassion was remarkable. The results, however, did not necessarily indicate that their noble behavior was related to benevolent exercise of power. As the authors of the study point out, it could have been a function of apathy, fear of retaliation by faculty, buck passing, or a lack of credibility in the experimental situation.[7]

There is, alas, a formidable array of evidence to justify James Madison's plea in the Federalist Papers that access to power should be limited because of potential ambitiousness and vindictiveness in powerholders. Long before the infamous Watergate incident during the Nixon presidency, some political ideologies actually advocated corruption as a justifiable means and end (see "Machiavellianism" in Chapter 9). And why not? If powerholders are able to influence others because of this power, they are likely to believe that their ideas and views are superior to those of others. Moreover, they will do everything that they can to increase the social distance between themselves and those others.[8] Other studies, especially in military and industrial settings, have clearly demonstrated that a powerholder rewards subordinates, not because of feelings of gratitude and affection, nor even because subordinates are perceived as a threat to position, but simply because the subordinate has engaged in *ingratiation behavior.* This includes a whole array of demeaning buttering-up tactics aimed at pleasing the powerholder.[9] Sad but true is the fact that flattery seems to get you everywhere with your boss—or nearly everywhere. Even good and honest bosses may find themselves in a situation where they simply cannot adhere to the rules of conventional morality. As economist John Kenneth Galbraith has pointed out, managers in large corpo-

[7]Harari, Bujarski, Houlné, & Wullner, 1975. [8]Kipnis, 1972. [9]Kipnis & Vanderveer, 1971.

rations are forced to make decisions that minimize risk to corporate investments, even if such decisions break the law and are against the interest of public welfare.[10]

COMPLIANCE
Fear: It does strange things to you

The dictionary defines the term *compliance* as "yielding, as to a request, wish, desire, proposal, or demand." How do you get another person to comply? Whatever you do, the other person must have some motivation to yield. You can ask, beg, cajole, or flatter. But if everything fails, you can always threaten. Threat induces fear, and fear, since time immemorial, has been used by some people to get other people to comply. Priests, shamans, and gurus of all denominations have often promoted the concept of the god-fearing person. The impact of such practices has even filtered down to present-day childrearing practices. For example, a comprehensive analysis of 367 families revealed that parental control through coalition with God (that is, parents tell children that God will punish them if they do not comply) occurs frequently.[11]

Psychologists have been less interested in the ethical aspects of threatening others than in the effectiveness of this method in achieving compliance. More than 20 years ago, psychologists Irving Janis and Seymour Feshbach conducted a study to demonstrate the effectiveness of threat in inducing attitude change. High school students were given an illustrated lecture aimed at promoting better dental hygiene. The subjects were randomly divided into three groups, with each group listening to a different fear-arousing threat aimed at producing a more positive attitude toward oral hygiene. Mild threat (pain from toothaches) produced 37% attitude change in the desired direction; moderately intense threat (having cavities filled; sore, swollen, inflamed gums) produced 22% change; and extremely intense threat (having teeth pulled; cancer; paralysis; blindness) produced only 8% change. Clearly, the likelihood for compliance to occur decreased as threat intensity increased.[12]

Subsequent studies have generally supported the original Janis and Feshbach findings.[13] Others, however, have found that the higher the induced fear level of a communication, the greater its acceptance.[14] Much of the confusion is probably due to the fact that what one experimenter perceives as extremely frightening may only be moderately fear arousing to another. Most likely, the relationship between fear arousal and attitude change is curvilinear: Up to a certain point, the more fear-inducing a message is, the more attitude change it will evoke; after that point, its effectiveness will decline.[15]

The experiment by Janis and Feshbach brings up several interesting points. It shows that fear does strange things to people. When a threat becomes too frightening, so much fear and anxiety is generated in individuals that they may defensively avoid the message altogether. Moreover, severe threats are often perceived as implausible and are therefore ignored by the listener. It is very likely that, 30 years ago, the high school students in the experiment simply did not believe that failing to brush their teeth would lead to blindness, paralysis, or cancer. It is equally likely that today's adolescents are immune to

[10]GALBRAITH, 1967. [11]NUNN, 1964. [12]JANIS & FESHBACH, 1953. [13]JANIS & FESHBACH, 1954; JANIS & TERWILLIGER, 1962. [14]LEVENTHAL, 1965, 1967; LEVENTHAL & NILES, 1965. [15]HIGBEE, 1969.

the threat that the use of marijuana inevitably leads to the use of heroin, as so many of the messages presented to them imply.

It seems, therefore, that a moderately intense threat (if some sort of consensus of what constitutes "moderate" can be reached) is effective in inducing attitude change. But does attitude change mean compliance? Several studies have shown that the two are not necessarily one and the same. Psychologist Howard Leventhal suggested that compliance to threat will occur only when fear is attached to the actions to be avoided and when the desired actions and attitudes are fear reducing.[16] For example, if you want your child to comply with your demand for daily tooth brushing, it is not enough to provide the fear-inducing message that sore and swollen gums are the other option. Such information may change the child's attitude, but not necessarily behavior. To achieve the latter, you must provide your child with specific information on how and when to brush teeth. To demonstrate this point, Leventhal and his associates tried to persuade college students to take tetanus inoculations under a variety of conditions. The dependent measure was the number of students who actually appeared at the student health center to be inoculated. Some of the subjects were exposed to a high-threat communication that maintained that tetanus is easily contracted. These communications described, in gory detail, the most distasteful aspects of tetanus symptoms. The subjects were also shown color photographs of a tetanus patient receiving a tracheotomy and having tubes inserted in different parts of the body. Other subjects were given low-fear instructions. These subjects read a message with the same content but with a less vivid and shocking description of the disease. In addition, some of the subjects in the high-fear group and some of the subjects in the low-fear group were given specific instructions about what course of action to take. These instructions went so far as to tell the students to check their schedule to determine what times of day they passed near the health center and provided a visual aid showing the location of the health center in relation to other campus buildings.

The results of the experiment were highly interesting. Subjects exposed to a strong fear-arousing message were more likely to report that they intended to take the shots than those exposed to a nonarousing communication. Specific instructions had no effect either on verbal reports of intentions to take the shots or on fear about tetanus. The effects of these two manipulations appear different, however, if action rather than words is counted. When records were examined to determine who actually came for the shots, it turned out that getting specific instructions was more important than fear arousal. Of those given specific instructions, 29% reported for the inoculation. Only 3% of those not given specific instructions came for the injections. All the groups subjected to threat, however, complied with the recommendation more than control groups who received no fear instructions.[17]

Taken together, these results are important for several reasons. First, some fear arousal appears to increase compliant behavior. Second, specific information aids in changing behavior but has little effect on attitudes. Fear arousal thus changes attitudes, but it is not too effective in increasing compliance

[16]LEVENTHAL, 1974. [17]LEVENTHAL, SINGER, & JONES, 1965.

unless it is paired with a specific plan of action. In these days of fear-arousing doomsday campaigns in many vital areas such as consumerism, ecology, and birth control, this two-step process between attitude change and actual compliance should be kept in mind.

Guilt: Do it for mother!

A husband sends his wife a beautiful bouquet of flowers. If this is an uncharacteristic gesture on his part, should the wife worry? If the guilt feeling principle is operating, she should. The wife wants flowers from her spouse. He knows what her desire is but is not too motivated to do anything about it. Then he does something that makes him feel guilty. Afterward, bingo—off to the florist shop!

Guilt has a powerful effect on people. Among other things, it can be manipulated to get one to comply. Several studies have demonstrated this effect rather conclusively. In one such study, subjects operated a machine that could be used to give electric shocks in the context of a learning experiment. It required a "teacher" to administer various degrees of shocks to "learners" whenever the latter made mistakes. The subjects in the experiment were always cast in the role of a teacher, and a confederate always drew the role of a learner. Half of the subjects were led to believe that they were really giving electric shocks to the learner, while the other half knew they were not shocking the confederate. After the supposed learning experiment, the confederate would turn to the subject and ask if he or she would be willing to volunteer some time for a campaign to save California's redwood trees.

According to the experimenter's hypothesis, the subjects who thought they had shocked the confederate should feel a little guilty. It was predicted that these subjects would be more willing to comply than the subjects who did not think they had shocked the confederate. This is precisely what happened. Seventy-five percent of the people who were made to feel guilty (or had delivered shocks) agreed to work for the campaign. Among those who had not been made to feel guilty, only 25% complied with the confederate's request.[18]

In another study, guilt was intensified by reprimanding subjects and then observing their helping behavior. Visitors to the Portland Art Museum were observed on three consecutive Sunday afternoons. During the first two Sundays, visitors who disregarded warning signs at the entrance of the museum telling them not to touch the displays were first reprimanded by a uniformed guard and later observed on their helping behavior to a confederate art student who "accidentally" dropped her pencils. Visitors who obeyed the sign were also subjected to the experimental confederate, as were those on the third Sunday, who broke the rule by disregarding the sign but were not reprimanded (and, presumably, may or may not have been aware of transgressing). The results showed that the combination of guilt inducement through transgression plus reprimand yielded the highest percentage (58%) of helping, as opposed to the transgression only condition (40%), or no transgression control condition (35%).[19]

The previous studies suggest that one way to manipulate people is to make

[18]CARLSMITH & GROSS, 1969. [19]KATZEV, EDELSACK, STEINMETZ, WALKER, & WRIGHT, 1978.

them feel guilty. Of course, advertisers are only too well aware of this principle. Television commercials often butter us up for a big pitch by making us aware of something we should have done. For example, the telephone company tries to get you to spend money on long-distance phone calls by asking you when the last time was that you talked to your family (especially your mother). You may not have talked to them in a while. Once reminded, you feel guilty and head for the telephone.

Sympathy: Have a heart!

Sympathy, as well as guilt, will increase compliance. This was demonstrated in an experiment conducted during five wet days in Toronto by psychologist Vladimir Konecni. The carefully planned scene went like this: a man walks down the street and drops some computer cards on the wet ground. The cards are always dropped just as a pedestrian approaches the scene. When the pedestrian closes in, the man who dropped the cards says "Please don't step on them" (the cards). The pedestrian is eventually asked to help pick up the cards (see Figure 4-2).

Figure 4-2.
Will this woman be more likely to help the man pick up his cards if she feels sympathy or guilt?

Before the request for help, however, several experimental manipulations take place. One condition attempts to induce sympathy in the pedestrian-subject. Just before approaching the scene, the subject sees another person (actually a confederate of the experimenter) slam into the man with the computer cards. That other person neither apologizes nor offers to help pick up the cards—just walks away briskly. Another condition aims at instilling a generalized feeling of guilt in the subject. Before reaching the man with the computer cards, an experimental confederate carrying a set of expensive-looking books bumps into the subject. The books are dropped, but before the subject can help, the confederate scoops them up while scolding the subject for carelessness. After this incident, the pedestrian-subject encounters the man with the computer cards.

In the sympathy condition, 64% of the pedestrian-subjects complied with the request to pick up the computer cards. The generalized guilt condition was also effective in getting people to comply. In this condition, 42% of the subjects complied. These figures are in contrast to the 16% of the subjects who complied in a control condition where neither guilt nor sympathy were aroused. The results of Konecni's study suggest that both guilt and sympathy can increase compliance.[20]

One of the most interesting examples of the use of generalized guilt to manipulate people comes from an analysis of brainwashing techniques used by the Chinese during the Korean War. American soldiers in prison camps were encouraged to confess all misdeeds. At first, the soldiers only confessed small things, but with encouragement they began to confess greater transgressions. After a while, they began to confess all sorts of very personal thoughts about themselves, their fellow soldiers, their captors, and their country. Because of these confessions, the soldiers developed tremendous feelings of guilt. Once the soldier had been made to feel guilty, the captors were more able to get their prisoners to comply with their requests than before.[21]

Force: The stick and the carrot

Can you imagine being paid $20 to carry out a boring task that makes no sense? This is what psychologists Leon Festinger and J. Merrill Carlsmith paid students to do. The task consisted of such activities as packing spools and turning screws. After they had packed the spools or turned the screws, the experimenter explained to the subjects that he was studying the effects of preconceived notions upon the performance of dull tasks. Each subject was therefore asked to tell another subject that the task had been a very enjoyable one. In other words, subjects who had just participated in a boring task were asked to tell someone else that it really was exciting. For telling this lie, the experimenter offered some of the subjects $1 and other subjects $20. Most of the subjects accepted the offer and went on to tell the next subject that the task had been exciting. Then the subjects were asked how much they themselves had enjoyed the task.

Before we continue on this track, we must take a short side trip into the realm of theory. Leon Festinger introduced his theory of **cognitive dissonance** in 1957. In its formulation it is similar to Fritz Heider's balance theory (see Chapter 1), but seems to be more appealing because of its elegant simplicity. Festinger suggested that every time a person is confronted with a logical inconsistency—for example, with a discrepancy between belief and daily

[20]KONECNI, 1972. [21]SCHEIN, 1956.

Is this man doing this boring task because he is paid well or because he enjoys it? The theory of cognitive dissonance has some answers.

practice—cognitive dissonance occurs.[22] If you are a heavy smoker and believe that smoking leads to cancer, you experience cognitive dissonance. If you stuff yourself with fattening food and believe that obesity causes health or social problems, you experience cognitive dissonance. It is an unpleasant state, one that people tend to avoid at all cost. One way to regain *consonance* is to change the original belief. If, for example, you can somehow convince yourself that smoking does not necessarily lead to cancer, your cognitive dissonance will disappear. The American Tobacco Institute can probably provide you with such information. If you are convinced, you can go on smoking with impunity. You are once again at peace with the world.

What has all this got to do with being paid $20 for a boring task, and then being asked to lie about it? The answer is that Festinger and Carlsmith proposed that their experiment was a test of the differences between dissonance theory and learning theory. Learning theory argues that the greater the incentive, the greater the attitude change. In other words, the more you get paid for lying, the more you will begin to believe your own lies. Thus, those who were paid $20 were expected to believe their lies about how enjoyable the task was more often than those who were paid a mere $1 for it. Dissonance theory predicts the exact opposite. It suggests that when the subjects realized

[22]FESTINGER, 1957.

Cognitive dissonance and health. Heavy smokers can relieve their dissonance by obtaining information that casts doubt on current research linking smoking and cancer.

that they were engaged in a boring task for the measly sum of $1, they experienced dissonance. To relieve this dissonance, they had to justify their actions. By attributing greater importance to the task than it really deserved, the subjects could regain consonance. So they would lie more often for $1 than for $20. And then they would believe their lies.

Now let us get back to the original experiment. The results showed that those who were paid $20 for lying did not believe what they were saying. They expressed virtually the same feelings as a control group of subjects who were not asked to lie. Those who said that they enjoyed the task most were the ones who had been paid $1.[23]

These results are in line with many other findings supportive of cognitive dissonance theory. People who find themselves committed voluntarily to behavior inconsistent with their beliefs are likely to experience dissonance. To relieve this dissonance, they will go to great lengths to justify their behavior. Horseplayers committed to betting on a certain horse attribute special qualities to it.[24] New car owners avoid reading advertisements of similar cars by another manufacturer lest they encounter features that are missing in their own cars.[25] Shoppers discovering that their favorite-brand product costs more than others nevertheless continue buying it because of its presumed superior quality.[26] Prospective group members increase their liking for the group that puts forth the greatest obstacles for joiners.[27] Young men with a negative attitude toward marriage who subsequently become engaged increase their expressed affection toward their fiancées.[28]

[23]FESTINGER & CARLSMITH, 1959. [24]KNOX & INKSTER, 1968. [25]EHRLICH, GUTTMAN, SCHONBACH, & MILLS, 1957. [26]DOOB, CARLSMITH, FREEDMAN, LANDAUER, & TOM, 1969. [27]ARONSON & MILLS, 1959. [28]BREHM & COHEN, 1962.

There are, however, other explanations for the results of Festinger and Carlsmith's experiment. One of the more interesting has been provided by psychologists Irving Janis and John Gilmore. They described the results of the Festinger and Carlsmith experiment in terms of *discombobulation*. That's right, discombobulation. According to Janis and Gilmore, it means interfering response. The discombobulation hypothesis was developed to explain why there was no attitude change in the high-incentive ($20) condition. According to the hypothesis, being paid $20 to do a boring task may have made the subjects suspicious about being exploited by the experimenter. In addition, the subjects in this condition may have felt more guilty about telling lies to another student. Because of this suspicion, the subjects would not change overt compliance (telling a lie) into private acceptance (believing the lie).[29] Although discombobulation is a fancy word, experiments have been unable to confirm this theory as a plausible explanation of the now-classic $1 and $20 study.[30]

Remember, however, that the studies cited so far had one thing in common: the subjects in them had *voluntarily* committed themselves to engage in something they really did not believe in; hence, they experienced dissonance. Clearly, if you lie for a measly sum of money, you would want to justify your behavior. You therefore change your original belief and begin to believe your own lies. This should not happen if you are *forced* into doing something you do not believe in (such as saying that a boring task has been enjoyable). In that case, you can always shift the blame for your predicament onto the people who forced you into it. There is simply no compelling reason for you to lie about how you feel about what you are doing.

The moral of this is that if you want another person to comply, using force is not as effective as handing that person enough rope to voluntarily hang himself (or herself). Unfortunately, it is virtually impossible to conduct experiments where you can force people into doing something they dislike. Subjects in psychological experiments know very well that they can quit and go home anytime. Experimenters have no stick to wield to make subjects participate. They can, however, wield different sorts of sticks once the subjects are ready to participate. For example, it is one thing to tell subjects repeatedly that they can quit at any point in the experiment. It is quite another thing to tell subjects in a matter-of-fact tone of voice to do this or that. Although it is true that in both cases subjects have the ultimate choice of quitting, there is, nevertheless, a lack of choice of sorts in the second condition. In any event, if it can be shown that the first condition (absolute free choice) produces different results than the second condition (relative lack of choice), we can justifiably say something meaningful about the use of force in inducing compliance.

Psychologists Darwyn Linder, Joel Cooper, and Edward Jones conducted an experiment that proceeded precisely along those lines. In the free-decision condition, each subject was told repeatedly "I want to explain to you what this task is all about. I want to make it clear, though, that the decision to perform the task will be entirely your own." In the no-choice (force) condition, each subject was merely told "I want to explain to you what this task you have volunteered for is all about." The task itself was assured to be unpleasant to

[29] Janis & Gilmore, 1965. [30] Collins, 1970.

the subjects. They were asked to write an essay *in favor* of a speaker-ban law on campus (previous informal opinion polls, fortified by the plausible expectations that, as college students themselves, the subjects would oppose the freedom to restrict their right to listen, led to the assumption that the subjects would strongly oppose the speaker-ban law). In addition, two types of incentives were offered to the subjects for complying: low (50¢) or high ($2.50). At the end of the experiment, an attitude scale was administered to all subjects to find out how they felt about the speaker-ban issue. The results showed that the free-choice condition coupled with the low incentive produced the highest amount of attitude change in favor of the speaker-ban position. Wielding a stick (not giving free choice) was clearly ineffective. But giving subjects all the rope they needed (free-choice) evidently caused them enough dissonance about their behavior (writing an essay opposing the speaker ban for a paltry 50¢) to make them justify that behavior (by beginning to favor the speaker ban).[31]

The previously cited study is one of many on the topic of *forced compliance*. We have already pointed out that the term "force" is rather relative. Moreover, most of these studies offer various kinds of incentives (money, grades, and the like) for complying. They present what is popularly known as the stick-and-carrot technique for achieving compliance. This mixture of force and bribery seems to work very well with stubborn mules. With people, the process is somewhat more complex. It depends on how the stick is applied and how big the carrot is. To demonstrate this point, psychologist Merrill Carlsworth and his associates forced subjects in an experiment to comply but also offered them various sums of money for acting this way. The subjects were first given reams of pages with random numbers and instructed to engage in the task of crossing out all the 2s and 6s. As part of the experiment, they were subsequently induced to say that they enjoyed the task. Some of the subjects were allowed to do so by writing anonymous essays on the joys of crossing out numbers. The other subjects were expected to express the same attitude in a face-to-face confrontation with their peers. In addition, there were three kinds of payoff. One-third of the subjects received $5 each for their participation, another third of the subjects received $1.50 each, and the final third of the subjects received 50¢ each.

By way of analogy, it can be said that the experiment featured two ways of applying the stick (anonymous essays and personal confrontation) and three carrots differing in size ($5, $1.50, 50¢). The ultimate test was the extent to which the subjects believed their own lies. This was done by asking the subjects how much they had enjoyed the task.

The results showed that, in the essay condition, the stick-and-carrot combination was very effective. As the payoff increased, so did compliance. Whereas 50¢ caused very little compliance, payoffs of $1.50 and $5 resulted increasingly in statements that crossing out numbers was fun. These results were expected because the relative safety in which the subjects had expressed themselves earlier (anonymous essays) minimized cognitive dissonance. In the face-to-face condition, the very opposite occurred. With increased payoff,

[31]LINDER, COOPER, & JONES, 1967.

compliance decreased. The idea of telling a lie for money was evidently inconsistent (dissonant) with the subjects' beliefs of being good and honest persons.[32]

What does this experiment tell us for our day-to-day living? You may have heard the old saying: if you tell a lie long enough, you will start to believe it yourself. There are many situations in which a person could be paid well for lying to others. In these days of political hush money and cover-ups, we are all too often aware that people will tell lies for the right fee. Whether or not they begin to believe in what they say depends on the degree of cognitive dissonance that these lies produce. If we are being paid off to tell a little white lie that is not likely to cause much harm, we may begin to believe this lie ourselves. If we are forced into an open confrontation with others, we are less likely to believe our own lies, regardless of payoff.

Guile: A foot in the door and low-balling

Have you ever heard about the foot-in-the-door technique of salesmanship? Two psychologists, Jonathan Freedman and Scott Fraser, ran a series of interesting experiments to show how people can be made to comply with a minimum of pressure. The guiding principle of their research is based on dissonance theory and goes as follows: if you get someone committed to do a minor favor for you, refusing to perform a greater favor for you will arouse dissonance in that person. To avoid this unpleasant state, he or she will comply again. Thus, commitment to do a favor will lead to more commitment, which in turn will lead to more commitment, and so on.

To demonstrate this foot-in-the-door technique, Freedman and Fraser ran two experiments. In both experiments, subjects were asked to comply with a small request and, some days later, to comply with a larger request. In the first experiment, citizens randomly chosen from the telephone directory in Palo Alto, California were called by "California Consumers' Group" (a made-up cover name) and asked to provide information for a survey about household goods. Those citizens who agreed to respond were then asked a series of eight innocuous questions about soaps. The caller thanked them for their cooperation and hung up.

A few days after the initial contact, the purported California Consumers' Group recontacted the citizens and presented them with a larger request. This time, the citizens were asked to participate in a more involved survey. Five or six men were to enter the subject's home for about two hours to enumerate and classify all household products. These persons were to have full freedom to go through all cupboards and storage places. The information they collected was to be used for a public service publication.

In addition to the citizens who were contacted twice, another group of people was only confronted with the second, larger request. In summary, there were two groups of subjects. One group was given a small request and then presented with a larger request. The other (control) group was only presented with the second, or larger, request.

The results of the experiment clearly showed that subjects were more likely

[32]CARLSMITH, COLLINS, & HELMREICH, 1966.

The foot-in-the-door technique. Compliance with a small request is followed by compliance with a larger one.

to comply with the larger request if they had formerly agreed to a lesser request. Of those contacted twice, 53% agreed to the large request. Only 22% of those who had been contacted once (control group) agreed to comply with the large request. The foot-in-the-door technique was thus shown to work.

Freedman and Fraser then ran another even more conclusive study. Experimental groups were once again contacted before the large request, whereas the control group was contacted only once for the same request. Depending on the experimental conditions under which they were placed, subjects were asked either to sign a petition to keep California beautiful, put up a sign in their windows that said "Keep California Beautiful," sign a petition about traffic safety, or put up a sign in their window that said "Drive Carefully." Later, all subjects were presented with the same large request. So were the control subjects, who had not been asked to comply with any previous requests.

The large request was a tall order, indeed. It called for the subjects to place in their front yards a big ugly sign reading "Drive Carefully!" To make this large request even less attractive, a sample picture was shown to the subjects. It showed the sign obscuring much of the view of an attractive house.

The results of the study were nothing less than astonishing. As expected, the control condition yielded very little compliance. Only 17% of the people who were asked directly to put up the ugly sign were willing to do so. The experimental conditions, however, yielded entirely different results. Softened up by the foot-in-the-door technique, subjects in those conditions were quite willing to comply with the request to put up the ugly sign. This was particularly evident in the case where both the issue (driving carefully) and the task (displaying a window sign) was similar for the two contacts. Under those conditions, 76% of the people were willing to put up the ugly sign in their front yards. This means an almost fivefold increase in compliance!

Freedman and Fraser chose to interpret the results as follows: "What may occur is a change in the person's feeling about getting involved in action. Once he has agreed to a request, his attitude may change. He may become, in his own eyes, the kind of person who does this sort of thing, who agrees to requests made by strangers, who takes action on things he believes in, who cooperates in good causes" (p. 201).[33] Important for our interest is the finding that any involvement in action may stimulate a person to be compliant in future action.

One final note on this topic. The foot-in-the-door technique is not to be confused with a similar technique, popularly known as **low-balling**. As many car salespeople worth their salt readily know, this technique can be highly effective. You begin by offering your prospective customer an excellent price, way below that of your competitor. Once the customer is hooked and begins to complete the appropriate form, you state that the price does not include certain options that can be added for a minimal price or, better yet, that your manager has voided the deal because the trade-in value for the customer's old car has been inflated, or because "We'll lose money," and so on. But with the customer's mind already made up that the car is appealing, the chances for consummating the sale anyway are far greater than if the more expensive price tag had been announced right away. According to psychologist Robert Cialdini, low-balling is different from the foot-in-the-door technique because the target behavior (such as buying a specific car) is introduced right from the start, rather than through a series of related but different behaviors as in the foot-in-the-door technique. Cialdini also found that, from a behavioral point of view—that is, not just saying that one would comply but actually complying—the low-ball technique seems to be superior to the foot-in-the-door technique.[34]

Concession: A door in the face

Involvement in action can take a different turn. Suppose you want someone to do you a favor. What would happen if you first present this person with an outrageous request (which that person is sure to reject), and *then* ask him or her to comply with your original favor? This approach is diametrically opposed to the foot-in-the-door technique. In fact, you may label it the **door-in-the-face technique.** Under certain circumstances, it can become very effective.

A group of psychologists headed by Robert Cialdini demonstrated this technique in a series of experiments conducted at Arizona State University. Subjects were male or female students who happened to be walking alone on campus during daylight hours. They were approached by another student (always of the same sex as the subject) and asked to volunteer as a nonpaid counselor for the County Juvenile Detention Center. The position, the subjects were told, would require about two unpaid hours per week for a minimum period of two *years*. As expected, not a single subject complied with this extreme request. The subjects were subsequently presented with a smaller request—namely, to act as a chaperone for a two-hour trip to the zoo with a group of children from the County Juvenile Detention Center. Some of

[33]Freedman & Fraser, 1966.   [34]Cialdini, Cacioppo, Basset, & Miller, 1978.

the subjects were presented with both requests and asked to perform either one, and other subjects were faced first with the large request and then with the small request. In addition, a group of subjects was presented only with the small request to establish a control baseline. The results showed that when subjects were asked to perform the smaller request (chaperone duty), only about 17% complied. When they were given a choice of either chaperoning or taking the two-year position, 25% of the subjects agreed to perform chaperone duty. But when they were first exposed to the extreme request for the two-year commitment and *then* asked to perform chaperone duty, 50% of the subjects were willing to act as chaperones. The door-in-the-face technique increased compliance from 17% to 50%!

Cialdini and his associates had a ready explanation for these findings. They suggested that the reason for the increased compliance of the subjects was their perception of concession on the part of the person making the request. In other words, because they realized that the person making the request "lowered the ante," so to speak, from a two-year service to a two-hour service, the subjects in turn felt obligated to make some concessions as well, hence their increased willingness to comply with the small request. To make sure that it was this process of reciprocal concessions that accounted for their results, Cialdini and his associates repeated the experiment with one person making the extreme request, thanking the subject, and walking away; then with *another* person making the small request. Under these conditions, subjects did not perceive the request for the smaller favor as a concession offered by the requester. Accordingly, only about 11% of the subjects complied with the small request, as opposed to 55% with the door-in-the-face technique (where both requests came from the *same* person).[35]

Which of the two techniques, foot-in-the-door or door-in-the-face, is more effective? The verdict is not yet in, for the results are conflicting.[36] As a college student, however, you may find at least one study of more than passing interest.[37] The authors of that study posed the following questions: should college students who ask their professor for academic help be advised to overstate their initial request, with the hope that refusal would induce their teachers to grant a subsequent moderate request? Or would it be more effective to try and "weasel their way" into the moderate request by means of a small preliminary request? Or, finally, should they forego any attempts to manipulate, and approach the professors with their moderate request in a straightforward manner? As the results in Table 4-2 show, your best bet is to overstate your request (door-in-the-face) and, as a second choice, be straightforward (control). Trying to weasel your way in gradually (foot-in-the-door) is a distant third choice in terms of effectiveness.

Impugnment: The art of name calling

The techniques for achieving compliance listed so far may be complex, but all share a logical basis. It is reasonable to assume that, if you capitalize on fear, guilt, sympathy, force, or guile, you may eventually get other people to comply

[35]Cialdini, Vincent, Lewis, Catalan, Wheeler, & Darby, 1975. [36]Brechner, Shippee, & Obitz, 1976; Cialdini & Ascani, 1976; Snyder & Cunningham, 1975. [37]Harari, Mohr, & Hosey, 1980.

TABLE 4-2 Faculty compliance to moderate request, by compliance technique used

Technique used	Response rates % Yes	% No
Door-in-the-face (large initial request) (n = 50)	78.0	22.0
Foot-in-the-door (small initial request) (n = 57)	33.3	66.7
Control (no initial request) (n = 44)	56.8	43.2
Overall (n = 151)	54.9	45.1

Source: Harari, Mohr, & Hosey, 1980.

with your wishes. Psychologist Claude Steele has now added another dimension that really stretches the imagination: if you want people to comply—insult them! To understand this strange suggestion, let us use Steele's own words:

> One day a liberal person was called a racist. The liberal was, of course, very hurt by this name and wanted to argue the name-caller into retracting it. But the name-caller went away before the liberal had a chance to speak. The liberal was left alone to brood. Another day, soon after, the liberal was asked by a friend if he would contribute some of his time and money for the development of a project to help the disadvantaged members of another race. The liberal paused for a moment. And then, he remembered that he had been called a racist. He also recalled the bad feeling that the name had caused him. Thus, he looked at his friend, and with the poise of a man with great conviction agreed to his request.[38] (p. 361)

The logic of all this, according to Steele, is that an insulted person loses self-esteem. To avoid any further threat to positive self-regard, that person will begin to comply with requests that restore and enhance self-image. To support his contention, Steele asked a group of 60 homemakers selected from the Salt Lake City telephone directory to answer a few questions in a preliminary poll taken by "Bill Glass of the National Polling Institute." While talking to the women, the bogus pollster told some of them that it was common knowledge that she (the homemaker) was not particularly oriented toward the betterment of others, that she was known to be self-centered and smug, and so on. Other homemakers were given a diametrically opposite treatment; that is, the bogus pollster complimented them on their concern, cooperation, and helpfulness. Two days later, the women were contacted once again and asked to prepare a lengthy list of food items and household goods for the purported establishment of a food cooperative for the needy in lower-income neighborhoods. This list was to be compiled within three days, and the experimenter actually called for it. Thus the experimenter had in his possession not only the number of women *willing* to comply, but also those who *actually* complied. In either case, insulting the compliers produced superior results. When

[38] STEELE, 1975.

insulted, subjects were both more willing to comply (93%) and to actually comply (66%), than when praised (65% and 57%, respectively).

One of the implications of Steele's study is that it would be a smart move on the part of extremists to insult their lukewarm supporters to get them to comply with requests for additional support. Calling liberals racists, or males chauvinist pigs, could pay dividends to the Black Power or Women's Liberation movements, just as labeling moderate conservatives Communists could pay dividends to members of the John Birch Society. This can also be effective on a personal level, provided the insulted party lets you have your say . . . or does not knock your teeth out. Perhaps it all depends on the style and delivery of the insult. In the previously described experiment, all insults were delivered politely and smoothly, and, according to Steele, the bogus pollster was "almost never" interrupted before completing his entire message.

Hypnosis: A matter of concentration

Down in San Diego, where we live, there is an exciting nightclub act that features an entertainer who puts people from the audience into a trance and then commands them to perform some unusual behaviors. He puts them horizontally between two chairs and stands on their rigid bodies, or tells them to laugh and to cry. He even tells them that they are famous nightclub entertainers and then lets the audience watch as they make fools of themselves attempting to perform. Characteristic of the people in the act is that they comply with everything the entertainer requests.

As you have probably guessed, the trance we are referring to is part of the process of *hypnosis*. Hypnosis is commonly thought of as a form of sleep. Although the term "hypnosis" comes from the root *hypnos*, which is Greek for sleep, we know now that the hypnotic trance is not ordinary sleep. When brain wave recordings are taken from hypnotized people, they look more like those of people awake than asleep.

Psychologist Ernest Hilgard of Stanford University has spent many years studying the phenomenon of hypnosis. He and his colleagues have compiled a list of characteristics of the hypnotic state (see Table 4-3).[39]

TABLE 4-3 Characteristics of hypnotized subjects

1. *Lack of initiative.*
   The subjects do not initiate activity but wait for the hypnotist to give them directions.
2. *Selective attention*
   The hypnotist makes the subjects pay attention to a specific matter, ignoring everything else.
3. *Reduction in reality testing.*
   The subjects are willing to accept hallucinations uncritically (that a chicken is sitting on their shoulder, for example).
4. *Readiness for role enactment.*
   The subjects are willing to enact roles of others, as well as their own at different stage of development (such as childhood or adolescence).
5. *Openness to suggestion.*
   The subjects show less hesitation in accepting suggestion than they would ordinarily exhibit.
6. *Selective memory.*
   Some subjects are able to forget what transpired during the hypnotic session if they are told to do so.

Source: Hilgard, Atkinson, & Atkinson, 1979.

[39] HILGARD, ATKINSON, & ATKINSON, 1979.

Psychologists have disagreed among themselves about many aspects of hypnotism, as well as about the methods by which it should be studied. Despite these disagreements, students of hypnotism seem to agree on certain points. The American Society of Clinical Hypnosis, in its *Handbook of Therapeutic Suggestions*, lists the subject's ability to concentrate as the primary factor in inducing hypnosis. Hypnotists must capture the subject's attention, the handbook warns, because "when attention is concentrated on an idea, the idea tends to be realized." (p. 3).[40]

A recent review describes some other points about which students of hypnosis are generally in agreement. First and foremost, it is understood that people who become hypnotized are willing to be hypnotized. If you do not want to go into a trance, you do not need to worry about someone sneakily putting you into one. Most theoretical treatments of hypnosis assert that those who become hypnotized are motivated to become hypnotized.

Once hypnotized, you will comply with the most dangerous demands—or so it seems. This was demonstrated in an experiment where subjects were hypnotized and asked to engage in dangerous behavior. Naturally, the experimenter-hypnotist had taken all the necessary precautions so nobody would get hurt. The hypnotized subjects, who did not know this, were nevertheless willing to handle rattlesnakes in a cage, dip their hands into a beaker of nitric acid, and even throw the acid in the experimenter's face. But so did subjects who were told to pretend that they were deeply hypnotized and subjects who were merely told that they were in an experiment (without mentioning hypnosis). Hypnotized or not, the subjects simply refused to believe that the conditions were for real. They took it as part of the experimental game, unlike another group of subjects who were not told that they were in an experiment. In that group, not a single person complied.[41]

Because of such findings, some people tend to dismiss hypnosis as nothing more than role playing. The interesting part about all this is that people's belief (or lack of it) in hypnosis is closely related to their susceptibility to the trance state. Those who are given positive information about hypnosis become more susceptible than those given no information, whereas those given adverse information become less susceptible.[42]

Another common finding is that hypnotic suggestions are more likely to be experienced when subjects have been stimulated to use their imagination. If imagination is directed along specific channels in which the hypnotist wants to induce compliance, this state is more likely to occur.[43] For example, if you want subjects under hypnosis to experience anesthesia, you will be more successful if you ask them to imagine novocaine being injected into their body than you would be if you had just asked them not to experience pain. It was also found that subjects who were asked to imagine anesthesia, stiffening of limbs, and arm levitation, were more likely to comply with the hypnotist.

In summary, hypnosis can be an effective way of getting people to comply, but it is not capable of doing what some people think it will do. First, a hypnotic subject must be ready and willing to be hypnotized in order to go under. Second, what one experiences is greatly influenced by the skills of the hypnotist and the subject's capacity to concentrate and imagine. Thus, hyp-

[40]HANDBOOK OF THERAPEUTIC SUGGESTIONS, 1974. [41]ORNE & EVANS, 1965. [42]SPANOS & BARBER, 1974. [43]SPANOS, 1971; ORNE, 1966; SPANOS & BARBER, 1972.

OBEDIENCE

Following orders: The road to atrocity

notism as a device to get people to comply can be regarded as effective only in a limited number of cases and under very special circumstances.

During the years 1933 to 1945, millions of innocent people were killed in Nazi Germany's gas chambers. The deaths of these people were engineered by a single person who, through a series of commands, gave orders to have these grim deeds carried out. The fabric that binds command to action is *obedience*. According to psychologist Stanley Milgram, "Obedience is the psychological mechanism that links individual action to political purpose. It is the dispositional cement that binds men to systems of authority" (p. 1).[44]

Because people tend to obey orders, history has been the witness of many atrocities. Some historians suggest that during the course of history more hideous crimes have resulted from obedience to authority than from any type of rebellion.[45] The problem with obedience to authority is age old and has been recognized for thousands of years. Obedience to authority is treated in the biblical story of Abraham and discussed in philosophical terms by Plato and Hobbs. Hobbs, for example, argued that the responsibility for crimes committed on command rests with the authority rather than with the person who carries out the order.

The problem of obedience to authority is still very much with us. An example of this is the following chilling interview between CBS reporter Mike Wallace and a participant in the My Lai incident during the war in Vietnam:

Q. How many men aboard each chopper?
A. Five of us. And we landed next to the village, and we all got on line and we started walking toward the village. And there was one man, one gook in the shelter, and he was all huddled up down in there, and the man called out and said there's a gook over there.
Q. How old a man was this? I mean was this a fighting man or an older man?
A. An older man. And the man hollered out and said that there's a gook over here, and then Sergeant Mitchell hollered back and said, "Shoot him."
Q. Sergeant Mitchell was in charge of the twenty of you?
A. He was in charge of the whole squad. And so then, the man shot him. So we moved into the village, and we started searching up the village and gathering people and running through the center of the village.
Q. How many people did you round up?
A. Well, there was about forty, fifty people that we gathered in the center of the village. And we placed them in there, and it was like a little island, right there in the center of the village, I'd say. . . . And . . .
Q. What kind of people—men, women, children?
A. Men, women, children.
Q. Babies?
A. Babies. And we huddled them up. We made them squat down and

[44]MILGRAM, 1974. [45]SNOW, 1961.

Lieutenant Calley came over and said, "You know what to do with them, don't you?" And I said, "Yes." So I took it for granted that he just wanted us to watch them. And he left, and came back about ten or fifteen minutes later and said, "How come you ain't killed them yet?" And I told him that I didn't think you wanted us to kill them, that you just wanted us to guard them. He said, "No. I want them dead." So?

Q. He told this to all of you, or to you particularly?
A. Well, I was facing him. So, but the other three, four guys heard it and so he stepped back about ten, fifteen feet, and he started shooting them. And he told me to start shooting. So I started shooting, I poured about four clips into the group.
Q. You fired four clips from your....
A. M-16.
Q. And that's about how many clips? I mean, how many?
A. I carried seventeen rounds to each clip.
Q. So you fired something like sixty-seven shots?
A. Right.
Q. And you killed how many? At that time?
A. Well, I fired them automatic, so you can't—You just spray the area on them and so you can't know how many you killed 'cause they were going fast. So I might have killed ten or fifteen of them.
Q. Men, women, and children?
A. Men, women and children.
Q. And babies?
A. And babies.
Q. Okay. Then what?
A. So we started to gather them up, more people, and we had about seven or eight people, that we was gonna put into the hootch, and we dropped a hand grenade in there with them.
Q. Now, you're rounding up more?
A. We're rounding up more, and we had about seven or eight people. And we was going to throw them in the hootch, and well, we put them in the hootch and then we dropped a hand grenade down there with them. And somebody holed up in the ravine, and told us to bring them over to the ravine, so we took them back out, and led them over to—and by that time, we already had them over there, and they had about seventy, seventy-five people all gathered up. So we threw ours in with them and Lieutenant Calley told me, he said "Soldier, we got another job to do." And so he walked over to the people, and he started pushing them off and started shooting....
Q. Started pushing them off into the ravine?
A. Off into the ravine. It was a ditch. And so we started pushing them off, and we started shooting them, so all together we just pushed them all off, and just started using automatics on them. And then....
Q. Again—men, women, and children?
A. Men, women, and children.
Q. And babies?

A. And babies. And so we started shooting them and somebody told us to switch off to single shot so that we could save ammo. So we switched off to single shot, and shot a few more rounds. . . .
Q. Why did you do it?
A. Why did I do it? Because I felt like I was ordered to do it, and it seemed like that, at the time I felt like I was doing the right thing, because, like I said, I lost buddies. I lost a damn good buddy, Bobby Wilson, and it was on my conscience. So, after I done it, I felt good, but later on that day, it was getting to me.
Q. You're married?
A. Right.
Q. Children?
A. Two.
Q. How old?
A. The boy is two and a half, and the little girl is a year and a half.
Q. Obviously, the question comes to mind . . . the father of two little kids like that . . . how can he shoot babies?
A. I didn't have the little girl. I just had the little boy at the time.
Q. Uh-huh. . . . How do you shoot babies?
A. I don't know. It's just one of these things.
Q. How many people would you imagine were killed that day?
A. I'd say about three hundred and seventy.
Q. How do you arrive at that figure?
A. Just looking.
Q. You say you think that many people, and you yourself were responsible for how many?
A. I couldn't say.
Q. Twenty-five? Fifty?
A. I couldn't say. Just too many.
Q. And how many men did the actual shooting?
A. Well, I really couldn't say that either. There was other . . . there was another platoon in there, and . . . but I just couldn't say how many.
Q. But these civilians were lined up and shot? They weren't killed by cross fire?
A. They weren't lined up. . . . They [were] just being pushed and they were doing what they was told to do.
Q. They weren't begging, or saying, "No . . . no," or. . . .
A. Right. They were begging and saying, "No, no." And the mothers was hugging their children, and . . . but they kept right on firing. Well, we kept right on firing. They was waving their arms and begging. . . .[46] (pp. 183–186)

You may be wondering whether these agonies of war bear any relationship to obedient behaviors in our everyday lives. The situations in My Lai or in Nazi Germany were obviously quite different from the ordinary situations most of us encounter. And, of course, it is easy to rationalize that the Nazi execution-

[46]MILGRAM, 1974.

ers were different sorts of people from us. But you still must ask yourself the question: would *I* blindly obey an authority, even though I knew I might be harming somebody innocent?

Breeding grounds for blind obedience

In the early 1960s, Stanley Milgram set out to explore the phenomenon of obedience. Before then, obedience had been widely recognized as an essential element of social life, yet nobody had attempted to study it systematically.

Milgram has now completed 18 separate experiments on the topic. In all of these experiments, the procedure has been similar. Let us imagine that you are a subject in one of the experiments. You just answered an ad in your local newspaper asking you to participate (for pay) in a scientific study of memory. When you arrive at the laboratory, you are introduced to another subject, a likable, mild-mannered, 47-year-old Irish-American accountant. Although you are not told this, this man is not really another subject. He is an actor working for the experimenter. After you meet this purported subject, the experimenter explains to both of you that the study you are involved in is about the effects of punishment on learning. One of you will be the teacher and the other will be the learner. To determine who gets to play each role, you draw from a hat. You are allowed to draw first and you pull out the word "teacher." Actually, this has been a rigged drawing. Both of the pieces of paper in the hat said "teacher" and because you drew first, you were assured of being assigned that role.

You watch as the learner (the actor) is taken to another room. He is first put in a chair and then strapped down to prevent excessive movement. As an electrode is strapped to his wrist, he is told that he must learn a list of word pairs. Each time he makes a mistake he will receive an electric shock of increasing intensity.

Now you are taken to another room and placed in front of a large and impressive-looking shock generator. The machine has 30 switches labeled 15 volts, 30 volts, 45 volts, and so on up to 450 volts in 15-volt increments. Near the switches for lower voltages is the label "Slight Shock." On the other side of the machine, near the switches associated with higher voltages, is another label, "Danger—Severe Shock." Your task is to give a learning test to the other subject. Each time he gives a right answer, you are to go on to the next word. Each time he gives a wrong answer, you are to punish him. The first time he misses an item, you are to give him a 15-volt shock. The next time, you must give him a 30-volt shock. You are to continue using a shock 15 volts higher than the preceding one each time the learner makes an error.

Things start out well, but soon you begin to realize that this is an uncomfortable situation. When you get to 75 volts, you hear the learner grunt. By the time you get to 120 volts, he has loudly complained about the situation. When you get to 150 volts, he wants to quit the experiment, and by the time you get to 285 volts, he screams in pain when you give the shock.

What would you do in this situation? Would you give the shocks? Probably you would first complain to the experimenter. The first time you complain, he says "Please continue" or "Please go on." The next time, he says "The experiment requires that you continue." The third time, he says "It is absolutely essential that you continue." If you continue to object, he will tell you "You have no other choice; you must go on." If you express worry about being liable for the learner's personal injury, the experimenter says "Although the shocks may be painful, there is no permanent tissue damage, so please go on."

How many shocks would you give to the learner before refusing to go on with the experiment? Go ahead and write the number in the margin of this book. Now let us see how your estimate compares to the predictions made by psychiatrists, college students, and middle-class adults.

Figure 4-3 shows a diagram of the control panel. There were 30 shock levels. The arrows point to the places that the three groups chose as predicted cutoff points. These are the points at which these people thought most subjects would say "I will not go on with the experiment." Notice that the psychiatrists were the ones who expected the subjects to be the most defiant. Everyone in each of the groups also predicted that the subjects would protest and stop the experiment before they had administered the 450-volt shock. Now that you have had the opportunity to review the predictions made by others, you may wish to revise your own predictions. You can do this by drawing an arrow on Figure 4-3 to show your own expectation.

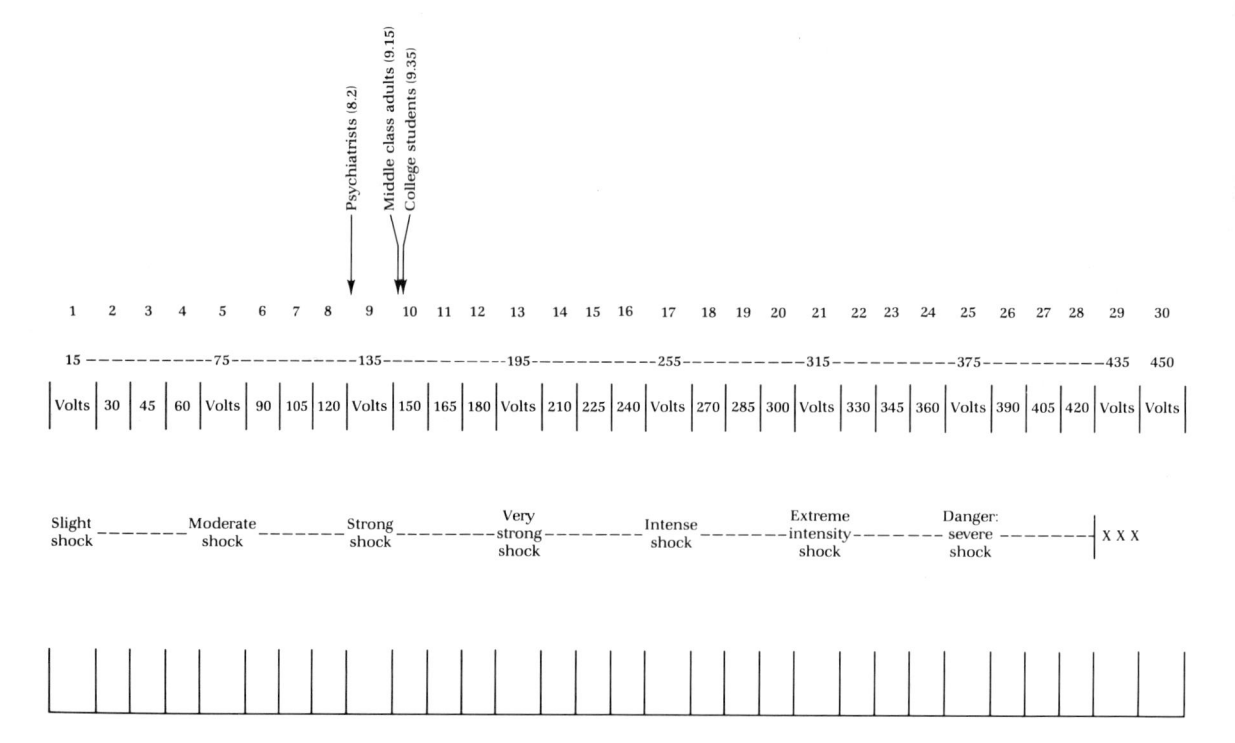

Figure 4-3. How far would you go? This is a diagram of the control panel used in Milgram's experiments (see text). The top row of numbers shows the levels of shock. The next row shows the voltage associated with each shock level. The strength of each level of shock is also indicated. The arrows show how far psychiatrists, college students, and middle-class adults thought the average subject would go. What is your estimate? *Source:* Milgram, 1974.

Now that we have your prediction, we can let you in on a secret. The learner in this experiment does not really receive shocks. The electrodes attached to his wrists do not actually deliver the electrical jolt. Any response he makes (such as yelling) is merely to make the subjects believe that they are really delivering the electric shocks. As a subject, you would think you were delivering the shock. You would have no idea that you were not really hurting the learner.

In his first experiment, Milgram found out something that should startle you. Sixty-five percent of the subjects obeyed the experimenter's demands and continued to give shocks until they had reached the final level—450 volts! No subject stopped the experiment before the 300-volt mark. At this point, they heard the learner pounding in agony on the wall of his room. Only 12.5% of the subjects who heard this refused to go on. The rest continued to obey!

All this is not to say that the task of obeying was easy on the subjects. Many of them protested, fumbled for cigarettes, mopped their sweating brows, and nervously turned in their chairs. Nevertheless, they continued to obey the orders. Remember, these were not war criminals. They were ordinary citizens like you or me.

Once Milgram had found this shocking evidence, he continued his research to find out exactly what conditions are most likely to increase or decrease obedience. Table 4-4 summarizes many of these experiments.

TABLE 4-4 Summary of Stanley Milgram's research on obedience[a]

Condition	Percentage obeying all the way
1. Subject plays subsidiary role to another subject (a confederate) who obeys. Subject can still refuse to obey at any point.	92.5
2. Victim is in a separate room but can be heard pounding on the wall.	65.0
3. Victim (with heart condition) is in a separate room but can be heard pounding on the wall.	65.0
4. One experimenter gives the orders, another experimenter acts as victim.	65.0
5. Subjects are women rather than men.	65.0
6. Victim is in a separate room but his vocal complaints can be heard.	62.5
7. Location of experiment is moved from prestigious Yale University premises to rundown industrial downtown area. No connection with the university is mentioned.	47.5
8. Experimenter is not very forceful and victim is rugged-looking.	47.5
9. Victim and subject are in the same room.	40.0
10. Victim stipulates at onset of experiment that he expects it to be halted upon his command because of his heart condition.	40.0
11. Subject is required to place victim's hand on a shock plate.	30.0
12. Experimenter is not in the room.	20.5
13. Experimenter leaves room and appoints another subject (a confederate) to act as experimenter.	20.0
14. Subject sits with two peers who refuse to punish victim.	10.0
15. Subject has choice of shock level for any trial.	2.5
16. One experimenter demands subject stop, another experimenter urges subject to go on.	0.0
17. Experimenter turns into victim and another subject gives orders.	0.0
18. Experimenter stops at 150 volts, but victim demands to go on.	0.0

[a]The left-hand column describes the experimental condition. The right-hand column shows the percentage of subjects obeying *all the way* to the command to shock the victim with 450 volts.
Source: Milgram, 1974.

Looking at the results of the Milgram studies, we can draw several conclusions about obedience to authority. To begin with, the closer the subject was to the victim, the less likely the subject was to obey. When they were required to put the victim's hand onto the shock plate, subjects became increasingly defiant. Another aspect of obedience to authority concerns the authority as such. Obedience was less likely to occur if the authority was not forceful (experiment 8), if the authority was absent from the room (experiment 12), or if a nonauthority figure gave the commands (experiment 13). When the authority himself was the victim, there was no obedient behavior (experiment 17). Obedience was also reduced when the authority's credibility was taken away by moving his laboratory out of a prestigious university into an unattractive downtown office complex (experiment 7). All subjects stopped giving shocks before they hit the 450-volt mark when the authority wanted to halt the experiment at a lower shock level (experiment 18), or when there were two authorities and one wanted the experiment stopped (experiment 16). Most of these experiments suggest that the word of an authority is taken seriously and that we are frightfully subservient to authority figures.

One of the most disturbing results of Milgram's experiment was discovered in experiment 1. In this experiment, the subject played a secondary role while another subject (actually a confederate) administered the shocks. In this situation, 92.5% of the subjects stood by without protest until the final 450-volt shock had been administered![47] In our modern bureaucratic society with its military organizations, most people do not actually engage in destructive behavior. Instead, they occupy secondary roles. People load guns, design weapons, provide support, shuffle papers, and so forth. Clearly, these people are part of the destructive effort. Yet, like the subjects in Milgram's experiment, they are not likely to do much about the wrongs they observe.

The Milgram experiments have been criticized because they may have been unethical, and because they may lack relevance to the real world.[48] Others have suggested that this criticism is based less on ethical considerations than on an unwillingness to accept the unflattering side of human nature that Milgram's studies have yielded. They claim that, if most of Milgram's subjects had disobeyed, his experiment would not have received as much condemnation.[49] Either way, Milgram's results say something profound and frightening about human nature. Their message is one we should all reflect upon with deep concern.

CONFORMITY

Can you be your own person?

Do your own thing! That is the type of advice we get from friends, counselors, and the Dear Abby column. Today people in all walks of life take pride in being resistant to the influence of others. Movies and television shows abound with young heroes bravely resisting evil influences to conform. As the heroes strike out on their own and tell others where to get off, the audience rewards them with frequent applause. In the popular movie *Serpico*, the audience is dazed by the true story of a New York policeman who resists tremendous pressures to conform to a corrupt system. For his lack of conformity, he becomes

[47]MILGRAM, 1974. [48]BAUMRIND, 1964. [49]BICKMAN & ZARANTONELLO, 1978.

disliked by the bad guys and admired by the good guys. Another area in which people like to proclaim their independence is politics. After the infamous Watergate incident, the most common cry from campaigning politicians was "I am my own person" or "I am not influenced by big money or political favors."

To put things in proper perspective, we must realize that very often conformity is the most adaptive form of behavior. Let us first look at the different definitions psychologists have given to the term **conformity**. Some psychologists arrive at a definition by pointing out what the term does *not* encompass. For example, to believe that the earth is not flat is uniformity, not conformity; or for men to wear pants rather than dresses is conventionality, not conformity. By the same token, excessively long hair in males is not necessarily an indication of independence. It could be a manifestation of rebellion (counterconformity), recently accepted conventionality, or even conformity to a counterculture.

Other psychologists make a distinction between *information-seeking* conformity and *norm-seeking* conformity. Norm-seeking individuals are true conformers. They conform because of the fear of exclusion, ridicule, or ostracism by others. Information-seeking individuals conform because they are confronted with unstructured or illogical situations that supply them with little or no information.[50] In a sense, such people only appear to conform. If you walk on a busy street and suddenly stop and glance up intensely at a tall building, it will take very little time for many others to conform to your behavior. Once they find out what it is all about, they will make up their own minds whether to continue with such behavior.

Sometimes the distinction between the two types of conformity is not entirely clear. The television show *Candid Camera*, where people were photographed without being aware of it, once provided a classical example of what appeared to be a display of conformity. The innocent victim was waiting on the second floor for an elevator to take him to the fifth floor. As the door opened, he saw three other passengers already occupying the elevator, which was on the way up from the first floor. The three people (confederates of the producer of the show) stood silently—facing the back wall of the elevator. The victim, faced with the strange sight of three immobile backs, first seemed hesitant. Then he shrugged his shoulders, pressed the button to the fifth floor, resignedly turned around and rode the elevator up to the fifth floor in the same position. If such behavior was motivated by fear of being ridiculed by the others, it would fall under the category of norm seeking. It is far more likely, however, that such behavior was spurred by the unstructured situation, which simply did not convey enough information. As such, it would fall under the category of information-seeking conformity (see Figure 4-4).

A widely accepted definition of conformity is that offered by psychologists Charles and Sara Kiesler. They suggest two forms of conformity: *compliance* and *private acceptance*. Compliance refers to actual changes in behavior in the direction that is desired by the influencing source. It does not take into consideration whether or not the conforming person believes in what he or

[50]DEUTSCH & GERARD, 1955.

Figure 4-4.
If the woman waiting for the elevator follows the example of the people already in it, it is likely that she is displaying information-seeking conformity (see text).

she is doing. Private acceptance refers to the internalization of group pressure. It occurs when the conforming person's beliefs and attitudes become the same as those of the influencing source.[51]

Compliance does not necessarily involve private acceptance. Imagine that you bump into someone while walking down the sidewalk. The person you bumped into turns and yells "You bumped into me! Apologize, you dirty...!" You might apologize and be on your way, thus complying with what was asked of you. There are several good reasons why you would want to handle the situation the way you did. Perhaps you did not want to make a scene. Or you might have been afraid of getting beaten up. Whatever the reason, if there was no private acceptance, your behavior is not going to change much. Your contacts with people in the street on future occasions will remain about the same. When the same situation occurs and involves your private acceptance, however, you would consider yourself clumsy and inconsiderate. Not only would you apologize, you would also be likely to change your behavior so that similar confrontations would be avoided in the future. After all, admission of clumsiness and inconsiderateness is damaging to your self-esteem. It is a painful process that we all try to avoid.

Let us now look at some of the research psychologists have done on conformity. You will soon find out that being your own person is easier said than done.

Look at the lines displayed in Figure 4-5. First look at the line in the left half of the figure. Now look at the three lines labeled comparison lines. Which of the comparison lines is the same length as the standard line?

Before you make your choice, we should tell you more about the situation. You are in a group consisting of eight students. All the students will judge the length of the lines and you will be the eighth person to respond. The first

[51]KIESLER & KIESLER, 1969.

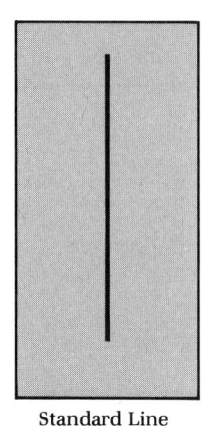

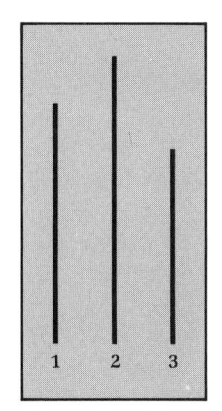

Figure 4-5.
A set of sample stimuli used in Asch's experiment on conformity. The standard line is the same length as line 2. When the experimental confederates said that either line 1 or line 3 was the same length as the standard line, subjects would conform by choosing the same incorrect line.

person chooses line 3. An honest mistake, you think, as you wait for the response of your next classmate. But she also chooses 3, and so does the third, fourth, and fifth student. Could this be, you ask yourself? Am I going crazy? After a few more students claim that 3 is the same length as the standard line, your turn comes. Which line do you choose? If you are like many of the people in an experiment conducted by Solomon Asch, you probably swing with the crowd and say that line 3 is the same length as the standard line. Actually, line 2 is the same length as the standard line, and the people who claimed line 3 was correct were confederates working for the experimenter. Asch found that about 33% of the judgments were incorrect. Of course, there is the possibility that humans do not make judgments about lines too accurately. To determine whether or not this was so, Asch included some subjects who were not exposed to group pressure. Among these people, 92% judged the length accurately.[52] Thus, there is solid evidence that people are easily influenced by pressures brought on by others.

Now that we know that you or your classmates would probably conform in the face of group pressure, you might be wondering *why* you would do it. Is it because you really believe that line 3 was the correct choice, or is it because you know line 3 was wrong but you did not want to rock the boat by deviating from the others? Some of the subjects in Asch's experiments later reported that they began to wonder about the adequacy of their eyesight or whether they were following instructions correctly. But many subjects knew they were giving the incorrect response but went ahead with it because they did not want to disagree openly with the others. For example, in one of Asch's later experiments he found less conformity if subjects responded privately.

If studies on line-judgment conformity do not overly impress you, consider the studies of psychologist Richard Crutchfield. He developed a mechanical device where people recorded their judgments and in turn were presented

[52]ASCH, 1952.

with the purported judgments of others. The advantage of this device was that it allowed for the expression of judgments in the choice of pictures, facts, opinions, and beliefs. For example, the statement "I doubt whether I would make a good leader" was rejected by every single Army officer under study. Under unanimous peer-group pressure (that is, when he was led to believe that fellow officers had endorsed this statement unanimously), 37% of the officers expressed agreement with the statement.[53] As an enlightened student, you may consider yourself immune to conformity. If so, you may be interested to know that college students under unanimous peer-group pressure have been known to agree to rather bizarre statements: that 60 to 70% of all Americans are over 65; that the average American male is about 8 to 9 inches taller than the average female but has a life expectancy of only 25 years; that the average American eats 6 meals a day but sleeps only 4 to 5 hours a night; and so on.[54]

Breeding grounds for conformity

What maximizes conformity? As we shall see later, some people are more conforming than others. It is part of their personality makeup. But there are also situational factors that operate across the board. Chief among those situational variables are the *size* of the pressure group, its degree of *unanimity*, its *competence*, and its general *cohesiveness*.

In Asch's original experiment, seven confederates served as the pressure group that tried to influence the subject to make an incorrect statement. Asch found out that with three confederates he achieved essentially the same results. Although more recent evidence indicates that, as the size of the pressure group increases, so does conformity to its norms,[55] the magic number 3 still remains. Two people are not sufficient to induce conformity.

A more important characteristic of the pressure group is its degree of unanimity, as, for example, in jury deliberations (see Box 4-1). Remember that all the confederates in the Asch experiment gave the same wrong answer. But just one dissenting opinion will greatly reduce conformity. Asch found that, when just one of the eight people broke rank and gave the correct response for each trial, the percentage of conforming subjects dropped from 32% to 5%. A more recent study showed that, even if the dissenting person's judgment could be perceived as highly questionable, the ensuing drop in conformity was still maintained. The dissenting person who broke rank and gave the correct answer was squinting through very thick glasses. The conclusion that this person might possibly be in error due to his poor eyesight did not faze the subjects. It still helped them to resist pressure to conform to the majority of the (no longer unanimous) group.[56]

A person's appraisal of the members of the pressure group will also affect the probability of conformity. If you are told that the others are very competent in judging lines (for example, you are told that they have been 90% correct on preceding trials), you are more likely to conform. If, on the other hand, you were told that the others are incompetent (that they have in the past been

---

[53]CRUTCHFIELD, 1955. [54]TUDDENHAM & MCBRIDE, 1959. [55]GERARD, WILHELMY, & CONNOLLEY, 1968. [56]ALLEN & LEVINE, 1971.

Box 4-1. Conformity pressure in the jury room

A few years ago, Alvin Leon Collins went on trial in San Diego for armed robbery. Although Collins had not been accused of threatening anyone with a weapon, it was alleged that he gave orders to another man to hold a knife to the throat of a young Marine and demand his wallet. The man who held the knife was given a lesser charge in exchange for testifying against Collins. The jury in the Collins trial deliberated for some time, with one juror holding out for a not guilty verdict against 11 others who favored conviction. Unable to deal with the situation, the dissenting juror asked to be released. When the judge consented to this request, a substitute juror who had watched the trial but had not experienced the deliberations was added to the jury. Within a few minutes, the jury decided on a guilty verdict.

Mr. Collins' lawyer was unhappy with this situation because he felt that the new juror had been put under undue pressure to conform to the majority view for conviction. California law requires that each juror make an independent judgment and that each juror have an equal chance of influencing the others. Accordingly, Collins' lawyer got in touch with social psychologists Robert Kaplan and Cathie Atkins[57] and asked them if any evidence in social psychology indicated that a new juror entering a group in which the others already unanimously favored one view was under any pressure to conform. The psychologists cited the Asch experiments and then performed a series of experimental simulations of the Collins trial. They found that the probability of a new juror's favoring conviction was a function of the number of jurors already favoring conviction when the alternate entered. Further, they found that a naive juror could easily be persuaded by a jury that had already had the experience of deliberation. When the case was appealed, the California Supreme Court agreed with the two psychologists. As a result, the procedure for introducing a new juror in California was changed. As for Collins, when the court reexamined the evidence against him, it still concluded that he belonged in jail.

---

wrong in 90% of the trials), you might be apt to *counterconform*. Counterconformity is not necessarily true independence of judgment. It is a deliberate disagreement with the group.[58]

Finally, your degree of conformity depends to a large extent on how you feel about the group as a working team. Groups where members feel close to one another and are functioning well together are known as cohesive groups. In such groups, members tend to feel loyal and dedicated to group goals. Former President Nixon considered public officials who conformed with a cover-up plot to deceive the public "good team players." Since Nixon's group was originally cohesive, many high-level officials did conform.

The case of former President Nixon is an example of how people will conform the more support they get from other group members to do so. Such support, however, is only one form of security. What happens when you know that other people in the group will like you, or dislike you, regardless of your intended course of action? Under such conditions, you are less likely to conform indiscriminately. One study demonstrated that subjects who felt

[57] KAPLAN & ATKINS, 1979. [58] WILLS & HOLLANDER, 1964.

most accepted *or* least accepted by the group conformed less than those who felt somewhat accepted.[59] Thus, it seems that fear of rejection may make you conform. This fear may increase in groups toward which you feel a special sense of closeness.

Profiles in conformity

Apart from situational factors, there are many personality characteristics associated with conforming behavior. Emotionally stable and intelligent people are most likely to resist group pressure to conform.[60] Individuals who perceive themselves as competent are less likely to conform than those who doubt their competency. Females are generally assumed to conform more than males, but these findings are confounded by methodical problems.[61]; primarily, however, it is a function of the degree they acquiesce to the traditional female role. Females who experience conflict about such a role, or who reject it, show a marked degree of independence.[62] An interesting, if somewhat complicated, relationship exists between achievement motivation and conformity. It was found that those with high motivation to achieve resist group pressure in unambiguous situations but conform more than unmotivated individuals as the situation becomes ambiguous.[63] In other words, as long as people are uncertain about the situation, they tend to depend on others in their judgment; as their certainty increases, they begin to depend on their own judgment. These findings provide further support for the need to separate information-seeking conformity from norm-seeking conformity.

Table 4-5 summarizes some self-perception patterns related to conformity.

BEHAVIOR MODIFICATION

Some principles of learning

Not too long ago, one of us attended a clinical staff conference at a community mental health center in his capacity as consultant. The discussion centered around the chartered course of psychotherapy for several previously diagnosed patients. Although the patients differed somewhat from one another in the diagnostic labels assigned to them, it was obvious from listening to those who had made the diagnosis that they considered their patients to be aggressive. Some of them spoke of dangerous aggression, and several even went so far as to mention homicidal forms of aggression.

At that point, someone suggested that the *behavior* of the aggressive patients be described. It soon became increasingly evident that many of the participants had used the identical label, aggression, for a variety of behaviors. The behavior of a child who threw temper tantrums was labeled aggressive. A supercritical father who belittled his son was labeled aggressive. A middle-aged handball player who played to win rather than for sportsmanlike competition was labeled aggressive. He was also considered to be aggressive in his (perfectly legal) business transactions. A high school student who engaged in senseless acts of property destruction was labeled aggressive. A young girl who kicked her parents' furniture was labeled aggressive, as was a man who on several occasions had wielded an ax over his wife's head. Naturally, the chartered course of psychotherapy, as well as the prognosis, for these patients had to differ considerably.

[59]DITTES & KELLEY, 1956. [60]DIVESTA, 1958. [61]ETTINGER, MARINO, ENDLER, GELLER, & NATZIUK, 1971; COOPER, 1979.
[62]TUDDENHAM & MCBRIDE, 1959. [63]MCDAVID & SISTRUNK, 1964.

TABLE 4-5 Some conformity variables

You are likely to conform if:	You are less likely to conform if:

You see yourself as
  modest
  tactful
  kind
  mannerly
  obliging
  helpful
  patient
	You see yourself as
	  moody
	  optimistic
	  logical
	  rational
	  demanding
	  humorous
	  original

Personality tests measure you as
  submissive-restrained
  cautious-controlled
  theoretical-intellectual
	Personality tests measure you as
	  outgoing-sociable
	  intelligent
	  self-confident
	  high in need-achievement

The experimenter tells you that
  your intelligence is being assessed
  you will be shocked for mistakes
  your group will be rewarded for cooperation
	The experimenter tells you that
	  you will be competing for an individual reward

Source: DiVesta, 1958.

The importance of behavioral terms is by no means limited to clinical situations. Over the course of the last quarter-century, there has been a dramatic growth in approaches to psychology that focus on behavior and minimize the role of thoughts, internal forces, and personality traits. B. F. Skinner has been the major advocate of behavioral psychology. He and his followers (generally referred to as behaviorists) believe that internal feelings, thoughts, and dispositions cannot be directly observed, cannot be measured accurately, and have no place in a scientific discipline such as psychology. Instead, psychologists are urged to study the relationship between the organism and its environment in stimulus and response terms, using precise behavioral descriptions to achieve this end. To say, for example, that you are hungry is meaningless for research, according to Skinner. To say that the stimulus is hunger and the response is eating is also not enough. In Skinnerian terms, your hunger must be described in terms of the elapsed time since you ate last. Eating must be described in terms of the amount of food consumed. Only with such rigorous descriptions, behaviorists say, is it possible to make predictions about the causes and effects of behavior. Table 4-6 lists several examples of behavioristic terminology.

Skinner is among the more radical behaviorists. His work has been frequently criticized, as has the method of manipulation that behaviorists use. Known as **behavior modification** (or behavior mod, to the in crowd), this method has assumed an all-powerful mystique which it may not deserve.[64] We shall address ourselves to this question later in the chapter. Regardless of such criticism, however, there is no denying that Skinner has had a tremendous impact on contemporary thought. His ideas have influenced such diverse fields as engineering, navigation, educational technology, psychotherapy, philosophy, and literature. But to understand Skinner, and behaviorism in general, it is necessary to have a rudimentary knowledge of some principles of

[64] "SENATE REPORT," 1975; "NIMH" REPORT, 1975.

TABLE 4-6 Talking in behavior terms. Behavioral psychologists define behavior in terms of the *operations* needed to observe it. Below are some examples of such operational definitions.

Behavior	Operational Definition
Hunger	Number of hours of food deprivation
Affection	Intensity of hugging response
Anxiety	Number of drops of sweat secreted into palms of hands
Aggression	Frequency of hitting, pushing, or shoving
Fear of heights	Number of steps a person will climb
Fear of dogs	Number of inches a person will allow between himself or herself and a dog
Intimacy of a couple	Amount of time spent in mutual eye contact

learning. (Don't let the number of unfamiliar terms in the next few pages discourage you, by the way; even if you have a problem remembering them, you will be able to finish the chapter with little difficulty.)

Classical conditioning: Learning the passive way

When a light is shined in your eyes, what do you do? You blink. The light is a *stimulus*. The blinking is your *response* to the stimulus. What happens to your blinking response if another stimulus is presented—say, the ringing of a bell? Whatever your response, blinking is not likely to be it. Suppose, however, that each time the light was flashed in your eyes, we rang a bell 1 second before the light came on. After a few rings, you would begin to blink your eyes as soon as you heard the bell. Getting you to blink your eyes when the bell is sounded is called **classical conditioning**, a method first developed around the turn of the century by a Russian physiologist named Ivan Pavlov. In classical conditioning, the stimulus that naturally evokes a response (in our example, the flash of light) is called the *unconditioned stimulus*, or *UCS*. The response (in our example, eye blinking) is called the *unconditioned response*, or *UCR*. The UCS leads to the UCR without any training: shining a light leads to blinking; presentation of food leads to salivating and so on.

After we find a UCS that produces a UCR, we can pair another stimulus with the unconditioned stimulus. This stimulus (in our example, the ringing of the bell) is called the *conditioned stimulus*, or CS. The CS may be associated with many responses, but it does not naturally lead to the response we wish to condition: ringing a bell does not ordinarily lead to blinking; sounding a buzzer does not ordinarily lead to salivating and so on. After we pair the conditioning stimulus with the unconditioned stimulus for several trials, the CS comes to elicit a response similar to the UCR. This response is called the *conditioned response*, or *CR*. The CR is similar to the UCR in many ways, but it is not exactly the same. Figure 4-6 shows an example of classical conditioning.

What happens when we stop pairing the CS with the UCS? That is, what would happen if we stopped pairing the flash of light (UCS) with the bell (CS)? Probably the CS would gradually lose its ability to evoke a conditioned response: you would gradually stop blinking when the bell sounded, or stop

1. UCS naturally leads to UCR:

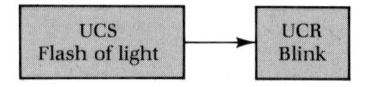

   UCS Flash of light → UCR Blink

2. CS is paired with UCS:

   CS Bell → UCS Flash of light → UCR Blink

3. CS elicits CR similar to UCR:

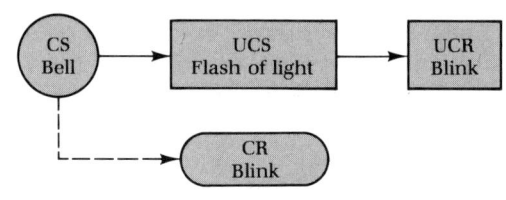

   CS Bell → UCS Flash of light → UCR Blink
         ↘ CR Blink

Figure 4-6.
An example of classical conditioning. The unconditioned stimulus (UCS) naturally produces an unconditioned response (UCR). By pairing the conditioned stimulus (CS) with the unconditioned stimulus (UCS), CS comes to elicit a conditioned response (CR).

salivating when the buzzer sounded. This process is called **extinction** because the potency of the CS gradually diminishes.

If bells, flashes of light, and eyeblinks do not excite you because their laboratorylike aspects are too scientific, consider an analogy from daily life. If you were the advertising director of a cigar company, one of your expected duties would be to get potential consumers to like your product. Suppose your company and your product, the El Bueno cigar, are new and unknown. You show your cigar for the first time on a television commercial. It is a stimulus presented to many viewers, among them potential buyers, but you have no way of knowing what kind of response this stimulus elicits. You are even less sure whether the responses are the kind you hoped for, such as liking or admiration. You know, however, that certain stimuli are almost guaranteed to evoke liking or admiration in television viewers—a celebrity, for example. Your interest, of course, is in a celebrity who evokes admiration in people who are cigar smokers, or at least potential cigar smokers. This limits the target group mostly to males over 30. Your celebrity, therefore, is not going to be Bozo the Clown or some character from a Walt Disney movie. You pick a well-endowed, sexy actress who, among other things, evokes admiration in your intended audience. You have found your UCS (the actress) who produces the UCR (admiration).

Now you pair the CS (El Bueno cigar) with the UCS (the actress) for a well-done commercial. Admiration is assured, if not for your cigar, then for your actress. You continue to pair them, all the time achieving the UCR of admiration. Then one day you show only the CS (El Bueno cigar) *without* the UCS (the actress). According to the concept of classical conditioning, the viewers' response will still be admiration (CR). The stimulus, El Bueno cigar, which before did not evoke the response that you wanted, is now admired by all. Of course, if you let go of the actress entirely, the CR may eventually face extinction. You run the danger that showing the El Bueno cigar without the actress may eventually lead to indifference. Just to make sure, once in a while you renew the conditioning process by re-pairing the CS (El Bueno cigar) and the UCS (the actress). Congratulations! Your potential customers are "learning"—the passive way, from the recesses of their armchairs with their eyes glued to the television screen—that El Bueno is a product to be admired.

Operant conditioning: Behaviors that pay off

In classical conditioning, the learner is passive. The learner, be it a person, an animal, or any living organism, can also be active. Organisms emit behavior that in effect performs some operation on the environment. The operation is called a response, and the learning process is known as **operant conditioning**. For example, a rat in a box with several levers in it seems to wander aimlessly around. Sooner or later, it hits one of the levers. Whether this response will occur again under the same circumstances depends largely on whether it is reinforced. Technically, a **reinforcement** is anything that, when presented after a response, strengthens that response. If the rat was hungry (and you know for how many hours it has been deprived of food), and if the lever hitting was followed by a food pellet, you can be sure that the lever will be pressed again and again. Your rat has learned to press a lever. Just make sure that the lever pressing will be followed by a food pellet at all times (*continuous reinforcement*), or sometimes (*partial reinforcement*). If no more pellets follow, the chances are high that the newly learned response will extinguish rapidly.

So far we have been discussing reinforcers as things that alleviate hunger or thirst. Hunger and thirst are *primary drives*. By primary drives, we mean drives which involve some tissue deficit.[65] These include hunger, thirst, sleep, and so on. Reinforcers that satisfy primary drives are called **primary reinforcers**. A characteristic of primary reinforcers is that they operate on a deprivation-satiation function. To be *satiated* means you have no need for a substance you would ordinarily consume. If you have a satiated food drive, for example, you have had enough to eat. When primary drives are satiated, we will not learn to get primary reinforcers. If Spot is not hungry, he will not learn to get the dog biscuit.

Besides primary drives, there are *secondary drives*. Secondary drives are learned, or acquired, drives satisfied by **secondary reinforcers**. Among such drives are those for power, achievement, affiliation, and approval. Although it was once believed that you can satiate a child's need for social approval,[66] later evidence suggests that social approval drives in children are not subject to satiation.[67] Thus, social approval can be one of the most effective forms of reinforcement because it is not affected by overuse.

[65]BOLLES, 1967; EISENBERGER, 1972. [66]GEWIRTZ & BAER, 1958. [67]EISENBERGER, KAPLAN, & SINGER, 1974.

Another principle of learning is **generalization**. Generalization occurs when we respond to a stimulus that is similar to, but not the same as, the stimulus we were trained on. For example, suppose you had learned to be afraid of a German Shepherd after it bit you. Generalization would refer to the extent to which you respond with fear to other dogs. Probably you would show the most fear in the presence of other German Shepherds. To a lesser extent, you might respond fearfully to all dogs. Behaviorists point out that generalization is one of the bases of prejudice: if a White person has had a bad experience with one Black person, that White person may generalize negative responses to other persons with similar skin coloration, and vice versa.[68]

The opposite of generalization is **discrimination**. Discrimination occurs when responses are stimulus specific. If you are afraid of the German Shepherd that bit you but are not afraid of any other dogs, you are demonstrating discrimination. Discrimination would occur if you respond to members of ethnic groups as individuals rather than generalizing the behaviors of one to others of the same group. (Ironically, "discrimination" as used by behaviorists can thus lead to the very opposite behavior of what the term usually connotes in race relations.)

The process of operant conditioning is far more complex than indicated in these examples. It involves an extensive terminology and a variety of conditions. Although an in-depth treatment of the process is beyond the scope of this book, numerous excellent textbooks are available on the topic of operant conditioning and behavioral psychology in general. For the beginning student, we strongly recommend a modest but thorough paperback text by William L. Mikulas, *Behavior Modification*.[69]

The power of social reinforcement

Behavior modification also refers to a variety of techniques for the application of learning theory to the change of behavior. Since the early 1960s, the growth of the movement has assumed astronomical dimensions. Leonard Ullman, one of the leaders in the field, has pointed out that the spread of behavior modification techniques has been like the development of a social movement.[70] At the same time, the movement has also come under criticism for a variety of reasons. Traditional psychotherapists have attacked behavioristic approaches as too simplistic, treating symptoms rather than underlying disturbances or disorders. Other psychologists have rejected the behavioristic notion that cognitive processes (such as opinions, judgments, decisions) are of little consequence. There is also a general uneasiness in public opinion about the use of behavior modification in prisons, mental institutions, and the like. It has sinister, dehumanizing overtones that conjure thoughts of control, punishment, deprivation, and shades of the oppressive society envisaged in George Orwell's *1984*.

Behaviorists have become acutely aware of these feelings. Recent publications by leaders in the field warn their colleagues to use the technique of behavior modification judiciously, to be aware of its limitations, and to engage in an active educational campaign to alleviate some of the common misper-

[68]McGinnis, 1970.   [69]Mikulas, 1974.   [70]Ullman, 1972.

ceptions about it.[71] There is little doubt, however, that behavior modification techniques do work. The problem, as we shall see later, is in deciding who does the manipulating and what is to be manipulated to maximize individual benefits and public welfare.

At this point in time, behavior modification is not a single technique but a series of methods that draw upon clinical, social, developmental, and experimental psychology. Psychologist Leonard Krasner has listed at least 15 streams of development in the field of behavior modification. Since the late 1960s, the streams have come increasingly together under the collective label of behavior modification. The merger of streams is not yet complete, and many of the approaches still remain distinct from one another.[72] The rest of this chapter will be a brief examination of some of the most common forms of behavior modification.

"Boy, do we have this guy conditioned. Every time I press the bar down he drops a pellet in."

Social psychologists, despite some limitations, have nevertheless made increasing use of behavior modification in the study of social issues (see Chapter 11) as well as social interaction. For example, several studies by psychologists have clearly demonstrated how our need for approval is manipulated in our daily interactions with others. You may have never heard of the *Greenspoon effect* or the *method of successive approximation* in conjunction with the need for approval. We shall dutifully explain these terms and describe the experiments that brought them about. Somehow, however, we have a feeling that, as you are reading along, you will come to realize that both terms are actually part of your daily routine, even though you may have been unfamiliar with their assigned technical labels.

[71]BANDURA, 1974. [72]KRASNER, 1971.

Psychologist Joel Greenspoon assigned 75 college students to five different groups of 15 subjects each. The students were individually asked to say all the words they could think of but to refrain from using sentences or phrases. The sounds "mm-hmm" and "huh-uh" made by the experimenter served as the intended reinforcing stimuli. The reinforcing stimuli were introduced in Group I ("mm-mm-hmm") and in Group II ("huh-uh") following each *plural* response during the first 25 minutes of the testing sessions. Similarly, they were introduced in Groups III and IV, but following each nonplural response. A fifth group served as a control, since no sounds were introduced during the entire session. Responses were scored in time blocks of 5-minute periods each. The results indicated that the "huh-uh" stimulus (presumably implying dissapproval) tended to decrease the frequency of the plural responses, whereas the "mm-mm-hmm" stimulus (presumably implying approval) tended to increase the frequency of both plural and nonplural responses.[73]

How important is the **Greenspoon effect**, which is the common term used to describe the findings just given? The fact that sounds of approval or disapproval can significantly alter the rate of another person's uttering of plural or nonplural words (in most cases, without that person's awareness of the reason for the change) is, in itself, not very earthshaking. Its implications and generalizations, however, are of considerable importance. If sounds of approval, or gestures of approval such as head nodding or smiling, can systematically alter *other* behaviors as well, then the Greenspoon effect is a milestone in social behavior modification. The evidence clearly points that way. For example, in one study 24 college students attending an experimental psychology class were chosen to reinforce the 550 students of their school by complimenting each student when wearing clothes of a particular color. Reinforcement took place at lunchtime, and every five days the inspection of clothes for color took place. The color blue was reinforced daily for about four weeks (from 25% of the students wearing blue to an average of 38% after the first five days), then extinguished (to 27%), then reinforced again (to 38%). Similarly, the color red was reinforced within five days (from 13% to 22%).[74]

The fact is that most of us simply do not realize the reinforcing potential of smiles, head nodding, or sounds of approval. The secret, of course, is to administer these reinforcers judiciously and systematically. Constant smiling and head nodding (continuous reinforcement) are not as effective as occasional gestures of this sort (partial reinforcement). In any event, the effects of these reinforcers are astonishing. If you observe successful salespersons, you will see a most effective use of a variety of such reinforcers (even though the salespersons themselves may not be aware that they are administering systematic reinforcement). If you ever have to address a group of people, you will find out immediately how important it is to see some of your listeners nodding their heads or smiling whenever you are trying to make a point. The cruelest joke anyone could play on you would be to preinstruct your listeners to gaze blankly at you, registering neither approval or disapproval. You are guaranteed to perspire and feel uneasy within a short time, and if your frantic search for at least some sort of reinforcer is in vain, you will begin to fumble for words. We are reminded of the time when members of a class taught by one of

[73]GREENSPOON, 1955. [74]CALVIN, 1962.

our colleagues decided to modify his behavior. The professor had the annoying habit of constantly pacing back and forth across the width of the room while lecturing. To modify his behavior, the students decided to smile or nod their heads only when the professor stood near his lectern. Every time he strayed from that location, he was met with blank stares. Within two weeks, they had him practically glued to the lectern. Most significant of all, until he was told about the students' behavior, he did not realize what was going one. His lectures, incidentally, dealt with the topic of behavior modification.

Closely related to these antics is the method of **successive approximation**. Before we describe the original experiment in this area, let us take you back to elementary school. At one time or another during those days, you and your friends were actually engaged in applying the method of successive approximation. The scenario may have been something like this: it is a beautiful spring day, the sun is shining, and you are aching to be outside playing. Somehow you are not in the mood to engage in serious study. Not too surprisingly, when the teacher announces that today's topic will be the structure of minerals, there is a collective groan from the class. The teacher has barely begun with "There is a considerable deposit of minerals in Mexico ..." when bright-eyed little Johnny's hand is up, inquiring whether the teacher has ever been to Mexico. Of course, says the teacher. Really, exclaim some amazed students, and did he, the teacher, actually watch a bullfight? Of course, says the teacher, enjoying the excitement generated by his statement. When little Jane bemoans the fact that bullfighting is cruel, the teacher tells her that it does not have to be so. When he was in Portugal, he saw bullfights that were bloodless. Another collective gasp of admiration. The teacher, basking in that admiration, tells the class how he backpacked across Portugal. An intense discussion of the relative merits of backpacking versus motoring follows. Then the features of the latest car models are discussed. Pretty soon the bell rings. The class ends on a happy note. Whatever the topic of discussion may have been, the structure of minerals was definitely not it.

Was the teacher aware that his students conned him, so to speak? Some teachers are aware but do not mind. Other teachers are not even aware of it. In either case, the student-produced stimuli (eagerness, interest, smiling, head nodding) satisfied the teachers' needs for approval. With some teachers, of course, you cannot get away with it. They will stick to the topic of the structure of minerals, just as some satiated rats will not press a lever when the food pellet appears. Yet sooner or later, when those rats are deprived of food or when the food pellet is especially delectable, they will press the lever. By the same token, sooner or later circumstances will make those stubborn teachers succumb to the delectable reinforcement of student admiration, interest, and gestures of approval.

Now for the experiment proper. Twenty-four individuals were administered worded reinforcements during ordinary conversation by 17 psychology students who were their roommates or friends. Once the conversation started, the experimenter tried to refrain from making any response to the subject's expressed opinions for the first 10 minutes. During the next 10 minutes, every expressed opinion was positively reinforced by such exclamations as "You're right" and "Yes, that's so" or by paraphrasing aloud the opinion that the subject had just expressed; during the last 10 minutes, extinction was attempted (once more, no responses were made to the expressed opinion of the subject). A control group was established in which the first 10-minute treatment (aimed at establishing a baseline) was eliminated, so that order effects were under control. In both groups, the administration of reinforcement significantly increased the number of expressed statements. The content of the conversation was thus manipulated by administering interpersonal approval and disapproval. The implication of the findings is clear: it is possible to set in advance a given target topic and, by successively administering the proper verbal reinforcement, to approximate the achievement of that target.[75]

A final word of caution. Rewarding people has its limits. There has been considerable evidence that offering rewards to a person engaged in otherwise enjoyable activity will undermine the person's subsequent interest in that activity when the reward is discontinued. Known as the **overjustification effect**,[76] it has the following logic: you are engaged in an enjoyable task—say, woodcarving—and your enjoyment is justified by just what you are doing (intrinsic incentive). If, however, you should now also get paid for it on a regular basis, there is a danger that you would infer that your woodcarving activity was motivated by the reward itself (extrinsic incentive) rather than by enjoyment, with the result that once payments stop, your interest in the task decreases. (You may wonder how psychologists manipulate intrinsic motivation in the laboratory, since it calls for subjects to be engaged in challenging but enjoyable tasks. One such task is the "Nina Puzzle," derived from drawings by cartoonist Al Hirschfeld. If you want to have a go at it, try solving the puzzle in Figure 4-7.)

SUMMARY HIGHLIGHTS

1. Attitudes do not necessarily predict actions. People frequently express preference for a product or a political candidate yet fail to vote or make purchases consistent with their expressed preference.
2. There are six types of *social power:* information power, coercive power, reward power, legitimate power, referent power, and expert power.
3. Many methods have been shown to increase compliance to a given demand. People comply more with requests that elicit guilt, sympathy, and fear. Some of the methods that have been shown to increase compliance, however, are counterintuitive. *Cognitive dissonance* studies show that people may comply to requests when they are not paid well to do it, when they have recently been insulted, or after they have engaged in counterattitudinal activities. *Hypnosis*, which is often thought of as a failproof method of increasing compliance, may have little effect unless the subject desires to be hypnotized.
4. *Obedience* is another form of yielding to social power. A series of experiments revealed that people are much more obedient under certain conditions than was predicted by either trained mental health specialists, laypersons, or college students. Factors associated with obedience

[75]VERPLANCK, 1955. [76]LEPPER, GREENE, & NISBETT, 1973; LEPPER & GREENE, 1978; HARACKIEWICZ, 1979.

Figure 4-7.
A Nina Puzzle. The name NINA is hidden in the picture eight times. *(Al Hirschfeld portrait of Joel Grey reproduced by special arrangement with the Margo Feiden Galleries, New York, New York.)*

include the degree of interaction between the subject and the victim, and the presence of an authority figure giving the orders.
5. *Conformity* studies show that social pressures to conform increase the likelihood that people will endorse views they are uncertain to be correct. The chances of conforming increase when pressure by others is unanimous. A unanimous majority of three elicits more pressure to conform than a larger nonunanimous majority. *Information-seeking conformity* only arises in ambiguous situations, but *norm-seeking conformity* is manifested when there are fears of group ridicule or retaliation for noncompliance.
6. Principles of *behavior modification* have also been used to get others to change their behaviors. These methods include *classical conditioning, operant conditioning,* and *social reinforcement. Overjustification effect* studies, however, have shown that people may lose interest in intrinsically well-liked activities once external rewards are withdrawn.

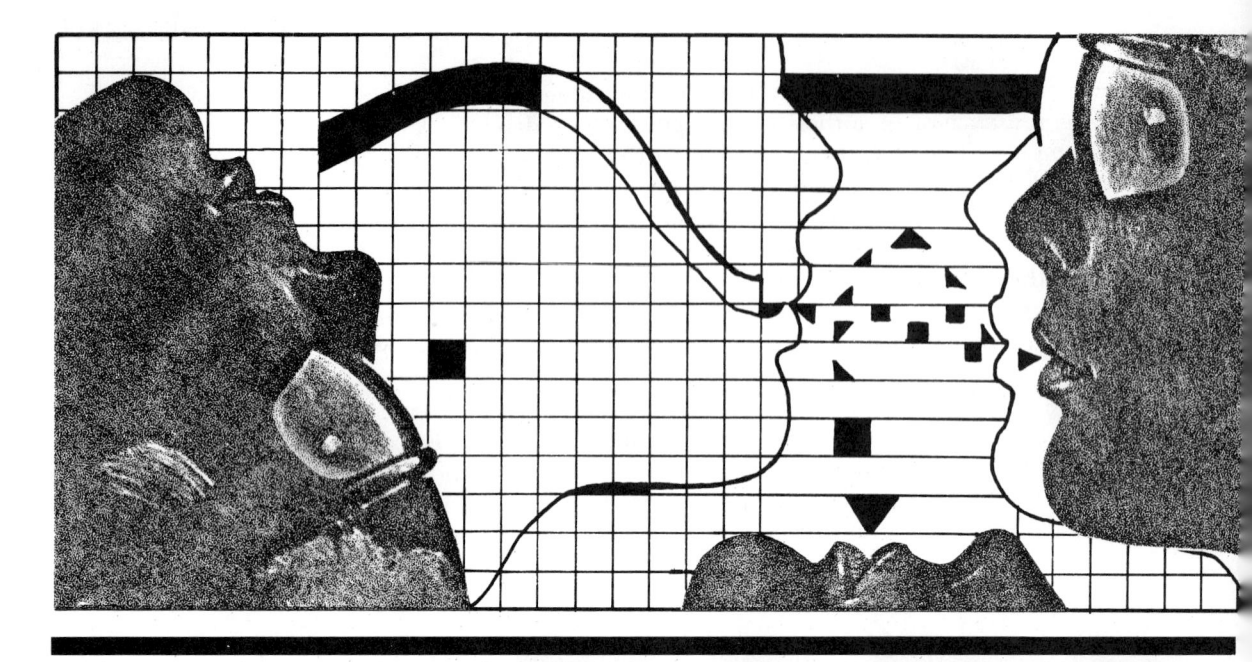

PART

SOCIAL

THREE

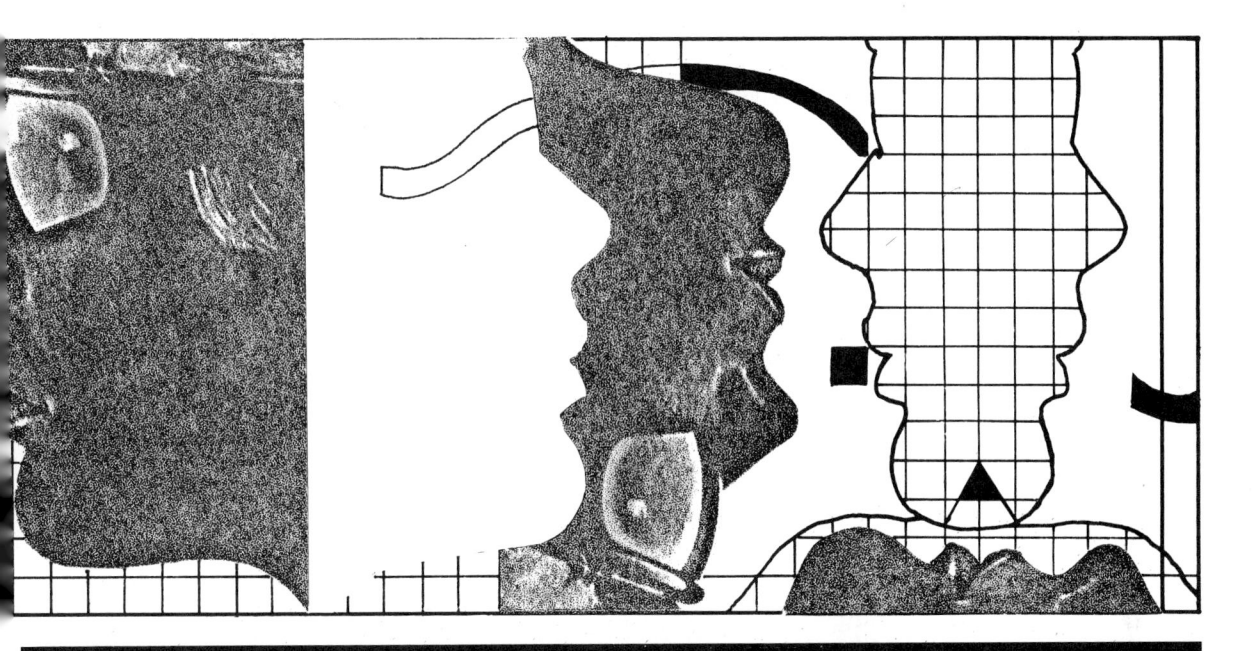

INTERACTION

CHAPTER 5 ATTRACTION AND INTIMACY

POPULARITY AND LIKING
    Popularity: Moving in (the right) circles
    Exchange: The interpersonal marketplace
    Exposure: Familiarity makes the heart grow fonder
    Propinquity: The folks next door
    Similarity: Birds of a feather flock together
    Self-perception: If the adrenalin flows, it must be love
    Climate: Cool temperatures and hot passions

DATING AND MATING
    The winners: Beautiful and adored
    The losers: Homely and ignored
    The trophy: Lots of love but few data
    The game plan: The girl next door who plays hard to get
    The penalties: No points for jealousy

MARRIAGE PROBLEMS
    Traditional: The law of infidelity
    Divorce: The end of the road

SUMMARY HIGHLIGHTS

"There is a law that man should love his neighbor as himself. In a few hundred years it should be as natural to mankind as breathing or the upright gait."[1] Thus spoke the famous psychologist Alfred Adler, who may have overstated his case. Not everyone is *that* loving. On the other hand, there are plenty of people who are loving but who are not exactly lovable. Adler was, nevertheless, on the right track. At least the *need* to be loved is critical to our personal and social adjustment. For these reasons alone, it seems that a closer look at such elusive terms as "popularity," "liking," and "love" is very much in order.

POPULARITY AND LIKING

Popularity: Moving in (the right) circles

Popular people are generally liked (although sometimes merely admired or respected). Popularity, however, differs from friendship. To be *liked*, one must be liked *by someone;* to be *popular*, one must be regarded collectively as attractive *by the members of a group*. Friendship always involves interaction between people. Popularity may or may not involve such interaction.

What makes some people more popular than others? It would be futile to attempt to find out what causes popularity. At best, we can talk about popularity correlates. For example, it has been clearly demonstrated that

[1]SELDES, 1966.

popularity is inversely related to accident proneness. First aid records of school nurses show that highly unpopular children sustain the most injuries, just as steelmill workers with low status among their peers display the greatest number of industrial accidents.[2] It is, however, not quite clear whether these unpopular individuals have such high rates of accidents because they are rejected by others, or whether they are rejected because they tend to sustain so many accidents.

Because of the circularity of the problem, we can only present you with a brief list of what it takes to be popular (but not necessarily how to go about it). In general, your chances of being popular increase as

You stay with people similar to you in socioeconomic status.
Your family relationship is marked by harmony.
You have physical skills.
You are relatively free from accidents.
You display scholastic achievement.
You have a moderate (as opposed to high or low) self-concept.
You have a common name.
You are physically attractive.[3]

(Incidentally, as far as scholastic achievement goes, brilliance alone may not be sufficient to earn popularity. Intellectual dullness, however, is no asset among young Americans whose social groups are often closely related to scholastic settings. In any event, it is more likely for a highly intelligent student to be unpopular than for a student of low intelligence to be popular.)

Exchange: The interpersonal marketplace

George Homans and Peter Blau, two well-known sociologists, have developed a theoretical framework for human interactions. Relationships between and among people are assumed to be based on fair exchanges. If I like to talk and you like to listen, we will get along fine—we have a fair exchange. But if I like to talk and you do not like to listen, we no longer have an even exchange. Life is essentially a series of such exchanges. You put up with school and teachers in exchange for a degree; you refrain from yelling at your boss in exchange for the chance to keep your job; and so forth.[4]

As Harvard psychologist Zick Rubin points out, you should not be surprised if you encounter a beautiful young woman draping her arms around a short, balding, but successful businessman. Each has something the other desires. She has beauty, and he has the capacity to take her to glamorous places and buy her nice things. Both parties, aware of their offerings, have negotiated a fair trade.[5]

When you buy something in the marketplace, you usually know the limits of your spending capacity. The more money you have, the more lavish you can be. Your dollars provide you with a precise estimate of your buying power. In

[2]FULLER & BAUNE, 1951; SPEROFF & KERR, 1952. [3]LOOMIS & PROCTOR, 1950; KUHLEN & BRETSCH, 1947; BRECK, 1950; FRENCH, 1951; GROSSMAN & WRIGHTER, 1948; BONNEY, 1955; REESE, 1961; MCDAVID & HARARI, 1966; DION, BERSCHEID, & WALSTER, 1972. [4]BLAU, 1955; HOMANS, 1961. [5]RUBIN, 1973.

the interpersonal marketplace, you must appraise your own buying power. There are no loans, and if you try to buy something beyond your assets, you may be flatly turned down. Psychologists use the term *self-esteem* to describe your appraisal of your own market value. Through a series of exchanges with other people, you eventually come to recognize your worth.

For women, physical attractiveness may be a quality that greatly enhances marketability. An important quality for men may be occupational status. Such sexist pricetagging may be deplorable, but this is what occurs even in supposedly enlightened interpersonal marketplaces such as universities and colleges. In one study, female university students were rated on their physical attractiveness. These women were asked in turn to rate how acceptable men in various occupations would be as dates. Most of the women felt that men in high-status fields would be acceptable. These high-status occupations included doctors, lawyers, and chemists. Almost all the college women thought that men in the low-status occupations of janitor or bartender would be unacceptable as dates. Attractive and unattractive women differed in their ratings of acceptability for medium-status occupations. The attractive women felt that electricians, bookkeepers, and plumbers would not be acceptable dates. The unattractive women felt that men in these occupations would be moderately acceptable. Thus, the women in this study had assessed their own market value in terms of physical beauty and had judged the acceptability of middle-status men according to their own "buying power."[6]

Psychologists Elaine Walster and Ellen Berscheid have provided a similar theoretical framework for exchange in human interaction. Their **equity theory** contains a number of propositions and formulas aimed at "making clear predictions of the impact that equity/inequity should have on intimate relationships."[7] In one of their studies, the responses of over 500 college men and women who described their dating relationships yielded three classes of subjects: (1) *underbenefitted* partners—those who felt that the relationship was inequitable because they were not getting enough from their partners when it came to decision making, including decisions regarding sex (when to engage in it, when to abstain, how to practice it, and so on); (2) *overbenefitted* partners—those who felt that the relationship was inequitable because they were getting too much from their partners; and (3) *equitable* partners—those who felt that there was a fair exchange in giving and taking. The results clearly showed that equitable love relationships were the happiest and most content. The inequitable relationships were volatile and unstable, with the underbenefitted feeling resentful and the overbenefitted feeling guilty. Moreoever, "both the underbenefitted, who have every reason to believe that something better will come along, and the overbenefitted, who have every reason to wish that their relationship could last, are well aware that their relationships are tenuous ones. If their relationships are not already in disarray, they expect that they soon will be!" (p. 91).

Equity, or the lack of it, almost always involves some sort of power relationship. In male-female interaction, the exercise of power is often dictated by sex role expectations. Psychologists Toni Falbo and Anne Peplau investigated

---

[6]VanGorp, Stempfle, & Olson, 1969. [7]Walster, Walster, & Berscheid, 1978; Walster, Walster, & Traupman, 1978.

various power strategies used by heterosexual and homosexual partners (studies on the latter were conducted under the assumption that sex role constraints would not be operative). As Table 5-1 shows, power strategies have aspects of interaction and directness. The results of the study showed gender differences only among the heterosexuals, with men more likely than women to report using bilateral and direct strategies. The results, according to the authors, reflect balance of power relationships. That is, people who preferred and perceived themselves as having more power than their partners, such as heterosexual men, were also more likely to use bilateral and direct strategies. No other differences were found between the heterosexual and homosexual groups.[8]

TABLE 5-1. Examples of various power strategies among intimate partners

	Interaction	
	Bilateral	Unilateral
Direct	"We talk about it. We discuss our differences and needs."	"I ask him/her to do what I want."
	"I reason with him/her. I argue my position logically."	"I tell him/her how important it is to me."
	"We usually negotiate something agreeable to both of us. We compromise."	"I tell him/her what I want. I state my needs."
	"I repeatedly remind him/her of what I want until he/she gives in."	
Indirect	"I smile a lot. I am especially affectionate."	"I pout or threaten to cry if I don't get my way."
	"I drop hints. I make suggestions."	"I clam up. I become silent."
		"We do our own thing. I just do it by myself."

Source: Falbo & Peplau, 1980.

As long as we are using the marketplace analogy, we may as well deal with such phenomena as rewardingness and gain-loss. In the interpersonal marketplace, you are trying to sell something. To get the most in exchange, you must be able to enhance your *rewardingness.* The day-to-day trading activity does not necessarily involve such traditional offerings as appearance or wealth. A simple exchange of friendship can be rewarding, such as verbal comments like "You look nice," "You are doing a good job," "I like you," or even a mere smile of approval (actually, these seemingly innocuous gestures can be come potent weapons when applied systematically; see Chapter 4).

Sometimes we like people just because they are involved with a situation that is rewarding for us. For example, psychologists Albert and Bernice Lott had children play games in small groups. Some of the children were given model cars in exchange for their participation. It was observed that these children liked the other group members more than children who did not receive rewards.[9] Other studies have shown that uncomfortably hot rooms

[8] Falbo & Peplau, 1980. [9] Lott & Lott, 1960.

can cause negative emotional responses that generalize to make those in the rooms appear less attractive.[10] These cases show the effects of rewards that do not come directly from a rewarding source.

The most powerful rewards, however, are based upon what people say. Equipped with a little background in behavioral psychology (see Chapter 4), you might be ready to flatter everyone in sight. Dale Carnegie, author of *How to Win Friends and Influence People*, recommends just such an approach. The Carnegie style is to use flattery and praise continually. The advice is: be ingratiating—flattery will get you anywhere![11]

Traditional folk wisdom, however, also teaches us that flattery should get you nowhere. In fact, many people shy away from flattery. One reason for this is that such praise may cause the receiver's head to swell. In response to a highly laudatory introduction, Adlai Stevenson once wryly remarked that "flattery is all right, as long as you don't inhale it." The Dale Carnegie approach to flattery could also be faulted because you might suspect that someone who praises you lavishly is out to manipulate you. The nice comments directed at you may be merely devices to get your money, your time, or your body.

The sad fact is that flattery *will* get you nearly everywhere. Psychologist Edward Jones has performed several experiments on *ingratiation* behavior. His findings generally support the notion that flattery will get you somewhere. After reviewing several of his own experiments, Jones found himself admiring the candor of Lord Chesterfield, who said:

> Vanity is, perhaps, the most universal principle of human actions. . . . If my insatiable thirst for popularity, applause, and admiration made me do some silly things on the one hand, it made me, on the other hand do all the right things I did. . . . With the men I was a Proteus, and assumed every shape to please them all: Among the gay I was the gayest: Among the grave, the gravest: and I never omitted the least attention to good breeding, to their least offices of friendship, that could either please or attach them to me. . . .[12] (p. 290)

Keeping the market analogy in mind, let us now turn to the **gain-loss phenomenon**. Many a nervous investor in stocks has found out that there is nothing stationary about his or her investments. Fortunes wax and wane, ranging from dizzying gains to abysmal losses. The interpersonal marketplace is no exception. The varying impact of interpersonal rewards was clearly demonstrated in an experiment by psychologists Elliot Aronson and Darwyn Linder.[13] In discussing the study, Aronson described it as analogous to what happens at the scene of a cocktail party.[14] According to the familiar script, you attend a party and talk to someone. After talking to you, this person wanders off and talks to someone else about you. On many occasions, you may actually hear yourself discussed as you listen to the snatches of conversation around you.

Place yourself now in each of the following conditions: (1) you overhear a person praising you at several different cocktail parties (gain); (2) the same person praises you at the early parties but at later parties becomes more negative (gain-loss); (3) the person speaks negatively about you at early parties but gradually becomes more positive (loss-gain); and (4) the person continues

---

[10]Griffitt, 1970.　[11]Carnegie, 1937.　[12]Jones, 1977.　[13]Aronson & Linder, 1965.　[14]Aronson, 1980.

to be negative about you throughout the parties (loss). Under which of these four conditions are you going to be most attracted to that cocktail party gossiper?

In the Aronson and Linder experiment, the cocktail-party circuit was simulated by giving each of the subjects (college women) a chance to eavesdrop on a conversation between another subject (an experimental confederate) and the experimenter over a period of seven meetings. The confederate, asked by the experimenter to give her reactions about the subject for a purported study on how people form impressions, described the subject differently in each of four series of meetings. In the positive-positive conditions, the subject heard herself described favorably (intelligent, likable) throughout the seven meetings. In the negative-negative condition, the subject heard herself described unfavorably (dull, ordinary) during the seven meetings. In the negative-positive condition, the subject heard a negative evaluation throughout the first three meetings; from the fourth meeting on, however, the evaluations became more positive until, in the seventh meeting, they became entirely positive. In the positive-negative conditions, the subject heard herself described positively during the first three meetings, but from the fourth meeting on, the evaluations became increasingly negative until, in the seventh meeting, they became entirely negative.

At the conclusion of the experiment, each of the subjects was asked to give her gut response about the person she had overheard. The average responses (on a scale ranging from –10 to +10) of the subjects in the various conditions are shown in Table 5-2. As the data demonstrate, the most remarkable gains occurred in the negative-positive condition. Apparently, hearing a gossiper's few negative comments can, so to speak, "ripen" you, so that subsequent positive comments increase your liking for that person.

TABLE 5-2. Gain-loss phenomenon in liking

Experimental condition	Average liking[a]
Negative-positive	+7.67
Positive-positive	+6.42
Negative-negative	+2.52
Positive-negative	+0.87

[a]The ratings are given by subjects who overhear another person (the evaluator) speaking of them. When the evaluation changes from negative to positive, the evaluator is liked more than when the evaluation is consistently positive. When the evaluation changes from positive to negative, the evaluator is liked least (see also Figure 5-1).
Source: Aronson & Linder, 1965.

Exposure: Familiarity makes the heart grow fonder

A few years ago, one of the authors of this book lived in a house with several other people. One of the roommates used to play the same acid-rock record over and over again. At first, the record got on the nerves of everyone in the house. "How can he listen to that junk?" they would ask one another indignantly. Gradually, however, something unexpected happened. The others actually began to like the ear-piercing rock music. As it turned out, those who

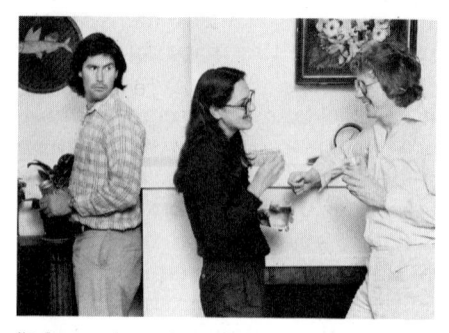

128 CHAPTER 5

"John can be so boring, don't you think?"

"Overall, I think John is a really nice person."

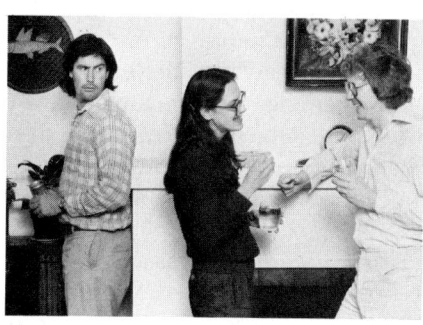

"John is nice...."

"John is so intelligent...."

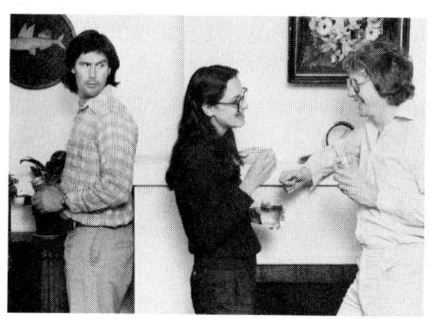

"In my opinion, John is not very likable."

"John is boring, period."

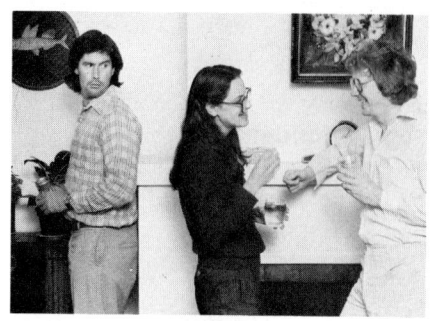

Figure 5-1.
The cocktail party gossip. How does John feel about her? (Refer to Table 5-2.).

"I think John is a nice person."

"John is absolutely dull."

were around most when it was played were also the ones who became fondest of the record. In fact, when this writer moved out of the house, he found himself going to the local music store to buy the same record.

A few years later, he was not surprised to learn that the same thing had happened to some very cultured rats. The rats, who grew up in a laboratory at Texas Technological College, were exposed to fine music for 12 hours daily while they spent 52 days in laboratory confinement. One group of rats listened to the soothing sounds of Mozart. Their listening diet included *The Magic Flute* as well as Violin Concerto no. 5 and Symphonies no. 40 and 41. A second group of rats heard a different sort of classical music. These animals heard atonal sounds created by Schoenberg, including *Pierrot Lunaire, A Survivor from Warsaw, Verklaerte Nacht,* and *Kol Nidre.* A third group of rats used as a control was not exposed to any music.

After hearing concert music for 52 consecutive days, the Texas rats were given 15 days of quiet and then tested for their musical preferences. To achieve this end, a preference test appropriate for rats had to be devised. Switches were rigged up in the cages which a rat could easily step on to activate a Mozart or a Schoenberg concert. The rats soon learned to use the switches. Since both switches were available in each cage, the rats could play whichever composer they preferred. The only catch was that these recordings contained different selections from the concerts that the rats had heard previously (although by the same composers).

Which music did the rats play most? It depended on what they were exposed to the most. Those raised on Mozart liked Mozart. Those who had grown up on Schoenberg preferred his compositions.*[15] What happened to the rats and the writer with the acid-rock roommate was essentially the same thing. Both came to like the music they were exposed to most. According to psychologist Robert Zajonc, these results should not be surprising. Zajonc has been studying the effects of exposure for quite some time. Psychologists have always been aware that people begin to like things more after repeated exposure. It was not until 1968, however, that Zajonc formally presented the theory of **mere exposure**. The principle is simply that repeated exposure to a stimulus is a sufficient condition to enhance a person's attitude toward it.[16]

One reason people come to like each other may be no different from the principle which makes rats like a certain composer. That is, you may like most those to whom you are most frequently exposed. In Robert Zajonc's study, pictures of men were taken from the Michigan State University yearbook and shown to University of Michigan students for periods of 2 seconds. Some pictures were shown for more 2-second periods than other pictures. When asked how much they might like the person in the picture, the students tended to display more favorable attitudes toward the men whose pictures were displayed most frequently.

A more recent study showed that mere exposure also enhanced attraction when the stimuli were people (instead of pictures). Women from the Univer-

---

[15]CROSS, HALCOMB, & MATTER, 1967. [16]ZAJONC, 1968

*Should you ever argue with your friends about who is the greater composer, we suggest (somewhat tongue-in-cheek) that you cite the following facts: the preference for Mozart among Mozart-reared rats was stronger than the preference for Schoenberg among Schoenberg-reared rats. In addition, rats raised without music tended to prefer Mozart. Thus, even rats are aware that Mozart created more likable sounds.

sity of Michigan signed up for an experiment purportedly dealing with the psychophysics of taste. While the women were being ushered from room to room to taste various liquids, the experimenters carefully arranged to allow each subject to be exposed to other subjects in the experiment. In fact, the room shuffles were planned so well that each subject encountered one person 10 times, another person 5 times, a third person 2 times and a fourth person once. After the tasting session, the women were brought to a large room, where they filled out questionnaires. Most of the questions concerned reactions to the tastes (which was of no interest to the experimenters). The experimenters also sneaked in some questions about how much the women liked other subjects in the experiment (which was what the experiment was really about). Even though the women had never seen one another before the experiment and were not allowed to talk to one another while it took place, they tended to like most those whom they had been exposed to most. The less frequently they had seen a particular person, the less likely they were to like her.[17]

Who will be exposed to us is often dictated by circumstances beyond our control. An example of such a setting is the Training Academy of the Maryland State Police. At the academy, students are assigned to rooms and seats in the classrooms according to the alphabetical placement of the first letters in their last names. As a result of this procedure, students with last names starting with the same letter have more exposure to one another than students with last names beginning with different letters. As the theory of mere exposure would have predicted, the alphabet influenced attraction. When asked to name their friends, students at the academy tended to choose people whose last names came from the same part of the alphabet as their own names.[18]

Before we leave the area of mere exposure, it is appropriate to relate the true story of a student who attended classes at Oregon State University covered by a big black bag. When the Black Bag came to class and sat on a small table at the back of the classroom, only his bare feet would show. At first other students reacted with hostility to the Bag. As the Bag continued to appear in class, however, the other students' hostility turned to curiosity and eventually to friendship.[19] Moral: If you must wear a black bag and you still want friends, just expose yourself—that is, your black bag—frequently.

Propinquity: The folks next door

If the theory of mere exposure is correct, we should become most attracted to those we are exposed to most often. This means that your friends are most likely to be the people who live near you. Research has demonstrated that if other things are equal, **propinquity** (proximity) is the most important determiner of friendship-formation.[20] More than a quarter-century ago, psychologists Leon Festinger, Stanley Schachter, and Kurt Back conducted a study that took place in two large university housing projects at the Massachusetts Institute of Technology. The residents in the complex were typical married graduate students. The students were assigned to housing units when they became available. All the housing units faced a grassy court except the end units, which faced the street (see Figure 5-2).

[17]SAEGERT, SWAP, & ZAJONC, 1973.   [18]SEGAL, 1974.   [19]ZAJONC, 1968.   [20]LUNDBERG, HERTZLER, & DICKSON, 1949.

The Black Bag and the theory of mere exposure. At Oregon State University, after being exposed to the Black Bag over a period of time, students' initial hostility gradually became curiosity, and then friendship.

When the psychologists examined who became friends with whom, they found two things to be important. The most important determiner of friendship was how far apart people lived. The second factor was the direction in which the house faced. Those residents whose apartments faced the street had only half as many friends as those whose homes faced the grassy court.

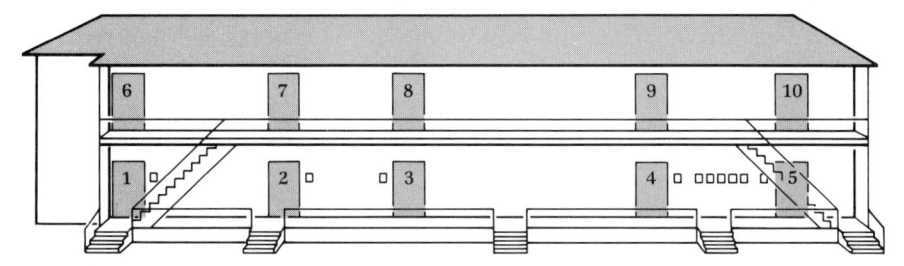

Figure 5-2.
Love thy neighbor! The building shown in the drawing is one of the Westgate Buildings studied by Festinger and his colleagues. Distance between dwelling units was the most important determiner of friendship formation in this complex. Also important, however, was the "functional distance" of the living arrangement which caused people to pass each other or come face-to-face with each other. In order for occupants of several apartments to get upstairs, they must pass by apartment 1. The stairs on the other side are near apartment 5, as are the mailboxes for upstairs occupants. Consequently, people living in apartments 1 and 5 had more friends upstairs than those who lived in the other first-floor apartments. *Source:* Festinger, Schachter, & Back, 1950.

These results suggest that you become friends with people you see most often.[21] The seeds of friendship are planted when you are taking out the garbage, sitting on the porch, getting your mail, and so on. The more exposure you get, the more seeds get planted.

Following the original study by Festinger and his associates, Robert Priest and Jack Sawyer, two sociologists, studied the formation of friendship in college dormitories at the University of Chicago. If you are familiar with campus life, you know that college dorm rooms are close together. Over the course of a school year, you should, therefore, get plenty of exposure to most of the people on your floor. Nevertheless, Priest and Sawyer still found that friendships were most likely to spring up between next-door neighbors. In interpreting their findings, Priest and Sawyer suggested that *perceived* distances influenced choice of friends more than inches, feet, or miles of physical distance. Perceived distance is based upon the number of people who live in between. If you live in the country, your next-door neighbor may live a mile down the road. Even so, you perceive the people down the road as your neighbors because no others are closer.

One of the reasons you may become friends with those you perceive to be close neighbors is that contact with them is more acceptable than with others. If you live in a dormitory, you might feel perfectly comfortable borrowing some notebook paper from the person next door. If you walked six doors down the hall to get the paper, you might feel awkward. After all, everyone has notebook paper. Why, then, did you not borrow some from the person who lives next to you? Moreover, you might not feel comfortable just taking the paper and going back to your own room. After asking for the paper, you talk for a while and, in the meantime, become friends.[22]

At this point, you are probably convinced that architecture influences friendships. Consequently, you may be ready to design new apartment buildings which have five or six front doors opening onto a common patio. Before you change your major to urban planning, you should stop to examine the other side of the coin. If you have to be exposed to others in order to like them, you may also have to be exposed to them in order to dislike them. If your next-door neighbors play their stereo full-blast at three in the morning, you will dislike them regardless of the number of times you see them in the hall.

In one study, choices of friends and enemies were studied among residents of a middle to upper-middle income condominium complex near Irvine, California. As was observed in the studies discussed earlier, friendships were most common among people who lived close together and among people who had the most face-to-face contact. It is important to remember, however, that studies such as these merely describe statistical relationships among variables. Although neighbors tend to be friends, we do not mean to say that all neighbors will be friends. In the Irvine study, people who were disliked were most often cited as such by their near neighbors. In fact, physical distance was a better predictor of disliking than liking. Frequency of face-to-face contact was unrelated to disliking. The psychologists who conducted this study suggested that liking and disliking may be the consequences of different social processes. Liking seems to result from mere exposure.

[21]Festinger, Schachter, & Back, 1950. [22]Priest & Sawyer, 1967.

Disliking, on the other hand, occurs when a specific person engages in behavior that makes the living environment less desirable. The closer you live to someone who spoils the living environment, the more you will be affected by that person's spoiling behaviors.[23]

Similarity: Birds of a feather flock together

Several years ago, a social psychologist named Theodore Newcomb rented a large house adjacent to the Ann Arbor campus of the University of Michigan. For each of two semesters, Newcomb offered college men the opportunity to live in the house. No rent was required; instead, the men spent several hours a week providing experimental data for the psychologist. All of the men chosen by Newcomb were transferring to the University of Michigan as juniors or sophomores, and no one knew anyone else before the study. None of the men had chosen a college major, and they were evenly distributed between the Colleges of Arts and Sciences and of Engineering. All of the men were White, eight of them were Protestant, four were Catholic, and five were Jewish.

The data provided by the men in this experiment concerned a variety of personality characteristics, attitudinal similarity, and interpersonal attraction. Newcomb was trying to determine whether interpersonal attraction was systematically related to similarity of attitudes among people. The results of the study showed that attitudinal similarity was the best predictor for eventual friendship. Those men for whom preacquaintance attitudinal similarity was high were more likely to be attracted to one another after living in the house than those for whom attitudes were dissimilar before their acquaintance. After about the second week of living together, friendships had already begun to form on the basis of attitude similarity. These preferences remained stable over the remainder of the 15-week experiment. People who were strongly attracted to one another tended to overestimate the strength of their attitudinal similarity—that is, they indicated that they were more similar than they actually were. Perceived rather than measured similarity seemed most related to friendship choice.[24]

The experimental commune created by Newcomb clearly demonstrated that birds of a feather flock together. Perhaps your personal experience has already told you this. The psychologists studying this flocking phenomenon over the last quarter-century also started with the belief about birds of a feather, but many of them wanted to get a more in-depth understanding of the phenomenon. Once they were sure that birds of a feather flock together, they wanted to know why they flock together and under what circumstances they do not.

A question examined in Newcomb's study of the experimental commune concerned the nature of the functional relationship between interpersonal attraction and attitudinal similarity. Do people just assume that their friends are similar to themselves, or do they eventually become attracted to those who actually are similar to themselves? Newcomb's experience suggested that the latter is true. As time passes, people become attracted to those who are attitudinally similar to themselves.

But what if you are similar to people on some attitudinal issues and

[23]EBBESEN, KJOS, & KONECNI, 1975. [24]NEWCOMB, 1961.

dissimilar to them on other issues? Psychologist Donn Byrne and his colleagues have shown that interpersonal attraction is "a linear function of the proportion of similar attitudes"—which means that the greater the proportion of similar attitudes people share, the more they will be attracted to one another.[25]

When you are choosing friends, you will probably pay more attention to some issues than to others. When you are looking for a new boyfriend or girlfriend, you may pay more attention to prospective dates' attitudes toward religion, politics, and sex than you do to their attitudes on checkers and television shows. Although the sheer number of similar attitudes influencing friendship choice is staggering, it has been observed that similar attitudes on some issues are more important than similar attitudes on other issues.[26] For example, to find out whether some attitudes were more important than others in the process of selecting and appreciating dates, one psychologist set up a computer dating system in which students were deliberately matched or mismatched with regard to sexual or religious attitudes. Some of the couples were paired up because they had similar opinions about sexual permissiveness; other couples were paired because they had dissimilar views of permissiveness. Still other couples were formed on the basis of similar or dissimilar religious values. Finally, some couples were formed at random. Which matches were most successful? As you can see in Table 5-3, the most important issue for men was not the most important issue for women. For men, sexual attitudes seemed to be most important. Men liked their dates most when the dates had similar beliefs on sex and liked them least when they had dissimilar sexual attitudes. For women, the most important factor affecting attraction was similar religious attitude.[27]

TABLE 5-3. Birds of a feather flock together—up to a point[a]

Type of attitudinal match	Attraction of male subjects toward date	Attraction of female subjects toward date
Random	9.51	9.78
Similar in sexual attitudes	11.33	10.23
Dissimilar in sexual attitudes	7.47	9.42
Similar in religious attitudes	9.97	11.22
Dissimilar in religious attitudes	8.93	9.07

[a]The scores reflect the degree of attraction dating college students felt for each other. Overall, similarity in attitudes was related to attraction. Males, however, put major emphasis on similarity in sexual attitudes while females put more emphasis on similarity in religious attitudes.
Source: Touhey, 1972.

Several experiments have attempted to determine whether racial or attitudinal similarity is the most important determinant of friendship. In these experiments subjects rate how much they would like hypothetical others who are either of the same race or of a different race. In addition, some of the hypothetical others have attitudes similar to those of the subject and some have attitudes dissimilar to those of the subject. Most (but not all) of these

[25]BYRNE & NELSON, 1965; BYRNE & GRIFFITT, 1966; GRIFFITT, NELSON, & LITTLEPAGE, 1972.   [26]CLORE & BALDRIDGE, 1968.   [27]TOUHEY, 1972.

experiments suggest that attitudinal similarity influences attraction more than does skin color.[28]

Box 5-1. Liking and disliking: Sketch of an alternative view

Under this provocative title, psychologist Miriam Rodin of San Diego State University has addressed herself to a theoretical issue with considerable implications for psychologists engaged in research on interpersonal attraction. Rodin's point is that liking and disliking are separate cognitions and therefore are not unidimensional judgments. You may find this out for yourself by conducting a simple experiment. You should collect data from several subjects, but it is important that you deal with them *one at a time*.

Condition 1. Ask your subjects to think of someone they like. When they have someone in mind (they do not need to tell you who it is), ask which one or two qualities they like best about that person. (The typical person will say something like "warm" and/or "open.")

Now ask your subjects whether they can think of anyone they *dislike* who has the same qualities. For example, "Can you think of someone who is warm whom you don't like?"

Condition 2. Ask your subjects to think of someone they dislike. When they have someone in mind, ask which one or two qualities they dislike most about the person. (The typical subject will indicate either something negative, such as "spiteful," or the absence of a critical positive, such as "isn't straight.")

Now ask your subjects whether they can think of anyone they like who has the same qualities. For example, "Can you think of someone who is spiteful whom you like?"

Results. According to Rodin's hypotheses and supporting data, the results should be highly predictable. Most of the subjects in Condition 1 (75% among Rodin's subjects) will give you an immediate affirmative response—that is, they can easily think of someone they dislike even though that person has admirable qualities. A few of your subjects may initially give negative responses, but these responses readily turn into the affirmative once you ask the subject to provide concrete instances of the characterization. Such delayed affirmatives (25% among Rodin's subjects) are generally linked to previous liking of the person. For example, when a friend inquires about a personal matter, it is evidence of "caring," whereas the same inquiry from someone who is not a friend is evidence of "nosiness."

Condition 2 may cause some problems, particularly if your subjects are females. Most will claim at first that there is no one they really dislike. If you give them enough time, they may eventually come up with someone, even if it is someone whom they "like least." There is practically no chance, however, that they will come up with someone they like who also has negative qualities, such as "vindictiveness." (Among Rodin's subjects, 100% came up with negative answers.)

Conclusion. From these and other examples, it is quite apparent that the grounds for liking and disliking are distinct. It just does not make sense to apply the term "like" to all persons for whom the term "dislike" is inappropriate. A positive answer to the question "Do you like your boss?" may

(continued)

---

[28]Byrne & Wong, 1962; Stein, Hardyck, & Smith, 1965; Rokeach & Mezei, 1966.

(Box 5-1 continued)

be an affirmation that you like that person, but it may also simply be a denial that you dislike him or her. Rodin's point is that the relationship between liking and disliking is uneven, or asymmetrical. Because of this fact, it seems somewhat futile to look for a single, universal criterion for likability. But this is precisely what psychologists have been doing. For example, the criterion of "similarity" has been the cornerstone of research on interpersonal attraction. Almost any kind of similarity will do as a determinant of liking—similarity of background, personality, attitude, and the like, as indicated throughout this chapter.

A more fruitful alternative, according to Rodin, is to assume that the criteria for liking or disliking are *context specific*. If psychologists do not provide a common criterion for their subjects, Rodin warns, then the subjects in their studies will be forced into arbitrary choices. For example, it is not really meaningful to ask how much you like an office mate, as opposed to a drinking companion, if no further information about the context is supplied. It would be like asking subjects to rate filet mignon and strawberry shortcake. Unless the experimenter specifies the context, the subjects have no way of knowing whether they are to consider the two items within the context of "which is a better item to skip in a meal" or "which is a better item for a potluck dinner."

Rodin's article raises thought-provoking questions. Pointing to the complexities of human cognitive judgments, it carries implications that go well beyond the interesting methodological issues that are its immediate concern.

Source: Rodin, 1978.

Before we uncritically accept these findings, however, we must look at the differences between these experiments and behavior in the real world. Studies comparing the relative importance of race and attitudinal similarity are a case in point. Most college students know that it is "uncool" to dislike someone just because of skin color. They take this into consideration when they fill out questionnaires, but when it really comes down to interacting with people of another race, their responses may be different. People will say that they would be attracted to someone described on paper but when faced with situations requiring them to interact with, live next door to, or marry someone of another race, the subtle forces of discrimination go into operation. For this reason, studies in which subjects are only required to rate someone they have never met are often held suspect. Unfortunately, much of our research on interpersonal attraction does not deal with people actually interacting with each other. For this reason alone, the work of psychologist Denise Kandel of the New York State Psychiatric Institute is of extraordinary importance.[29] To test the hypothesis that similarity and liking are closely related, she observed the actual friendship patterns of close to 2000 adolescents (average age 16.2) and compared them for similarity on a wide array of demographic characteristics, behaviors, and attitudes. All relationships were statistically significant and are listed in Table 5-4.

[29]KANDEL, 1978.

TABLE 5-4. Similarity of demographic characteristics, behaviors, and attitudes within adolescent friendship dyads.[a*]

Characteristic	All pairs (n = 1879)	Characteristic	All pairs (n = 1879)
Sociodemographic		Other activities	
Grade in school		Index of peer activity	
Sex		Attending religious services	
Ethnicity		Participating in political activities	
Age		Listening to records	
Religion		Index of minor delinquency	
Program in school		Index of serious delinquency	
Father's birthplace		Time spent reading for pleasure	
Mother's birthplace		Time spent watching television	
Father's education			
Mother's education		Relationships with parents	
Family income		Closeness to father	
		Closeness to mother	
Use of illegal drugs ever		Parent-peer orientation	
Marijuana			
LSD		Intrapersonal	
Psychedelics		Political orientation	
Methedrine		Depression	
Heroin		Self-esteem	
Downs		Normlessness	
Cocaine		Social isolation	
Ups			
Tranquilizers		Drug-related attitudes	
Other narcotics		Marijuana use few times harmful	
Inhalents		Marijuana should be legalized	
Use of legal drugs		Heroin use a few times harmful	
Smoking			
Drinking hard liquor		Selected attitudes	
Drinking beer or wine		Conformity to adult expectations index	
		Materialistic career orientation index	
Drug-related activities		Teachers not interested in teenagers	
Number of friends reported to be using marijuana		Bored in class	
Number of hard drugs purchased		Teachers are friendly	
Ever sold marijuana		Teachers willing to help in activities	
		Personal career orientation index	
School activities			
Educational expectations			
Overall self-reported grade average			
Classes cut per week			
Time spent on homework			
Days absent from school			

[a*]*All* similarities are statistically significant and are presented in descending order. Thus, similarity of grade in school is more related to friendship than similarity of religion, similarity in attending religious services is more related to friendship than similarity in listening to records, and so on.
Source: Kandel, 1978.

Self-perception: If the adrenalin flows, it must be love

Can you imagine the following scene? You look up from behind your buttered popcorn to see your hero on the screen having his nose cut off by a bad guy. The people in Hollywood have really done a good job this time. The blood looks real and you can almost feel the pain yourself. Your heart begins to pound in anguish. Suddenly you drop your box of popcorn and reach for your date's hand. Your heart is beating faster now, and then it hits you. You are in love!

Does all this make sense? Can you suddenly find love during a blood and guts exhibition? The answer is yes. In a book offering advice to first-century Roman males, Ovid suggested that taking a woman to a gladiator match was a good way to arouse passion. Ovid was in the business of giving advice but did not get bogged down in how his principles worked. He simply knew that going to the gladiator matches got things going.[30]

Nearly 2000 years later, social psychologists began to explain why Ovid made sense. Several years ago, Stanley Schachter and Jerome Singer performed an experiment in which some subjects were injected with a substance that aroused them emotionally. These subjects were then placed in a room with either a happy or an angry experimental confederate. Schachter and Singer observed that those who were exposed to the happy confederate felt happy and those exposed to the angry confederate felt angry. For those subjects who understood that it was the shot which had made them emotional, however, the presence of confederates had little bearing on how they rated their own moods.

These results are not nearly as confusing as they seem to be. When people do not clearly understand what is making them emotional, they tend to search for reasons to explain their emotional state. As they become less certain about what their bodies are telling them, they begin to seek information from the world outside their bodies to account for their internal state. If the external world seems happy, they label their own emotions as happy, and vice versa.[31] Some recent research has raised questions about the Schachter and Singer findings,[32] making it necessary to perform new experiments to validate competing interpretations of the data. Because tighter restrictions now regulate research involving human subjects, however, we do not expect a resolution of this problem in the near future.

Let us now go back to Ovid at the gladiator arena—and you at the show. When you (and your date) begin to experience a change in heartbeat rate, you may not immediately attribute your bodily changes to the gory movie you have seen. In this case, not understanding your internal state, you may begin to look for external clues to explain what is happening to you. Turning to your partner and realizing the racing pace of your heart, you might conclude that it's love that has made your heartbeat change.

Several years ago psychologist Stuart Valins collected a group of college men and had them view some slides of seminude women. A microphone was taped to the heart of each man so that he could hear his own heartbeat while he was watching the slides. In actuality, the men did not hear their real heartbeats. Valins had rigged the system so that he could control the beat rate fed back to the men. When some of the slides came on, Valins made it sound as though the heartbeat rate had increased. When other slides came on, he made it sound as though the heartbeat rate decreased. With still other slides the heartbeat rate was made to stay the same. Based on their own ratings of their

[30]Rubin, 1973. [31]Schachter & Singer, 1962. [32]Maslach, 1979; Marshall & Zimbardo, 1979; Schachter & Singer, 1979.

liking of the women in the pictures, the men were most attracted to the women they thought had caused their hearts to either speed up or slow down. They were least attracted to women they thought had not "moved" them (by affecting their supposed heartbeat rate). The preference for women associated with heartbeat rate change persisted as long as four weeks after the experiment.[33]

Climate: Cool temperatures and hot passions

Sometimes we engage in elaborate behaviors to stay warm. If it gets too cold, we put on more clothes, ignite heaters, build fires, and sometimes try to get close to other people. The last in this list of behaviors is probably of greatest interest to social psychologists.

Folklore tells us that cool temperatures ripen affections. We have all heard what happens on long, cold winter nights, or how young lovers behave during the crisp, cool days of springtime. The suggestion is that cool temperatures cause hot passions. On the other hand, folklore also tells us that hot temperatures are associated with instant attractions. These stories glorify the hot-blooded Italian lover who uses the Mediterranean sun as an ingredient of his own charm. Romantic vacation spots include Hawaii, the Caribbean, Tahiti, and other tropical locations.

What do we know about the effects of heat upon attraction? Well, not much. Psychologist William Griffitt, however, has provided us with some preliminary data on the topic. Griffitt had subjects dress in cotton shirts or blouses (to reduce the effect of clothes on heat sensations) and then sent them into either a cool (67.5°F) or a hot (90.6°F) room. After a 45-minute exposure to these environments, Griffitt showed the subjects an attitude scale that had been completed by a "stranger." The scale revealed that the stranger had either similar or dissimilar attitudes to the subject. When the subjects rated their attraction for the stranger, it was found that those in the hot environment were less attracted to the stranger than those in the cool surroundings. This finding was particularly strong for those strangers who were attitudinally dissimilar to the subjects.[34] Although research in this area is currently incomplete, it appears that hot environments detract from interpersonal attraction.

The winners: Beautiful and adored

DATING AND MATING

Do physically attractive people get all the breaks? They do. As we have pointed out in Chapter 1, the benefits of beauty accrue early. Beginning with nursery school, beautiful children are liked more by adults and classmates, get away with mischievous behavior, and are attributed with a host of positive personality characteristics. They are even perceived as more competent than their less attractive counterparts.

In view of all this, how does physical appearance affect the dating and mating process? Before we examine the evidence, a word of caution is due. There are few areas of human interaction where hypocrisy is practiced as often as in the area of dating and mating. What they really like and what they say they like are far apart whenever people are interrogated about their dating

[33]VALINS, 1966. [34]GRIFFITT, 1970.

patterns. If you ask your college friends what they look for in a girlfriend or boyfriend, they will probably tell you that their first priority is to find someone who is intelligent, friendly, and sincere. Take it with a grain of salt. When confronted with real-life situations, these same people are most likely to base their dating choices on physical rather than on personality characteristics. Perhaps they were just fooling themselves. More likely, college students think that, if they judge someone by their looks, they will be regarded as superficial people. Even though they are judging books by their covers, they are embarrassed to admit it.[35] One study on physical attractiveness and dating preference involved a computer dating dance. Freshmen at the University of Minnesota purchased tickets to a dance for which a computer would find them a date. Actually, there was no computer and the students were paired randomly. When the students picked up their tickets, the physical attractiveness of the subjects was rated by a panel of judges. In the middle of the evening, the band was stopped so that the social psychologists could pass out questionnaires. The questionnaires asked how well the students liked their dates and whether they wanted to see the date again. Both men and women who had attractive dates liked them most and wanted future interaction with them.[36]

This finding came as a surprise. In dating situations, you might expect people who are *equally* attractive to pair up. In the computer dating study, this is not how things worked out; everyone wanted to pair up with the most attractive participants. Perhaps the reason that the subjects did not prefer dates with appearances they judged equal to their own was because there was no possibility of rejection. In the real world, there may be a greater chance of being turned down if you pursue the homecoming queen than if you ask out the girl next door. To check out this notion, a second computer dance was set up. This time the subjects had the chance to meet their dates before the dance and to indicate how much they were attracted to their prospective dates. They also knew that their prospective dates would be rating them. When the possibility for rejection existed, preferences tended to be greatest for people of equal attractiveness.[37] Although we are most attracted to the most beautiful members of the opposite sex, we *can* assess our own attractiveness and pursue someone who is equally as attractive as we are.[38] And we do, evidently. A recent study involved two samples of married couples, one from the mainland United States (55 couples) and one from Hawaii (72 couples), and included young and recently married, middle-aged, and older couples. Each individual was photographed separately and rated independently by judges for physical attractiveness. The results showed significant "matching" for attractiveness—that is, similarity of ratings—between couples well into middle age and beyond.[39]

The losers: Homely and ignored

What happens to those not blessed with physical attractiveness? A study by psychologists Dennis Krebs and Allen Adinolfi investigated the relationship among physical attractiveness, personality, and social relations among 60

---

[35]Vreeland, 1972. [36]Walster, Aronson, Abrahams, & Rottmann, 1966. [37]Walster & Walster, 1969. [38]Berscheid, Dion, Walster, & Walster, 1971. [39]Price & Vandenberg, 1979.

male and 60 female student-dormitory residents. As expected, physical attractiveness in women was associated with frequency of dating. For men, appearance was unrelated to dating frequency. Evidently, men who date attractive women run the gamut of physical attractiveness.

Do physically attractive people get more breaks? Research says they do.

One interesting finding in the study concerned the reactions of residents in the same dormitory (who were of the same sex as the subjects). The most attractive males and females were *rejected* most often by their dormmates. Evidently, there are some limits even for beautiful people. Perhaps they evoked jealousy in the others or may have become aloof as a result of being so desirable. All this, however, is scarcely a consolation for those who are homely. The fact that only *some* attractive people were rejected (moderately attractive people were in fact most accepted) did not mean that the least attractive persons were accepted with open arms. Contrary to expectation, these homely people were not even rejected. They were simply ignored. Although we cannot say for sure, it is reasonable to assume that the indifference shown by peers can cause these unfortunate people to turn inward and become social isolates.[40]

The unhappy lot of homely people is aggravated by the fact that they are caught in a bind. Because they are ignored, they become isolates whose self-esteem is low. Ironically, this may cause them to try even harder to associate with the beautiful people, since this is one of the ways by which people can raise their self-esteem. Men like to be seen with beautiful women and women like to be seen with handsome men. One possible reason for this is that the attractiveness of a partner may be taken as an indication of one's own worth.

Along these lines, psychologists Harold Sigall and David Landy wondered if

[40] KREBS & ADINOLFI, 1975.

beauty "radiates." In other words, can the beauty of one person radiate to persons associated with him or her? In one experiment, they had college students form impressions of a young man. When the students saw the man, he was always with the same woman, who was described in some cases as his girlfriend and in other cases as someone unassociated with him. Half the time, the woman was made to look very attractive. The rest of the time, she was made to appear quite unattractive. The man was evaluated most favorably when he was believed to have an attractive girlfriend. When just seen with (but not associated with) a woman, her attractiveness seemed not to make much difference.

This experiment tells us what other people will think of us when we are seen with attractive or unattractive partners. Another factor that may contribute to our desire to find attractive partners is that we think more highly of ourselves if we have attractive mates. To demonstrate how this process might work, Sigall and Landy asked college men to help them in an experiment in which they would be introduced to another student as the boyfriend of either an attractive or an unattractive woman. The men met their partners and were then asked to predict what sort of impression another student would have of them. As expected, the men thought they would be evaluated most favorably if they posed as the boyfriend of an attractive woman and least favorably if they posed as the boyfriend of an unattractive woman.[41] Clearly, part of the reason for our desire for attractive partners is to enhance our own status and self-esteem.

The trophy: Lots of love but few data

As the frenzy of the mating and dating games continues unabashedly around us, it seems somewhat naive to ask what it is really all about. The obvious answer, of course, is love and romance. Throughout history, men and women have written about and sung about love more than any other topic. The index of *Bartlett's Familiar Quotations* shows that love is the second most commonly referred to term ("love" is cited 769 times, "man" is cited 843 times).[42] All this preoccupation with love has not, however, led to a better understanding of what it really is. Perhaps it is something we can feel but not necessarily understand well enough to describe in a definite way.

All of us have romantic ideals. Some regard love as feelings of togetherness. The poet Shelley proclaimed, "Soul meets soul on lover's lips." Erich Fromm points out the complexity of this togetherness: "In love the paradox occurs that two things become one yet remain two."

For other people, feelings of love seem to be related to the love they get in return. An old Turkish proverb says "All women are perfection, especially she who loves you." This need for reciprocation seems to be prevalent across cultures, as suggested by the German adage, "Love unreciprocated is like a question without an answer."

Still other people seem to feel love most intensely when they are faced with the possibility that their lover may be taken away. According to G. K. Chesterton, "The way to love anything is to realize that it might be lost." Finally, some

[41] SIGALL & LANDY, 1973. [42] RUBIN, 1973.

have questioned whether love exists. Ernest Hemingway asked "Is love possible? Every man knows that for himself. For me it is."[43]

As scientists, we have almost completely neglected the topic of love. Few studies have gone beyond asking what people think love is. Since we have never been quite certain what love is, we have never been able to measure it.[44] In the words of folk singer Joan Baez, "Love is just a four-letter word." Few of us would have trouble measuring the length of a table because we know exactly what the table is. In addition, our measurement of the table length would be fairly constant from one measurement to the next, despite the fact that tables are often spilled upon, pounded on, and pushed around.

Contrast this situation with love. We do not know exactly what love is; we have no yardstick with which to measure it. And even if we could measure love, different situations might affect the outcome of our measures.

A few years ago, Zick Rubin became the first psychologist to make a serious attempt at the measurement of romantic love. The technique he used is called *construct validation*. Construct validation is used to develop measures of poorly understood psychological concepts. When we use construct validation, we simultaneously define a concept and develop an instrument to measure it.[44]

To prepare his measure, Rubin read extensively about love. You can get a feel for the diversity of statements about love that Rubin encountered by consulting Table 5-5. The most succinct statement is probably that by Elizabeth Barrett Browning, who once said "How do I love thee? Let me count the ways." Indeed, after reading the many diverse views of love, Rubin hardly knew where to begin counting. One thing, however, was clear in his mind: all the people who had written about love were probably talking about something different than what had been studied in the psychological laboratory.

TABLE 5-5. What is this thing called love? Some famous statements.

Author	Quotation
Elizabeth Barrett Browning	"How do I love thee? Let me count the ways."
Erich Segal	"Love is never having to say you're sorry."
Voltaire	"There are so many sorts of love, that one does not know where to seek a definition of it."
William Shakespeare	"Love is a spirit all compact of fire."
Samuel Daniel	"Love is a sickness full of woes."
Erich Fromm	"Love is the active concern for the life and growth of that which we love."
Harry Stack Sullivan	"When the satisfaction or the security of another person becomes as significant as one's own satisfaction or security, then the state of love exists."
David Orlinsky	"Love is when attachment and caring form a dual feeling of impulse."

Source: Rubin, 1973.

Rubin began his study by condensing conventional wisdom about loving and liking into sets of statements to which people could respond on a scale

[43]MONTAPERT, 1964. [44]CRONBACH & MEEHL, 1955.

ranging from disagreement to agreement. Some of the items were intended to measure love, others were supposed to tap liking. Next, he gave the pool of items to 198 students from the University of Michigan. Each of the items had a blank in which a name could be filled in. The students responded to the questions twice, one time filling in the name of their boyfriend or girlfriend, and another time filling in the name of a platonic friend.

The data from these scales were subjected to several statistical procedures that helped to discriminate between responses of girlfriends, boyfriends, and platonic friends, and eventually led to the establishment of two measures (a love scale and a liking scale). The items making up the love scale were composed of three components: attachment ("If I were lonely, my first thoughts would be to seek _____ out"); caring ("If _____ were feeling bad, my first duty would be to cheer him [her] up"); and intimacy ("I feel that I can confide in _____ about virtually everything"). The items on the liking scale focused on favorable aspects of the other person along such dimensions as adjustment, maturity, good judgment, and intelligence.

Now that measures of liking and loving were available, it was necessary to determine whether they were really measuring what they were supposed to measure. One study, using dating couples, suggested that loving and liking were not necessarily related. There was a modest relationship between scores on the two scales, weaker for women than for men. This suggested, especially for women, that it is possible to love someone whom one may not particularly like.

There were several indications that the love scale really was measuring "love." For example, men and women scored higher on the love scale when they filled in the names of their boyfriends or girlfriends than when they filled in the name of a same-sex friend. There was also a substantial correlation between love scale scores and estimates of the likelihood of marriage. The greater the love score, the more probable marriage was considered to be.

Finally, some of the dating couples were separated into strong love (high love scores) or weak love (low love scores) groups. From behind a one-way mirror, the researchers noted how much eye contact the lovers had with one another. Strong lovers, it was observed, spent more time simply gazing into each other's eyes than did weak lovers. When paired with a strong opposite-sex lover from another couple, mutual eye contact was no greater than it was for people who were weak lovers.

This, then, is the yeoman's work of psychologist Zick Rubin, which finally allowed the elusive concepts of love and liking to be measured.[45] Some examples of items from the Love and Liking Scales are given in Table 5-6.

We do not want to leave you with the impression that psychologists have found the definition of love. Indeed, Rubin's work is only a beginning. For example, it has been suggested that the absence of any reference to interpersonal sexual behavior within the Love Scale is inappropriate, particularly since samples of college students (on whom the scale is often used) have shown that at least 56% of respondents "in love" were also having sexual intercourse. The inclusion of "erotica" (sexually oriented material) has led to increased reliability and validity of the scale.[46] On the other hand, some

---

[45]RUBIN, 1970. [46]DERMER & PYSZCZYNSKI, 1978.

TABLE 5-6. Examples of items from Rubin's love and liking scales[a]

Love scale items
I feel that I can confide in _____ about virtually everything.
I would forgive _____ for practically anything.

Liking scale items
I think _____ is unusually well-adjusted.
I would recommend _____ for a responsible job.
_____ is one of the most likable people I know.

[a] If you were responding to the items, you would fill the blanks with the name of your boyfriend or girlfriend. Then you would read each statement and indicate your agreement or disagreement on the following scale.

```
    1    2    3    4    5    6    7    8    9
   Strongly disagree    Neutral    Strongly agree
```

Source: Rubin, 1973.

people feel that the Love Scale measures infatuation rather than love. An adult couple, after years of partnership, may feel very much in love. Their scores on Love Scale items, however, may not be very high, and it is unlikely that they would spend long periods of time simply staring into each other's eyes. Does this mean that they do not love each other? Of course not. It only means that the Love Scale emphasizes the aspects of love characterized by Hollywood movies and deemphasizes aspects of love experienced by many mature couples in the course of ongoing relationships.

Since the Love and Liking Scales are only in their infancy stages of development, Rubin has been cautious in recommending that people use them. He warns that they are currently research instruments and they should not be used as self-administered "test-your-love" measures. Before we can use the scales as clinical tools, we will need many more studies.

Over the course of time, we hope an empirical bridge will be built between these scales and vague theoretical notions of love.

The game plan: The girl next door who plays hard to get

Dating and mating being a fact of life, is there a game plan best suited for successful mate selection? Regardless of your political orientation, you are probably pleased by one characteristic of American society—you have the freedom to marry someone of your own choice. In India, or in Japan, marriages are still frequently arranged by families (though because these cultures are becoming more Westernized, it should be noted, prearranged marriages are becoming less common). These cultures, however, still put less emphasis on romantic ideals of love and more on companionship.

Most of us would disapprove of having someone else choose a marriage partner for us, especially if parents do the choosing. Interestingly, however, most of us choose marriage partners who generally meet with the approval of our parents. We often hear about interracial marriages, but such marriages are rare indeed. Whites marry Whites (99.8%) and Blacks with Blacks (99%). Common religion is also a characteristic of contemporary marriages. In 93.6% of

American marriages, husband and wife belong to the same major religious group. In some of these cases, however, one spouse may have been brought up in another religion and converted to the same religion as her or his partner.[47]

Religion and race are just two things that people who choose each other as partners have in common. Sociologist Eloise Snyder examined attitudes of couples who would later become married. Their predating attitudes were available from high school records and the like. Fourteen areas of behavior were investigated: attending dances, attending church, loafing, dating, divorce, social drinking, smoking, playing cards, staying out late, going to Sunday movies, working on the sabbath, doing badly in school, spending money, and using makeup. As you might have predicted from what you learned earlier, birds of a feather flock together. Those couples who eventually married had considerably more similar attitudes than could have been expected by chance.[48]

With all the people in the world, where do you find someone so similar to yourself? You might try next door. The folklore image of the girl or boy next door is meant to symbolize someone who has the same values as your parents. In fact, he or she probably does. People intentionally buy homes in areas where the neighbors share common values. This ensures that their children will make the "right" kind of friends. Add to this the effects of propinquity and mere exposure, and the boy or girl next door are no longer unlikely selections. In one analysis of 5000 marriage license applications 35 years ago, sociologist James Bossard found that a third of the couples were people who lived within five blocks of each other.[49] Although automobiles have made us more mobile in recent years, it is still most likely we will marry someone who lives nearby.[50]

North American parents do not choose mates for their children. Not directly, anyway. By sending you to certain schools, giving you certain skills, and instilling certain values in you, they may be doing the same thing. How many of you would not submit your prospective bride or groom to your family for approval?

There are, however, cases where parents can exert too much influence. In the famous and touching love story *Romeo and Juliet*, parental opposition was used to try to squelch the flame of true love. Perhaps the parents used the wrong substance to put out the fire. Psychologists Richard Driscoll, Keith Davis, and Milton Lipetz found evidence that parental opposition can make the flame grow stronger. In their study, married and unmarried (dating) couples were studied over a period of up to 10 months on their degree of expressed romantic love and parental interference. Parental interference was defined as the perception that parents are a bad influence, are hurting the couple's relationship, take advantage of the woman, do not accept the man, try to make the man look bad, and so on. In both married and unmarried couples, parental interference was strongly related to mutual feelings of love. Moreover, akin to the classic Romeo and Juliet situation, the relationship grew progressively stronger over time.[51]

[47]SNYDER, 1973. [48]SNYDER, 1973. [49]BOSSARD, 1931. [50]RAMSY, 1966. [51]DRISCOLL, DAVIS, & LIPETZ, 1972.

In his study on dating couples, Zick Rubin also observed the "Romeo and Juliet effect." Couples of different religions showed higher love scores than those who had the same religious affiliations. This was only true, however, for couples who had recently started dating. Among long-term couples, including most sets who intended to marry, love scores were higher for same-religion pairs.

Several alternative explanations can be given for these results. One is that parental pressure was successful in extinguishing the flame of romance. Another, and perhaps more likely, explanation is that parental pressure actually provided the energy for the love relationship. When parental pressure was overcome, there was no fuel left for the fire.[52] In any case, parental opposition seems to have a unifying effect. This effect becomes weaker when parents are not around. Had Romeo and Juliet been able to elope and escape the influence of their folks, they might have had at least the chance for a divorce!

In these days of sexual liberation, it is not too surprising that the effectiveness of parental pressure is on the decline. Parents may set the stage for the selection of someone next door, but the rest is assumed to be up to their offspring. Ordinarily, this would mean that it is up to you to devise a proper strategy to attract your mate. The trouble is that such strategies are often based on popular misconceptions. A case in point is the strategy of the woman who plays hard-to-get.

If there is one thing that Ovid, Terence, the *Kama Sutra*, and Dear Abby agree on, it is that women should be hard to get. Easy women are not considered much of a prize. Ovid summed it up as follows:

> Fool, if you feel no need to guard your girl for her own sake, see that you guard her for mine, so I may want her the more. Easy things nobody wants, but what is forbidden is tempting.... Anyone who can love the wife of an indolent cuckold, I should suppose, would steal buckets of sand from the shore.

As social psychologists often do, Elaine Walster, William Walster, Jane Piliavin, and Lynn Schmidt decided to look into the phenomenon of playing hard to get in order to see if there is any truth behind this maxim.

Before they entered into a series of experiments, Walster and her colleagues asked a group of college men why they preferred women who were hard to get. They found that men preferred hard-to-get women because a woman in this category was presumably more valuable, could afford to be choosier because of her good looks, and would give prestige to a man who could get her to go out with him. The woman who was easy to get was seen as making too many demands or being too desperate for a man. Some of the men saw the easy women as even more of a threat. They feared she would want to get serious too soon, or even (believe it or not) have a "disease." In short, most of the men seemed to agree that a woman who is hard to get should be prized and that a woman who is easy to get should be avoided at all costs.

Walster and her associates were still not entirely convinced, so they decided to put the issue to a real-world test. They recruited 71 male summer school students at the University of Wisconsin and told them they were going

---

[52] RUBIN, 1973.

to be in a computer dating experiment. The men were told to come to the computer dating center to choose a date from five potential candidates.

All of the men had filled out questionnaires giving their own backgrounds. When they came to the computer dating center, they were given five folders that contained questionnaires filled out by five women. Actually, the questionnaires had been filled out by the experimenters and the women were fictitious. In the folders for three of the five women were date selection forms. These women, it was explained, had already had the opportunity to study the men's folders and to select with whom they wanted to go out. The selections for the other two had not yet been made. For those who had filled out the date selection forms, each of five men was rated on a numerical scale which ranged from –10 (or "definitely do not want to date") to +10 (or "definitely want to date"). These forms allowed the experimenters to manipulate the elusiveness of the woman.

By controlling the elusiveness of the women, Walster and her colleagues were able to give the young men choices among women who differed in difficulty to get. First, there was the woman who was uniformly hard to get. Her questionnaire showed that none of her choices turned her on—although she would go out with any of them. All of her choices were given a rating of between +1 and +2. The male subject always found himself rated as a +1.75.

In contrast to this hard-to-get woman, there was a woman who was easy to get. This woman wanted to out with everyone and anyone. In her folder all of the five men were rated higher (from +7 to +9), including the subject, who always got +8.

Which of these women do you think was chosen for a date most often? Would it be the hard-to-get woman, with all her charms and mystique, or the easy-to-get woman, who would boost egos and probably provide a hassle-free evening? As it turned out, neither of these women was chosen very often.

What we have not told you thus far is that the men had some other choices. Most important of these was the woman who was *selectively* hard to get. This woman was hard to get for everyone except one person. And who do you think that one person was? You guessed it—the subject. This alleged woman gave the subject a fantastic +8 rating, and rated everyone else below +3. In turn, these selectively hard-to-get women were chosen almost four times as often as the other women![53]

The application of these findings is entirely up to you. If you are like some people, you will be glad to know that the proven-effective strategy for a woman to attract a man is to acquire a reputation of being hard to get, and then, by her behavior, make it clear to the intended man that she is attracted to him. If you are like some other people, all this will leave you indifferent because you feel that there is something demeaning in deliberate tactics and game plans to "catch" a mate.

The penalties: No points for jealousy

Chances are that you will have experienced jealousy in some form during your adolescent or college years. In fact, jealousy is one of the most common human emotions and a prime motivator of social behavior. Despite its obvious

[53]WALSTER, WALSTER, PILIAVIN, & SCHMIDT, 1973.

importance, very little systematic research has been devoted to jealousy. According to psychologist Jeff Bryson, "the lack of research on jealousy is such that it seems fair to assert that some future historian reviewing our scientific literature, would feel justified in presuming that jealousy was either non-existent in our society, or at most experienced by an isolated subset of pathological individuals."

Bryson's research has been among the few efforts systematically to define and measure sexual jealousy. Bryson defines jealousy as a "complex of emotional and behavioral reactions to the perception of real or imagined threat by a rival to the existence or quality of an ongoing attractive relationship."[54] In one study, he showed that college students differ greatly in the way they express jealousy. He found eight distinct patterns, which are summarized in Table 5-7. Later, he was able to classify jealousy reactions as related to two specific goals. Some jealous reactions are attempts to improve the relationship. For example, when made to feel jealous, some people report that they try to make themselves more attractive to their partner. The other reaction to jealousy provocation involves attempts to improve self-esteem, or sense of self-worth. Jealousy-provoking reactions can be a heavy blow to the ego and many people react by protecting themselves before protecting the relationship. For example, some ego-defensive responses might include verbal or even physical attacks on the partner. As we will see in Chapter 6, jealousy is one of the major motivations for murder.

TABLE 5-7. Factors in social jealousy. Psychologist Jeff Bryson used various statistical analyses to identify eight independent patterns of reaction to jealousy-provoking situations.

Factor	Representative Items
Emotional devastation	"Feel helpless" "Feel depressed"
Reactive retribution	"Do something to get my partner jealous" "Start going out with other people"
Arousal	"Feel more sexually aroused by my partner" "Pay more attention to my partner than before"
Need for social support	"Talk to close friends about my feelings" "Cry when I'm alone"
Intropunitiveness	"Feel angry toward myself" "Feel guilty about being jealous"
Confrontation	"Ask my partner to explain the situation" "Confront the other person directly"
Anger	"Feel angry toward my partner" "Feel angry toward the other person"
Impression management	"Try to make other people think I don't care" "Get drunk or high"

Source: Bryson, 1977.

In addition to studies on the dimensions of jealousy, Bryson has developed a method for creating jealousy in the laboratory. In a typical study, college

[54]BRYSON, 1977.

men were asked to identify with the male in a videotaped scene in which a couple is affectionately involved on a couch. When the man in the film gets up to refill some wine glasses, his partner's old boyfriend enters. The man then returns to discover his girlfriend intimately touching and kissing her old boyfriend. For female subjects, the film was identical except that the woman in the film leaves the room and returns to find her boyfriend kissing his old girlfriend. The attractiveness of the former lover also varied. In half of the cases, he or she was very attractive, and in the other half very unattractive.

When the former lover was unattractive, and presumably not much of a threat, men and women said they would react very much in the same way. When the former lover was attractive, however, men and women responded differently. Men reported that they would be more likely to start going out with other women and would be more sexually active with other women. The opposite pattern was found for women, who reported that they would be less likely to go out with others or be sexually aggressive toward them. In other words, men are more likely to respond in a way that will protect their self-esteem, and women are more likely to respond in a way that will protect the relationship.[55]

A strategy as old as the activity of dating is to try to make your partner jealous so that he or she will pay more attention to you. Many women, however, may have developed this strategy on the basis of their own jealousy reactions. As we have seen in this experiment, you should not assume that an opposite-sex partner will respond to jealousy the same way you do.

MARRIAGE PROBLEMS

Traditional: The law of infidelity

Infidelity is one of the greatest threats to the marital bond. Each time an act of infidelity comes into the open, people begin to speculate about the morality (or immorality) of the people involved. Psychologist Elliot Aronson, however, has a new insight into this perplexing phenomenon. He explains infidelity in terms of simple social rewards and exchanges.

To illustrate Aronson's "law of infidelity," consider the following example. A husband who loves his wife tells her time and again that she looks nice. She knows he loves her and expects these comments. When she hears what she expects, the comments fail to boost her ego. The exchange value of her husband's comments has been discounted. When another man makes the same comments, she is caught by surprise. She does not expect to hear these things. She is flattered. Thus, the same compliments are more potent if they are given by someone other than the husband.

Since the husband's love is expected, negative comments made by him may have a more harmful impact than when the same criticisms are made by someone else. In some relationships, a hurt person may work hard to reestablish admiration (offsetting Aronson's law). Other people want to avoid those who can hurt them. So the loving husband is really in a bind: by saying the same things, he can reward less and hurt more than someone else. Infidelity often follows.[56]

Infidelity, of course, is only one of many symptoms of a troubled marriage.

[55]SHETTEL-NEUBER, BRYSON, & YOUNG, 1978. [56]ARONSON, 1969, 1980.

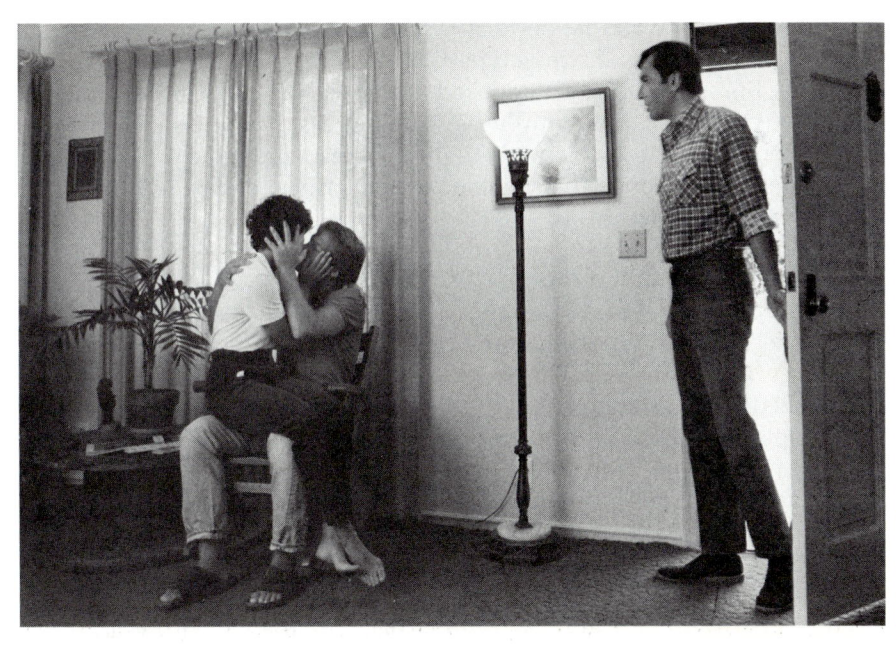

Reactions to sexual jealousy. Men are more likely to respond in a way that protects their self-esteem. Women respond in a way to protect and maintain a relationship.

Sociologically speaking, people with less education and income are particularly susceptible to marital unhappiness. People presently raising children report more dissatisfaction than people whose children have already left home or people who have never had children. Marital satisfaction also seems to be further related to a positive view of one's own health. Those with physical disabilities report more dissatisfaction than physically healthy individuals. Marital happiness is also associated with job satisfaction and is less common among those who drink heavily.[57] Finally, there is evidence that the marital relationship might be strengthened when both partners are working.[58]

Although extensive literature exists on marriage counseling and intervention techniques,[59] psychologists have devoted little study to the behavior of those involved in marital discord. Most of the available literature includes case studies and attitudinal studies.[60] These studies do not include systematic observations of those involved in the conflict, nor do they show how the conflicts develop. In assessing marital situations, verbal reports are often unsatisfactory because the people involved are so close to the situation that their emotions shade their reports.

One recent attempt by psychologists to study marital discord systematically at the behavioral level was conducted in Oregon. Newspaper advertisements explained that the University of Oregon was looking for both couples experiencing marital distress and happily married couples for a marriage research project. Self-report measures and observation interviews were used to confirm that the couples were indeed either distressed or nondistressed.

[57]Renne, 1973; [58]Orden & Bradburn, 1973. [59]Knox, 1971; Patterson & Hops, 1972; Stuart, 1969; Weiss, Hops, & Patterson, 1973; Sussman, 1974. [60]Levinger & Breedlove, 1966; Ryder, 1968.

Overall results showed that nondistressed partners tended to engage seven times more often than distressed partners in pleasing behavior (agreement, approval, humor, smiling) as opposed to displeasing behavior (complaints, criticism, putdowns, inattentiveness). Nondistressed couples also engaged more often than distressed couples in mutual recreational activities.[61] (There is also general evidence that people become critical of each other as they become more intimate.)[62]

Divorce: The end of the road

When conflict gets too severe, the option of ending the marriage is still available. Today more people than ever before are exercising that option.

Divorce has been available as an option for some time. When it was introduced to Protestant populations in Europe, centuries passed with only a few people pursuing legal separateness. Divorce was something sinful that only the rich and powerful dared to risk. In the early nineteenth century, the American divorce rate was maintained at round 1%! Since then, the divorce rate has steadily risen. Today, two out of three California couples currently taking their vows will someday face the divorce court judge (for the nation at large, the divorce rate is about one in three marriages). Half of all divorces occur within the first eight years of marriage. By the fifteenth year, three-quarters of the couples who will separate have done so.[63]

With the increase in divorce has come an increase in the acceptability and desirability of changing social lifestyles. Most bookstores carry such books as *Creative Divorce, The World of the Formerly Married,* and *How to Do Your Own Divorce in California.*

Divorce is no fun. It is a major shakeup that cannot be shrugged off as no big deal. It *is* a big deal. Divorce can affect every aspect of your life. The newly divorced will rapidly find out that this new status will make changes in what they think, with whom they sleep, with whom they eat, where they go, and what the future holds. Just as physical collisions may cause broken bones and tissues that prevent proper functioning, emotional collisions leave their own brand of wounds. But, like bones and tissues, emotional wounds heal quickly in most cases. As divorce has become more acceptable, an increasing number of people have begun to find divorce a positive experience that stimulates personal growth. Mel Krantzler, the author of *Creative Divorce,* describes this process in terms of his own divorce:

> Today I look back on the last three years as the most personally enriching period in my life. Through a painful emotional crisis, I have become a happier and stronger person than I was before. I learned that what I went through was what all divorced people, men and women, go through to a greater or lesser extent—a period of mourning, and finally a slow, painful emotional readjustment to the facts of single life. I experienced the pitfalls along the way—the wallowing in self-pity, the refusal to let go of the old relationship, the repetition of old ways in relating to new people, the confusion of past emotions with present reality—and I emerged the better for it. (pp. 27–28)

Learning about dating for newly separated people is often difficult. Because

---

[61]Birchler, Weiss, & Vincent, 1975. [62]Winter, Ferreira, & Bowers, 1973. [63]Life and Health, 1972.

of their age and accumulation of experiences, the formerly married become more selective than they were in their youth. There is a tendency to search for someone who has had common experiences. For instance, most prefer to date people who have also been divorced. Among mature people, emotional and physical involvement seem to advance more quickly than during adolescent courtship. After some exposure to the world of the formerly married, and some readjustment to life, most people are once again ready to enter into a marital bond.[64]

SUMMARY HIGHLIGHTS

1. Popularity is associated with certain characteristics and behaviors. Popular people tend to have physical skills, be relatively free from accidents, come from harmonious families, be physically attractive, and have common names, among other traits.
2. *Exchange theory* and *equity theory* use a marketplace analogy to conceptualize interpersonal relationships. Social relationships are viewed as fair exchanges between rational participants in the marketplace. Self-esteem is the appraisal of one's own exchange value in the interpersonal market.
3. The value of social rewards can be altered by previous interactions. The *gain-loss phenomenon* occurs when someone dislikes you at first—but comes to like you after repeated exposure. When this happens, you may develop in turn a greater attraction for the other person.
4. Other things being equal, the more you are exposed to someone, the more you will like that person. This is known as the theory of *mere exposure*.
5. Perhaps as a result of mere exposure, there is a tendency to come to like people who live nearby. This effect is known as *propinquity*.
6. Most research suggests that people with *similar attitudes* and beliefs will like each other. There is evidence, however, that under some conditions, opposites attract.
7. Liking can also be influenced by beliefs about the causes of changes in physiological states. Self-perception theory suggests that we become aroused (wild heartbeat, short breath) while in the presence of other persons. We will come to like these persons more because we attribute the cause of the arousal to them.
8. Physical attractiveness is one of the most important factors in interpersonal relationships. In general, couples tend to be matched on physical attractiveness. There is also a tendency, however, for the most attractive people (particularly women) to have greater opportunity for social relationships with members of the opposite sex. At the same time, the most attractive members of each sex may come to be the most rejected by members of their own sex. Markedly unattractive men and women may be neither accepted nor rejected; instead, they tend to be ignored.
9. Attempts to measure romantic love have suggested that loving may be

[64]KRANTZLER, 1975; HUNT, 1966; SHERMAN, 1972.

something other than intense liking. A measuring device has been developed that can predict certain aspects of romantic love, such as how much time couples will spend staring into each other's eyes, and so on. The scale has been less successful in predicting couples' break-ups, however.

10. Experiments tend to confirm some folklore about interpersonal relationships. People tend to marry those who live nearby ("the girl next door"); a woman may gain some favor if she creates the image of being "hard to get." Being hard to get, however, is only useful if the woman is easy to get for the person interested in her.

11. Psychologists have only recently begun to study *sexual jealousy*. Some jealousy responses are designed to maintain the relationship; others are attempts to maintain self-esteem. When threatened, women tend to opt for the former response, and men are more likely to use self-defensive coping strategies.

12. Systematic studies of marriage and divorce, as of jealousy, are relatively rare. Happy couples do appear to be more active in self-fulfilling activities than couples experiencing discord.

CHAPTER 6 ANGER AND AGGRESSION

AGGRESSION DEFINED
  Outcome, intent, means to an end, and plain meanness

AGGRESSION DETERMINANTS
  Organic: Bad brains, mean genes, instincts, and evolution
  Psychological: Anger, arousal, and provocation
  Learning: Conditioning and imitation

AGGRESSION PREDICTION
  From birth to maturity

AGGRESSION REDUCTION
  Catharsis: Drain it off!
  Cognition: Think cool!
  Empathy: How would you like it?
  Humor: The right jokes

AGGRESSION EFFECTS
  Television and aggression: A complicated picture

SUMMARY HIGHLIGHTS

It was an intense battle between two strong men. Ray felt a burning sensation from the large cut that came from the blow to his eye. Blood dripped down his face, and he cringed at the strong salty taste as the thick red liquid mixed with sweat entered his mouth. Then Ray saw his chance to stop his opponent. A strong left jab, followed by a flurry of hard punches . . . (and so on, and so on).

Is this grim scene repugnant to you? You would certainly not enjoy being the victim of Ray's brutal assault. Most people would condemn a public fist fight as unacceptable by the standards of modern society. Yet the scene was modeled after a televised boxing match featuring Sugar Ray Leonard. The reaction of the audience revealed little condemnation of the successful fighter. Instead, he left the ring to loud cheers of adulation.

Throughout recorded history, aggressive behavior has remained one of the most intriguing mysteries of human behavior. Nearly all human societies have condemned aggression and fighting. Yet these same cultures made heroes out of individuals who were brutally aggressive—in appropriate *areas*. Ray's assault could have got him time in prison if it had occurred in the alley behind Joe's bar. Because it occurred in the acceptable environment of the sports arena, however, it was rewarded with an outlandish sum of money, fame, and glory.

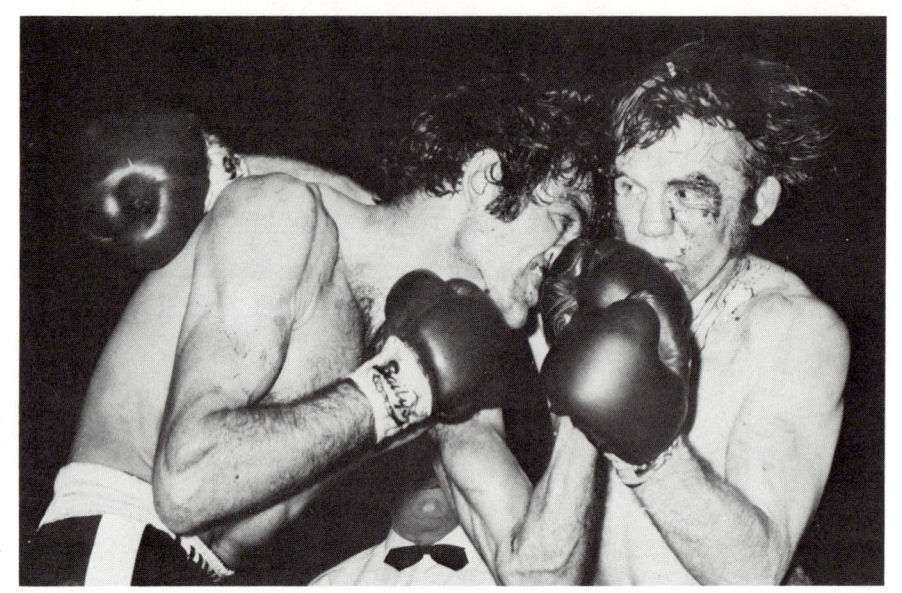

Although the public accepts violence in the form of public events, such as boxing matches, similar behaviors are condemned in other situations.

AGGRESSION DEFINED

Biologists tell us that aggression has played an important role in the evolution of mankind. Animals incapable of self-defense simply do not survive. Yet at the same time, humankind has felt heightened concern over its own undesirable acts of aggression. If growing trends in violence cannot be controlled, civilization may be doomed.

During the past two decades, the crime rate in the United States alone grew much more rapidly than the population! Table 6-1 is based on the Federal Bureau of Investigation (FBI) *Uniform Crime Reports* on violent crimes between 1960 and 1980. The increases between 1970 and 1980, though not as staggering as in the previous decade, are still frightening. Although FBI statistics have been held suspect by some (police records, for example, are sometimes doctored to scare taxpayers into supporting law enforcement),[1] these data are alarming.

TABLE 6-1. Increases in violent crimes between 1960 and 1980[a]

Crime	Percent Increase 1960–1970	Percent Increase 1970–1980
Murder	44	28
Forcible Rape	93	84
Aggravated Assault	79	79
Robbery	146	13

[a] Figures take population increase into consideration.
Source: Estimated from FBI Uniform Crime Report.

What is causing all this violence and aggression? Psychologists have several possible explanations that we will look at shortly. But first we must decide what types of behavior should be called aggressive.

[1] JOHNSON, 1972.

Outcome, intent, means to an end, and plain meanness

Most of us would agree that aggression is behavior that results in harm to another person. But what if we hurt someone we did not intend to hurt? Have we been aggressive? Confusion often results from situations that cause injury to an individual although injury had not been the original goal. Consider the football lineman who, while attempting to block a punt, lands on the kicker, breaking his leg. Here, the *intent* of the behavior was to block the kick, not to harm the kicker. If we defined aggression as behavior that results in harm, then this incident would be classified as aggression. Employing the intent definition, however, the incident would not be called aggression.

On the other hand, there are situations in which intent to injure is present yet no injury occurs. For example, suppose a young boy throws a rock at a school rival, but the rock misses its mark. Here is intent to harm, yet no harm results. Whether or not the rock-throwing incident is aggression depends on which definition of aggression we employ. But if we stress only *outcome* (harm), we exclude behavior that could be identical to that which has destructive consequences. Suppose the young boy throws two rocks at his school rival. The rival ducks and avoids the first rock, but the second one hits him. The rock thrower's behavior would only be called aggressive for the second toss even though his behavior was the same on both occasions.

Intent definitions have also met with criticism. It is so difficult to observe what other people intend to do that some psychologists have written detailed treatises arguing that aggression cannot be defined. For the purpose of this discussion, we will follow those who refer to aggression as "behavior designed to result in harm to a person or his property."[2]

The question of outcome and intent is not the only problem facing research on aggression. A distinction has to be made between instrumental and hostile aggression. Instrumental aggression is aggressive behavior as a means to an end. This type of aggression is used to obtain a "nonaggressive goal" such as money, power, or sexual enjoyment. In pure cases of instrumental aggression, anger and hostility are at a minimum. A wife who kills her husband solely to cash in his life insurance policy or a boxer who fights for titles and prizes may be exhibiting instrumental aggression. The act of injuring someone else is not what sustains or motivates this aggressive behavior. The behavior is sustained by some other reward, or the expectation of one.

Sometimes people act aggressively just because they are mad. This is hostile aggression. Instead of being an instrumental act to obtain nonaggressive goals, this type of aggression occurs because people are furious or plain mad and are rewarded when the person they are mad at gets hurt. The goal is the infliction of pain or injury on another person, group, or object. For example, each year hundreds of murders are committed by jealous lovers. Such acts exemplify hostile aggression.

Most aggressive acts contain elements of both hostile and instrumental aggression. Although it is rare for either type to occur in its pure form, psychologists have found it useful to keep these concepts separate.[3] In any event, the definition of aggression is at least partially a matter of value judgment. Different communities can hold different opinions about the

[2]Freedman, Sears, & Carlsmith, 1978. [3]Feshbach, 1964.

nature of aggressive behavior. This was demonstrated by psychologist Robert Kahn, who works at the Institute of Social Research at the University of Michigan. Part of the Institute, the Center for Survey Research, frequently conducts national surveys. In one such survey, a sample of 1400 White and Black American men were asked what behavior they would consider violent. The results showed that Black and White men differ considerably in their perception, as illustrated in Table 6-2.

Table 6-2. White and Black views on violence

Situation	Percentage of White men classifying situation as violent	Percentage of Black men classifying situation as violent
Police beating students	52	82[a]
Police shooting looters	32	59[a]
Police stopping people to frisk them	13	34
Denying people's civil rights	46	70
Looting	87	74
Burglary	64	70
Student protest	39[a]	23
Sit-ins	23	15
Draft-card burning	59	51

[a]Blacks are more likely than Whites to view police assertiveness as aggressive. Whites are more likely than Blacks to perceive assertive behavior by middle-class college students as violent.
Source: Kahn, 1972.

The survey demonstrates that aggression, as most people use the term, is in part a value judgment.[4] Different people may have different values. For the purposes of this book, however, we will stick to behaviorally related definitions of aggression.

AGGRESSION DETERMINANTS

Organic: Bad brains, mean genes, instincts, and evolution

In 1966, a University of Texas student named Charles Whitman killed his wife and mother. The next day he got up, took his rifle, climbed the University tower, and for 90 minutes blasted away at everything that moved. He hit 38 people (14 of whom died) and even got one airplane.

Before this bizarre incident, Whitman had not been a particularly brutal person. What could have been responsible for this outrage? In his case, we may have an answer: it appears that Whitman suffered from an organic brain tumor. Experiments with animals have shown that several areas of the brain seem to be associated with aggressive behavior. When these brain centers are damaged or stimulated, the animals will behave violently. When these areas are damaged in a human brain, the person can become violent or even a killer.

Charles Whitman was just such a case. He had some damage in his brain that produced uncontrollable impulses to destroy and kill. He was aware that something was wrong. This awareness is apparent in the note Whitman wrote, which described his problem and his unsuccessful attempt to get help:

[4]Kahn, 1972.

Charles Whitman at age 18. What made this all-American boy go beserk?

I don't quite understand what it is that compels me to type this letter. Perhaps it is to leave some vague reason for the actions I have recently performed. [At this point Whitman had harmed no one; his wife and mother were elsewhere in the city, still alive.]

I don't really understand myself these days. I am supposed to be an average, reasonable and intelligent young man. However, lately (I can't recall when it started) I have been a victim of many unusual and irrational thoughts. These thoughts constantly recur, and it requires a tremendous mental effort to concentrate on useful and progressive tasks. In March when my parents made a physical break I noticed a great deal of stress. I consulted a Dr. Cochrum at the University Health Center and asked him to recommend someone that I could consult with about some psychiatric disorders I felt I had. I talked with a Doctor once for about two hours and tried to convey to him my fears that I felt overcome by overwhelming violent impulses. After one session I never saw the Doctor again, and since then I have been fighting my mental turmoil alone, and seemingly to no avail. After my death I wish that an autopsy would be performed on me to see if there is any visible physical disorder. I have had some tremendous headaches in the past and have consumed two large bottles of Excedrin in the past three months.

It was after much thought that I decided to kill my wife, Kathy, tonight after I pick her up from work. . . . I love her dearly, and she has been a fine wife to me as any man could ever hope to have. I cannot rationally pinpoint any specific reason for doing this. I don't know whether it is selfishness, or if I don't want her to have to face the embarrassment my actions would surely cause her. At this time though, the prominent reason in my mind is that I truly do not consider this world worth living in, and am prepared to die, and I do not want to leave her to suffer alone in it. I intend to kill her as painlessly as possible.

Later in the night he killed both his mother and wife, and then wrote.

> I imagine it appears that I brutally killed both of my loved ones. I was only trying to do a good thorough job.
>
> If my life insurance policy is valid please see that all the worthless checks I wrote this weekend are made good. Please pay off all my debts. I am 25 years old and have never been financially independent. Donate the rest anonymously to a mental health foundation. Maybe research can prevent further tragedies of this type. (p. 78)[5]

Whitman's mass murders occurred the day after this second note had been written. According to his request, an autopsy was performed on Whitman's brain. The autopsy revealed a huge tumor in an area of the brain that had been identified in animal studies as associated with aggressive behavior.[6]

Psychiatrists estimate that as many as 10 million Americans have obvious brain damage and another 5 million may have some form of brain disease that is not detectable. Some experts believe that we can help certain violent people by subjecting them to brain surgery. Such surgery, however, can turn a functioning individual into a vegetable, and such psychosurgery techniques have become very controversial in recent years.[7]

Genetically speaking, most of us have 46 chromosomes. These chromosomes come in pairs. We have 23 pairs; half from our fathers and half from our mothers. Of these 23 pairs of chromosomes, one pair determines our sex. For this pair, females have two chromosomes that look like Xs. Females are referred to conventionally by the label XX. Males have one chromosome that looks like an X and another shorter one that looks more like a Y. Males, therefore, are referred to by geneticists as XY. The short Y chromosome seems to be associated with male hormones, male sex organs, and the behavior commonly related to those structures.

Sometimes the process of forming normal males and females gets fouled up. For example, sometimes there will only be one X chromosome and nothing from the other parent (XO). This is called *Turner's syndrome* and people with these syndromes are females who develop abnormally. The other side of the coin is *Klinefelter's syndrome*, where there is an extra X chromosome. People with Klinefelter's syndrome (XXY) have male genitals but also may develop many female characteristics, such as breasts.

Recently it has been shown that a certain genetic disorder, the XYY or **supermale syndrome**, may be associated with violent behavior. These men have the regular genetic characteristics of males along with an additional Y or male chromosome, and often are physically strong, sometimes display homosexual tendencies, and frequently exhibit severe behavior problems.[8] A review of the literature of the XYY syndrome estimated that about 13 in every 10,000 newborn males have this chromosomal condition,[9] whereas criminal males are much more likely to have this abnormality. In fact, criminals are 15 times as likely to have the XYY pattern. It has also been shown that inmates in several institutions for the criminally insane displayed XYY abnormalities more than 20 times as often as samples from the general population.

[5]JOHNSON, 1972. [6]SWEET, ERVIN, & MARK, 1969. [7]MARK, 1974. [8]DALY, 1969. [9]JARVICK, KLODIN, & MATSUYAMA, 1973.

Does this mean that all violent criminals have the XYY problem? It does not. In fact, most violent acts are more likely to be caused by something in the environment, as we shall see later on. Nevertheless, some biologically oriented scientists still feel that aggression is an instinct. Sigmund Freud, for example, felt that there is a drive in all individuals to behave aggressively—but he did not feel this way in his early writings (before 1918), when he believed that aggression was a way of expressing frustration. After World War I, however, during which he saw people killed or mutilated without good reason, he decided that humans must have an innate drive to destroy themselves and that this drive is expressed through aggression.

Like Freud, European *ethologists* (students of animal behavior) such as Konrad Lorenz believe that aggression has an instinctive base. Lorenz thinks that aggressive impulses build up until they can be released.[10] Lorenz's work has more recently been expanded on by scientists representing a new field known as **sociobiology**. Sociobiologists tend to be strict believers in Darwin's theory of evolution. They believe that an overproduction of all animals occurs in every generation and that, because of high levels of genetic mutation, there is great diversity among members of all species. When the environment changes, those animals most suited for the new environment survive and those less suited die off. Over the course of generations, only the fittest survive.

Most scientists have accepted Darwin's explanation of the evolutionary significance of most physical characteristics. More controversial has been his belief that many social behaviors are also inherited.[11] Sociobiologists believe that fighting, like all other social behaviors, has a biological basis. Over the course of many generations, those animals that were toughest and best able to defend their territories survived—the weaker and poorer fighters did not live to reproduce. Baboon breeding provides some evidence for this position. In baboon colonies, each female animal is only sexually receptive for a few days of her estrous cycle. During this relatively brief period, a great deal of competition goes on among the males for the opportunity to mate with her. At the height of her receptivity, which is the time when she is most likely to become pregnant, the competition among the males is severe and only the strongest and toughest male gains the opportunity of sexual advance. The toughest male's ability to outfight his rivals assures that the strongest animals have the best opportunity to reproduce.

It is important to realize that sociobiologists do not make evaluative judgments about aggression among animals. They regard aggression as an adaptive pattern of behavior that allows aggressive groups of animals to survive. Those species that are able to defend their territories survive and those incapable of defending their territories are killed by predators.[12] Fighting among members of the same species also has adaptive advantages. It assures that animals do not get too close to one another, which reduces the chances of spreading communicable diseases and of overconsuming the food supply in a particular area. Moreover, although animals fight with members of their own species, *killing* members of their own species is very rare in the animal kingdom.

[10]LORENZ, 1966. [11]WILSON, 1975. [12]DALY & WILSON, 1978; PATTERSON & PETRINOVICH, 1980.

Human beings differ from other animals in the degree to which they will pursue an attack—only humans commonly kill members of their own species. Most animals have some sort of ritual that can be used to call off a death-threatening attack. For example, a dog will roll over and expose its neck as a signal to an attacking animal that he concedes victory in the fight. To curtail violence, Lorenz thinks, people should engage in aggressive rituals as animals do. (We will talk more about Lorenz's idea when we discuss catharsis later in this chapter.)

Psychological: Anger, arousal, and provocation

Have you ever thought you would behave differently if nobody around knew who you were? Would you be more impulsive if you felt nobody would be able to identify you? The conclusion of some prominent psychologists is that you would.

Psychologist Philip Zimbardo has shown how anonymity can be related to aggression. He claims that people can lose their feelings of identifiability when they become members of a large group or mob. Without their feelings of personal identity, they no longer feel responsible for their own behavior. They are **deindividuated**. Arousal produced by the excitement of a crowd, by drugs, or by alcohol is a case in point. Under these conditions, people do not evaluate their own behavior or feel bound by guilt, shame, or consistency with things done in the past.

To test some of these ideas, Zimbardo conducted an experiment in which college women served as subjects (see Figure 6-1). Half of the women were made to feel a sense of identifiability by being met at the door and given large nametags to wear. Another group was made to feel anonymous. During the experiment, these women wore large lab coats (size 44) and hoods over their heads. All the women then heard tape recordings of another woman who seemed to be either nice (accepting, sweet, and altruistic) or obnoxious (self-centered, conceited). The women were then placed in a situation where they would have to give electric shocks to the nice or the obnoxious woman. The women who had been allowed to feel anonymous gave longer shocks to the victim than the women with a sense of identifiability. The obnoxious victim also received longer punishment from them. The individuated group gave shorter shocks, and it made little difference if the victim was obnoxious or nice.[13]

Zimbardo feels that his theory describes much of the aggression we see in our everyday lives. He suggests that Army uniforms, Ku Klux Klan outfits, and police uniforms are all covers that make people lose their feelings of identity. Other things that might make people feel deindividuated could be the stresses of urban life and the breakdown of the primary family. (See also the concept of *alienation* in Chapter 9.)

Other psychologists have made use of the term **catharsis**. Catharsis is a Greek word that means "purification" or "cleansing." Within the study of social sciences, however, catharsis has taken on a much more specific meaning. It refers to the process by which a person exhibits an emotion and is

[13]ZIMBARDO, 1970.

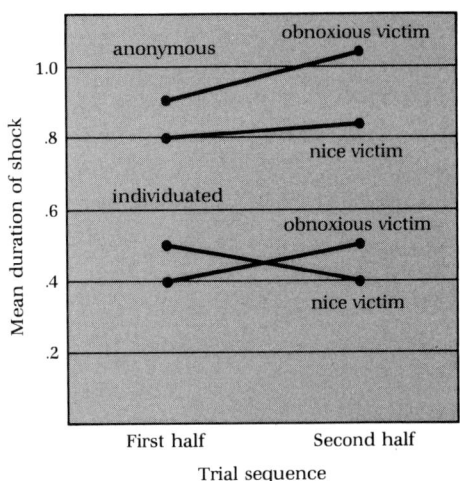

Figure 6-1.
Deindividuation and aggression. On the left side is a picture of "deindividuated" subjects in an experiment: college women dressed in baggy lab coats, head hooded, and never referred to by name. On the right side is a graph depicting the duration of electric shocks administered (as part of the experiment) to these anonymous subjects as opposed to "individuated" subjects (college women in ordinary clothing wearing name tags). Clearly, aggression towards obnoxiously-acting subjects increased over time. More important, however, is the fact that as a group, the deindividuated subjects were given more shocks than their counterparts. *Source:* Zimbardo, 1969.

thereby purged or cleansed of it. The most frequent reference to catharsis is in relation to aggressive behavior. It is widely believed that expressing aggression or hostility makes an angry person less angry and thus reduces his or her drive to behave aggressively.

Leonard Berkowitz, a noted authority on aggression research, points out that the validity of the catharsis concept is widely accepted by both the layperson and the social scientist.[14] A close look at experimental and theoretical treatments of catharsis, however, would suggest that a blanket acceptance of the concept may not be justified. It has, in fact, become a controversial issue among psychologists because some maintain that, rather than reducing aggressive behavior, catharsis actually increases it.

The dispute over the existence of "emotional purges" is not really new. It dates back to the fourth century B.C., when catharsis was discussed in terms of the effects of observing emotion-laden plays. Aristotle believed that watching tragic drama "operates psychologically to relieve us of the oppressive emotions of pity and fear, just as a catharter purges the body of excessive humor." Aristotle's mentor, Plato, had a different view on the effects of tragic drama. He believed that plays ". . . arouse violent emotions and stir men to all sorts of passions." Plato further contended that artists were deceitful, dangerous, and deserving of censorship.[15]

Plato and Aristotle discussed catharsis nearly 2300 years ago. In contempor-

[14]BERKOWITZ, 1962, 1980. [15]JONES, 1969.

ary psychology, the concept of catharsis was introduced via psychoanalysis. Josef Breuer and Sigmund Freud used the term in their discussions of hysteria, which were originally published between 1893 and 1895. *Hysteria* is a condition in which people complain about physical symptoms for which no physiological reasons exist. The problem usually involves guilt. Breuer and Freud originally viewed hysteria as the result of a repressed traumatic event. They found that the event could be recalled under hypnosis, and that such recollection was accompanied by an intense reproduction of the original emotion. Following the emotional reexperience, the symptoms disappeared. This therapeutic process was labeled *abreaction*. Catharsis was the name given to the method.[16]

It can be readily seen that the Greek philosophers and Freud were assigning the same name to totally different processes. The Greek philosophers perceived catharsis as an emotional purge brought on by vicarious experiences, such as witnessing others involved in emotional upheaval. Freud postulated that catharsis was an intrapsychic process—something originating solely within the person. Most subsequent descriptions of catharsis have been more similar to the Freudian than to the Aristotelian definition.

Some psychologists, psychiatrists, and ethologists have found it more useful to define the concept of catharsis by way of analogy. In proposing a "hydraulic model" of aggression, the somewhat crude but effective analogy is that of the process of urine storing up in the bladder. It is a process which gradually builds up until release has to occur. The assumption here is that, in a similar manner, a drive to "aggress" can build up until aggression is expressed. Releasing the aggression (catharsis) then returns the drive to a lower level. Typical of such thinking is the monograph entitled *Frustration and Aggression* published in 1939 by a group of psychologists at Yale University headed by John Dollard.[17] Their work has been the prime instigator of aggression research over the last 30 years. The major reason for their impact was that the Yale researchers' statement of hypotheses was couched in testable terms. The publication of *Frustration and Aggression* was clearly a turning point in the study of catharsis and aggression because it stated the problem in a form that could be adapted for experimental tests.

In their discussion of aggression, Dollard and his coworkers generally follow the hydraulic model. They suggest a circular process that works somewhat like this: aggression (or the drive to aggress) is a direct function of frustration. Inhibiting aggressive behavior merely serves to increase the drive to aggress, which facilitates the expression of aggression. The expression of aggression in turn reduces the chances for aggression to continue, or, as the Yale group put it, "the occurrence of any act of aggression is assumed to reduce the instigation of aggression." This instigation to aggress represents catharsis, or a "cathartic effect."[18]

In summary, here is what these various theoretical frameworks suggest. Aristotle's theory is simple: you become less nasty after watching others acting nastily. Freud and Dollard and his Yale colleagues say you must go

---

[16]BREUER & FREUD, 1957. [17]DOLLARD, DOOB, MILLER, MOWRER, & SEARS, 1939. [18]DOLLARD, DOOB, MILLER, MOWRER, & SEARS, 1939.

through catharsis within yourself. The Yale group says that, when your frustrations build up, you release them by means of aggression, thereby reducing chances for further aggression. Freud says essentially the same thing, except that he feels that aggressive behavior has to be an emotional reexperience. The only trouble with these theories is that they tend to classify as aggressive such diverse behaviors as acts of physical violence, spreading rumors, masochism, or aggression in dreams. Many researchers since then have followed this line of reasoning without first determining whether it is justifiable to lump everything together in one equivalent package. As a result, some glaring inconsistencies have emerged in many studies of catharsis.

Then there are psychologists who do not accept the concept of catharsis in the first place. In fact, they suggest that expressions of aggression, anger, or hostility lead to increases rather than decreases in aggression.[19] One explanation of such views fits within the theory of cognitive dissonance (see Chapter 4). Briefly, it assumes that expressing hostility toward someone may or may not involve emotional upheaval but is virtually certain to be accompanied by cognitions (thoughts, judgments, and the like) within the aggressor. For example, did you ever wonder if the target of your anger might be a good and reasonable person who really should not be attacked? Or weren't you ever surprised that a peaceful and friendly person like yourself could be engaged in an act of aggression? In such cases, your judgment of the situation is simply dissonant (inconsistent) with the behavior you are displaying. The resulting doubts can be disturbing to your self-perception.

The theory of cognitive dissonance suggests several ways out of this cognitive fix. For example, if you are convinced that the target of your aggression *deserves* punishment, you are off the hook—after all, punishment is precisely what you are administering. Finding reasons to justify your attack by denigrating or putting down your victim thus becomes common practice. Once denigrated, a person or group is obviously even more likely to be attacked than before. They "deserve" to be attacked. Not too surprisingly, evidence tends to show that disliked persons or groups are the most likely targets for continuing aggression. The dissonance view can be summed up by the dictum that violence does not reduce the tendency toward violence; violence breeds *more* violence.

Catharsis and frustration are closely tied to the experience of anger. In fact, anger is the best known predictor of aggressive behavior. Experiments rarely show that any manipulation has much effect upon aggression if it is not combined with anger.[20] Experiments that compare aggression between angry and nonangry subjects virtually always demonstrate that people are more aggressive when they are angry than when they are not.

We doubt if you will be surprised to learn that people fight more when they are mad. Yet only within the last few years have psychologists attempted to explore the nature of the emotions most responsible for serious crimes of violence. Many years ago, Wolfgang showed that close friends and relatives were involved in more than half of the solved murders. A staggering 84% of the female and 59% of the male victims were killed by someone with whom they

[19] KAHN, 1966; MALLICK & McCANDLESS, 1966. [20] KAPLAN & SINGER, 1976; KONECNI, 1982.

had a close relationship.[21] Although there is an increasing tendency for victims to be killed by someone they do not know, Wolfgang's findings tend to reflect modern trends.[22]

Most murders are not committed by mad people who randomly jump out of bushes to destroy someone previously unknown to them. A murder victim is more likely to be killed by a jealous lover or by someone who has a particular grudge against him or her. In most cases, the murderer is in an aroused emotional state. Despite the importance of anger, however, psychologists have devoted scant attention to the formal study of anger states.

One exception is the work of psychologist Ray Novaco, who has made a career out of studying angry people. Novaco views anger as a form of stress reaction. Anger, he believes, occurs as a response to perceived environmental events. Most commonly, the events are unpleasant psychosocial situations. These situations cause physiological arousal, and anger results when the person begins to label his or her own arousal "anger," "annoyance," "irritation," and so on.[23]

Anger most often results from some sort of *provocation*—as when someone insults us or interferes with our ability to control important situations. Many experiments have demonstrated that the amount of anger experimental subjects experience is a function of the perceived intentions of the anger instigator.

Perhaps the most common reason for murder is sexual jealousy. Most homicides are crimes of passion. The typical scenario runs as follows: a husband learns that his wife (frequently estranged) is sexually involved with another man. He follows her and discovers her with the other lover. On confirming that she has indeed found someone else, he confronts her, loses all control, and shoots her.

Not all attacks on spouses result from jealousy. One of the crimes reportedly on the increase in recent years is spousal abuse. Although the term could also refer to husband beating, there are many fewer cases of a wife beating a husband than vice versa. The apparent increase in the number of reported wife beatings, however, may be somewhat illusory. Although the number of cases reported to the police has been increasing, this may reflect the greater likelihood that today's woman will report the problem. In the past, most incidents of spousal abuse simply went unreported.

An interesting line of research on wife abuse concerns determining who is responsible for the assault. In most cases, observers will report that the husband is more to blame for an assault than his victim wife. It is interesting, however, to see what happens when the observers are given some excuse for the husband's behavior. A common legal defense has been that the husband was drunk, since criminal law acknowledges drunkenness as an extenuating circumstance.[24] In one study, college students read an alleged newspaper account of a wife abuse incident in which either the husband, the wife, or both were drunk. The subjects were then given the opportunity to blame the incident on either the man, the woman, the situation, or chance. Although

---

[21]WOLFGANG, 1958.   [22]HERJANIC & MEYER, 1976.   [23]KONECNI, 1975; NOVACO, 1979.   [24]AMIR, 1971.

there was a greater tendency to blame the incident on the man, the results differed for male and female subjects. As expected, men were more likely than women to cite situational factors as a cause of the problem.

The effects of one partner's drunkenness provide a more ironic twist. When the abusing husband was described as a drunk, there was a tendency to excuse him by citing situational factors. When the wife was drunk, however, the tendency was to assign greater personal responsibility to her. In other words, being drunk provides an excuse for the abusing husband. For the victim wife, being drunk provides justification for her beating.[25]

Among the leading explanations for the increase in incidents of violence against women is the increase of pornography. The last few decades have seen an enormous growth in the number of pornographic publications and films. At the same time, access to these materials has been made easier. As early as the 1960s, a Presidential commission was formed to investigate the effect of pornography. After an extensive investigation that included a series of original studies, the commission concluded that pornography did not have adverse effects upon human behavior.[26] The commission was later criticized, however, for failing to distinguish among different types of pornography. Although the effects of viewing sexual materials may not be strong, there was particular concern about *violent* portrayals of sexual behavior.[27]

Concern about violent pornography has come from many quarters. Feminists call it "hate literature" and law enforcement officers cite increases in crime in areas where violent pornography is distributed. One systematic study demonstrated that violent sexuality in *Playboy* and *Penthouse* magazines pictures has increased significantly between 1974 and 1977 (see Figure 6-2). About 13% of all of the cartoons in *Penthouse* included some reference to sexual violence; the comparable figure for *Playboy* was 6%.[28]

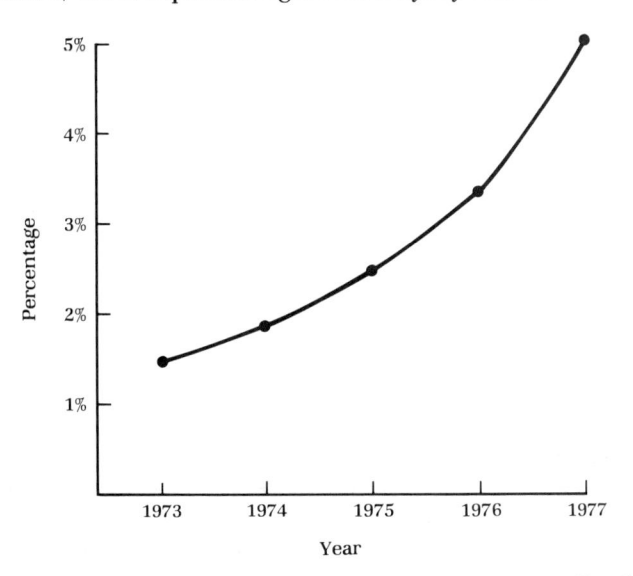

Figure 6-2. Percentage of sexual violence in the pictorials of *Penthouse* and *Playboy* magazines as a function of year of publication. *Source:* Malamuth & Spinner, 1980.

[25]RICHARDSON & CAMPBELL, 1980. [26]COMMISSION ON OBSENITY AND PORNOGRAPHY, 1970. [27]DAVIS & BRAUCHT, 1973; CLINE, 1973. [28]MALAMUTH & SPINNER, 1980.

Many studies have demonstrated that violent pornography has greater impact upon the viewer than nonviolent sexual material. In one experiment, subjects watched narrated slide shows depicting either intercourse between two mutually consenting partners or a violent rape. Those who had been exposed to the rape had more sexual fantasies than those who had witnessed the sexual scenes without violence.[29] Other experiments lend support to the belief that violent pornography leads to an increase in violence against women.[30] In one such study, male subjects were shown either a neutral, an erotic, or a violent erotic film and then had the opportunity to give painful electric shocks to either males or females. If the men were angry at the time they watched the film, there was a clear tendency for those who had seen the violent erotic film to aggress more against a female victim. The violent erotic film did not increase aggression toward men, nor did the erotic film without violence have much effect upon aggression.[31] Thus, it appears that the new pornography making women the victims of cruel punishments may increase the number of female victims in the real world.

Of course, violent pornography is only one of many causes of rape and violence against women. One of the most disturbing reports about rape is that one-half of a sample of college males reported that they themselves might rape if they were assured they would not be punished! Further, both male and female college students believe that a substantial percentage of "other" women would enjoy being raped. Evidence clearly suggests, however, that women do not enjoy being raped and very few college women believe that they personally would enjoy being a rape victim.[32]

Learning: Conditioning and imitation

Do you remember how some of the kids in elementary school were always tougher than others? And when the tough kids got mean, they also got their way. It didn't take them long to learn that if the teacher wasn't around, they could get what they wanted by being tough. Thus, the tough bully got rewarded for aggression and learned to behave aggressively on future occasions.

Let us now examine some of the ways in which the expression of hostility or acts of aggression may make it more likely that further aggression will occur. Once again, we are dealing with the notion that violence breeds more violence.

Psychologist Seymour Feshbach of UCLA believes that an aggressive drive can produce a motivation to injure others.[33] If we hurt someone we want to injure, it may be rewarding. In learning terms, the *reinforcement* of the hostile behavior increases the strength of a hostile habit. As a result, hostile behavior is likely to reoccur on future occasions.

Another psychologist, Arnold Buss, also believes that aggressive behavior, especially in males, is often reinforced, leading to strengthened aggressive habit strength. Buss noted that aggressive acts often enhance the status and position of the aggressor. As examples, Buss mentioned that aggression is reinforced by (1) organized crime, where destruction of property and murder

---

[29]MALAMUTH, 1980. [30]DONNERSTEIN & HALLAM, 1978; DONNERSTEIN & BARRETT, 1978. [31]DONNERSTEIN & BARRETT, 1978. [32]MALAMUTH, HABER, & FESHBACH, 1980. [33]FESHBACH, 1971.

are rewarded with money; (2) national myths and war legends, which make heroes of those who kill on a mass scale during battles; and (3) the model for the masculine role in society, which emphasizes dominance, competitiveness, and aggression. In short, aggression is often rewarded with money, prestige, and status.[34] The evidence that aggressive behavior can be increased by rewarding aggressive response is overwhelming.[35]

Another model to account for the learning of aggressive behavior among young children has been proposed and developed by Albert Bandura and other psychologists at Stanford University. Bandura's views are couched in terms of his theory of social learning and imitation. According to the theory, a child learns some behavior (in this case, aggressive behavior) by observing a model. The child may then imitate or reproduce the behavior to a lesser or greater extent, depending on whether it leads to, or is expected to lead to, reward or punishment. If the consequences of the observationally learned behavior are rewarded, the behavior is expected to recur with greater frequency; if they are punished, the behavior will be expressed to a lesser extent.

To test this theory, Bandura and his associates had preschool children observe an adult aggressive model, either live or on film. A third group watched a film of an aggressive cartoon character. No film was shown to a control group. In the live and film conditions, the young boys and girls watched an adult model attack a large Bobo doll while screaming, "Sock him in the nose . . . hit him down . . . throw him in the air . . ." and "Pow!" Children in the cartoon test group watched "Herman the Cat" assault a Bobo doll as the adult had done in the other conditions.

The children were then led to another room, where they found the Bobo doll and the instruments the model had used to attack it. The experimenter mildly frustrated her subjects by giving them some fancy toys to play with and then taking the toys away. The results showed that children can learn aggressive behavior by just watching a model. Children who had observed an aggressive model attack a Bobo doll were nearly twice as likely as all other groups to aggress against the doll in an identical or similar manner. A second experiment revealed that the children's aggression was more likely to be expressed when they had observed a model who was rewarded than if they had seen a model who was punished for his aggression.

In summary, Bandura's imitation theory holds that, once an aggressive response is acquired, it is not weakened or strengthened simply by the act of expression. Only the consequences of expression are important. The response is held in reserve for situations in which it may be reinforced. According to Bandura, aggression by children often leads to positive consequences; therefore, aggression is often followed by more aggression.[36] Other studies show that the experience of making the doll move strengthens the tendency to be aggressive.[37]

One of the most important theories of aggression is that of Leonard Berkowitz, a psychologist who proposes that impulsive responses may become conditioned to situational stimuli in a person's environment. Aggression functions as a conditioned response to certain stimuli, provided such stimuli

[34]Buss, 1971. [35]Geen & Pigg, 1970; Geen & Stonner, 1971; Geen, 1972; Loew, 1967. [36]Bandura, 1977, 1965, 1973; Bandura, Ross, & Ross, 1961, 1963a, 1963b, 1963c. [37]Hayes, 1980.

Imitation of aggression. After witnessing an adult behave aggressively, children will imitate the aggression. In the sequence shown on the top row an adult attacks a large BoBo doll. In the sequences shown in the next two rows, children are shown imitating the aggressive attacks on the doll. *Source:* Bandura, Ross, & Ross, 1961.

are associated with violent scenes the individual has encountered previously. This process, known as classical conditioning, can lead to heightened hostile reactions. For example, by associating names with unpleasant words, psychologists were able to condition students to dislike certain names. Each student then participated in a discussion with two other students (actually confederates of Berkowitz), one of whom actually possessed the name associated with the conditioning. Ratings demonstrated that the students showed greater hostility toward the person who bore the disliked name than toward the confederate having a neutral name. The unpleasant effect conditioned to the name had been generalized to the person bearing the label.[38]

The classical conditioning model implies that "stimuli having aggressive meaning should be capable of eliciting aggressive responses from people who, for one reason or another, are ready to act aggressively." To demonstrate this principle, a confederate of Berkowitz delivered either one or several shocks to each of a group of college students. The students were then allowed to administer shocks to the confederates. While they were administering the shocks, some of the subjects saw weapons on the table near the shock machine. Half of the subjects were told that the weapons were left there by the

[38]BERKOWITZ, 1968, 1971, 1980.

confederate, and the other half were told that the weapon had been left by the previous experimenter. As controls, some angered and nonangered subjects returned the shocks when no weapon was present. Another group of angered and nonangered subjects returned the shocks in the presence of a badminton racket and shuttlecocks.

The angered subjects gave more shocks than the nonangered subjects. The subjects who delivered shocks in the presence of a weapon gave more shocks than those with either a neutral object (badminton racket) or no object present. The students believing that the weapon belonged to the confederate did not give reliably more shocks than the subjects believing that the weapon had been left by a previous experimenter. Thus, the hypothesis that angered subjects will shock their provokers more in the presence of weapons was supported.[39]

In another study, a confederate who was introduced as a boxer or a college speech major either insulted or did not insult a group of college students. Half of these students then watched a boxing film; the others watched a nonaggressive control film. When given an opportunity to shock the confederate, insulted subjects showed aggression most often toward the confederate who had been introduced as a boxer. It was argued that the association between the filmed boxer's aggression and the label of "boxer" for the confederate was responsible for these increases in aggression.

Extensions of the Berkowitz studies showed that subjects would give more shocks to a confederate who bore the same name as one of the filmed boxers[40] and that even more shocks would be administered to a confederate who bore the same name as the filmed victim instead of the filmed victor.[41] Responses to filmed violence, however, can be greatly influenced by the viewer's understanding of what he or she is watching. For example, people will respond more aggressively when they feel that the violence is justified. In justified violence, the aggressors "have the right" to aggress because someone has treated them wrongly, or because someone has broken the law. This type of violence is commonly shown in Clint Eastwood movies and in television police stories. Experiments show that viewers are not stimulated to aggression by unjustified violence.[42] According to Berkowitz, then, anger arousal is the energizer for aggressive behavior and creates a readiness to respond aggressively. For aggression to occur, stimuli associated with a present or a previous anger instigator must be present. These "aggressive cues" activate the angered person's aggressive thoughts or aggressive behavior.

From birth to maturity

Parents are notorious in exaggerating the virtues of their children. Yet all parents will sooner or later agree that some little devils justly deserve to be labeled aggressive. Is there a parent, though, who has not wondered what kind of adult a certain 4-year-old will turn into, especially when this precious child consistently tends to strike parents, throw temper tantrums, attack other children physically or verbally without provocation, or display uncontrollable destructive activity?

AGGRESSION PREDICTION

[39]BERKOWITZ & LEPAGE, 1967. [40]BERKOWITZ & GEEN, 1966. [41]GEEN & BERKOWITZ, 1966. [42]BERKOWITZ & POWERS, 1979.

Psychologists can provide some answers to such parental worries. One way of looking into the future is based on *cross-sectional* research. By studying large samples of children at various ages, it is possible to arrive at some typical behavior for that age. Parents can thus obtain an authoritative book on "The Child at 5," "The Child at 10," or "The Child at 14," from which they can learn whether their child displays normal behavior and whether this kind of behavior is likely to be maintained as the child grows older.

Another way of making predictions about children is to follow the behavior of the same children over a long period of time. This is known as *longitudinal* research, which is costly, difficult to carry out, and, therefore, rarely conducted. The advantages, however, are obvious. The psychologist observes the child at the age of, say, 2 and makes certain predictions about him or her. The *same* child is then observed at the age of 4, or 10, or 13, or 16—in fact, right into adulthood. With each observation it is possible to verify the extent to which the previous prediction was accurate.

One of the classical longitudinal studies, appropriately labeled *Birth to Maturity: A Study in Psychological Development*, was conducted between 1929 and 1954—a period of 25 years! As reported by psychologists Jerome Kagan and Howard Moss, careful observations and interviews with the subjects were conducted during periodic visits at home, at school, at play, and at work over that entire period. The children—subsequently, the adults—were checked for a variety of behavior patterns, among them passivity, dependency, achievement, and aggression.

The major finding of Kagan and Moss was that if we want to make predictions about the future behavior of children, the safest bet is to rely on the traditional definition of sex-appropriate behavior. In other words, since society tolerates, or in fact encourages, aggressive behavior in boys, it is a safe bet that aggressive boys will turn into aggressive adults. When it is not tolerated, or is discouraged, as in the case of girls, it is far more difficult to predict the stability of the child's initial behavior. In Kagan and Moss's study, at least, the findings were extremely stable for boys. Those boys who during their childhoods showed such behavior patterns as aggression toward peers, tantrums, rage reactions, and low levels of frustration tolerance turned into excessively aggressive and irritable adults. Many of the excessively aggressive girls, on the other hand, failed to show such behavior as adults because of the continuing pattern of reward and punishment by parents, teachers, friends, and, in fact, our entire culture, which discourages such behavior in females.[43]

Although this study shows that aggressive boys are likely to turn into aggressive men far more often than aggressive girls into aggressive women, a word of caution is due. Let us not forget that cultural norms do change, and what was sex appropriate between 1929 and 1954 is not necessarily sex appropriate between 1982 and 1999! Undoubtedly, the behavior of many young girls and women today would then have been labeled aggressive and therefore inappropriate for females (just as a lot of accepted behavior for males nowadays would then have been labeled dependent and inappropriate). But the current liberation of the sexes does not really invalidate the

[43]KAGAN & MOSS, 1962.

basic findings of Kagan and Moss: what society wants, society gets. Parents attempting to make a prediction about their child's future behavior should always bear that in mind.

AGGRESSION REDUCTION

Without carefully detailed operational definitions, aggression as a concept may lose all meaning. With such definitions included, it becomes possible to separate aggressive behavior that is socially acceptable, perhaps even desirable (as in sports or business), from that which is not. Most aggressive behavior falls in the latter category and is not socially approved. Throwing tantrums, insulting others, physically attacking others, or just being plain nasty to others is frowned upon. It is also destructive, even self-destructive behavior. The reduction of aggression thus becomes a vital issue in interpersonal adjustment and mental health. Few psychologists or psychiatrists will dispute this point. Where they differ, however, is on the clinical approaches and techniques to achieve aggression reduction.

Catharsis: Drain it off!

As pointed out earlier, Sigmund Freud and other noted psychoanalysts made extensive use of abreaction, or emotional reexperience. They felt that an intense reproduction of a person's original emotion—say, aggression—would lead to its reduction with subsequent benefit (such as guilt removal) to the person expressing that emotion. Since effective abreaction in psychoanalysis must occur only at a particular point in time during the charted course of psychotherapy, it often becomes part of a time-consuming process.

Contemporary psychotherapy has several approaches that consider the expression of emotion essential but, unlike psychoanalysis, are less time consuming and complex. These approaches seem adequate for those who neither are nor should be candidates for psychoanalysis. Most of us fall under this category.

Reevaluation therapy is based on the premise that effective functioning is obstructed by psychological distresses. The distresses can be removed through emotional discharges. After the distress has been discharged, reevaluation can take place. In the case of anger, the anger blocks a rational evaluation of the arousing incident. Anger expression during counseling leads to discharge, which in turn leads to reevaluation of the anger-arousing incident.[44] The implication applies, therefore, to noncounseling situations as well: kick a can, pound a door, or break a dish—only *then* will you be able to effectively evaluate the situation that led up to this behavior.

Psychologist Arthur Janov advocates an even greater return to basics. **Primal therapy** maintains that severe psychological disturbances become repressed.[45] The prescription (somewhat oversimplified) for getting rid of this repression: find yourself a therapist who will make you aware of your repressed feelings and scream at the top of your lungs! Janov maintains that this violent emotional discharge facilitates the eventual recognition of the disturbance, and as such becomes the core of the healing process.

It is important to note that both reevaluation therapy and primal therapy

[44]JACKINS, 1965.   [45]JANOV, 1970

maintain that anger needs only be expressed. It does not need to be directed toward a particular person or instigator. Several approaches to psychotherapy based on a cathartic model, especially those involving marriage counseling, take a different approach. Controversial psychologist George Bach claims that the expression of anger is not enough; it must be directed against another person or instigator. Partners are taught to allow each other to vent their hostility in the context of a fair but harmless fight. For example, you and your spouse may grab pillows or "batacas" (pillow-type clubs) and by mutual agreement beat each other mercilessly, with little danger of incurring physical damage. After all is over, both of you will feel great. The assumption is that the expression of aggression will exercise a purging effect.

But that is not all venting your anger in such harmless fashion does for you. Think of what it means in terms of improved communication. According to Bach, while belting each other, both you and your partner have considerable control over the location, duration, and intensity with which you express your aggressive behavior. The manner in which you or your partner dish out punishment provides subtle clues that are not lost on the recipient. Many partners who either will not or cannot communicate effectively via speech or gentle touch suddenly find that they get the message this way.[46]

We must point out, however, that although many psychotherapists believe that cathartic psychotherapies help people release pent-up emotions, we were unable to find experimental studies to support this claim. In fact, one of us found that the expression of emotion increases aggression.[47]

Cognition: Think cool!

Psychologist Seymour Feshbach has described three processes through which anger and aggressive drive can be reduced.[48] The first involves the infliction of injury upon the anger instigator—a form of displaced aggression. This modality of reduction is similar to the previously discussed catharsis models.

The second process Feshbach proposes is similar to the previously discussed reevaluation therapy but does not necessarily call for the expression of emotion. The assumption is simply that anger and hostility reduction involves a rational reevaluation of the threat value of the anger-producing stimulus. For example, suppose a college student is intentionally insulted during a psychology experiment. As many students do, the insulted subject may see through the guise of the experiment and realize that the insult scene was contrived. With the insult no longer a threat, the student's initial anger reaction to the attack will dissipate.

Feshbach's third process is the most intriguing one. It minimizes the role of emotion (and hence the cathartic approach) by focusing almost entirely on mental events. To demonstrate this principle experimentally, subjects read a case history about a juvenile delinquent with an extensive record who attacked an elderly man with brass knuckles and took the man's money. Different groups of subjects were then given different information about the

[46]BACH & WYDEN, 1969. [47]KAPLAN, 1975a. [48]FESHBACH, 1964.

ANGER AND AGGRESSION 175

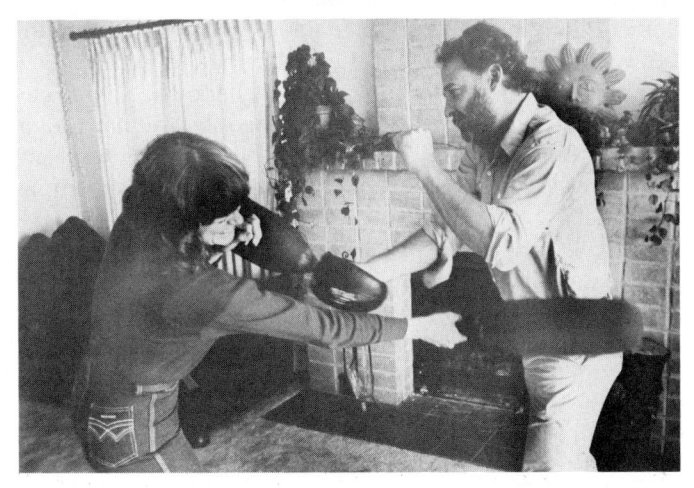

Get it out of your system! Partners engage in a fair and harmless fight using *batacas* (pillow-type clubs), thereby reducing aggression and hostility.

delinquent's family background. The severity of the criminal sentence the subjects recommended for the delinquent was used as a measure of hostile behavior. The lightest sentences were prescribed by subjects who believed the delinquent had been the victim of bad circumstances and had come from a broken home. In this case, a hostile response (recommended punishment) was diminished by the strengthening of a nonhostile thought (sympathy).[49]

Does this mean that a deliberate effort to "think cool" can be effective in reducing hot anger? Apparently so. At least Feshbach believes that reduction in the anger-hostility impulse constellation (in addition to aggressive behavior) involves the thoughts or fantasies that work in opposition to aggressive drive or anger. For example, anger-hostility reduction may be accomplished by facilitating anger-inhibiting cognitions such as "anger breeds destruction" or "love thine enemy." These thoughts may result in such behaviors as withdrawal or pacification.

Clinical psychologist Ray Novaco has made great advances in using cognitive methods with angry people. He has been working with individuals who have serious anger control problems. These people lose their tempers frequently and may become involved in violent activities such as barroom fighting. Novaco's approach is to study what angry people say to themselves when they are provoked, because angry people talk to themselves in a way that stimulates more rage ("I'm not going to put up with any of the crap from that S.O.B"). In a series of sessions, Novaco trains these persons to relax whenever they want. Then he modifies the private conversations they might have internally after having been provoked. For example, the person might learn to say "I can work out a plan to handle this. Easy does it," or "He probably wants me to get angry, but I'm going to deal with it constructively." Novaco has reported impressive results working with anger-prone persons as well with people such as police officers who must frequently confront provocations.[50]

Empathy: How would you like it?

Sometimes, when you are mad at others, you may want to see them get hurt. But what would happen if they really had to experience agony? Would you feel sorry for them? Perhaps. Strangely enough, there is evidence to suggest that merely witnessing the agony of people who have angered you is likely to reduce your own aggressive drive, even though their grief was caused by someone else.[51] Moreover, you do not have to show compassion and mercy at the time!

In one study, subjects were insulted by a confederate and then allowed to overhear another person insult the confederate. After overhearing someone insult their provoker, subjects were less hostile toward that person than a control group who had not heard the confederate being insulted.[52] In a similar group of studies, subjects appeared to become less hostile after watching the anger instigator suffer. For example, male college students heard a tape recording of an experimenter who had just insulted or not

[49]KAUFMANN & FESHBACH, 1963.   [50]NOVACO, 1976, 1979.   [51]STAUB, 1971.   [52]ROSENBAUM & DECHARMES, 1960.

insulted them. The tapes were purported to be made while the experimenter was a subject in a drug study. Each of the three groups heard a different version of the tape. One group heard the experimenter having a euphoric reaction to the drug. The second group heard a neutral reaction; the third group heard the experimenter suffering miserably. In comparison to the other two groups, those who had heard the experimenter suffer were subsequently less punitive when rating the experimenter on verbal scales.[53]

Another type of abuse involves financial damage. One experimenter had his confederates insult the subjects. Some of the subjects then watched as the experimenter took money away from the confederate in the context of an experimental task. In comparison to subjects who had not watched the money being taken away, those who had witnessed the financial abuse were less aggressive, as measured by the number of shocks they would give to the confederate.[54]

Each of the previously described experiments demonstrates a decrease in hostility and aggression after the witness of abuse. It does not appear, however, that such reduction in aggression is tied in with a cathartic draining off of emotion. At best, it shows some sort of understanding on the part of the witness (perhaps this is what is meant by "it takes one to know one"). This is the process of **empathy**, which is the capacity "... to view events from the standpoint of others and experience vicariously others' emotions."[55] As such, empathy has come to be recognized as an important inhibitor of aggressive behavior.

Despite the importance of empathy as a means of controlling aggression, very little research has been devoted to empathy training.[56] It does appear, however, that empathy can be taught if you catch children early enough. Research has consistently demonstrated that girls are more empathic than boys. Evidence suggests that this difference in empathy results from socialization practices. For example, in some homes little girls are socialized and taught to solve problems in the same way as litte boys. In these homes, it has been observed that the girls turn out to behave as aggressively as the boys do. As a solution to the problem of increasing violence, it has therefore been suggested that boys be socialized in a manner comparable to what our society has always provided for girls. Teaching boys to be tender, sensitive, and cooperative may indeed hold great promise, because these qualities have been shown to be incompatible with aggressive behavior.[57] Indeed, one program in the Los Angeles area provides empathy training for elementary school children. Early results suggest that the program has been successful in limiting the amount of aggression among the children.[58]

Humor: The right jokes

People like to laugh. We laugh at parties, when we are with our friends, and in general associate laughing with having a good time. Laughter may also be a way of helping us avoid certain personal problems and as such provides at least a hint about how to control aggression.

[53]Bramel, Taub, & Blum, 1968. [54]Doob, 1970. [55]Breuer & Freud, 1957. [56]Clark, 1980. [57]Eron, 1980. [58]Feshbach, 1980.

Psychologists Robert Baron and Rodney Ball conducted a unique experiment on humor and aggressive behavior. They created two groups of male college students and had their assistant anger one group and not anger the other. Half the students in each of these groups were then exposed to humorous cartoons. The other half were shown pictures of furniture, abstract art, and other nonhumorous scenes. After they had seen the pictures, all of the students were given the opportunity to give electric shocks to the confederate. Interestingly, Baron found that angry subjects become less aggressive after seeing funny cartoons than subjects who had seen neutral pictures.[59]

One of the problems with using humor to reduce aggression is that cartoons may also include hostile or sexual information, and each of these may have its own effect. Baron found that nonhostile humor may lower aggression, but exposure to hostile humor may actually serve to increase it among subjects who are already angry. An example of hostile humor was a cartoon depicting a woman speaking on the telephone while a body hanging from a rope dangles in sight behind her. The caption reads "It turned out just like you said it would, Mother." One of the reasons why this cartoon was associated with increased aggression among angry subjects is that the hostile message may have been stronger than the humor. On the other hand, the nonhostile humor may have distracted them.[60] Things that take our minds away from aggressive activities may help reduce anger, whereas those that remind us of our anger may increase aggression.[61]

If this is true, then what about sexual humor? Sexual humor is becoming commonplace, both on television and in magazine cartoons. Some sexual humor clearly exploits women and is overtly hostile. Yet at the same time it does not involve aggression in the sense of physical attack. In one study, Baron attempted to separate the effects of exploitative and nonexploitative sexual humor by exposing subjects to humorous cartoons of both types.[62] The problem, of course, is that what is exploitative or not is often in the eye of the beholder. One cartoon showed a young woman sitting across the table from a physician, remarking "Have I had any side effects from the Pill? Only promiscuity." In view of the fact that promiscuity is a term (often clinical) almost exclusively designated to label women's free sexual behavior, many women would consider this an exploitative cartoon, although in the study it was not regarded as exploitative. On the other hand, this cartoon is clearly not in the same class as another featured in the study, in which a partially dressed young woman in an executive's office is about to don her clothes when the executive, speaking on the phone, turns toward her and remarks "Don't get dressed yet, Miss Collins . . . I'm not through hiring you!" Some humor is also more sophisticated than other kinds and thus may be more distracting. Perhaps these confounding factors contributed to the surprising finding that nonexploitative humor caused a decline in subjects' aggressive responses. In general, however, this line of research has suggested that sexual and nonhostile humor can be used to lower the likelihood of aggressive behavior on the part of an angered person. Hostile humor that depicts violence may have the opposite effect.

[59]BARON & BALL, 1974. [60]BARON, 1978a. [61]KAPLAN, 1975; KONECNI, 1975. [62]BARON, 1978b.

AGGRESSION EFFECTS

Television and aggression: A complicated picture

Experiments on social learning and classical conditioning suggest that children can learn to behave aggressively by watching television. Indeed, an enormous amount of research effort and attention has been directed toward the possibility that much of the violence we confront in contemporary society results from exposure to violence on television. Concern has been stimulated by public trials of well-known criminals. When Ronnie Zamora went on trial in Florida for killing an elderly woman in cold blood, his attorney argued that it was not Ronnie's fault. Rather the blame rested with ABC, NBC, and CBS, who had saturated the poor child's brain with a steady diet of violence. When a San Diego youth murdered members of his family, the district attorney attributed the incident to the boy's viewing of a similar crime on a television program about Lizzie Borden. The similarities between the slasher slayings in Los Angeles and a telecast of NBC's "Police Story" have also been regarded as suspiciously close. Similarly, some people have attributed the gasoline dousing and burning of a derelict in Boston, the rape of two preteenagers with a broom handle, the death of a youngster attempting a mock hanging, and a child's lacing the family dinner with ground glass to television programs depicting similar behaviors. Yet after careful inspection, courts of law have never found any of these arguments compelling enough to suggest any form of censorship.

Most experimental studies do support the belief that television causes aggressive behavior.[63] There are some dissenting views, however, that are important to consider because many observers have already called for reme-

Ronnie Zamora on trial for killing an elderly woman: "TV made me do it!"

[63]GEEN, 1976.

dial action.[64] Remedial action may eventually result in censorship and could adversely affect the First Amendment right to freedom of expression.

To date, most research that attempts to establish a causal link between television and aggression has been conducted in laboratory environments. Unfortunately, these laboratory situations are not representative of the life situations to which we wish to generalize. The measures of aggression used for these studies may be unrelated to the forms of violence with which we are so concerned. For instance, the laboratory studies have typically inferred increases in aggression from attacks on Bobo dolls or from willingness to give shocks with bogus punishment machines. These measures would be acceptable if they could be shown to be related to assault, murder, or rape. The research evidence, however, has not established a reliable association between laboratory measures and serious destructive behavior in the real world.

Even with laboratory research, the results are not as clear-cut as the public has been led to believe. A common practice in aggression experiments has been to increase arousal by angering or frustrating subjects. This has sometimes been done because many of the experiments have been designed to test whether exposure to television violence reduces aggression. Several of the studies that concern us here have tested the effects of frustration or anger by arousing half the subjects and not arousing the others. In these experiments, the results have usually shown that television only affects subjects who are angered immediately before exposure to television.[65] Indeed, very little experimental data exist showing televised violence has any effect upon people who are not angered immediately before viewing.

Do children learn to imitate the violence they see on television?

[64]Liebert, Neale, & Davidson, 1973; Rothenberg, 1975; Sommers, 1976.   [65]Hanratty, O'Neal, & Sulzer, 1972.

Studies that purportedly show that television increases aggression typically make this inference because angry subjects who had viewed violence exhibit more laboratory aggression than angry subjects who had viewed neutral material. What is not well publicized is that the "increase" in aggression may actually represent a slight decrease. Communication specialists Dolf Zillman and Roland Johnson of the University of Indiana have shown that, in comparison to subjects shown no film at all, the tendency to aggress decreases slightly when angry people are shown violent films and decreases more rapidly when they are shown neutral films. It is from these differences in rate of decrease that some psychologists have inferred that television violence increases aggression.[66]

The effects of televised violence that have been demonstrated appear specific to certain types of programs. For example, there is a difference in the influence of fantasy violence and real violence—as may be portrayed on news shows—on aggressive behavior. Fantasy violence, presented in the form of fictional programs, has not been shown to instigate aggression. Real violence, however, such as that shown on television news programs, has influenced aggression in viewers who were intentionally angered by experimenters immediately before viewing.[67]

Experiments conducted in more natural settings have tended not to demonstrate that television has a significant effect upon aggression.[68] It is worth noting that some well-known reports about naturalistic experiments do claim to have demonstrated a disinhibitory effect on television violence.[69] A careful reanalysis of the data from these reports conducted by sociologist David Armor of the Rand Corporation, however, failed to demonstrate any reliable relationship between watching violence and behaving aggressively.[70]

There still remains the possibility that violence on television may contribute to violent behavior by "disturbed" viewers. Unfortunately, the literature and current methodology do not permit us to evaluate such possiblities clearly. At present, the best evidence on this issue comes from a series of 12 studies conducted by Melvin Heller and Samuel Polsky at Temple University. These investigators concluded that televised violence did not have significant effects upon the amount of aggression committed by pathological and highly assaultive youths.[71]

We do not want to be interpreted as saying that television has no effect upon aggression. Rather, we are suggesting that research evidence has not conclusively demonstrated a causal link. Ultimately, well-planned psychological research should guide us toward the appropriate conclusion.[72]

SUMMARY HIGHLIGHTS

1. The term *aggression* is semantically complex. In this chapter, it is defined as behavior designed to result in harm to a person or his or her property.
2. There are different explanations for why humans and other animals are aggressive. Aggression can be caused by biological factors such as

---

[66]Zillman & Johnson, 1973. [67]Feshbach, 1972; Berkowitz & Alioto, 1973. [68]Milgram & Shortland, 1973; Feshbach & Singer, 1971. [69]Eron, Huesmann, Lefkowitz, & Walder, 1972. [70]Armor, 1976. [71]Heller & Polsky, 1976. [72]Kaplan & Singer, 1976, 1977.

brain tumors or hormonal surplus. Biologically oriented theorists think that most aggression is instinctual rather than caused by specific environmental factors.

3. One way to increase the amount of aggression in someone is to provoke that person. Insults, for example, cause anger and physiological arousal, greatly increasing the probability of an attack.
4. Aggression can also be taught. Studies have shown that aggressive behavior can be conditioned to certain arousal states and then be learned by watching aggressive models who are rewarded for their actions.
5. Being an aggressive boy may be predictive of being an aggressive man. On the other hand, being an aggressive girl is a less accurate predictor of being an aggressive woman.
6. *Catharsis* is the notion that expression of aggression will drain off some anger and lead to lower levels of aggressive behavior. Although this idea has been widely endorsed by clinical psychologists, research evidence tends to show that expression of aggression or anger may lead to higher (rather than lower) levels of aggression.
7. *Cognitive controls*, such as talking to yourself in a positive way (as "I'm not going to let this guy get to me," "I can control my temper") have been shown to be effective in controlling the tempers of some very angry people.
8. A similar technique for controlling aggression is to create *empathy* by having aggressors identify with the victims of aggression.
9. Humor can also help reduce aggression. Sexual and nonhostile humor are particularly effective in distracting angry people. Hostile humor, however, may actually increase aggression.
10. The relationship between watching violence on television and behaving aggressively is complicated. Most studies show that televised violence does stimulate aggression. Studies conducted in natural settings, however, and studies in which subjects are not already angry while watching violence, do not show a relationship between viewing violence and behaving aggressively.

CHAPTER 7 ALTRUISM AND HELPING

HELP: A MATTER OF DEFINITION
    The prosocial altruist

WHEN HELP IS NEEDED
    People in distress
    Ripped-off institutions

WHEN HELP IS GIVEN OR WITHHELD
    Clarity: Social comparison
    Responsibility: Diffusing it
    Reciprocity: Mutual backscratching
    Imitation: Following the leader

    Reinforcement: Cost and reward
    Location: Urban and rural

HELP-GIVERS AND RECEIVERS
    Race: To each his own?
    Sex: Is chivalry dead?
    Physical handicap: Is there a credibility gap?
    Lifestyle: Is hipness kindness?
    Request style: Accentuate the positive

SUMMARY HIGHLIGHTS

HELP: A MATTER OF DEFINITION

The prosocial altruist

The willingness to express concern and care for others is a deeply ingrained humanistic value. When translated into action it can become a source of satisfaction in many ways to the one who cares. That is why it is important to draw a distinction between altruism and **prosocial behavior**. Both behaviors are socially desirable and benefit others. The term *altruism,* however, describes helpful acts for which nothing is expected in return. A volunteer who spends a great deal of time and effort aiding the handicapped is regarded as a selfless, altruistic individual who does not expect something tangible in return. (Of course, there is an intrinsic payoff of sorts. In a sense, helpers reward themselves by gratifying their own needs.)

Contrast such altruistic behavior with the prosocial behavior of the donor to a charity foundation for the purpose of changing a tax bracket, or of the doctor who stops to help an accident victim and then presents a hefty bill. Clearly, both individuals have been helpful. But because they expected something tangible in return for their help, their behavior can hardly be characterized as altruistic.

WHEN HELP IS NEEDED

People in distress

A French proverb proclaims "We must assist one another, it is the law of nature." These words of wisdom are not always heeded. On March 26, 1975, the *Los Angeles Times* carried the following story:

> Hundreds of carnival-goers looked on as six young thugs pummeled, stabbed and fatally shot the father of five at a crowded church fair in the Bronx. But

Mass media have attributed the behavior of Treglia's friends to apathy, indifference, dehumanization, and similar collective responsibilities. But studies by psychologists have shown more subtle forces at work (see text).

> **50 in Area of Murder, But No One is Talking**
>
> NEW YORK, Oct. 25 (UPI) — Police say they have been stymied in their efforts to solve the murder of a 42-year-old Brooklyn plumber because none of the 50 persons who may have witnessed the slaying has been willing to talk.
>
> Angelo Treglia was getting into his truck, which was parked down the street from his home Saturday, when a car pulled alongside and a gunman shot him three times in the head and once in the shoulder.
>
> Police said about 50 of Treglia's friends and neighbors were in the area at the time, but that subsequent questioning of them failed to provide any clues to the gunman's identity. Police said that the slaying apparently was over a private matter.
>
> From the *Washington Post* 10/26/77. Reprinted by permission of United Press International.

police say they can find only three or four people who are willing to admit they saw anything. All are co-workers of the victim.

Bartolo Rivera, the victim in this instance, could have been helped by any of the hundreds who witnessed the murder. He was not. Only his coworkers, who had passively witnessed the murder, took the time to describe the incident to the police. If you are shocked by this bystander apathy, prepare yourself for some more disturbing examples:

> A man bursts into an office, grabs the switchboard operator, and proceeds to beat and rape her. She temporarily escapes. Naked and bleeding, she runs into the street and begs for help. A group of 40 people stops to check out the situation. Not one of them tries to stop the assailant, who recaptures the girl and attempts to drag her back into the office. Finally, two policemen stumble upon the incident and arrest the assailant.[1]

> A young woman by the name of Kitty Genovese returns at 3:00 A.M. to her home in the Kew Gardens area of New York City. Just outside the building she is attacked by an assailant with a knife. But Kitty does not give up without a fight. Her screams and cries attract the attention of 38 neighbors who come to their windows, listen, and watch as Kitty fights with her attacker for more than a half-hour. Finally, Kitty Genovese is dead. Not one of her 38 witnessing neighbors has even bothered to pick up the telephone to call the police.[2]

These are not fictitious scenes from Hollywood movies; they are real incidents involving ordinary people. Why is it that the witnesses did so little to help someone in an emergency? To what should we attribute this? Is it alienation, apathy, indifference, future shock, breakdown of the family, or lack of religion? All of these have been proposed as explanations at one time or another, but, as we shall see, psychologists have come up with other explanations as well.

[1] Latané & Darley, 1970. [2] Latané & Darley, 1970.

Ripped-off institutions

People in distress need help. As we have seen, they do not always get it. Institutions sometimes need help, too; they are even less likely to get it. For one thing, there is something impersonal about institutions and organizations. How can you help a department store that is systematically looted by shoplifters? Some people even pose the question: Why help the store at all (see Chapter 9). The fact remains, however, that thievery is on the rise. Stores get little help from customers who witness the most brazen forms of shoplifting. The "ripoff" (which sounds infinitely better than "theft") is blithely ignored (in the long run, of course, this is self-defeating, since the customer ultimately pays for all losses incurred).

A typical example of the phenomenon of the ripped-off institution was provided by psychologist Max Dertke and his associates at a bookstore in a Southern university. Shoppers were observed while browsing in the paperback book section of the campus bookstore. Each of the 129 male and 111 female shoppers were at one time observed alone (no other shoppers within 50 to 60 feet) in a particular section of the store. When that occurred, an experimental confederate approached the spot and staged a theft in full view of the observed subject. The "thief" reached in front of the subject, picked up a book, placed it inside his or her shirt, and then retreated to another area of the store. Another confederate, dressed as a bookstore employee, then moved to within 3 to 4 feet of the subject, either waiting for the subject's report or (if none was forthcoming) questioning him or her about the theft.

As expected, there was a significant difference between reporting the crime spontaneously (without prompting) or confirming it (prompted by questioning). In either case, however, the rate was extremely low. No subject spontane-

Would you turn this shoplifter over to the authorities? Stores get little help from customers who witness shoplifting.

ously reported the theft, and only 6.7 percent did so upon prompting.[3] Evidently, the institution of the campus bookstore is generally regarded as a ripoff (having an excessive profit margin) to be ripped off in return. Similar studies have shown a rate of reporting ranging from 23% (in variety-drug stores)[4] to 65% (in discount beer stores).*

Can anything be done to improve this unhappy state of affairs? Psychologist Leonard Bickman, taking an optimistic view of human nature,[5] suggests that, when prompting is clear and explicit, people will report the transgression. Using 125 shoppers in a supermarket as subjects, he exposed them individually to a clear-cut case of shoplifting (carried out by an experimental confederate) and, subsequently, to one of five types of prompting.

> The Notice Prompt: "Say, look at her" (the shoplifter in the act of shoplifting).
> The Noncrime Prompt: "Say, look at her. Oh, it's hers. No one would shoplift here."
> The Crime Prompt: "Say, look at her. She's shoplifting. She put that in her purse."
> The Nonreport Prompt: "Say, look at her. She's shoplifting. She put that in her purse. But it's the store's problem. They have security people here."
> The Report Prompt: "Say, look at her. She's shoplifting. She put that in her purse. We saw it. We should report it. It's our responsibility."

As expected, the Noncrime Prompt yielded the lowest amount of reporting (16%). Just putting the shoppers on notice that something was going on (without mentioning shoplifting), however, increased the rate of intervention (32%). From that point on, intervention increased steadily in the Crime Prompt (38%), even when it was suggested to the shopper that the store would probably take care of matters (42%), as the Nonreport Prompt stated. Moreover, when the shoppers were confronted by the Report Prompt, which appealed directly to their sense of responsibility, an even more dramatic increase in intervention (74%) occurred.

WHEN HELP IS GIVEN OR WITHHELD

As the previous study indicates, people are probably more willing to help than they are given credit for. We certainly do not want to leave you with the impression that nobody would help if you were left bleeding by the side of the road somewhere. People help each other out all the time. They donate blood, contribute to charity, help each other move, and so on. The list of helping behaviors is virtually endless. But why is it that helping people will sometimes abandon a Kitty Genovese when she so desperately needs assistance? Does

---

[3]Dertke, Penner, & Ulrich, 1972. [4]Gelfand, Hartman, Walder, & Page, 1973. [5]Bickman, 1979.

*The psychologists who conduct such studies, incidentally, have to plan their studies as craftily as experienced criminals do their planning. It takes some planning (and audacity, to say the least) to "rob" a liquor store,[6] to steal a portable radio on a public beach, or to repeatedly lift a suitcase from a public place.[7] Though the information from witnesses of this behavior may be of interest to the North American public, some people are puzzled or even disturbed by such capers. Upon reading Dertke's study on the campus bookstore ripoff in a psychology textbook, an indignant British bookstore owner wrote the publisher that "such examples of social behavior are a little irresponsible. The book no doubt will be read by psychology and sociology students throughout the U.K. and will only serve to give them further ideas as to a standard behavioural pattern.... One would have thought that your editorial staff might have been slightly more responsible in the U.S.A."[8]

[6]Latané & Darley, 1969. [7]Moriarty, 1975. [8]McDavid & Harari, 1974.

helping depend on the situation at hand, on the characteristics of the helper, or on the characteristics of the victim?

We shall attempt to answer some of these questions from the point of view of the psychologist. Unlike the mass media, which can blithely attribute such incidents as the Kitty Genovese case to apathy, indifference, dehumanization, and loss of concern for our fellow person, psychologists cannot accept value judgments. In assigning collective responsibility to society, the media representatives often sound as if they are isolates in a sea of moral bankruptcy. A growing number of psychologists, on the other hand, find it useful to study the issue carefully under highly controlled conditions. Some of them have gone so far as to create a model of the outside world inside the laboratory before studying helping behavior (this artificial approximation of the outside world is known as *simulation*, which has its methodological problems [see Box 7-1]).

Clarity: Social comparison

Psychologists Bibb Latané and John Darley simulated situations analogous to the Kitty Genovese incident to discover why bystanders do not intervene in emergencies. In their first experiment, they invited male students from Columbia University to discuss some of the problems associated with student life at an urban university. While the subjects were filling out questionnaires and waiting to be interviewed in a small room, smoke was pumped into the room through a wall vent. Not all of the subjects faced this crisis under the same circumstances. In one condition, the subject was in the room by himself. In a second condition, the subject was with two experimental confederates (employed by Latané and Darley) who remained nonreactive during the incident—that is, as the smoke came into the room, they just shrugged their shoulders and turned their attention back to the questionnaires. If the subject asked about the situation, the confederates were instructed to reply "I dunno." Then they would wave away some smoke and continue to fill out their questionnaires. In the final condition, three naive subjects who did not know one another were in the room. The smoke was pumped into the room as the two-page questionnaire was being completed. The experimenters then observed to see how many of the subjects left the room to report the smoke within a 6-minute period.

Subjects left alone acted very reasonably in this situation. Typically, they would act a bit startled, check out the situation, and calmly go to report it. Out of the 24 people in this condition, 75% reported the smoke within 6 minutes. Subjects placed with the two nonreactive confederates acted differently. Latané and Darley were surprised to find that, under these circumstances, helping occurred only 10% of the time. The subjects coughed, choked, brushed smoke away from their faces, but did not report the emergency.

The most interesting findings concerned the three naive subjects. One could expect, under these conditions, that the crisis would be reported on almost all occasions. If three out of four subjects reported it when they were alone, the chances of reporting the incident should be three times as great when the three subjects were together. In fact, it turned out just the opposite.

If three naive people were available to report the incident, it was less likely that any one of the three would do so. In only 38% of the cases did even one member of a three-person group get up to report the incident. Thus, it seems that the more people available to report an emergency, the less likely it is that anyone will report it. But why? There are several explanations. One is that people become less fearful in the presence of companions. Another is that people want to hide their fear from others so they will not be perceived as "chicken."[9]

Later experiments showed that neither of these explanations was correct. Rather, it seems that we depend upon the reactions of others to clarify the situation for us. As we become less and less certain what is going on, we depend increasingly on others to clarify the situation for us. This is what psychologist Leon Festinger calls *social comparison theory* (see Chapter 8).

Although the smoke-filled room may have been an ambiguous situation that prevented help from being offered, nonambiguous situations evoke considerable help. In one study, subjects heard a maintenance man fall and cry in agony. In this situation, *all* of the subjects (either alone or in two- or five-person groups) offered help. When subjects heard an identical fall but without the verbal cues of pain, only 30% offered help. Presumably, the latter situation was more ambiguous. In another set of experiments, 96% of the subjects (regardless of the number of subjects around) helped in nonambiguous situations. When the same situations were made slightly more ambiguous, only 29% of the subjects offered help.[10] In short, if other people make you think the incident is not serious (as the nonreacting confederates did in these experiments), then you may interpret the situation as not being serious enough to get involved.[11]

To demonstrate how people depend upon each other's reactions, Bibb Latané and Judith Rodin created situations in which there was no danger for the helper and someone other than the helper required assistance. Subjects were recruited and brought to a testing room by a pleasant young woman. The woman (actually a confederate) left the subjects to fill out some questionnaires while she went into the next room to work. Then an emergency was created. From their room the subjects could clearly hear the woman climb on a chair to reach something on top of a bookcase. Then they heard a loud crash of the chair collapsing. The woman, after crashing to the ground, could be heard moaning "Oh my God, my foot . . . I . . . can't move . . . it. Oh my ankle . . . I . . . can't get this . . . thing . . . off . . . me." She continued to moan over the course of the next 2 minutes, gradually becoming subdued. Finally, she could be heard pulling herself to her feet and exiting. Clearly, the woman was in distress. The question was whether the subjects in the next room would do anything about it. More specifically, *under what circumstances* would the people in the next room do something about the emergency?

The subjects, in fact, did not hear this event under the same circumstances. Four experimental conditions varied the relationship between the subjects and the others in the room with him or her. The subjects heard the incident in the company of either a friend, a stranger, a stranger who was an experimental

[9]Latané & Darley, 1968.   [10]Clark & Word, 1972.   [11]Clark & Word, 1974.

confederate (preprogrammed not to react to the emergency), or nobody (the subject was alone).

Now, in which case was the woman most likely to receive help? First, let us look at the situation in which she was least likely to get help. When the subject waited with a nonreactive stranger, only 7% helped. When two naive subjects were together, the woman got help from *either* person in 40% of the cases. Her chances of receiving help increased considerably when two friends were together. In that case, *and* in the case when the subject was alone, help was offered in 70% of the cases.[12] Although the conditions involving friends and those in which subjects were alone appear to have yielded the same results, we must recognize that, in the "friends" condition, twice as many people were available to act. In both this study and the smoky room experiment, people were more likely to act if they were by themselves. In both cases, the presence of a passive confederate greatly inhibited intervention. Their behavior defined the seriousness (or rather, lack of seriousness) of the situation for the potential helper.

In another study, psychologist Leonard Bickman demonstrated that people will help in the same situation if the victim's need is clarified. The arranged situation was similar to the one just described. In this experiment, however, the subject was always with one confederate who interpreted the incident in one of three ways. In one condition, the confederate clearly acknowledged the emergency ("She must really be hurt"). In a second condition, a possible emergency was acknowledged ("She might be hurt"). In the third condition the confederate interpreted the fall as not serious ("Well, I guess it's okay"). Subjects in this experiment responded much sooner when the confederate clarified that the woman was hurt.[13] (But just think of the incongruity of the third statement. You have just heard a woman fall, crash to the ground, and moan in pain. Then someone you don't know tells you "It's okay.")

Responsibility: Diffusing it

Imagine driving down a crowded country road. You are cautiously watching for other cars with one eye and for police cars with the other. As you scan for radar traps, you spot a distressed motorist who clearly needs help. But then, there are so many other people who could do something. "After all," you think to yourself, "with my meager knowledge of auto mechanics, this person is better off waiting for someone else." Feeling little, if any, guilt, you pass on.

Now imagine driving on the same country road. There are no other cars in sight. When you come upon the distressed motorist, you recognize that nobody else is available to render help. You think about passing by, but as you do, you are overcome by feelings of guilt—so you stop.

If these scenarios are accurate in describing how we behave, they suggest that the more people are available to help, the less likely it is that anyone will.

The effects of **diffusion of responsibility** were demonstrated by psychologists John Darley and Bibb Latané. In this simulation, subjects were brought to the laboratory to discuss problems associated with urban living. They were put in individual rooms so that they could say whatever they wanted without

[12]LATANÉ & RODIN, 1969. [13]BICKMAN, 1972.

getting embarrassed. The subjects listened through an intercom as a confederate (presumably another subject) spoke about his experiences in New York City. With obvious embarrassment, he mentioned that he was prone to seizures when under the pressures of school. Then several other subjects (actually prerecorded voices) talked for 2 minutes. Finally, the real subject was given the opportunity to talk last.

The experimenter had explained that he would not listen to the introductory comments and that a switching device regulated the discussion. The device switched on a different microphone every 2 minutes. When the microphone was switched back to the student with a history of seizures, a voice, which gradually became louder and more incoherent muttered: ". . . because-er-er a-cause I-er I-uh I've got a one of the-er sei—er er things coming on and and I could really-er use some help so if somebody would-er give me a little h-help uh er-er-er-er-er- c-could somebody er-er help uh-uh-uh [choking sounds] . . . I'm gonna die er-er I'm . . . gonna die er-help er-er seizure-er" [chokes, then quiet].

There was little question about this person's need for help. The major factor varied by the experimenters was the number of people who the subject was led to believe also heard the distressed voice. The major measure was the time that elapsed between the beginning of the seizure until the subject left the cubicle in which he or she was seated in order to help. In settings in which the subject believed that he or she alone knew about the seizure, the incident was typically reported before the victim's voice was cut off. Conversely, less than one-third of the subjects helped this quickly if they believed that four others were available for help. Comparing groups that the subject believed to consist of one, three, or five subjects, it was found that the more people the subject thought were available to help, the less likely did he or she take prompt and decisive action. There seemed to be a diffusion of responsibility; as the number of potential helpers increased, the personal responsibility felt by any one subject decreased.[14] The old notion that there is safety in numbers may not be correct. In fact, you may be safer with fewer people around.

Reciprocity: Mutual backscratching

The movie hit *The Godfather* opened with a scene in which a mortician comes to Marlon Brando, in the role of gangster Vito Corleone, asking for a favor. Brando agrees to help the man who makes it clear that someday he will expect a favor in return. Favors are exchanged throughout the film and into *Godfather II* (the sequel). Eventually, when favors are no longer traded, the Mafia family tumbles.

The old adage "I'll scratch your back if you will scratch mine" describes what psychologists call the reciprocity norm. People, businesses, and nations expect returns for their favors. Sometimes, too, exchanges that are politically sensitive are fictitious (but politically expedient) labels. As pointed out by psychologists Philip Brickman and Amy Stearns, upper- and middle-class people often resent direct welfare payment to the poor but are willing to accept vast sums themselves in the form of such exchange fictions as help for

[14]DARLEY & LATANÉ, 1968.

the farmer through crop subsidies, help for higher education through tax exemption, or help to a business enterprise through tax incentives.[15] In a related experiment, people were asked to contribute to a fund for perceptually handicapped children. The greatest willingness to spend money for that purpose was when candles were offered for sale with the understanding that $1.00 of the purchase price would go to the fund. Less willingness to spend money was exhibited when asked to give help directly, or just to buy candles.[16] Whether it's just candles for the handicapped or an elaborate charity ball, the principle for help in this case is the same: "something for something."

Of course, if you receive too many favors without reciprocating, you will develop a social debt. In other words, you will owe favors. An experiment demonstrating the reciprocity norm was conducted by psychologists Richard Goranson and Leonard Berkowitz at the University of Wisconsin. In the experiment, college women were required to work for someone who had previously either refused, volunteered, or was forced to assist them. The results showed that the women worked hardest to assist peers who had previously helped them of their own free will. When asked why they had worked hard for someone who had aided them, the women explained that is what people *ought* to do.[17] Thus, one reason for helping could be feelings of social obligation.[18]

Although godfathers and other gangsters deal in the exchange of favors, this does not mean that all people do. Certain life circumstances make some classes of people more dependent upon exchanges of favors than other classes. Consider, for example, some differences between members of the entrepreneurial middle class (in business for themselves), members of the bureaucratic middle class (working for others), and the working class. People of the entrepreneurial middle class are involved in business and thus depend on the exchange of favors. Members of the bureaucratic middle class and members of the working class do not have the same need to exchange favors. They work for the government or for strong businesses that do not depend on anyone's whims. People from each of these social strata have been used in experiments on receiving and giving help. As you might expect, members of the entrepreneurial middle class are more apt to help someone who has just helped them. In other words, these business-oriented people know how to return a favor. Representatives from the bureaucratic middle and the working classes tended to give help when they thought help was needed; their helping was less dependent on whether the person they were helping had previously helped them. Instead of operating on a norm of reciprocity, the bureaucratic middle- and working-class people seemed to use a **responsibility norm**.[19]

Imitation: Following the leader

People around us give all sorts of hints about the way we should behave. As we have seen in the previous chapter, people can learn vicariously by observing a model. If we are already capable of performing a response, observing a model may increase our motivation to perform the same response. Ample evidence

---

[15]Brickman & Stearns, 1978. [16]Lerner, Miller, & Holmes, 1976. [17]Goranson & Berkowitz, 1966. [18]Pruitt, 1968; Wilke & Lanzetta, 1970. [19]Berkowitz & Friedman, 1967.

suggests that people are more likely to help if they have recently observed someone else helping.[20] Two examples of this modeling influence on helping behavior were provided in natural settings. In one study, a young female was put in a situation that implied the need for help: she was stationed by a 1964 Ford Mustang with a flat rear tire and an inflated tire leaning on the left side of her car. The model situation consisted of a 1965 Oldsmobile located about 400 yards behind the first car, raised by a jack, and a girl watching a man changing a flat tire. Of 4000 cars that passed, only 93 (virtually all makes) stopped to help the woman fix her Mustang. There were, however, almost twice as many offers of help from those who had passed the Oldsmobile than when it was absent.

The second study was conducted around Christmas, when Salvation Army kettles were placed on the sidewalk in various shopping centers. The solicitors were two females who rang the Salvation Army bell at regular intervals but did not engage in verbal pleas or eye contact with the shoppers. Once every minute, a male dressed as a white-collar worker approached the kettle from within the store and contributed a nickel. The 20-second period following the model's return to the store was designated as the observation time for the number of people who made a donation. Donations were made by 112 out of 365 people, with about twice as many donations made when the model was present as when he was absent. Subsequent studies that varied the sex and race of both solicitor and model produced essentially the same results, except for a tendency for Black solicitors to elicit a lower percentage of donors than Whites.[21]

Although we are influenced by models, not all models have an equal effect. Probably you will be most influenced by a model you respect or one who is similar to you. This was demonstrated by Harvey Hornstein, Elidra Fisch, and Michael Holmes, social psychologists who chose the streets of Manhattan as their laboratory and used wallets full of money as their props. The subjects were unsuspecting New York pedestrians who discovered a wallet, half protruding from an envelope, lying on the sidewalk. If they picked up the envelope, they also found a note from someone who had found the wallet and was returning it to the owner. To summarize the scene, the subject found an envelope containing a wallet and a note. The note led them to believe that someone else had found the wallet before they had and then lost it again. The note, purportedly written by the first finder, served as a model to the subject. One-third of the people who found the wallet also found a note that made positive and courteous comments about being able to help. Another one-third encountered a note that contained negative comments and complaints about helping. The remaining subjects found a note with neutral comments about helping.

To determine the age, sex, and other characteristics of the people who picked up the wallet, the experimenters stationed spies nearby. Then they waited to see how many people actually returned the wallet and the money in it. Nearly two-thirds of the wallets were returned when the note-writing model made positive or neutral comments about helping. When the model made negative comments about helping, only 10 percent returned the wallet.

[20]Rosenhan & White, 1967; Wagner & Wheeler, 1969; Aderman & Berkowitz, 1970.   [21]Bryan & Test, 1967.

Now we come to the part concerning the similarity between the subjects and the model. The results we have just reported are for notes which were written in plain, clear English. For example, the neutral note read "I found your wallet which I am returning. Everything is here just as I found it." But would people copy the behavior of neutral or positive models if they were unable to identify with the model? To test this, Hornstein and his associates created some notes as though they had been written by a visitor to the United States. For example, one read "I am visit your country finding your ways not familiar and strange. But I find your wallet which I here return. Everything is here just as I find it." Since the note appeared to have been written by someone dissimilar to the subjects, we might not expect the subjects to imitate the model's behavior. In fact, this is what the researchers observed. When the note had apparently been written by a foreigner, it had no more effect when it was positive or negative than it did when it was neutral. Thus, models have an effect on helping behavior—when they are similar to us. When they are dissimilar, they may not influence our helping behavior.[22]

The best model, of course, is someone who is an acknowledged leader. Helping in emergencies requires quick and decisive action. Studies have shown that groups headed by assertive leaders take more rapid, decisive action than groups headed by a leader who was arbitrarily picked by the experimenter. Under the latter form of leadership, groups often had to redefine leadership before they could take the appropriate action.[23] This slow process of transitory leadership could be costly to a needy victim. In emergencies, the one who hesitates is lost.

Reinforcement: Cost and reward
Your decision to help others may depend upon the consequences of your helping. According to learning theory, you will help when your action is followed by positive events. You will not help if there are negative consequences for your intervention. In the case of Kitty Genovese, neighbors may have avoided direct intervention because the cost was too high. Perhaps they feared that the assailant might turn his knife upon them. The negative consequences of helping may have outweighed the positive benefits.

A demonstration of these cost and reward considerations was conducted by two psychologists who used the streets of Dayton, Ohio as their laboratory. The subjects in the experiment were unsuspecting citizens who, while walking along the street, were approached by a female confederate who asked for directions to a local department store. After the unsuspecting citizen had given the directions, the confederate responded in one of three ways. Sometimes she gave the positive reply "Thank you very much, I really appreciate this," and rewarded the subject with a smile. On other occasions, she would give the negative reply "I can't understand what you're saying. Never mind, I'll ask someone else," and frown accordingly. To some subjects, she gave the simple neutral reply "Okay."

After this incident, the subject continued down the street about 75 feet. Here he encountered a second confederate. This confederate looked in a store

[22]HORNSTEIN, FISCH, & HOLMES, 1968. [23]FIRESTONE, LICHTMAN, & COLAMOSCA, 1975.

window as the subject approached. When the subject was about 6 feet away, she turned and walked toward him. As she approached, a small paper bag fell to the ground and the confederate continued on as though she hadn't noticed. The results showed that almost all of the subjects who had received positive or neutral feedback for helping the first confederate also helped the second confederate. Among those who had received negative feedback for their previous efforts to help, only 40% offered their assistance to the second confederate.[24]

Success, in particular, is a rewarding experience that seems to increase helping behavior. This was demonstrated by psychologist Alice Isen, who had schoolteachers take perceptual and psychomotor skill tests. Isen told her subjects that she was measuring the relationship between psychomotor skills and creativity. Then she told some of the teachers they had done extremely well and others they had done very poorly. A third group was given no feedback about their performance. The type of feedback was determined randomly—it had nothing to do with actual performance.

After their experiences with success, failure, or no feedback, the teachers were given an opportunity to contribute money anonymously for an air conditioner to make the school library more comfortable. Those who had been told they had succeeded on the tests donated an average of 46 cents. Those who believed they had done poorly gave an average of 7 cents. In a similar study, college students who thought they had succeeded on a task were more likely to offer assistance to another person who was struggling with an armload of books. It seems, therefore, that "the warm glow of success" can make you a more helping person.[25]

Under certain circumstances, however, even failure can induce helping. This happens when a person fails to maintain a positive self-image. In one study, personality tests were administered to college students in introductory psychology courses. These were followed by a 50-item multiple-choice test in psychology, which purportedly served as a self-improvement program for those courses. Each subject was assured that the test would not affect his or her course grade unless he or she made a very high score. In half the cases, an experimental confederate posing as a student who had already taken the test gave each subject the chance to cheat by disclosing that most of the correct answers were choice B (which in fact they were not). Half the subjects were also given bogus feedback designed to bolster their self-images: Subjects about to conclude the multiple-choice test were given a written interpretation of their performance on the personality test that was highly complimentary (for example, saying that they were poised, self-assured, resourceful, flexible).

In all conditions, each subject was then asked to comply with a request for help that involved the scoring of a stack of about 500 tests. The highest rate of helping behavior was displayed by students who cheated but had received no bogus feedback. The offered explanation was that a person's act of cheating is inconsistent with positive self-image, and by complying with a request a person can restore that image. The subjects who received the bogus feedback before the request for help had their positive self-images restored that way and thus did not feel the need to comply.[26]

[24]Moss & Page, 1972. [25]Isen, 1970. [26]McMillen, 1971.

Not only does success cause good moods and warm glows, it also causes feelings of competence. Perhaps telling people that they have succeeded on a test may make them more helpful than otherwise merely because they feel that since they are more competent, they are also more able to give help.

To explore this issue, psychologists Alice Isen and Paula Levin decided to manipulate mood in a way that did not affect people's feelings of competence. To create a good mood, individuals studying in several university and college libraries were given . . . cookies. After a while, a person came into the libraries and asked the students to volunteer as assistants in an experiment. As experimental assistants, they were given the choice of playing either a helpful, positive role or a distracting, negative role. Those who had received cookies volunteered most often for the helpful role; those who had not received cookies volunteered most frequently for the distracting role.[27]

If nothing else, Isen and Levin established the first empirical link between cookies and kindness. More specifically (and seriously), they showed that mood, not just feelings of competence, can produce altruism. Isen and some of her colleagues also demonstrated that the ensuing willingness to help is not a passing whim. Subjects were given small "free sample" packets of stationery by a confederate who went from door to door and then were contacted over the phone for help by means of the "wrong number technique" (see p. 201). Not only were the subjects who received the free gift more willing to help than those who were not contacted, but this mood effect lasted up to 20 minutes.[28] Perhaps, with greater elation (and probably a greater incentive than a packet of stationery), this willingness to help could have been extended to longer time periods. From an applied point of view, these findings are reflected in the activities of various fundraising organizations who sometimes enclose small gifts in their solicitations.

There are, of course, still other explanations for this effect. Perhaps cookies caused kindness because subjects in that study may have been imitating an altruistic cookie-dispensing model. To eliminate this alternative explanation, Isen and Levin created an on-the-spot laboratory in telephone booths of San Francisco and Philadelphia shopping centers. Half of the people who came to use the phones found a dime planted by the experimenters in the coin-return tray. The other half did not find a dime. This situation allowed for people to have an unexpected pleasant surprise without being exposed to an altruistic model. As the subjects left the phone booth, a female confederate approached and dropped a folder full of papers in the subject's path. Those who found dimes were more likely to help the experimenter pick up her papers than those who had not found dimes. This study shows that, in the absence of altruistic models or manipulated feelings of competence, a positive mood can make helping more likely. A little bit of cheer always helps!

Location: Urban and rural

Psychologist Stanley Milgram has spent the last few years studying the psychological consequences of living in big cities. One such consequence, according to Milgram, is that people are continually exposed to the needs of others. To protect their own private lives, people in big cities learn to tune out

[27]ISEN & LEVIN, 1972. [28]ISEN, CLARK, & SCHWARTZ, 1976.

the needs of other people. They engage in self-protecting maneuvers that minimize their involvement with others. Rising crime rates, especially in urban areas, have resulted in urban behavior that is often marked by caution, incivility, distrust, and unwillingness to help others based on the (probably correct) perception that interactions with others, especially strangers, can be dangerous.[29] This does not mean that the city folks would not be truly concerned if they got involved. If, somehow, people are forced to help, the social and psychological forces of genuine warmth and concern will take over. In other words, city dwellers may not volunteer to help as often as rural people. When they do help, however, the quality of their help may be no worse.[30]

An experiment conducted on the streets of Cambridge, Massachusetts demonstrates how some city dwellers will avoid helping if they can get away with it. The situation in the experiment was natural and realistic. As people walked down a city street, someone (actually a confederate of the experimenters) collapsed on the street. In one condition, the confederate collapsed right in the path of an oncoming person. Under these circumstances, escape is difficult—it is hard to pretend you have not observed what is happening. In another condition, the confederate collapsed on the other side of the street. Here escape is easy and it is no problem to pretend that you did not see what happened. In the experiment, observers from a car made sure that everyone they counted as a subject had at least noticed the victim. If a subject approached the victim, he or she was requested to place a call to the victim's roommate. In contrast to those who had an easy escape, those for whom escape was difficult were more likely to approach the victim, and the probability that they would place the phone call was more than five times as great.[31] Perhaps one way to get an increase in the amount of helping behavior is to make it hard for people to escape from the situation.

As a postscript to this section, let us briefly discuss the circumstances under which kindness and help, although offered, are rejected.

If people do favors for you, they will probably become more attractive to you.[32] There are occasions, however, when people try so hard to persuade with favors that their efforts have just the opposite effect because they are seen as manipulative and insincere.

Psychologists Jack Brehm and Ann Cole demonstrated this type of reaction. In their experiment, college students sat in a room with another student (actually a confederate), about whom they would soon be asked to give their first impressions. While they were waiting, the confederate asked permission to leave the room. In some cases, he returned to the room carrying a soft drink for himself and one for the subject (to whom he was a complete stranger). In other cases, he simply returned and took his seat. When asked to help the confederate to perform a dull task, it was observed that those who were given the Coke were less likely to help than those not given a soft drink.[33] Presumably, the subjects in this experiment thought the gift of a Coke was being used as a means of manipulation. Perceived as such, the act of "kindness" had the opposite effect.

[29]House & Wolf, 1978. [30]Milgram, 1970. [31]Staub & Baer, 1974. [32]Nemeth, 1970. [33]Brehm & Cole, 1966.

Box 7-1. Is there safety in numbers?

The answer is no, according to psychologist Bibb Latané and his colleagues. Even a sole bystander is more likely to provide help than a group of bystanders. Explanations for *why* people behave in this curious manner may vary from lack of clarity to the diffusion of responsibility (see discussion in text), but the lack of safety of numbers has been demonstrated in many experiments.

The brutal murder of Kitty Genovese (see text) has probably been the major impetus behind the widely cited research by Latané and his colleagues. It is generally acknowledged that these researchers have been successful in their simulation of the situational variables that governed the violent assault on Kitty Genovese, such as the lack of communication among the bystanders who were out of one another's sight, the lack of a clear observation of the victim's plight, and other factors. Ironically, however, despite faithful approximations of all these conditions, most subsequent studies on bystander intervention have involved *nonviolent* emergencies such as car breakdowns,[34] falling bookcases,[35] sick or drunk victims,[36] nonviolent thefts,[37] bursting grocery bags,[38] and the like.

Many psychologists nowadays believe that the only way to find out whether there is safety in numbers is to recreate, preferably in a natural setting, the situations in which help is needed. Evidence also suggests that when the situation is such that bystanders are in a familiar setting, can see and communicate with one another, and can clearly observe the victim's plight, there is an increasing willingness by groups of bystanders to help.[39] Once again, explanations for this behavior may vary. Perhaps under such conditions it is more likely that one bystander in a group will adhere to the norm of social responsibility, take action, and serve as a model for others (see text). It is possible that potential helpers are more likely, in the company of others, to become aware that any *lack* of intervention may generate social disapproval.

Perhaps what is really needed to clear the confusion is an introduction of new situational factors into the simulation of a *violent* emergency. Violence, after all, is what got psychologists interested in the topic of helping behavior in the first place. But here's the rub: to recreate faithfully a violent emergency poses so many ethical, technical, and even economic difficulties that most studies apparently follow the resigned advice of a pair of investigators, who, after attempting to simulate a violent emergency in a natural setting with adequate controls, gave up and suggested that the most productive avenue would be a return to the "nonthreatening laboratory situation"[40] (p. 149). One of the few exceptions to the latter has been the innovative violent emergency laboratory study by Shalom Schwartz and Avi Gottlieb, but even in that experiment the alleged crime of robbery was out of the sight of the subjects who could only hear it.[41]

Rape is one of the most violent crimes that can be committed. It is, in fact, more an act of hostility, aggression, and intimidation than an act of sexual passion. To any potential victim, therefore, the issue of whether there is safety in numbers is more than academic. The victim's life may literally depend on the knowledge that the greater the awareness of the situation by surrounding bystanders, the greater the likelihood of receiving help. But how are

(continued)

---

[34]GRUDER, ROMER, & KORTH, 1978. [35]LATANÉ & RODIN, 1969. [36]PILIAVIN, RODIN, & PILIAVIN, 1969. [37]MORIARTY, 1975. [38]WISPÉ & FRESHLEY, 1971. [39]PILIAVIN, PILIAVIN, & RODIN, 1975. [40]WEGNER & SCHAEFER, 1978. [41]SCHWARTZ & GOTTLIEB, 1976.

(Box 7-1 continued)

psychologists to recreate a rape incident realistically? The logistics are formidable, not to mention the potential legal problems. On the other hand, consider the validity of results derived from studies in nonnatural settings, such as when feigned assaults in a psychodrama session led to the conclusion that male subjects did not help a woman attacked by another male "because they were deriving some kind of vicarious sexual and/or hostile gratification from seeing a man injure a woman?"[42] (p. 312).

A recent study, "Rape and Bystander Intervention: Is There Safety in Numbers?",[43] attempted to recreate a rape incident in a natural setting. Male college students who were walking alone or in the presence of other males witnessed a simulated rape attempt on campus. The location of the rape was chosen on the advice of campus police (who cooperated in the conduct of the entire study) because several assaults had taken place there previously. The rape attempt was carried out realistically by two experimental confederates with considerable acting experience. The incident occurred in full view of the subjects at a vantage point that was chosen because its topography allowed each subject one of three options: not to intervene by walking away on an alternate path, to intervene indirectly by summoning a nearby (and presumably unaware) policeman, or to intervene directly. The table shows the frequency of intervention as monitored.

Bystanders	Help	No help
Group	34[a]	6
Individual	26[b]	14

[a] Direct = 28, indirect = 6.
[b] Direct = 20, indirect = 6.

These results present an optimistic picture: the overall number of helpers exceeded the number of nonhelpers 75% to 25%. This finding seems to contradict the frequent charge of callousness, indifference, or vicarious enjoyment among bystanders witnessing a violent crime such as rape. The data also indicate clearly that more help was forthcoming from bystanders in groups than from bystanders alone.

Does all this mean that there *is* safety in numbers? The answer, according to the authors, is a qualified yes. The fact that the study was conducted on a college campus could have confounded the results somewhat. For example, even though the subjects in the group condition did not know each other personally, the campus setting most likely made them perceive the other subjects, as well as the victim, as college students similar to themselves; both conditions would increase the probability of intervention. Yet the results are so clear-cut that they suggest, at the very least, that we should refrain from attempts to offer single global explanations to the dynamics of bystander intervention, as has often been done since the Genovese case, to violent emergencies such as rape. The results suggest instead that the most fruitful avenues for future research are studies in a variety of settings, despite the many inherent problems that mark such an approach.

---

[42] BOROFSKY, STOLLACK, & MESSE, 1971. [43] HARARI, HARARI, & WHITE, 1982.

HELP-GIVERS AND RECEIVERS

Who helps whom? Psychologists have addressed themselves at length to this question but have been less than successful in coming up with the answer. Numerous studies have been conducted in which the sex, race, or age of the helpers and the helped were varied. The net result of these studies has been a mixed bag of findings that makes it almost impossible to make generalizations. At first glance, it appears that people of the same race help each other more often than people of different races; that men are more helpful than women; and that women are helped more often than men. But then the plot thickens. The same-race tendency to help occurs when the victim is drunk, but not when he or she is seriously ill. It also occurs more often among the politically conservative than among liberals. Black men are more helpful than Black women, whereas White men and women do not differ in their willingness to help. Men help people similar to themselves more often than women do. Whether women are helped more than men depends on geographic locations. And so on.

Evidently, it is easier to find out *why* people help each other than who helps whom. We are nevertheless going to cite some studies on helpers and "helpees," if only because some of the techniques used by the investigators are interesting or even amusing. But you will have to draw your own conclusions about exactly what the results mean.

Race: To each his own?

Who is the Good Samaritan? Psychologist Jane Piliavin and her associates conducted an extensive study in which about 4450 men and women who traveled on a New York subway during a 9-week period were observed. This particular train was chosen because it typically carried a composition of riders that was 55% White and 45% Black. On different occasions, each of four informally dressed young men (three Whites and one Black) simulated emergency situations that called for help. About a minute after the train passed the first station, the "victim" staggered forward, collapsed, and remained supine on the floor looking at the ceiling. To simulate the effect of intoxication, he smelled of liquor and carried a liquor bottle tightly wrapped in a brown paper bag. On other occasions, illness was simulated by having the victim carry a cane. On several occasions, each of four young White men acted as models who administered immediate or delayed help. Observers noted the race, sex, and location of every person who helped the victim and of every person who was in an adjacent area to the victim, and in all cases tried to elicit comments from these people. Helping behavior occurred with rather high frequency (about 60%), and was mostly exhibited by males, with a same-race tendency to help when the victim appeared drunk. The victim who appeared ill received help more frequently than the one who appeared drunk. The number of bystanders had little effect on the speed of helping, and the impact of models dissipated the longer the emergency lasted without help being offered.

Despite the complexity of the results, Piliavin and her colleagues agreed that the extent of help given can best be measured by the anticipated result for the helper: praise, censure, self-blame, effort, embarrassment, disgust, possible physical harm, and so on. The major implication of this view is that

What are this person's chances of getting help? (Refer to p. 201.)

What are this person's chances of getting help? (Refer to p. 201.)

positive, altruistic behavior is largely governed by a selfish desire to rid oneself of unpleasant emotions.[44]

For another study on the effects of the race of the victim, a "wrong number" research method was developed. Two groups of New York-registered voters (230 Liberal Party members and 217 Conservative Party members) were matched as closely as possible on their election districts and types of dwelling units. Each subject received an apparent wrong-number telephone call in which the caller (a male or a female posing as a stranded motorist) asked for help in an easily identifiable White or Black accent. The caller asked for Ralph's Garage and immediately informed the subject that he was stuck on the parkway. Upon being informed that he had the wrong number, the caller then indicated that he was out of change to make an additional call and asked the subject to relay the message to the garage. The frequency of calls to the number provided by the stranded motorist (actually to a telephone attended by the experimenter) served as the measure for helping behavior.

Who helped whom? Males tended to render assistance more frequently than females, but females were not assisted more frequently than were males. In all cases, Whites received more help than Blacks, but the extent to which Blacks were helped less than Whites was greater among conservatives than among liberals.[45]

To complicate matters further, let us combine race and sex. Suppose it is Friday evening and you are ready for a weekend of fun. Before you get going, you have to stop at the store for some groceries. As you head for the front of the store, the bottom of someone's grocery bag breaks right in front of you and the contents spill onto the ground. Question: will you help? A further question: will you be affected by the race and sex of the person with the broken bag?

In one study, Black and White experimental confederates of both sexes dropped bags of groceries in the paths of subjects of both races. Black men, it was observed, helped more than Black women. White men and women did not differ in the degree to which they helped. Women of both races were more likely to ignore someone of their own race. Overall, White women received no more help than Black women, and Whites helped no more than Blacks.[46]

More recently, a group of psychologists from Florida State University arranged for Black or White motorists to have engine trouble in neighborhoods with either predominantly Black or predominantly White inhabitants. Distressed female motorists were helped much sooner than male victims. The Black motorists were helped sooner in areas housing primarily Blacks, whereas the White motorists got the fastest help in White neighborhoods. In most cases, the helpers were male and of the same race as the victim. The results differed, however, when the scene shifted to areas surrounding college campuses. On that occasion, White motorists got help sooner near a predominantly Black college than near a White campus. Conversely, Black students received help faster near campuses with predominantly White students.[47]

Sex: Is chivalry dead?

Is chivalry dead? What about the days in which gentlemen were expected to help ladies, and ladies were expected to accept the assistance with a curtsy

[44]PILIAVIN, RODIN, & PILIAVIN, 1969. [45]GAERTNER, 1970. [46]WISPÉ & FRESHLEY, 1971. [47]WEST, WHITNEY, & SCHNEDLER, 1975.

and a blush? The trend for change in sex roles has led some to speculate that chivalry is no longer with us.

To check on the health status of chivalry, psychologist Bibb Latané arranged to have men and women drop coins in public elevators in a Southern U.S. city (Atlanta), a Western city (Seattle), and a Midwestern city (Columbus). Observations were made to determine how often these coin-dropping men and women would get assistance from members of the opposite sex. In Columbus, women helped men almost as often as men helped women. In either case helping was uncommon. In Atlanta, men usually helped women, but women rarely helped men. Seattle fell in between the two extremes.[48] These results suggest that chivalry is alive and well in Atlanta, choking and coughing in Seattle, and almost dead in Columbus (see Figure 7-1).

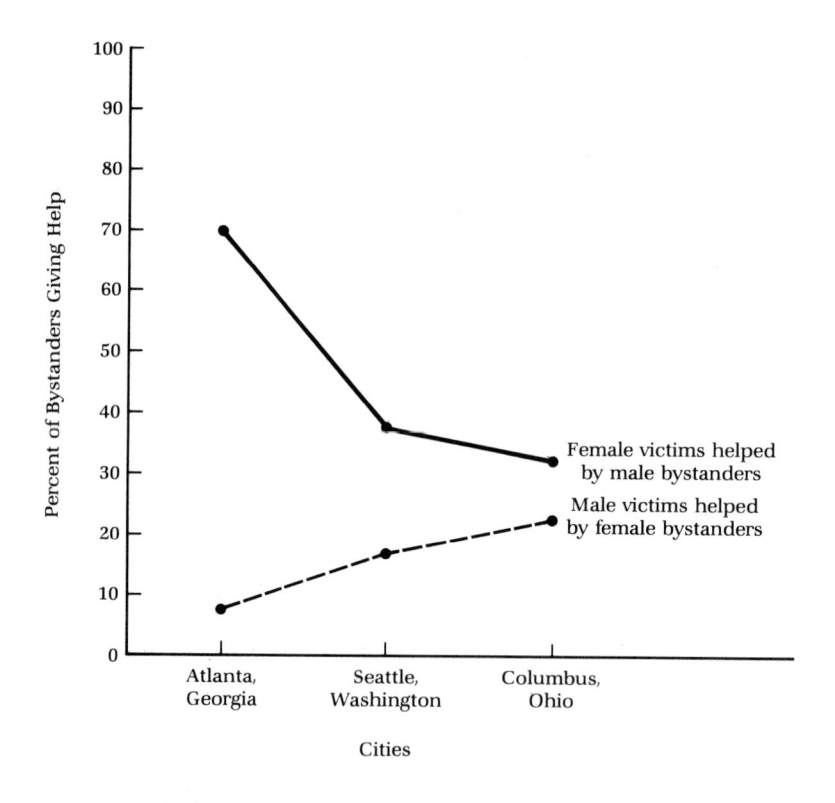

Figure 7-1. Is chivalry dead? If judged by the degree males helped females to retrieve dropped pencils or coins, chivalry is alive and well in Atlanta, choking and coughing in Seattle, and almost dead in Columbus. *Source:* Latané, 1972.

Physical handicap: Is there a credibility gap?

As we pointed out in Chapter 1, physical handicaps generate perceptions that lead to discomfort and inhibition in both handicapped and nonhandicapped interacting individuals. How does this affect the willingness to help the handicapped? A study conducted by Michigan's Department of Vocational Rehabilitation showed that, in general, behavioral predictions based on reciprocity and exchange were supported: subjects were willing to help greater numbers of handicapped persons when costs, in time and effort, were rela-

[48]LATANÉ, 1972.

tively low. This pattern is neither unusual nor limited to helping the handicapped.[49]

There are, however, important implications to helping the handicapped as a result of the feedback that handicapped persons receive from the nonhandicapped. In a study conducted at Stanford University, an experimental confederate was given feedback about his performance on a series of experimental trials in a labyrinth game, in which a metal ball is made to slide through various holes in a maze. The confederate was presented as either able-bodied or handicapped (leg braces). The results showed the existence of a "norm to be kind" toward the handicapped: even when the expectations for good performance by the handicapped individual were low, the actual positive feedback provided to him was significantly higher than when he was in the role of a nonhandicapped performer. This tendency to provide less critical feedback to the handicapped than to normal people may have some serious implications, according to the authors of the study. If a handicapped person continually receives unrealistic positive feedback regardless of performance, he or she may either attribute it to a favorable attitude on the part of the nonhandicapped feedback dispenser, or simply ignore it. On the other hand, at the first sign of even a hint of negative feedback, the handicapped recipient may regard it as truly reflecting the quality of performance. The net result is a credibility gap: the handicapped person will pay attention only to negative feedback, which in turn may affect socialization differences between handicapped and nonhandicapped individuals.[50]

The findings of the previous study also indicate that helping the handicapped can be a double-edged sword. If the feedback implied by the helping act is perceived by the handicapped person that he or she is doing better than before and should now be encouraged to engage in new activities that require initial help, it may be dismissed as kindness or pity, and as such probably be ignored. But if the feedback leads to the belief, however erroneous, that helping occurred because the helper thinks that the handicapped person's performance is inadequate, the handicapped person may accept it as the true state of affairs. The negative impact on the handicapped individual's self-esteem may be disastrous, even though the helper never meant to convey this kind of message at all.

Lifestyle: Is hipness kindness?

Birds of a feather flock together, as was pointed out in Chapter 5. Because we are attracted to people like us, we might expect to get more help from similar people than from people who are dissimilar. To investigate this issue, three psychologists at Purdue University defined criteria to identify some students as hippies and others as straights. Then they had hippies and straights of both sexes go up to students who fell into the same four categories and say "Excuse me, could I borrow a dime for a long-distance phone call? It's kind of important." Both male and female subjects tended to help someone similar to themselves. This trend, however, was more evident for men than for women. In general, women helped men more often than they helped women. Straight women were also more willing than straight men to give help to hippie men.[51]

The reluctance of straights to help hippies (as they were called then) was

[49]Cowan & Inskeep, 1978. [50]Hastorf, Northcraft, & Picciotto, 1979. [51]Emswiller, Deaux, & Willits, 1971.

demonstrated in a study completed by our colleagues Richard Graf and Jeanne Riddell. The scene once again involved a stranded motorist (hippie or straight, male or female, Black or White, military or civilian). Helping responses were then compared. The results indicated that Blacks and hippies were helpful to all. The military people, on the other hand, only helped distressed motorists who had "acceptable" (nonhippie) physical characteristics.[52]

Request style: Accentuate the positive

If you needed help, how would you ask for it? You could use a positive approach and tell the person how nice it would be if he or she would help. Or you might try a negative approach and explain what a bad person he or she would be by refusing to help.

Psychologists Mitchell Kriss, Eugene Indenbaum, and Frederick Tesch investigated this issue using the previously described "wrong number" method. To refresh your memory: if you were a subject, your phone would ring, and when you picked it up, someone would say "Hello, Ralph's Garage?" Most likely, you would then explain that you were not Ralph's Garage and that the caller had reached the wrong number. Before you could hang up, however, the caller would say "Oh, I'm sorry to have disturbed you. Oh, wait a minute! That was my last dime and I'm stuck out here. My car has broken down and I think it's really serious."

Now comes the caller's appeal for help. What type of request will be most likely to elicit your help? Let us look at three possibilities:

Negative appeal: "Look, think how you would feel if you were in a similar position and you weren't helped. So would you please call my garage for me?"
Positive appeal: "If you help me, I'd appreciate it and you'd know that you helped someone out of a really tough spot. So would you please call my garage for me?"
Neutral (simple) appeal: "Would you please call my garage for me?"

Which of these calls would get you to call the garage for them? According to Kriss and his colleagues, positive and simple appeals evoked more helping than negative appeals. The results, however, were complicated by the curious finding that the type of appeal only has an effect when the caller's status is unknown or when his or her status is opposite that of the receiver of the call.[53]

If you need help, you can focus your appeal in at least two ways. You can emphasize your own need for help, or you can direct attention to your potential helper's feelings of duty and obligation. In other words, it is either "I need help" or "You should help me." Research has shown that victim-centered ("I need help") appeals were most effective when the requested favor was legitimate (such as if victim is injured, asks for a letter to be mailed), but ineffective when the favor was not seen as legitimate (victim is in a hurry to go shopping, asks letter to be mailed). Helper-centered appeals ("You should help") were found to be only moderately effective in all cases.[54]

[52]Graf & Riddell, 1972. [53]Kriss, Indenbaum & Tesch, 1974. [54]Langer & Abelson, 1972.

If nothing else works, you may consider recruiting a third party. One such study engaged subjects in a complex gambling task culminated by requests for help in the form of donation of chips in order to stay in the game.[55] Requests were made either directly by the loser or through a third party. It was expected that third-party requests for help would be honored more often, and they were. Among the possible reasons for this pattern: third-party requests are more likely to induce the norm of social responsibility (see earlier in this chapter) in helpers; third parties have greater credibility because their requests are seen as less self-serving than those made by potential beneficiaries; and third parties are liked more than those who appeal directly because they are perceived as showing concern for the need of others.

SUMMARY HIGHLIGHTS

1. A behavior that benefits another person is *prosocial*. A special class of prosocial behavior is *altruism*, a helpful act for which nothing is expected in return.
2. There are many documented incidents in which someone was allowed to suffer even though others were available to help. The best known of these is the New York case of Kitty Genovese, who was brutally stabbed, and eventually killed, by an assailant in front of her apartment building. While the incident occurred, her neighbors watched from the windows of their apartments, and not one of them bothered to call the police.
3. Many explanations have been given for why people do not offer help when it is required. The *social comparison* explanation suggests that when people are uncertain about whether an emergency is actually taking place, they look to others to help them clarify their own reactions. If the others react as though no emergency exists, they may conclude that there indeed is not much to be concerned about.
4. *Diffusion of responsibility* is another explanation for why help is not always offered in emergency situations. If others are available to help in an emergency situation, we may conclude that someone else will help.
5. *Reciprocity* is a third explanation for helping. We have a tendency to help those who have helped us in the past. This is particularly true for people who are self-employed. Those who work for others show a tendency not to let past interactions affect future helping.
6. The principles of *social learning* and *imitation* also apply to helping. Helping is more likely to occur when a model similar to ourselves has been rewarded for a similar helping behavior.
7. Having just succeeded in some task or having unexpectedly received a gift can increase the chances that the recipient will offer help to others.
8. Some research suggests that we consider the costs to ourselves in trying to decide when to offer help. Helping is most likely when we are praised and when it is not too difficult to render. Helping is avoided, however, when efforts could cause embarrassment, disgust, or danger.
9. Although helping tends to be an act of kindness, there are cases when the intention is misdirected. People will help a handicapped person

[55] ENZLE & HARVEY, 1978.

more than someone who is in lesser need. There is a tendency, however, to give false positive feedback to those with handicaps. This sort of feedback makes it less likely that such persons will be able to solve future problems on their own.
10. Helping can also be influenced by style of request, race, sex, and lifestyle of help-givers and receivers.

CHAPTER 8   GROUPS AND LEADERSHIP

GROUP FORMATION
    Diads, triads, and small groups in general
    The joiners: Anxious, curious, or just shopping around
    Role, position, and status
    Group communication: Circles, chains, wheels, and Ys

GROUP OUTPUT
    Quality: Groupthink failures
    Size: How many cooks spoil the broth?
    Activity: A case of social loafing?

    Composition: To mix or not to mix?
    Climate: Autocratic, democratic, or doing your thing
    Style: Cautious or risky?

LEADERSHIP
    Leadership and personality: Are leaders born or made?
    Effective leadership: The contingency model
    Leaders and followers: Banking idiosyncracy credit

SUMMARY HIGHLIGHTS

Diads, triads, and small groups in general

GROUP FORMATION

To live alone, one must be either an animal or a god.
Aristotle, in *Politics*, 350 B.C.

Social behavior is as old as humankind. So are the speculations that try to explain it. Perhaps, as Aristotle suggested, people get together simply because they share a gregarious instinct. Then again, as suggested by another ancient philosopher, it could be because of practical considerations: "No one is self-sufficing, but all of us have many wants" (Plato, in *The Republic*, 350 B.C.). Perhaps, too, being with others alleviates what psychologist Carl Rogers calls the prevailing "inner loneliness" in all of us.[1] Whatever brought it on in the first place, this much is certain: togetherness is here to stay. Being with others can mean your membership in a formally established organization, or just being a part of a crowd, a mob, or an audience. In each case, your behavior will be markedly affected as a result. The main purpose of this chapter is to focus on small, informal groups. Such groups constitute an integral part of the daily activities of virtually every one of us. Whether at home, at work, or at play, we are all group members. There are family groups, work groups, classroom groups, social groups, encounter groups, therapy groups—the possibilities are limitless.

Despite their diversity, *all* groups share some common characteristics, or "dynamics." You can be sure, for example, that, as the size of any group

[1] ROGERS, 1970.

increases, there is a corresponding increment of talking done by fewer and fewer members; or as the size of the group increases, its leader inevitably becomes more autocratic and directive. Social psychologists in their studies of *group dynamics* have made extensive observations of such small, informal groups.

You will notice that relatively little space in this chapter is devoted to the encounter group and human growth movements, typical of the 1960s and 1970s. You may wonder about this apparently glaring omission in a book purporting to deal with human interaction. If you believe, as psychologist Carl Rogers does, that the encounter movement is "the most rapidly spreading social invention of the century, and probably the most potent," you may even be outraged by our omission.

There is no denying that encounter groups and growth centers have been going strong in some areas. In fact, this is just about the only thing upon which the supporters and detractors of the encounter movement seem to agree. They strongly disagree about whether encounter groups are here to stay, and how much, if at all, they achieve what they claim they can do (the claims range from vague promises of beneficial change for those who join to the ultimate solution of all personal and social adjustment problems).

Carl Rogers, the eminent supporter of the encounter movement, has provided us with some clues on what goes on in the "basic encounter." His vivid description lists in detail the benefits for those who join an encounter group, beginning with the breakdown of their initial resistance and ending with the helpful group providing individual serenity and self-acceptance.[2] Among the detractors are social psychologists such as Kurt Back, eminent in his own right, who cite potential dangers of what they consider to be essentially a fad ("cocktail parties are out, encounter groups are in....").[3] Then there are psychologists such as John Campbell and Marvin Dunnette, who bemoan the fact that encounter groups are based on ill-defined concepts that make any meaningful assessment of such groups virtually impossible.[4]

We chose not to enter this controversy for several reasons. For one, very little remains that has not been said about the topic. Jumping into the fray will not bring on a solution (we can assure you, however, that the debates among the just-mentioned scholars are interesting and provide fascinating reading). We did mention encounter groups on several occasions, primarily within the context of self-disclosure (Chapter 2). Above all, we believe that encountering others is a highly personal experience. These experiences vary so much that any attempt to put them into a uniform experimental framework (as follows from Campbell and Dunnette) is doomed to fail. If you have not done so by now, we suggest you try a growth experience group, but do so with a "let the buyer beware" attitude.

How small is "small," then? Obviously, the smallest group is a two-person group, or *diad*. Much of our previous discussion on aggression and helping behavior (see Chapters 6 and 7) involved primarily one-to-one relationships and thus was diadic. But for the purpose of exploring the effects of being with more than one other person, diads simply won't do. Three-person groups, or *triads*, have properties that diads lack. For example, two members can form a coalition and gang up on the third member; one member can mediate

[2]ROGERS, 1970. [3]BACK, 1972. [4]CAMPBELL & DUNNETTE, 1968.

conflicts between the two others; and there is greater probability of more suspicion (and less self-disclosure) among three group members than between two.[5] Obviously, the larger the group, the more complex the interaction possibilities. Although psychologists set no hard and fast rules about the size of the groups they study, these usually range from five to nine persons in membership.

The joiners: Anxious, curious, or just shopping around

Suppose you have just volunteered for a psychology experiment—be it for credit, grades, money, or sheer curiosity. On a given day, you arrive at the assigned location on time. The room looks like something out of a science fiction movie, with electronic paraphernalia and other laboratory equipment strewn around. As you are waiting with other students, you almost expect the "mad scientist" to enter the room momentarily. And, indeed, a stern figure in a white smock appears and introduces himself with a heavy foreign accent (always sinister!) as Dr. Gregor Zillstein of the Medical School, Department of Psychiatry and Neurology. He thanks all of you for agreeing to undergo a series of electric shocks while having your pulse rate taken. Some of the shocks are intense, he suggests, but they won't hurt—not much, anyway. Besides, there is no danger of permanent tissue damage. He then announces a 10-minute delay to set up the equipment and gives each of you the chance to wait either in a private room alone or in another classroom with some of the other students in the experiment.

What would your choice be? Would you prefer to be alone or with a group of other individuals who are essentially strangers to you? The chances are that you would prefer to wait with the others. At least, that is what psychologist

Triads have characteristics that are lacking in diads, such as two members excluding the third member.

[5]MILLS, 1953; TAYLOR, DE SOTO, & LIEB, 1979.

Stanley Schachter found when he subjected female undergraduates at the University of Minnesota to this condition.[6] Two-thirds of his subjects became highly anxious after Dr. Zillstein's appearance. Somehow, joining others in the same predicament may help alleviate anxiety. At least, this is what the subjects may have had in mind. When a similar group of subjects were met by Dr. Zillstein acting in a far less alarming manner (and presumably causing little or no anxiety), two-thirds of the subjects preferred either to wait alone or did not care one way or the other. It seems that misery loves company, or, to be more accurate, misery loves *miserable* company!

Despite Schachter's dramatic findings, there is no unanimity of opinion among psychologists who have conducted similar experiments. Although their findings generally support those of Schachter, especially in the case of firstborns (who show the highest degree of affiliative tendencies), the underlying motivation has not as yet been clearly established.[7] Whether threats of electric shock really induce anxiety is debatable, because joining others may have occurred either to fulfill the experimenter's expectation or, perhaps, out of curiosity.

If people join others out of curiosity, the question arises: curiosity about what? As early as 1954, psychologist Leon Festinger proposed that being with others provides individuals with "social reality." In his **social comparison theory**, Festinger suggested that groups can convey feedback to those who join them and thus provide them with a better understanding of the world around them.[8] In the case of Schachter's subjects, they may have been not so much anxious as uncertain about what was going on, hoping subsequently to get more information from the reactions of others. At least one study that largely replicated Schachter's but varied the subjects' certainty about their own reactions (by making a supposedly accurate gauge fluctuate wildly during physical measurements) clearly established that the greatest need to affiliate occurred among those subjects receiving the most uncertain feedback.[9]

It seems that both Schachter and his critics are on the right track. People may join groups merely because they are curious about others, perhaps even hoping to be stimulated by new associations. But the process of getting your kicks from new acquaintances seems to be tempered with a heavy dose of anxiety. In a study purporting to engage in dream research, each of 160 college students who enlisted for the experiment was told that he or she had been assigned (as the only outsider) to another work group. Before joining, the other group was described to the subject as either similar or dissimilar to him or her. Three additional experimental conditions were then established. In the first condition, no further information was given to the subject, presumably evoking concern in the subject about whether or not he or she would be liked by the new group. In the second condition, the subject was told that, for plausible reasons, he or she would be introduced to the new group in a most favorable manner. It was assumed that the subject, having been assured of being liked, would thus have little or no concern. In the third condition, the subject was told that, for plausible reasons, he or she would be introduced to

---

[6]SCHACHTER, 1959. [7]ZIMBARDO & FORMICA, 1963; RING, LIPINSKI, & BRAGINSKI, 1965; MACDONALD, 1970. [8]FESTINGER, 1954. [9]GERARD, 1963.

the new group in a rather unfavorable manner, thus increasing the subject's concern for being disliked.

Given the choice of joining, which group do you suppose was most frequently cited by the subjects? The obvious answer would be: groups with members similar to the subject. We already know that birds of a feather flock together from previous studies of attitudinal similarity and interpersonal attraction (see Chapter 5). But similarity does not always breed contentment. As expected, when the subjects were concerned about being liked by members of the group they were about to join (conditions 1 and 3), they chose similar groups. The subjects who were assured of being liked (condition 2), however, showed a marked interest in joining *dissimilar* groups.[10] Apparently, with anxiety out of the way people are curious and willing to take their chances with strangers.

Finally, there is the matter of difficulty in joining. Did you ever try to join a fraternity or a sorority, an athletic team, a religious group, or social club? Obviously, people join groups for many reasons. But one reason is so paradoxical that it almost defies explanation. It seems that as it becomes harder for some individuals to join the group of their choice, they not only increase their efforts to join, but their liking for the group as well! The explanation of this phenomenon is rooted in the cognitive process of individuals, as postulated by the theory of *cognitive dissonance* (see Chapter 4). In their classic experiment, psychologists Elliot Aronson and Judson Mills subjected college women who volunteered to participate in discussion groups to three kinds of initiation. Those who underwent severe initiation were required to read aloud to a male experimenter some embarrassing material before joining the group. In the mild initiation condition, the subjects were required to read aloud some material that was not embarrassing, whereas in the third condition (the control) they were not required to read anything. Each subject then listened to a tape recording of the group she was about to join and then evaluated the group and its discussants. The subjects who underwent severe initiation judged their respective group as significantly more attractive than did those who underwent mild initiation or no initiation.[11] According to the theory of cognitive dissonance, this choice was to be expected because the subjects had to justify the pain and effort they had experienced during the severe initiation. Of course, there are other possible explanations besides cognitive dissonance. Perhaps the subjects were pleased with themselves for mastering such a difficult task and thus chose the group that offered them this challenge. One way or another, it seems that roadblocks thrown by the group provide a certain attraction for some joiners.

Role, position, and status

To understand the effect of groups on individuals, it is important to know how the group is structured. Many psychologists have addressed themselves to this task by coming up with descriptions of the individual's role, position, and status in the group. Unfortunately, these concepts are frequently used in a vague, nebulous, and confusing manner.[12] Let us be as specific as possible.

---

[10]WALSTER & WALSTER, 1963. [11]ARONSON & MILLS, 1959. [12]FOA, 1958; THIBAUT & KELLEY, 1959.

Position refers to a specific slot occupied by an individual in a group, and *role* refers to the behavior displayed by an individual in a certain position. For example, a family consisting of parents and two children is a group in which the position of the female parent is that of a mother. So we have a mother position, a father position (also a husband position and a wife position), and a child position (or a son position, daughter position, and so on). The typical pattern of behavior of the position's occupant is his or her role. The dominant father, the caring mother, and the obedient child display the typical *father role*, *mother role*, and *child role*.

Do they really? What about the father who is not dominant, the mother who does not care, and the child who is not obedient? Obviously *role* needs further definition. Suppose you are a friend of the family and also consider yourself an objective observer. You describe the father's behavior as somewhat meek and subdued. This would refer to the father's actual behavior, or *enacted role*. But this may or may not coincide with the way the other members of the family, including the father himself, perceive the same behavior. If the mother considers the father to be meek and henpecked (and thus essentially agrees with you) even though the father considers himself a dominant John Wayne type, we can safely assume that there is quite a difference in the *perceived role* of the father. But this is not all. Take the case where the mother's actual behavior, as assessed by objective observers (and hence enacted role) and as perceived by her family (and hence perceived role), shows callousness and indifference toward her children. The enacted role and the perceived role of the mother are thus identical. But such behavior is contrary to the expectations that most people hold about the mother position. Thus the mother's enacted role and perceived role differ considerably from her *prescribed role*, or, in other words, what society says her behavior ought to be. Given a great deal of information about the mother's past behavior, we can even speak of a *predicted role*. That is, if we know that she has been arrested many times for child abuse and has shown no significant attempts to change, her callousness toward her children is not too surprising.

Finally, *status* refers to an evaluation of the contribution of particular roles to the welfare of the group. In the family group example, the prescribed role for the man in the husband-father position is to be the breadwinner and provider. This may differ from his enacted role if he is lazy, unambitious, and unemployed. His perceived role depends on who does the judging: in his own eyes, he may think that he does more than his share in providing for his family; his family, however, views him in line with his predicted role, which is based on his past record as an inadequate provider. The net result is low status within the family for the father (though he may not even be aware of it).

Although these examples were designed to clear up the confusion in the usage of the term *role*, a serious real-life problem arises from the matter of role confusion. All of us display a variety of role behaviors because of the many positions that we occupy at home, at work, and at play. Sex roles involve different perceptions and sometimes different expectations for and by men and women (see Chapter 10). The same holds true for practically every role, often resulting in confusion and stress for the individuals concerned. Experimental studies have shown that minor neuroses can originate from such role conflicts as those between homemaker and career woman, military chaplain and officer, or Black and middle-class Black.[13] Fortunately, under normal conditions role confusion tends to be minimal, since most individuals can control their voluntary participation in various groups. Men or women who belong to the Knights of Columbus, a Catholic organization, are not likely to become participants in the Planned Parenthood League, which advocates contraception and birth control. Furthermore, since an individual is ordinarily engaged in one group at a time, only one set of roles is dominant at a given occasion, reducing the chance of conflict even more.

Clearly defined positions and roles are not always a hedge against role confusion. They often degenerate into a rigid format that only increases defensive behavior and stress. A study on the role behavior of professionals in mental institutions is a case in point. This study showed the close relationship that exists between role rigidity and interdisciplinary squabbles. Social workers in such institutions have lower status than psychologists because they usually do not hold a doctoral degree. As a result, they attempt to enact the role of psychologists by increasing their usage of standard psychological jargon. Psychologists keep developing new mystical professional jargon to differentiate themselves from the social workers. Psychologists also zealously guard what they consider their own professional domain (psychotherapy and testing). Enjoying top status as physicians, psychiatrists tend to draw on the secret magic of both psychology and medicine, so that, when challenged by an expert in one discipline, they can always use counterarguments involving the jargon of the other discipline. General physicians' initial perceived role and status are high, but subsequent enacted role behavior shows that they are assigned routine jobs that most nurses can and do handle as well. The inevitable result—loss of status and the emergence of stress among the general physicians.[14] Altogether, not a very happy scene.

Even when positions and roles are not clearly spelled out, they emerge anyway. Studies of small, informal groups show that, sooner or later, members display systematic patterns of role behavior even though their positions are not clearly defined. For example, in a discussion group with no formally assigned leader some members will show task-oriented behavior and others will show maintenance-oriented behavior. Group *task roles* are directed toward solving the group's problems and involve such behavior as initiating new ideas, providing useful information, or coordinating the efforts and contributions of individual members of the group. *Maintenance roles* are concerned with group morale and involve such behavior as encouraging others, promoting general harmony, and catering to individual members' problems. In addition, there are instances of what psychologist Bernard Bass calls *self-oriented roles:* individual roles that are primarily self-centered in nature and perhaps irrelevant to the group's task or maintenance (such as the behavior of a recognition-seeking playboy).[15] Bass believes that it is possible to

[13]ELLIS, 1952; BURCHARD, 1954; FRAZIER, 1957.   [14]HARSHBARGER, 1970.   [15]BASS, 1965(a).

make certain generalizations about the personality characteristics of people on the basis of role behavior (to be described later on), but this brings up the thorny issue of role and personality.

Have you ever noticed that college instructors are pompous individuals? Before you enthusiastically endorse this proposition—beware! You may be expressing bias, prejudice, or, at best, some harmless stereotyping. But suppose that, with the aid of objective observers, you had conducted careful observations of a wide array of college instructors and, using a good operational definition for "pomposity," you found that college instructors *are* pompous. You are then immediately faced with the circular question of whether role affects personality or vice versa. In other words, since the expected (and probably enacted) role of the instructor makes him or her the important dispenser of knowledge and grades, is it really surprising that such omnipotence takes its toll and creates a pompous individual? On the other hand, perhaps individuals who are pompous to begin with gravitate toward those professions that allow, and in fact maximize, role behavior that is pompous. These circular questions permeate practically every occupational field. It could be argued, for example, that most psychotherapists are themselves neurotic. But is it because of the toll-taking constant emotional involvement in the delusional system of their patients, or is it because they actively seek out a profession where they can express their own neuroticism freely and legitimately?

Because of the circularity problem, few studies have been conducted on the relationship between role and personality. One investigator asked rank-and-file workers in an appliance factory to respond to an attitude questionnaire dealing with management and union. During the year, 23 of the respondents were promoted to foremen and 35 were elected union stewards. Fifteen months after taking the first test, they took the test once again, as did a control group consisting of workers who had not been promoted. Those whose positions had changed also underwent systematic shifts in attitude, whereas those who experienced no change in position displayed little or none in attitude. The foremen's attitudes toward management became more favorable, whereas that of the union stewards became more favorable toward the union.[16] It is possible that the change in positions and roles demonstrated the influence of roles upon attitudes rather than the selection of people for a position on the basis of their attitude. But despite this suggestive study, the question still remains unanswered. The choice of people who became foremen or union stewards (or a choice of no promotion, for that matter) was probably not made in an arbitrary manner. Conceivably, those people may all along have displayed abilities, attitudes, and general personality characteristics compatible with the position in which they eventually landed and were therefore chosen accordingly.

Nevertheless, some psychologists believe that roles can generate attitudes and behavior. One of the most concrete examples of roles changing personality comes from a fascinating study about prisons. The experiment, known as the Stanford County Prison experiment, was conducted by psychologist

[16]LIEBERMAN, 1956.

Philip Zimbardo and his students at Stanford University. A mock prison was created in the basement of the Stanford psychology building. Earlier, the subject population, consisting of normal, middle-class college men, had been randomly assigned as guards or prisoners.

The experiment itself started in a way that took the prisoners by surprise. Without warning they were picked up at their homes and taken to the police station to be searched, fingerprinted, and booked. Then they were blindfolded and taken to the simulated prison. The prison was not a literal replication of prison conditions, but it contained many elements that made it similar to a real prison. It had no windows or clocks, and it forced the prisoners to be almost totally dependent upon their guards. The guards were told to maintain strict law and order. They carried billy clubs, wore khaki uniforms, had access to handcuffs, blew their whistles, and wore sunglasses to hide their emotions.[17]

The experiment was originally scheduled to last for two weeks. After only six days, however, it had to be halted because the subjects became too much involved in the roles to which they had been randomly assigned. The prisoners became dehumanized, lacking all sense of unity and self-esteem. Only their hatred for the guards somehow kept them hanging on. As the prisoners became more passive, the guards became more assertive. They greatly increased the frequency of their commands, insults, and other incidents of debasing behavior. It was not uncommon for them to use threats and to actually enjoy bullying the prisoners into controllable behavior. One guard expressed his feelings this way: "I was surprised at myself... I made them call each other names and clean toilets out with their bare hands. I practically considered the prisoners cattle, and I kept thinking that I have to watch out for them in case they try something" (p. 54).[18] Remember, at the beginning of the study the young men were randomly assigned to their respective roles of prisoners and guards. In the end, they played their roles too well—so well, in fact, that the study had to be discontinued before it ran its originally planned course (see Figure 8-1).

Some psychologists have gone even further. They believe that entire populations show personality, attitudinal, and behavioral characteristics as a function of their particular roles. Psychologist Bernard Bass, reviewing about 60 studies in which his *Orientation Inventory (ORI)* had been employed, suggested that maintenance role behavior is displayed by *interaction-oriented* individuals whose personality is marked by a strong need to be accepted and to share things with others. Women, younger persons, Baptists, Catholics, student teachers, counselors, hospital attendants and social workers tend to be interaction oriented. *Task-oriented* individuals show high degrees of persistence, confidence, and tolerance. They are predominantly men, older persons, Unitarians, engineers, managers, people with fewer personal problems and ... weight-lifters (!) Finally, *self-oriented* people are portrayed as easily irritated individuals striving for extrinsic rewards, expecting to be endorsed by others on the basis of past performance rather than future potential, and concerned more with their own needs than with those of

[17]ZIMBARDO, 1973. [18]ZIMBARDO, HANEY, BANKS, & JAFFEE, 1972.

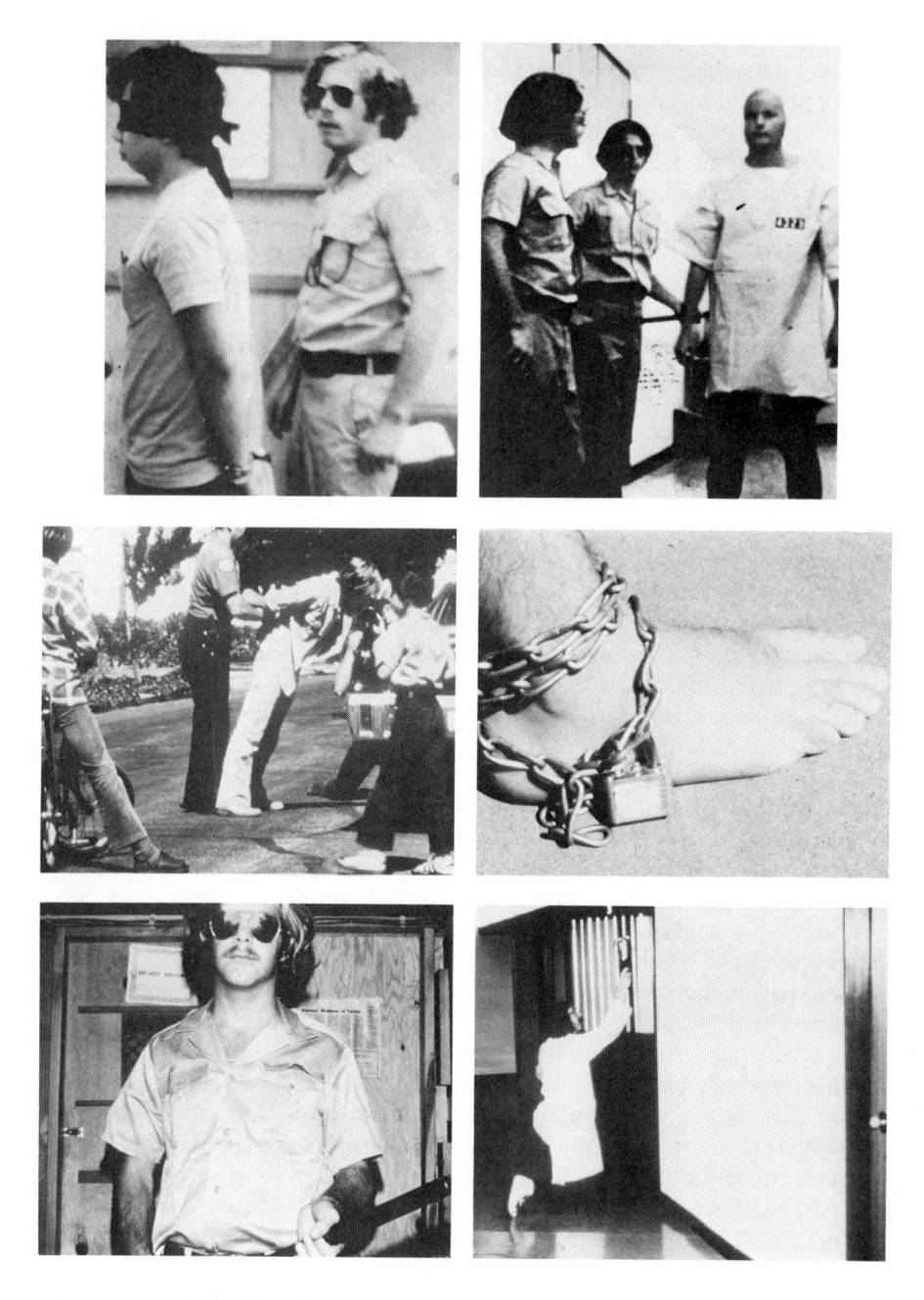

Figure 8-1. Roles generate behavior. This sequence of pictures shows scenes from the now-classic experiment of simulated prison conditions by psychologist Philip Zimbardo. At the beginning of the study, the young men were randomly assigned to their respective roles of prisoners and guards. In the end, roles were played well enough as to affect the men's behavior—so well, in fact, that the study had to be discontinued before it ran its originally planned course (see text). *Source:* Zimbardo, 1973.

others. According to Bass, self-oriented individuals are predominantly Northern students as opposed to Southerners, high-level supervisory personnel as opposed to lower-level foremen, and . . . football players and beauty queens.[19]

Despite Bass's extensive research, most of his reasoning remains circular. It is, however, not necessarily problematical. In the case of our clinician who displays neurotic behavior (enacted role), it may not be a professional handicap—at least if you believe in the adage "It takes one to know one."

Group communication: Circles, chains, wheels, and Ys

One interesting aspect of role behavior and status is that certain modes of communication emerge accordingly. In formal organizations such as the military or the world of big business, modes of communication are clearly spelled out. A person knows when, where, what, and how to communicate with his or her superiors or subordinates. Observe the resplendent boxes, squares, and intersecting lines in organizational flowcharts tended to by loving bureaucratic hands. What they really do is spell out with whom and how organization members are to communicate.

If you think that small, informal groups are not burdened by such limitations in communication, you have a big surprise coming. As soon as you join such a group, you become part of a relentless process in which your role relationship with others defines your modes of communication with them. Psychologist Harold Kelley observed many such groups and found that who says what depends to a large extent on the status or prestige of the member involved. High-status members not only feel freer than low-status members to make negative comments about the group but, when dissatisfied, tend to communicate primarily to other high-status members. Low-status members address themselves to high-status members more often than to members of their own level.[20] In fact, there is even a relationship between where you sit with others and how you communicate! In a study involving five-person groups, seating arrangements were observed from behind a one-way mirror as follows: member 1 sat on the left side of the table near the door; members 2, 3, and 4 along the long side of the table opposite the mirror; and member 5 on the right side, farthest from the door. The members opposite each other (1 and 5) and the member in the central position (3) were recipients of the most communications and also did most of the talking. Members who chose seats 1 and 5 showed role behavior marked by an orientation toward the group's task, whereas member 3 displayed a marked tendency to limit his role to the social-emotional aspects of maintaining group morale. The more inhibited and somewhat anxious members, who avoided the "high-talking seats," chose seats 2 and 4. When the situation was purely social, most of the communications occurred between members in adjacent seats (see Figure 8-2).[21]

Being with others in small, informal groups does not, therefore, imply spontaneity or arbitrariness in communication. In fact, one can observe and experiment with such groups to make certain predictions about more formal occasions. Studies of mock juries are a case in point. Subjects drawn from a regular jury pool who engaged in mock jury deliberations concerning an auto

[19]Bass, 1965(b). [20]Kelley, 1951. [21]Hare & Bales, 1963.

Figure 8-2. Who talks to whom? It depends where you sit. Seats 2 and 4 are "low-talking" seats occupied by the more inhibited group members. Occupants of seats 1 and 5 tend to be task oriented. Occupants of seat 3 usually tend to the problems of group morale. The behavior of the group members is recorded by an observer from behind a one-way mirror.

negligence case showed marked sex differences in their role behavior. Male jurors tended to be active and task oriented, whereas female jurors were reactive and maintenance oriented. Female jurors also tended to be less competent than males in discussing issues of negligence and damages,[22] an enacted role behavior that may have been the result of a prescribed role—which nowadays many women reject.

What it all amounts to, then, is that once people get together, even informally, their role relationships tend to define stable channels of communication. Among the most frequently studied communication networks are the circle, the chain, the Y, and the wheel (see Figure 8-3). In the circle, A talks to B, B to C, C to D, D to E, and E to A. There is a whole lot of talking going on under this arrangement. In the wheel network, on the other hand, only A does the talking. In the general sequence from circle to chain to Y to wheel networks, the circle example is related to activity and more enjoyment by the members—but also to lack of leadership and direction. The wheel at the other extreme shows the opposite characteristics[23]—which boils down to the fact that a lot of talk may be enjoyable but not necessarily productive.

Fortunately, the dynamics of the group are such that, as time passes, communication networks settle into a pattern that is most conducive to the goals of the group. If you join a group of people with a definite task in mind, sooner or later the communication network will have to assume some central

[22]STRODBOCK & MANN, 1956.   [23]LEAVITT, 1951.

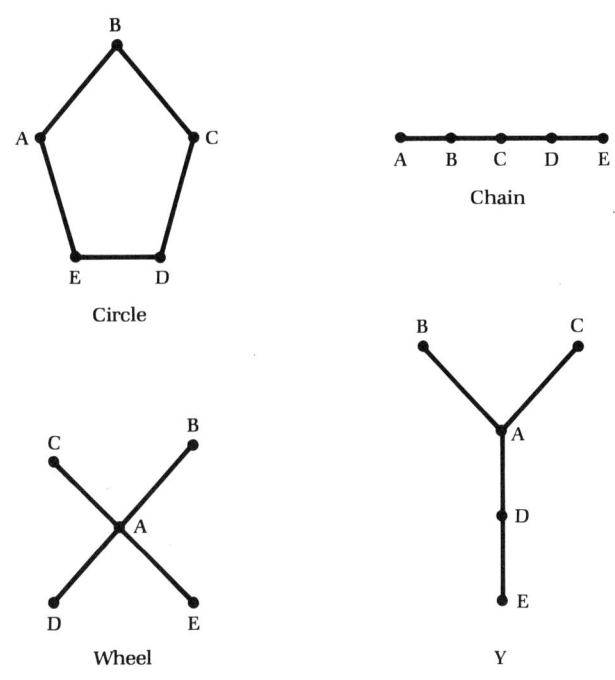

Figure 8-3.
Five-person group communication patterns. In the circle, there is a lot of talking and enjoyment—as well as a lack of direction and leadership. The wheel at the other extreme shows the opposite characteristics. The chain and the Y are compromise arrangements.

characteristics (such as the Y or the wheel) or the group will never realize its goal. On the other hand, if you are with a group of people whose only goal is to enjoy one another socially, the communication pattern is going to be more flexible. It may even begin as an all-channel network, with everybody talking to everyone else and enjoying it. Eventually, however, even in such happy, egalitarian groups, positions, roles, and status emerge, resulting in a more restricted communication network.

Quality: Groupthink failures

Winston Churchill, the noted British statesman, must have had little faith in certain group experiences, as witnessed by his famous quote "A committee is the organized result of a group of incompetents who have been appointed by the uninformed to accomplish the unnecessary." Certain psychologists take a similar jaundiced view of what happens in groups. Psychologist Irving Janis, who brought the concept of **Groupthink** into the 1970s, has consistently argued that group-inherent pressures toward conformity can lead to serious interference with efficient decision making.[24] One study of archival records of public statements by leading decision makers in five American foreign policy crises is a case in point. The five crises involved support and

GROUP OUTPUT

[24] JANIS, 1972.

opposition to the Marshall Plan, the invasion of North Korea, the Bay of Pigs invasion, the Cuban missile crisis, and the decision to escalate the Vietnam War. The analysis involved public statements by the decision makers and subsequent outcomes of the crises. In each case, the decision makers were rated on the degree to which they identified with their group and the "integrative complexity" of their decision. The latter involved the ability of the decision makers to distinguish among the various characteristics of the problem situation as well as their ability to integrate these characteristics into a meaningful whole. Table 8-1 shows integrative complexity ranged from 1.0 (very low) to 5.9 (out of a possible 7.0, thus fairly high).

TABLE 8-1. Groupthink and non-Groupthink decisions.

Crisis	Decision Maker	Integrative Complexity	Group Identification
Marshall Plan	Truman (1947)	3.66	low
	Acheson (1947)	4.50	non-Groupthink
	Marshall (1947)	5.90	
Cuban missile crisis	Kennedy (1962)	4.33	low
	Rusk (1962)	3.16	non-Groupthink
Invasion of North Korea	Truman (1950)	1.00	high
	Acheson (1950)	1.83	Groupthink
Bay of Pigs invasion	Kennedy (1961)	2.16	high
	Rusk (1961)	2.58	Groupthink
Vietnam War escalation	Johnson (1964–1965)	2.16	high
	Rusk (1964–1965)	2.50	Groupthink

Source: Tetlock, 1979.

The three Groupthink crises (where identification with the group was high) also reflected the poorest quality of decision (low integrative complexity): to pursue the defeated North Korean army beyond the 38th Parallel in 1950, to launch the Bay of Pigs invasion of Cuba in 1961, and to escalate the war in Vietnam in 1964-1965. On the other hand, non-groupthink decisions, such as the launching the Marshall Plan in 1947 or the handling of the Cuban missile crisis in 1962, were highly successful and beneficial (high levels of integrative complexity).

In a more satirical vein, psychologist Christian Buys has argued that "humans would do better without groups" since being in groups has been shown to cause loss of individual responsiblity, to increase risk taking and conformity, and frequently to induce panic behavior.[25] Other social psychologists, perhaps less humorously inclined, have heatedly argued in favor of the positive functions of the group experience.[26]

What, then, constitutes a "good group"? One way of answering the question is to measure how effective the group is in attaining its task-related objectives. Measure such as the quantity or quality of items produced by a group of factory workers, the number of puzzles solved by a problem-solving group in a laboratory investigation, or the ingenuity of new ideas produced in a meeting of advertising executives—all would constitute measures of group effective-

[25]Buys, 1978. [26]Anderson, 1978; Green & Mack, 1978.

ness. Another way of evaluating group performance is to measure the extent to which a group satisfies the needs of its members. Such measures as the extent to which the group satisfies individual needs, the degree to which group members like one another and the activities of the group, or the degree of willingness to remain in the group voluntarily would provide evaluation of group satisfaction.

These two dimensions of evaluation of group performance (production and satisfaction) are largely, though not completely, independent. It is possible to have an effective but dissatisfied group, in the sense that members can be forced to produce while participating unhappily in a group. It is even possible to have a satisfied but ineffective group that has little success in achieving task-related goals: a well-oiled machine that never squeaks but produces nothing. Research evidence clearly shows, however, that each limits the other. Even in highly successful groups, individual members do not remain indefinitely attracted to the group when their own personal needs are not satisfied; similarly, people do not remain attracted to a group that chronically fails in all its efforts.

Size: How many cooks spoil the broth?

Several studies have shown that, compared to larger groups, smaller groups are more creative, express more ideas, show more mutual influence, need less guidance from higher authority, and display greater morale.[27] If so, are two heads better than one, or do too many cooks spoil the broth? In evaluating group output, both rather different adages are, paradoxically, true. There is evidence that two heads are indeed better than one in problem solving.[28]

Two heads are better than one—up to a point. Group output increases with more participants, but at a given point the group may become so large and unwieldy that the quality and quantity of its output will decline.

[27]MARRIOT, 1949; BAUMGARTEL & SOBEL, 1959; MCGRATH, 1962.   [28]GOLDMAN, 1966.

Simple logic, however, will convince you that any such increase in the quality or quantity of group output is only good *up to a point*. For example, if one person can solve a problem in 50 minutes, two may require 20 minutes (rather than 25), and five require 15 minutes (rather than 10). Eventually, however, a point of no further gain may be reached, so that the addition of even an infinite number of members may produce no further increment in group output. In fact, there is evidence that under some circumstances the group may become so large and unwieldy and require so much investment of its energy in communication and maintenance of morale that the solution may require an even greater amount of time. Psychologist Jack Gibb studied groups ranging in size from 2 to 96 members and found that with increase in group size there were progressively smaller increments in the number of ideas produced for the solution of the problem. Not too surprisingly, he found out from post-experimental questioning that, as the group increased in size, many members began to experience feelings of threat and inhibition, which in turn created obstacles in the completion of tasks in the larger groups.[29]

It is, therefore, impossible to state categorically the exact number of group members needed to achieve maximum effectiveness in group output. At best, we must adopt what some experimenters call the **principle of least group size,** which states that the optimum group size for the performance of an interactive task is the minimum number of individuals required to make available to the group all of the resources required for the execution of its task.[30]

The data in Table 8-2 illustrate the point. Subjects in groups of various sizes were presented with three problems varying in difficulty (easy, medium, difficult). Groups solving the low-difficulty and medium-difficulty tasks were observed to do as well as had been statistically predicted. As Table 8-2 demonstrates, however, as the size of the groups solving the difficult task increased, they began to perform below what had been expected. The results also show that, as group size increases from two to six, solution time began to drop. Six members appear to be the optimum composition, since six-person groups were quickest to reach a solution. With ten-person groups, solution time increased once again.

Activity: A case of social loafing

Closely related to the issue of group size and group output is the case of **social loafing.** Consider, for example, the saying "Many hands make light the work." If you are an optimist, your interpretation of this statement will dwell on the blessings of collective action, which in turn makes the attainment of goals easier. If you are a pessimist, you are more likely to interpret the saying literally—namely, that when many hands are available, people actually work less hard than they could and ought. In other words, they loaf.

There is evidence to support the pessimistic view of social loafing. As early as 50 years ago, a German psychologist named Ringelman asked subjects to pull a rope as hard as they could, either alone, or with one, two, or seven other people. He then used a strain gauge to measure how hard they pulled in

[29]GIBB, 1951. [30]THELEN, 1949.

TABLE 8-2. Group size and productivity

Group Size	Solution Time (All Tasks)	Observed Solutions (Difficult Task)	Predicted Solutions (Difficult Task)
2	288.45 seconds	4.00	4.95
3	247.48 seconds	4.00	6.75
6	206.06 seconds	3.00	10.50
10	221.26 seconds	6.00	12.90

Source: Bray, Kerr, & Atkin, 1978.

kilograms of pressure. He found that with increased group size the collective performance of its members became increasingly less than the sum of the individual efforts.

More recent studies have replicated Ringelman's effect with other tasks. In one study, subjects were asked to evaluate critically a poem or an editorial. Depending on the experimental condition, they were told that they were the only evaluators, or 1 of 4, or 1 of 16. When subsequently asked to report the degree of effort they had put into their task, the least amount reported was in the 16-person group and the greatest amount in the individual condition.[31] In another study, subjects were asked to perform physically exerting tasks such as handclapping or shouting. In both tasks there was a similar sizable decrease in individual effort when performing in groups as compared to solo performance.[32] Even nonphysical activities such as cognitive decision making

The Ringelman effect of social loafing. As more people become available for a collective task, individual efforts decline. Each one of these people would pull harder if the other two were absent.

[31] PETTY, HARKINS, WILLIAMS, & LATANÉ, 1977.   [32] LATANÉ, WILLIAMS, & HARKINS, 1979.

are subject to social loafing. These experiments clearly show that social loafing exists, but its manifestation in real life seems to depend on the cultural context in which it occurs. For example, Russian collective farms *(kolkhoz)* have had a long history of social loafing and abdication of individual responsibility, whereas Israeli collective farms *(kibbutzim)* have always been highly productive.

There is a final touch of irony in the case of social loafing. Psychologists Michael Ross and Fiore Sicoly studied married couples, basketball players, and discussants in planning groups and found that individuals made a disproportionate attribution of their own role in their group's output. Perhaps individual group members are not even aware that an increase in group size produces a decrease in individual effort, because each of Ross and Fiore's subjects always took more credit for the joint group output than any of their fellow group members would attribute to them.[33]

Composition: To mix or not to mix?

Do you prefer to be with friends or with strangers? This seems like a silly question because the answer seems obvious. Of course you want to be with friends. You like your friends, and (you hope) they like you. Remember, however, that the question at hand deals with evaluating group output. As we shall see, being with friends does not always lead to beneficial results.

Groups composed of friends frequently display a high degree of satisfaction and productivity. But it is not necessarily friendship as such that accounts for this happy state. Rather, it is the probability that friends are likely to be compatible on a wide range of interests, attitudes, and, most likely, abilities and personality characteristics as well. As every hostess knows, compatible people make happy groups. And happy groups deliver, as demonstrated in a study by psychologist William Schutz while working with naval trainees. He divided his subjects into five-man groups and asked them to compete against one another on a series of experimental tasks. The groups were composed of either "personal" members (who preferred close and intimate relations with others), "counterpersonal" members (who preferred to keep others at a distance), or mixed types. The results showed that groups compatible in terms of member need (all of the same type) were more productive than were incompatible groups (mixed type.)[34]

Schutz's study seems to suggest that it is not advisable to mix different types of individuals, at least as far as group output is concerned. Indeed, at work people do prefer to be with others who are compatible in terms of belief, age, race, seniority, and marital status.[35] Moreover, on simple tasks that require speed, such as on an assembly line, compatible groups show the highest morale and productivity. On the other hand, once compatibility leads to the formation of friendships on the job, there is always the risk that increased talking and sociability may interfere with productivity.[36]

The notion of compatibility in itself is complex. Take the matter of ability grouping. You may remember the times in grade school when the teacher divided the class into reading groups euphemistically labeled Bluebirds,

[33]Ross & Sicoly, 1979.   [34]Schutz, 1955.   [35]Pfiffner, 1951.   [36]Horsfall & Arensberg, 1949.

Blackbirds, Redbirds, and so on. Of course, this subterfuge never fooled students. You asked a youngster who he was, and he would say "I'm a dumb Bluebird" or "a smart Blackbird." Whether such ability grouping was beneficial to the individual student is not clear. Neither is the evidence in terms of group output. In one study, respondents were divided on the basis of their scores on a standard intelligence test into three categories: high (H), medium (M), and low (L) intelligence. Three-person groups based on combinations of compatibility (such as MMM, LLL) were then compared on a cognitive task with groups based on combinations of possible incompatibility (HML). To nobody's surprise (considering the nature of the task), the compatible group of highly intelligent members (HHH) achieved the highest score. In all other combinations, however, the supposedly incompatible groups did better (for instance, HML did better than MMM).[37]

To mix or not to mix with others? By all means mix, but first decide on your goal. If your aim is simply to join others in a context of sociability, mix with people of your own kind. Joining such compatible groups will bring you the greatest amount of satisfaction. But if you want something done beyond a simple task, such as a nonroutine activity requiring creativity and originality, mix with people differing in ability and opinion as often as you can.[38] In fact, you are better off mixing with the opposite sex. In a study of same-sex and mixed-sex groups, subjects were presented with a series of problems involving logistics (getting a group of people across a mined road), finances (distributing $3000 to a group of students), and human relations (settling an argument between two group members). The quality of problem solution was scored for all-male groups, groups composed of three males and one female, and groups composed of two or three females and one or two males. On all three problems, mixed-sex groups performed better than same-sex groups.[39]

Climate: Autocratic, democratic, or doing your thing

When a group of people meet, be it for purely social purposes or for tackling a specific problem, the climate in which the group operates can become a critical factor in the group's productivity and the satisfaction of its members. To a large extent the social climate in a group is initiated by its most prominent members (see subsequent section on leadership), but it takes the response of the entire membership to set the social climate in its totality.

One of the most famous studies on the social climate of groups was conducted by social psychologist Kurt Lewin, beginning as early as 1938 and continued by his associates throughout the 1950s. Using groups of 10-year-old boys as subjects, they varied the leadership style of the adults in charge of an after-school hobby club to which the group members belonged. Three conditions of leadership shifted from group to group every six weeks and were aimed at generating the following respective climates: *autocratic, democratic,* and *laissez faire.* In the autocratic condition, the supervising adult dictated all work tasks and assignments, tended to be highly personal in his praise or criticism, and generally remained aloof from active group participation except when demonstrating. In the democratic condition, all policies were set

[37]LAUGHLIN, BRANCH, & JOHNSON, 1969. [38]ZILLER, BEHRINGER, & GOODCHILDS, 1962. [39]HOFFMAN & MAIER, 1961.

by group discussion, members were free to work with whomever they chose, criticism or praise was objective, and the leader attempted to be more of a group member than a task-imposing authority. In the laissez faire condition, members were essentially doing their own thing: complete freedom for groups or individual decision, with neither praise or criticism offered.

How did the groups respond to the social climates thus generated? In terms of productivity, the autocratic group scored highest—but only when the leader was in the room. The democratic group, on the other hand, maintained high work motivation and steady productivity throughout. The laissez faire group showed poor productivity, both in quantity and in quality. The most dramatic differences occurred in group morale and satisfaction. In the democratic group there was little discontent, few dropouts, and a great deal of friendliness and spontaneity. In the autocratic group, members were either hostile and destructive or meek and submissive; in both cases, morale was low and discontent was high. In the laissez faire condition, there was a lot of horsing around but little satisfaction, as witnessed by the members' preference for democratic leadership.[40]

Does this mean that democracy is the best system for getting things done and keeping people happy? Perhaps so, at least in our society, which is preconditioned to a democratic social climate. Some psychologists have even extended Lewin's findings to the North American educational system, advocating a change from the traditional teacher-centered classroom climate to a more democratic learner-centered climate.[41] Nevertheless, Lewin's findings are far from universal. In a later study of preadolescent Hindu boys living in northern India, which was closely modeled after the original U.S. study, the autocratic social climate elicited greater productivity and satisfaction than did the democratic social climate.[42]

Style: Cautious or risky?

> Mr. A, an electrical engineer who is married and has one child, has been working for a large electronics corporation since graduating from college five years ago. He is assured of a lifetime job with a modest, although adequate, salary, and liberal pension benefits on retirement. It is very unlikely that his salary will increase much before he retires. While attending a convention, Mr. A is offered a job with a small, new company that has a highly uncertain future. The new job would pay more to start and would offer the possibility of a share in the ownership if the company survived the competition of the larger firms.
>
> Imagine that you are adivising Mr. A. Listed are several probabilities or odds of the new company's proving financially sound. Please decide the *lowest* probability that you would consider acceptable to make it worthwhile for Mr. A to take the new job.
>
> 1. The chances are 1 in 10 that the company will prove financially sound.
> 2. The chances are 3 in 10 that the company will prove financially sound.
> 3. The chances are 5 in 10 that the company will prove financially sound.
> 4. The chances are 7 in 10 that the company will prove financially sound.

[40]LIPPIT, 1940; WHITE & LIPPIT, 1960. [41]BEVARD, 1951; FLANDERS, 1954. [42]MEADE, 1967.

5. The chances are 9 in 10 that the company will prove financially sound.
6. Mr. A should not take the new job no matter what the probabilities.

What is *your* choice, given this situation? If you regard the new job as acceptable under choice 1, you are obviously more of a risk taker than if you had picked choice 2, and even more so had you picked choice 3. If you are a cautious person who refuses to take *any* risk, your choice would obviously be the one advising against taking the new job, regardless of the odds (choice 6).

Individual choices, however, differ from group choices. Regardless of size, composition, and social climate, the manner of style of a group's decision making differs from that of the individuals who comprise it. A considerable body of research has shown a consistent tendency of groups to make decisions by consensus that, when compared to individual decisions, are characterized by being more risky. This phenomenon is known as the **risky shift**. (In a very few instances, group decisions are more cautious than individual decisions. Because of these *cautious shifts*, some psychologists refer instead to all such group decisions as *choice shifts*.)

Why is it that people who are *less* willing to express unorthodox ideas or opinions as individuals are *more* willing to do so collectively, in the name of the group? At the time of this writing, no clear-cut answer can be provided. Some psychologists contend that when people get together there is a "diffusion of responsibility"—that is, since individual group members know that the responsibility for the decision is spread among several others, their own sense of personal responsibility diminishes and they can therefore advocate a riskier course than they would ordinarily.[43] Other explanations for the risky shift phenomenon suggest familiarization (group discussion reduces individual uncertainty), pluralistic ignorance (erroneously having assumed that others are cautious), or leadership (the leader's ability to persuade individual members).[44] Some psychologists point out that responses to risk-taking questionnaires (as in the case of the hypothetical electrical engineer) only indicate what you *think* you will do, rather than what you will *actually* do.[45] This is known as the Walter Mitty effect, named after the James Thurber fictional hero who lived a sedate life but in his fantasies engaged in risky adventures.

In summary, it is entirely possible that, when a group of people come up with a risky decision, they may not necessarily act accordingly. But then again, they may. The implication that decision-making groups are prone to take greater risks than their individual members can scarcely be ignored when world leaders and their advisors gather to make vital decisions under the shadow of nuclear threat.

LEADERSHIP

Leadership and personality: Are leaders born or made?

It is a beautiful day in the city of Linz, Austria. The year is 1896. Mrs. Alois Schickelgruber, six months pregnant, is on her way to the market. As she crosses the street, she slips on a banana peel and falls. Later, in the hospital, she is given the sad news that she suffered a miscarriage. The result: Adolf Hitler never existed.

[43]WALLACH, KOGAN, & BEM, 1962, 1964, 1965. [44]PRUITT, 1971. [45]HIGBEE, 1971.

Would the course of history have been altered? Could it be that, in the absence of that spellbinding demagogue, Germany and the rest of the world would have been spared the agonies of World War II and genocide? If you think so, consider yourself a **Great Man** theorist on leadership (the label *person* was not common at the time this phrase was coined).

Or do you think that it really would have made no difference, since the time was ripe in the 1920s and 1930s for someone *like* Hitler to appear? Do you believe that the German national character, the humiliating experience of losing World War I, and the economic chaos prevailing at that time would have sprouted a Schultz, or a Krantz, or some other *Fuehrer* (leader) who would not differ significantly from the original product? If so, consider yourself a **Zeitgeist** (ironically, a German word denoting "spirit of the times") theorist on leadership.

It boils down essentially to the question of whether leaders are made (*Zeitgeist*) or born (Great Man). Like so many other maddening problems in human behavior, this poses a circular question that is almost impossible to answer. Yet psychologists have spent an inordinate amount of time and effort on this question, and their findings, as you may very well guess, depend to a large extent on their original stance. Most of the studies have focused on the personality characteristics of leaders and are thus prone to support the Great Man notion. A comprehensive review of such studies revealed that certain personality variables show a consistent relationship with displays of leadership: high intelligence, large physical size, great sociability and friendliness, self-confidence and self-assurance, and great will and energy.[46]

The single and most predominant leadership characteristic is the ability to talk and converse. Numerous studies have consistently shown a positive relationship exists between verbal participation rates in a group and leadership status.[47] Once again, however, we are confronted with the circular question: do leaders come into the group with the ability of verbal expression, or does their acquired leadership status require that they speak more often than others?

Effective leadership: The contingency model

Although it is possible that certain personality characteristics are associated with leadership, it is not a fruitful avenue of research. Apart from the circularity of the Great Man/*Zeitgeist* problem, there is ample research evidence to show that leadership is a function of personal traits of the leader *as perceived by the follower*. As the situation changes, so do the perceived traits of the leader.[48] Ask any politician who suddenly discovers that his or her charisma is gone!

Other studies on leadership take a more productive avenue of research. They focus on the contingent circumstances of the situation in which effective leadership is displayed. Psychologist Fred Fiedler first focused on the relationship between leaders and their *least* preferred group member in a variety of settings, such as infantry squads, bomber crews, basketball teams, and church groups. Leaders who described their least preferred coworkers in

[46]BERELSON & STEINER, 1964.   [47]STEIN & HELLER, 1979.   [48]CLIFFORD & COHN, 1964.

relatively unfavorable terms (low LPC scorers) tended to be controlling, directive, active, punitive, task oriented, and relatively uninterested in furthering good interpersonal relations.[49]

In his subsequent **contingency model** of leadership, Fiedler clearly spelled out the circumstances that particularly influence effective leadership: affective relationships (liking) between leader and followers; task structure (or ambiguity) in which the group is involved; and power of position (the legitimacy—or lack of it—of the leader's power). Extensive studies of a variety of groups and organizations have shown the consistency of effective leadership patterns. When things are going well for the group *or* when things do not go well, the leader who is a task-oriented, low LPC scorer is most effective; in the first case, because the group has no reason to reject him or her, and in the second case, because only his or her directive leadership saves the group from falling apart. When things are going neither very well nor very badly for the group (moderately favorable), however, then the socially oriented, high LPC-scoring leader becomes most effective.[50]

Leaders and followers: Banking idiosyncracy credit

As we have seen earlier, leadership is to a large extent a function of followers' perception. Studies in this area show an amazing degree of latitude on the part of followers in tolerating their leader's transgressions. People will allow their leaders to get away with murder, figuratively speaking—but only after the leaders have given ample evidence of their competence. This odd phenomenon has been thoroughly investigated by psychologist Edwin Hollander, who labeled it **idiosyncracy credit**. Idiosyncracy refers to a quality or habit peculiar to an individual. Hollander suggested that leaders who are initially perceived as conforming to the group's expectancies and subsequently show competence are awarded "credits" in the form of positive impressions by the group. These credits accrue over time until the leader reaches a point where he or she can engage in idiosyncratic behavior—even though such behavior may be at odds with the norms of the group. In short, once established, leaders can do their thing—and get away with it!

To demonstrate how leaders can cash in on idiosyncracy credit bestowed on them by their followers, Hollander had 12 groups of subjects engage in a choice task requiring 15 trials. Each of the four-person groups first agreed on certain procedures that would constitute the group's norms—such things as majority rule, order of choices, and the manner in which winnings would be divided. A confederate subject in each group contrived to be correct on all but 4 trials, thus reflecting considerable task competence. To achieve this competence, however, the confederate systematically violated practically every procedure to which the group had previously agreed. Despite such lack of conformity, the confederate received increasingly higher positive ratings by the others in his group.[51]

The fact that higher-status group members are allowed to nonconform with relative impunity has been demonstrated in many studies.[52] Not everyone is

---

[49]FIEDLER, 1958. [50]FIEDLER, 1963, 1967. [51]HOLLANDER, 1960. [52]BERKOWITZ & MACAULAY, 1961; JULIAN & STEINER, 1961; SABATH, 1964; WIGGINS, DILL, & SCHWARTZ, 1965.

that lucky, though. An interesting experiment by psychologists Harvey and Consalvi showed what happens to conformity in a status hierarchy. Groups of delinquent boys were asked to estimate the distance between two simultaneous flashes of light in a dark room. Unknown to the subjects, the leader and either the second highest or the lowest member in status were exposed to two flashes 48 inches apart, as compared to the two flashes 12 inches apart observed by the rest of the group. To increase motivation, group rewards for accuracy were promised to the subjects. Under the assumption that all were seeing the same light, verbal pressure against those who strayed in their judgments occurred since the judgments were made aloud. As expected, the leader strayed considerably. He simply called out what he saw, despite possible punishment by the group. Perhaps not too surprisingly, so did the lowest-status member (after all, what did he have to lose?). The second-in-status member did not dare to stray from the group's expectations and conformed accordingly.[53] No wonder that Number 2 in many a group or organization is so uptight—he or she simply has to try harder to meet the group's norms!

SUMMARY HIGHLIGHTS

1. Individual behavior is greatly influenced by the many social groups in which one participates. All groups share common characteristics known as *dynamics*.
2. People join groups for various reasons. When people are made anxious, they prefer to be with others who have undergone the same anxiety-arousing experience. In general, people will join groups of similar individuals, but if they are assured of a positive introduction into the group, they may choose to satisfy their curiosity by joining a group of dissimilar individuals.
3. The specific slot occupied by a particular individual in a group is a *position*. The behavior displayed by the occupants of a position is a *role*. The prestige associated with the position is *status*.
4. Studies such as the Stanford prison experiment demonstrate how behavior can be shaped by *social roles*. In that study, students were assigned as prisoners or guards in a simulated prison. After a brief time, "guards" came to behave like real prison guards, and "prisoners" came to act like real prisoners.
5. *Group communication* patterns have been simulated in experimental studies and have been described as *circles*, *wheels*, *Ys*, and other shapes. Experimental studies specify how group productivity and group morale are associated with the number of persons in a group and the extent that they are able to communicate with each other.
6. Bad decisions sometimes come out of group discussion. This problem, which has been labeled *Groupthink*, is most likely to occur when the group is highly cohesive and its members identify strongly with it.
7. Studies tend to show that small groups are more creative and effective than large groups. The *principle of least group size* suggests that the optimum group size for the performance of a task is the minimum

[53]Harvey & Consalvi, 1960.

number of individuals required to make available to the group all of the resources required for the execution of the task.
8. One of the reasons large groups may be ineffective is the phenomenon of *social loafing*. As more people are added to a group, the amount of effort exerted by individual group members decreases.
9. Another problem in the study of groups is whether or not to mix different types of individuals. The most effective groups will be those with the most capable people. A group with a high-, a medium-, and a low-ability member, however, is probably more effective than a group with three medium-ability participants.
10. *Social climate* studies have shown that both democratic and autocratic group climates are effective for accomplishing group tasks but that satisfaction in the former tends to be higher. Laissez faire group climates lead to neither high productivity nor high satisfaction.
11. Groups tend to make riskier decisions than individuals, a phenomenon known as the *risky shift*. Some groups also exercise *cautious shifts*.
12. Whether leaders are born (*Great Man* theory) or made (*Zeitgeist* theory) is not as productive a research focus as the study of the conditions that maximize leadership effectiveness. There is a tendency for followers to let a leader get away from the group norm after he or she has established competence. This effect is known as *idiosyncratic credit* for leaders.

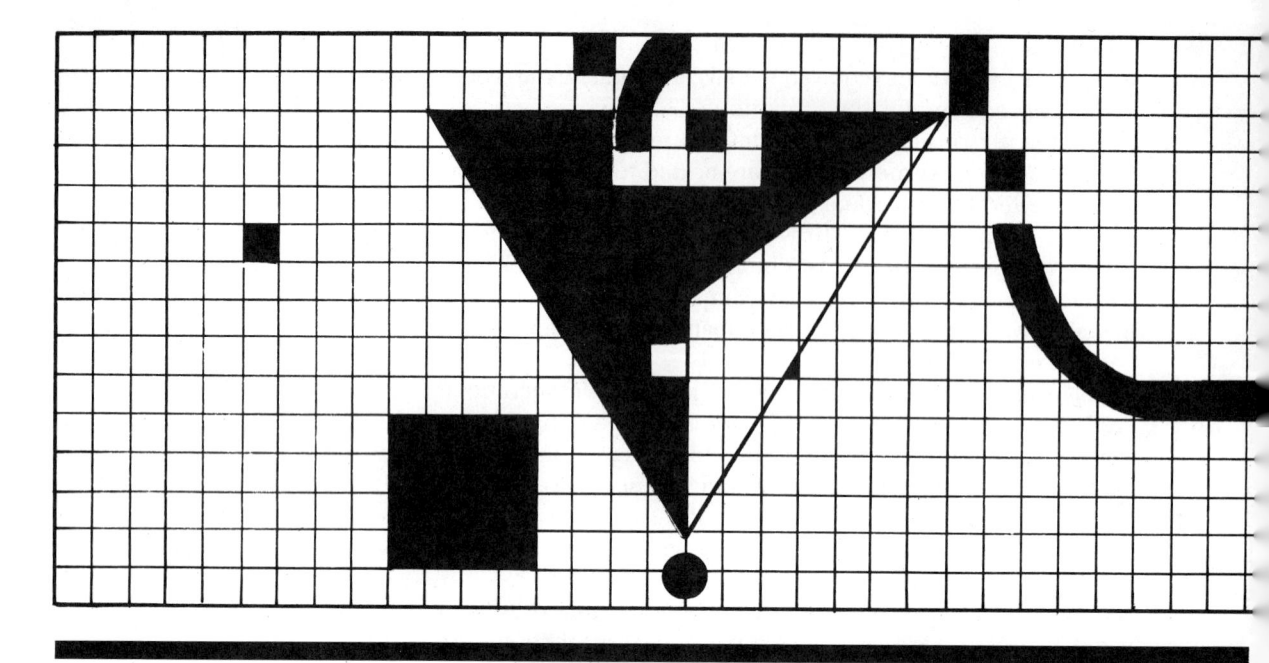

PART

SOCIAL

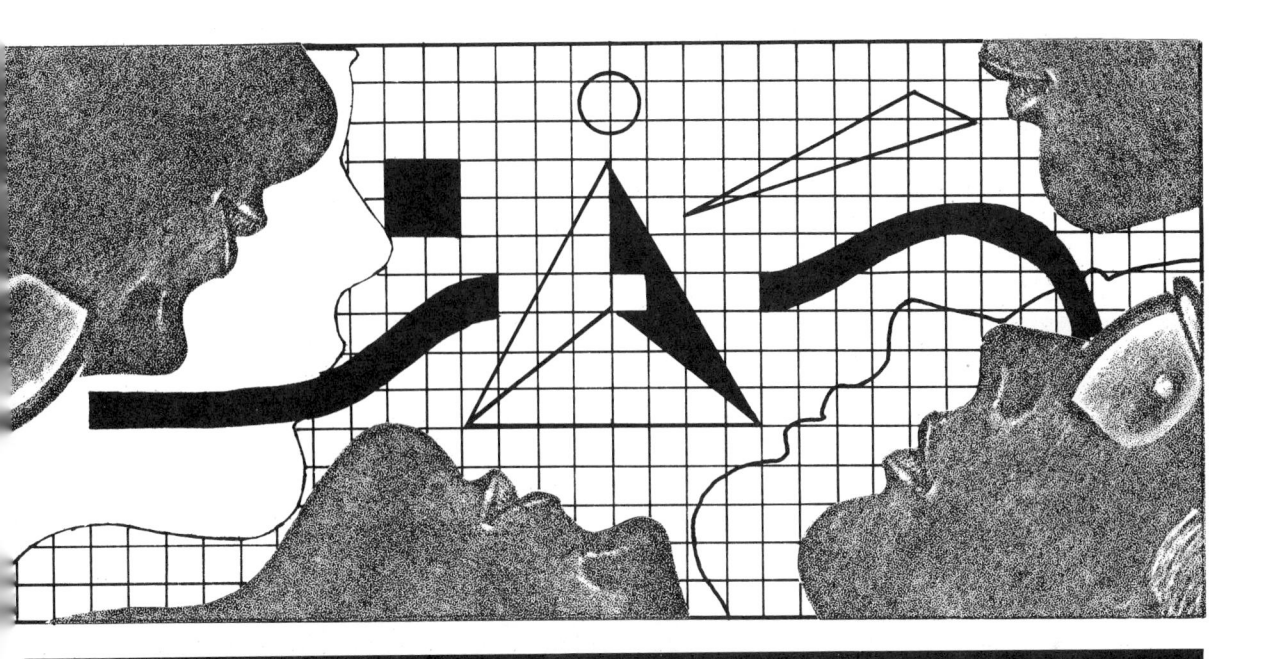

FOUR

I S S U E S

CHAPTER 9　PREJUDICE AND MORALITY

MISPERCEPTIONS AND PREJUDICE
　In search of "true" perception
　Halo wearers, stereotypers, and bigots
MORALITY: INDIVIDUAL DEVELOPMENT
　Moving through stages
　Machiavellianism: Any means to an end

MORALITY: SOCIAL DEVELOPMENT
　Law and order versus personal conscience
　Morality, politics, and religion
　Alienation: Getting away from it all
SUMMARY HIGHLIGHTS

MISPERCEPTIONS AND PREJUDICE

In search of "true" perception

Do you consider yourself an accurate perceiver? The evidence, on the whole, does little to support the notion that the ability to read character of others is a stable, measurable attribute. There are simply too many variables involved. Chief among these are the characteristics of the perceiver, the characteristics of the perceived person, and the situational context in which the perception takes place.

Before we deal with these issues, there remains the problem of what constitutes "true" perception. Because we are talking about accuracy of perception, it would imply that some absolute standard exists by which we can gauge people's perception. Unfortunately, there are no absolute standards. At best, we can say that "true" perception is a joint function of the degree to which the perceiver approximates the way others perceive a target person and the latter's perception of himself or herself. The following study is a good illustration of how psychologists obtain "true" perception criteria.

To study the effects of training and experience on perception accuracy, subjects were presented with 25 hypothetical situations and asked how they would react to them. At the same time, their close friends indicated how they thought these individuals would react. Subjects who showed the greatest consistency in their replies and whose friends judged them most accurately were subsequently chosen as target persons to be perceived. Judging these target persons were graduate and undergraduate students majoring in psychology, classics, and the natural sciences. Their task was to respond to the same 25 situations *as if* they were the target person, after the latter gave a 10-minute speech about labor relations. The actual responses of the target persons, which were already on record, thus served as a criterion. Accuracy of perception was measured by counting the number of times the friend's responses agreed with those of the target person.

The findings of the study suggested that relatively few people possess high perceptual accuracy: only 14% of the judges showed relatively high accuracy in their estimates of how the target person would react. Training and experience did not seem to be a critical factor: graduates were no more accurate than undergraduates, nor was any group of majors superior to others. It appears that some people are simply more accurate than others, but that this ability is limited to relatively few individuals.[1]

Nevertheless, it is possible to pinpoint some characteristics and attributes affecting a perceiver's accuracy. Most studies show that emotionally well-adjusted people show greater perceptual accuracy than their maladjusted counterparts.[2] People who are sociable, secure, and show a high degree of self-acceptance, however, often fall into a **leniency effect** trap that distorts their perception. They judge others too benevolently along the same dimensions that characterize them as perceivers. For example, on presentation of 200 photographs of persons to be judged either favorably (warm) or unfavorably (cold), perceivers rated as "very secure" made significantly more positive judgments than perceivers rated as "very insecure."[3]

Intellectually dull individuals tend to judge others inaccurately, but intellectual brilliance is no guarantee of accurate judgment. At best, perceivers who are above average in intelligence are more accurate than others in their judgment of people's intellectual abilities.[4]

Probably the most intriguing attributes in person perception relate to the sex or race of the perceiver. Although earlier studies have suggested that there are essentially no differences between the perceptual accuracy of males and females, more recent studies have shown differences in the way the sexes perceive each other. We shall deal with this issue at great length in the next chapter. When the effects of sex and race are combined, the results clearly favor race. In one study, 160 college students were equally divided by race and sex and asked to judge the emotions (anger, happiness, surprise, fear, disgust, pain, and sadness) portrayed by several Black and White professional actors of both sexes. Black perceivers, regardless of sex, were more accurate than their White counterparts. The experimenters concluded that these results could be expected because Blacks have developed a cultural sensitivity to emotional nuances during their long history of oppression in the United States.[5]

Accuracy in perceiving emotions does not necessarily mean that Blacks are more accurate in perceiving the *attitudes* of Whites. In one study, Black, Mexican-American, and White high school students were asked to fill out an attitude questionnaire concerning such issues as aggression, impulsiveness, and sex roles. Some of the people in each racial group simply replied to the questions and received no special instructions. Others filled out the questionnaire while playing the role of someone in one of the other racial groups. For example, some Black students filled out the questionnaire as themselves, other Black students filled it out as they thought White students would fill it out, still other Black students filled it out as they thought Mexican-American students would, and so on. The results were then examined to see how accurately the various groups were able to play the role of

[1]KREMERS, 1960. [2]NORMAN, 1953. [3]BOSSOM & MARLOW, 1957. [4]TAFT, 1955. [5]BLACK, 1969.

students in the other groups (this was done by comparing each group's scores when they were playing a role with the scores of the group that was filling out the questionnaires as themselves). The results showed that White students were the most accurate in their perceptions and Black students were the least accurate. The Black and Mexican-American students were quite inaccurate in playing the White role, and the White and Black students were fairly accurate in playing the Mexican-American role. The results, however, may be merely indicative of the fact that the White role is more ambiguous. After all, the label "White" applies to groups as diverse as Jews, Italians, Irish, and others.[6]

In any event, a word of caution is due because of the suggestion that oppressed minorities are more sensitive, and therefore more accurate, in their perception. Prejudice is a two-way street, and prejudiced individuals are notoriously inaccurate perceivers. In clinical settings, for example, Black patients tend to label Black therapists indiscriminately as servile collaborators of the White power structure, while White therapists are labeled in the same manner as patronizing reinforcers of the "Uncle Tom" tradition. Black therapists are no more accurate than their White counterparts. Depending on their attitudes toward Whites in general, Black therapists are either exceedingly punitive or permissive toward their White patients. White therapists, on the other hand, blanket-label their Black patients as hostile and uncommunicative.[7] Actually, contrary to popular belief, extreme and bigoted individuals are inaccurate even in their perception of the objects of their prejudice. The highly anti-Semitic individual, for example, will attribute the label "Jew" indiscriminately to others, just as the political extremist will attribute others with the undeserved label of "Red" or "Fascist."[8]

The characteristics of the perceived person are equally important in assessing perceptual accuracy. As we shall see later, the most important variable in perceptual accuracy is the willingness of the perceived person to expose himself or herself to others and the manner in which this is done. But there are other factors that are independent of one's willingness to be exposed. We have already seen that the perceived person's physical attributes, as well as any label applied to that person (name, occupation, and so on), can generate expectations and faulty perceptions. The perceived person's sex is just as important as the perceiver's sex as a factor in perceptual accuracy. There is evidence that females are more accepted than males as expressors of emotion because our society is more tolerant of such behavior in females than in males. As a result, females are generally judged more accurately than males.[9]

Sometimes the perceptual situation as such can have an effect on perceptual accuracy. How would you interpret the emotions of the person pictured in Figure 9-1? Pain? Passion? Anger? Elation? Determination? Meanness? Now turn the page and look at the picture in Figure 9-2. It shows a woman running in a track race. Her face is the same one you were asked to judge in Figure 9-1. Because you are now aware of the context of the situation, your judgment is more precise. You are likely to perceive determination or pain rather than anger or passion. As early as the 1930s, it was shown that additional knowledge of the situational context in which facial expressions occur will increase perceptual accuracy.[10]

[6]Kaplan & Goldman, 1973. [7]Sattler, 1970. [8]Scodel, 1957. [9]Manis, 1955. [10]Hulin & Katz, 1935.

Figure 9-1.
What are this person's emotions? Pain? Passion? Anger? Elation? Determination? Meanness?

Finally, there is some evidence that facial expression readings are overrated and that greater accuracy can be derived from bodily cues.[11]

Halo wearers, stereotypers, and bigots

You may have realized by now that not only are people's inferences and judgments governed by what they perceive, but that such perceptions are frequently inaccurate. Good-looking people are considered interesting and competent; people who wear glasses are perceived as intelligent and industrious. It appears that there is a tendency to blur one characteristic into another based on some speculative associations. This tendency is known as the **halo effect**. A person may convincingly display a certain socially desirable or valued characteristic—as, say, kindness, or dependability. His or her attributed halo allows for inferences that are by no means justifiable: kind, therefore trustworthy; dependable, therefore intelligent; good-looking, therefore interesting; and so on. Of course, not all halos are positive. He or she is dirty, also unreliable; lazy, and also stupid—are examples of negative halo effects.

Even though halo effects may be harmless in most daily interactions, they can become devastating under certain conditions. Think about what they can do when a person's job future depends on the evaluation of superiors, or when academic success depends upon the evaluation of instructors. The evaluators, of course, will always maintain that they perceive objectively on the basis of performance. Unfortunately, the halo effect may operate so subtly that the perceiver-evaluator is not even aware of it. If you were a teacher about to grade two papers of equal quality (as established by several outside objective judges), could you withstand the halo effect? That is, if one paper is delivered in a plastic cover, neatly typed by an electric typewriter on crackling bond paper, and the other is a handwritten, grease-stained, frequently erased

[11]LITTLEPAGE & PINEAULT, 1979.

Figure 9-2.
What are this person's emotions? (Compare with Figure 9-1.)

production—would you grade them equally? The temptation to deduce that the one writer is neat *and* intelligent *and* a good student must be great, just as it would be hard to resist the perception that the other is dirty *and* flighty *and* not a very good student. Some may even go as far as to suggest this is one of the reasons why, in our sexist society, girls (especially in elementary and junior high schools) often receive better grades than boys. After all, it is more enjoyable for the teacher to receive a neatly written paper accompanied by an occasional pressed flower than a grease-stained paper accompanied by an occasional frog.

Inaccurate perception of and by people is generally associated with the process of **stereotyping**. It refers to a relatively rigid and oversimplified perception or conception of an aspect of reality, especially of persons or social groups. The perception of "bankers," or "women," or "Irish," in general and without discrimination (except possibly for a particular banker, woman, or Irishman), is known as stereotyping. The term comes from printing—it is difficult to make changes once the metal *stereotype* is cast—and, as experimental data have shown, the process follows a systematic sequence (see Box 9-1).

Psychologist John Brigham has defined an ethnic stereotype as "a generalization made about an ethnic group concerning a trait attribution, which is considered to be unjust by the observer" (p. 31).[12] This definition distinguishes between stereotyping and other forms of generalization. The important defining characteristic of stereotyping is that the observer knows that the characterization is unjust.[13]

[12]BRIGHAM, 1971.   [13]MCCAULEY, STITT, & SEGAL, 1980.

Box 9-1. Five steps in the stereotyping process

Step 1. *The categorization and organization of incoming information:* People are being categorized on physical and social dimensions such as "male," "Black," "laborer," and the like.

Step 2. *The minimization of within-group differences and the exaggeration of between-group differences:* This step is reflected in judgments such as "Blacks are similar to each other and different than Whites."

Step 3. *The use of stereotypical terms for within-group members' behavior:* In employing stereotypical grouping, "warm" is perceived as female behavior and therefore "motherly"; or "aggressive" as male behavior and thus "macho," and so on.

Step 4. *The exaggeration of within-group attributes in inverse proportion to the size of the minority group:* For example, people will selectively distinguish (recall, or differentiate) Blacks better and Whites worse if they judge a group of two Blacks and four Whites than if they judge a group of four Blacks and two Whites.

Step 5. *The attribution of similarity in inverse proportion to familiarity with the grouped objects:* The more familiar people are with their own subgroups, the better their ability to differentiate within their own subgroup. For example, White subjects do not distinguish among Black faces nearly as well as among White faces, and thus the notion "They (Blacks) all look alike."

Source: Taylor, Fiske, Etcoff, & Ruderman, 1978.

The negative by-products of stereotyping are reflected most dramatically in racial, ethnic, and sexist discriminatory practices. At this point we would like to demonstrate stereotyping in seemingly harmless and innocuous areas remote from potential prejudice and bigotry.

A name is a label and as such generates certain expectations. Names such as Jim, Herman, Adrian, Michael, Elmer, Susie, or Bertha generate certain expectations. Could these expectations carry with them serious consequences for the bearers of those names? Unfortunately, the answer is yes.

To begin with, there is evidence that grade school children with unattractive names are less popular than those with attractive names. To rule out the possibility that these findings were a result of the children's attitudes toward their classmates rather than vice versa, ratings for the names were also taken from children in other classes. The results were the same. Whether merely names or people, Adelle, Elmer and Sanford were rated lower than Jim, Karen, and Michael.[14] As if being unpopular with their classmates were not enough, bearers of unattractive names also face trouble from their teachers. Names of students can lead to nondeliberate bias in teachers' judgments of academic performance, as shown in an experiment involving blind grading of essays by fifth-grade teachers. The essays were linked to fifth-grade authors by first names only. The same essays were randomly associated with four names stereotyped by teachers as attractive and favorable (David, Michael, Karen, and Lisa) and four regarded as unattractive and unfavorable (Elmer, Hubert,

[14] McDavid & Harari, 1966.

Bertha, and Adelle). Even though the same essays were associated with different names for different teachers, those reported to be authored by favorable names were graded a full letter grade higher than those reported to be authored by unfavorable names![15]

What does all this mean? Are people called Elmer, or Hubert, or Bertha losers who are doomed to fail? Not necessarily. A name is just a label and, along with the other labels attributed to us, can constitute either an asset or a liability. As a rule, a first name is a relatively small asset or liability. A person called Ebenezer can still be the most popular person with his peers and teachers and display no sign of stress. By way of analogy, a thoroughbred race horse can be handicapped with additional weights and still come in first every time. But not all horses are thoroughbreds, nor are all people perennial winners. Just as some horses will fall behind as the weight on them increases, so will people who carry various labels that handicap them. Sometimes as small a handicap as an unattractive name can assume major proportions in a person's adjustment problems, just like the proverbial straw that broke the camel's back. The evidence shows, especially among males, that common names are more positively evaluated than uncommon names, and that people who dislike their first names have less positive attitudes toward themselves than people who like their first names. Studies of clinical institutions have shown that people with uncommon names (e.g., Horace and Allison) tend to have more severe problems than those with common names.[16] One study has shown that males named after their fathers (Jr., II, or III) perceive their fathers as dominant and controlling.[17]

Despite this evidence, the problem of names and their consequences should be kept in perspective. Since stereotypes are not constant, neither are name preferences. They change with time and location. The late Senator Hubert Horatio Humphrey has been quoted as saying "My name has never been a problem to me."[18] This is probably true, considering his age at the time and Midwestern origin. But will it be true of his grandson, Hubert Horatio IV? The real problem is that, in the process of naming their offspring, parents often succumb to what is a fad at the time, the need to be original, or the desire to be cute. One has only to glance at the following actually documented named to perceive parental folly:

Adam Apple
Hard Ware
Quick Silver
Sunny Rainday
Pansie Pickenpaugh

In addition, there are such documented first names as Dink, Rhebus, Derwin, Fourth-of-July, and Halloween.[19] Can you imagine the childhood of these people before they had the good sense (and authority) to change their names?

Changing the handicapping name is probably the best solution, even though some people prefer to fight back, as "A Boy Named Sue" did in Johnny Cash's famous song. In any event, if you are dissatisfied with your name but

[15]Harari & McDavid, 1973. [16]Kibler & Harari, 1974. [17]Bennet, 1974. [18]Names can hurt, 1974. [19]Kibler & Harari, 1974.

intend to keep it, you may be heartened to know about the activities of the Harvey Liberation Movement. Cartoons, television, movies, and sometimes advertisements have made the name "Harvey" the symbol of the fumbling and inept male. In the spring of 1965, Harvey Edwards organized 150 prominent Harveys for support in a campaign to end this denigration of the good Harvey name. As a result, three television commercials were retired by their ad agencies.[20] This is Harvey Power!

As pointed out earlier, given the human tendency to make such statements as "Women are . . . ," "College students are . . . ," "Blacks are . . . ," and so on, it is not too surprising that stereotyping has been intimately linked with prejudice and bigotry. If the term *prejudice* refers to rendering a judgment on the basis of limited and incomplete information, then stereotyping is indeed related to prejudice (but not necessarily the "negative" kind, since one can also prejudge favorably). If the term implies bigotry (as it generally does, and as we shall refer to it henceforth), stereotyping begins to assume more complex dimensions. But then the entire issue of prejudice and bigotry is complex and highly sensitive. Perhaps a better way to deal with the problem is to ask ourselves the following questions:

Is stereotyping invariably related to bigotry? If so, how? If not, where do the two terms differ?
Are stereotypes based on truth? If so, can they be eliminated, changed, or reduced?
What are the practical results and effects of stereotyping?

The relationship between prejudice and stereotyping can be summed up best by the following dictum: *people who are prejudiced stereotype, but people who stereotype are not necessarily prejudiced.* In a study appropriately entitled "Race and Belief: An Open and Shut Case," it was shown conclusively that the major differentiating factor in the perception of others was belief similarity (for example, the other person was perceived more positively if he or she resembled the perceiver in academic status or interests), rather than race. Only when information about belief was lacking did race become the major differentiating factor. Presumably this happened because the perceivers were forced to fall back on partial information supplied by racial stereotyping.[21]

The matter of information is crucial here. Although stereotypes lead to bias, they provide *some* information to help us to make accurate predictions about others. For example, the belief that males perform better on tasks requiring physical strength is not simply an illusion. Thus, knowing a person's gender may help you to predict how much weight an individual can lift. If you take time to learn more about that person, however, you will also find that you would have been a much better predictor with more information. Some women can lift more than the average, or the above-average, man. Using the information gained from the stereotype only helps prediction when more complete information is unavailable.[22]

In another study, White subjects presented with photos of Blacks persisted in stereotyping their features as "Black" as long as the Blacks were recogniza-

[20]Don't Tread on Harvey, 1965. [21]Stein, Hardyck, & Smith, 1965. [22]McCauley, Stitt, & Segal, 1980.

ble as such. The process continued regardless of the extent to which Caucasian physical features were discernible. Still, there were so many individual differences in the kind of attributes being judged as characteristic of Blacks that the investigators had to conclude that, in addition to stereotyping by consensus, many individuals have their own personality theories by which they judge others.[23] Some of these "theories" may be of such obscure origin as to be virtually undetectable. How can one explain *why* Adrian is perceived as artistic, Jim as athletic, and poor Herman as stupid?

Though stereotyping may thus be an inescapable fact of life, it does not mean that the bases from which positive or negative traits are attributed to a group are identical. A study involving 80 Black and 80 White college students in the Washington, D.C. area showed significant differences in the way Blacks and Whites, regardless of the social class to which they assign themselves (middle or lower), stereotype race and social class (see Table 9-1). The White subjects' stereotyping was solely on the basis of class: middle class is perceived positively (high) and lower class is perceived negatively (low), regardless of race. The Black subjects' stereotyping was primarily on the basis of race: Blacks are perceived positively (high) regardless of class; Whites are perceived less positively (fair) if they are of middle class, and negatively (low) if they are of lower class.[24]

Table 9-1. Favorability ratings (stereotyping) by Blacks and Whites

		Blacks Middle Class	Blacks Lower Class	Whites Middle Class	Whites Lower Class
RATERS — Blacks	Higher class (self-assigned)	high	high	fair	low
	Lower class (self-assigned)	high	high	fair	low
RATERS — Whites	Higher class (self-assigned)	high	low	high	low
	Lower class (self-assigned)	high	low	high	low

Source: Smedley & Bayton, 1978.

Are stereotypes based on truth? This is a critical question, considering that so much racial and ethnic prejudice involves stereotyped perception. The answer, alas, is that there is a kernel of truth in stereotypes. It is possible to show that many (*never* all) Blacks are educationally inferior by pointing to their poor academic performance.[25] It is possible to show that Jews are overachievers and overrepresented in the college population.[26] It is possible to show that many men display high levels of career achievement and many women display the lack of same.[27] It is, however, a serious mistake to assume that these relationships are invariant, or "fixed." They are merely the product of social training that produces behavior that validates social expectations

[23]Secord, 1959. [24]Smedley & Bayton, 1978. [25]Jensen, 1969, 1980. [26]Clark, 1949; Jospe, 1965. [27]Horner, 1969.

generation after generation. For example, among American farmers and infantry soldiers, the percentage of Jews is probably exceedingly small, whereas among American business executives their percentage is relatively large (referring to small retail businesses rather than industries such as oil, steel, and automobiles). To understand this phenomenon, one must know something about the history of the Jewish people. Centuries of persecution and denial of opportunities for jobs and land inevitably take their toll. Jews were forced to fall back on their own meager resources—to live by their wits, so to speak. The ensuing reverence for knowledge, learning, and the entire educational process is, therefore, not too surprising. A rabbi is revered for his knowledge; he is a learned man rather than a middleman between congregants and God. The intrusive Jewish mother who trains her children to revere education is an inevitable by-product of such a milieu. The proud Jewish mother who tells her neighbor, on being asked how old her children are, that "the lawyer is 7 and the doctor is 9," is far from atypical. Little wonder, then, that evidence consistently shows that Jewish children are overachievers in school.

The fact of the matter is, however, that all of these traits are not a "fixed" characteristic of Jews wherever they are. Could the American-Jewish stereotype of the unadapting farmer, poor soldier, and shrewd business executive be applied to the Jew in Israel? Obviously not. Each of these stereotypes is, in fact, reversed in Israel. The stereotype there (once again, based on a kernel of truth) is of the Jew as a first-class farmer and fighting soldier. The constant bankruptcy facing that country certainly does nothing to further the image of its inhabitants as efficient and affluent business managers.

The moral of this example should be obvious: as conditions change, so do stereotypes. Those who discriminate and those who are objects of prejudice can do much to change conditions, which in turn will change the direction of stereotyping. But it is difficult to expect the impetus for such change to come primarily from those who discriminate. Such expectations may be based on strong ethical foundations, but they are hardly realistic. People who exercise their privilege to discriminate are often reluctant to give up this practice. Only if the objects of discrimination actively do something about the conditions that breed prejudice does stereotyping take a different direction. The impressive results achieved over the past decade by the so-called power movements (Blacks, Mexican-Americans, Native Americans, Asian-Americans, women, gays, and senior citizens) have already radically changed the content of many common stereotypes.[28]

In their zeal to combat injustice, however, many of the power movements do not always exercise wisdom in the manner in which they allocate their meager resources. Too often, they spend more time and effort fighting the stereotyped image rather than the actual conditions that gave rise to it in the first place. Both types of action are important, but without changing conditions stereotyping will persist. As long as people are aligned with an identifiable social entity, there will be stereotyping. Old stereotypes never die. They just fade away—*but new ones emerge immediately* (see Table 9-2).[29]

The saddest and most disturbing effect of stereotypes is that they may become **self-fulfilling prophecies.** If you throw a person in the gutter and

[28]McDavid & Harari, 1974. [29]Karlins, Coffman, & Walters, 1969.

TABLE 9-2. Three generations of stereotypes: as old ones fade away, new ones emerge

	Percentage of attributed traits		
	1933	1951	1967
AMERICANS			
Industrious	48	30	23
Intelligent	47	32	20
Materialistic	33	37	67 [a]
Ambitious	33	21	42 [a]
GERMANS			
Stolid	44	10	9
Aggressive	—	27	30 [a]
IRISH			
Pugnacious	45	24	13
Extremely nationalistic	21	20	41 [a]
ITALIANS			
Artistic	53	28	30
Passionate	37	25	44 [a]
JAPANESE			
Sly	20	21	3
Industrious	43	12	57 [a]
JEWS			
Shrewd	79	47	30
Mercenary	49	28	15
Ambitious	21	28	48 [a]
BLACKS			
Superstitious	83	41	13
Lazy	75	31	26
Musical	26	33	47 [a]

[a] Newly emerging stereotypes.
Source: Karlins, Coffman, & Walters, 1969.

forcibly hold him there for some time, you will be telling nothing but the truth if you label him dirty. Coupled with the fact that you will continue to treat him as a dirty person, there is little wonder that the person in the gutter begins to accept this label as a fact of life. Many eminent clinicians have pointed out that a patient with the label of say, schizophrenic, causes all others to treat him or her according to certain expectations, until this person resignedly becomes what the label implies.[30] Nowhere has the devastating effect of the self-fulfilling prophecy of expectations been better demonstrated than in the area of education. In their classic experiment, psychologists Robert Rosenthal and Lenore Jacobson demonstrated an effect they appropriately called "Pygmalion in the Classroom." After selecting a group of children randomly from several classes, their teachers were told that these children were "intellectual bloomers who will show unusual intellectual gains during the academic year." And they did! The teachers *expected* them to do better and therefore treated them accordingly (spoke to them more often, listened to them more often, presented them with more challenging tasks, and so on).[31] It seems that if teachers have certain expectations about the poor academic performance of ghetto children, their treatment of them will result in poor academic performance. If a student is expected to go to trade school, the chances are that his or her academic performance will justify such expectations.

[30] Szasz, 1970. [31] Rosenthal & Jacobson, 1968.

Discriminatory practices in the United States that arose as a function of widely believed stereotypes about Black inferiority may have produced an inferior subculture into which Blacks continue to be assimilated. The social consequences can even be powerful enough to resist perceivers' expectations. A study involving White teachers-in-training showed, as expected, that, when interacting with supposedly gifted White students, the teachers bestowed upon them the most favorable preferential treatment. Surprising—and disturbing—was the fact that supposedly gifted Black students got the worst treatment (even worse than the ordinary Black students). These findings are significant even though (or perhaps because) the description of the supposedly gifted Black students did not fit the conventional negative stereotype of the Black student.[32]

With the exception of the few bigots whose blatant discriminatory practices involve no apologies on their part, those who practice exclusion of others generally do so under the protective mantle of some higher-order morality. For example, six all-Black and all-White groups of adolescents were observed playing a game in which "Humanus," a voice on a tape recorder, informed them that they were "the last surviving people on earth after a disaster." Humanus then gave them choices that required group discussion and decision on several issues, including whether or not to let a possible contaminated survivor join them in their safe area. The groups of Whites decided not to permit the survivor to join them but the Black groups did. *All* groups invoked moral considerations, but of different kinds: the Whites' morality was humanity oriented, and the Blacks' was people oriented. The White groups contended that it was their responsibility to survive as the sole remaining representatives of the entire human race, whereas the Black groups insisted that they take a chance on the survivor because he was still alive and because they were not absolutely sure whether they themselves were contaminated or not.[33]

Moving through stages

MORALITY: INDIVIDUAL DEVELOPMENT

Question (to you, the reader): Are you a liar?
Answer (indignantly): Of course not!
Question: Have you ever lied?
Answer: Well . . .
Question: Yes or no?
Answer: Yes, on occasions . . .
Question: Doesn't that make you a liar?
Answer: Of course not! Everyone lies once in a while. Didn't you ever hear of "white lies"?
Question: What are those for?
Answer: If you don't want to hurt someone's feelings . . . or in a case where lying won't cause as much harm as telling the truth.

Congratulations! You have just demonstrated that you are past the stage of **moral realism**. According to the late psychologist Jean Piaget, up to age 7 or 8

[32]Rubovits & Maehr, 1973. [33]Haan, 1978.

your conception of justice is based on rigid and inflexible standards of right and wrong. Lying is wrong under all circumstances. As you grow older, the absolute standards of moral realism turn into those of **moral relativism**. Your concept of justice becomes tempered with notions of equity and fairness. You realize that under certain circumstances lying is justified. You may lie to save others embarrassment. You may lie to prevent a worsening situation from turning into a disaster. You recognize the utility of fibs and white lies.[34]

Piaget's original formulations have recently been extended by psychologist Lawrence Kohlberg, who suggests that there are three general levels of moral development, each marked by two stages:

Preconventional, Stage 1. This stage is characterized by punishment and obedience. You do the right thing because of fear of punishment. Your morality is determined by the physical consequences of your action. Typical age: up to about 7.

Preconventional, Stage 2. Your morality is determined by your personal needs and satisfaction. It is a selfish approach that considers the needs of others only to the extent that favors will be returned. It is a "scratch my back and I'll scratch yours" type of morality. Loyalty, gratitude, and justice hardly enter the picture at this stage. Typical age: 7 to 10.

Conventional, Stage 3. Your morality is determined by conventional role expectations. You do what a good boy or a nice girl should do. Typical age: 10 to 13.

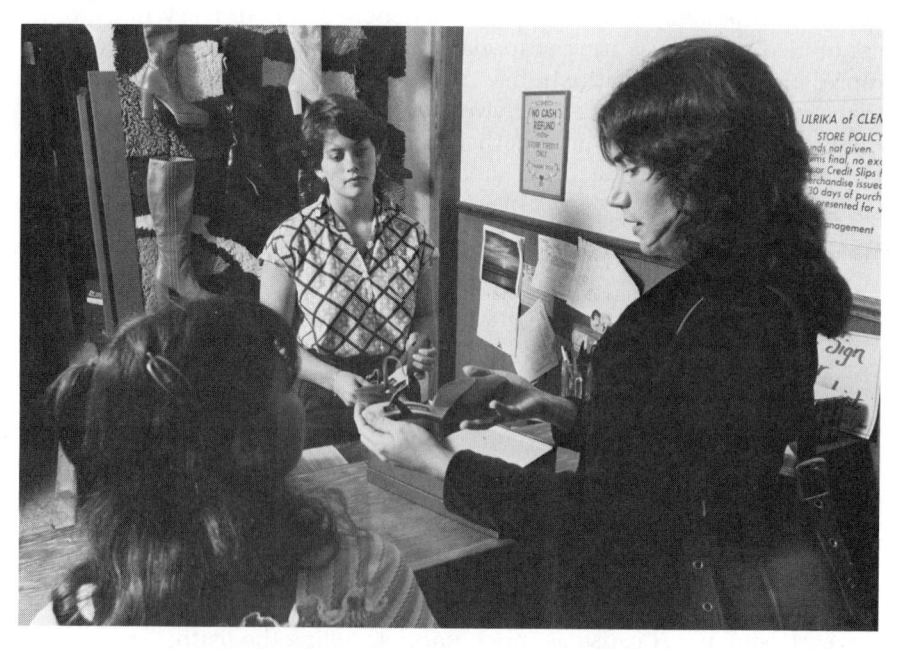

"I bought these shoes two weeks ago but I never wore them because they didn't fit. I would like a refund, please." The mother's little white lie is not acceptable to her young morally realistic daughter. As she grows into a moral relativist, such lies are accepted as a matter of course.

[34]PIAGET, 1932.

Conventional, Stage 4. This stage involves broader concepts such as conventional rules of behavior, community standards, and the requirements of law and order. Your morality is determined by duty, respect, and maintenance of social order. Typical age: 13 to 16.

Postconventional, Stage 5. Moral codes are no longer perceived as absolute. If they can be amended to serve the good of the community adequately, they should. Your morality is determined by conventional rules serving as means to an end, not ends in themselves. Typical (ideal) age: adulthood.

Postconventional, Stage 6. Your morality is determined by universal principles of justice and human rights. Typical (ideal) age: adulthood.[35]

Kohlberg does not suggest that all of us go through this sequence. In fact, *relatively few people ever reach stage 5, and even fewer pass into stage 6.* Many adults remain fixated at certain levels, and many others often regress to lower levels. Kohlberg's method of scoring people's responses is also very complicated and cumbersome. To simplify matters, psychologists Karen Maitland and Jacqueline Goldman have developed a Moral Judgment Scale (MJS) and an abbreviated scoring method.[36] First, consider the following situation:

> Your mother is near death from a special form of cancer. There is one drug that the doctors think might save her. It is a form of radium that a druggist in your town has recently discovered. The drug is expensive to make, but the druggist is charging ten times what the drug cost him to make. He pays $200 for the radium and charges $2000 for a small dose of the drug. You have gone to everyone you know to borrow the money, but you can only get together about $1000, which is half of what it costs. You tell the druggist that your mother is dying and ask him to sell it to you cheaper or let you pay later. But the druggist says, "No, I discovered the drug and I'm going to make money from it." So you get desperate and break into the man's store and steal the drug for your mother. *Why shouldn't you steal the drug?*

Notice that the question refers to why you should *not* steal the drug. It does not necessarily assume that you will do so. The six listed answers that follow, according to Maitland and Goldman, correspond to the six stages of development formulated by Kohlberg. For greater clarity, we have italicized key phrases for each stage.

1. I am quite desperate in this situation and I may not truly realize I'm doing wrong when I steal the drug. *But I'll certainly know I've done wrong after I'm punished and sent to jail.* I'll always feel guilty about being dishonest and breaking the law (the effect of punishment).
2. I may not get much of a jail term if I steal the drug, but my mother will probably die before I get out, *so it won't do me much good.* If my mother dies, I shouldn't blame myself, it isn't *my* fault if she has cancer (self-centered needs).
3. I'll get caught and sent to jail if I do. If I get away, *my conscience will bother me thinking how police will catch up with me any minute* (not living up to role of honest citizen).
4. It isn't just the druggist who will think that I am a criminal, *everyone else will too.*

---

[35]KOHLBERG, 1968. [36]MAITLAND & GOLDMAN, 1974.

After I steal it, I'll feel bad thinking *how I brought dishonor on my family and myself;* I won't be able to face anyone again (regard for social convention).
5. If I stole the drug, *I wouldn't be blamed by other people, but I'd condemn myself* because I wouldn't have lived up to my own standards of conscience and standards of honesty (disregard of social convention).
6. I would lose my standing and respect in the community and *violate the law.* I'd lose respect for myself *if I'm carried away by emotion* and forget the long-term effects of my action (total adherence to the justice principle).

In comparing Piaget's and Kohlberg's notions of moral development, you may be wondering who is more flexible: the immature youngster who condemns lying under *all* circumstances or the adult in the exalted sixth stage who would *never* steal a drug for his fatally ill mother. It is clear, though, that the morality of young children is based on primitive conceptualizations. Consider the following two situations:

1. John is in his room when his mother calls him to dinner. John goes down and opens the door to the dining room. But behind the door is a chair, and on the chair is a tray with 15 cups on it. John does not know the cups are behind the door. He opens the door, the door hits the tray, bang go the 15 cups, and they all get broken.
2. On a day when Henry's mother is out, Henry tries to get some cookies out of the cupboard. He climbs up on a chair, but the cookie jar is still too high, and he can't reach it. But while he is trying to get to the cookie jar, he knocks over a cup. The cup falls down and breaks.

Clearly, John's and Henry's positions are not alike. John has committed a well-intentioned act (following mother's call for dinner) that, however, resulted in considerable damage. Henry has committed a transgression (trying to get to the cookies while his mother was absent) that resulted in only minor damage. According to Piaget, young children under about the age of 8 display a strong tendency to ignore the intent behind an action. In their rigid way, they espouse *objective responsibility.* That is, when faced with the John and Henry situation and asked "Who did the naughtier thing?" they regard John as the real culprit simply because of the great damage he had caused. Older children, on the other hand, endorse *subjective responsibility:* despite the fact that he caused so much damage, John is seen as less guilty than Henry because John's good intents are weighed heavily in this case.

In all fairness to the rigidity of Piaget's morally realistic youngsters, it must be admitted that the greater flexibility of the morally relativistic older children and adults is not always colored by noble motives. That is, not all our fibs and white lies are caused by a wish to protect others from harm. A selective process seems to be operating because of possible conflict over what constitutes a transgression. Consider, for example, the moral dilemma of preadolescents. At this age, youngsters are already past their rigid morally realistic code. They nevertheless face a serious problem when they learn that one of their peers has committed a transgression. On one hand, there is the implicit commandment "Thou Shalt Tell Authority (parent, teacher, law enforcement

According to Piaget, young children display objective responsibility. They judge the seriousness of a transgression by how much damage is done. As the children grow older, they develop a sense of subjective responsibility. Thus, this boy's actions would not be judged as naughty unless he intended to break the cups.

agency, and so on) When Your Peer Does Wrong." On the other hand, there is the well-known norm "Thou Shalt Not Fink On Your Friend."

One of these writers, along with psychologist John McDavid, conducted a study that forced preadolescents to make this moral choice. Two experimental confederates were recruited among the youngsters to act as transgressors. One of them was very popular with his peers and as such was assigned to be the high-status transgressor. The other confederate was not very popular with his peers and thus was assigned to be the low-status transgressor. The witnessed transgression was either theft of money from the teacher or a deliberate erasure from an important series of tapes. In both staged transgressions, the malicious intent of the transgressors was obvious. The subjects were then called in by adult authority (school principal) and interrogated about their knowledge of what they had witnessed earlier.[37]

What does a youngster do under the circumstances? There is good evidence that the moral judgment of children can be modified into various directions by adult models[38] even more than by peers.[39] Since the model in this case (the principal) indicated that transgression must be reported, the subjects could be expected to do so. They did indeed—as long as they were interrogated alone. *Then* all subjects finked freely about both transgressors, regardless of their status. When interrogated in pairs, however, the subjects

[37]HARARI & MCDAVID, 1973.   [38]BANDURA & MCDONALD, 1963.   [39]DORR & FEY, 1974.

showed a curious type of flexibility. They protected the high-status transgressor to the end by refusing to divulge any information to the adult authority. Little of this consideration was evident when they were queried about the low-status transgressor: they reported his transgression without hesitation. The motive for this kind of behavior is obvious: because the subjects were interrogated in pairs, each subject knew that his behavior could easily become common knowledge among his peers. Finking on a popular peer can lead to unpleasant results. The unpopular peer can be thrown to the dogs, so to speak.

This twisted type of morality is by no means limited to children and adolescents. Adults excel in it, too. Psychologist Karen Dion showed adults pictures of children who had previously been rated as physically attractive or unattractive. The subjects were then told that the children had committed various transgressions, such as torturing a dog or deliberately injuring another child. Compared to the unattractive children for identical transgressions, the attractive children fared much better in the adult evaluation. The attractive children not only received less blame, but their transgressions were seen as less severe.[40]

Twisted morality, however, is not necessarily limited to a pervasive belief in the excellence of attractiveness. Take the case of shoplifting (as shown earlier, see Chapter 7): the evidence shows that the number of people who report shoplifters after witnessing the crime is incredibly low (from 6% to 28%).[41] This breach of the moral code should not be too surprising in view of the fact that corporate victims arouse little sympathy.[42] Ripping off the corporation is, more often than not, perceived as a righteous act by the exploited against the exploiter. Even if you condemn shoplifting and do not want to fault the victim, you can always minimize the transgression. You can argue that if the crime were *really* serious, the store's security forces, who use a one-way observation window for scanning the area, would have arrested the thief without waiting for anyone to report him or her. Besides, the potential rewards for reporting shoplifting are notoriously minimal. Corporations offer little if any monetary rewards or generous expressions of thanks for the conscientious customer who reports the crime. On the other hand, taking action is bound to be time consuming, inconvenient, and perhaps even dangerous.[43]

Machiavellianism: Any means to an end

Throughout history, many prominent people have taken a rather jaundiced view of morality and conscience. Charles Pierce, the well-known American physicist and logician, suggested that, because morality and conscience mean nothing more than blind obedience to the traditional maxims of one's community, "morality is—I will not say immoral, that would be going too far—composed of the very substance of immorality." Friedrich Nietzche, the German philosopher, equated conscience with stupidity because "at every failure, conscience finds an excuse as an encouragement in itself. That is why there are so many conscientious and so few intelligent people." Fyodor

[40]Dion, 1972. [41]Dertke, Penner, & Ulrich, 1972; Gelfand, Hartman, Walder, & Page, 1973. [42]Shaver, 1970. [43]Gelfand, Hartman, Walder, & Page, 1973.

Dostoyevski, the Russian novelist, bemoaned the fact that freedom of conscience is not only seductive, "but nothing is a greater cause of suffering." The notorious German leader, Adolf Hitler, simplified the entire problem by promising his followers: "I am liberating man from the degrading absurdity known as conscience."

Despite their frontal attack on morality, none of these men ever took the time for a systematic promotion of *immorality* as a political philosophy. That dubious honor remains with Niccoló Machiavelli, the Italian statesman and political writer (1469–1527). Machiavelli's cynical views of how leaders successfully manipulate their followers suggest that immorality can be elevated to a fine art. The ideal leader, according to Machiavelli, "should know how to color his nature well, and how to be a great hypocrite . . . for men are so simple, and yield so much to immediate necessity." Moreover, since "common people are always taken by appearances and results," as long as the leader pretends to be on a "friendly footing with the vulgar mass that constitutes the world" he can be sure that "the means which he employs for his end will always be accounted honorable, and will be praised by everybody." Open force should be used sparingly as a means to an end, not because of moral reasons, but because "I do not believe that there was ever a man who from obscure condition arrived at great power; but there are many who have succeeded by fraud alone." As a final exercise in utter perversity, Machiavelli recommends that moral beliefs should be promoted in the interest of immorality: "Anything that tends to favor religion (even though it were believed false), should be received and availed to strengthen it . . . for it is easy to keep the people religious, and consequently well conducted."[44]

Turning back to present times, it would be a mistake to assume that morality and conscience are on the way out. Granted, the morality of believers in a just world or a capricious world is obviously based on some twisted logic. But it is also a tortured morality, in the literal sense of the word. The derogation and loathing of an innocent victim is not done out of joy, or as a result of deliberate planning, or because of some deep-seated personal philosophy. It is the result of anxiety, guilt, shame, or fear for one's fate. All these are part of what is known as "conscience." To label such people (who, in fact, constitute a majority) as immoral would be incorrect.

Still, there is a little bit of Machiavelli in all of us. Psychologists Richard Christie and Florence Geis have used simple paper and pencil tests to measure **Machiavellian** attitudes. You can test yourself on the sampler provided in Table 9-3.

One of the more encouraging findings by Christie and Geis was that, by and large, most of their subjects were able to strike a reasonable balance between expressing high and low Machiavellian attitudes.[45] High Machiavellians were more likely to be males than females, to come from urban backgrounds, and to be relatively young members of society. They tended to be cool and detached, resistant to social pressures, rational and logical. They were able to cheat on tests and deny it while staring the accuser coolly in the eye.[46] When given the

---

[44]Seldes, 1966. [45]Christie & Geis, 1970. [46]Geis & Christie, 1970.

TABLE 9-3. Are you a Machiavellian?[a]

		Disagree a lot	Disagree a little	Neutral	Agree a little	Agree a lot
1.	The best way to handle people is to tell them what they want to hear.	1	2	3	4	5
2.	When you ask someone to do something for you, it is best to give the real reasons rather than giving reasons that might carry more weight.	5	4	3	2	1
3.	Anyone who completely trusts anyone else is asking for trouble.	1	2	3	4	5
4.	It is hard to get ahead without cutting corners here and there.	1	2	3	4	5
5.	It is safest to assume that all people have a vicious streak and it will come out when they are given a chance.	1	2	3	4	5
6.	One should take action only when sure it is morally right.	5	4	3	2	1
7.	Most people are basically good and kind.	5	4	3	2	1
8.	There is no excuse for lying to someone.	5	4	3	2	1
9.	Most men forget more easily the death of their fathers than the loss of their property.	1	2	3	4	5
10.	Generally speaking, men won't work hard unless they're forced to.	1	2	3	4	5

[a]Check the point on the scale that most closely represents your attitude. To find your Mach score, add the numbers that you have checked in each column. The National Opinion Research Center, which used a form very similar to this in a random sample of American adults, found that the national average was 25.
Source: Christie and Geis, 1970.

chance for offensive manipulation, such as license to confuse or distract other subjects engaged in a complex embedded-figures test, low Machiavellians were simply no match for high Machiavellians in devilish ingenuity. The low Machiavellians came up with a limited number of tactics which, as they later reported, they did not even find enjoyable. The high Machiavellians greatly enjoyed innovative manipulations such as using makeshift springs to send ballpoint pens flying across the room, knocking over tables to send papers flying in all directions (while profusely apologizing at the same time), tapping pencils rhythmically on the table, jingling contents of pockets noisily, and so on.[47]

One of the most interesting findings by Geis and Christie was that professions that require the manipulation of people tend to have high Machiavellian clusters: for example, psychiatrists as opposed to surgeons; social psychologists as opposed to physicists; and so on. The cynical view reflected in the stereotype of the American politician is, of course, not new. In view of recent events, from the packaged *Selling of the President*[48] through the Abscam scandal in which members of the House of Representatives were filmed taking bribes, Machiavellianism seems to have made a remarkable comeback. Even

[47]GEIS, CHRISTIE, & NELSON, 1970. [48]MCGINNIS, 1969.

American business and industry may have to take a second look at their highly touted job enrichment programs. The purported aim of such programs has been to humanize the dreary boredom of routine jobs like the assembly line by providing the workers with some interesting and meaningful, if costly, additional activities. Laurence Zeitlin, an industrial psychologist, tells us now that a little larceny can do a lot for employee morale. After reviewing the pilfering and cheating by employees in jobs ranging from bakeries through clothing stores to toll booths, Zeitlin claims that not only do employees find such activities highly enriching and satisfying, but management gets a bargain to boot. Theft serves as a safety valve to employee frustration and costs the management, on the average, no more than $1.50 per worker a day. Permitting a controlled amount of theft can thus get management off the hook from such costly items as job enrichment or wage increases.[49] The perfect Machiavellian solution!

Law and order versus personal conscience

MORALITY: SOCIAL DEVELOPMENT

From the evidence presented so far, you may have concluded that morality is a relative matter. Despite individual fluctuations, however, the overall framework is quite stable for our society. The Judeo-Christian code of justice and compassion for others is accepted as a product of normal social development. Differences of opinion are largely confined to *how* best to implement this code of ethics.

The law-and-order viewpoint is best summarized by Sigmund Freud:

> Human life in common is only made possible when a majority comes together which is stronger than any separate individual and which remains united against all separate individuals.... The first requisite of civilization, therefore, is that of justice—that is, the assurance that a law once made will not be broken in favor of an individual.[50]

The personal conscience viewpoint is put forth by Carl Jung, a disciple of Freud who later parted ways with his teacher:

> Morality was not brought down on tables of stone from Sinai and imposed on people, but is a function of the human soul, as old as humanity itself.... We have it in ourselves from the start—not the law, but our moral nature without which the collective life of human society would be impossible.[51]

These two viewpoints are, of course, diametrically opposite. They exemplify two extreme philosophies that serve as rallying points for all shades of in-between opinions. Psychologists Robert Hogan and Ellen Dickstein have developed a measure that can assess your own viewpoint in this matter. For example, if you are a strong law-and-order advocate, you are likely to endorse an item such as "Right or wrong can be meaningfully defined only by law." If you believe in a personal conscience, you are more likely to endorse items such as "All civil law should be judged against a higher moral law," or "An unjust law should not be obeyed."[52]

There is evidence in support of both viewpoints. Those who believe in a

[49]ZEITLIN, 1971. [50]FREUD, 1961. [51]JUNG, 1956. [52]HOGAN & DICKSTEIN, 1972.

personal conscience can cite a remarkable survey on morality among college students. The survey was taken on various college campuses throughout the nation during the years 1939, 1949, 1958, and 1969. On all occasions, the students rated the wrongness of 50 acts, all of which could be considered immoral. Examples of the acts included killing a person in defense of one's life, forging a check, and advertising a medicine to cure a disease known to be incurable by such a remedy. Sexual behavior, religious behavior, corporate responsibility, and a host of other topics were covered as well.

The alarming decline in morality frequently cited by the law-and-order proponents was not reflected in this survey. In fact, throughout the many years there was a remarkable stability in the expression of high moralistic principles. Frowned-on behavior ranged from misrepresentation (such as a student allowed to grade his or her own paper reports a higher grade than the one earned) to the immorality of war (such as nations at war using poison gas on the homes and cities of its enemy behind the lines). The only marked change was in the area of sexual morality (such as having sex relations while unmarried). As expected, contemporary college students did not rate these items as severely as their predecessors did. The ratings on this topic by contemporary students suggested that both males and females tended to reduce the previously held double standard in sex roles. In the overall ratings of the items, however, the females tended to be more severe than the males. This, too, was in line with previous findings.[53]

In contrast to this optimistic view of morality, proponents of law and order pointedly refer to two other studies on morality among college students. The first study shows that college students experience moral conflict in a variety of areas but are highly selective about which area to apply mature solutions. Reported conflicts with moral overtones were in the area of social relations (35%), honesty (19%), sexuality (14%) and politics (12%). In line with Kohlberg's previously discussed model, the quality of solutions were found to range from the immature, selfish type of preconventional morality to the noble, selfless type of postconventional morality. The findings also indicated that the students were willing to apply mature solutions in the rather detached political-ideological conflict areas. When it came to personal and concrete areas of conflict such as honesty, solutions were more often marked by selfish immaturity.[54] According to the law-and-order proponents, these results should not surprise us. When college students were put in a position where they could cheat in class, moral appeals to refrain from doing so were totally useless. On the other hand, there was a "clear and substantial effect" when threat of sanction was invoked.[55] Sanction, as defined by the dictionary, means "making certain that the law will be obeyed."

Morality, politics, and religion

To apply lofty principles of morality to the game of politics is either futile, as many cynics contend, or downright stupid, as practical Machiavellians will readily tell you. Political ideology, however, is a horse of a different color. All of us have certain ideas of what good government is or should be, which is what

[53]GORSUCH & SMITH, 1972. [54]BUTLER & SEIDENBERG, 1973. [55]TITTLE & ROWE, 1973.

political ideology is all about. Even those who are so alienated as to drop out from the political scene express, as we shall see later, a political ideology of sorts.

As for the perception of those who practice good citizenship and vote within the system, it is colored by sentiments: those who admire a candidate tend to see him or her as promoting policies they themselves favor (*assimilation*), and those displeased with a candidate show the opposite tendency (*contrast*). There is, however, a lack of balance in people's political choices. The assimilation effect is very powerful since it is essential for citizens to see candidates they like (and have chosen) as holding positions similar to their own on *all* issues; disliked candidates, on the other hand, do not need to be seen as uniformly dissimilar. Thus, if a candidate has a lone positive attribute (for example, is a good leader), it may not be sufficient to induce liking and support, whereas even a single negative attribute (for example, is a wheeler-dealer) is sufficient to induce dislike and lack of support.[56]

Psychologists, unlike political scientists or sociologists, are understandably more interested in various personality characteristics used to express political beliefs. One of the earliest studies was conducted in the 1950s by a group of psychologists at the University of California headed by T. W. Adorno. Their findings, summarized in *The Authoritarian Personality*, were based on a comprehensive study of college students, public school teachers, public health nurses, prison inmates, mental patients, veteran groups, labor union members, and members of the Kiwanis Club. The study originally was aimed at investigating the roots of anti-Semitism, but as time went on it became increasingly evident that extreme anti-Semitic attitudes did not exist in isolation. Closely related to such attitudes was an implicit antidemocratic ideology which, among other things, advocated political and economic conservatism, antagonism to out-group members (such as minorities), unbounded patriotism, and a reverence for power.[57]

The morality of the **authoritarian** personality is exemplified by some of the statements he or she endorses. The authoritarian is clearly a rigid and punitive believer in law and order[58] but also advocates values that are part of personal conscience, such as a strong belief in the perfection of the American way of living. The overall profile of the authoritarian is not flattering, though. He or she emerges as a rigid, power-oriented, crusty right-winger. This is precisely one of the reasons why the findings of Adorno and his colleagues have come under increasing criticism. Obviously, many law-and-order conservatives do not fit this caricature of rigidity, just as many extreme liberals do fit it. Thus, psychologist Milton Rokeach prefers the term **dogmatism** or *ideological dogmatism*, to describe a relatively rigid outlook on life with intolerance toward those with opposing beliefs. Rokeach found that both authoritarian left-of-center groups (Communists and religious nonbelievers) and authoritarian right-of-center groups (devout Catholics) tend to embrace similar dogmatic values (see Table 9-4).[59] Rokeach's reasoning seems to be based on solid foundations. Evidently, political extremism has an appeal for its own sake. A poll by the American Institute for Public Opinion in 1971

[56]KINDER, 1978. [57]ADORNO, FRENKEL-BRUNSWICK, LEVINSON, & SANFORD, 1950. [58]BRAY & NOBLE, 1978. [59]ROKEACH, 1960.

among a wide sample of college students and a standard sample of the United States adult population showed that a significant portion of sympathizers with far-right organizations such as the John Birch Society and the Ku Klux Klan gave favorable ratings to far-left organizations such as the Students for Democratic Society, the Weathermen, and the Black Panthers; and vice versa.

TABLE 9-4. Typical statements endorsed by authoritarians and dogmatists

AUTHORITARIANS
Obedience and respect for authority are the most important virtues children should learn.
Young people sometimes get rebellious ideas, but as they grow up they ought to get over them and settle down.
Every person should have complete faith in some supernatural power whose decisions he obeys without question.
When a person has a problem or worry, it is best for him not to think about it but to keep busy with more cheerful things.
Nowadays, when so many different kinds of people move around and mix together so much, a person has to protect himself especially carefully against catching an infection or disease from them.
Wars and social troubles may someday be ended by an earthquake or flood that will destroy the whole world.
People are divided into two distinct classes: the weak and the strong.
Homosexuals are hardly better than criminals and ought to be severely punished.
The wild sex life of the old Greeks and Romans was tame compared to some of the goings-on in this country, even in places where people might least expect it.
Certain religious sects that refuse to salute the flag should be forced to conform to such patriotic action or else be abolished.
America may not be perfect, but the American Way has brought us as close as human beings can get to a perfect society.

DOGMATISTS
Most people just don't give a damn for others.
It is only natural for a person to be rather fearful of the future.
It is better to be a dead hero than a live coward.
If I had to choose between happiness and greatness, I'd choose greatness.
Once I get wound up in a heated discussion, I just can't stop.
I have often felt that strangers are looking at me critically.
To compromise with our political opponents is dangerous because it usually leads to the betrayal of our own side.
It's all too true that people just won't practice what they preach.
There are two kinds of people in the world: those who are for the truth and those who are against the truth.

Source: Adorno, Frenkel-Brunswick, Levinson, & Sanford, 1950; Rokeach, 1960.

The same survey also produced the encouraging findings that, by and large, the American public rejects extremism. Both far-left and far-right extremists were rejected by an overwhelming margin (95%). The morality of extremists should thus be kept in proper perspective, because they appeal to a relatively small segment of our society. As for most of us, consider the following items:

Duties are more important than rights.
You can't change human nature.
The heart is as good a guide as the head.
No matter what people think, a few people run things anyway.
Few people know what is in their best interest in the long run.

Do you agree with these statements? Do they constitute part of your value system, which guides your moral code? You may be interested to know that authoritarian and dogmatic individuals generally endorse such statements. If you did so, does this label you as an authoritarian or dogmatic person? Of course not. Even if you endorsed some of the items in Table 9-4, you do not necessarily qualify as a highly authoritarian person. The key word, obviously, is "highly." Authoritarianism is a matter of degree, with very high scoring individuals comprising a minority segment of the population.

If political ideology is not sufficient to promote equality and brotherhood, righteousness and justice, humanitarianism and compassion—what else is there? The obvious answer that comes to mind is religion. Few people will disagree that religion performs a key role in our society. Philosophically speaking, the disagreement may center on whether religion, as sociologist Emile Durkheim claimed, maintains social solidarity by "sacredizing" the structure of society,[60] or, as Karl Marx maintained, by being a corrupting "opiate of the people."[61] Psychologists, however, are less interested in philosophical speculations than in the personality and behavioral correlates of religious beliefs and practice. Here we encounter what psychologist Gordon Allport has called the great paradox. Whereas many great figures whose lives embodied the highest moral precepts—Christ, St. Ambrose, Mahatma Gandhi, Martin Luther King, and many others—were religiously motivated, religious practice as such has consistently been associated with rigidity, intolerance, and downright bigotry.[62]

To begin with, religious people in general have been found to be less humanitarian than nonreligious people. They have more punitive attitudes toward criminals, delinquents, prostitutes, homosexuals, and those in need of psychiatric treatment.[63] If this sounds similar to the description of the authoritarian personality, you are on the right track. One of the major characteristics of the latter is the expression of deep religiosity and unbounded faith (see Table 9-4). On the average, religious people show more intolerance than nonreligious people, not only toward ethnic groups but to any ideological group that does not conform to in-group standards.[64] It has also been shown that, whereas frequent church attendance is associated with high socioeconomic status and college education,[65] highly educated nonattenders are less prejudiced than attenders.[66] Clearly, the poor humanitarian record of the churchgoer cannot simply be attributed to low education.

Fortunately, the dismal picture of religion and morality is open to further interpretation. Think, for example, of some religious people that you know and ask yourself: are their religious beliefs intrinsic or extrinsic? Allport, who coined these phrases, suggested that intrinsic believers *live* their religion, since they have fully internalized religion's high moral precepts. They are practicing what religion preaches, but they do so out of deep moral convictions rather than as a means for their own ends. Extrinsic believers *use* religion for a variety of needs—to provide security and solace, sociability and distraction, status and self-justification, and so on. Other investigators using

---

[60]Durkheim, 1965. [61]Marx & Engels, 1964. [62]Allport & Ross, 1967. [63]Kirkpatrick, 1949. [64]Stouffer, 1955. [65]Demerath, 1965. [66]Struening, 1963.

similar descriptions, such as nuclear, devout, associational (seeking the deeper value of faith), modal, or communal (for the purpose of sociability and status), have shown that the intrinsic believer is *not* prejudiced or intolerant.[67]

Let us now reexamine the findings of the relationship among prejudice, intolerance, lack of humanitarianism, and the personal practice of religion. Extrinsic believers attend church infrequently—just enough to satisfy their personal or social needs. Intrinsic believers attend church regularly, because it is part of their internalized code of living rather than a means for their own ends. Thus, the overall findings that church attenders are more prejudiced than others is only true up to a point. Statistically speaking, this is known as a curvilinear relationship. It means that, although it is true that most attenders are more prejudiced than nonattenders, a significant minority of them are *less* prejudiced (see Figure 9-3).

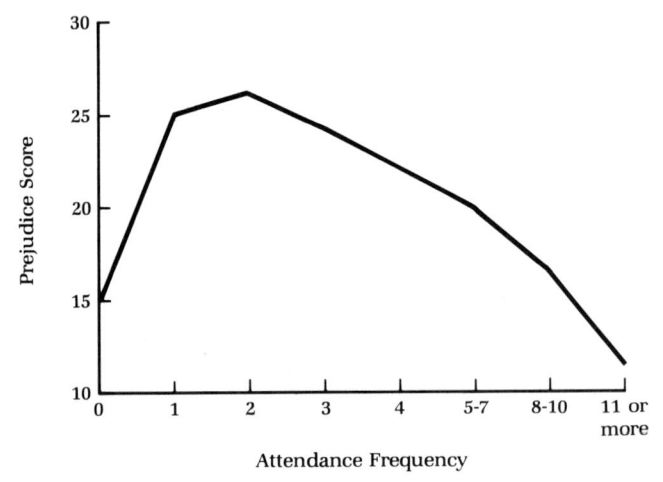

Figure 9-3. Church attendance and prejudice among faculty members of a Midwestern university. Source: Allport & Ross, 1967.

In summary, the evidence suggests that those who have either given up on religion or who cynically disparage it may be acting too hastily. Religion *can* be an effective vehicle for promoting human welfare and morality. The behavior of the devout, intrinsic believer is living proof of this contention.

Alienation: Getting away from it all

"Those were the days, the good old days!" is a stock phrase with which you are undoubtedly familiar. Sooner or later, somebody you meet will extoll the merits of the past, when men were men (whatever that means), when the family gathered around the piano in close harmony, when house doors remained unlocked, and when trust, honesty, and the fear of God were the order of the day.

Many people, disenchanted with the lack of old-fashioned virtue and morality in our present society, yearn for those good old times. Just how good those times really were is open to speculation. Nostalgia has a way of making things in the past seem better than they actually were. It is true, however, that

[67]FICHTER, 1954; LENSKI, 1961.

our complex technological society carries with it the potential of alienation. There is increasing evidence of *powerlessness*—a feeling of inability to understand or to influence events occurring in the mass societies of the twentieth century; of *normlessness* (anomie)—a lack of purpose and direction to life; and of social isolation—a feeling of separation from society and its standards.[68] Many political writers, philosophers, sociologists, and psychologists have addressed themselves to the problem of alienation. It has become almost routine to define all of our troubles, and to seek solutions, in the language of alienation—so routine, in fact, that some writers feel that the term *alienation* has been overrated, is of dubious validity, and should be divested of its mystique.[69]

Be that as it may, there was a time when alienation could be dealt with in a relatively simple manner. Look at the previously described components of alienation (powerlessness, normlessness, and social alienation). Would you be surprised if you were told that these feelings increase with advancing age? Would you be surprised if you were told that, with higher levels of occupational prestige, education, and income, there is less alienation? Probably not. Indeed, until recently, alienation was seen as the exclusive domain of the aged, the poor, and the uneducated.

Until the 1960s, that is. At that time, *youth* began to enter the picture. It was the decade of the counterculture that dictated "Don't trust anyone over 30." It was the decade of a pointless war in Vietnam, of long hair, of the Woodstock festival, of rejection of traditional values, of the generation gap. Suddenly, alienation was no longer limited to the old and the poor. Psychiatrists, psychologists, sociologists, and educators vied with one another in invoking the concept of alienation to explain the baffling behavior of the young, affluent, college-educated rebels.

What was myth and what was reality about the alienation of young people in the 1960s? Now, in the 1980s, when materialism seems to flourish and university business colleges are flooded with applications, the alienation of the young in the 1960s may seem somewhat quaint and arouse only mild interest (see Box 9-2). Psychologically speaking, however, the topic reflects a wider historical perspective. There existed a curious paradox in the lifestyle of the young rebels of the 1960s. On one hand, there were feelings of alienation from society, which dictated apathy, withdrawal, "doing your own thing." On the other hand, this was the time when student activism to produce social change was at its peak. Prodded by the injustices of the Vietnam War and the hypocrisy of their elders, student activists literally mounted the barricades to achieve the kind of world they wanted. The content, industrious, apathetic, and somewhat ridiculous panty-raiding student of the 1950s simply disappeared. The newly emerging activists, as described in the glowing accounts of those who studied them, were liberal, intelligent, tolerant, and sensitive to poverty, injustice, and the misfortunes of others.[70]

There were, of course, some discordant notes here and there. Political activism can easily produce extremism, and, as we have already seen, extremism of both the far left and the far right is often associated with rigidity and

[68]DEAN, 1961. [69]SEEMAN, 1971. [70]FLACKS, 1967; BLOCK, HAAN, & SMITH, 1968; HAAN, SMITH, & BLOCK, 1968.

intolerance. Several studies had also shown that the so-called generation gap came close to being a myth. One such study, involving over 3000 young people between the ages of 12 and 18 from all walks of life, showed a remarkable amiability in the relationship between young people and their parents.[71] Other studies showed a marked similarity between young people and their parents on practically every aspect of daily life, ranging from ways to raise children, career choices, religious beliefs, and voting behavior.[72] It became increasingly evident that, at best, the student activists represented a rather narrow segment of the college population. Even though their impact upon fostering an ideological gap was undoubtedly great, the generation gap as such may not have been as formidable as it once appeared to be.

Box 9-2. The times they are a changin'

During the 1960s, a number of young people became media stars for fighting the establishment. Some of the best known of the student radicals were Jerry Rubin, Abbie Hoffman, and Tom Hayden. During the 1970s, these men who had worked so hard to radicalize others became deradicalized themselves. The seventies seemed to mellow them out.

Jerry Rubin was perhaps the most emotional of the sixties radicals. In 1967, Rubin singlehandedly stopped the New York Stock Exchange by throwing dollar bills from the visitors' gallery and watching the "pigs" scramble for the bucks. In 1968, Rubin led the drive to run a symbolic pig for the United States Presidency as a comment on the other candidates.

By 1980, Rubin had changed significantly. He accepted a job with John Muir and Co., a New York securities firm. Rubin, who cast aside his Yippie garb for a three-piece suit, commented "Welcome Wall Street, here I come! Let's make millions of dollars together" (p. 23)[73]

Most humorous of the sixties radicals was *Abbie Hoffman*. Hoffman became famous for his mockery of public figures and his books. One of his books, titled *Steal This Book*, advised people on methods for "ripping off" the system and avoiding the capitalistic way of life. In 1973, Hoffman ran into trouble with the New York police when he attempted to sell 3 pounds of cocaine to an undercover officer. Rather than face charges, Hoffman went underground. In 1980, seven years later, he came forward to turn himself in. During his time as a fugitive, Hoffman spent a quiet life on a tiny island in the St. Lawrence River; living under the name "Barry Freed," he worked as a writer and attracted little attention.

Although Hoffman went through the seventies attracting little attention, his friend *Tom Hayden* continued to attract headlines. Like Rubin, Hayden switched his attire to a three-piece suit. He married actress Jane Fonda and began an organization to fight for social and economic change from within the system. He even ran (unsuccessfully) for the United States Senate. By the early 1980s, Hayden had attracted a strong following from a variety of political groups.

Another discordant note was in the findings that alienation and violence were often closely related. This paradoxical finding was clearly established in

[71]DOUVAN & ADELSON, 1966.   [72]CROSS, 1968; LUBELL, 1968; ADELSON, 1970.   [73]RUBIN RELENTS, 1980.

Jerry Rubin as a Yippie in the 1960s and as a Wall Street securities broker in 1980.

a study of Black males between the ages of 18 and 35. Unlike middle-class Blacks who participated in organized civil rights protests, the population in this study (65% of which fell in the "highly alienated" category) seemed to have lost faith in their leaders. They had little hope for improvement through organized protest and viewed violence as the only realistic recourse for obtaining racial justice.[74]

Although student activism is presently in decline, there is little doubt that the young counterculture of the 1960s has left its impact. To some extent, alienation is part of that legacy. An extensive survey of American college students between the years of 1950 and 1970 on what constitutes "the good life" provides some insight in this matter. The major finding of the study is that there has been a continuing rejection of what the authors call "conservatism in the finest sense": the idea that, to preserve the best man has attained, it is best to exercise social restraint, self-control, and avoid radical changes in society. There was also a continuing tendency among the students to favor withdrawal ("meditating on the inner life") and self-sufficiency ("cultivate independence of person and things"). Almost one-half of the respondents did not believe that present-day American society is favorable for realizing the life they would like to live.[75]

Recent studies in alienation have turned from the problems of society to problems of individual adjustment. Alienation is now being studied primarily in the context of depression, narcissism, aggression, suicide, and a variety of other psychiatric disorders.[76] This brings up a final point. Since the 1960s, it has been common practice to link alienation and drug abuse, in line with the

[74]RANSFORD, 1968.   [75]MORRIS & SMALL, 1971.   [76]LEONARD, 1973; MEISSNER, 1974.

dropping-out and turning-on syndrome of the counterculture. Several studies have documented the fact that heavy users of marijuana and psychedelic drugs experience alienation.[77] It is important, however, to make a distinction between societal alienation and personal alienation. One study of marijuana usage divided 168 college students into four categories: nonusers, experimenters, recreational users, and "potheads." Alienation from conventional standards was directly associated with degree of marijuana usage. But this collective alienation from socially accepted goals and standards (**societal alienation**) is not the same as **personal alienation**, which is marked by individual feelings of isolation, remoteness, cynicism, distrust, and apathy. Such personal alienation, with its clinical overtones, is unrelated to either marijuana usage or the use of hard narcotics. The student who uses marijuana does not necessarily view himself or herself as different from the nonuser, nor does he or she feel any more personally estranged and isolated. The most that can be said about this student is that he or she operates within a "hang-loose" ethic marked by a degree of societal alienation, causing rejection of some conventional social norms.[78]

SUMMARY HIGHLIGHTS

1. Relatively few people are able to perceive accurately the emotions of others. Some studies have shown that Blacks are more accurate than Whites in perceiving the emotions of others but are less accurate in perceiving attitudinal and behavioral characteristics of Whites than Whites are of Blacks.
2. The tendency to infer that one characteristic of an individual is positive because another characteristic is desirable is called the *halo effect*. *Stereotyping* is a relatively rigid and oversimplified perception or conception of persons or social groups. The tendency to judge others merely on the basis of their gender, religion, or race is an example of stereotyping.
3. *Prejudice* involves making judgments on the basis of limited and incomplete information. Bigoted and prejudiced people almost always make judgments of others on the basis of stereotypes, but not everyone who stereotypes is bigoted or prejudiced.
4. Stereotyping alters cognitive closure, cannot be eliminated, has a kernel of truth to it, and has the potential for turning into self-fulfilling prophecies.
5. Moral development goes through certain defined stages. The best-known stages of development have been outlined by Kohlberg, who suggests that there are three general levels of moral development, each marked by two stages. The last level, *postconventional reasoning*, involves moral reasoning that may be beyond that of most members of society. Studies also show that there are situational determinants for moral reasoning. For example, children are more likely to "fink" on a classmate when they are interrogated without witnesses and when they are telling on an unpopular classmate.

[77]JESSOR, JESSOR, & FINNEY, 1973; KNIGHT, SHEPOSH, & BRYSON, 1974.   [78]HORMAN, 1973; KNIGHT, SHEPOSH, & BRYSON, 1974.

6. *Machiavellian* individuals believe that anything is useful as long as it accomplishes the desired goal. The morality of an *authoritarian personality* is characterized by antidemocratic ideologies, antagonism toward minorities, unbounded patriotism, and a reverence for power. A similar type of morality is exhibited by those scoring high on *dogmatism*. Dogmatists, however, come from either end of the political spectrum, whereas authoritarians tend to be right wingers.
7. Religious beliefs appear to be related to morality. People who attend church for extrinsic reasons, however, do not hold beliefs advocated in the teachings of the church. People who attend church very frequently or very infrequently score lower on measures of prejudice than people who attend church occasionally.
8. *Powerlessness* is the label for personal feelings of inability to understand, or to influence events, occurring in the mass societies of the twentieth century. *Normlessness* or *anomie* is the sensation of lack of purpose and direction caused by same. *Social isolation* is a feeling of separation from society and its standards. All these feelings may lead to personal or societal *alienation*.

CHAPTER 10   SEX ROLES AND SEXISM

SEX TYPING
    The battle of the sexes
    What men think women think—and vice versa

SEXIST STUDIES
    Monkeymen and women
    The body watchers

WOMEN'S LIBERATION
    Women's lib begins in the crib
    Is anatomy destiny?

SEXIST GAMES
    Will Anne succeed in medical school?
    Who was that doctor?
    Who does the housework?

ADJUSTMENT PROBLEMS AND SOLUTIONS
    Healthy for women—sick for men
    The solution: Psychological androgyny?

SUMMARY HIGHLIGHTS

SEX TYPING

The battle of the sexes

Nicolas Chauvin was a French soldier and a follower of Napoleon. After the fall of Napoleon, Chauvin became known for his grotesque gestures of attachment to his deposed leader, including extreme discrimination against any foreigners, in the belief that the French were superior. Little did Chauvin know that a few hundred years later his name would be included in a phrase people use to refer to men they believe to be obnoxious. As Chauvin believed the French were all-powerful, some people believe the male sex is superior. The term *male chauvinist* has come to refer to a man who holds the belief that women are creatures inferior to men.

From Nicolas Chauvin, let us turn to Bobby Riggs. On September 20, 1973, Bobby Riggs faced Billie Jean King in a tennis match billed as "the battle of the sexes." The 55-year-old Riggs had received considerable attention in the press for being a hustler and self-proclaimed male chauvinist. He claimed women were not fit to compete against men. King had also been in the public light. She had been cited both for her excellence on the tennis court and for her leadership in the establishment of equal rights and rewards for female tennis players. As the date of the event approached, the match took on a symbolic meaning. The Riggs image became synonymous with the attitude that women should know their place and should not be allowed to compete in a man's world, and King's image became fused with the ideals of Women's Liberation.

Social psychologists like to take advantage of real-life events, and this tennis match seemed like a good chance to collect such data. The study that was subsequently designed operated under the reasonable premise that preference for Riggs might be a good index of male chauvinism and preference for King might reflect feminist beliefs. It was a real opportunity to study what men thought women thought (and vice versa) about a well-known and controversial issue.

A reciprocal role-play method for the study of intergroup perceptions was chosen as the method of investigation, requiring some students to play the role of an average classmate of the opposite sex. Because subjects were responding as average males or females, the measured perceptions could be considered an index of intersex stereotypes. The reciprocal role-play method thus allowed for the assessment both of the nature and the accuracy of intergroup stereotypes.

On the day of the match, 18 male and 18 female college students were asked (1) to predict the outcome of the match, and (2) whom they preferred to win. They were also asked how strongly they felt about their beliefs and preferences. Half of the male and half of the female respondents answered the questions as themselves; the others played the role of a member of the opposite sex when responding. After the match, subjects chose a reason for King's victory.

The results of this study indicated that men and women differed in their attitudes and beliefs about the King-Riggs tennis match. Both men and women answering wanted King to win. Women, however, had stronger preferences for King. Compared to the average man, the average woman was viewed by both sexes as being more supportive of Billie Jean King. This was apparent from attitudes about the preferred victor in the match, predictions about the outcome of the match, and postmatch attributions about the cause of King's victory.

Another aspect of the study dealt with **sex typing**. If you have ever heard people's behavior described as "typically male" or "typically female," then you know what sex typing means. It is the tendency to assess behavior on the basis of expectations derived solely from the fact that people are male or female. Men are commonly sex typed as more traditional and less flexible than women on the issue of sex roles. If this is true, they can be expected to engage more frequently in sex typing than women. This somewhat circular reasoning was not supported by the results of the study. Contrary to expectations, the women perceived the greatest dissimilarity between the men and the women in terms of whom they preferred to win the match.

The study also suggested that men can play the role of women with greater success than women can play the role of men (see Figure 10-1). Such a finding may point to an accomplishment of the women's movement, at least among college men. By letting people know where they stand, women have educated men about their beliefs and attitudes.

What about the question the Riggs/King match brought to public attention in the first place: does Billie Jean King have the ability to compete against a man? Although the data from the study did not permit this question to be answered directly, some speculations about the opinions of college men and women can be made. Most college students would say yes to the question. Agreement by women, however, would be more frequent than by men. Furth-

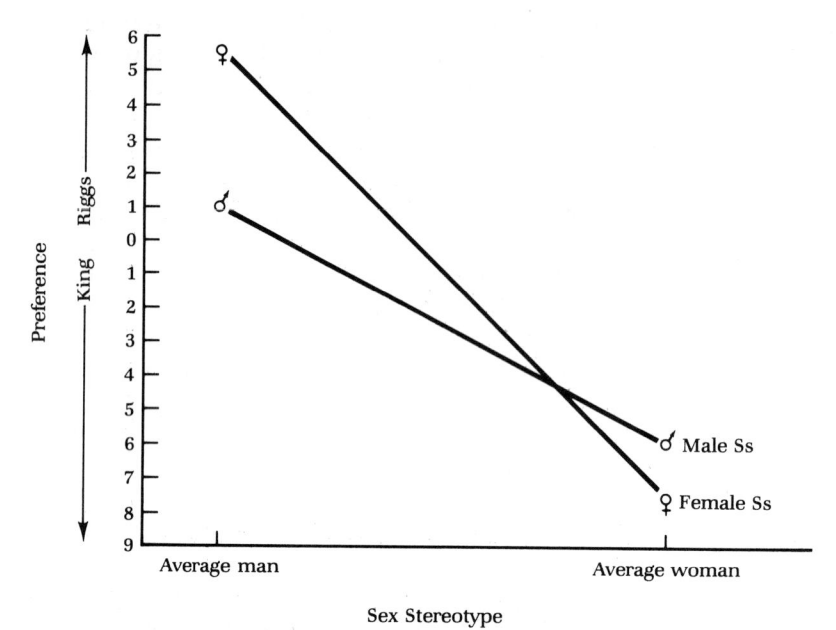

Figure 10-1. Intersex perception and the Riggs/King tennis match. On the day of the match, male and female college students were asked to indicate whom they preferred to win. In addition, some were asked to estimate the preferences of average members of the opposite sex. (Upper scores on the vertical axis represent strength of preference for Riggs. Lower scores represent strength of support for King.) As the graph shows, female respondents perceived more dissimilarity in the preferences of males and females than male respondents. In terms of stereotype accuracy, men can evidently play the role of women with greater success than women can play the role of men (as evidenced in the graph by the proximity of the points above "average woman" and the distance between points above "average man"). *Source:* Kaplan, 1975.

ermore, the men appeared to be more aware of the women's position in the matter than the women were of the men's position.[1]

What men think women think—and vice versa

In what ways do you think women are affected by what men think? If you are a college woman, do you think you are making important decisions in your life completely on your own? Or do your decisions rely upon what important men in your life think you should do? Peggy Hawley, a counseling psychologist, has provided evidence that what women think men think may make a difference in what women choose to do with their lives.

Hawley developed a 35-item questionnaire dealing with attitudes toward women's role in society (see Table 10-1). From these questions, five key areas were determined:

1. Woman as Partner: division of responsibility, power, and labor between the sexes in work and the conjugal relationship.

[1] KAPLAN, 1975b.

2. Woman as Ingenue: woman in her most dependent state, as a possession, a decorative item, and a sex symbol.
3. Woman as Homemaker: emphasis on the traditional role as keeper of the home.
4. Woman as Competitor: woman's right to compete, with implications for the man-woman relationship.
5. Woman as Knower: appropriate ways of knowing; for instance, the assumption that women are naturally intuitive and men naturally rational.

As a first step, Hawley asked college women to indicate the degree to which they thought significant men in their lives would agree or disagree with the items in the questionnaire. Next, Hawley found out what sort of careers the college women were planning and what they were studying in college.

The results of the study showed that women who were studying mathematics or science thought that significant men in their lives saw little difference in what men's and women's roles ought to be. For example, these women felt that significant men in their lives did *not* think women should just hang around the house and do the dishes. Their men did not think women should be traditional and they were not planning traditionally feminine careers.

How about the women whose men believed women should stay in their place? According to the study, these women were not planning to rock the boat. They were more likely to be planning occupations in traditional female occupations such as teaching or housekeeping.[2]

What men think about a woman's career can translate into encouragement or discouragement for achievement-related behaviors. One study demonstrated that women planning for careers received more encouragement from teachers and significant men in their lives than women who were not planning careers.[3]

It is not clear whether traditional men influence their women to become traditional or whether traditional women consider traditional men to be the most influential. Nevertheless, the relationship exists. What women think men think does make a difference.

And although what women think men think can influence career plans, it may not determine who does the housework. Even women with nontraditional attitudes and women who are employed in professional jobs report that they and their husbands divide household tasks in a traditional sex-role fashion. Activity in the world of work may not mean that less is expected of a woman at home. In other words, for working women, the more you have, the more you do![4]

SEXIST STUDIES

Monkeymen and women

Men and women are different. They have different appearances, different preferences, and different lifestyles. Some of the differences between men and women are clearly anatomical and physiological. Others are more difficult to

[2]HAWLEY, 1971. [3]STAKE & LEVITZ, 1979. [4]BECKMAN & HOUSER, 1979.

TABLE 10-1. Attitudes toward women's role in society

Instructions: Indicate the degree to which you disagree or agree with the statements using the following scale (circle the appropriate number for each item). Then score.[a]

1 = strongly disagree   2 = disagree   3 = neither agree nor disagree   4 = agree
5 = strongly agree

#	Scale	Statement
1.	1 2 3 4 5	Men and women should share both the responsibilities and privileges of life equally.
2.	1 2 3 4 5	Women should be the "power behind the man" and not the one "out in front."
3.	1 2 3 4 5	Women should let the man believe he is the dominant one even if this is not true.
4.	1 2 3 4 5	Women should always be honest when they are asked an opinion, even if this opinion is in disagreement with a man.
5.	1 2 3 4 5	There should be a division of labor between the sexes, as women and men have different abilities.
6.	1 2 3 4 5	Women should be paid the same salary as would be paid to a man in the same position.
7.	1 2 3 4 5	Men should make the decisions regarding important financial matters and women should make decisions regarding home and children.
8.	1 2 3 4 5	Women are expected to be slightly illogical.
9.	1 2 3 4 5	Women should be helpless because this is flattering to men.
10.	1 2 3 4 5	Women who are easily impressed and somewhat naive are especially feminine.
11.	1 2 3 4 5	Men like women who use "feminine wiles" to accomplish their aims.
12.	1 2 3 4 5	Men dislike women who act like "sex pots" in every situation.
13.	1 2 3 4 5	The one single most important thing a wife can do to insure a good marriage is to subordinate her own needs to those of her husband.
14.	1 2 3 4 5	It is extremely important to marry a woman who is physically desirable in the eyes of other men.
15.	1 2 3 4 5	Women should never let outside interests or activities interfere with their domestic duties.
16.	1 2 3 4 5	The best way for women to express their love for their families is to perform the small services, e.g., lay out clothes, cook favorite dishes, etc.
17.	1 2 3 4 5	It is possible for women to handle both a home and an outside career and do justice to them both.
18.	1 2 3 4 5	Women do not belong in business and professional life because they act inappropriately; for example, they burst into tears when things go wrong, they demand equal treatment with men in some cases and insist on their feminine prerogatives in others.
19.	1 2 3 4 5	Women who engage in activities outside the home are more interesting than those who do not.

(continued)

attribute to hormones or body structure. Until recently, feminine psychology was often the subject of jokes. Men would simply imply that women were impossible to understand. For example, Harry Harlow, a well-known and respected psychologist, included the following poem in one of his research articles:

> No one really understands
> The females' head or heart or glands
> Perhaps it's just as well for us
> That they remain mysterious

Of course, feminists were angered by Harlow's poem. But then Harlow has never gotten along well with supporters of the feminist movement. The

(Table 10-1 continued)

20.	1 2 3 4 5	Women are naturally "people-centered" and men are naturally "idea-centered."
21.	1 2 3 4 5	Women's place is in the home.
22.	1 2 3 4 5	Modern woman is too competitive.
23.	1 2 3 4 5	Women should be able to follow any vocation or profession they wish, even if it violates tradition.
24.	1 2 3 4 5	Women should not compete for top-salaried positions.
25.	1 2 3 4 5	Men do not want women to be highly successful in areas where their own egos are deeply involved.
26.	1 2 3 4 5	Women can be competitive in all endeavors without appearing masculine.
27.	1 2 3 4 5	Women should never be placed in positions of authority over men, even if they are qualified.
28.	1 2 3 4 5	The relationship between husbands and wives can be good even if both are competing in the same area.
29.	1 2 3 4 5	The intellectual capacity of men and women is equal but different.
30.	1 2 3 4 5	It is more important for a truly feminine woman to be beautiful than to be intelligent.
31.	1 2 3 4 5	Women should limit themselves to friendships with other women.
32.	1 2 3 4 5	Men think it is just as important to educate their daughters as to educate their sons.
33.	1 2 3 4 5	It is important for a woman to be articulate and verbally fluent.
34.	1 2 3 4 5	It would be perfectly appropriate to have a woman president of the United States if she were qualified.
35.	1 2 3 4 5	There are no genetically based differences in the way men and women think.

[a]Scoring Directions: For items 1, 4, 6, 12, 17, 19, 23, 25, 26, 28, 32, 33, 34, and 35, you must change your answer using the following transformation: 1 = 5; 2 = 4; 4 = 2; 1 = 5 (if your answer was 3, leave it as it is).

There are five subscales. You can get your score for each one by adding up your responses to the items which make up the scale. The subscales are:

1. Woman as Partner — items 1–7
2. Woman as Ingenue — items 8–14
3. Woman as Homemaker — items 15–21
4. Woman as Competitor — items 22–28
5. Woman as Knower — items 29–35

(The subscales are fully described in the text)

Now compare your scores to the averages obtained from students at the University of California, Riverside.

SUBSCALE	AVERAGE SCORES	
	Men	Women
1. Woman as Partner	19.00	14.65
2. Woman as Ingenue	18.62	17.13
3. Woman as Homemaker	20.54	15.86
4. Woman as Competitor	21.16	17.04
5. Woman as Knower	20.66	17.08

Higher scores indicate more traditional attitudes.
Source: Hawley, 1972; Kaplan & Goldman, 1973.

dispute goes back to 1959, when Harlow reported a very interesting set of experiments designed to determine whether infants gain attachment to their mothers because the mothers provide food and oral gratification. (Remember that Freudian psychologists believe that oral stimulation is the most important form of gratification for a young infant.) Harlow set up a laboratory situation in which young rhesus monkeys were raised with artificial mothers. One of the mothers was a structure covered with soft terry cloth, cuddly and warm, called the cloth mother. Besides the cloth mother, there was a wire mother, simply a wire frame with a head. The two types of mothers are shown in Figure 10-2.

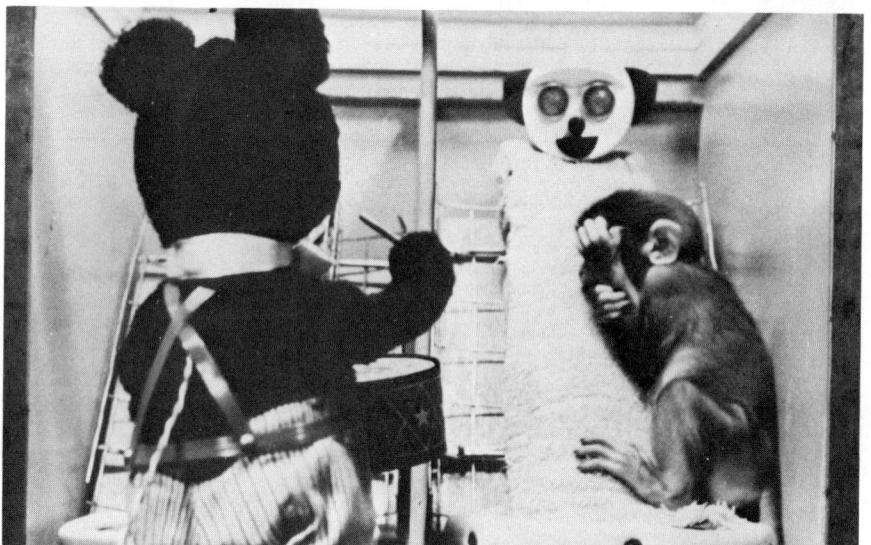

Figure 10-2. Artificial mothers. The first picture shows the wire and cloth mothers used in Harlow's experiments. Although fed by the wire mother, the infant monkey prefers to cling to the cloth mother (second picture). Having been raised in social isolation, the infant monkey becomes fearful when confronted with novel stimuli (third picture). *Source:* Harlow & Harlow, 1965.

In Harlow's experiment, some of the infant monkeys were fed by the cloth mother and others were fed by the wire mother. Feeding was accomplished by placing a milk bottle on the chest of the surrogate mothers. The results of the experiment clearly showed that the monkeys developed an attachment to the cloth mother, regardless of which mother fed them. Moreover, when the infant was placed in a frightening environment, he or she would cling to the cloth mother for security. All this suggested that contact-comfort is more important than oral gratification in the development of mother/infant relationships.

What would happen if there were no cloth mother? Harlow tested this, too. He found that young monkeys raised with just a wire mother or alone in plain wire cages turned out to be severely disturbed animals. These monkeys became *autistic:* they would sit in their cages and rock back and forth, often banging their heads against the sides of their cages; they rarely showed appropriate sexual responses as adults. Later experiments showed that although infants raised with cloth mothers fared a little better, inadequate experience with other live monkeys during the first six months of life had disastrous effects upon social development.[5]

All this tells us that monkeys who do not grow up under normal circumstances grow up to be maladjusted. But what does it have to do with the dispute between Professor Harlow and the feminists? The answer, basically, is that feminists feel that Harlow is pushing the notion that infants need full-time mothers. That is, mothers must spend time providing contact-comfort for their infants—not working or developing themselves as unique individuals. Many modern women reject the notion that women are created to be mothers. Instead of confining themselves solely to motherhood, they strive also for fulfilling careers.[*]

The body watchers

Zoologist Desmond Morris has provided us with extensive speculation about characteristics of female anatomy in two books, *The Naked Ape* and *Intimate Behavior*. Morris was particularly interested in the evolutionary significance of certain anatomical features—for example, female breasts. It is clear that our culture associates breasts with sexuality. There is also historical evidence that some cultures have recognized the strong sensuality associated with breasts and, for puritanical reasons, tried to discourage what they considered unacceptable thoughts by keeping breasts confined. Early English Puritans used a tight bodice to flatten breasts completely; seventeenth-century Spaniards put lead plates across the chests of young girls to prevent their bosoms from developing. In our culture a person engaged in such medieval practices would be considered weird or crazy. In fact, now pieces of clothing are often used to expose breasts by pushing them up, pushing them together to accentuate the cleavage.

Another feature of the anatomy that has been of some concern in our culture is female buttocks. This region is more pronounced in females than males and seems to be a uniquely human feature that does not protrude in any other primate species. Many sexual connotations are associated with the

---

[5]Harlow & Harlow, 1965.
[*]Actually, the dispute between supporters of the feminist movement and Harlow runs deeper. Harlow's argument is that men and women differ and women will never be able to do many men's jobs. Even Harlow's explanation of his idea for the cloth and wire study sounds somewhat sexist. He claimed that he got the idea for the experiment while on a plane flight from Washington, D.C. to Wisconsin: "Somewhere over Detroit I realized I was sitting next to a cloth surrogate mother—an inanimate female with a wire body covered by terrycloth.[6]
[6]Tavris, 1973.

buttocks. Some men are stimulated by a woman whose gait accentuates the sway of her buttocks. The effect of protruding buttocks is also thought to be stimulating.

In addition to breasts and buttocks, legs are also believed to be a symbol of sexiness. Female thighs have greater fat deposits than do male thighs, and at various times in history the thickness of thighs has been considered a symbol of sexiness. Morris points out that long legs, characteristic of adolescent maturation, have been associated with sexual appeal, since the young, maturing female is thought to be sexy. This may be a reason albeit an unconscious one, that many women are disposed toward making their legs look longer by wearing high-heeled shoes, which tilt the foot down and make the leg appear longer.

Morris has lots of theories about why parts of the female body have evolved as they have. One of these concerns the evolutionary significance of female breasts. Our male ancestors (typically monkeys and apes) approached their mates from the rear during sexual intercourse. The female's buttocks were the real sexual stimulus. When hunting societies developed, Morris argues, it became more important to form stable pair (male/female) relationships. This was accomplished by making sex more personal. The personalness came with face-to-face exposure. Females with a chest that reminded the male of buttocks were selected because they were more sexy in a face-to-face confrontation.[7]

Most psychologists would not put much faith in what Morris said. Psychology is an empirical science and usually likes to base its generalizations on more solid evidence than he presents. And how can we study a theory that sounds as far out as what Morris has proposed? The answer is that we cannot. We can, however, study how males are attracted to parts of the female anatomy, and vice versa.

A particular type of biased study is based on cultural beliefs about the personality characteristics of men (and, to a lesser extent, women) who prefer different parts of the anatomy of their opposite-sex counterparts. For example, for some reason it is assumed that men who prefer large breasts are more dependent than men who prefer small breasts. Surprisingly, a study designed to investigate this common notion showed just the opposite to be true.[8]

A few years ago, psychologists Jerry and Nancy Wiggins and J. C. Conger decided to do a systematic study of male preferences for female anatomy. They presented 95 male college students with pairs of nude female silhouettes such as those shown in Figure 10-3. The silhouettes were systematically varied to include five sizes of breasts, buttocks, and legs.

The male students who participated in the study came to the laboratory twice. The first time, they rated the attractiveness of each of the silhouettes. During their second visit (which they believed was for a different experiment), the men filled out a variety of personality tests. In addition, they answered a detailed questionnaire about their personal habits and backgrounds. Finally, they rated the concepts of buttocks, legs, and breasts on semantic differential scales (semantic differential scales are designed to measure meaning along

[7]MORRIS, 1967, 1971. [8]SCODEL, 1957.

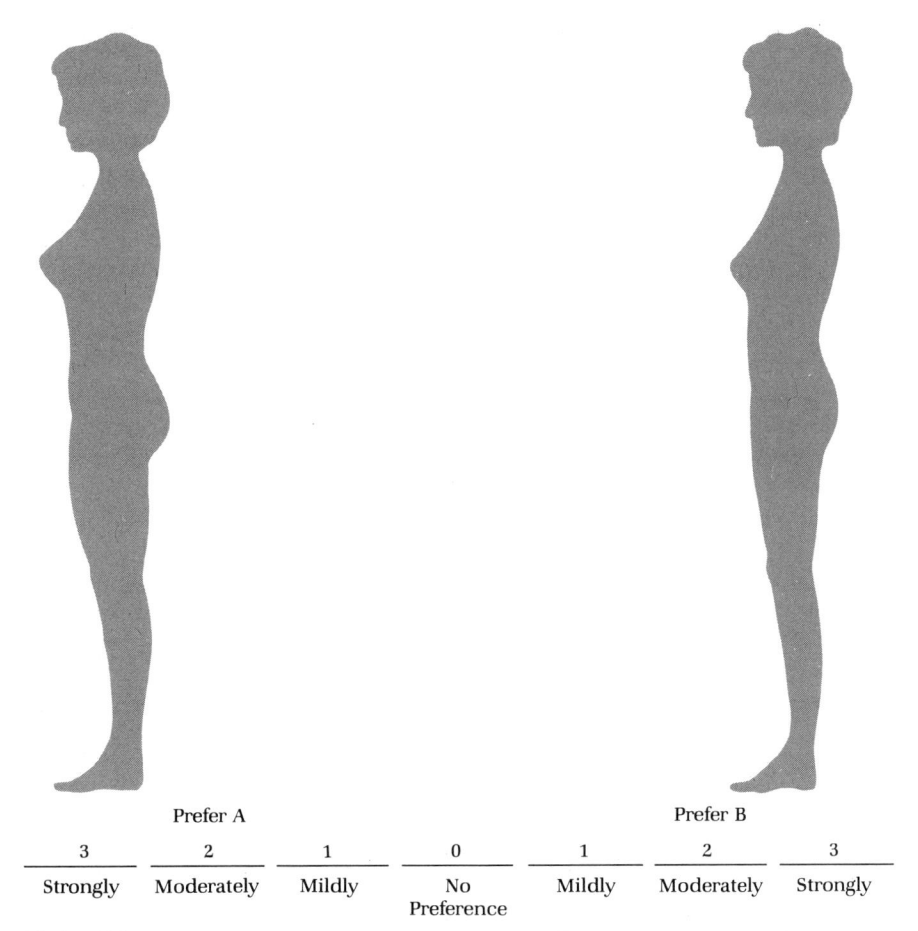

Prefer A				Prefer B		
3	2	1	0	1	2	3
Strongly	Moderately	Mildly	No Preference	Mildly	Moderately	Strongly

Figure 10-3.
Sexist stimuli. An example of a stimulus pair (in this case, breast size difference) used in the study of heterosexual somatic preference. Similar comparisons of legs and buttocks were found to be associated with certain behaviors and personality characteristics. *Source:* Wiggins, Wiggins, & Conger, 1968.

the dimensions of potency, activity, and evaluation). The results of the study revealed that preferences for various sizes of breasts, buttocks, and legs were associated with personality characteristics and personal history. For example, men who preferred large breasts tended to favor *Playboy* magazine, sports, and physical contact with women. In contrast, those who preferred small breasts tended to be nondrinkers who held fundamentalist religious beliefs. Preference for large buttocks was associated with high scores on measure of guilt and self-blame whereas preference for small buttocks was not associated with guilt. Leg preference was associated with quiet men who tended not to drink and preferred a slow tempo of life.[9]

Some may find this study a disgusting example of sexist research. Yet others, even in this enlightened age, still engage in locker room discussions

[9]Wiggins, Wiggins, & Conger, 1968.

about breast size, shapes of legs, and other female characteristics. What has changed is the discussion in the women's dressing room. To parallel sexist studies in which men rate their preferences for female anatomy, there are now studies on aspects of the male body that appeal to women. A striking finding in these studies is that men appear to be uninformed about what physical characteristics appeal to women. The left-hand column of Table 10-2 lists 11 male physical characteristics. The middle column shows the percentage of 100 women who felt this characteristic was a real "turn on." The right-hand column shows the percentage of 100 men who thought each characteristic would turn women on. As you can see, the men were very inaccurate. For example, the men thought muscular chest and shoulders would be the most appealing physical characteristic to women. Instead, women appear to favor "small and sexy" buttocks and slimness.[10]

TABLE 10-2. What is sexy about men's bodies?

Characteristic	% Women	% Men
Buttocks (small)	39	4
Slimness	15	7
Flat stomach	13	9
Eyes	11	4
Long legs	6	3
Tallness	5	13
Hair	5	4
Neck	3	2
Penis	2	15
Muscular chest and shoulders	1	21
Muscular arms	0	18

Source: Smith, 1975, p. 112.

WOMEN'S LIBERATION

Do you strongly believe that men and women differ in their attitudes, values, interests, and behavior as well as in their anatomy? If so, you are probably right. Your opinion will probably earn you some unflattering comments, such as "male chauvinist" or "Aunt Jemima" (the oppressed-female counterpart of "Uncle Tom") from outraged peers. Despite the outcry, you will not find it difficult to provide empirical evidence that this difference between the sexes does indeed exist.

After the furor dies down, you can point out to your indignant friends that the real issue is not the existence of sex differences. What is really at stake is first, to what extent are such differences inculcated into our value system by the society in which we live? The answer is that we are exposed to this conditioning from birth to maturity to death. Second, what are the implications of such practices? The answer is that not only do they lead to discriminatory actions toward individuals of both sexes who do not fit society's value system, most of all they lead to wholesale discrimination toward one sex. Women's Lib should begin in the crib, because it is there that discriminatory practices begin.

[10]SMITH, 1975.

Women's lib begins in the crib

Do you realize that you were subjected to discriminatory practices as early as six weeks after your birth? There is evidence that, even at such an early age, girls are talked to more often than boys and boys are handled more often than girls.[11] By the time you were 6 years old, the accumulated effects of socialization practices must have left their mark on your self-concept. Like so many other children of that age who were shown pictures of "animals that are like you," you chose a tiger if you were a boy and a lamb if you were a girl.[12] As an adult, you agreed that males are stronger, more aggressive, and more daring than women. You probably also agreed to what does not necessarily follow from such comparisons—namely, that males are less inadequate, more mature, and more competent than females.[13]

All this happened to you provided you were subjected to typical North American socialization practices. If you happened to be born into one of the Latin American cultures stressing *machismo* (a tradition that accords practically no autonomy to women), the process would be shorter and less complicated. As a man, you would "own" a woman, who would be an object for your personal use (unless she belonged to another man); as a woman, you would have no right to do anything about this state of affairs.[14]

It is common for us to think of the days of strong sex-role socialization as the "old days." Yet recent studies suggest that many factors continue to operate to shape sex-role behaviors. An analysis of children's picture books, which are important transmitters of sex-role information, was conducted for books published before and after the beginning of the present-day women's movement. Contrary to expectation, children's books did not radically change with the beginning of the women's movement. Women continue to be under represented in the titles of the books and in the central roles. In fact, the percentage of books with males on the front cover and in central roles increased, whereas the comparable percentages for women decreased. According to psychologist Shirley St. Peter, the author of this study, "when Jack goes up the hill, Jill stays home" (p. 260).[15]

Formal organizations to help socialize young boys into the male role also continue to attract a strong following. One of these is the historic Boy Scouts of America. First organized in 1910, the Boy Scouts thereafter experienced rapid recognition and growth. By the end of their first decade, they had the President of the United States as an honorary president and were the largest male organization in American history. Sociologist Jeffrey Hantover maintains that the Boy Scouts were organized because adult men at the turn of the century felt too many restrictions had been placed on the development of masculinity and that scouting was needed to counteract the developing forces of feminization. Hantover's analysis of the social motivations of scoutmasters suggested that scouting provided for the adults (not necessarily the children) an opportunity to validate the traditional male sex role that may have been denied to them through their occupations.[16]

Another way sex-role stereotypes can be introduced is through subtle

[11]Kagan, 1971.   [12]Kagan, Hoskin, & Watson, 1961.   [13]Bennett & Cohen, 1959.   [14]Aramoni, 1972.   [15]St. Peter, 1979.   [16]Hantover, 1978.

communications between teacher and students. In one study, teachers were asked to call upon children in their classes to demonstrate new toys. When the plaything was a "masculine" toy such as a truck, the teachers called upon boys to demonstrate it significantly more often than when it was a "feminine" toy. The type of introduction a toy is given can affect which gender will play with it. Three and 4-year-old boys and girls are equally likely to play with dolls and trucks when the instructions to play with them do not include sex-role stereotyping. When the instructions include typical sex-role references, however, boys tend to choose to play with trucks and girls tend to play with dolls.[17]

Box 10-1. Sex hormones and behavior: The other side of the argument

This chapter has presented considerable evidence that differences in sex role behaviors are the result of socialization practices. Although most psychologists would probably agree with us, it is also necessary to point out that there is another side to the argument. Some researchers believe that sex-role differences are the result of biological, not social, influences.

A major biological difference between males and females is the activity of male and female sex hormones. Males have greater activity of androgens (male sex hormones) and females have greater activity of estrogens (female sex hormones). People afflicted with rare medical problems, however, may get overexposed to the hormone that is not appropriate for their gender. One example is *adrenal hyperplasia*, a congenital problem that causes a fetus to be exposed to unusual doses of male sex hormones before birth.

Researchers John Money and Anke Ehrhardt have followed a group of children with adrenal hyperplasia from birth through adolescence. They observe that girls who are exposed to the male hormone before birth tend to be tomboys during childhood. Despite socializing influences, they reject playing with dolls in favor of rougher play activities common to young boys. The girls ovulate when they come of age, however, and they do identify themselves as female. The boys with this condition are not significantly different from other boys.

More unusual evidence comes from research by endocrinologist Julianne Imperato-McGinley, who has been studying 38 males in two small Santo Domingo towns. These males have a peculiar enzyme deficiency that causes their genitals to look female at birth. At puberty, however, the boys begin to make testosterone normally for the first time and their bodies undergo a transformation. All of a sudden, these young children believed to be girls turn into boys! Their voices change, their testes descend, their clitorises are transformed into penises, and their musculature develops accordingly.

Even though these 38 males had been reared as females, Imperato-McGinley observed that they took on male identities and sexual behaviors at puberty. In these cases, neither the boys nor their parents suspected the abnormality and the children were raised as though they were female.

Although the rare condition experienced by these 38 boys does occur in other countries, some medical intervention usually occurs earlier in life than this. In the United States, for example, doctors prefer to change the boys surgically into girls at the time of puberty. The reason for doing the study in

(continued)

---

[17]SERBIN, CONNOR, & ILER, 1979.

(Box 10-1 continued)

Santo Domingo was that these surgical procedures have been unavailable there. Imperato-McGinley, however, has found cases in France, England, and Italy in which there was no surgical intervention and the persons involved took on masculine-like behavior at the time they became physically and hormonally male—even though they had been raised to be female.[18] These findings contradict the notion that socialization of a young child into the female sex role locks the child into a lifetime of sex-typed behaviors.

Is anatomy destiny?

We have seen that what society values can lead to different destinies for men and women. This is not to say that anatomical differences as such must lead to different destinies for men and women. During the past decade, many enlightened people have rejected this notion, as well as the second-class citizenship for women that it usually entails.

Historically speaking, though, psychology has fostered and tolerated chauvinistic beliefs. Sigmund Freud, the father of psychoanalysis and insight therapy, believed that there were psychological consequences of the anatomical distinction between men and women. Thus, the implication arises that anatomy *is* destiny. Of course, one obvious physical distinction between the sexes is that women do not have penises. During the stage in development that Freud referred to as the phallic stage (which occurs around age 5), the child discovers his or her sexual organs. According to Freudian theory, little girls recognize at this stage in their lives that their sexual apparatus is simple—not fancy like that of their fathers. They envy their fathers but, recognizing they cannot be like them, identify with their mothers and take on behaviors and attitudes characteristic of females. Freud referred to this process as penis envy. From these beliefs, Freud derived the notion that both men and women regard the female as an inferior being.

Karen Horney, a former disciple of Freud, departed from him on the issue of penis envy. She believed that neurotic problems in women were not rooted in envy over genitals but rather in overdependencies on love relationships.[19] Feminist psychology was born in Horney's writings.

Politically, too, it was inevitable that many women would embrace the concept of consciousness raising and initiate action to put an end to the injustices of discrimination. Women's organizations such as the National Organization of Women (NOW) and the National Women's Political Caucus (NWPC) pointed out some time ago that even though over one-half of the 63 million women in the United States between the ages of 18 and 63 are working, only one-third are married to men who theoretically could support a family. The majority of working women are separated, widowed, or divorced (many of them with children), and are underrepresented (three times less than men) in full-time jobs that pay more than the median national income annually. To add insult to injury, women occupying the same jobs as men are usually given different titles and lower pay, and their professional skills are generally underutilized.[20]

[18]KOLATA, 1979. [19]HORNEY, 1939. [20]FLEXNER, 1971.

Common belief holds that the status of women in the labor force is rapidly changing for the better. Is this true? Not exactly, according to a survey of women having professions between 1870 and 1970. The results indicated that the number of women in professions reached a high in the 1930s and then declined for the next two decades. In the last decade, the number of women in professions went up again, but not to the 1930 high.[21]

Most psychologists were not too surprised by the findings in the survey. The evidence shows that even supposedly enlightened college students of both sexes find it difficult to shed latent prejudices. One study asked a sample of college students to rate the status of several highly prestigious professional titles: architect, professor, lawyer, and physician. Some of the students were also given the information that these professions are increasingly open to women. To those students, this small bit of additional information was sufficient to produce a marked decrease in their prestige ratings of these professions![22]

One of the reasons women may have had difficulty gaining acceptance as workers is that men *and* women assume that work done by women is inferior. If enough people make this assumption, women will have greater difficulty in getting jobs. There is convincing evidence that people do indeed devalue female performance.

One of the first studies in this area was done by psychologist Philip Goldberg. The study involved getting college women to rate professionally written articles for such considerations as value, competence, style, and convincingness. The articles were put in booklets, each of which featured one of six technical topics: linguistics, law, art, history, dietetics, education, and city planning. Goldberg arranged the books so that, for each article, half of the subjects were told the author was a male (for example, John T. McKay) and others were told the author was a female (Joan T. McKay).

Goldberg was not surprised to find that articles about traditionally masculine endeavors (law and city planning) were judged to be better if the subjects thought they had been written by men. He was, however, surprised to find that articles about traditionally female domains (dietetics and education) were also seen as better if the female subjects were told they had been written by men.[23] Psychologists Sandra and Daryl Bem repeated this study with their students at Stanford University and found that both men and women regard the writings of female authors to be inferior to the writings of male authors—even when the articles are about things society expects women to know more about. As the Bems point out, these studies suggest that college students of the twentieth century subconsciously agree with what Aristotle claimed 2300 years ago—that "we should regard the female character as afflicted with natural defectiveness."[24]

Actually, things are somewhat more complex than the Bems suggest. Earlier, psychologist Gail Pheterson had failed to replicate Goldberg's findings when she presented articles purportedly authored by either males or females to groups of uneducated middle-aged women. In contrast to Goldberg, she observed that if the author of the article was purportedly female, the women

[21]BLITZ, 1974. [22]TOUHEY, 1974. [23]GOLDBERG, 1968. [24]BEM & BEM, 1973.

rated it as good or better than if it had been written by a male.[25] Why? Perhaps it was because Pheterson told her subjects that the article had been published. The female subjects may have thought that if a woman can get something published, she must be really outstanding—even better than an average man who can get his work published!

To reconcile the differences between the two previously cited studies, Pheterson and some associates conducted another study. They asked 120 students from an Eastern women's college to play the role of judges in an art contest. Each subject saw slides of eight paintings and in each case read a biographical sketch about the painter. For each painting, half the subjects were told it had been painted by a male artist and the other half that it had been painted by a female artist. For example, the artist in one case was identified as "Bob (or Barbara) Soulman, born in 1941 in Cleveland, Ohio, teaches English in a progressive program of adult education." For each subject, half of the paintings were described as entries in a contest and the others were described as winners of the contest.

The results clearly showed that, if the painting was identified as an entry in a contest, it would receive higher ratings if the artist was identified to be male. Just the opposite occurred if the painting was supposed to be a winner of a contest. In this case, the same painting was judged to be better by subjects who thought it had been painted by a female than by subjects who thought it had been painted by a male.[26] Does this odd finding make sense? Yes, it may. It seems that females will discriminate against other females when the others are just ordinary people. Once a woman "makes it," however, she will probably gain the respect and admiration of other women. Perhaps they believe that such a woman deserves respect for transcending all the barriers.

Another example of selective discrimination was demonstrated in a study of male and female undergraduate students at the University of South Florida. They were shown videotapes of other undergraduates who were being trained as psychological experimenters. The subjects' task was to give their impressions of the person they saw on the videotape.

Supposedly, the person on the tape was conducting an experiment about people's physiological reactions to stress. There were several versions of the tape. In one version the student-experimenter appeared competent—relaxed, calm, and self-assured. In another version the experimenter seemed incompetent. He or she started the experimental session late, had the wrong list of subjects' names, did not have chairs for the subjects to sit on, and did not know how to operate the equipment. Some of the subjects saw a male experimenter on the videotape; others saw a female.

If an experimenter is competent, does gender make a difference in judgments about the quality of his or her work? According to this study, it does not. But what happened when the experimenter appeared to be incompetent? In this case, women were perceived to be less competent than men who had engaged in identical behavior.[27] In a similar study, male and female college students were asked to make judgments about the suitability of identical male and female applicants for law school. There were no differences between the

[25]PHETERSON, 1969. [26]PHETERSON, KIESLER, & GOLDBERG, 1971. [27]PIACENTE, 1974.

judged qualifications of male and female applicants on objective criteria such as adequacy of grades and test scores. When given the chance to rate personality characteristics and employment alternatives, however, a prejudicial pattern of responding began to emerge. There was a greater tendency to ascribe the traits *ambitious, competitive,* and *well-adjusted* to the male applicant and to regard the female applicant as a less healthy person who overestimates her own potential.[28] Even though discrimination appears to be less when objective criteria are used, it is difficult to eliminate the "hidden" factors employers and graduate admissions committees think about when they consider male and female applicants.

SEXIST GAMES

Some men and women freely admit their sexist attitudes and biases. Should you ask them about their adjustment problems, they will strongly deny any link between such problems and sexist biases. Then there are men and women who are truly liberated from sex-typing practices and beliefs. You are likely to find that their adjustment problems, if any, are not related to sexist biases. Finally, there are those who *profess* liberation from sexist bias. The main problem of these people is their inability to recognize in themselves sexist attitudes, since they are not consciously aware of them. To solve the problem, here are some word games that may be of help.

Will Anne succeed in medical school?

This game was developed by Martina Horner of Radcliffe College. She asked college women, most of whom were heading for professional careers, to complete the following story:

> "After first term finals, Anne finds herself at the top of her medical school class."[29]

Before we look at Horner's results, go ahead and complete the story yourself. Write anything that comes to your mind about Anne, her feelings, her future, and so forth.

Now for Horner's results. In her study, she examined the stories about Anne for internal conflicts about success and failure. You may wish to compare your results with Horner's findings of women's "fear of success." This fear was evident when the story depicted Anne at the top of her medical school class, but not when the story depicted *John* in an identical situation. The bulk of Horner's evidence has been summarized by psychologists Sandra and Daryl Bem:

> *The most common "fear-of-success" stories showed strong fears of social rejection as a result of success. The women in this group showed anxiety about becoming unpopular, unmarriageable, and lonely:*
> Anne starts proclaiming her surprise and joy. Her fellow classmates are so disgusted with her behavior that they jump on her in a body and beat her. She is maimed for life.
>
> Anne is an acne-faced bookworm. . . . She studies twelve hours a day, and lives

[28]BEATTIE & DIEHL, 1979. [29]HORNER, 1971.

at home to save money. "Well, it certainly paid off. All the Friday and Saturday nights without dates, fun—I'll be the best woman doctor alive." And yet a twinge of sadness comes through—she wonders what she really has. . . .

Although Anne is happy with her success, she fears what will happen to her social life. The male med students don't seem to think very highly of a female who has beaten them in their field. . . . She will be a proud and successful but alas a very lonely doctor.

Anne is pretty darn proud of herself, but everyone hates and envies her.

Anne doesn't want to be number one in her class. . . . She feels she shouldn't rank so high because of social reasons. She drops to ninth and then marries the boy who graduates number one.

In the second "fear of success" category were stories in which the women seemed concerned about definitions of womanhood. These stories expressed guilt and despair over success and doubts about femininity and normality:
Unfortunately Anne no longer feels so certain that she really wants to be a doctor. She is worried about herself and wonders if perhaps she is not normal. . . . Anne decides not to continue with her medical work but to take courses that have a deeper personal meaning for her.

Anne feels guilty. . . . She will finally have a nervous breakdown and quit medical school and marry a successful young doctor.

A third group of stories could not even face up to the conflict between having a career and being a woman. These stories simply denied the possibility that any woman could be so successful:
Anne is a code name for a nonexistent person created by a group of medical students. They take turns writing for Anne.

Anne is really happy she's on top, though Tom is higher than she—though that's as it should be. Anne doesn't mind Tom winning.

Anne is talking to her counselor. Counselor says she will make a fine nurse.

It was luck that Anne came out on top because she didn't want to go to medical school anyway.

By way of contrast, here is a typical story written not about Anne, but about John:
John has worked very hard and his long hours of study have paid off. . . . He is thinking about his girl, Cheri, whom he will marry at the end of med school. He realizes he can give her all the things she desires after he becomes established. He will go on in med school and be successful in the long run.

Nevertheless, there were a few women in the study who welcomed the prospect of success.
Anne is quite a lady—not only is she top academically, but she is liked and admired by her fellow students—quite a trick in a male-dominated field. She is brilliant—but she is also a woman. She will continue to be at or near the top. And . . . always a lady.

Hopefully the day is approaching when as many "Anne" stories as "John" stories will have happy endings. (pp. 296-297)[30]

[30]Bem & Bem, 1973.

As you might expect, the Horner study has not been viewed by psychologists as a methodological masterpiece. The study has been criticized because there was no male control group and because it is difficult to quantify the projective measures (stories of Anne and John) that Horner used. Newer studies have shown that both men and women tend to reject anyone (male or female) who violates expected sex-role behavior.[31] Such findings suggest that *both* men and women fear stepping out of line with their sex-role prescription. Unfortunately, the prevailing sex-role expectation for women is still not geared to have them at the top of their classes in medical school.

One note is worth adding here. It concerns a problem with Horner's definition of success.[32] Bessie Stanley wrote in 1904 "He has achieved success who has lived well, laughed often, and loved much." It is not clear that this includes the ability to solve anagrams or to end up first in a medical-school class. In short, we must clearly specify what we mean by success and fear of it.

Who was that doctor?

See if you can solve this riddle. The correct answer is in the footnote on page 285.

> A boy and his father are in an automobile accident. The father is killed, and the boy is seriously injured. The boy is rushed to the hospital and taken into the operating room. A few minutes later, the surgeon comes out of the operating room and says, "I cannot operate on this boy; he is my son." Justify this set of facts.

Regardless of your own ability to solve this riddle, how many people do you think can solve it? And who do you think these people are? These are some of the questions that Karen Folmar, a student at the University of California in San Diego, tried to answer. She presented the riddle to a wide array of male and female students on campus. Of the total responses obtained, 12.5% were correct and 87.5% were inaccurate to varying degrees and therefore incorrect. Amazingly, not a single male was able to solve this riddle. All the correct responses were given by females!

Folmar also presented students with two similar riddles, as follows:

> *Second Version*
> A girl and her father are in an automobile accident. The father is killed, and the girl is seriously injured. The girl is rushed to the hospital and taken into the operating room. A few minutes later, the surgeon comes out of the operating room and says, "I cannot operate on this girl; she is my daughter." Justify this set of facts.
>
> *Third Version*
> A girl and her mother are in an automobile accident. The mother is killed, and the girl is seriously injured. The girl is rushed to the hospital and taken into the operating room. A few minutes later, the surgeon comes out of the operating room and says, "I cannot operate on this girl; she is my daughter." Justify this set of facts.

The third version was included to test whether a riddle of this nature is comprehensible. As you can see, it is about a girl and her mother and allows

[31]WEITZ, 1977.   [32]TRESEMER, 1974.

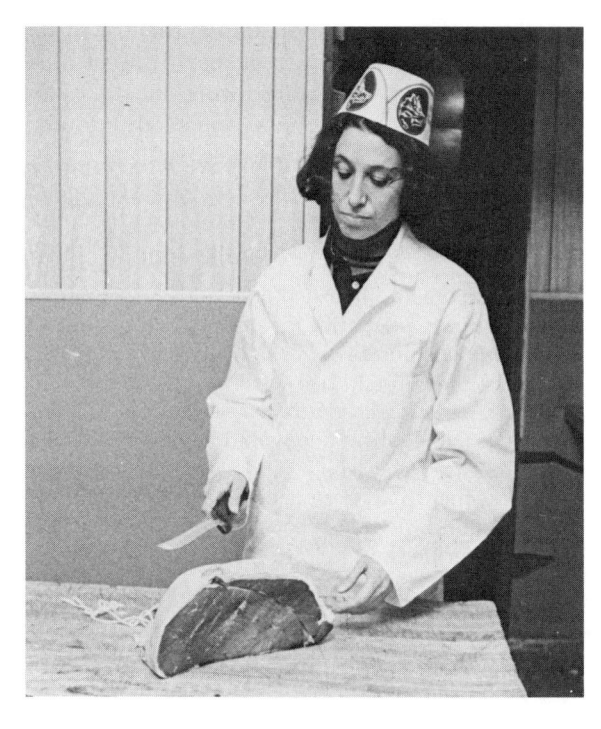

Women are entering professions that for centuries have been dominated by men. This butcher represents the new trend.

for the surgeon to be a male. With this version, *all* respondents gave the correct answer. The surgeon was expected to be a man, and the correct answers came to the respondents naturally.

Now look at the second version of the riddle. The correct answer to this version is still that the surgeon is a woman, but it shows that the accident involves a girl and her father. Although this version should be equally as difficult to solve as the original one, the inclusion of a female (the girl) evidently provided the respondents with a hint for the correct solution. Upon presentation of this riddle, 30% of the respondents came up with the correct answer. Once again, the female respondents provided the correct solution more often than did the male respondents.

So far, then, the experiment had shown that the availability of feminine clues increased the likelihood of a correct response to the riddle. There were also other factors related to responding correctly. For example, the occupation of the respondents' mothers was associated with correct responses. About half of the sons or daughters of professional women were able to give a correct response to either one of the first two versions of the riddle, whereas only 15% of the offspring of housewives could do so. Children of professional women are evidently more attuned to the fact that a woman can perform the role of a surgeon.

Folmar also analyzed the various types of incorrect responses. She found the marital status of the respondents' parents to be a related factor, suggesting, perhaps, that coming from a broken home may open one's mind to the possibility of female professionalism in a male-oriented society. For example, the incorrect responses of those who had grown up with both natural parents usually involved a complete denial that the riddle had a correct solution. On the other hand, the incorrect responses of those whose parents had been divorced were often justifications for suggesting alternatives to the male surgeon, such as stepfathers, priests, or adopted fathers.[33]

Who does the housework?

Here is another game you can play. Read the following passage describing the relationship between two people of equal status:

> Both my wife and I earned college degrees in our respective disciplines. I turned down a superior job offer in Oregon and accepted a slightly less desirable position in New York where my wife would have more opportunities for part-time work in her specialty. Although I would have preferred to live in a suburb, we purchased a home near my wife's job so that she could have an office at home where she would be when the children returned from school. Because my wife earns a good salary, she can easily afford to pay a housekeeper to do her major household chores. My wife and I share all other tasks around the house equally. For example, she cooks the meals, but I do the laundry for her and help her with many of her other household tasks.

Does the marriage described in this passage imply interpersonal equality? Is everything divided in a manner that each partner makes a fair and equal contribution? There is a rather simple way to find out if the passage portrays a truly egalitarian relationship. Switch the partners' roles around! If they are of equal status to begin with, it should not sound funny when the roles of husband and wife are substituted for one another:

> Both my husband and I earned college degrees in our respective disciplines. I turned down a superior job offer in Oregon and accepted a slightly less desirable position in New York where my husband would have more opportunities for part-time work in his specialty. Although I would have preferred to live in a suburb, we purchased a home near my husband's job so that he could have an office at home where he would be when the children returned from school. Because my husband earns a good salary, he can easily afford to pay a housekeeper to do his major household chores. My husband and I share all other tasks around the house equally. For example, he cooks the meals, but I do the laundry for him and help him with many of his other household tasks.

Somehow it sounds so different, and yet only the pronouns have been changed to protect the powerful! Certainly no one would ever mistake the marriage just described as egalitarian or even very desirable, and thus it becomes apparent that the ideology about the woman's "natural" place unconsciously permeates the entire fabric of such "pseudoegalitarian" marriages. It is true the wife gains some measure of equality when she can have a career rather than a job and when her career can influence the final place of residence. But why is it the unquestioned assumption that the husband's career solely determines the initial set of alternatives to be considered? Why is it the wife who automatically seeks the part-time position? Why is it *her* housekeeper rather than *their* housekeeper? Why *her* household tasks? And so on throughout the entire relationship.[34]

[33]Folmar & Kaplan, 1974. [34]Bem & Bem, 1973.

In an egalitarian relationship the household tasks are not assigned exclusively to one sex.

ADJUSTMENT PROBLEMS AND SOLUTIONS

Healthy for women—sick for men

Several years ago, a group of clinical psychologists set out to study whether traits characteristic of females were judged to be as healthy as those characteristic of males. The research group consisted of Inge K. Broverman, Donald M. Broverman, Frank E. Clarkson, Paul S. Rosenkrantz, and Susan R. Vogel. The purpose of the study was to determine whether people in the helping professions maintained a double standard about ideal concepts of mental health. The researchers did this by comparing the professionals' ideal concept of mental health for a mature adult whose sex was unspecified with their ideal concept for either a man or a woman.

The subjects in the study were 79 psychologists, psychiatrists, and social workers—all clinically trained and working in clinical settings. All subjects responded to a questionnaire with 122 short descriptions of traits. The trait descriptors were made up of two words that were opposite in nature, one designed to represent the male stereotype and the other designed to portray the female stereotype. Of these descriptors, 38 were either male-valued or female-valued traits considered to be of particular importance. Male-valued items were ones for which the male "pole" (category) was seen as most socially desirable (very aggressive or very logical). Female-valued items were those for which the female pole was seen as most desirable (very gentle, very quiet). The items are shown in Table 10-3.

About a third of the clinicians were given the questionnaire and asked to

Answer to the riddle on page 282: The surgeon is the boy's mother.

TABLE 10-3. Stereotypic traits

Feminine Pole	Masculine Pole
\multicolumn{2}{c}{Male-Valued Items[a]}
Not at all aggressive	Very aggressive
Not at all independent	Very independent
Very emotional	Not at all emotional
Does not hide emotions at all	Almost always hides emotions
Very subjective	Very objective
Very easily influenced	Not at all easily influenced
Very submissive	Very dominant
Dislikes math and science very much	Likes math and science very much
Very excitable in a minor crisis	Not at all excitable in a minor crisis
Very passive	Very active
Not at all competitive	Very competitive
Very illogical	Very logical
Very home oriented	Very worldly
Not at all skilled in business	Very skilled in business
Very sneaky	Very direct
Does not know the way of the world	Knows the way of the world
Feelings easily hurt	Feelings not easily hurt
Not at all adventurous	Very adventurous
Has difficulty making decisions	Can make decisions easily
Cries very easily	Never cries
Almost never acts as a leader	Almost always acts as a leader
Not at all self-confident	Very self-confident
Very uncomfortable about being aggressive	Not at all uncomfortable about being aggressive
Not at all ambitious	Very ambitious
Unable to separate feelings from ideas	Easily able to separate feelings from ideas
Very dependent	Not at all dependent
Very conceited about appearance	Never conceited about appearance
\multicolumn{2}{c}{Female-Valued Items[a]}
Very talkative	Not at all talkative
Very tactful	Very blunt
Very gentle	Very rough
Very aware of feelings of others	Not at all aware of feelings of others
Very religious	Not at all religious
Very interested in own appearance	Not at all interested in own appearance
Very neat in habits	Very sloppy in habits
Very quiet	Very loud
Very strong need for security	Very little need for security
Enjoys art and literature very much	Does not enjoy art and literature at all
Easily expresses tender feelings	Does not express tender feelings at all

[a]Clinically trained psychologists, psychiatrists and social workers value some behaviors as healthy for men but not for women. The "male-valued" items are traits for which the masculine pole was judged as descriptive of a mentally healthy man. The "female-valued" items are traits for which the feminine pole was judged as descriptive of a mentally healthy woman.
Source: Broverman, Broverman, Clarkson, Rosenkrantz, & Vogel, 1970.

indicate which side of the trait descriptor fit the "mature, healthy, socially competent adult male." Another third of the clinicians was asked to do the same for the "mature, healthy, socially competent adult female." The final group was asked to do the same for the "mature, healthy, socially competent adult." For this last group, the sex of the target person was unspecified.

The results of the study showed that people playing active roles in the mental health professions have different values for what is healthy for men and what is healthy for women. The healthy man and the healthy adult with sex unspecified were judged about the same. Traits considered characteristic of the healthy adult were more often attributed to the healthy male than to the healthy female. In fact, traits that were considered healthy for females were judged as neurotic for males.[35]

For many years, psychologists believed that this study demonstrated that women would receive biased treatment by counselors and psychotherapists. More recent research shows, however, that men and women can now expect to be treated about the same by a competent therapist. Recently, educational psychologist Mary Lee Smith reviewed all published and unpublished studies on sex bias in counseling and psychotherapy and found very little evidence that women received discriminatory treatment. Although there was a small bias in the published studies, the unpublished studies revealed a slight bias toward discriminating against *men*.[36] Thus, even though early studies had produced good reason for alarm, recent and more thorough evidence suggests that good counselors will not be unduly influenced by stereotyped beliefs.

Even though women may now receive fairer treatment than before from well-trained psychotherapists, strong social pressures are still exerted on women who deviate from the norm. In the eyes of traditionalists, nothing is healthier for women than having babies. Yet a growing number of women (and men) are questioning whether or not they really want children. Surveys of American adults suggest that childfree couples are no less happy on the average, and in many cases are more satisfied with their lives, than couples with children.[37] If you choose to be a childfree adult, however, be prepared to be the target of negative stereotyping. In one study, a voluntarily childfree wife was rated as less sensitive and loving, less typical, less happy, less well-adjusted, and less likely to get along with parents as compared to an otherwise identically described mother of two children. The subjects also suggested that the childfree woman would be less happy as an older adult. Being a childfree man is also atypical, and there is evidence that men who decide not to have children can also become the victims of negative stereotyping.[38]

Thus, women who choose to be different may suffer negative stereotyping, which in turn may produce self-fulfilling prophecies (see Chapter 9), resulting in women with less self-confidence and less self-esteem. This may suggest that it is important to fight back and attempt to alter some of the socializing agents. For example, one important socializer that reinforces traditional sex roles is the television commercial. Most commercials depict the major role for the American woman as attracting or feeding men, and cleaning the house. Constant exposure to these models may teach women to be subservient to men and not to trust their own judgment. One experiment attempted to reverse this problem by exposing a group of women to commercials in which a male played the subservient role. A control group watched the same commercials with a woman playing the typical female role. Those who had watched the nontraditional commercials later displayed more independence in a conformity experiment and were more self-confident when giving a

[35]BROVERMAN, BROVERMAN, CLARKSON, ROSENKRANTZ, & VOGEL, 1970. [36]SMITH, 1980. [37]CAMPBELL, 1975. [38]JAMISON, FRANZINI, & KAPLAN, 1979.

speech.[39] Television commercials can be important sources of social information, and it is possible that repeated exposure to nonstereotypic commercials may help women gain greater independence and self-confidence.

Another serious problem facing women is in the area of professional accomplishment. Because this is undoubtedly a source of personal satisfaction or dissatisfaction, studies relating a woman's competence to her femininity seem to be especially interesting. The results, alas, are far from encouraging. It has been shown that, when women are judged as competent, they are viewed as less feminine. When they engage in incompetent behavior, their ratings of femininity go up.[40] Thus, when a woman achieves competency in a chosen field, she may do so at the cost of decreasing her appeal to members of the opposite sex. Perhaps this is the reason women are more likely than men to drop out of graduate school[41] and are sparsely represented on the faculties of prestigious educational institutions.[42] Perhaps the most shocking evidence of all concerns the suicide rate among women professionals. Women psychologists, for example, commit suicide about three times as often as women in the general population. Cited among the reasons for this tragedy is that successful women scare men and, therefore, have troubled personal affairs.[43]

The solution: Psychological androgyny?

By now it must be apparent to you that, even though sex may be fun, sex roles and sex typing can be the root of much unhappiness. Yet, incredible as it may seem, most of the solutions offered to alleviate the situation contain elements that in themselves bring about unhappiness.

The reasoning behind those solutions goes something like this: little girls should play with dolls, wear pretty dresses, and act quietly around the house. When they grow up, they should love children, be susceptible to flattery, and above all be understanding. After all, that is what being a woman is all about. Boys, on the other hand, should play with footballs and frogs, and engage in rough-and-tumble play. When they grow up, they should be competitive, forceful, and make instant decisions. If a little boy enjoys girlish activities, he is a sissy most likely to turn into a "fag," and his female counterpart is a tomboy most likely to become a "dyke."

You may find the foregoing paragraph funny or even absurd. It is, nevertheless, the essence of a commonly advocated solution for better adjustment. It suggests that it is healthy for men to act masculine and women to act feminine. Moreover, this view is by no means limited to the man on the street. Until recently, psychologists by and large tended to divide the world into male and female subsections. Sigmund Freud, of course, had already stated this belief that men should be masculine and women should be feminine. In fact, he maintained that if sex roles were not played "correctly," something was wrong. Many current forms of psychotherapy also emphasize the need for adjusting the person to his or her assigned sex role.

Despite such good advice, men and women continue to experience unhappiness about their respective sex roles. The question thus arises

[39]Jennings, Geis, & Brown, 1980. [40]Piacente, 1974. [41]Creager, 1971. [42]Kimmel, 1974. [43]Schaar, 1974.

whether we may have been incorrect in our assumptions about the benefits of the male and female roles. An increasing amount of evidence tends to support such doubts. For women, high scores on "femininity" measures were found to be related to poor self-esteem, low acceptance by others, and high anxiety.[44] Extensive studies by Eleanor Maccoby of Stanford University have shown that boys and girls who identify strongly with their own sex roles tend to be *less* intelligent and creative than children who do not identify as strongly with members of their own sex.[45] Although there is some evidence that during high school years the more masculine males are the better-adjusted boys,[46] there is also evidence to show that sex-typed identification among adult males is associated with low self-acceptance, high anxiety, and neuroticism.[47] In short, grown men who still feel that they must prove themselves on the football field have problems.

If you do not identify solely with members of your own sex, what else is there? Androgyny, for one thing. To be androgynous literally means to be both male and female at the same time. Our interest, of course, is in individuals who are **psychologically androgynous**—those who do not identify exclusively with either the male or the female sex role. To make any such statements, we must first find a way to measure psychological androgyny. Considerable progress in this direction has been made by psychologist Sandra Bem of Cornell University.

Bem began her studies by developing a psychological measure for masculinity, femininity, and androgyny. The common assumption has always been that masculinity and femininity were mutually exclusive terms. If you were a

Male or female? Individuals who are *psychologically* androgynous do not identify exclusively with either the male or female sex-role. Experiments have demonstrated that such individuals can adapt themselves more comfortably to a variety of situations.

[44]Cosentino & Heilbrun, 1964; Gray, 1957; Webb, 1963; Sears, 1970. [45]Maccoby, 1966. [46]Mussen, 1961. [47]Mussen, 1962; Harford, Willis, & Deabler, 1967.

feminine person, for example, you could not be masculine. In constructing her measures, Bem disregarded this assumption of inverse relationships between the sex roles. In fact, there is little evidence that masculinity and femininity are at opposite ends of the same continuum.[48] Instead, she asked a group of Stanford undergraduates which traits would be more desirable in U.S. society for men and which for women. Table 10-4 shows some of the traits so judged.

TABLE 10-4. Sample traits judged as desirable of the sexes

Masculine Items	Feminine Items
Aggressive	Cheerful
Analytical	Compassionate
Forceful	Gullible
Self-reliant	Sympathetic

Source: Bem, 1974.

In summarizing her research, Bem concluded that psychologically androgynous people are capable of adapting their behavior to either masculine or feminine situations. In other words, they behave appropriately to a given situation without regard for what is considered correct for a member of their sex to do.[49] To demonstrate this, Bem performed two experiments on that topic. Typically, in such studies males are found to be less conforming than females. To be less conforming is also assumed to be indicative of better personal adaptation and adjustment. In Bem's conformity study, the androgynous men and women behaved just as the masculine subjects did: they showed independence when under pressure to conform. In the second study, Bem gave her subjects the opportunity to engage in feminine behavior —playing with a little kitten. In this situation, the androgynous male and female subjects responded more like the feminine subjects and proceeded to play with the kitten. Together, these experiments demonstrate that people who do not identify exclusively with either the male or the female role can adapt themselves more comfortably than others to a variety of situations.[50]

Another study related androgyny to nonverbal behavior (see Chapter 1 for a discussion of nonverbal behavior). Among the many ways we communicate nonverbally, some behaviors are more common among women (gazing and smiling) and others are more frequently seen among men (interrupting and filling pauses). Masculine, feminine, and androgynous individuals were divided into same-sex pairs and observed as they performed several tasks. Those who had scored androgynous on Bem's Sex Role Inventory were observed using a better blend of masculine and feminine nonverbal behaviors than the subjects in either sex-typed group. As in Bem's studies, these results show that androgynous individuals can better adapt their behavior to situations than people who identify exclusively with one sex role.[51]

[48]BERNARD, 1980. [49]BEM, 1974. [50]BEM, 1975. [51]LA FRANCE & CARMEN, 1980.

Men who score high on psychological tests for masculinity will not engage in the "feminine" activity of playing with a small kitten. However, men who score high on androgyny can adapt their role and enjoy this activity.

We need to be adaptable to have successful social relationships. Studies have shown that, when masculine males and feminine females are paired up, they may not hit it off, presumably because each has an inflexible identification with his or her role. Social encounters between two androgynous members of opposite sexes seem to go more smoothly.[52] Still another study on androgyny examined responses to an invitation to participate in a study on erotic films. Actually, subjects were contacted by telephone and asked if they would volunteer for an experiment involving either watching an erotic film or the perception of geometric figures. In general, women were found less likely than men to volunteer for the erotic film study. When the data were inspected more closely, however, it was determined that only women who scored high on femininity volunteered less. Androgynous women were no less likely to volunteer for the erotic film experiment than were men. Although men and women may be equally responsive to erotic films,[53] traditional women may have learned to avoid erotic films because they were not supposed to like them. The more adaptable androgynous women may be better able to express their preference without concern for "what is proper."[54]

We must point out that the study of sex roles is a new and rapidly developing area. Many psychologists doubt that androgyny will solve the many problems associated with sex-role identification,[55] and others have criticized methods for measuring androgyny.[56] Thus, the area of androgyny and sex-role

[52]ICKES & BARNES, 1978. [53]FISHER & BYRNE, 1978. [54]KENDRICK, STRINGFIELD, WAGENHALS, DAHL, & RANSDELL, 1980. [55]PURSELL & BANIKIOTES, 1978; BERNARD, 1980. [56]JACKSON & PAUNONEN, 1980; KELLY & WORELL, 1977; HINRICHSEN & STONE, 1978; WALKUP & ABBOTT, 1978.

adaptability represents a challenging and important set of opportunities for young psychologists new to the field. In the meantime, however, we must remember that sexism has been the cause of many adjustment problems. Think of your own life. Surely you must recall more than one instance when your behavior was influenced by the process of sex typing. In other words, you acted manly in situations that supposedly tested your bravery as a male or tenderly in situations that supposedly tested your warmth and understanding as a female. On those occasions, you let your behavior be influenced by the expectations of others, or perhaps even by the expectations of society at large. You also may have harbored some resentment at the time. You may have felt that you should have been judged by others on the basis of your qualities as a *person*. Why, then, did you behave the way you did? Most likely because sex typing is an unfortunate fact of life. It is difficult to eradicate because, apart from anatomical differences, there are also many documented differences in attitudes, interests, beliefs, and behavior patterns between the sexes.

So what? We submit to you that the existence of such differences is not necessarily the crucial issue here. What one should really ask is, first, to what extent are such differences inculcated into our personal value systems by the society in which we live? Second, what are the implications of the existence of such differences?

The answer to both questions is clear, as the evidence presented in this chapter shows. Society is the primary force that sets in motion, then zealously guards, the process of sex typing. From birth through maturity to death, in fact. The unfortunate individuals of both sexes who do not fit this process are usually subjected to discriminatory treatment. In other words, the feminine male and masculine female are headed for trouble. The strait jacket of sex roles that society bestows upon us is so tight and so oppressive that even those who follow the rules have problems. The feminine female and the masculine male have their own share of troubles in living up to expectations.

What have psychologists and other social scientists contributed to our knowledge of this problem? Quite a lot, as you can gather from this chapter. The numerous studies that we have presented may be regarded as more than mere evidence for the existence of sexism in the form of male chauvinism. They are, in fact, an indictment of the entirely male-dominated society in which we live. One might argue, however, that it is not necessarily the task of social scientists to offer solutions along with their research findings. It may very well be the task of legislators, organizers, or political activists. It is precisely because of such considerations that psychologist Sandra Bem's research is so meaningful. Her findings clearly show that, despite societal sex typing and sex-role pressures, psychologically androgynous individuals show the greatest sex-role adaptability. Becoming androgynous may not be easy, however, particularly if you are male. A study showed that college students felt a woman performing a masculine task was more deserving of a reward than a man performing the same task. Men, however, were not seen as more deserving of rewards than women for performing feminine tasks.[57] Striving for androgyny is not a simple solution, but we feel it is a good one.

[57]Bem, 1975.

Box 10-2. How to combat sexism: An "editorial."

As a rule, textbook writers in psychology are not supposed to editorialize. To the extent that their personal views are expressed, it is always done discreetly in parenthetical asides. What follows began as a footnote, but its size became unmanageable and so it appears in its present form. It reflects our concern as two male psychologists on the lack of studies (with the notable exception of one recent issue of the *Journal of Social Issues*) on the damaging effect of sexism on males. If sexism affects women adversely, it must also affect men who live according to equally rigorous societal dictates.

Yet studies on discrimination against women keep pouring in. Psychologists have practically been falling over themselves in their crusading zeal to expose the evils of sexism. At the time this is being written, the damning pile of evidence for male-chauvinistic discriminatory practices has increased to gigantic proportions. Most of the studies, incidentally, have ignored the issue of what to *do* about sexism. They simply report the lamentable facts without offering solutions.

Lately, we have been wondering if all this mounting evidence may not constitute a classic case of overkill. If so, such studies may in a way be a disservice to those who are trying to work out their sex-role adjustment problems. Those unfortunate people are presented—in fact, bombarded—with what they have known and experienced most of their lives. Consider, for example, what happens if you are a female victim of the system: initially, there is solid evidence to show that you are being discriminated against solely because you are female, knowledge that is supportive and reassuring. You say to yourself: now *they* know what I have known all along. After a while, however, the novelty wears off. You begin to get tired of hearing how oppressed you are. You want solutions. If none is forthcoming, despair, desperation, and depression are sure to follow. (We do not mean to imply that presentation of information about sexist practices is not important. It is a necessary *first step* of great educational value, particularly because many of the oppressors and the oppressed are not even aware of their status.)

The oppressor, on the other hand, soon becomes immune to the avalanche of damning evidence. All he has to do is weather the shock and guilt he experiences upon first being confronted with that evidence. In the absence of any offered solution and plan of action, even those men most sympathetic to feminism will shrug their shoulders and return to the sexist fold and its comfortable payoffs. (Perhaps they never left the fold: many feminists are justifiably suspicious of liberal and sympathetic males who ease their guilt through words rather than action.)

Bem's research actually offers a solution of sorts. You can consult Table 10-4 and try to incorporate into your value system both types of featured items. If you do this sincerely and consistently, you may very well be on the way to joining, as Bem puts it, "a distinct class of people who can be appropriately termed androgynous, and whose sex-role adaptation enables them to engage in situationally effective behavior without regard for its stereotype as masculine or feminine" (p. 643).[58]

[58]BEM, 1975.

SUMMARY HIGHLIGHTS

1. The gender roles played by male and female participants have important consequences in their lives because they are *sex typed*. The evidence is not convincing, however, that men and women truly understand the roles, needs, and requirements of the opposite sex.

2. Many of the early studies on *sex roles* would be judged as *sexist* by contemporary standards. Experiments in which infant monkeys were found to prefer cloth to wire mothers were interpreted to mean that young children need to have a mother at home to provide contact comfort for them. Other sexist studies were used to demonstrate that personality characteristics of men were associated with preference for large or small dimensions of the female anatomy. Similar studies on female preferences for the male anatomy suggest that men are not aware of the characteristics that stimulate women.

3. The predominant explanation for the differences in behaviors between men and women is rooted in sex-role *socialization*. From a very early age, boys and girls are subjected to different experiences in line with what is thought to be appropriate to their sex (such as mechanical toys for boys, dolls for girls, and so on).

4. Despite the overwhelming evidence that sex roles are learned, some biologically oriented psychologists believe that differences in sex-typed behaviors are a product of hormonal differences.

5. Both men and women discriminate against women. The same product may be judged as superior, if the judges are led to believe it was done by a man, by both sexes. Competent women, however, gain some protection because these results are most often obtained for samples of equally poor work. In fact, women may even have an edge in judgments of equally distinguished work.

6. When asked what traits are healthy for men, for women, and adults (sex unspecified), mental health professionals tend to identify a different set of traits for each sex. Traits judged to be healthy for women include some of the same ones considered neurotic for men. There is little evidence, however, that women receive biased treatment from competent psychotherapists.

7. Many pressures on adult women force them into situations that might increase the chances that they will have less self-esteem and less self-confidence. Pressures on women to become mothers, and the depiction of women as housewives in television commercials, are among the many normative socializing pressures facing contemporary women.

8. To be *psychologically andrognynous* is to be able to adopt either sex role, depending on the demands of a given situation. A growing number of young adults are able to ignore how a "man" or a "woman" should behave in a given situation.

CHAPTER 11 SOCIAL ECOLOGY

STRESS AND ENVIRONMENTS
    Classifying environments
    The nature of stress: Frustration, conflict, and pressure
    Stressful environments can kill!

ENVIRONMENTAL SOURCES OF STRESS
    Future shock: Too many changes
    Noise: Quiet, you're disturbing my blood pressure!
    Heat: Hot tempers and big tips
    Crowds: Are they maddening?
    Proxemics: Getting too close
    The moon: It doesn't cause lunacy
    The economy: Recession inflates problems

COPING WITH ENVIRONMENTS
    Ecological psychology: The study of behavioral settings
    The medical environment: Coping with pain
    General adaptation: Nature's own way

MODIFYING ENVIRONMENTS
    Therapeutic environments and sick societies
    Disarming the population bomb
    Cash for trash
    Nutritional balance acts
    Modifying the energy crisis

SUMMARY HIGHLIGHTS

STRESS AND ENVIRONMENTS

Ecology is the branch of biology that studies the relationship between living organisms and their environments. Organisms must adapt to the physical environment to survive. Similarly, environments can have an impact on the social lives of their inhabitants. Thus, psychologists have recently come to recognize the importance of studying people within natural environments and analyzing the impact physical environments have upon social behavior.[1] This field of study is called **environmental psychology**. A related area, *ecological psychology*, focuses on things that happen in a behavioral setting. We will refer to these areas of study jointly as **social ecology**. As well-known environmental psychologist Dan Stokols proclaims, "At a time when environmentalists and economists are proclaiming that 'small is beautiful,' the research literature on human behavior in relation to its environmental settings continues to expand at a staggering rate" (p. 253).[2] Currently, environmental psychology or social ecology is a combination of many different research fields. Some social ecologists study the nature of social and physical environments; others focus on psychological stress, the most common response when we are unable to control the environment. Other social ecologists concentrate on the relationship among environmental change, stress response, and the mechanisms for coping with stress.

[1]WICKER, 1979. [2]STOKOLS, 1978.

This woman's harried working conditions are typical of psychological, stress-evoking situations studied by environmental psychologists.

Classifying environments

How do different environments affect your behavior? Are you happier when the sun is out? Or do you get into more fights and arguments on hot days? Most of social psychology is based on the premise that behavior is influenced by situations. Some of the early work in the field of environmental psychology involved building classification systems for various situations. You might think of this as similar to the work done by many early personality psychologists who built elaborate systems to classify personality types (such as aggressive, masculine). The environmental psychologists built elaborate systems to classify the characteristics of environments that had been shown to affect individual or group behavior. Table 11-1, a classification system created by psychologist Rudolf Moos,[3] shows six characteristics of social environments and gives examples of how they can affect your behavior. For example, many studies demonstrate that characteristics of the social climate (*milieu*) of your environment will affect your behavior. The likelihood that a high school girl will begin to drink, for example, can be greatly influenced by the number of other girls who already drink or who approve of social drinking. Other characteristics of the environment are physical, such as the density of housing, the amount of noise, or the climate.

Until the 1960s, people seemed unconcerned about many rapid changes in the physical environment. Then, suddenly, people began to consider the potential dangers of overpopulation, overuse of the wilderness, urban noise, dumping of dangerous chemicals, and air pollution. Popular books such as Rachel Carson's *Silent Spring*[4] and Paul Ehrlich's *The Population Bomb*[5] stimulated mass public concern that became reflected in major public events like Earth Day. Public concern was followed by rapid growth in environmental

[3]Moos, 1973. [4]Carson, 1962. [5]Ehrlich, 1971.

TABLE 11-1. Six characteristics of environments

Characteristics	Examples
1. Ecological dimensions	Architectural design, geographic location, weather conditions
2. Behavior setting	Office, home, store
3. Organizational structure	Percentage of women in the student body, number of people per household, average age of group
4. Characteristics of milieu inhabitants	Proportion of students in university who date, drink, or vote
5. Psychosocial and organization climate	Work pressure, encouragement of participation, orientation toward helping with personal problems
6. Functional or reinforcing properties of the environment	Is aggression reinforced on the football field, is it reinforced at home?

Source: Moos, 1973.

psychology as a field of research.[6] One of the major themes in the area of environmental psychology is that the objectionable parts of the environment cause psychological stress. Before we review the particular causes of environmental stress, however, it is best to discuss the notion of psychological stress and its basic causes.

The nature of stress: Frustration, conflict, and pressure

Psychological stress is something that all of us have experienced at one time or another. It is virtually impossible to escape its effects. No matter who you are or where you are, sooner or later stress will bear down on you. It can come in many forms, depending on the situation. Its intensity may vary. But its effects are never in doubt. It will force you to change, to adapt, or to cope with the situation facing you. And when the cumulative effects of frustration, conflict, and pressure reach a certain point, stress can even kill you—*literally*, not just as a figure of speech.

Psychologist James Coleman considers frustration, conflict, and pressure to be integral parts of psychological stress.[7] *Frustration* occurs when you are blocked from obtaining something you want. It may take different forms, but the principle remains the same. If, after being a pre-med student for four years, you are rejected by all major medical schools, you become frustrated. If you want to get into a rock concert and the doorman refuses to honor your ticket, you become frustrated. You may become aggressive as the result of these frustrations (see Chapter 6), but, as we shall see later in the chapter, there are more constructive ways to cope with such situations. Finally, we shall deal with stress caused by *pressure* to speed up activities. This could be in the form of external pressure, as when your professor assigns a lot of extra reading right before the midterm exam; or in the form of internal pressure, as when no such reading is assigned, but you take it upon yourself because it fits your style and aspirations.

Then, of course, there is always *anxiety*. The term anxiety usually refers to

[6]ALTMAN, 1976; STOKOLS, 1978. [7]COLEMAN, 1973.

observable reactions to stress. It is an unpleasant emotional state marked by worry, apprehension, and tension. When you are anxious, your autonomic nervous system becomes activated: your heart beats faster; your pulse goes up; your hands tend to sweat. The amount of anxiety you experience will, in part, depend on the intensity of the stress-producing stimuli as perceived by you. How potentially harmful is the situation? How threatening? How dangerous?[8]

Actually, there are two types of anxiety. Anxiety as described in the last paragraph is actually **state anxiety**. State anxiety is an emotional reaction to a situation and will vary from one situation to another. **Trait anxiety** is a personality characteristic, reflecting the noticeable differences among individuals in the frequencies and intensities of emotional reactions to stress. For example, it was shown that patients who had undergone major surgery showed less state anxiety after they had been told they were recovering well than they did before the operation. Trait anxiety was not affected by the situation: it remained the same before and after surgery.[9] People high in trait anxiety simply continue to respond in an anxious way, even in situations that evoke little or no anxiety among people low in trait anxiety.[10]

Both types of anxiety are closely related to effective coping with life situations. People who are high in trait anxiety are prone to look at the world as a threatening and dangerous place, which is similar to the perception of many psychoneurotic individuals.[11] State anxiety can turn into an acute *traumatic neurosis*, a temporary personality change due to some emotional shakeup (such as involvement in an accident or escape from one). This emotional shakeup is not necessarily the result of a one-time experience. It could very well be the accumulation of several less traumatic experiences. Psychologists suggest that most of us have, or will experience, some form of traumatic neurosis during our lifetimes.[12]

Much of what we know about traumatic neuroses comes from studies of American soldiers during World War II. Battlefields are stressful environments known to cause trauma (psychological and/or physical damage). The condition experienced by these soldiers was battle fatigue or shell shock, which affected the men in different ways. Some wandered around the battlefield all day long not knowing quite where they were or what they were doing. Others went into fits of rage, attacking anything in sight. Still others went into panic and fled from the battle area. After this initial reaction to the stress, a variety of symptoms followed. The three types of symptoms observed most often were:

1. Spells of uncontrollable emotion—usually anxiety, but sometimes rage and depression
2. Sleep disturbance, including insomnia and terrifying dreams in which the traumatic event is relived
3. Blocking or partial loss of various personal skills, inability to concentrate, and loss of other "ego functions"[13]

[8]SPIELBERGER, 1972. [9]SPIELBERGER, AUERBACH, WADSWORTH, DUNN, & TAULBEE, 1975. [10]SPIELBERGER, 1966. [11]SPIELBERGER, 1976. [12]MASLOW & MITTLEMAN, 1951. [13]JANIS, MAHL, KAGAN, & HOLT, 1969.

The bulk of the evidence from other studies related to war environments indicates that severe anxiety reactions were observed in soldiers exposed to front-line combat, in pilots flying combat missions, and in people whose relatives were killed in air raids.[14] Some lasting effects of wartime stress are described in Figure 11-1. It is noteworthy that 70% of those who had anxiety reactions were still experiencing some symptoms 20 years later. Evidence from Korean War veterans also suggests that combat anxiety may interfere with activities later in life; men who had experienced anxiety during combat were more often unemployed years after returning to civilian life.[15]

The difficulties faced by World War II veterans may have been minor in comparison to those experienced by the veterans of the Vietnam War. In comparison to World War II vets, those who participated in the Vietnam War faced greater uncertainty on the battle lines. For example, in contrast to many earlier wars, soldiers in the Vietnam conflict did not know for certain who the enemy was. The enemy did not wear uniforms or march in organized groups.

Many other factors made it difficult for the Vietnam veterans to return home. On returning, many found their friends and families were very much against the war, greeting them with such questions as "Did you kill any babies?" The exact impact of the war upon American participants is difficult to determine. A report by the Center for Policy Studies showed that 75% of the Vietnam veterans experienced nightmares, marital difficulties, and problems on the job. The report suggested that nearly half of the veterans faced physical and psychological ailments long after the war, including nervous disorders and drug abuse.[16]

One could argue that the type of person who experienced combat anxiety would have developed these problems anyway. This is entirely possible (see Box 11-1). But the fact that such problems were less frequent among noncombat psychiatric patients suggests that combat neuroses will endure and cause continued adjustment problems. A more important question is whether reactions to traumatic catastrophies such as earthquakes, fires, and automobile accidents are grossly different from reactions to battlefield traumas. The most common symptoms among survivors of such catastrophic events are nausea, diarrhea, short temper, and the inability to sleep and concentrate.[17] Fortunately, these symptoms are usually short lived, do not affect realistic responses to the disaster, and rarely lead to chronic states of severe mental disturbance.[18]

Stressful environments can kill!

Let us turn from battlefields and earthquakes to more common affairs of daily life. Johnny Jones wanted to do well on his final exams. He studied hard. He also worried a lot. On the day of the exams, he felt reasonably ready. Then, just as he was preparing to answer the first test question, he became engulfed in a wave of nausea. He could not concentrate. He sat frozen at his desk but finally managed to leave the room. The test questions remained unanswered.

[14]Fraser, Leslie, & Phelps, 1943; Star, 1949; Tompkins, 1959. [15]Archibald & Tuddenham, 1965. [16]Viet Vets, 1979. [17]Leff, 1975. [18]Janis, Mahl, Kagan, & Holt, 1969.

> **Box 11-1. Did the war cause his problems?**
>
> Eric was a captain in Vietnam. During his tour of duty, he had the responsibility for a large number of men. When his tour of duty was over in 1970, Eric returned home to a small Midwestern farming town. Most of Eric's friends thought he would be happy to be home. During his first six months back in the United States, however, Eric suffered severe depression.
>
> Was Eric's depression caused by the war? This is difficult to determine. There are many reasons why a person might feel upset or depressed. It thus becomes necessary to determine whether the incidence of depression is greater among veterans than would be expected for an equivalent group of men.
>
> One study of Vietnam veterans was conducted by psychologists John Helzer, Lee Robins, Eric Wish, and Michi Hesselbrock. They found that, immediately after returning from duty in Vietnam, those who had experienced combat duty showed noticeably more symptoms of depression than a matched control group of nonveterans. When the same veterans were followed three years later, however, they no longer experienced more depression than the matched control group.
>
> Now the question remains, why did Eric continue to experience depression? Although Eric participated in the war, we cannot say with certainty that the war was the cause of his problems. The probability of being depressed three years after the war appeared to be about the same for those who served in Vietnam as for those who did not. In each group, a fair number of individuals experienced the symptoms of depression.
>
> Another problem has been whether the control group was really equivalent to the group of individuals who served in Vietnam. The only way to assure equivalence would be to assign people randomly to serve in the armed services. This is not likely to happen. Because of this problem, it is difficult to determine whether any similarities of differences between the groups were the result of war experiences, or just differences between the two groups of people that existed before the war.
>
> *Source:* Viet Vets, 1979.

Was Johnny merely the victim of fate? Perhaps so. But we do know that our defenses against disease are not very efficient when we are under stress. We also know that many disorders are caused or aggravated by emotional upset. Among problems that have been linked to stress are tension headaches, warts, hives, stomach ulcers, high blood pressure, heart attacks, and a host of psychological disorders.

More than three centuries ago, French philosopher René Descartes wrote about the connection between mind and body, being aware that one could affect the other. Because he was a religious man, Descartes thought of the mind as the human soul—our link to the divine. He postulated that the nonphysical mind made connection with the physical body through the pineal gland in the brain. The human being could thus be viewed as partly

| Symptoms | Percent displaying symptoms |

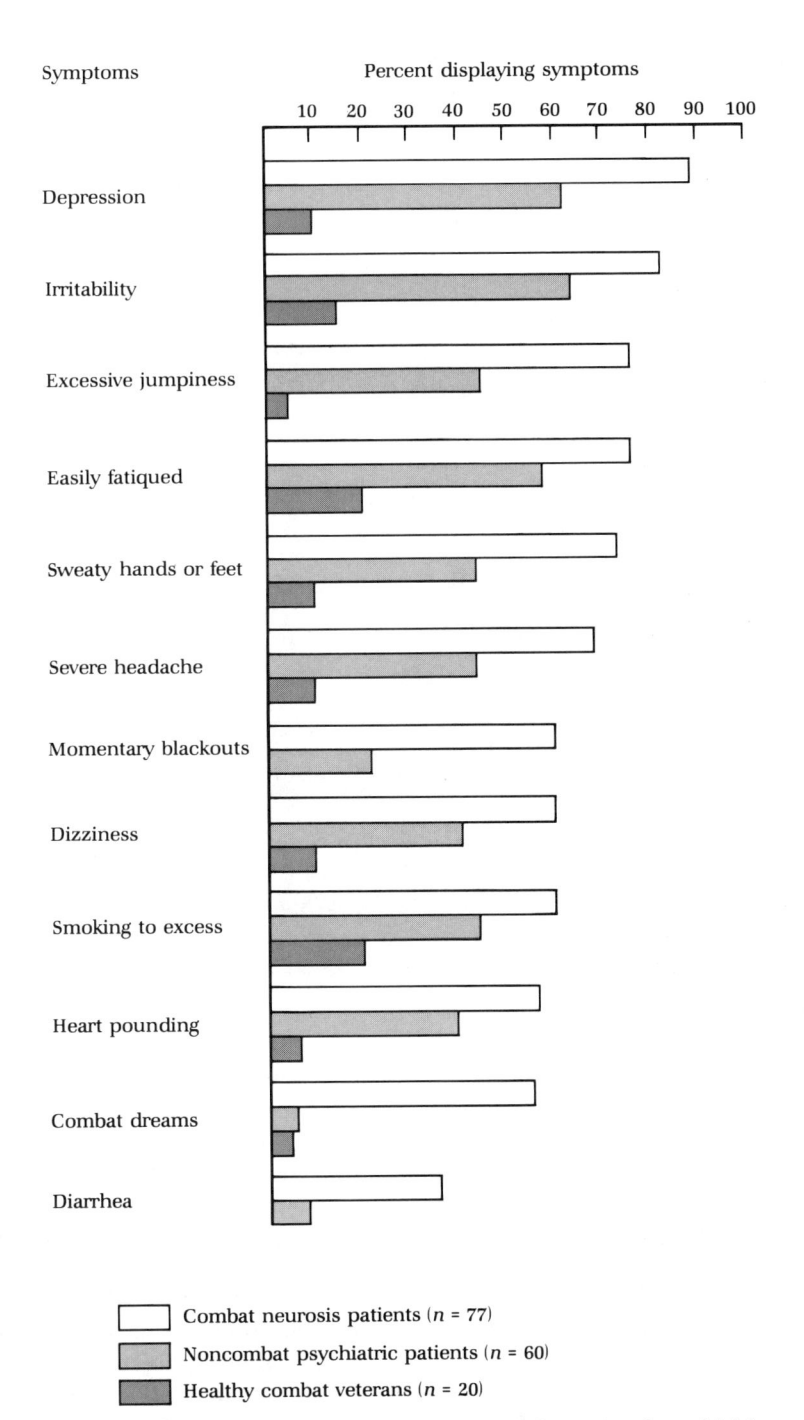

Figure 11-1. Lasting effects of battlefield environments. Twenty years after World War II, many veterans still suffered from stress. Notice especially the lasting symptoms of combat neurosis patients. *Source:* Archibald & Tuddenham, 1965.

Symptoms (top to bottom): Depression, Irritability, Excessive jumpiness, Easily fatigued, Sweaty hands or feet, Severe headache, Momentary blackouts, Dizziness, Smoking to excess, Heart pounding, Combat dreams, Diarrhea.

Legend:
- Combat neurosis patients (n = 77)
- Noncombat psychiatric patients (n = 60)
- Healthy combat veterans (n = 20)

divine (through the soul) and partly a member of the animal world (through the body). Physiologists later showed that Descartes' theory about the pineal gland was wrong. Nevertheless, he was influential in getting people to consider ways in which the mind affects the body, and vice versa.

In a best-selling book, *Type A Behavior and Your Heart*, the authors argue that certain individuals maintain a lifestyle that stress is practically built into. Typical of such people is the hard-driving, competitive individual whose calendar shows something scheduled for every hour of the day. (see Figure 11-2). Over a period of ten years, the authors were able to predict with great accuracy the number of heart attacks these people would suffer.[19]

Figure 11-2.
Type A individuals are hard-driving and competitive. They maintain a lifestyle with built-in stress—with fatal results (see text).

If you have a Type A behavior pattern, you are about twice as likely to develop coronary heart disease as individuals who are classified Type B.[20] The Type A pattern has three components: achievement striving, time urgency, and aggressiveness.[21] Psychologist David Glass and his associates have shown the achievement-striving component by demonstrating how the individual prone to heart attack will persist at tasks even when he or she feels tired.[22] The need for the Type A person to do things quickly (time urgency) has been demonstrated in experiments showing that Type A individuals do more poorly than Type Bs on tasks requiring a low rate of responding for reinforcement.[23] The third component of the Type A behavior pattern is aggressiveness. In one series of experiments, Type A and Type B individuals were either treated neutrally or exposed to an instigation designed to threaten their sense of well-being. Later, the subjects were given the opportunity to give electric shocks to a confederate who had been involved in the threat. Type As and Type Bs did not differ in the amount of aggression observed when there had

---

[19]Friedman & Rosenman, 1974. [20]Rosenman, Brand, Jenkins, Friedman, Strauss, & Wurm, 1975. [21]Glass, 1977.
[22]Carver, Coleman, & Glass, 1976. [23]Glass, Snyder, & Hollis, 1974.

been no threat. In response to threat, however, Type As reacted with significantly more aggression. One explanation for the Type A pattern of behavior is that it is a response style for maintaining heightened personal control over the physical and social environment.

The most notorious product of stressful environments is still the stomach ulcer. Considering its painful symptoms and potential dangers, it seems incredible that having an ulcer was once considered a badge of honor among business executives, a testimonial to their dedication to their work. Hopefully, such stupidity in value judgment is no longer around. Just consider what happens when you develop an ulcer.

Whenever you are under stress, your body is likely to produce excessive amounts of hydrochloric acid (HCL), which is normally used in the process of digesting food by breaking it down into substances your body can use. In addition, HCL activates other digestive enzymes.

The worst combination for you is stress and the consumption of acid-producing items such as spicy foods and coffee. The resulting "acid stomach" and heartburn cause considerable discomfort. When the acid gets out of control, there is insufficient mucus production to protect your stomach lining from small sores or lesions. When those occur, you have developed an ulcer.

Having an ulcer is not fun. You must avoid spicy foods, coffee, and other substances that irritate the lesions. Milk or antacids usually help to alleviate discomfort somewhat. Drugs such as Tagamet may also be prescribed. But ulcers can be very dangerous—the lesions can erode a blood vessel, causing internal bleeding. Even worse, ulcers can get so bad that they gnaw a hole through the gastric wall of the stomach, allowing its contents to empty into the abdominal cavity. This is a very dangerous condition that can cause infection of other internal organs and, eventually, death.

Although stress is probably not the sole cause of ulcers (genetic factors may be involved), it is a potent factor in causing the disorder. Experiments have shown that ulcers can be produced in rats in as short a period as two weeks. The rats were deprived of food and water to make them hungry and thirsty. When food and water were made available, shocks were given each time a rat tried to eat or drink. Thus, there was a conflict between the tendency to approach food and the tendency to avoid shock. Not only did the rats rapidly develop ulcers, many of them died of internal hemorrhaging within a few weeks.[25]

As a postscript to the topic of ulcers, you may be interested in the following observation. Franz Alexander, a proponent of psychoanalytic theory, believes that ulcers are caused by the conflict between the need for love and affection and the need to be strong, assertive, and independent. This is the reason, according to Alexander, that men have been more likely to develop ulcers than women. The liberation of women may change all that. It may create some of the same conflicts and pressures upon women that men have experienced in the past. One study, for example, showed that the proportion of ulcers among men greatly increased during the years of the 1930s Depression. Thus, with equal rights women may also attain equal ulcers.[26]

[24]CARVER & GLASS, 1978.   [25]SAWREY & WEISZ, 1956.   [26]MITTLEMAN & WOLFF, 1942; DAVISON & NEALE, 1974.

ENVIRONMENTAL SOURCES OF STRESS

Future shock: Too many changes

Society is changing, and changing fast. We are a society on the go—much more so than in any other period in history. Throwaway containers save the time spent on washing dishes, car radios give the news while we are traveling between activities, and jet planes deliver us in a few hours to places that formerly required months of travel to reach. While we are bouncing around from one place to the next, we can drive through the bank, the hamburger place, and in some cities even the mortuary. There has been an increase in mobile homes and portable buildings. People used to want to settle in one place forever; now it is not uncommon to have several homes in different locations, such as a cabin in the mountains and an apartment on the beach. Some people live in one place and work in another. One Wall Street executive lives in Columbus, Ohio and travels between his home and New York each week. A retired Stanford professor leaves his California home each Monday to travel to Ohio State University. He teaches a class there and returns home the next day. Love is also an inspiration for travel. A romance was reported in which the man lived in San Francisco and the woman lived in Honolulu. Each weekend, one or the other would board a jet plane to cross the 2000 miles of water so they could be together again.[27] In short, our world is becoming one in which time means everything and distance means nothing.

What effect do all these changes have? According to journalist Alvin Toffler, they cause a psychological state called *future shock*. Future shock is caused by the inability to adapt to the rapid rate of change in the pace of life. As Toffler puts it:

> *Future shock* will not be found in *Index Medicus* or in any listing of psychological abnormalities. Yet, unless intelligent steps are taken to combat it, millions of human beings will find themselves increasingly disoriented, progressively incompetent to deal rationally with their environments. The malaise, mass neurosis, irrationality, and free-floating violence already apparent in contemporary life are merely a foretaste of what may lie ahead unless we come to understand and treat this disease. (p. 13)[28]

Toffler explains that the changing world makes reality seem like a "kaleidoscope run wild." The resulting future shock is manifested in many symptoms. Some 12-year-old children act like adults and some 50-year-old adults act like 12 year olds. Simple pleasures are no longer exciting. They are being replaced with cocaine . . . Zen . . . porn movies . . . tranquilizers . . . Playboy Clubs . . . pop art. Future shock has been proposed as the cause of fractured families, psychological confusion, wife swapping, and "flipping out." It has created business for hard drug dealers, psychotherapists, and those who sell unique experiences. The long and the short of it is that the change in the pace of life is a stress that can be expected to get increasingly worse in the future.

Let us personalize the concept of life change for you. Take a look at Table 11-2. Go down the list of life change events and put a check mark beside each event that happened to you during the last six months. For each of these events look up the corresponding Life Change Units (LCUs) in the right-hand column. Now add up these scores.

[27]TOFFLER, 1970. [28]TOFFLER, 1970.

TABLE 11-2. Values of life change events [a]

	LCU Values
FAMILY	
Death of spouse	100
Divorce	73
Marital separation	65
Death of close family member	63
Marriage	50
Marital reconciliation	45
Major change in health of family	44
Pregnancy	40
Addition of new family member	39
Major change in arguments with spouse	35
Son or daughter leaving home	29
In-law troubles	29
Spouse starting or ending work	26
Major change in family get-togethers	15
PERSONAL	
Detention in jail	63
Major personal injury or illness	53
Sexual difficulties	39
Death of a close friend	37
Outstanding personal achievement	28
Start or end of formal schooling	26
Major change in living conditions	25
Major revision of personal habits	24
Changing to a new school	20
Change in residence	20
Major change in recreation	19
Major change in church activities	19
Major change in sleeping habits	16
Major change in eating habits	15
Vacation	13
Christmas	12
Minor violations of the law	11
WORK	
Being fired from work	47
Retirement from work	45
Major business adjustment	39
Changing to different line of work	36
Major change in work responsibilities	29
Trouble with boss	23
Major change in working conditions	20
FINANCIAL	
Major change in financial state	38
Mortgage or loan over $10,000	31
Mortgage foreclosure	30
Mortgage or loan less than $10,000	17

[a] *Scoring directions:* Mark the changes which may have happened in your life within the last six months. Add up the Life Change Unit (LCU) values associated with each of the events you have checked. People who experience the most life changes also experience the most illness (see text).
Source: Rahe, 1972.

How high is your score? The higher your score, the greater the likelihood that you will become ill. If your life change score is between 0 and 100, you would, on the average, probably report around 1.4 illnesses during the last six months. If your score is higher—say, 300 to 400—you would probably report more illnesses (around 1.9 on the average). Perhaps there have been a lot of life changes for you during the last six months and your score is between 500 and 600. In this case you would be likely to experience even more illness (an average of 2.1). These predictions have been taken from the actual findings of investigators studying the effects of life change. These investigators demonstrated that people who have had many life changes packed into a short period of time are more likely to develop symptoms of physical illness and stress than those who have experienced fewer life changes.[29]

To get the values listed in Table 11-2 under the heading LCU, social values had to be measured. It is easy to see that all of the events listed in the table represent life changes. But obviously each life change event cannot be counted as having the same effect. Getting a traffic ticket cannot be considered as disrupting as getting a divorce. To determine how much weight each of the events had, the investigators had people of different social backgrounds rate the degree of turmoil, upheaval, and social readjustment each of the events would require of a person. Each event was rated in comparison to the life change of getting married, which was arbitrarily assigned the score of 50. For example, people who were asked to give a number to the readjustment required by the death of a spouse (if the amount of readjustment necessitated by marriage is 50). Remarkably, there was little disagreement about these values among raters differing in age, sex, marital status, education, social class, race, and creed. In addition, there was substantial agreement among people from different cultures. Swedes, Danes, Japanese, and North Americans appear to regard the impact of life changes in similar ways. Once the scoring system had been developed, it was possible to create life stress scores and to compare these scores to types and amounts of illnesses contracted.[30]

In one study conducted with U.S. Navy personnel, life stress scores were obtained for entire crews before their vessels were sent out to sea. After six months, the sailors and their health records were examined. It was observed that sailors who were in the top 10% in life change scores were twice as likely to become ill as sailors in the bottom 10%. Life crises may have weakened the bodies of those sailors and made them easier targets for disease.

One of the most interesting aspects of the life change studies is that positive as well as negative life changes are considered to be potentially hazardous. We have all heard that people can die of broken hearts. This research shows that too many positive changes (getting married, outstanding personal achievement, starting a new job, and the like) may add up to produce the same effect.

Some of the work on life change and onset of illness has come under attack for methodological reasons.[31] Nevertheless, it is an exciting and interesting line of research that can at any point become focal to people's well-being.

Noise: Quiet, you're disturbing my blood pressure!

Another stress-producing aspect of modern society is increased urbanization. Living in the city means living with noise. The 87 million cars and nearly 20 million trucks in America are all equipped with loud engines and ear-piercing horns. Motorcycles (2.6 million of them) are, pound for pound, the highest

---

[29]Holmes & Rahe, 1967; Rahe, 1969a; Rahe, Mahan, & Arthur, 1970; Pugh, Gunderson, Erikson, Rahe, & Rubin, 1972; Rubin, Gunderson, & Arthur, 1969; Rahe, 1972. [30]Komaroff, Masuda, & Holmes, 1968; Rahe, 1969b; Rahe, Lundberg, Bennett, & Theorell, 1971. [31]Sarason & Hunt, 1974.

noise pollutants. Airplanes at takeoff produce a sound level of 105 decibels at a distance of 1000 feet. We are also confronted with the loud sounds of construction (a jackhammer produces 98 decibels at 50 feet), the sounds of garbage trucks, barking dogs, and human voices. Even within our own homes we are confronted with the sounds of vacuum cleaners, food blenders, and garbage disposals (all producing between 60 and 94 decibels at 3 feet).[32]

Psychologists David Glass and Jerome Singer have made extensive studies on the effects of noise upon the human psyche. They concluded that urban sounds are arousing, annoying, and stress-producing. Too much noise can affect your performance on the job, shake up your emotions, and cause physiological disturbances.

For many of their experiments, Glass and Singer created a simulation of a 108-decibel sound by tape recording some common noises superimposed upon each other, such as a typewriter, a desk calculator, a mimeograph machine, and several people talking in foreign languages. Subjects were seated in front of a panel of lights and buttons. For some of the subjects, the noise was presented in bursts occurring at predictable times and durations. Other subjects experienced interruptions of unpredictable duration on a random time schedule. To determine the effects of exposure to noise, Glass and Singer took a variety of physiological measures, including electrical conductivity of the skin, muscle tension, and the constriction of blood vessels in the finger. All of these measures are commonly used as indicators of stress.

The results of the study were somewhat perplexing. Initial noise exposure clearly produced stress, as indicated by the physiological changes in the responding subjects. On repeated presentation, however, stress responses diminished until they reached a point where there was no difference between being exposed to noise and not experiencing noise at all. It also made no difference whether noise exposure was on schedule or unpredictable, or whether the subjects thought they could control the noise.[33]

If all this causes you to rush to your stereo set for some blasts of loud rock music without fear of consequences—beware! Although it is true that Glass and Singer demonstrated the remarkable ability of people to adapt to noise, their findings about the *aftereffects* of exposure to noise spell out an altogether different message. They discovered a great number of detrimental consequences for those who had been exposed to noise, such as an inability to concentrate or tolerate frustration. These undesirable aftereffects were most pronounced for those who had been exposed to the unpredictable blasts of noise.

Besides these psychological symptoms, exposure to unpredictable noise may also lead to an increase in physical symptoms. In one study, subjects were presented with either predictable or unpredictable bursts of noise. Afterwards it was shown that those exposed to unpredictable noise had slower reaction times and reported more physical symptoms (such as upset stomach, ringing ears, shortness of breath, and so on). One of the fascinating aspects of this study, however, is that these aftereffects of noise were only observed for subjects who were told not to pay attention to the unexpected bursts. A noisy environment will affect you most when the noise is unpredic-

[32]U.S. Environmental Protection Agency, 1972. [33]Glass & Singer, 1972.

table and when it comes while you are paying attention to something else.[34] Still, long-term exposure to very loud noises regardless of your attention can have other serious physical consequences. In fact, overindulgence in loud music can lead to temporary, and sometimes permanent, hearing loss.[35]

On the social side, Glass and Singer found that noise, especially when unexpected, uncontrollable, and perceived as irritating, tended to decrease altruistic behavior. In Chapter 7, we reported that people will be more altruistic when they have recently succeeded at a task. This warm glow of success can, however, be wiped out when loud noise is added to the positive feedback. In the presence of this irritant, people who have just experienced success will be no more helpful than those who have just failed. Other investigators have shown that angry people are less able to deal with complex noises and that increased noise levels can actually heighten aggressive behavior.[36]

In summary, laboratory studies have suggested that living in noisy environments may not be desirable. Overexposure to noise can disrupt performance on mental tasks,[37] make you less sensitive to others,[38] and increase your blood pressure.[39] These findings might make you want to choose a quieter environment in which to live, or to fight for changes within your neighborhood to keep the noise level down. One group who has expressed concern about noise pollution are people who live near major airports. It is estimated that 8 million people in the United States are exposed to aircraft noise[40] (U.S. Environmental Protection Agency, 1974). A recent study demonstrated why these people have a good reason to be concerned. The subjects were school children who attended schools located under the flight paths of the Los Angeles International Airport. The air traffic over these elementary schools sometimes includes over 300 flights per day, or about one flight every 2.5 minutes, during the hours the children are attending school. For purposes of comparison, a sample of three schools in a quiet area was chosen and an extensive effort was made to ensure that the children in the quiet schools were similar to the airport area children in grade level, ethnic background, number of families receiving public aid, and the like.

The results, frequently observed in the laboratory, were replicated in the observations of the children. Children from schools under the flight paths had higher average blood pressure than those who attended quieter schools, and were less persistent in attempts to solve problems. Figure 11-3 shows the relationship between the time it took to solve a puzzle as a function of the number of years children had attended either quiet or noisy schools. As you can see, the longer children had been enrolled in the noisy school, the longer it took them to solve the puzzle. This was not the case for the children from the quiet schools. In fact, they needed less time to solve the puzzle as a function of years in the quiet environment.[41]

Heat: Hot tempers and big tips

Besides noise, heat is another pollutant related to the stressful effects of urban living. It is in the heat of the summer when riots are supposed to happen, tempers expected to flare, and people expected to lose their cool. Journalists

[34]MATTHEWS, SCHEIER, BRUNSON, & CARDUCCI, 1980. [35]DEY, 1970. [36]ISEN, 1970; YINON & BIZMAN, 1980; GEEN & O'NEAL, 1969; KONECNI, CROZIER, & DOOB, 1975. [37]BROADBENT, 1978; LOEB, 1979. [38]COHEN & LEZAK, 1977. [39]JONSSON & HANSSON, 1977. [40]U.S. ENVIRONMENTAL PROTECTION AGENCY, 1972. [41]COHEN, EVANS, KRANTZ, & STOKOLS, 1980.

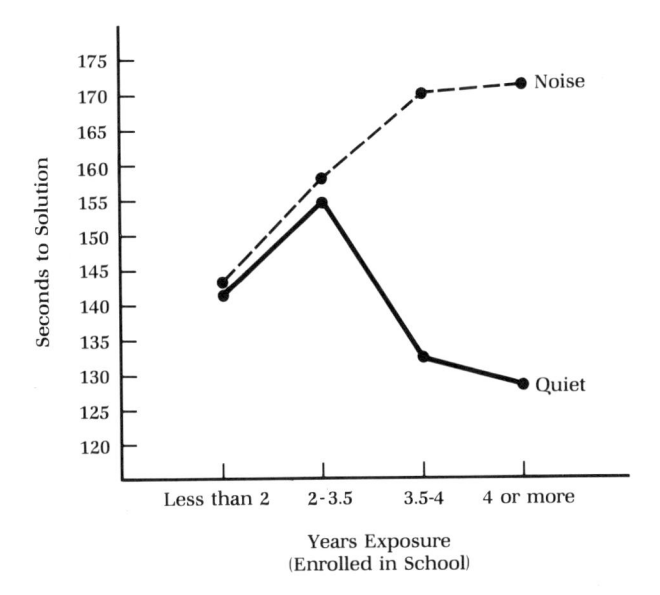

Figure 11-3.
Children attending a school under a flight path take longer to solve a puzzle than comparable children who attend quiet schools. This problem becomes apparent after 3.5 years of exposure. *Source:* Cohen, Evans, Krantz, & Stokols, 1980.

have speculated for years that intra-city troubles are most likely to occur during the "long hot summer" periods. But if such city riots are primarily caused by the poor social and economic conditions of a population segment, why this concern with summer months? The depressed conditions, after all, exist all year round.

Research by psychologists tends to confirm the journalistic speculations. A study was conducted comparing temperatures on days on which there had been riots to temperatures on the days before and after the riots occurred. Also compared were the normal daily baseline temperatures from years in which there had been no riots. The results of this study demonstrate that temperatures on the days of the riots were much higher than on the preceding or following days. Riot days were also warmer than their calendar equivalents in preceding years.[42]

Finding the relationship between heat and temperature can be confusing because there are many more days of average heat than there are extremely hot or extremely cold days. To test out the relationship between heat and rioting, it is necessary to take into consideration how rare very hot days are compared to average temperature days. For example, more riots do occur on days between 81° and 85° F.[43] However, many more such days fall in an average summer than days that are 95° F or higher. When psychologists J. Merrill Carlsmith and Craig Anderson took this into consideration by making a statistical adjustment, they found a clear relationship between temperature and chances of a riot. The graph in Figure 11-4 is based on reports of 102 separate riots that occurred between 1967 and 1971. Among these riots, 16 were judged to be directly related to the assassination of Martin Luther King on April 4, 1968 (14 occurred within two days of his death, and 2 occurred on the anniversary of his assassination). The analysis was done including and excluding the riots associated with Dr. King's death because it was believed

[42] GORANSON & KING, 1970. [43] BARON & RANSBERGER, 1978.

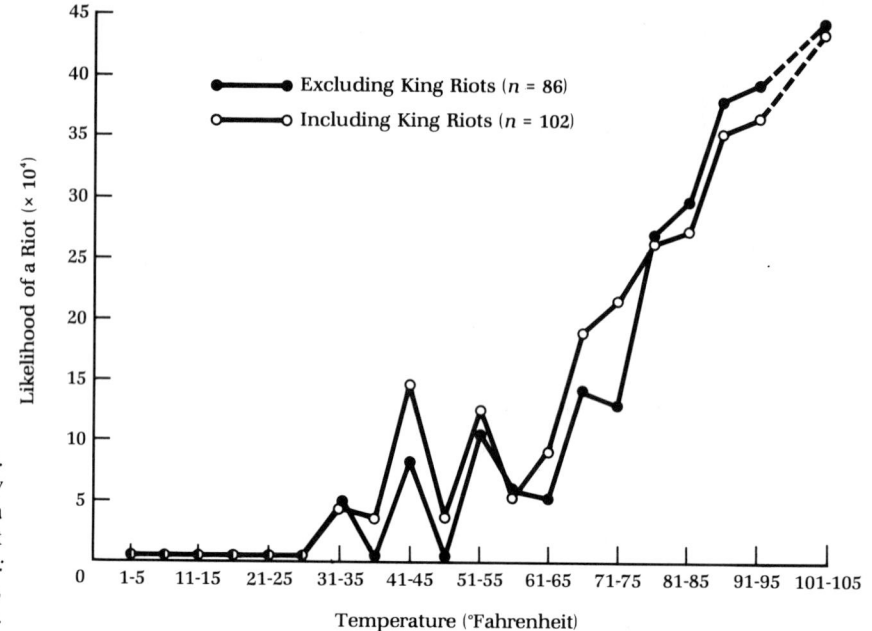

Figure 11-4. Conditional probability (likelihood) of a riot as a function of ambient temperature. *Source:* Carlsmith & Anderson, 1979.

that these riots may have been provoked by the specific incident rather than by heat. As you can see, either way riots are more likely on hot days.[44]

These findings do not necessarily indicate that heat causes riots. There are at least two explanations for the relationship between rioting and temperature. One explanation suggests that high temperatures aggravate existing conditions. Added to the ongoing frustrations of ghetto life, heat just caused the pot to boil over. The other explanation is that the heat caused people to get out of their homes into the streets. The excess of people in the streets provided an available mob to get involved in even minor disorders.[45]

The apparent relationship between heat and rioting suggests that heat can be a strong psychological stress agent. This, in turn, brought social psychologists into the laboratory for a closer look at the heat/aggression relationship.

In the first experiment, psychologist Robert Baron placed angered or non-angered subjects into either a hot (80° F) or a cool (69° F) room. Each room contained an aggression machine (see Chapter 4). When Baron asked the subjects to operate the aggression machine, he found just the opposite of what he had expected. Subjects in the cool environment gave shocks of greater intensity than subjects in the hot environment. One possible explanation was that the subjects in the hot room were so uncomfortable that they did not want to concentrate on the game.[46]

Thinking over his results and looking back at the riot situation, Baron reasoned that hot temperatures alone may not cause aggression, but that heat may make people more susceptible to the influences of a model. In his second experiment, the subjects were either exposed or not exposed to an aggressive model (see Chapter 6) and then allowed to use the aggression machine. The

[44]CARLSMITH & ANDERSON, 1979. [45]GORANSON & KING, 1970. [46]BARON, 1972.

results showed that hot temperatures decreased aggression when there was no model but increased aggression when there was a model. These findings allow for certain speculations about the relationship between heat and riots: hot temperatures may drive people into the streets, where they are susceptible to the influences of rioting models.[47]

Aggression is not the only social behavior affected by weather. Other research shows that the right weather can affect the helping mood. In one study, 540 pedestrians walking off campus near the University of Minnesota were observed for their willingness to submit themselves to a lengthy interview for a survey of social opinions. In another study, 130 restaurant patrons were observed on their tipping behavior. Both studies were conducted over a year, covering all seasons, with weather conditions such as amount of sunshine, temperature, relative humidity, and wind velocity carefully monitored. The most consistent statistical predictor for willingness to assist in the poll, or for generous tipping, was amount of sunshine. Because the study was a correlational one, it is not possible to draw the clear conclusion that good weather causes helping behavior. Nevertheless, say the authors, sunshine level could influence mood through its connection with pleasant events: "Thus sunshine could increase mood by stimulating thoughts of swimming, picnics, and other outings, whereas cloudy days could be associated with the annoyance of rain and snow" (p. 1954).[48]

Crowds: Are they maddening?

Unlike groups or organizations, crowds imply a minimum of individual interaction with others. In fact, the frequently repeated phrase "the faceless crowd" suggests individual anonymity. Nevertheless, under certain conditions being part of a crowd can have a significant impact on the individual. Many findings, however, tend to dispel commonly held stereotypes and old adages.

Take the notion of the "madding" crowd, for instance. What is the effect of people being crowded in relatively small areas? Perhaps not as bad as you may think. Psychologist Jonathan Freedman and his associates varied density by placing people in rooms of 160, 80, and 35 square feet. Groups of five to nine subjects were placed in the rooms and given various tasks (such as group discussion, cross-out task, memory task). In the extreme density condition, where nine subjects were seated in chairs with desk-type arms in the 35-square-foot room, there was just enough space for the subjects not to touch each other. Regardless of density, the productivity and quality of output of the various groups did not differ significantly.[49]

Although Freedman's contention that the crowd is not so maddening after all was popular just a few years ago, more recent research has turned up some clearly undesirable effects of overpopulating a small environment. In various studies, crowding has been linked to increased blood pressure, physiological arousal, physical discomfort, and an increase in the number of symptoms of illness people report.[50] People living in crowded environments experience

[47]Baron & Byrne, 1981; Baron & Lawton, 1972. [48]Cunningham, 1979. [49]Freedman, 1971; Freedman, Klevansky, & Ehrlich, 1971. [50]Aiello, Epstein, & Karlin, 1975; D'Atri, 1975; McCain, Cox, & Paulus, 1976.

The population explosion. Increasing evidence suggests that excessive population density and crowding can lead to a wide range of mental and physical health problems.

greater alienation,[51] and in some cases crowding has been associated with premature death.[52] Thus, the more recent evidence suggests that excessive population density is an undesirable human condition.[53]

Of course, not all humans react to crowded environments in the same way. Some people actually cope with crowded spaces extremely well, whereas others have much greater difficulty. The difference between coping and not coping well with crowded environments has been related to how much control people feel they have over the crowded environment.[54] If you feel you have some personal control, you may be able to cope with crowded environments. If you feel you have no control, however, the crowd is more likely to get to you. Thus, one key to helping people cope with crowded environments is to design environments that give them a feeling of personal control.

Within college dormitories, one of the most important types of personal control is social control. If you live in a dormitory, you probably want to be able to regulate the kind of people you will talk to or form social ties with. A common complaint among students who live in large dormitories is that it is difficult to be with people you care about and, at the same time, to avoid people you really don't care to be around. Figure 11-5 shows several dormitory floor plans. Floor plan A requires more than 40 students to share the same long corridor. If you have lived in such an environment, you probably know that it is undesirable. Studies have shown that students prefer floor plan B. This plan has only about 20 students sharing a space, and it allows for regula-

[51]McCarthy & Seagert, 1979. [52]Paulus, McCain, & Cox, 1978. [53]Sundstrom, 1978. [54]Baron & Rodin, 1978; Baum & Valins, 1979; Stokols, 1978.

tion of social life. If your college has already built dormitories using a model like floor plan A, it is unlikely that they will change over to the other plan because of the enormous cost. They can, however, follow the suggestions of psychologists Andrew Baum and Glenn Davis. These researchers convinced a small residential liberal arts college to place dividers in the middle of the corridor in a dormitory built along the lines of floor plan A. What resulted was two spaces, each serving about 20 students (see floor plan C in Figure 11-5).

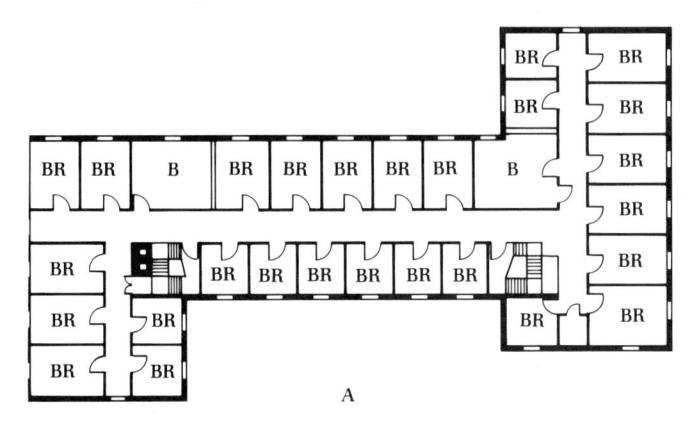

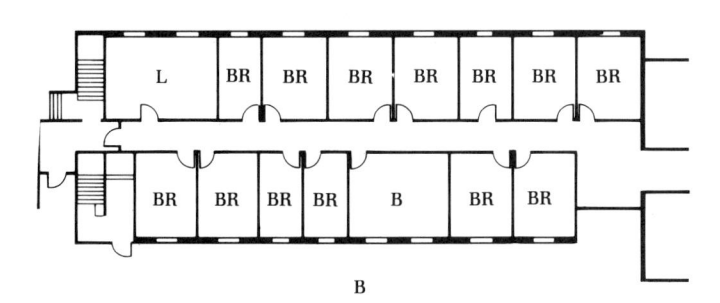

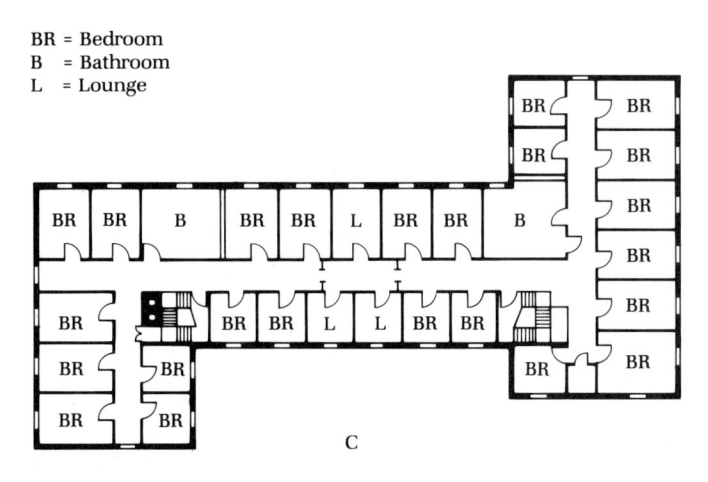

BR = Bedroom
B = Bathroom
L = Lounge

Figure 11-5.
Floor plans of the dormitory floors. (Plan A is the long corridor floor, B is the short corridor floor, and C is the intervention floor.) *Source:* Baum & Davis, 1980.

Then they made comparisons of the social behavior and personal reports of students living in the three different types of dormitories featured in the study. Although there were no differences between the groups when they first moved in, those in the long corridor dorm quickly grew dissatisfied. In contrast, those in the modified dorm reported less crowding and fewer social problems. In fact, they seemed to be about as satisfied as those living on a floor serving only 20 students.[55]

Although people may be able to adapt to crowded environments in laboratory experiments,[56] the best evidence suggests that privacy and social control are very important in choosing residential environment. Odds are that you will be happiest living in a not-too-crowded environment where you have some personal control over your interactions with others.

Proxemics: Getting too close

Other people are also part of your environment. The way you divide the environment between yourself and others is another aspect of social ecology. On certain occasions, people will avoid others by literally fleeing from them. They do this without any evidence of threat of violence to them. People avoid others simply because they cherish their own *personal space*.

Personal space. People like being with other people, but not too closely. When experiencing invasion of their personal space, people either flee the intruder or fight for their personal space.

You, too, have your personal space. If you are a White, middle-class North American, the chances are that, when another person who is talking to you stands closer than 5½ feet from you, you will feel uncomfortable. If you are a Black North American or a Latin American, this is not likely to bother you.[57] An

[55]BAUM & DAVIS, 1980. [56]PAULUS & MATTHEWS, 1980. [57]HALL, 1960; AIELLO & JONES, 1971.

interesting study of the interaction between Arabs and Americans showed that the Arabs' preference for standing close to the Americans caused considerable anxiety in the latter. The Arabs' touch, voice level, and warm, moist breath caused discomfort for the Americans and led to numerous attempts on their part to extricate themselves from the position.[58]

The term **proxemics** has been coined to describe the manner in which people structure and organize their personal space.[59] Obviously, this process involves several types of behavior. If people have to defend their personal space, other people must be bent on invading it. All of us have been guilty of the latter behavior at some time or another. In the language of proxemics, we have displayed *territorial behavior.* **Territoriality** is the act of staking out psychological and physical space, ranging from national boundaries to the habitat of communities, right down to the personal space of each and every individual. Territoriality spells out a message to the invader: Stay out—unless given permission!

When the territorial markers are clearly and legally defined, such as in the case of national boundaries or an individual's home, unauthorized intrusion will most likely be met with an active defense. When it comes to less structured markers, however, the overwhelming reaction is to flee the intruder. Psychologists Nancy Russo and Robert Sommer clearly demonstrated this phenomenon when they studied individuals' reactions to the intrusion of personal space in a university library (see Figure 11-6).[60] Studies conducted in settings such as cafeterias, public beaches, and other public places have shown similar results.[61] In short, people like being with other people, but not *too* closely.

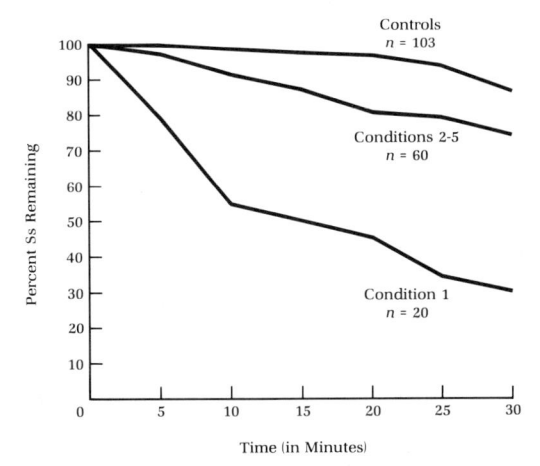

Figure 11-6.
Flight! This figure shows what happened to "victims" in a study hall of a university library when an experimental confederate invaded their personal space. It shows the percentage of people remaining in the hall after condition 1 (maximum intrusion—confederate takes seat less than 15 inches from the victim), conditions 2 through 5 (four less intrusive arrangements), and control condition (no intrusion—observed person stays and leaves at will). *Source:* Redrawn from Russo & Sommer, 1966.

[58]Watson & Graves, 1966. [59]Hall, 1963. [60]Russo & Sommer, 1966. [61]Becker & Mayo, 1971; Edney & Jordan-Edney, 1974.

One aspect of proxemics, however, if carried out properly and systematically, actually *increases* human interaction. It is the aspect dealing with architectural space organization. For example, it has been shown that furniture arrangements in homes, bus depots, theaters, hotel lobbies, hospital recreation rooms, and other locales can be detrimental to positive social interaction. But a few corrective measures such as removing couches from along the wall and replacing them with small tables around the room, or introducing conversation pieces (such as abstract sculpture), can lead to dramatic changes.[62] Even the dreariest places can once again become pleasurable environments.

The moon: It doesn't cause lunacy

Studies on the effects of noise and heat help document what many people already believe—that environmental influences can have undesirable side effects. Research is also needed, however, to refute folklore concerning other environmental influences. One widely held belief is that our behavior can be influenced by the phases of the moon. For example, in folklore, and even in some legal circles, it is believed that crime and violence are more common under a full moon than at other times of the month. A few years ago, psychologists David Campbell and John Beets had a careful look at all of the empirical studies attempting to relate phases of the moon to human behavior. They found no evidence that moon phase was related to psychiatric hospital admissions, suicides, or murders. The many reported instances of specific incidents occurring during a certain cycle were found to be about what would be expected by chance. As for lunacy and the moon—there appears to be no connection.[63]

The economy: Recession inflates problems

One of the most important variations in our lives is the ups and downs in the economy. During good economic times, employment is high and most people have enough money to get by. Yet, at the same time, economic growth often produces inflation, which eats away at the buying power of your dollar. The economy has a regular cycle: following periods of high inflation, it goes into recessions. Recessions are usually associated with reduced spending power and high unemployment. Economic fluctuations are bound to have profound impact on many aspects of our lives.

Several years ago, sociologist Harvey Brenner demonstrated a relationship between economic downturns and admissions to mental hospitals.[64] Each time the economy went bad, mental problems increased a certain number of years later. This finding has been followed up by economist Ray Catalano and psychologist David Dooley, who have been keeping tabs on the interrelationships among the economy, psychological stress, and illness. They found that psychological stress goes up during downturns in the economy. Then, some time later, the impact of the stress becomes apparent in lower health status among members of the community.

[62]SOMMER, 1969; MEHRABIAN & DIAMOND, 1971.   [63]CAMPBELL & BEETS, 1978.   [64]BRENNER, 1973; DOOLEY & CATALANO, 1980.

COPING WITH ENVIRONMENTS

Ecological psychology: The study of behavioral settings

Each day, you participate in a variety of behavioral settings. For example, your social psychology class is a behavioral setting. The program for this setting might include a lecturer who comes to deliver a prepared talk to a group of students. The lecturer might arrive 2 to 3 minutes late and enter a room in which students are conversing casually. On the arrival of the lecturer, however, the room grows quiet and, as the presentation begins, attention is focused on the speaker. Physical arrangements in the room facilitate this social interaction. For example, chairs are pointed toward the front of the room and a blackboard is available for the lecturer's use. Psychologist Roger Barker has made the study of behavioral settings his life work. For many years, he and his colleagues described the publicly available behavioral settings in two small towns: Oskaloosa, Kansas, and Leyburn, England. Each of these towns housed many behavioral settings such as card games, court sessions, special businesses, and the like. Barker's work involved documenting each setting by describing how long interactions lasted, who participated, sex of the participants, and so on.[65]

The study of behavioral settings reveals a great deal about the social rules of the environments. For example, in both the small towns (Oskaloosa and Leyburn), women spent less time in public behavioral settings than men. The studies also confirmed what many feminists have been saying all along—that participation for women is limited to certain behavioral settings. For example, women in both towns were observed most often in such settings as churches and schools. They were also often found in settings that favored social talking, and less often in business and governmental settings.

Behavioral settings are truly self-regulating ecologies. When some component of the system is missing, the activities in the program will be changed to correct the imbalance. For example, if you go to your social psychology class and there are no chairs, students will probably go out looking for chairs to bring the situation into balance. If someone in the class makes too much noise, social forces will come into operation to eliminate the disruption.[66] Thus, to avoid social condemnation, you must act according to the rules for that behavioral setting. A catcall during psychology class might bring you strange and rejecting looks because it is out of place. Yet in the behavioral setting of a rock concert it is perfectly appropriate. Social adjustment requires that you know the rules of many social settings and follow them.

The study of behavioral settings also involves the relationship between work satisfaction and the requirements of the job. Psychologists Alan Wicker and Sandy Kirmeyer used this approach in a study of coping among rangers in Yosemite National Park. During the summer, the work load for the rangers varies greatly because the number of people entering the behavioral setting differs. When the workload increases, the rangers feel more challenged, and needed on the job. However, the rangers in the study also used more strategies to cope with their jobs as the number of visitors increased. By the end of the summer, when the workload was heaviest, the challenge of heavy crowds was no longer associated with job satisfaction. Instead, the rangers were less

[65]BARKER & SCHOGGEN, 1973; BARKER, 1979; SCHOGGEN, 1979; WICKER, 1979.   [66]WICKER, 1979.

able to cope than before and felt physically and emotionally drained.[67] To understand the relationship between work setting and satisfaction, many aspects of the environment must be considered. These include workload, coping strategies, and the duration of work overload.

The medical environment: Coping with pain

Studies in ecological psychology examine adaptation to many different behavioral environments. An alternative approach is to study how people adapt and cope with specific stressful environments. One environment that is highly stressful to individuals is the medical examining room. In fact, a very high proportion of patients report tensing up when they go into the medical examining room or when they climb into a dental chair. The situation is little better for doctors and nurses who have to confront tense patients who would much rather be somewhere else. Because of these problems, several social psychologists have devoted their attention to developing strategies to help patients cope with these particularly stressful environments. Most of these approaches attempt to get patients to think differently as a method for controlling pain.

More than 30 years ago, the psychologist team of John Dollard and Neal Miller suggested that *avoidant thinking* was a way to cope with stress. People can avoid stress, they suggested, by turning their attention away from the stress-causing situations and thinking about other things.[68] More recently, several studies have lent initial support to the notion that avoidant thinking may be a useful coping strategy. In one such demonstration, subjects were told that they would receive electric shocks. They were not told, however, when they would receive the shocks or how often they would get them. The subjects' self-reports about coping strategies indicated that the use of avoidant thinking was associated with less psychophysiological activity and distress than was paying attention to the threatening situation.[69]

Unfortunately, there is also evidence to the contrary. In one experiment, subjects were informed that they would receive a shock at some time within a 6-minute period. Once again, they were not told when within the period they would receive the shock. The uncertainty, as expected, was stress producing. The subjects were then given an opportunity either to engage in an avoidant-thinking activity (listening to music) or to attend to the threat (listening for a tone that was emitted 5 seconds before each shock was presented). The results indicated that those who chose to avoid thinking about the shock showed the greatest amount of psychophysiological activity and distress.[70]

Because the findings of those experiments had been contradictory, psychologists Kent Houston and David Holmes decided to devote more study to the issue. They were aware that the earlier studies had been correlational in nature, with the question of causation remaining largely unanswered. That is, it was not clear whether avoidant thinking caused psychophysiological distress or if psychophysiological distress caused avoidant thinking.

To clarify the causal relationship, Houston and Holmes began with the

[67]WICKER & KIRMEYER, 1976. [68]DOLLARD & MILLER, 1950. [69]MONAT, AVERILL, & LAZARUS, 1972. [70]AVERILL & ROSENN, 1972.

hypothesis that avoidant thinking *is* an effective coping mechanism. Subjects were told that they would either receive, or not receive, electric shocks at some time during the experiment. For half of the subjects, distraction was created by having them read an interesting story while they were waiting for the experiment to get underway. Reading the stories, it was presumed, would cause avoidant thinking. The other half of the subjects did not read the distracting material. Among the subjects who thought they were to receive the shocks, psychophysiological reactions were highest for those who had read the distracting story. These findings were just the opposite of what was expected. After further analysis, Houston and Holmes discovered that those who were not given the distracting reading material used the time to reappraise the seriousness of the threat. On reappraisal, their stress level went down. Subjects who had engaged in avoidant thinking did not have the opportunity for reappraisal, and, therefore, their stress level remained high. In any event, it became clear that avoidant thinking seemed to increase, rather than decrease, stress reactions.[71]

If, as the evidence seems to indicate, avoidant thinking is not very effective for coping with stress, what about meeting the threat head on? In other words, rather than avoiding information about the stress-producing situation, how about gathering *more* information about it? Medical and dental examinations are cases in point. How many times have you gone for those examinations almost scared out of your wits? Your fears may not even have been groundless. It is possible that, at least in some cases, you would be subjected to painful experiences, such as being jabbed by a needle or cut by an instrument. How, then, would you react if you were told in advance the gory details of the forthcoming experience? "I don't even want to hear about it" is a common response. The evidence suggests that you should listen—information is one of the best treatments for stress.

Psychologist Jean Johnson has probed deeply into mechanisms for coping with pain and distressing experiences. Her belief is that fear comes about as the result of inaccurate expectations about the sensations we experience. In one experiment, she exposed two groups of subjects to blood pressure tests. She told one group that the cuff used in the blood pressure tests would cause pressure, tingling of the hand, aching, and blueness—which, in fact, it does. These people were given accurate information. The other group was told how the cuff would be placed on and inflated but were not told exactly what sensations to expect. Those who knew what sensations to expect gave significantly lower ratings when asked to indicate how distressful the situation had been.[72] In a similar experiment, it was shown that subjects were less distressed by an electric shock if they had accurate expectations of what the shock would feel like.[73]

One detailed study examined reactions to an endoscopic medical examination. The endoscopic examination is a noxious and distressing procedure in which a tube is sent down the throat to allow visual and photographic inspection of the upper gastrointestinal tract. If you were to go in for this test, your throat would be swabbed with an anesthetic, followed by an injection

[71]HOUSTON & HOLMES, 1974. [72]JOHNSON, 1973. [73]STAUB & KELLETT, 1972.

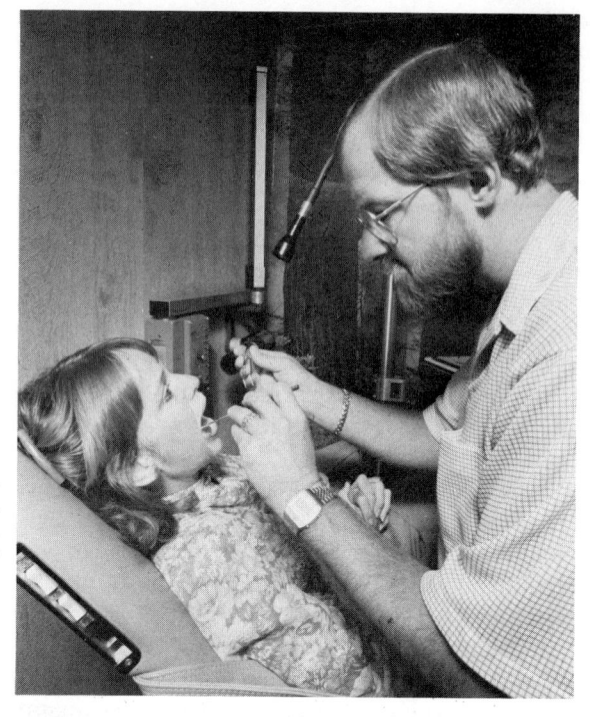

Coping with pain. Providing patients with advance information about what to expect in dreaded dental or medical procedures is one of the best techniques for the reduction of anxiety and stress.

directly into a vein; then a tube would be sent down your throat, and you would be asked to hold the tube there for 15 or 20 minutes. Under any circumstances, it would not be much fun. In a study on reactions to endoscopic examinations, Jean Johnson and Howard Leventhal prepared 48 hospitalized patients for the procedure by giving them either one of two types of preparatory instructions, both types of instructions, or no instructions at all. One type of instruction described the specific set of sensations that would be experienced: what would be seen, heard, felt, and tasted. The other instructions told the subjects what they would have to do during the examination: keep the chin down and make swallowing motions. These were called danger-control instructions.

The results of the experiment showed that the instructions giving a description of the expected sensations reduced scores on selected measures of emotional stress. The danger-control instructions were only successful when they were used in combination with the sensory description instructions.[74] These findings show how simple and accurate information can increase coping with potentially stressful situations.

Another benefit of information, also in a medical setting, has been described by psychologists David Vernon and Douglas Bigelow. These investigators tested the effect of giving accurate information about a hernia-repair operation to 80 men who were about to enter such surgery. They found that those given the information: (1) were more able to concentrate on the specific

[74] JOHNSON & LEVENTHAL, 1974.

problems involved in the operation; (2) had greater confidence in the physician and (3) were less likely to have fits of anger after the operation. The instructions, however, did not immunize the men against fear and worry.[75]

Some other approaches involve getting people to change the way they talk to themselves. For example, psychologists Dennis Turk and Donald Meichenbaum use an approach known as *cognitive behavior modification* to help patients cope with painful experiences.[76] People are taught to relax their muscles and then say things to themselves such as "I'm not going to let this get to me" or "Just relax, this will be over soon." Various applications of this method have been shown to help patients experiencing stressful medical procedures such as rectal examinations, neurological exams that require patients to receive painful electric shocks, and children's dentistry.[77] As we mentioned in Chapter 6, similar methods have been helpful in teaching people to control their tempers.

General adaptation: Nature's own way

We arrive now at the last approach to coping with stress, the "naturalistic" option. This is really a misnomer, because it suggests that nothing happens. In fact, plenty does—only it is an automatic process involving biological and physiological functions in addition to your cognitive control.

Hans Selye has been a pioneer in the field of stress research. An endocrinologist and physician, Selye published his views nearly three decades ago in a book called *The Stress of Life*, which has maintained its status as a classic to this day. Selye proposed that we adapt to stress by manifesting a set of reactions labeled the **general adaptation syndrome** (GAS). The sources of stress may vary, according to Selye—they could be too many life changes, too much frustration, too much heat, or anything else—but the reaction will vary little. The GAS is specific, and its reactions are essentially always of the same pattern.

Let us look at the characteristics of the GAS through its three well-defined stages: alarm, resistance, and exhaustion. This sequence describes the manner in which your body adapts to stress. Before we describe the phases, however, it will be necessary to give you some information about the major mechanisms of adaptation.

Selye is an endocrinologist and is consequently most interested in the operations of glands that secrete hormones into the blood stream. For coping with stress, one hormone is very important. This is the adrenocorticotropic hormone, better known as ACTH. The release of ACTH by the pituitary gland stimulates the adrenal cortex, which in turn releases two hormones. One of these hormones produces inflammation of tissue and the other leads to reduction of inflammation. Inflammation can occur anyplace in the body; it is a natural process that functions to check an attacking agent and prevents it from spreading to other parts of the body.

During the *alarm* phase of the GAS, a considerable amount of ACTH is released into the bloodstream. Large portions of the body are affected, but no specific organ is as yet involved.

[75]VERNON & BIGELOW, 1974. [76]MEICHENBAUM & TURK, 1976. [77]KAPLAN, 1981.

The second phase is *resistance.* During this stage, ACTH secretion drops a little below normal. Only those organs and systems that are most appropriate to cope with a particular stress agent become activated. As a result, resistance to a particular disease may go up during this phase. At the same time, however, the resistance to disease in general tends to decrease.

The last phase is *exhaustion.* This phase occurs when the organ system that is handling the stress gets tired and breaks down. ACTH secretion occurs while the specific organs are relieved of their workload. Nonspecific body areas take over once again, as in the original alarm phase.

In case you are wondering how all this ties in with psychological stress, it is because psychological stress manifests so many similarities to biological stress. The GAS has been observed in rats that had their legs tied or were exposed to variations in temperature. The autopsies of the animals that had experienced these stressful conditions showed enlarged adrenal glands and bleeding ulcers in the stomach linings and intestinal tracts.

Selye is convinced that many disorders attributed to psychological stress occur because of exhaustion of the GAS mechanism. He contends that high blood pressure, allergic reactions, ulcers, sexual malfunctioning, and various mental disorders are associated with general nonadaptation to stress. Since GAS reactions are specific and predictable, it should be possible to deal effectively with the stress-producing situations.[78]

But what happens if the original stress-producing situations are not easily identifiable? This is particularly true in medicine, which accounts for the fact that the GAS was for many years largely ignored as a diagnostic tool by physicians. If, as Selye contends, all stresses produce essentially the same reaction, no clues are provided about the specific irritating agent. Selye's model has also been criticized for its lack of a description of specific reactions to social-psychological events.[79] Nevertheless, Selye's theory has revolutionized many aspects of medical practice and reflects one of the best attempts to integrate the disciplines of psychology, physiology, biochemistry, and medicine.

MODIFYING ENVIRONMENTS

In Chapter 4, we introduced some principles of learning and behavior modification and demonstrated how these can be used to modify the behaviors of individuals. These same principles can also be used to modify the behavior of societies. In other words, behavioral programs can be used to help solve some important environmental problems.

Therapeutic environments and sick societies

Behavior modification involves the manipulation of others through the manipulation of their environment. Most often, this is accomplished by controlling the contingencies within a small environment, such as a hospital ward or a classroom.

Another approach has been to provide a total environment that may have therapeutic effects. Psychologist George W. Fairweather has made some attempts in that direction.

[78]SELYE, 1956. [79]MOSS, 1973.

Fairweather was aware of two problems with our current mental health system: (1) that mental patients, on their release from institutions, are often ill-equipped to function outside; after years of hospitalization, they have lost the skills necessary to make it in the cold, competitive atmosphere of society; and (2) that at a certain point patients must learn to function with minimal assistance from mental health professionals.

Fairweather was aware that sending patients directly from the hospital into the community was a serious mistake. Many of the patients lasted only a short time before they returned to the hospital. As an alternative, Fairweather created a community lodge that functioned as a halfway house between the hospital and the community. Located in the community, the lodge was collectively run and operated by the patients, with minimal intervention by the hospital staff.

Before going to the lodge, patients gathered at the hospital and were required as a group to make decisions about rules for their future community. Initially, the decisions were about simple things such as grooming and self-care. Later they involved important aspects of community management. The patients as a group were held responsible for the behavior of each member. A series of graded steps was established, with each step requiring more responsibility. When success at one step had been achieved, the group was reinforced by being allowed to go on to the next step (and have more responsibility).

Eventually the group moved into the lodge. At first they were assisted by hospital personnel. Gradually, as the group became more self-sufficient, these hospital employees were replaced by volunteers from the community. The group began to organize several activities that would teach them the necessary skills to become self-sufficient. Some members hired themselves out as janitors, and others kept the records and managed the project. All members of the community had some responsibility. When the community had been in operation for three years, all the external assistants were removed. The community established its own self-management and business structure.[80]

Evaluations of the *therapeutic community* concept showed it to be successful along a variety of dimensions. After five years of operation, lodge patients were compared to patients who had not been sent to the lodge. Those participating in the therapeutic community were more satisfied with their setting, made better impressions upon the hospital staff, were more capable of obtaining employment, and were less likely to require further hospitalization than nonparticipating patients. Besides being a treatment success, the lodge was considerably less expensive than hospitalization. The average daily cost for a patient to stay in the lodge was less than $5. At the time the experiment was conducted, hospital costs were from three to ten times this amount; today they would be even more. The community lodge experience demonstrated that, with the creation of a therapeutic environment, former mental patients can treat themselves while enjoying the advantages of first-class citizenship. In therapeutic environments, they can determine their own destinies and function as productive members of society. All this is achieved for a fraction of the cost of traditional therapy.[81]

[80]FAIRWEATHER, 1964; 1967; FAIRWEATHER, SANDERS, CRESSLER, & MAYNARD, 1969. [81]FAIRWEATHER, 1973.

If communities can serve as therapeutic entities, what about "sick" societies? People who apply that label are actually engaged in diagnostic work. Just as doctors examine their patients and determine that they have the flu, people examine society and explain that it has a population explosion, an energy crisis, or stagflation.

There are, however, some differences between the way your doctor treats you and the way we treat society. When you are ill, the doctor usually has some remedy that he or she is willing to try. For society's ills, however, things tend to come to a dead end at the point of diagnosis. An example was provided shortly after President Ford took office. The President was greatly concerned about the economy. Inflation was getting out of control, while at the same time a recession seemed imminent. As a new president, Mr. Ford knew he must get the problem diagnosed. Columnist-humorist Art Buchwald was quick to make the analogy between a sick person and a sick economy. He explained that the economy had to go to the doctor because its inflation had risen steadily overnight and it could not move its gross national product. To assess the problem, the President called the nation's leading economists to a summit meeting. The economists disagreed on many issues. "Galloping inflation," said one. "Ordinary growth and business cycles," said another. "Nonsense," said a third, "it is stagflation." All of these were diagnoses. Some of the diagnosticians used standard terms to describe the situation. Others invented new terms. Although each diagnostician at the summit suggested some worthwhile treatment, the meeting closed without a clear-cut plan of action.

Behaviorally oriented psychologists suggest that we should get away from diagnosing society's illnesses. Instead, they recommend a *functional analysis* to examine behavior in terms of its antecedents and consequences. A functional analysis of economic conditions, for example, could involve society as a whole as well as the behavior of the individuals in it. Consider the inflationary practice of price raising by store owners. Among the possible antecedent events could be listed employee demands for higher wages or increases in wholesale costs. Among the possible consequences of the price hike are customers' anger or even boycott of the store. If the consequences are severe enough (people stopping to buy), the storeowner's behavior (raising prices) will not occur. (A somewhat simplistic solution to inflation, to say the least.)

Disarming the population bomb

Another area where functional analysis could be of use is the current societal problem of population overgrowth. Psychologists Steven Zifferblatt and Carroll Hendricks started with the belief that the goal of family planning should be the solution of the population problem rather than the development of a theory of what causes it. Their action-oriented approach to societal problems is heavily infused with behavioral concepts. To eliminate unwanted births, Zifferblatt and Hendricks say, problem behaviors and appropriate behaviors must first be identified. These behaviors cannot be considered "good" or "bad," since they have to be viewed within the context of a given society. What precedes sexual intercourse in one culture, for example, might be quite different from the antecedents of intercourse in another culture. In Malaysia, where families are crowded in a single room, intercourse might occur spontaneously when there is privacy. In rural Canada, where people enjoy plenty of privacy, the antecedents of sexual behavior might be quite different. There the climate and those long winter nights may be the antecedents triggering sexual behavior. If we train health workers to identify such antecedents, it becomes possible to modify the consequences (the population explosion).[82] Again, a somewhat simplistic solution.

Cash for trash

Functional analyses for the solution of formidable societal problems seem to be oversimplified to the point of being ludicrous. Some of them may indeed be so. It would, however, be a serious mistake to dismiss them all offhandedly. Some do work. You can talk about ecology forever, just like you talk about the weather. But what can you do about it? For example, is there too much trash lying around in your town? For most of us, there is. A major factor in environmental deterioration is that trash is left everywhere. Since all of us want a beautiful environment, why is it that campaigns to clean up parks and roadsides of beer cans, lunch bags, and soft drink bottles have been only minimally effective? The recent "you got to pitch in to clean up America" effort provided catchy jingles for radio commercials, but otherwise had little effect on the amount of trash left around. Another approach has been to pay children in neighborhoods to pick up trash. Despite overtones of behavior modification, paying these children seemed to have little effect on the amount of trash remaining around.

Enter now the behavioral psychologists and functional analysis. They define exactly what behaviors are to be rewarded. They notice that the children were highly rewarded for picking up large pieces of litter and less rewarded for turning in small, but still unsightly, items. They also notice that some of the craftier children found out that they could be rewarded for raiding trash cans or industrial trash bins. And so the behavioral psychologists develop specific rates for cleaning specific areas. Used this way, the procedure led to effective litter reduction in an urban high-density area.[83] It also shows that children between the ages of 4 and 13 can be an effective labor force in solving the mounting urban trash problems. Similar experiments have demonstrated that simple reward strategies can also effectively increase newspaper recycling.[84]

Nutritional balance acts

While we are on the topic of children, there is a critical problem in our society involving nutrition. People of lower socioeconomic status do not get proper nutritional balance in their meals. Beyond the problem that good food is unavailable to minority children is the fact that children will not consume unfamiliar food. Experience with Head Start programs bears this out. The normal diets of children in these programs were deficient in nutritional requirements, so these rural and economically impoverished children were

[82] ZIFFERBLATT & HENDRICKS, 1974. [83] PIERCE & RISLEY, 1974. [84] REID, LUYBEN, RAWERS, & BAILEY, 1976.

provided with free breakfasts that contained adequate nutrition. Unfortunately, the children found the nutritionally adequate food unfamiliar and often refused to eat it. To remedy this problem, one group of researchers had teachers reward eating behaviors with sugar-coated cereal, small candies, and praise. Children who finished their entire meal were given more goodies and praise than those who had not cleaned their plates. This simple behavior technique greatly increased the proportion of meals consumed and the number of children who would eat.[85]

Modifying the energy crisis

Let us now look at behavior modification and another societal problem, the urban transportation issue. Because of the energy crisis, it is very important that we conserve fuel in every way possible. One way to do this is to increase the utilization of public transportation systems. In view of the notorious love affair between average North Americans and their automobiles, this seems to be an almost insurmountable task. Despite a widely publicized educational program and various price reduction gimmicks by bus companies, public transportation is still vastly underused. An experiment by a group of behavioral psychologists may provide some answers to the problem. In that study, tokens were given to all persons who rode on a campus bus. The tokens could be exchanged for a variety of items such as ice cream, beer, pizza, flowers, records, and the like. In addition, a token could be exchanged for another bus ride. The introduction of the token system increased ridership by 150%! Moreover, most of the people exchanged their tokens for another bus ride, thus ensuring continued bus operation. Although it may seem expensive to pay people for riding the bus, the token system appeared to be less costly than other approaches aimed at increased bus utilization.[86] This behavioral approach has also been effective when expanded from college campuses to larger community settings.[87]

Using public transportation is not the only type of positive environmental behavior that can be modified with behavioral strategies. Some studies now show that reinforcement can help decrease the amount of energy consumers use in their cars and in their homes. These same studies tend to show that merely giving people energy conservation manuals does not work well.[88] The rewards used to encourage energy conservation do not necessarily have to be financial. Social praise works fairly well.[89] Giving feedback to the family about the usage of energy can also help decrease the amount of electricity used.[90]

Our energy problems will best be solved by gaining independence from foreign energy suppliers and by stepping up energy exploration. In the meantime, we must learn to use what we have and to conserve. Psychological interventions hold great potential for helping us do this.

SUMMARY HIGHLIGHTS

1. To a large extent, behavior is determined by the physical and social environments in which we live. *Environmental psychology* and *social ecology*, which focus on the relationship between environment and behavior, are relatively new areas of study within social psychology.

[85]MADSEN, MADSEN, & THOMPSON, 1974. [86]EVERETT, HAYWARD, & MEYERS, 1974. [87]EVERETT, STUDER, & DOUGLAS, 1978; EVERETT, DESLAURIES, NEWSOM, & ANDERSON, 1978. [88]HAYES & CONE, 1978. [89]SEAVER & PATTERSON, 1976. [90]SELIGMAN & DARLEY, 1978.

2. A major effect of the environment on humans is stress. Stress is usually a response to frustration, conflict, and pressure. It can have effects upon both mental functioning and on physical health, as studies linking environmental stress to stomach ulcers and heart disease have shown.
3. A growing number of research studies link specific environmental factors to stress reactions. One type of stress reaction, labeled *future shock*, is caused by experiencing too many life changes.
4. Noise, another environmental stressor, can have many undesirable effects—from disrupting concentration to increasing blood pressure. These effects are most prominent when the noise is unpredictable and disrupts some activity.
5. High temperature can also have adverse effects on humans. Riots are more likely on the hottest summer days. Sunny days, however, may also put some people in a more generous mood, as evidenced by their willingness to leave large tips in restaurants, assist in street polls, and similar behavior.
6. With a few exceptions, evidence suggests that *crowding* is undesirable because it takes social control away from the individual. Environments that are designed to allow people control over social situations help people cope with crowding.
7. *Proxemics* is the use of space to regulate social behavior. It includes the use of *personal space* and *territorial behavior*. If someone else comes too close, one may feel uncomfortable, yet just how close "too close" is depends on the culture.
8. Some less obvious environmental factors have been studied as causes of social stress. For example, when the economy goes bad, subsequent admissions to mental hospitals have been shown to increase. The effect of phases of the moon on changes in social behavior has yet to be demonstrated, however.
9. Certain environments are known to be more stressful than others. *Psychological ecology* is the study of *behavioral settings*. Certain behaviors are appropriate in some environments but not in others. The study of behavioral settings provides information about the social rules dictated by these environments.
10. The medical examining room is one behavioral setting that produces stress for a number of patients. Research has shown that certain cognitive interventions help patients cope with these undesirable experiences. Among the more successful interventions are distractions, accurate information about what sensory information is expected, and learning to talk to oneself in a positive way.
11. *Behavior modification* strategies can be used to help change many environmentally relevant behaviors. Reinforcement strategies can be used to get children to clean up the environment and recycle newspapers. For adults, behavioral strategies can get people to do such things as eat a balanced diet, conserve energy, and use public transportation.

CHAPTER 12 RESEARCH METHODS IN SOCIAL PSYCHOLOGY

RESEARCH BASIS OF SOCIAL PSYCHOLOGY
    Rational and empirical approaches

RESEARCH CONSIDERATIONS
    Methodological, economical, and ethical issues

RESEARCH DESIGNS
    Experimental and control groups
    Validity and reliability
    Evaluating experimental designs
    Problem experiments
    True experiments
    Quasi-experiments
    Confounding factors

RESEARCH SETTINGS
    Field studies
    Natural experiments
    Field experiments
    Laboratory experiments
    Simulation experiments

RESEARCH TECHNIQUES
    Interviews and surveys
    Attitude studies
    Interaction analyses
    Content analyses

RESEARCH STATISTICS
    Types of data
    Correlational methods
    Parametric and nonparametric statistics
    Univariate and multivariate statistics
    Some examples of specific procedures

Notice to the Student Reader

This chapter presents research methods in social psychology. Some of the sections require a degree of sophistication that may be beyond your present level. We advise you to ask your instructor which of the sections you could possibly omit.

RESEARCH BASIS OF SOCIAL PSYCHOLOGY

Rational and empirical approaches

From time to time, there are outcries of public indignation about government inefficiency and wastefulness. Such protestations are part and parcel of the democratic process and more often than not are based on solid facts. That in such cases politicians are eager to pounce on every possibility to garner newspaper headlines is also part of the democratic process. The unfortunate aspect of such headline hunting, however, is that sometimes worthwhile projects and individuals are victimized.

The National Science Foundation (NSF) is one of the most vulnerable targets for criticism. Many funded research projects are no more than a collection of segmented efforts to reach an understanding of a larger, overall problem. Project titles are often couched in professional jargon that facilitates communication among researchers but may alienate outsiders. Also, the very nature of a good portion of ongoing research precludes its immediate applicability. It is, therefore, easy for a critic to take a project out of context and submit it to public derision. Not too surprisingly, many politicians find it useful to boost their own popularity by "viewing with alarm" the financial excesses of the scientific community (while undoubtedly pointing with pride at their own frugality).

Some time ago, Senator William Proxmire made headlines by scolding the NSF for funding costly research projects on "why people like one another," or "why people fall in love." The gist of Proxmire's criticism was that studying something that everyone knows intuitively is a waste of resources. Moreover, Proxmire argued, it is best to leave the present mystery of liking and loving undisturbed. The romantic reasoning of this argument may appeal to many, but it is still only a subjective value judgment by Senator Proxmire. The very nature of science, after all, is to shed mysteries and mystiques.

What about Proxmire's argument that *everyone* knows intuitively what there is to know about loving and liking? Take the following example: your friend has just graduated with honors and received her Ph.D. in psychology. You ask her about one of her career highlights so far: her doctoral dissertation. What was it all about? What did she discover? Somewhat reluctantly (she may have become pompous in the process of getting her education), she mumbles something about "effects of propinquity on interpersonal attraction." You press her further, and she cites observations, statistical inferences, critical ratios, analyses of variance, and (the ultimate!) computer data. But suppose you are one of those pesky individuals who never gives up. You force her to tell you, in a nutshell and in layperson's terms, what her research was all about. After some hedging, she tells you that she found out that the more people are separated from each other, the more their liking for each other increases.

Now you are really stunned. Not only by the innocuousness of this ordinary problem, but by the fact that your friend had been spending a seemingly endless time in graduate school poring over books, journals, abstracts, computer printouts, to come up with—this! Moreover, you and probably a million others already *know* that absence makes the heart grow fonder.

Before you condemn your poor friend, the fallen idol, consider for a moment that, while you and others *said* that you knew that absence makes the heart grow fonder, your friend went out and *did* something about it—just in case you're from Missouri and want to be shown. In short, your friend used an *empirical* approach.

Your friend did not use the *rational* approach, which is based on logical considerations that minimize, or even frown upon, empirical evidence. During the Middle Ages, however, the rational method flourished. You may have heard of the venerable scholars who spent considerable time trying to establish how many angels were able to dance on top of a pin. From the writings of Francis Bacon in 1494, we have information on how the early empiricist fared among the scholars, as when they discussed the formidable question of how many teeth a horse has:

> In the year of our Lord 1432, there arose a grievous quarrel among the brethren over the number of teeth in the mouth of a horse. For thirteen days the disputation raged without ceasing. All the ancient books and chronicles were fetched out, and wonderful and ponderous erudition, such as was never heard before in the region, was made manifest. At the beginning of the fourteenth day, a youthful friar of goodly bearing asked his learned superiors to add a word, and straightaway, to the wonderment of the disputants whose deep wisdom he sorely vexed, he beseeched them to unbend in a manner coarse and unheard of, and to look in the open mouth of a horse and find answer to the questioning. At this, their dignity being exceedingly hurt, they waxed exceedingly wroth; and joining in a mighty uproar, they flew upon him and smote his hip and thigh, and cast him out forewith . . .

Despite the quaintness of the language, the narrative makes abundantly clear that our empiricist, the youthful friar of goodly bearing, must have had the wind knocked out of him by his zealous colleagues for daring to propose to look inside a horse's mouth. In turn, after declaring that "surely Satan hath tempted this bold neophyte," they unanimously agreed that the problem (the number of teeth in a horse's mouth) must be "an everlasting mystery."

All this does not mean that the rational approach is without merits. A college student, whether a psychology major or not, would do very well taking courses in philosophy that offer logic, truth tables, syllogisms, and the like. Philosophy, after all, is the parent discipline of psychology. The rational method is also useful in forming hypotheses before undertaking research. As a modern science, however, psychology must rely on empirical evidence.

There is an even more compelling reason why your friend deserves credit for her findings. Suppose she came up with the opposite results. Would she have impressed you then? Probably not. You and a million others *also* know that out of sight is out of mind. In fact, all of us know that

> You are never too old to learn *and* You can't teach an old dog new tricks.
> Clothes make the man *and* You can't judge a book by its cover.
> Look before you leap *and* He who hesitates is lost.

Well, which is it—one, the other, or both? Even a cursory observation of daily activities will show us that *all* these assertions are justified. But the psychologist who studies these topics by the scientific method can at least come up with a good estimate of which type of behavior, under what conditions, is more likely to occur than the other. In other words, psychologists predict the probability of the occurrence of a given behavior (this, incidentally, is where statistics enter the picture, as you will find out as you progress in your study of psychology).

As for Senator Proxmire, he quickly found out that "nobody is as good as psychologists at fighting dirty," as one writer has ironically suggested. For example, one of the targets of the Senator's derision made pointed reference to the Senator's own rocky marriage.[1] To add insult to injury, in 1980, the courts decided in favor of another target who had sued him for defamation of character and made the Senator apologize publicly.

Methodological, economical, and ethical issues

RESEARCH CONSIDERATIONS

When Stanley Milgram conducted his famous study on obedience, he reaped not only fame but a great deal of criticism as well. Among other things were accusations that his studies lack relevance to the real world and are unethical (see Chapter 4).

How valid are such criticisms? Before we attempt to answer this question, let us engage in the following scenario:

> You are a member of a blue ribbon commission appointed by the President of the United States. Your mandate is to decide, with other members of the commission, whether any recommended medication for the cure of the common cold is based on valid scientific claims. A man who introduces himself as Dr. James Brown appears before the entire commission, pulls out a pill from his pocket, shows it triumphantly, and declares "This pill will end the common cold once and for all!" You are asked to fulfill your mandate by either accepting or rejecting the claim.

Obviously, you would reject the claim. Apart from the man's fuzzy credentials, there are a host of other things to consider. There has to be an *operational definition* of the common cold, stating exactly what the term denotes: a pattern of respiratory symptoms with a given length, intensity, possible side effects, and so on. There has to be a proper *sample*, both in size and representativeness, of common cold sufferers who took the pill and found relief. There have to be *control* samples, such as common cold sufferers who received a placebo (harmless inactive pill) that looks like the new pill; or a sample of common cold sufferers who were measured for relief after having taken no pills at all; and so on. Only if the manipulation (taking the new pill) in the *experimental* sample shows *statistically significant* (greater than chance) relief than that achieved in the control samples would you begin to consider whether the claims for the new pill have validity. Anything short of such solid evidence should make you reject the claims outright. If you do all this, you have employed *methodological* considerations in deciding the merits of this particular research in the quest for the common cold cure.

There are, however, other considerations. Suppose that Dr. Brown satisfied you on all the methodological issues just described and then some, yet his final findings show that, with the new pill, seven out of ten sufferers got well, whereas if they took a placebo, or even nothing at all, six out of ten found relief anyway. He also shows you, however, by means of statistics, that the difference between the relief attained by the new pill takers and the others is not one of chance but represents a real difference.

Would you accept the new pill? If you refuse, since it merely helps 70% of the

[1] BOFFEY, 1975.

cases, as opposed to 60% who find relief without it, Dr. Brown may justifiably accuse you of overstepping your mandate. The commission, if you recall, was appointed for the purpose of confirming whether the claim for the pill's effectiveness was valid, not whether it is worthwhile to research or produce it. Your decision in this case is clearly based on *economical* considerations. Unlike the objective methodological considerations, economical considerations are entirely subjective. *Your* marketing savvy may tell you that, with Dr. Brown's nonspectacular results, the new pill will never sell. Why buy it and get a 70% chance of relief, when you have a 60% chance of getting relief without taking anything? It is conceivable, however, that an enterprising drug company, using effective packaging and advertising, might wish to take a chance on marketing the new pill, despite the nonspectacular results.

What if the results are not only based on sound methodological considerations but actually do prove spectacular as well? For example, what if nine out of ten people find relief with the new pill, as opposed to only six out of ten who find relief without it? Most everyone would agree that such research findings are economically sound. Suppose, however, that under those conditions (nine out of ten attaining relief), the tenth person taking the new pill promptly drops dead! Worse yet, autopsies clearly show death to be attributable to the new pill. There is little doubt that, under those conditions, regardless of their sound methodological and economic aspects, this pill will not be marketed.

Would *you* stick by the decision to reject the new pill if research shows that "only" one out of 100 new pill takers drops dead? One out of 1000? One out of 100,000? One out of 1,000,000? The chances are that you would. After all, you wouldn't want to have a dead person on your conscience. But what if only one out of 100 million cold sufferers died and untold millions found relief? Undoubtedly, some people would say to go ahead and take the risk. Such questions are clearly based on *ethical* considerations, which are highly subjective. If, for example, instead of the common cold, the new pill were to alleviate heart trouble, you can be assured the odds would drop dramatically. For the trivial "common" cold, one death out of 1000 is rejected outright, but it may be an entirely acceptable sacrifice if a serious problem like heart disease can be overcome. In either case, there are undoubtedly some who, notwithstanding spectacular curative results in any area, would ban the use of a new product as long as it causes even one casualty. Equally predictable is the emergence of risk-taking decision makers who, after examining the benefits derived from the product, would lower the casualty acceptance odds drastically. In a society where there is freedom of choice and a free flow of true information, it may be difficult to designate one risk ratio proponent over another as being "better," or even more ethical.

These three considerations—methodological, economical, and ethical—govern all research in psychology. The first and foremost question in evaluating a study should be how methodologically sound it is. If it can be shown that the study is poorly designed, lacks adequate controls, uses faulty statistics, and offers conclusions not warranted by the data, it is of little, if any value. Even if it is methodologically sound, the question always remains whether the study is economical. As shown in the common cold example, this is an area of personal judgment. As social psychologists, we may, for example, think that any research on the conditioning of a cockroach's extremities is trivial. The psychologist engaged in this type of research would not only consider it extremely interesting, but would most likely be able to present evidence about its importance as well. But all this is beside the point, really. Who is to judge a fellow psychologist on whether a given type of research is warranted, as long as it is methodologically sound? Naturally, if this psychologist worked for a drug company, for example, the employer may fire him or her for economic reasons. In no way, however, would that detract from the soundness of the scientific procedures employed, which is, after all, our main concern. In a similar vein, most people would be unperturbed if the researcher on that project happened to kill thousands of cockroaches in the process. The ethics of that act would hardly bother anyone. If the experiment involved dogs, however, it would be an entirely different story. Again, different value systems are at work.

The problem with research in social psychology is that it deals primarily with complex issues of interpersonal behavior, which makes coming up with all the necessary controls for methodological soundness a difficult task. At the same time, there is a much greater lack of unanimity in social-psychological research on what is economical and/or ethical than in studies dealing with animal behavior, verbal learning, and the like. Another major problem is that social-psychological studies are often criticized and condemned by scientists on grounds that are not scientific at all. To return to the Milgram study, for example, just how sound was it methodologically? Was it really valid to draw such formidable conclusions about human obedience on the basis of a series of isolated studies involving deception and make believe? Milgram and many other social psychologists would undoubtedly claim that his experiments, in the settings in which they were conducted, were methodologically sound (as you will see later in this chapter, different research settings dictate different degrees of control and precision); and, as far as the make-belive aspect of those studies, the fact is indisputable that, at the time they were administering shocks as ordered, the subjects *did not know* that there were no real victims. Yet much of the criticism against Milgram does not address itself to those issues but rather to ethical considerations: the potential damage to the psyche of the subjects who had experienced the agony of inflicting pain and suffering, the violation of trust of unsuspecting subjects, and so on. This type of criticism is certainly valid, but it tends to ignore differences in value systems held by people, which in turn makes it difficult to state who is "right" and who is "wrong." Moreover, as has been pointed out earlier (see Chapter 4), there is always the possiblity that such criticism is motivated less by ethical considerations than by an unwillingness to accept the unflattering side of human nature that Milgram's studies have yielded. The problem of deception, however, cannot be dismissed lightly by social psychologists. Apart from those who think it is unethical,[2] there are those who think that the ensuing loss of subjects' trust will be counterproductive to future research,[3] and still others suggest that methods devoid of deception (role playing, for example) are equally as effective in social-psychological research.[4]

[2]BAUMRIND, 1964. [3]KELMAN, 1967. [4]MIXON, 1977.

RESEARCH DESIGNS Experimental and control groups

Determining the cause of behavior is at the heart of most social psychological research. We are constantly asking the question "Why?" Why do people fight? Why are people unwilling to help a stranger in distress? Why are small groups more productive than large groups? All of these are basic research questions and there are many ways to answer them. The *experiment* is unique among these many approaches because it attempts to gain control over all the other whys. In other words, the experimental method is defined as the research method that asks questions under controlled conditions.

There are many types of experiments and there are many well-known pitfalls associated with experimental inquiry. In fact, graduate students in psychology typically spend at least one whole year studying experimental design and methodology. Despite the complexities of experimental methodology, there are a few basic ideas you can master to become a good consumer of experimental results. To accomplish this, you will need to learn a little basic terminology.

Experiments involve both constants and variables. Most things are the same or are constant for all the participants in the study. The experimenter, however, usually manipulates one or more *variables* and attempts to determine what effects this tinkering produced. A variable is a score that may take on different values for different participants in the experiment. The variable manipulated by the experimenter is known as the *independent variable*. Thus, in experimental studies, it is appropriate to think of the independent variable as the manipulation. Of course, to determine what effect the manipulation has had, we must measure some other variable, known as the *dependent variable*. Try to remember that independent variable = manipulation, and dependent variable = outcome measure.

Sometimes, the manipulation of the independent variable involves the administration of experimental *treatments*. Subjects are given different treatments, each of which may have several *levels*. For example, we may give the treatment to one group and withhold it from another group. In this example, the independent variable has two treatment levels. The group that received the treatment is called the *experimental group*, and the group that did not receive the treatment is called the *control group*. Some experiments have several levels of the experimental treatment; these experiments have several experimental groups.

In good experiments, the experimental and control groups differ only for random reasons before the administration of the experimental treatments. If, after the administration of the treatment, the experimental and control groups come to differ, then the differences can be attributed to the treatment. It is possible to make this causal statement because *extraneous* variables have been controlled. An extraneous variable is one that might affect the relationship between an independent and a dependent variable. The purpose of control in experimental studies is to exclude the influence of extraneous variables.

Let us take the example of a research study on the effects of television violence on aggressive behavior among children. Correlational evidence suggests that those children who watch excessive violence on television tend to be highly aggressive themselves. These studies, however, do not show that television *causes* aggression. It may be that exposure to television violence causes aggression or it is equally likely that violent children prefer to watch violent television shows. To determine the direction of causation, it is necessary to control extraneous variables as well as the exposure to television.

In an experimental setting, we might begin by dividing children into two groups. The division has to be done in a way that would not produce systematic differences between the groups. By dividing randomly, the experimenter uses the process of *random assignment*. This is done to eliminate systematic biases in the way the subjects are assigned to the various conditions in the experiment (which in this case corresponds to the experimental group and the control group). The control group would not be shown television violence but might be exposed to equally exciting nonviolent television. It is necessary to have a control group to determine the level of aggressive behavior that occurs as a function of television exposure that is nonviolent in nature. The experimental group would be exposed to television violence. Later, both groups of children would be observed on the playground and the number of their physical and verbal aggressive behaviors would be recorded by trained observers.

In this experiment, the manipulation of television exposure is the independent variable. The violence-viewing and nonviolence-viewing groups are the experimental groups and define the levels of the independent variable. The measures of physical and verbal aggression on the playground are the dependent variables. Extraneous variables, such as the amount of violence the children usually watch, are controlled because each child has an equal chance of being assigned to either the experimental or the control group. Because the children were assigned to the two experimental groups by a random process, the groups differ only by chance before the experimental treatment.

After the treatment, the groups are compared. Statistical methods are then used to determine the chances that any observed differences between the groups after the treatment were the result of chance. If we are confident that the differences were not the result of chance, we conclude that it was the exposure to television that *caused* the two groups to differ in aggression.

It is important to emphasize that true experiments require that subjects be assigned to experimental and control groups by some random process. If the assignment is not random, then the statistical methods cannot adequately specify the chances the groups differ prior to the experimental treatments. This should become more obvious as we look at some of the variations on the experimental method.

Validity and reliability

Psychometrics is the area of psychology that deals with measurement. Several concepts from psychometrics are of importance for social psychology. Two of the most important concepts are validity and reliability.

Validity defines the range of inferences you can make on the basis of an observation. For example, if you observe that children will attack a Bobo doll after watching an adult attack the doll, you may want to infer that the children will also attack other children. You have not really observed the children hitting other children, however. Instead, you make an inference. The evidence that allows you to make this inference is the validity of the measure.

One well-known example of validity comes from the use of standardized tests such as the Scholastic Aptitude Test, or SAT. College administrators do not know how well you will do when you get to college before they accept you. To predict how well you will do, they use the SAT. Studies showing the correlation between the SAT and first-year college performance define the validity of the test. In other words, they tell the administrator what inferences can be made on the basis of the test scores.

Psychometricians used to refer to many different types of validity, such as *content*, *criterion*, and *construct*. There is now a move, however, to stop separating types of validity into categories and simply use the term *validity*.[5]

Reliability is the degree to which a score is free from measurement error. For example, most psychological measures are contaminated because a portion of the score is attributable to error. Methods have been developed to estimate the proportion of the variation of a score that is what the researcher wants to measure and the proportion that is error. The smaller the error, the higher the reliability. Reliability is important in psychological research because a measure that is not reliable cannot be associated with other measures. The lower the reliability, the more the measure reflects chance or random variation.

Evaluating experimental designs

Becoming an educated person requires learning how to be an astute consumer of information. Much of the information we have about the world comes from experimental research studies, yet the value of these studies is not always the same. By learning about experimental designs, you should be able to judge for yourself whether such information should be taken seriously. And, we hope, you will be less influenced by the credentials of the scientist than by the soundness of the method he or she employed.

Experimental design pioneers Donald Campbell and Julian Stanley outlined eight classes of extraneous variables that might call the results of an experimental investigation into question. Table 12-1 presents these eight "threats to internal validity" in the form of a series of questions you can ask about an experiment. All of these factors concern experiments in which observations are made before and after a treatment, followed by statements about change caused by the treatment.

The importance of these factors will become obvious as we discuss various experimental designs.

Problem experiments

Some "experiments" present many obvious problems. Take, for example, what some psychologists have called the "one-shot case study."[6] This is the approach most often used in journalistic studies of science. Typically, a reporter interviews someone who appears to have benefitted from therapeu-

---

[5] MESSICK, 1980.   [6] CAMPBELL & STANLEY, 1966.

TABLE 12-1. Questions you should ask about experiments.

Extraneous Variable	Question
History	Did any specific events (other than the experimental treatment) occur between a first and second observation that might account for the observed change?
Maturation	Could some natural process, such as growing older, getting tired, and so on, have been responsible for the observed change?
Testing	Were scores on the dependent measure affected by the experience gained by taking the test before the treatment?
Instrumentation	Were different tests, or different observers, used to collect the data after the treatment?
Statistical regression	Statisticians have noted that, when an extreme value is observed, the next time the same measure is taken it tends to be less extreme. Were the groups selected on the basis of extreme values or scores?
Selection	Was there any bias in the way subjects were selected for the experimental and control groups?
Mortality	Did more subjects drop out of one of the experimental treatments than the other?
Selection-maturation interaction	Might the rate of change for one experimental group be different than the rate of change expected for another comparison group—without any treatment?

Source: Campbell & Stanley, 1966.

tic treatment. For example, consider a television program featuring a patient who claims improvement because of exposure to an encounter group experience. We would like to believe that the group experience caused the change. We cannot rule out many other explanations, however, such as history (something else caused the change), maturation (the person might have changed without the treatment), selection (this was an unusual person), and so on.

Studies in which one group is observed before and after a treatment do more to bolster our confidence in the results than the one-shot case study. For example, we might study racial attitudes before and after a second grade class is desegregated. If racial attitudes change as a function of the desegregation, it would be nice to conclude that the change in attitudes was *caused* by the change in racial composition. History, maturation, testing, instrumentation, and the selection-maturation interaction, however, serve as rival explanations.

A common problem experiment is what some people call the *pseudo-experiment*. This is not an experiment at all. It is a study that only appears to be experimental. For example, suppose we want to learn how homosexuality affects attitudes toward abortion. A group of homosexuals serve as an "experimental group" and a group of heterosexuals function as a "control group." The dependent variable is the attitude measure. All this does not add up to an experiment because no independent variable was manipulated. Instead, groups of homosexuals and heterosexuals were chosen with the assumption that differences between them in attitudes toward abortion resulted from their sexual orientation. The two groups, however, may differ in many other ways that make it impossible to rule out other causal explanations based on the different social experiences that accompany the homosexual role in society.

True experiments

For many research problems, the best research method is the *true experiment*. In a true experiment, subjects are *randomly assigned* to experimental and control groups. Experimental designs are available to handle any number of experimental groups. For illustrative purposes, we will stick with the simple two-group concept.

When subjects are randomly assigned to experimental groups, we know that any differences between the groups before treatment is likely to be the result of chance. Although we cannot say for sure that the groups are the same, we can be assured that the probability that the groups differ is small and specifiable. After the treatment, we can test the groups and compare the differences between them. Statistical methods tell us the chances that the observed differences after treatment are the result of chance. If the chances are very small (usually less than 5 in 100), we conclude that the differences were caused by the treatment.

The major advantage of the true experiment is that we can assume that the experimental and the control groups were essentially the same before the treatment. Thus, differences cannot be attributed to testing, instrumentation, selection, or the interaction between instrumentation and testing, because both groups were treated the same. Further, we can rule out history and maturation because the control group tells what would have happened without the treatment. Regression and mortality are usually not problems in true experiments. They do cause severe difficulties in quasi-experiments, however.

Quasi-experiments

Quasi-experiments are studies that are not true experiments, even though they attempt to evaluate the effect of an experimental treatment. The major difference between the two types of experiments is that in a quasi-experiment subjects are not assigned to the experimental treatments by a random process. For example, in Chapter 3 we discussed a quasi-experiment on the effects of humorous examples in lectures. The lectures were presented to intact classes of college students. Some of the classes heard serious lectures and others were exposed to various versions of funny presentations. The reason this study was a quasi-experiment is that the subjects were not assigned to the lecture conditions by a random process. Instead, whole classes of students were assigned to hear a particular lecture. This procedure may pose some problems because there may be a systematic link between being a particular type of student and enrollment in a particular class. For instance, working students may be more likely to sign up for late afternoon classes. Thus, the type of person in the class, rather than the experimental treatment, might be related to any change in behavior.

Confounding factors

Wise consumers of experimental results must always be on the lookout for *confounding factors*. Confounding occurs when the experimenter simultaneously manipulates two factors at once. When this happens, it is impossible to determine which factor accounts for the experimental results. For example, imagine an experiment that attempts to evaluate the effect of a persuasive communication on attitude change. One group is exposed to a confederate who attempts to get them to buy U.S. Savings Bonds. The other group is not given this presentation and simply waits in a room until the dependent measure is given.

The problem with this study is that the experimental treatment involves the simultaneous manipulation of two factors. First, there is the persuasive message (to buy the bonds). The experimental group also gets personal contact, however. Thus, a difference between the two groups in the number of bonds purchased could be attributed to either the message *or* the contact. Usually, another experiment that separates these two factors is needed to unravel the true cause.

RESEARCH SETTINGS

Field studies

Is it possible to study social interaction by merely observing people, without manipulating or influencing them? It is, although many psychologists would claim that such studies are methodologically suspect: if no variable is manipulated, this reasoning runs, how could one infer what or who caused the experimental results? On the other hand, many psychologists believe that this lack of manipulation is a blessing because it fosters a real-life atmosphere and avoids artificial behavior by subjects who know they are part of an ongoing study or observation.

The investigation of interpersonal attraction among residents of a housing project (see Chapter 5) is typical of this type of research. It involved primarily observations of friendship patterns but also included some inevitable contact between investigator and subject. This is why the issue of *unobtrusive measures*, also known as *nonreactive research*, has become important in relation to field studies. For example, some purists, in their efforts totally to eliminate subjects' awareness of being studied, may even dispense with observing them. Instead of observing, say, alcohol consumers in various places to study drinking behavior, these investigators may resort simply to recording the number and kind of alcoholic beverage containers in refuse pickups from different neighborhoods; (more on nonreactive research under "Field Experiments").

With or without subjects, such *field studies* are difficult to interpret, despite their real-life authenticity. Some writers have suggested that field studies are particularly useful either at the very early stages of research on a given issue (to get a "feel" of potential variables for more formal research) or at the very late stages (to validate in real-life settings results from formal research).[7]

Natural experiments

Natural experiments are those in which nature and circumstance combine to change conditions critically in field study settings. For example, psychologist Seymour Lieberman observed workers' job behavior before and after a prescheduled change known to him and management but not to the workers. This change, a critical event in the workers' lives, called for some workers to be promoted to foremen and others to union stewards. The hypothesis was that the new occupational role would lead to different role behavior among the new foremen and union stewards, as opposed to the precritical event behavior, when all subjects were workers.[8] The problem, of course, is that, unlike Lieberman, who knew of the critical event about to occur, it is generally impossible to anticipate such events before they occur. The study of panic behavior during natural disasters is a case in point. Most of such research occurs after the fact, with data coming from people who have survived the flood, the earthquake, or other upheaval.[9] The validity of such data may be questionable because the survivors' recollections may be colored by self-serving or socially desirable motives. If, however, the timing of the natural disaster could have been predicted, "before" and "after" measures of people's behavior could be of considerable validity because it is reasonable to assume that any changes (such as panic) can be attributed to the natural disaster. One could thus make some sort of causal inference, which field studies do not allow. Not too surprisingly, because of their requirement for fortuitous combinations of circumstances, natural experiments are a rarity in social-psychological research.

Field experiments

Field experiments try to overcome the inadequate controls and manipulation that characterize field studies. Like natural experiments, they include some critical change in conditions from which causal inferences are made. Unlike natural experiments, however, rather than waiting for the critical change to occur naturally, the experimenter intrudes into the natural situation and causes some event to occur (the independent variable) in order to study its effect on the behavior under observation (the dependent variable).

When properly conducted, field experiments are especially useful in social psychology because they preserve all the advantages of a real-life situation while incorporating some of the refinement of laboratory control and manipulation. Kurt Lewin's classic study of social climate in groups (see Chapter 8) was the forerunner of many other now-famous field experiments in social psychology. There are, however, some disturbing problems associated with this type of research. The ethical-methodological dilemma for the researcher is as follows: Do I keep subjects in the dark about what is being done to them, risking possible psychological injuries to them, or even legal action against myself; or do I assume the ethical responsibility for the consequences of my

[7]McDavid & Harari, 1974. [8]Lieberman, 1956. [9]Fritz, 1961.

research by making subjects aware that the manipulations are only experimental, with the risk that awareness may cause artificial behavior that in turn will seriously confound the experimental results and conclusions?

As in other ethical aspects of psychological research, different value systems emerge. Some psychologists conduct field experiments without ever briefing or debriefing their subjects, under the assumption that "what they don't know won't hurt them." Others choose organizational frameworks such as industry, the military, or schools, where there are powers who can grant permission to do research, thus minimizing any ethical and legal complications. For this very reason, children are favorite subjects in field experiments, because parents are the ones who grant the permission for their children's participation in research. Then there are those researchers who scrupulously debrief their subjects about some, but not all, aspects of their study, and those who supply their subjects with general but vague information about what is going on in the various stages of the research. Still others do administer manipulations but find solace in the fact that their research may be in the *nonreactive* category (see "Field Studies" earlier in this chapter) which they believe somehow relieves them of ethical responsibility because of the "unobtrusiveness" of their measures. Finally, there are those who say that the ethical-methodological dilemma inherent in field experiments can never be solved and new methods should be employed, such as role playing, in which subjects are aware at all times of what is being done to them.[10]

In summary, field experiments are excellent vehicles for studying social-psychological behavior, provided they manifest some reasonably defensible ethical procedures (never satisfying all critics) but, more importantly, are methodologically sound. The latter is easier said than done, since real-life settings are so complex that it is often doubtful whether the manipulations and controls employed in field experiments can truly be maximally effective.

Laboratory experiments

The term *laboratory* conjures visions of precision, manipulation, and total control. It also suggests that, by attaining this formidable scientific goal, laboratory research inevitably foregoes the real-life quality of natural conditions. In short, laboratories appear sterile.

One may readily disagree with this view. Laboratory behavior is not unreal, for an individual's behavior there is as real as his or her behavior in other settings. As for the charge of sterility, consider this example. Before the introduction of instrument sterilization, it may have been quite possible that surgical procedures were invariably associated with skin infections, perhaps to the extent that this perception reflected real life. Of course, with the introduction of precise sterilization procedures, it became possible to minimize or eliminate infection risks, creating a new reality. Likewise, even if subjects may never encounter precisely the same conditions outside the laboratory, the findings may pinpoint relevant independent variables that may help the investigator make predictions about what to anticipate outside the laboratory under certain crucial conditions. Still, there is no denying that

[10]MIXON, 1977.

subjects in social-psychological laboratory research are often forced into specially contrived choices and decisions that seem somewhat devoid of reality (such as most of the attitude change studies in Chapter 3).

In terms of the effectiveness of research, the optimum probably lies somewhere between the two extreme views. Critics who advocate the abolishment of laboratory studies because of their artificiality can be compared to those who "throw out the baby with the bath water." They ignore the fact that even the best field experiment will have problems of control maximization, or that laboratory behavior is real and relevant. Moreover, laboratory research greatly facilitates the handling of potential ethical problems because, if nothing else, subjects at least *know* that they are part of some experimental manipulation. The most productive approach, it seems, is to study a particular issue under both methods—the laboratory for precision and the field for generalizability.

Simulation experiments

When it becomes impossible or impractical to duplicate natural conditions in the laboratory, it is sometimes possible to improvise by simulating some features of a natural situation through the use of audio and video tapes or "faked" messages. In general, however, simulation experiments refer to studies designed to *reproduce* the most essential features of real-life tasks outside the laboratory. In social psychology, certain *gaming* procedures have been employed in research on decision making, conflict, and strategy planning. Chief among such procedures are the *mixed-motives games*, of which the Prisoner's Dilemma (PD) is the best known. For example, two subjects may play a game on an electronic board in which they have the choice of pushing a red or black button, according to the following matrix:

		Player B	
		Red	Black
Player A	Red	A wins 15 (C) B wins 15 (C)	A wins 1 (S) B wins 20 (T)
	Black	A wins 20 (T) B wins 1 (S)	A wins 10 (P) B wins 10 (P)

A "Red" strategy of cooperation (pushing the red button) is one of Cooperation (C), since it maximizes both player's winnings. Such rational considerations, however, may not necessarily govern the players' responses. Because the matrix deliberately does not equate wins and losses, other strategies may be chosen: Temptation (T), where each player tries to maximize his or her own winnings at the expense of the other; Sucker (S), where each player loses for trusting the other; and Punishment (P), where both players end up winning less for yielding to temptation.

As you can see, this game is a simple, convenient, but very precise means for measuring some complex interpersonal behavior. Whether the results from such studies are generalizable outside the game setting is open to question. As you might expect, those who engage in this type of research do consider it relevant and generalizable. Chief among the critics of this method has been psychologist Phillip Gallo, who feels that the entire procedure is so sensitive to variations in payoff size and other related variables to make any meaningful generalization impossible.[11] Gallo's criticism is especially noteworthy because he had been one of the earliest and major contributors to research in the area of Prisoner Dilemma games.

Interviews and surveys

RESEARCH TECHNIQUES

Survey research is used to find out information about a population when such information cannot be obtained more cheaply by some other source. We would probably not do a survey to find out how many people live in the United States because the Bureau of the Census provides this information every decade. Sometimes, however, we need to have information and do not have the resources to question every single person. In such cases, we use survey methods to help us estimate how, on the basis of interviews of a smaller sample drawn from it, a large group would respond.

One example of the use of survey methods is the way television networks determine how many people watch their programs. You have probably never been contacted by a television pollster, yet they estimate your television viewing habits every week. The Nielsen Company, the major television viewership assessment organization, places electronic devices on the television sets of a limited number of American families. The devices record which stations are watched at all hours of the day and night. On the basis of a very small sample of households (about 1200 nationwide), Nielsen can make a fairly accurate estimate of the number of persons watching particular programs.

The major principle in survey research is that the sample be representative. This assures that all types of viewers are represented. When the samples are not randomly selected, results become very inaccurate. In a famous case, a magazine called the *Literary Digest* attempted to forecast the outcome of the 1936 presidential contest between Roosevelt and Landon. The magazine drew its sample from its readers, from automobile registrations, and from telephone directories. In 1936, all these sources overrepresented the wealthy, most of whom were Republicans. The poll showed that Landon would win by a landslide. The results of the election were, however, just the opposite. Roosevelt won by one of the greatest margins in American history. Thus, survey results will be of little value if the sample is not random. Election day polls using as few as 2000 respondents to represent all of the voters in the nation have repeatedly been shown to be very accurate when the small samples are drawn randomly.

Nonrandom selection of respondents is not the only type of problem encountered in survey research. Writing survey questions that do not suggest a certain response to the interviewee has become an art in itself (see Table 12-2). Further studies have also demonstrated that the behavior of an interviewer can have a big impact upon the response obtained in survey

[11]Gallo, 1968.

research. For example, respondents will agree with more statements if the interviewer reinforces each agreeing response by nodding, smiling, and similar positive feedback.

TABLE 12-2. Problems in phrasing survey questions

Phrasing Problem	Example
Connotative meaning	"Are you a fair reader?" Poor reader? Impartial reader?
Brevity and clarity	"Do you believe that no Black person should be deprived of a franchise except for reasons which would disenfranchise a White person, regardless of whether this occurs south or north of the Mason-Dixon line?" Most likely to be incomprehensible.
Projection	"What do most people think of the United Nations?" What does the respondent think about the United Nations? What does the respondent think other people think about the United Nations?
Specification	"How did you feel about this issue when you were young?" In your childhood? In your teens? During first year of marriage? "Are promotions in your office based on merit?" Are favoritism or seniority to be ignored if answer is positive?
Unfamiliar vocabulary or jargon[a]	"Do you believe that autistic children should be continuously retarded?"
Social desirability[a]	"Do you think that children should be taught not to fight with each other?" Is this socially acceptable? How do others feel about it? Better phrasing: "Some parents feel it's terribly important to teach a child not to fight with other children. Others feel that in some circumstances, a child must learn to fight. How do you feel about this?"
Euphemisms[a]	"What are your methods for punishing your children?" Substitute: "disciplining" for "punishing."
Partiality/impartiality[a]	"What do you like least about your boss?" should be preceded by "What do you like best about your boss?"
Face saving[a]	"Before leaving Russia, were you a Communist?" if asked of a Russian refugee, will not elicit a positive response as easily as "Before leaving Russia, were you able to keep out of the Communist Party?"

[a]Especially important in sensitive issues demanding reduction of personal defensiveness.
Source: McDavid & Harari, 1968.

It is important to note that even the most scientifically conducted polls do not always forecast election results. Public opinion may change during the course of a campaign, yet polls only reflect opinions at a specific point in time. For a poll to reflect how voters feel on election day, it would have to be conducted on that same day among a representative sample of those who voted. One glaring example of poll fallibility was the 1980 presidential election. Pollsters had predicted Carter and Reagan would be running neck and neck. In reality, Reagan won by a landslide.

Attitude studies

Attitude scales are mechanisms to assign numbers to attitudes according to a well-defined set of rules. There are many types and formats for attitude scales, but the most common are the Likert format and the Thurstone format.

Likert Format

The *Likert scale* presents subjects with a group of statements and asks the extent to which they agree or disagree. For example, you might be given a group of statements, such as:

The more noise at a party, the more fun it is.
Most married men would cheat on their wives if given the opportunity.

For each of these items, you would be asked to express the extent to which you agree or disagree on a 5-point scale with the options: strongly agree, agree, neither agree nor disagree, disagree, strongly disagree. Each of these alternatives is assigned a number (1 for strongly agree through 5 for strongly disagree) and a subject's score on the scale is the sum of the responses over all of the items in the scale. These scores can then be interpreted in relation to established norms by giving the same items to many people representing well-defined groups.

In constructing a Likert scale, the researcher must be sure that the scale is *unidimensional*, or represents only a single attitude. The two sample items given previously do not represent the same attitudinal dimension and would not be included in the same scale. Scale constructors usually need to employ complex statistical methods, such as factor analysis, to determine whether their scales are indeed unidimensional.

The Thurstone Format

Construction of a *Thurstone scale* is more complex. This method was developed by psychologist L. L. Thurstone, who adopted methods used by experimental psychologists in the field of psychophysics. The first stage in the development of a Thurstone scale requires assembling a large number of statements about a particular attitude. For example, one of Thurstone's best-known studies considers attitudes toward the church. Each statement is printed on an individual card and a group of judges is asked to sort them into 11 piles representing differing degrees of the attitude. The first pile might be used for statements expressing the highest appreciation for the values of the church, successive piles might represent increasing degrees of disfavor toward the church, and so on until the final pile, which would be the strongest depreciation of the church.

The purpose of this exercise is to establish scale values for each item. The scale values reflect the judgment of the group that originally rated the items. During this process, many ambiguous or irrelevant items are thrown out, so the scale becomes refined. Once the scale values are established, we can learn about the attitudes of other people by summing the scale values of items they are willing to endorse.

Interaction analyses

Interaction analysis is a general term reserved for a series of minimally intrusive methods for the observation of ongoing interpersonal behavior. The most critical problem facing such analyses is that of defining the unit of observation. That is, regardless of whether subjects are observed directly or indirectly (as from behind a one-way mirror), how does the experimenter convert the continuing flow of observed activity into measurable units without being arbitrary about it? For example, if verbal behavior is being recorded, should it be the number of sentences that express one complete thought, or the time it took to achieve the latter? If nonverbal behavior is being recorded, how, for example, should a subject's drumming fingers on the table be categorized? As impatience? Embarrassment? Relaxing to some recalled musical beat?

The most widely used interaction analysis has been developed by psychologist Robert Bales. Also known as the *Interaction Process Analysis*, it defines the basic unit of observation as "the smallest discriminable segment of verbal or nonverbal behavior to which the observer, using the present set of categories after proper training, can assign a classification under conditions of continuous serial scoring" (p. 37).[12] Figure 12-1 shows the twelve discrete categories of the Bales system, which are subsumed within four broad categories (A, B, C, and D). The observer is instructed to classify each instance of categorizable behavior in terms of its presumed significance for the *observed* person. Frequency computations are carried out either by checking off categories from a list within given time blocks or by the use of a mechanical device known as a *chronograph* where buttons (corresponding to the 12 categories of behavior) are pushed to activate a stylus marking the appropriate spot on a roll of paper unfurling at a set speed rate. Although one observer could conceivably observe an entire group, maximum effectiveness can be attained by assigning each group member to several observers and then checking the degree to which there is agreement on their categorization (observer interreliability).

After the frequencies of behavior are computed, it is possible to obtain a profile for either an individual in a group or the group itself. The profile can show the degree of harmony within a group, or the amount of interpersonal tension, or the extent to which the group and its members are oriented towards its tasks. Because Bales has provided his users with an elaborate manual for coding, the Interaction Process Analysis has become a well-known and handy tool in social-psychological research.

Content analyses

Interviews, surveys, attitude studies, even interaction analyses—all of these techniques, at some time or another, call for at least minimal interaction between investigators and their subjects. There is, however, a unique method that allows for the scientific investigation of social-psychological topics without the occurrence of such interactions. In fact, this method dispenses with subjects altogether. Known as *content analysis*, it focuses instead on the manifest content of communications.

There are several versions of content analyses, depending on the investigator's purpose. Some focus on written material such as newspapers or books, others on visual material such as movies or theatre plays, and still others emphasize auditory material such as musical compositions or word-of-

[12]BALES, 1950.

RESEARCH METHODS IN SOCIAL PSYCHOLOGY 347

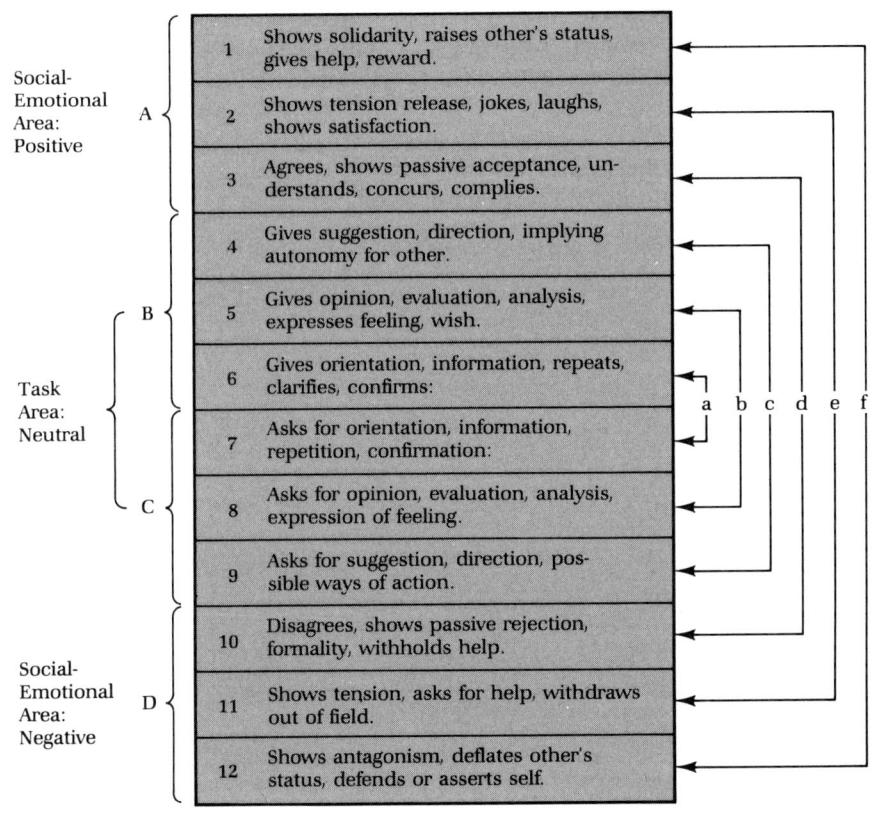

Social-Emotional Area: Positive	A	1	Shows solidarity, raises other's status, gives help, reward.
		2	Shows tension release, jokes, laughs, shows satisfaction.
		3	Agrees, shows passive acceptance, understands, concurs, complies.
Task Area: Neutral	B	4	Gives suggestion, direction, implying autonomy for other.
		5	Gives opinion, evaluation, analysis, expresses feeling, wish.
		6	Gives orientation, information, repeats, clarifies, confirms:
	C	7	Asks for orientation, information, repetition, confirmation:
		8	Asks for opinion, evaluation, analysis, expression of feeling.
		9	Asks for suggestion, direction, possible ways of action.
Social-Emotional Area: Negative	D	10	Disagrees, shows passive rejection, formality, withholds help.
		11	Shows tension, asks for help, withdraws out of field.
		12	Shows antagonism, deflates other's status, defends or asserts self.

KEY:

a Problems of Communication
b Problems of Evaluation
c Problems of Control
d Problems of Decision
e Problems of Tension Reduction
f Problems of Reintegration

A Positive Reactions
B Attempted Answers
C Questions
D Negative Reactions

Figure 12-1.
The Bales Interaction Process Analysis. *Source:* Bales, 1950.

mouth folklore. What they have in common is the employment of a frequency count of certain predesignated communication units of analysis. For example, if the unit of analysis is a space-and-time measure, we could compare cross-cultural values on any given topic by simply counting the allocated number of newspaper pages, or column inches, or film footage, or minutes of radio or television viewing, that are allocated to this topic within a given time period within a particular culture or country. Content analyses have also political and clinical applications. By counting and comparing themes (a larger unit about which an inference is made) in projective measures such as the *Thematic Apperception Test (TAT)*, norms can be generated and clinical diagnoses be made meaningful. By checking school textbooks for instances in which the persons around which the narratives are woven (such as Jane and Dick) engage in particular behaviors such as doll play and toy train assembly, or display docility or the lack of it, it is possible to show whether sexist practices are on the rise or on the decline. It is even possible to do a psychopolitical diagnosis of entire nations by means of content analyses. Political scientist Ivo Feierabend and psychologist Rosalind Feierabend were successful in determining psychopolitical profiles of over 100 nations, not by visiting them and surveying the people's beliefs and opinions, but by statistical analyses of archival information (in this case, from the United Nations). Consider, for example, the following profile of a mid-twentieth-century nation:

> gross national product (GNP) of $300 or more per person per year (note: inflation may have upped the ante in this case, since the original study was conducted in the 1960s)
> 45% or more of the population living in urban centers
> 90% or more literacy
> 2% or more of the population having telephones
> 65 or more radios and 120 or more newspapers per 100 population
> 2525 or more calories consumed per day per person
> not more than 1900 persons per physician

With this count as a minimal requirement, according to the Feierabends, a nation can be pronounced "healthy"—that is, relatively stable and not prone to violence. The degree of stability is established by a count of archive and mass media reports on political violence, such as the number of mass demonstrations, riots, purges, violations of civil rights, anti-foreign demonstrations, and the like.[13]

RESEARCH STATISTICS

Statistical methods are a major part of research in social psychology. Statistical models are important because they allow us to interpret our data in relation to well-understood rules of probability. For example, in experimental studies it is very unlikely that the scores for the experimental and control subjects will be exactly the same. The problem is to determine how much of a difference between the groups we should get excited about. To do this, we create a *statistical decision rule*. The statistical model tells us the probability that differences observed could have occurred by chance alone. If it appears unlikely that the differences could have happened by chance (say, less than 5 in 100), then we might conclude that the observed differences most probably resulted from the experimental treatment.

Most statistical methods apply the same logic. They create a ratio between an average or mean score and the average deviation from the mean score. For example, the *t test* is a ratio of the observed difference between means for two groups and the standard error—that is, the expected difference—between means. The larger the ratio becomes, the greater the *t* statistic; and the larger the *t* statistic, the smaller the probability that the observed difference can be attributed to chance. There are many different statistical methods. The choice of a particular method depends upon the type of *data* involved.

[13]FEIERABEND, FEIERABEND, & GURR, 1972.

Types of data

Data come in many different forms. Sometimes we obtain *qualitative* information, such as the ethnic group to which someone belongs. This type of information is "unscaled" and in the form of a *nominal* scale of measurement—that is, the scale of measurement only provides identification of categories. If we do a survey and ask respondents to which sex they belong, we can classify their responses as 1 if they are female and 2 if they are male. These numbers, however, only help us identify the categories; we cannot average them, add them, or use them for any other mathematical operation.

Much of the data we use in social sciences is *quantitative* or *scaled*. Quantitative data differ in the degree to which the scale is refined. *Ordinal scales* give the property of "moreness" by ranking objects according to some rule. For example, if we ranked children according to their height, we would have an ordinal scale. An ordinal scale does not consider the distance between the objects. If John is 5'6", Fred is 5'1", and Bill 5'0", an ordinal scale for height would rank John 1, Fred 2, and Bill 3. It would not consider that John is 5 inches taller than Fred, or that Fred is only an inch taller than Bill.

Distances among ranks are considered in *interval* and *ratio scales*. The difference between interval and ratio scales is that the latter has a meaningful starting point, whereas the former does not. For example, the temperature scale of Fahrenheit is an interval scale, because the 0 on the scale does not have a well-defined meaning. Water freezes at 32° and boils at 212°. Zero itself, however, does not define any particular atmospheric condition. When scales do not have a meaningful starting point, they cannot be used for mathematical operations that involve ratios. For example, we cannot say that 70° is twice as warm as 35° Fahrenheit because the zero point was picked arbitrarily. Ratio scales that do have a meaningful zero point, however, can be used for any mathematical operation.

Correlational methods

A *correlation coefficient* is a mathematical index used to express the degree to which two variables are associated. For example, suppose you believe that watching violent television programs is associated with behaving aggressively. To test this hypothesis, aggression is measured for a group of children. The amount of violence these same children watch on television is also recorded. Using this information, you attempt to make a precise statement about the association between watching television violence and behaving aggressively. The correlation coefficient can be used to evaluate the degree to which these variables are associated.

The correlation coefficient takes on values between –1.0 and 1.0. The value –1.0 represents perfect negative correlation and the value 1.0 represents perfect positive correlation. These values almost never occur in practice. A perfect correlation means that the two variables are perfectly associated so that the one variable can be completely predicted from knowledge of the other. Correlations between –1.0 and 1.0 describe relationships that are less than perfect. An example of a near-perfect correlation might be when the most aggressive child also watches the greatest amount of television violence, the second most aggressive child is second in the amount of violence he or she watches, and so on, until the least aggressive child watches the least amount of violence. This would yield a near-perfect (if not perfect) positive correlation. A correlation of 0 means that the variables are unrelated or related to one another in a random way. A variety of correlation coefficients are shown graphically in Figure 12-2.

Another way to evaluate a correlation is to ask how much variation in one variable can be explained by knowing about its correlation with another variable; that is, how well one can predict the other variable. (This is found by squaring the correlation coefficient.) If the correlation between aggression and televised violence is 1.0, *all* of the variation in aggression is explained by how much violence the child watches on television. Perfect correlations, however, are actually quite rare. In social psychology, the magnitude of correlations is usually less than .30. Thus, if the correlation between aggression and television was .30, squaring the results would make it .09 (.30 × .30 = .09). This tells us that about 9% of the variation in aggression is explained by how much violence children watch on television, but that 91% cannot be explained by known television viewing patterns.

Before we leave the topic of correlation, it is important to point out one well-known but often overlooked fact. It is *not* possible to determine causation from correlation. If amount of exposure to television violence is correlated with the degree of aggression a child displays, we cannot infer that exposure to television violence caused the aggression. Instead, we are left with many alternative explanations such as (1) television causes aggression, (2) being aggressive causes a preference for violent television programs, or (3) some other variable(s) cause both television preference and aggression (such as conflict with parents might cause both aggressive behavior and preference for violent television). The three causal explanations are diagrammed in Figure 12-3.

There are some situations in which one direction of causation can be ruled out as highly improbable. For example, a known correlation exists between

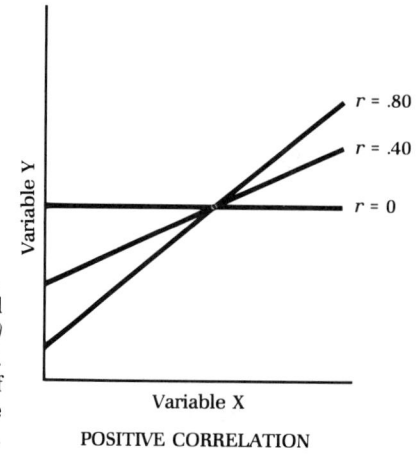

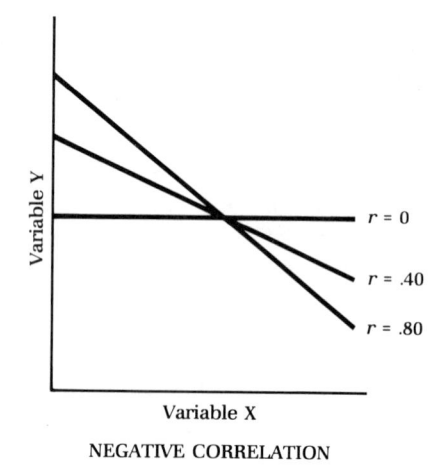

Figure 12-2. Examples of positive and negative correlations (r) of different magnitude. The steeper the slope of the line, the higher the correlation.

POSITIVE CORRELATION

$r = .80$
$r = .40$
$r = 0$

NEGATIVE CORRELATION

$r = 0$
$r = .40$
$r = .80$

1. Aggression ⟶ TV
   Aggression causes TV viewing.

2. Aggression ⟵ TV
   TV causes aggression.

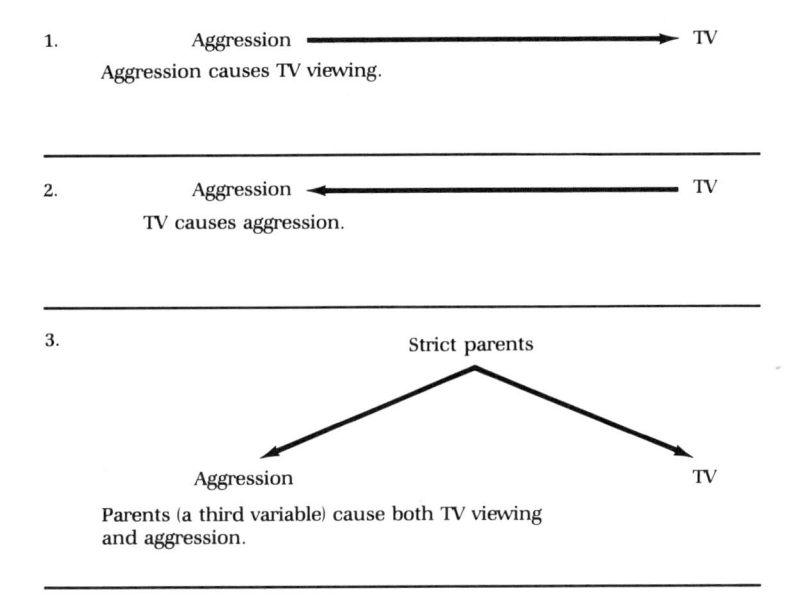

3. Strict parents ⟶ Aggression / TV
   Parents (a third variable) cause both TV viewing and aggression.

Figure 12-3. Three causal interpretations to explain the correlation between television and aggression. Arrows indicate the direction of causation.

rainfall and traffic accidents: the more it rains, the more accidents are reported. In this situation, one direction of causation is more plausible than the other. It is quite likely that rainfall causes accidents—and not very likely that accidents cause rainfall. In personality research, there are very few circumstances in which one causal explanation is so easily ruled out. As a result, many psychologists prefer experimental research in which they intentionally cause variation in one of the variables and maintain strict control over the situation to rule out third variable explanations.

Parametric and nonparametric statistics

The statistical methods most commonly used in social psychology test for differences between average, or mean, scores. Using these methods, however, requires that we make several assumptions. For example, it is necessary to assume that other statistical characteristics of the scores are the same, in particular that the scores vary the same way for all groups under comparison. These methods typically compare measures of the average scores for the groups and measures of the way scores vary within the groups. These are also known as parameters of the populations, and the methods used to compare them are called *parametric*.

Sometimes it is difficult to meet the assumptions that are required to use parametric statistics. Under these circumstances, researchers often opt for *nonparametric* methods that require different and sometimes fewer assumptions. These methods are also called *distribution-free* tests because they do not rest on any assumptions about the normality of the distribution of scores. Examples of nonparametric methods include the *chi square*, the *Mann-Whitney U Test*, the *Kruskal-Wallis Test*, and the *Spearman Rank Order Correlation*.

Univariate and multivariate statistics

Most of the methods discussed thus far consider relationships between one independent variable and one dependent variable. We gave an example of the effects of exposure to television violence (independent variable) on aggressive behavior (dependent variable). This is an example of a *univariate* problem because the focus is upon one variable (effects of television).

Multivariate analysis considers the relationship between combinations of three or more variables. For example, the prediction of success in the first year of college from the Scholastic Aptitude Test Verbal (SAT-V), Mathematics (SAT-M) scales, and Aptitude Test Quantitative would be a problem for multivariate analysis. The field of multivariate analysis is a technical one and it requires an understanding of linear and matrix algebra. Therefore, a detailed discussion of multivariate analysis is beyond the scope of this book. On the other hand, multivariate analysis is becoming common in social psychology and so it is important that you have a general idea of what the different methods entail.

Multivariate methods have advantages for the study of social behavior because they permit us to study the relationships among many variables. The correlational techniques only describe the relationship between one pair of observations. For example, they might only consider the relationship between stress and illness. To understand more fully the causes of illness, we need to consider many other potential factors in addition to stress. Multivariate analysis allows us to study the relationship between many predictors and an outcome. In addition, the methods allow us to study the relationship among the predictors.

Some examples of specific procedures

1. *t* test

The *t* test is a univariate, parametric method used to test for the difference between two means. Usually this is the difference between two experimental groups, but versions of the *t* test are also available to examine differences between two observations taken from the same group at different points in time.

Example. The experimental group is exposed to a persuasive communication and the control group is exposed to a neutral communication. The dependent measure is attitude change. The *t* test is used to determine whether the experimental and control groups differ significantly in attitude change.

2. One-Way Analysis of Variance (ANOVA)

The one-way analysis of variance is also a univariate, parametric method used to test for the differences between two or *more* means.

Example. Three groups participate in an attitude change experiment. Group 1 receives a positive communication, group 2 a neutral communication, and group 3 a negative communication. Attitude change is used as a dependent measure. Analysis of variance is used to determine whether there were any differences between the three groups in attitude change.

3. Multiple Range Post Hoc Comparisons

A significant result in the analysis of variance tells us only that there is a difference among the groups. Post hoc tests are then needed to determine exactly where the differences lie.

Example. An attitude change experiment is conducted using a positive, neutral, and negative message. The one-way analysis of variance shows that there is a difference among the three groups. Multiple range post hoc comparisons are used to show exactly where the differences lie. They might show that the positive communication produced significantly more attitude change than either the neutral or the negative communication, but that the neutral and the negative groups did not differ from one another.

4. Factorial Analysis of Variance

Factorial analysis of variance is used when there is more than one independent variable and the experimenter is interested in the effects of each independent variable by itself and in combination with the other independent variables.

Example. An experimenter wants to determine the effects of physical attractiveness and sex of rater upon evaluations of talent. Male and female judges rate work attributed to either attractive or unattractive women. Factorial analysis of variance is used to determine whether: (1) males and females differed in their ratings of talent; (2) ratings were different when the work was attributed to an attractive author; and (3) the effect of attractiveness had a different effect for male and female subjects.

5. Chi-Square

Chi-square is a univariate, nonparametric method. It has many uses, including the comparison of qualitative responses in different groups.

Example. A social psychologist conducts a survey and finds that 73% of single college students favor legalized abortion whereas only 46% of married college women favor abortion. Chi-square is used to determine whether the differences in these proportions is statistically significant.

6. Multiple Regression

In the last decade, social psychologists have shown a growing interest in multivariate statistical methods. Multiple regression is a multivariate method used to predict a quantitative variable on the basis of two or more predictor variables.

Example. A law school admissions board wants to determine whether it can predict first-year law school grade point average on the basis of three variables: undergraduate grade point average, ratings by former professors, and age. Using multiple regression, they are able to determine that law school performance can be predicted fairly accurately on the basis of the three predictors, and that undergraduate grade point average gives the most information among the three.

7. Discriminant Analysis

Multiple regression is appropriate when the variable the researcher wants to predict is scaled. There are many cases in social psychology, however, when we want to find out which variables can describe or predict the differences between groups. Discriminant analysis is appropriate for these purposes. The difference between discriminant analysis and multiple regression is that discriminant analysis uses a qualitative rather than a quantitative criterion variable.

Example. Male and female college students are asked about their preferences for different types of work. Discriminant analysis is used to determine whether the composite of the preferences is different for the two sexes and which specific preferences are most important in distinguishing between men and women.

GLOSSARY

Adaptation Level The notion that perceivers respond to three types of stimuli: focal, background, and residual. The focal stimulus is what faces the perceiver directly; the background stimulus serves as such for the focal stimulus; and the residual stimulus is a function of the perceiver's past experience with the other two stimuli.

Anomie A feeling of normlessness; a lack of purpose in direction to life.

Attitude A state of mind or conduct of a person regarding some matter; a predisposition to act.

Attribution Theory A broad cognitive approach that attempts to understand the basis of perceptual inferences on the causes of events or the causes of people's behavior.

Audience Sensitization A concept that assumes that arousal and distraction prevent the recipients of a persuasive message from forming counterarguments to its content.

Authoritarianism A personality trait marked by an implicit antidemocratic ideology, antagonism to outgroup members (ethnocentrism), and a reverence for power.

Balance Theories Several theories that assume that perceivers want logical consistency. If what is perceived does not make sense, the situation becomes "imbalanced" and perceivers will do their best to avoid such situations or change their perceptions to regain balance. One of the better known balance theories is Fritz Heider's *p-o-x* theory.

Behavior Modification A variety of techniques for the application of learning theory to the change of behavior. It is not a single technique, but a series of methods that draw on clinical, social, developmental, and experimental psychology.

Catharsis The process by which a person exhibits an emotion and is thereby purged or cleansed of it.

Classical Conditioning The repeated pairing of a neutral stimulus (conditioned stimulus, or CS) with a stimulus that elicits a response (the unconditioned response, or UR), so that the neutral stimulus eventually becomes capable of eliciting a similar response (the conditioned response, or CR).

Coercive Power Power derived from the ability to control punishments.

Cognitive Dissonance A theory that holds that the more effort a person exerts to attain a goal, the more dissonance and discomfort is aroused if logical inconsistency is perceived (as, for example, if the goal turns out to be less valuable than expected). One way to reduce dissonance is to change the original belief through the acquisition of new cognitive input.

Conformity When social pressure increases the likelihood that people will endorse a particular view. *Information-seeking conformity* is due to uncertainties in ambiguous situations, but *norm-seeking conformity* is manifested when there are fears of ridicule or retaliation by others for noncompliance.

Contingency Model A theory that spells out the circumstances influencing effective leadership. Circumstances include affective relationships between leader and followers, task structure, and power of position.

Defensive Attribution A hypothesis that suggests that people's perceptions are governed by self-serving biases. For example, the desire not to attribute another person's severe accident to chance is overridden by the fear that the accident could also happen to the perceiver.

Deindividuation A behavior manifested when individuals become members of a large group or mob. Lacking feelings of identity, they may no longer feel responsible for their behavior.

Diffusion of Responsibility The notion that the presence of others, such as in situations requiring help, diminishes a bystander's motivation to act.

Discrimination Learning or conditioning based on stimulus-specific responses.

Dogmatism A personality trait marked by a relatively rigid outlook on life with an intolerance toward those with opposing beliefs. As measured by the Dogmatism Scale (Rokeach), both left-of-center and right-of-center extremists show similar dogmatic values.

Door-in-the-face Technique A bargaining approach whereby the persuader first presents a person with an extreme request (likely to be rejected) and then asks that person to comply with the original favor.

Empathy The capacity to view events from the standpoint of others without bringing personal feelings into the process.

Environmental Psychology The study of people within natural environments and the impact of physical environments upon their social behavior.

Equity Theory A theory that contains a number of propositions and formulas aimed at making clear predictions of the impact that equity and inequity have on intimate relationships. Equity, or the lack of it, almost always involves some type of power relationship.

Exchange Theory The concept that, through a series of exchanges with other people, a person comes to recognize his or her own worth.

Expert Power Power that does not depend on the content of a communication but arises from the manipulator's credentials as an expert.

Extinction Any procedure in which the stimuli that elicit or maintain a behavior are omitted in an effort to reduce or eliminate that behavior.

Foot-in-the-door Technique A principle based on dissonance theory that states that, to commit someone to doing a favor, he or she should first be confronted with a request for a smaller favor.

Fundamental Attribution Error The persistent tendency to overestimate the importance of traits and to underestimate the importance of situations.

Gain-loss Phenomenon A phenomenon in personal interactions wherein, as a result of one person's evaluation of another changing from negative to positive, the evaluator is liked more than when the evaluation is consistently positive. When the evaluation changes from positive to negative, the evaluator is liked least.

General Adaptation Syndrome (GAS) The concept of adaptation to stress by the manifestation of a set of reactions. GAS phases are alarm, resistance, and exhaustion.

Generalization The extent to which a person who has been trained to respond to a certain stimulus will respond to new stimuli of varying similarity to the original stimulus.

Great Man Theory A theory of leadership that proposes that leaders are born (part of their personality), not made (a product of circumstances).

Greenspoon Effect Behavior modification based on verbal approval or disapproval.

Groupthink A process whereby bad decisions sometimes come out of group discussions. Groupthink is most likely to occur when a group is highly cohesive and its members identify strongly with the group.

Halo Effect In stereotyping, the tendency to blur one characteristic into another, based on some speculative associations (for example: he is honest, thus intelligent).

Hostile Aggression Aggression that occurs because people are furious or plain mean and are rewarded when the persons they are mad at get hurt.

Idiosyncracy Credit The phenomenon wherein people will allow their leaders to get away with norm-deviating behavior, but only after the leaders have given ample evidence of their competence. Leaders who are initially perceived as conforming to the group's expectancies and subsequently show competence are awarded "credits" in the form of positive impressions by the group.

Informational Power Power derived from manipulation based on the content of a message.

Instrumental Aggression Aggressive behavior as a means to an end. This type of aggression is used to obtain a nonaggressive goal such as money, power, or sexual enjoyment.

Interaction Theory The proposal that neither trait nor situation, but rather the interaction between the two, is the primary source of influence on variation in behavior.

Just World Hypothesis A hypothesis leading to misattribution and perceptual inaccuracy. The belief that we live in a just world where people get what they deserve can lead to the attribution of fault to innocent victims by perceivers who are trying to disassociate themselves from the fate of those victims.

Learned Helplessness A condition manifested by people or animals who are put in situations over which they have no control and then seem unable to learn new responses. In many cases, this can lead to apathy and depression.

Least Group Size Principle A principle that states that the optimum group size for the performance of an interactive task is the minimum number of individuals required to make available to the group all of the resources required for the execution of its task.

Legitimate Power A power stemming from an internalization of values advocated by an authoritative source. One yields to the manipulator by virtue of his or her recognized authority.

Leniency Effect The situation wherein people who are sociable, secure, and show a high degree of self-acceptance judge others too benevolently along the same dimensions that characterize them as perceivers.

Locus of Control A concept used to categorize those who believe they have control over important events in their lives (internals) as opposed to those who believe that what happens to them is primarily the result of environmental or chance events (externals).

Low-balling A persuasion technique, often confused with the foot-in-the-door technique, in which the target behavior is introduced in a tempting manner right from the start rather than through a sequence of smaller requests.

Machiavellianism The systematic promotion of immorality as a political philosophy or method of persuasion. It is based on a cynical view of how leaders successfully manipulate their followers.

Mere Exposure Theory The principle that repeated exposure to a stimulus is a sufficient condition to enhance a person's attitude toward it.

Moral Realism A conception of justice based on rigid and inflexible standards of right and wrong.

Moral Relativism A concept of justice that is tempered with notions of equity, fairness, and expediency.

Motivational Research (MR) A controversial and frequently criticized method of manipulation, especially of buying behavior. Its basic assumption is that people's buying patterns are based on deeply ingrained needs of which they may not even be aware.

Nonverbal Perception (Communication) Perception or communication based on the observation of stimuli other than the verbal content of oral communication, such as smile, posture, eye contact, and so on.

Operant Conditioning A learning procedure in which the subject's own behavior determines whether or not punishment, reward, or neither should be administered.

Overjustification Effect The notion that offering rewards to persons engaged in an otherwise enjoyable activity will undermine their subsequent interest in that activity when the reward is discontinued.

Personal Alienation Individual feelings of isolation, remoteness, cynicism, distrust, and apathy.

Position A specific slot occupied by an individual in a group, organization, or society (such as leader, boss, mother, student).

Power The six types of social power that are used as manipulators are: informational, coercive, reward, legitimate, referent, and expert power. (See separate listings.)

p-o-x model
See balance theories.

Primacy Effect The notion that the first perceived stimulus causes the greatest change (for instance, when people are judged on the basis of first impressions).

Primal Therapy A therapy that maintains that severe psychological problems are repressed and that violent discharges (such as screaming) facilitate the eventual recognition of these problems.

Primary Reinforcers Reinforcers that satisfy a primary drive or tissue deficit, such as hunger, thirst, or sleep.

Propaganda Any attempt to influence the development of attitudes or to change them.

Propinquity The notion that mere physical proximity can be an important determinant of interpersonal attraction.

Prosocial Behavior Any behavior that is socially desirable and benefits others. It may or may not be altruistic (helpful acts for which nothing explicit is expected in return).

Proxemics The manner in which people structure and organize their personal space; the study of territorial behavior.

Psychological Androgyny The ability to function psychologically as male and female at the same time, characteristic of those who do not identify exclusively with either male or female sex roles.

Recency Effect The notion that the last perceived stimulus causes the greatest change (for instance, when people are judged on the basis of last impressions). The effect increases considerably when perceivers are forewarned of the fallacies of first impressions.

Reciprocity Norm A norm based on the assumption that people expect reciprocity for their actions, such as when they are doing favors or helping others in distress.

Reevaluation Therapy A therapy based on the premise that effective functioning is obstructed by psychological distresses that can be removed through emotional discharges. After the discharge, reevaluation can take place.

Referent Power A power marked by yielding because of the prestige of the manipulator.

Reinforcement A set of operations, such as the presentation of a positive stimulus or the removal of a negative stimulus, designed to increase the measured strength of some behavior after a response of interest has occurred.

Responsibility Norm A norm based on the assumption that people act to help when they think it is needed, rather than as an exchange of favors.

Reward Power Power derived from the ability to give rewards.

Risky Shift The consistent tendency of groups to make decisions by consensus which, compared to individual decisions, are characterized by being more risky.

Role The behavior displayed by an individual in a certain position. This role can be enacted (actual behavior), perceived (by the role player or by others), prescribed (what society says the behavior should be), or predicted (on the basis of past behavior).

Secondary Reinforcers Reinforcers that satisfy secondary drives (learned or acquired) such as power, achievement, affiliation, and approval.

Self-efficacy A concept based on the assumption that, beyond knowing that something *should* be done, people need to know what they *can* do to function efficiently in the future.

Self-fulfilling Prophecy ("Rosenthal Effect") The finding that, when people are expecting others to behave in a certain way, they treat others accordingly. As a result of the treatment, others eventually conform to expectations.

Self-monitoring A type of self-management in which a person tries to maintain behavior appropriate to the situation at hand.

Self-schemata Cognitive generalizations about the self, derived from past experience.

Sex Typing The tendency to assess behavior on the basis of expectations derived solely from the fact that people are male or female.

Social Comparison A theory based on the assumption that perceptual clarity of a situation can be achieved by evaluating the reactions of others to that situation.

Social Ecology An area of study consisting of environmental psychology, ecological psychology, public policy, and related topics.

Social Influence Therapy A therapy based on manipulatory techniques derived from various social-psychological findings in the area of persuasion and attitude change. Adherents of this approach consider the therapist/client relationship to be just another ordinary social interaction rather than the unique relationship that many therapists and clients think it is.

Social Loafing The notion that the presence of many people for a given task will cause them to work less hard than they ought to, or could, if they wanted to exert themselves.

Social Self The notion that the self is a product of the perception of others.

Societal Alienation A collective alienation from socially accepted goals and standards.

Sociobiology A recently expanded field whose advocates tend to be strict believers in Darwin's theory of evolution. Their belief that many social behaviors are also inherited is controversial.

State Anxiety Anxiety as an emotional reaction to a situation that will vary from one situation to another.

Status The prestige associated with particular positions and roles.

Stereotyping A relatively rigid and overgeneralized perception using broad categories of persons or social groups.

Subliminal Advertising Attempts to induce attitude and behavior change by communicating with the consumer at a subconscious level.

Successive Approximation A conditioning technique for training a subject to perform a behavior that is not in the subject's behavioral repertoire. Simple behaviors and crude approximations to it are reinforced until the desired behavior is achieved.

Supermale Syndrome The XYY syndrome. Present in some men who have the regular genetic characteristics of males, along with an additional Y or male chromosome, and who are often physically strong, sometimes display homosexual tendencies, and frequently exhibit severe behavior problems. It may be associated with violent behavior.Template-matching

Template-matching Technique A descriptive system for the prediction of personal behavior in a given situation. A template in this technique consists of a description of how a hypothetical person would behave in a certain setting. After listening to various templates, people can then predict their own behavior in that setting by matching their own reactions to those of others.

Territoriality The act of staking out psychological and physical space, ranging from natural boundaries to the habitat of communities, down to the personal space of each and every individual.

Trait Anxiety Anxiety as a relatively stable personality characteristic.

Zeitgeist Theory A theory of leadership that proposes that leaders are made (a product of circumstances), not born (part of their personality).

REFERENCES

Abelson, R. P. Script processing in attitude formation and decision making. Unpublished manuscript, Yale University, 1975.

Adelson, J. What generation gap? *New York Times Magazine,* January 18, 1970, 1-11.

Aderman, D., & Berkowitz, L. Observational set, empathy, and helping. *Journal of Personality and Social Psychology,* 1970, *14,* 141-148.

Adorno, T. W., Frenkel-Brunswick, E., Levinson, D. J., & Sanford, R. N. *The authoritarian personality: Studies in prejudice.* New York: Harper & Row, 1950.

Aiello, J. R., Epstein, Y., & Karlin, R. Effects of crowding on electrodermal activity. *Sociological Symposium,* 1975, *14,* 43-57.

Aiello, J. R., & Jones, S. A. Field study of the proxemic behavior of young school children in three subcultural groups. *Journal of Personality and Social Psychology,* 1971, *19,* 351-356.

Ajzen, I., & Fishbein, M. The prediction of behavior from attitudinal and normative variables. *Journal of Experimental Psychology,* 1970, *6,* 466-487.

Allen, V., & Levine, J. M. Social support and conformity: The role of independent assessment of reality. *Journal of Experimental Social Psychology,* 1971, *7,* 48-58.

Allport, G. W., & Ross, M. J. Personal religious orientation and prejudice. *Journal of Personality and Social Psychology,* 1967, *5,* 432-443.

Altman, I. Environmental psychology and social psychology. *Personality and Social Psychology Bulletin,* 1976, *2,* 96-113.

Altman, I., & Taylor, D. A. *Social penetration: The development of interpersonal relationships.* New York: Holt, Rinehart & Winston, 1973.

Amir, M. *Patterns in forcible rape.* Chicago: University of Chicago Press, 1971.

Anderson, L. R. Groups would do better without humans. *Personality and Social Psychology Bulletin,* 1978, *4,* 557-558.

Anisfeld, M., Bogo, N., & Lambert, W. E. Evaluation reactions to accented English speech. *Journal of Abnormal and Social Psychology,* 1962, *65,* 223-231.

Apple, W., Streeter, L. A., & Krauss, R. M. Effects of pitch and speech rate on personal attributions. *Journal of Personality and Social Psychology,* 1979, *37,* 715-727.

Aramoni, A. Machismo. *Psychology Today,* January, 1972.

Archibald, H. C., & Tuddenham, R. D. Persistent stress reaction after combat. *Archives of General Psychiatry,* 1965, *12,* 475-481.

Armor, D. J. *Measuring the effects of television on aggressive behavior.* Santa Monica: Rand Corporation, 1976.

Aronson, E. Some antecedents of interpersonal attraction. In W. Arnold & D. Levine (Eds.), *Nebraska symposium on motivation,* 1969, *17,* 143-173.

Aronson, E. *The social animal.* San Francisco: W. H. Freeman, 1980.

Aronson, E., & Linder, D. Gain and loss of esteem as determinants of interpersonal attractiveness. *Journal of Experimental Social Psychology*, 1965, *1*, 156-171.

Aronson, E., & Mills, J. The effect of severity of initiation on liking for a group. *Journal of Abnormal and Social Psychology*, 1959, *59*, 177-181.

Asch, S. E. *Social psychology*. Englewood Cliffs, N.J.: Prentice-Hall, 1952.

Asch, S. E. Effects of group pressure upon the modification and distortion of judgments. In E. E. Maccoby, T. M. Newcomb, & E. L. Hartley (Eds.), *Readings in social psychology* (3rd ed.). New York: Holt, Rinehart & Winston, 1968.

Averill, J. R., & Rosenn, M. Vigilant and nonvigilant coping strategies and psychophysiological stress reactions during the anticipation of electric shocks. *Journal of Personality and Social Psychology*, 1972, *23*, 128-141.

Ayllon, T., & Azrin, N. *The token economy: A motivational system for therapy and rehabilitation*. New York: Appleton-Century-Crofts, 1968.

Bach, G., & Wyden, P. *The intimate enemy*. New York: Morrow, 1969.

Back, K. *Beyond words: The story of sensitivity training and the encounter movement*. New York: Russell Sage Foundation, 1972.

Bacon, M., & Jones, M. B. *Teen-age drinking*. New York: Thomas Y. Crowell, 1968.

Bales, F. F. *Interaction process analysis: A method for the study of small groups*. Reading, Mass.: Addison-Wesley, 1950.

Bandura, A. Vicarious processes: A case of no-trial learning. In L. Berkowitz (Ed.), *Advances in experimental social psychology* (Vol. 2). New York: Academic Press, 1965.

Bandura, A. *Principles of behavior modification*. New York: Holt, Rinehart & Winston, 1969.

Bandura, A. *Social learning theory*. Morristown, N.J.: General Learning Press, 1971.(a)

Bandura, A. Vicarious and self-reinforcement processes. In R. Glaser (Ed.), *The nature of reinforcement*. New York: Academic Press, 1971.(b)

Bandura, A. *Aggression: A social learning analysis*. Englewood Cliffs, N.J.: Prentice-Hall, 1973.

Bandura, A. Behavior theory and the models of man. *American Psychologist*, 1974, *29*, 859-869.

Bandura, A. Self-efficacy: Toward a unifying theory of behavior change. *Psychological Review*, 1977, *84*, 191-215.

Bandura, A., Adams, N. E., & Beyer, J. Cognitive processes mediating behavioral change. *Journal of Personality and Social Psychology*, 1977, *35*, 125-139.

Bandura, A., & McDonald, F. J. The influence of social reinforcement and the behavior of models in shaping children's moral judgments. *Journal of Abnormal and Social Psychology*, 1963, *67*, 274-281.

Bandura, A., Ross, D., & Ross, S. A. Transmission of aggression through imitation and aggressive models. *Journal of Abnormal and Social Psychology*, 1961, *63*, 575-592.

Bandura, A., Ross, D., & Ross, S. A. A comparative test of the status envy, social power, and secondary reinforcement theories of identificatory learning. *Journal of Abnormal and Social Psychology*, 1963, *67*, 527-534.(a)

Bandura, A., Ross, D., & Ross, S. A. Imitation of film-mediated aggressive models. *Journal of Abnormal and Social Psychology*, 1963, *66*, 3-11.(b)

Bandura, A., Ross, D., & Ross, S. A. Vicarious reinforcement and imitative learning. *Journal of Abnormal and Social Psychology*, 1963, *67*, 601-607.(c)

Barker, R. G. Settings of a professional lifetime. *Journal of Personality and Social Psychology*, 1979, *37*, 2137-2157.

Baron, R. A. Aggression as a function of ambient temperature and prior anger arousal. *Journal of Personality and Social Psychology*, 1972, *21*, 183-189.

Baron, R. A. Aggression-inhibiting influence of sexual humor. *Journal of Personality and Social Psychology*, 1978, *36*, 189-197.(a)

Baron, R. A. The influence of hostile and nonhostile humor upon physical aggression. *Personality and Social Psychology Bulletin*, 1978, *4*, 77-80.(b)

Baron, R. A., & Ball, R. L. The aggression-inhibiting influence of nonhostile humor. *Journal of Experimental Social Psychology*, 1974, *10*, 23-33.

Baron, R. A., & Byrne, D. *Social psychology: Understanding human interaction* (3rd ed.). Boston: Allyn & Bacon, 1981.

Baron, R. A., & Lawton, S. F. Environmental influences on aggression: The facilitation of modeling effects by high ambient temperatures. *Psychonomic Science*, 1972, *26*, 80-82.

Baron, R. A., & Ransberger, V. M. Ambient temperature and the occurrence of collective violence: The "long, hot summer" revisited. *Journal of Personality and Social Psychology*, 1978, *36*, 351-360.

Baron, R., & Rodin, J. Perceived control and crowding stress: Processes mediating the impact of spatial and social density. In A. Baum & Y. Epstein (Eds.), *Human response to crowding*. Hillsdale, N.J.: Erlbaum, 1978.

Bass, B. M. *Organizational psychology*. Boston: Allyn & Bacon, 1965.(a)

Bass, B. M. Social behavior and the orientation inventory: A review. (Tech. Rep. G, Contract NONR- 624, 14), November, 1965.(b)

Baum, A., & Davis, G. E. Reducing stress of high density living: An architectural intervention. *Journal of Personality and Social Psychology*, 1980, *38*, 471-481.

Baum, A., & Valins, S. Architectural mediation of residential density and control: Crowding and the regulation of social contact. In L. Berkowitz (Ed.), *Advances in experimental social psychology* (Vol. 12). New York: Academic Press, 1979.

Baumgartel, H., & Sobel, R. Background and organizational factors in absenteeism. *Personnel Psychology*, 1959, *12*, 141-143.

Baumrind, D. Some thoughts of ethics of research: After reading Milgram's behavioral study of obedience. *American Psychologist*, 1964, *19*, 421-423.

Beardslee, D. C., & O'Dowd, D. D. Students and the occupational world. In N. Sanford (Ed.), *The American college*. New York: Wiley, 1962.

Beattie, M. Y., & Diehl, L. A. Effects of social conditions on the expression of sex-role stereotypes. *Psychology of Women Quarterly*, 1979, *4*, 241-255.

Becker, F. D., & Mayo, C. Delineating personal distance and territoriality. *Environment and Behavior*, December 1971.

Beckman, L. J., & Houser, B. B. The more you have, the more you do: The relationship between wife's employment, sex-role attitudes, and household behavior. *Psychology of Women Quarterly*, 1979, *4*, 160-174.

Bem, D. J. Self-perception theory. In L. Berkowitz (Ed.), *Advances in experimental social psychology* (Vol. 6). New York: Academic Press, 1972.

Bem, D. J., & Allen, A. On predicting some of the people some of the time: The search for cross-situational consistencies in behavior. *Psychological Review*, 1974, *81*, 506-520.

Bem, D. J., & Funder, D. C. Predicting more of the people more of the time. *Psychological Review*, 1978, *85*, 485-561.

Bem, S. L. The measurement of psychological androgyny. *Journal of Consulting and Clinical Psychology*, 1974, *42*, 155-162.

Bem, S. L. Sex-role adaptability: One consequence of psychological androgyny. *Journal of Personality and Social Psychology*, 1975, *31*, 634-643.

Bem, S. L., & Bem, D. J. Training the woman to know her place: The power of a nonconscious ideology. In L. S. Wrightsman & J. C. Brigham (Eds.), *Contemporary issues in social psychology* (2nd ed.). Monterey, Calif.: Brooks/Cole, 1973.

Bennett, C. C. What price privacy? *American Psychologist*, 1967, *22*, 371-376.

Bennett, E. M. & Cohen, L. R. Men and women: Personality patterns and contrasts. *Genetic Psychology Monographs*, 1959, *59*, 101-155.

Bennet, T. S. Fathers and their namesake sons: Personality characteristics of actual and perceived similarity to each other. Unpublished master's thesis, Georgia State University, 1974.

Berelson, B., & Steiner, G. A. *Human Behavior: An inventory of scientific findings*. New York: Harcourt, Brace & World, 1964.

Berkowitz, L. *Aggression: A social-psychological analysis*. New York: McGraw-Hill, 1962.

Berkowitz, L. The frustration-aggression hypothesis revisited. In L. Berkowitz (Ed.), *Roots of aggression: A re-examination of the frustration-aggression hypothesis*. New York: Atherton Press, 1968.

Berkowitz, L. The contagion of violence: An S-R meditational analysis of some effects of observed aggression, 1970. In W. Arnold & D. Levine (Eds.), *Nebraska symposium on motivation*, 1971, 95-135.

Berkowitz, L. *A survey of social psychology* (2nd ed.). New York: Holt, Rinehart & Winston, 1980.

Berkowitz, L., & Alioto, J. T. The meaning of an observed event as a determinant of its aggressive consequences. *Journal of Personality and Social Psychology*, 1973, *28*, 206-217.

Berkowitz, L., & Friedman, P. Some social class differences in helping behavior. *Journal of Personality and Social Psychology*, 1967, *5*, 217-225.

Berkowitz, L., & Geen, R. G. Film violence and cue properties of available targets. *Journal of Personality and Social Psychology*, 1966, *3*, 525-530.

Berkowitz, L., & LePage, A. Weapons as aggression-eliciting stimuli. *Journal of Personality and Social Psychology*, 1967, *7*, 202-207.

Berkowitz, L., & Lundy, R. M. Personality characteristics related to susceptibility to influence by peers or authority figures. *Journal of Personality*, 1957, *25*, 306-316.

Berkowitz, L., & Macaulay, J. R. Some effects of differences in status level and status stability. *Human Relations*, 1961, *14*, 135-148.

Berkowitz, L., & Powers, P. C. Effects of timing and justification of witnessed aggression on the observers' punitiveness. *Journal of Research in Personality*, 1979, *13*, 71-80.

Berle, A. A. *Power*. New York: Harcourt, Brace & World, 1967.

Bernard, L. C. Multivariate analysis of new sex role formulations and personality. *Journal of Personality and Social Psychology*, 1980, *38*, 323-336.

Berscheid, E. Opinion change and communicator-communicatee similarity and dissimilarity. *Journal of Personality and Social Psychology*, 1966, *4*, 670-680.

Berscheid, E., Dion, K., Walster, E., & Walster, G. W. Physical attractiveness and dating choice: A test of the matching hypothesis. *Journal of Experimental Social Psychology*, 1971, *7*, 173-179.

Berscheid, E., & Walster, E. Beauty and the best. *Psychology Today*, 1972, *5*, 42-46.

Bevard, E. W., Jr. Group structure and perception. *Journal of Abnormal and Social Psychology*, 1951, *46*, 398-405.

Bickman, B. Social influence and diffusion of responsibility in an emergency. *Journal of Experimental Social Psychology*, 1972, *8*, 438-445.

Bickman, L. Interpersonal influence and the reporting of a crime. *Personality and Social Psychology Bulletin,* 1979, *5,* 32-35.

Bickman, L., & Zarantonello, M. The effects of deception and level of obedience on subjects' ratings of the Milgram study. *Personality and Social Psychology Bulletin,* 1978, *4,* 81-85.

Birchler, G. R., Weiss, R. L., & Vincent, J. P. Multimethod analysis of social reinforcement exchange between maritally distressed and nondistressed spouse and stranger dyads. *Journal of Personality and Social Psychology,* 1975, *31,* 349-360.

Black, H. Race and sex factors influencing the correct and erroneous perception of emotion. *Proceedings, 77th Annual American Psychological Association Convention,* 1969, 363-364.

Blau, P. *The dynamics of bureaucracy.* Chicago: University of Chicago Press, 1955.

Bleecker, E. R., & Engel, B. T. Learned control of cardiac rate and cardiac conduction in the Wolff-Parkinson-White Syndrome. In L. Birk (Ed.), *Biofeedback: Behavioral medicine.* New York: Grune & Stratton, 1973.

Blitz, R. C. Women in the professions, 1870-1970. *Monthly Labor Review,* 39, May 1974.

Block, J., Haan, N., & Smith, M. B. Activism and apathy in contemporary adolescents. In J. F. Adams (Ed.), *Understanding adolescents: Current developments in adolescent psychology.* Boston: Allyn & Bacon, 1968.

Bobrow, D. G., & Norman, D. A. Some principles of memory schemata. In D. G. Bobrow & A. Collins (Eds.), *Representation and understanding: Studies in cognitive science.* New York: Academic Press, 1975.

Boffey, P. M. Love and Senator Proxmire. *The Chronicle of Higher Education,* March 24, 1975, 5.

Bolles, R. C. *Theory of motivation.* New York: Harper & Row, 1967.

Bonney, M. E. Social behavior differences between second-grade children of high and low sociometric status. *Journal of Educational Research,* 1955, *48,* 481-495.

Borgida, E., & Nisbett, R. The differential impact of abstract vs. concrete information on decisions. *Journal of Applied Social Psychology,* 1977, *7,* 258-271.

Borofsky, G. L., Stollack, E. G., & Messe, L. A. Sex differences in bystander reactions to physical assault. *Journal of Experimental Social Psychology,* 1971, *7,* 313-318.

Bossard, J. H. S. Residential propinquity as a factor in marriage selection. *American Journal of Sociology,* 1931, *38,* 219-224.

Bossom, J., & Maslow, A. H. Security of judges as a factor in impression of warmth of others. *Journal of Abnormal and Social Psychology,* 1957, *55,* 147-148.

Bowers, K. S. Situationalism in psychology: An analysis and critique. *Psychological Review,* 1973, *80,* 307-336.

Bradley, G. W. Self-serving biases in the attribution process: A reexamination of the fact or fiction question. *Journal of Personality and Social Psychology,* 1978, *36,* 56-71.

Bramel, D., Taub, B., & Blum, B. An observer's reaction to the suffering of his enemy. *Journal of Personality and Social Psychology,* 1968, *8,* 384-392.

Bray, R. M., Kerr, N. L., & Atkin, R. S. Effects of group size, problem difficulty, and sex on group performance and member reactions. *Journal of Personality and Social Psychology,* 1978, *36,* 1224-1240.

Bray, R. M., & Noble, A. M. Authoritarianism and decisions of mock juries: Evidence of jury bias and group polarization. *Journal of Personality and Social Psychology,* 1978, *36,* 1424-1430.

Brechner, K., Shippee, G., & Obitz, F. W. Compliance techniques to increase mailed questionnaire return rates from alcoholics. *Journal of Studies on Alcohol, 1976, 37,* 995-996.

Breck, S. J. A sociometric measurement of status in physical education classes. *Research Quarterly: The American Association of Health, Physical Education, and Recreation, 1950, 21,* 75-82.

Brehm, J. W., & Cohen, A. R. *Explorations in cognitive dissonance.* New York: Wiley, 1962.

Brehm, J. W., & Cole, A. H. Effect of a favor which reduces freedom. *Journal of Personality and Social Psychology, 1966, 3,* 420-426.

Brenner, M. H. *Mental illness and the economy.* Cambridge, Mass.: Harvard University Press, 1973.

Breuer, J., & Freud, S. *Studies on hysteria.* New York: Basic Books, 1957.

Brickman, P., & Stearns, A. Help that is not called help. *Personality and Social Psychology Bulletin, 1978, 4,* 314-317.

Briggs, S. R., Cheek, J. M., & Buss, A. H. An analysis of the self-monitoring scale. *Journal of Personality and Social Personality, 1980, 38,* 679-686.

Brigham, J. C. Ethnic stereotypes. *Psychological Bulletin, 1971, 76,* 15-38.

Broadbent, D. E. The current state of noise research: Reply to Poulton. *Psychological Bulletin, 1978, 85,* 1052-1067.

Broverman, I. K., Broverman, D. M., Clarkson, F. E., Rosenkrantz, P. S., & Vogel, S. S. R. Sex-role stereotypes and clinical judgments of mental health. *Journal of Consulting and Clinical Psychology, 1970, 34,* 1-7.

Bryan, J. H., & Test, M. A. Models and helping: Naturalistic studies in aiding behavior. *Journal of Personality and Social Psychology, 1967, 6,* 400-407.

Bryson, J. B. Situational determinants of expression of jealousy. Paper presented at the meeting of the American Psychological Association, San Francisco, 1977.

Bugenthal, D. E. Interpretations of naturally occurring discrepancies between words and intonations. *Journal of Personality and Social Psychology, 1974, 30,* 125-133.

Burchard, W. W. Role conflicts in military chaplains. *American Sociological Review, 1954, 19,* 528-535

Buss, A. H. Aggression pays. In J. L. Singer (Ed.), *The control of aggression and violence.* New York: Academic Press, 1971.

Butler, C. J., & Seidenberg, B. Manifestations of moral development in concrete situations. *Social Behavior and Personality, 1973, 1,* 64-70.

Buys, C. J. Humans would do better without groups. *Personality and Social Psychology Bulletin, 1978, 4,* 123-125.

Byrne, D. The effect of a subliminal food stimulus on verbal response. *Journal of Applied Psychology, 1959, 43,* 249-252.

Byrne, D. & Griffitt, W. A developmental investigation of the law of attraction. *Journal of Personality and Social Psychology, 1966, 4,* 699-702.

Byrne, D., & Nelson, D. Attraction as a linear function of proportion of positive reinforcements. *Journal of Personality and Social Psychology, 1965, 1,* 659-663.

Byrne, D., & Wong, T. J. Racial prejudice, interpersonal attraction and assumed dissimilarity of attitudes. *Journal of Abnormal and Social Psychology, 1962, 65,* 246-253.

Cacioppo, J. T., & Petty, R. E. Effects of message repetition and position on cognitive response, recall, and persuasion. *Journal of Personality and Social Psychology, 1979, 37,* 97-109.

Calvin, A. D. Social reinforcement. *Journal of Social Psychology*, 1962, *56*, 15-19.

Campbell, A. The American way of mating, marriage, si, children only maybe. *Psychology Today*, May 1975, 37-42.

Campbell, D. E., & Beets, J. L. Lunacy and the moon. *Psychological Bulletin*, 1978, *85*, 1123-1129.

Campbell, D. T., & Stanley, J. C. *Experimental and quasi-experimental designs for research*. Chicago: Rand-McNally, 1966.

Campbell, J., & Dunnette, M. Effectiveness of T group experiences in managerial training and development. *Psychological Bulletin*, 1968, *70*, 73-104.

Carlsmith, J. M., & Anderson, C. A. Ambient temperature and the occurrence of collective violence: A new analysis. *Journal of Personality and Social Psychology*, 1979, *37*, 337-344.

Carlsmith, J. M., Collins, B. E., & Helmreich, R. L. Studies in forced compliance: I. The effect of pressure for compliance on attitude change produced by face-to-face role-playing and anonymous essay-writing. *Journal of Personality and Social Psychology*, 1966, *4*, 1-13.

Carlsmith, J. M., & Gross, A. Some effects of guilt on compliance. *Journal of Personality and Social Psychology*, 1969, *11*, 232-239.

Carmet, D. W., Miles, C. G., & Cervin, V. B. Persuasiveness and persuasibility as related to intelligence and extraversion. *British Journal of Social and Clinical Psychology*, 1965, *4*, 1-7.

Carnegie, D. *How to win friends and influence people*. New York: Simon & Schuster, 1937.

Carson, R. *Silent spring*. Boston: Houghton Mifflin, 1962.

Cartwright, D., & Zander, A. *Group dynamics* (3rd ed.). New York: Harper & Row, 1968.

Carver, C. S., Coleman, A. E., & Glass, D. C. The coronary-prone behavior pattern and the suppression of fatigue on a treadmill test. *Journal of Personality and Social Psychology*, 1976, *36*, 367-379.

Carver, C. S., & Glass, D. C. The coronary-prone behavior pattern and interpersonal aggression. *Journal of Personality and Social Psychology*, 1978, *36*, 361-366.

Chaikin, A. L., & Darley, J. M. Victim or perpetrator? *Journal of Personality and Social Psychology*, 1973, *25*, 268-275.

Chittick, E. V., & Himmelstein, P. The manipulation of self-disclosure. *Journal of Psychology*, 1967, *65*, 117-121.

Christie, R., & Geis, F. L. *Studies in Machiavellianism*. New York: Academic Press, 1970.

Cialdini, R. B., & Ascani, K. Test of a concession procedure for inducing verbal, behavioral and further compliance with a request to give blood. *Journal of Applied Psychology*, 1976, *61*, 295-300.

Cialdini, R. B., Cacioppo, J. T., Basset, R., & Miller, J. A. Low-ball procedure for producing compliance: Commitment to cost. *Journal of Personality and Social Psychology*, 1978, *36*, 463-476.

Cialdini, R. B., Vincent, J. E., Lewis, S. K., Catalan, J., Wheeler, D., & Darby, B. L. Reciprocal concessions for inducing compliance: The door-in-the-face technique. *Journal of Personality and Social Psychology*, 1975, *31*, 206-215.

Clark, E. L. Motivation of Jewish students. *Journal of Social Psychology*, 1949, *129*, 113-117.

Clark, K. B. Empathy: A neglected topic in psychological research. *American Psychologist*, 1980, *35*, 187-190.

Clark, R. D., III, & Word, L. E. Why don't bystanders help? Because of ambiguity? *Journal of Personality and Social Psychology*, 1972, *24*, 392–400.

Clark, R. D., III, & Word, L. E. Where is the apathetic bystander? Situational characteristics of the emergency. *Journal of Personality and Social Psychology*, 1974, *29*, 279–287.

Clifford, C., & Cohn, T. S. The relationship between leadership and personality attributes perceived by followers. *Journal of Social Psychology*, 1964, *64*, 57–64.

Clifford, M. M., & Walster, E. The effects of physical attractiveness on teachers' expectations. *Sociology of Education*, 1973, *46*, 248–258.

Cline, V. B. Another view: Pornography effects, the state of the art. In V. B. Cline (Ed.), *Where do you draw the line?* Provo, Utah: Brigham Young University Press, 1973.

Clore, G. L., & Baldridge, B. Interpersonal attraction: The role of agreement and topic interest. *Journal of Personality and Social Psychology*, 1968, *9*, 340–349.

Cohen, S., Evans, G. W., Krantz, D. S., & Stokols, D. Physiological, motivational, and cognitive effects of aircraft noise on children: Moving from laboratory to the field. *American Psychologist*, 1980, *35*, 321–343.

Cohen, S., & Lezak, A. Noise and inattentiveness to social cues. *Environment and Behavior*, 1977, *9*, 559–572.

Coleman, J. C. Life stress and maladaptive behavior. *American Journal of Occupational Therapy*, 1973, *27*, 169–180.

Collins, B. E. *Social psychology*. Reading, Mass.: Addison-Wesley, 1970.

Collins, B. E., & Raven, B. H. Group structure: Attraction, coalitions, communication, and power. In G. Lindzey and E. Aronson (Eds.), *Handbook of social psychology* (2nd ed.). New York: Addison-Wesley, 1969, 102–204.

Commission on Obscenity and Pornography. *The report of the Commission on Obscenity and Pornography*. New York: Bantam Books, 1970.

Cooley, C. H. *Human nature and the social order*. New York: Scribner's, 1902.

Cooper, H. M. Statistically combining independent studies: A meta-analysis of sex differences in conformity research. *Journal of Personality and Social Psychology*, 1979, *37*, 131–146.

Cooper, J., & Jones, R. A. Self-esteem and consistency as determinants of anticipatory opinion change. *Journal of Personality and Social Psychology*, 1970, *4*, 312–320.

Cosentino, F., & Heilbrun, A. B. Anxiety correlates of sex-role identity in college students. *Psychological Reports*, 1964, *14*, 729–730.

Cowan, G., & Inskeep, R. Commitments to help among the disabled-disadvantaged. *Personality and Social Psychology Bulletin*, 1978, *4*, 92–95.

Cox, D. F. & Bauer, R. A. Self-confidence and persuasibility in women. *Public Opinion Quarterly*, 1964, *28*, 453–466.

Cozby, P. C. Self-disclosure: A literature review. *Psychological Bulletin*, 1973, *79*, 73–91.

Creager, J. A. *The American graduate student: A normative description*. Washington, D.C.: American Council on Education, 1971.

Crockett, W. H. Balance, agreement, and subjective evaluations of the *p-o-x* triads. *Journal of Personality and Social Psychology*, 1974, *29*, 102–110.

Cronbach, L. J. Beyond the two disciplines of scientific psychology. *American Psychologist*, 1975, *30*, 116–127.

Cronbach, L. J., & Meehl, P. E. Construct validity in psychological tests. *Psychological Bulletin*, 1955, *52*, 281–302.

Cross, H. A., Halcomb, C. G., & Matter, W. W. Imprinting or exposure learning in rats given early auditory stimulation. *Psychonomic Science,* 1967, *7,* 233-234.

Cross, K. Is there a generation gap? *Journal of the National Association of Women Deans and Counselors,* 1968, *31,* 53-56.

Crutchfield, R. S. Conformity and character. *American Psychologist,* 1955, *10,* 191-198.

Cunningham, M. R. Weather, mood, and helping behavior: Quasi experiments with the Sunshine Samaritan. *Journal of Personality and Social Psychology,* 1979, *37,* 1947-1956.

Daly, M., & Wilson, M. *Sex, evolution, and behavior.* Boston: Duxbury, 1978.

Daly, R. F. Mental illness and patterns of behaviour in 10 XYY males. *Journal of Nervous and Mental Disorders,* 1969, *149,* 318-327.

Darley, J. M., & Latané, B. Bystander intervention in emergencies: Diffusion of responsibility. *Journal of Personality and Social Psychology,* 1968, *8,* 377-383.

D'Atri, D. Psychophysiological responses to crowding. *Environment and Behavior,* 1975, *7,* 237-252.

Davis, K. E., & Braucht, G. N. Exposure to pornography, character, and sexual deviance: A retrospective survey. *Journal of Social Issues,* 1973, *29,* 183-196.

Davison, G. C., & Neale, J. N. *Abnormal psychology: An experimental clinical approach.* New York: Wiley, 1974.

Davison, G. C., & Stuart, R. B. Behavior therapy and civil liberties. *American Psychologist,* 1975, *30,* 755-763.

Dean, D. G. Alienation: Its meaning and measurement. *American Sociological Review,* 1961, *26,* 753-758.

DeFleur, M., & Petranoff, R. A televised test of subliminal persuasion. *Public Opinion Quarterly,* 1959, *23,* 168-180.

Demerath, N. J., Ill. *Social class in American Protestantism.* Chicago: Rand McNally, 1965.

Dermer, M., & Pyszczynski, T. A. Effects of erotica upon men's loving and liking responses for women they love. *Journal of Personality and Social Psychology,* 1978, *36,* 1302-1309.

Dermer, M., & Thiel, D. L. When beauty may fail. *Journal of Personality and Social Psychology,* 1975, *31,* 1168-1176.

Dertke, M. C., Penner, L. A., & Ulrich, K. "Ripping off" the college bookstore: Race, sex, and the reporting of shoplifting. Paper presented at the meeting of the Southeastern Psychological Association, Atlanta, Georgia, 1972.

Deutsch, M., & Gerard, H. B. A study of normative and informational social influences upon individual judgment. *Journal of Abnormal and Social Psychology,* 1955, *51,* 629-636.

Dey, F. L. Auditory fatigue and predicted permanent hearing defects from rock-and-roll music. *The New England Journal of Medicine,* 1970, *282,* 467-469.

Dichter, E. Depth interviewing. Address presented to Market Research Council, October 15, 1943.

DiMatteo, M. R. A social psychological analysis of physician-patient rapport: Toward a science of the art of medicine. In H. Friedman, & M. R. DiMatteo, (Eds.), *Interpersonal relations in health care.* New York: Academic Press. 1981.

DiMatteo, M. R., Friedman, H. S., & Taranta, A. Sensitivity to bodily nonverbal communication as a factor in practitioner–patient rapport. *Journal of Nonverbal Behavior,* 1979, *4,* 18-26.

DiMatteo, M. R., & Hall, J. A. Nonverbal decoding skill and attention to nonverbal cues: A research note. *Environmental Psychology and Nonverbal Behavior,* 1979, *3,* 188-192.

DiMatteo, M. R., Prince, L. M., & Taranta, A. Patients' perceptions of physicians' behavior: Determinants of patient commitment to the therapeutic relationship. *Journal of Community Health*, 1979, *4*, 280-290.

Dion, K. Physical attractiveness and evaluations of children's transgressions. *Journal of Personality and Social Psychology*, 1972, *24*, 207-213.

Dion, K., Berscheid, E., & Walster, E. What is beautiful is good. *Journal of Personality and Social Psychology*, 1972, *24*, 285-290.

Dipboye, R., Fromkin, H., & Wiback, K. Relative importance of applicant sex, attractiveness, and scholastic standing in evaluation of job applicant resumes. *Journal of Applied Psychology*, 1975, *60*, 39-43.

Dittes, J., & Kelley, H. H. Effects of different conditions of acceptance upon conformity to group norms. *Journal of Abnormal and Social Psychology*, 1956, *53*, 100-107.

DiVesta, F. J. Susceptibility to pressures toward uniformity of behavior in social situations: A study of task, motivational and personality factors in conformity behavior. AFSOR Tr. 58-70. Washington, D.C.: U.S. Air Force, Office of Scientific Research, Behavioral Science Division, 1958.

Dollard, J., Doob, L. W., Miller, N. E., Mowrer, O. H., & Sears, R. R. *Frustration and aggression*. New Haven: Yale University Press, 1939.

Dollard, J., & Miller, N. *Personality and psychotherapy*. New York: McGraw-Hill, 1950.

Donnerstein, E., & Barrett, G. The effects of erotic stimuli on male aggression toward females. *Journal of Personality and Social Psychology*, 1978, *36*, 180-188.

Donnerstein, E., & Hallam, H. Facilitating effects of erotica on aggression against women. *Journal of Personality and Social Psychology*, 1978, *36*, 1270-1277.

Don't tread on Harvey. *Newsweek*, 1965, *66*, 75-76.

Doob, A. N. Catharsis and aggression: The effects of hurting one's enemy. *Journal of Experimental Research in Personality*, 1970, *4*, 291-296.

Doob, A. N., Carlsmith, J. M., Freedman, J. L., Landauer, T. K., & Tom, S. Effect of initial selling price on subsequent sales. *Journal of Personality and Social Psychology*, 1969, *4*, 345-350.

Dooley, D., & Catalano, R. Economic change as a cause of behavioral disorder. *Psychological Bulletin*, 1980, *87*, 450-468.

Dorr, D., & Fey, S. Relative power of symbolic adult and peer models in the modification of children's moral choice behavior. *Journal of Personality and Social Psychology*, 1974, *29*, 335-341.

Douvan, E. A. & Adelson, J. *The adolescent experience*. New York: Wiley, 1966.

Drag, R. H. Self-disclosure as a function of group size and experimenter behavior. *Dissertation Abstracts International*, 1969, *30* (5-6), 2416.

Driscoll, R., Davis, K. E., & Lipetz, M. E. Parental interference and romantic love: The Romeo and Juliet effect. *Journal of Personality and Social Psychology*, 1972, *24*, 1-10.

Durkheim, E. *Suicide*. (2nd ed. reprint, trans. J. A. Spaulding & G. Simpson). New York: Free Press, 1951.

Durkheim, E. *Elementary forms of religious life*. New York: Free Press of Glencoe, 1965.

Ebbesen, E. B., Kjos, G. L., & Konecni, V. J. Spatial ecology: Its effects on the choice of friends and enemies. Unpublished manuscript, University of California, San Diego, 1975.

Edney, J. J., & Jordan-Edney, N. L. Territorial spacing on a beach. *Sociometry*, 1974, *37*, 92-104.

Efran, M. G. The effect of physical attractiveness on the judgment of guilt, interpersonal attraction, and severity of recommended punishment in a simulated jury task. *Journal of Research in Personality*, 1974, *8*, 45-54.

Ehrlich, D., Guttman, I., Schonbach, P., & Mills, J. Post-decision exposure to relevant information. *Journal of Abnormal and Social Psychology*, 1957, *54*, 98-102.

Ehrlich, H. J., & Graeven, D. B. Reciprocal self-disclosure in a dyad. *Journal of Experimental Social Psychology*, 1971, *7*, 389-400.

Ehrlich, P. R. *The population bomb.* New York: Ballantine, 1971.

Eisenberg, L. Doing better and feeling worse: Health care in the United States. *Daedalus*, 1977, *106*, 235-246.

Eisenberger, R. Explanation of rewards that do not reduce tissue needs. *Psychological Bulletin*, 1972, *77*, 319-339.

Eisenberger, R., Kaplan, R. M., & Singer, R. D. Decremental and non-decremental effects of noncontingent social approval. *Journal of Personality and Social Psychology*, 1974, *30*, 716-722.

Ekman, P., & Friesen, W. V. *Unmasking the face.* Englewood Cliffs, N.J.: Prentice-Hall, 1975.

Ellis, E. Social psychological correlates of upward social mobility groups among unmarried career women. *American Sociological Review*, 1952, *17*, 558-563.

Ellsworth, P., & Carlsmith, H. Effects of eye contact and verbal content on affective response to a dyadic interaction. *Journal of Personality and Social Psychology*, 1968, *10*, 15-20.

Ellsworth, P., Carlsmith, J., & Henson. A. The stare as a stimulus to flight in human subjects: A series of field experiments. *Journal of Personality and Social Psychology*, 1972, *21*, 302-311.

Elms, A. Influence of fantasy ability on attitude change through role playing. *Journal of Personality and Social Psychology*, 1966, *4*, 36-43.

Emswiller, T., Deaux, K., & Willits, J. E. Similarity, sex, and requests for small favors. *Journal of Applied Social Psychology*, 1971, *1*, 284-291.

Endler, N. S. The person versus the situation—a pseudo issue? A response to Alker. *Journal of Personality*, 1973, *41*, 287-303.

Endler, N. S., & Hunt, J. McV. S-R inventories of hostility and comparisons of the proportions of variance from persons, responses, and situations for hostility and anxiousness. *Journal of Personality and Social Psychology*, 1968, *9*, 309-315.

Endler, N. S., & Magnussen, D. *Interactional psychology and personality.* Washington, D.C.: Hemisphere, 1976.

Engel, B. T. Clinical applications of operant techniques in the control of the cardiac arrhythmias. In L. Birk (Ed.), *Biofeedback: Behavioral medicine.* New York: Grune & Stratton, 1973.

English, H. B., & English, A. C. *A comprehensive dictionary of psychological and psychoanalytical terms.* New York: Longmans, Green and Co., 1958.

Enzle, M. E., & Harvey, M. D. Recipient vs. third-party requests, recipient need, and helping behavior. *Personality and Social Psychology Bulletin*, 1978, *4*, 620-623.

Eron, L. D. Prescription for reduction of aggression. *American Psychologist*, 1980, *35*, 244-252.

Eron, L. D., Huesmann, L. R., Lefkowitz, M. M., & Walder, L. O. Does television violence cause aggression? *American Psychologist*, 1972, *27*, 253-263.

Ettinger, R. F., Marino, C. J., Endler, N. S., Geller, S. H., & Natziuk, T. Effects of agreement and correctness on relative competence and conformity. *Journal of Personality and Social Psychology*, 1971, *19*, 204-212.

Everett, P. B., Deslauries, B. C., Newsom, T. J., & Anderson, V. B. Increasing the effectiveness of free transit. *Transit Journal*, 1978.

Everett, P. B., Hayward, S. C., & Meyers, A. W. The effects of a token reinforcement procedure on bus ridership. *Journal of Applied Behavior Analysis*, 1974, *7*, 1-9.

Everett, P. B., Studer, P. G., & Douglas, T. J. Gaming simulation to pretest operant-based community interventions: An urban transportation example. *American Journal of Community Psychology*, 1978.

Exline, R. V., Gray, D., & Schuette, D. Visual behavior in a dyad as affected by interview content and sex of respondent. *Journal of Personality and Social Psychology*, 1965, *1*, 201-209.

Fairweather, G. W. (Ed.). *Social psychology in treating mental illness: An experimental approach.* New York: Wiley, 1964.

Fairweather, G. W. *Methods for experimental social innovation.* New York: Wiley, 1967.

Fairweather, G. W. Innovation: A necessary but insufficient condition for change. *Innovations*, 1973, *1*, 25-27.

Fairweather, G. W., Sanders, D. H., Cressler, D. L., & Maynard, H. *Community life for the mentally ill: An alternative to institutional care.* Chicago: Aldine, 1969.

Falbo, T., & Peplau, L. A. Power strategies in intimate relationships. *Journal of Personality and Social Psychology*, 1980, *38*, 618-628.

Feierabend, I. K., Feierabend, R. L., & Gurr, T. R. *Anger, violence, and politics.* Englewood Cliffs, N.J.: Prentice-Hall, 1972.

Fendrich, J. M. A study of the association among verbal attitudes, commitment, and overt behavior in different experimental situations. *Social Forces*, 1967, *45*, 347-355.

Feshbach, N. D. Psychology of empathy and empathy of psychology. Presidential address to Western Psychological Association Convention, Honolulu, 1980.

Feshbach, S. The function of aggression and the regulation of aggressive drive. *Psychological Review*, 1964, *71*, 257-272.

Feshbach, S. Dynamics and morality of violence and aggression: Some psychological considerations. *American Psychologist*, 1971, *26*, 281-292.

Feshbach, S. Reality and fantasy in filmed violence. In J. P. Murray, E. A. Rubinstein, & G. A. Comstock (Eds.), *Television and social behavior* (Vol. 2). Washington, D.C.: U.S. Government Printing Office, 1972.

Feshbach, S., & Singer, R. D. *Television and aggression.* San Francisco: Jossey-Bass, 1971.

Festinger, L. A theory of social comparison processes. *Human Relations*, 1954, *7*, 117-140.

Festinger, L. *A theory of cognitive dissonance.* Stanford, Calif.: Stanford University Press, 1957.

Festinger, L., & Carlsmith, J. M. Cognitive consequences of forced compliance. *Journal of Abnormal and Social Psychology*, 1959, *58*, 203-210.

Festinger, L., & Maccoby, N. On resistance to persuasive communications. *Journal of Abnormal and Social Psychology*, 1964, *68*, 359-366.

Festinger, L., Schachter, S., & Back, K. W. *Social pressures in informal groups: A study of human factors in housing.* Palo Alto: Stanford University Press, 1950.

Fichter, J. H. *Social relations in the urban parish.* Chicago: University of Chicago Press, 1954.

Fiedler, F. *Leader attitudes and group effectiveness.* Urbana: University of Illinois Press, 1958.

Fiedler, F. A contingency model for the prediction of leadership effectiveness. (Tech. Rep. No. 10, ONR Contract. Nour-1834, 36), 1963.

Fiedler, F. *A theory of leadership effectiveness.* New York: McGraw-Hill, 1967.

Firestone, I. J., Lichtman, C. M., & Colamosca, J. V. Leader effectiveness and leader conferral as determinants of helping in a medical emergency. *Journal of Personality and Social Psychology,* 1975, *31,* 343-348.

Fishbein, M. The prediction of behavior from attitudinal variables. In K. K. Sereno & C. C. Mortenson (Eds.), *Advances in communication research.* New York: Harper & Row, 1972.

Fisher, W. A., & Byrne, D. Sex differences in response to erotica? Love versus lust. *Journal of Personality and Social Psychology,* 1978, *36,* 117-125.

Flacks, R. The liberated generation: An exploration of the roots of student protest. *Journal of Social Issues,* 1967, *23* (3), 52-75.

Flanders, N. A. *Teaching with groups.* Minneapolis: Burgess, 1954.

Flexner, E. *Women's rights—unfinished business.* New York: Public Affairs Committee, 1971.

Foa, V. G. The contiguity principle in the structure of interpersonal relations. *Human Relations,* 1958, *11,* 229-237.

Foersterling, F. Sex differences in risk taking: Effects of subjective and objective probability of success. *Personality and Social Psychology Bulletin,* 1979, *4,* 149-152.

Folmar, K., & Kaplan, R. M. Nonconscious ideologies and solutions to a riddle. Unpublished manuscript, University of California, San Diego, 1974.

Fraser, R., Leslie, I., & Phelps, D. Psychiatric effects of severe personal experiences during bombing. *Proceedings of the Royal Society of Medicine,* 1943, *36,* 119-123.

Frazier, E. F. The Negro middle class and desegregation. *Social Problems,* 1957, *4,* 291-301.

Freedman, J. L. The crowd—maybe not so maddening after all. *Psychology Today,* 1971, *5,* 58-61, 86.

Freedman, J. L., & Fraser, S. Compliance without pressure: The foot-in-the-door technique. *Journal of Personality and Social Psychology,* 1966, *4,* 195-202.

Freedman, J. L., Klevansky, S., & Ehrlich, P. R. The effect of crowding in human task performance. *Journal of Applied Social Psychology,* 1971, *1,* 7-25.

Freedman, J. L., Sears, D. O., & Carlsmith, J. M. *Social psychology* (3rd ed.). Englewood Cliffs, N.J.: Prentice-Hall, 1978.

French, J. R. P., Jr., & Raven, B. H. The bases of social power. In D. Cartwright (Ed.), *Studies in social power.* Ann Arbor: University of Michigan, 1959.

French, R. L. Sociometric status and individual adjustment among naval recruits. *Journal of Abnormal and Social Psychology,* 1951, *46,* 64-72.

Freud, S. *Civilization and its discontents.* New York: Norton, 1961.

Friedan, B. *The feminine mystique.* New York: Dell, 1963.

Friedman, H. Nonverbal communication between patients and medical practitioners. In H. Friedman & M. R. DiMatteo (Eds.), *Interpersonal relations in health care.* New York: Academic Press, 1981.

Friedman, M. & Rosenman, R. H. *Type A behavior and your heart.* New York: Knopf, 1974.

Frieze, I. H., & Snyder, H. N. Children's beliefs about the causes of success and failure in school settings. *Journal of Educational Psychology,* 1980, *72,* 186-196.

Fritz, C. E. Disaster. In R. K. Merton and R. Nisbett (Eds.), *Contemporary social problems.* New York: Harcourt Brace Jovanovich, 1961.

Fuller, E. M., & Baune, H. B. Injury proneness and adjustment in a second grade. *Sociometry,* 1951, *14,* 210-225.

Gabrenya, W. K., & Arkin, R. M. Self-monitoring scale: Factor structure and correlates. *Personality and Social Psychology Bulletin*, 1980, *6*, 13–22.

Gaertner, S. L. A "call" for help: Helping behavior extended to black and white victims by New York City liberal and conservative party members. *Proceedings, 78th Annual Convention, American Psychological Association*. 1970, 441–442.

Galbraith, J. K. *The new industrial state*. Boston: Houghton Mifflin, 1967.

Gallo, P. S. Prisoners of our own dilemma? Paper presented at Western Psychological Association, San Diego, 1968.

Geen, R. G. *Aggression*. Morristown, N.J.: General Learning Press, 1972.

Geen, R. G. Observing violence in the mass media: Implications of basic research. In R. Geen & E. O'Neal (Eds.), *Perspectives on aggression*. New York: Academic Press, 1976.

Geen, R. G., & Berkowitz, L. Name-mediated aggressive cue properties. *Journal of Personality*, 1966, *34*, 456–465.

Geen, R. G., & O'Neal, E. C. Activation of one elicited aggression by general arousal. *Journal of Personality and Social Psychology*, 1969, *11*, 289–292.

Geen, R. G., & Pigg, R. Acquisition of an aggressive response and its generalizations to verbal behavior. *Journal of Personality and Social Psychology*, 1970, *15*, 165–170.

Geen, R. G., & Stonner, D. Effects of aggressiveness habit strength on behavior in the presence of aggressive-related stimuli. *Journal of Personality and Social Psychology*, 1971, *17*, 149–153.

Geis, F. L., & Christie, R. Machiavellianism and the manipulation of one's fellow man. In D. Marlowe & K. J. Gergen (Eds.), *Personality and social behavior*. New York: Addison-Wesley, 1970.

Geis, F. L., Christie, R., & Nelson, C. In search of the Machiavel. In R. Christie & F. L. Geis (Eds.), *Studies in Machiavellianism*. New York: Academic Press, 1970.

Gelfand, D. M., Hartman, D. P., Walder, P., & Page, B. Who reports shoplifters? A field-experimental study. *Journal of Personality and Social Psychology*, 1973, *25*, 276–285.

Gerard, H. B. Emotional uncertainty and social comparison. *Journal of Abnormal and Social Psychology*, 1963, *66*, 568–573.

Gerard, H. B., Wilhelmy, R. A., & Connolley, E. S. Conformity and group size. *Journal of Personality and Social Psychology*, 1968, *8*, 79–82.

Gerwirtz, J. L., & Baer, D. M. Deprivation and satiation of social reinforcers as drive conditions. *Journal of Abnormal and Social Psychology*, 1958, *57*, 165–172.

Gibb, J. R. The effects of group size and of threat reduction upon creativity in a problem-solving situation. *American Psychologist*, 1951, *61*, 324.

Gibbins, K. Communication aspects of women's clothes and their relation to fashion ability. *British Journal of Social and Clinical Psychology*, 1969, *8*, 301–312.

Gillig, P. M., & Greenwald, A. G. Is it time to lay the sleeper effect to rest? *Journal of Personality and Social Psychology*, 1974, *29*, 132–139.

Gillis, J. S. Social influence therapy: The therapist as manipulator. *Psychology Today*, 1974, *12*, 91–95.

Glass, D. C. *Behavior patterns, stress, and coronary disease*. Hillsdale, N.J.: Erlbaum 1977.

Glass, D. C., & Singer, J. E. *Urban stress*. New York: Academic Press, 1972.

Glass, D. C., Snyder, M. L., & Hollis, J. F. Time urgency and the Type A coronary-prone behavior pattern. *Journal of Applied Social Psychology*, 1974, *4*, 125–140.

Goffman, E. *Encounters*. Indianapolis, Ind.: Bobbs-Merrill, 1961.

Goffman, E. *Interaction ritual: Essays in face-to-face behavior.* Chicago: Aldine, 1967.

Goldberg, L. R. Differential attribution of trait-descriptive terms to oneself as compared to well-liked, neutral, and disliked others: A psychometric analysis. *Journal of Personality and Social Psychology,* 1978, *36,* 1012–1028.

Goldberg, P. A. Are women prejudiced against women? *Trans-Action,* 1968, *5,* 28–30.

Goldiamond, I. Statement in subliminal advertising. In R. Ulrich, T. Stachnik, & J. Mabry (Eds.), *Control of human behavior.* Glenview, Ill.: Scott, Foresman, 1966.

Goldman, M. A comparison of group and individual performance where subjects have varying tendencies to solve problems. *Journal of Personality and Social Psychology,* 1966, *3,* 604–607.

Goranson, R. E., & Berkowitz, L. Reciprocity and responsibility reactions to prior help. *Journal of Personality and Social Psychology,* 1966, *3,* 227–232.

Goranson, R. E., & King, D. Rioting and daily temperature: Analysis of the U.S. riots in 1967. Unpublished manuscript, York University, Toronto, 1970.

Gordon, S. K., & Hallauer, D. S. Implementing a friendly visiting program on attitudes of college students toward the aged. *The Gerontologist,* 1976, *16,* 371–376.

Gorsuch, R. L., & Smith, R. A. Changes in college students' evaluation of moral behavior: 1969 versus 1939, 1949, and 1958. *Journal of Personality and Social Psychology,* 1972, *24,* 381–391.

Graf, R. G., & Riddell, J. Helping behavior as a function of interpersonal perception. *Journal of Social Psychology,* 1972, *86,* 227–231.

Gray, S. W. Masculinity-femininity in relation to anxiety and social acceptance. *Child Development,* 1957, *28,* 203–214.

Green, R. B., & Mack, J. Would groups do better without social psychologists? A response to Buys. *Personality and Social Psychology Bulletin,* 1978, *4,* 561–563.

Greenspoon, J. The reinforcing effect of two spoken sounds on the frequency of two responses. *American Journal of Psychology,* 1955, *68,* 409–416.

Griffitt, W. Environmental effects on interpersonal affective behavior: Ambient effective temperature and attraction. *Journal of Personality and Social Psychology,* 1970, *15,* 240–244.

Griffitt, W., Nelson, J., & Littlepage, G. Old age and response to agreement-disagreement. *Journal of Gerontology,* 1972, *27,* 269–274.

Grossman, B., & Wrighter, J. The relationship between selection-rejection and intelligence, social status, and personality amongst sixth grade children. *Sociometry.* 1948, *11,* 346–355.

Gruder, C. L., Cook, T. D., Hennigan, K. M., Flay, B. R., Alessis, C., & Halamaj, J. Empirical tests of the absolute sleeper effect predicted from the discounting cue hypothesis. *Journal of Personality and Social Psychology,* 1978, *36,* 1061–1074.

Gruder, C. L., Romer, D., & Korth, B. Dependency and fault as determinants of helping. *Journal of Experimental Social Psychology,* 1978, *14,* 227–235.

Gruner, C. An experimental study of satire as persuasion. *Speech Monographs,* 1965, *32,* 149–153.

Gruner, C. Effect of humor on speaker ethos and audience information. *Journal of Communication,* 1967, *17,* 228–233.

Haan, N. Two moralities in action contexts: Relationships to thought, ego regulation, and development. *Journal of Personality and Social Psychology,* 1978, *36,* 286–305.

Haan, N., Smith, M. B., & Block, J. Moral reasoning of young adults: Political-social behavior, family background, and personality correlates. *Journal of Personality and Social Psychology,* 1968, *10,* 183-201.

Hall, C. The language of space. *Landscape,* Autumn 1960, 41-44.

Hall, E. T. A system of notation of proxemic behavior. *American Anthropologist,* 1963, *65,* 1003-1026.

A handbook of therapeutic suggestions. American Society of Clinical Hypnosis, Education and Research Foundation, 1974.

Hanratty, M. A., O'Neal, E., & Sulzer, J. L. Effects of frustration upon imitation of aggression. *Journal of Personality and Social Psychology,* 1972, *21,* 30-34.

Hantover, J. P. The boy scouts and the validation of masculinity. *Journal of Social Issues,* 1978, *34* (1), 184-195.

Harackiewicz, J. M. The effects of reward contingency and performance feedback on intrinsic motivation. *Journal of Personality and Social Psychology,* 1979, *37,* 1352-1363.

Harari, H. An experimental evaluation of Heider's balance theory with respect to situational and predispositional variables. *Journal of Social Psychology,* 1967, *78,* 177-189.

Harari, H. Interpersonal models in psychotherapy and counseling. *Journal of Abnormal Psychology,* 1971, *78,* 127-133.

Harari, H. Cognitive manipulations with delinquent adolescents in group therapy. *Psychotherapy: Theory, Practice, and Research,* 1972, *2,* 303-307.

Harari, H., Bujarski, R., Houlné, S., & Wullner, K. Student power and faculty evaluation. *Journal of College Student Personnel,* 1975, *16,* 75-79.

Harari, H., Harari, O., & White, R. V. Group processes in bystander intervention in violent emergencies: A field experiment. Unpublished manuscript. San Diego State Unversity, 1982.

Harari, H., & Hosey, K. Locus of control and occupational role as determinants of clinical prognoses. *Journal of Clinical Psychology,* 1979, *35,* 145-147.

Harari, H., & Kaplan, R. M. *Psychology: Personal and social adjustment.* New York: Harper & Row, 1977.

Harari, H., & McDavid, J. W. Situational influence on moral justice: A study of "finking." *Journal of Personality and Social Psychology,* 1969, *3,* 240-244.

Harari, H., & McDavid, J. W. Teachers' expectations and name stereotypes. *Journal of Educational Psychology,* 1973, *65,* 222-225.

Harari, H., Mohr, D., & Hosey, K. Faculty helpfulness to students: A comparison of compliance techniques. *Personality and Social Psychology Bulletin,* 1980, *6,* 373-377.

Hare, A. P., & Bales, R. F. Seating position and small group interaction. *Sociometry,* 1963, *26,* 480-486.

Harford, T. C., Willis, C. H., & Deabler, H. L. Personality correlates of masculinity-femininity. *Psychological Reports,* 1967, *21,* 881-884.

Harlow, H. F., & Harlow, M. K. The affectional systems. In A. M. Schrier, H. F. Harlow, & F. Stollmitz (Eds.), *Behavior of non-human primates* (Vol. 2). New York: Academic Press, 1965.

Harshbarger, D. High priests of hospitaldom. *Hospital and Community Psychiatry,* May 1970, 156-159.

Harvey, O. J., & Consalvi, C. Status and conformity to pressures in informal groups. *Journal of Abnormal and Social Psychology,* 1960, *60,* 182-187.

Hastorf, A. H., Northcraft, G. B., & Picciotto, S. R. Helping the handicapped: How realistic is the performance feedback received by the physically handicapped? *Personality and Social Psychology Bulletin,* 1979, *5,* 373-376.

Hastorf, A. H., Wildfogel, J., & Cassman, T. Acknowledgement of handicap as a tactic in social interaction. *Journal of Personality and Social Psychology,* 1979, *37,* 1790–1797.

Hawley, P. What women think men think: Does it affect career choice? *Journal of Counseling Psychology,* 1971, *18,* 193–199.

Hayes, S. C., Rincover, A., & Volosin, D. Variables influencing the acquisition and maintenance of aggressive behavior: Modeling vs. sensory reinforcement. *Journal of Abnormal Psychology,* 1980, *89,* 254–262.

Hayes, S. C., & Cone, J. D. Reducing residential electrical energy use: Payments, information, and feedback. *Journal of Applied Behavioral Analysis,* 1978.

Haynes, R. B., & Sackett, D. L. *An annotated bibliography on the compliance of patients with therapeutic regimens.* Hamilton, Ontario: McMaster University, 1974.

Heider, F. Social perception and phenomenal causation. *Psychological Review,* 1944, *51,* 358–374.

Heider, F. *The psychology of interpersonal relations.* New York: Wiley, 1958.

Heller, M. S., & Polsky, S. *Studies in violence and television.* New York: American Broadcasting Company, 1976.

Helson, H. Adaptation level as a basis for a quantitative theory of frames of reference. *Psychological Review,* 1948, *55,* 297–313.

Helson, H., Dworkin, R. S., & Michels, W. C. Quantitative denotations of common words as a function of background. *American Journal of Psychology,* 1956, *69,* 194–208.

Hereford, C. *Changing parental attitudes through group discussion.* Austin: University of Texas Press, 1963.

Herjanic, M., & Meyer, D. A. Notes on epidemiology of homicide in an urban area. *Forensic Science,* 1976, *8,* 235–245.

Higbee, K. L. Fifteen years of fear arousal: Research on threat appeals: 1953-1968. *Psychological Bulletin,* 1969, *72,* 426–444.

Higbee, K. L. Expression of "Walter Mitty-ness" in actual behavior. *Journal of Personality and Social Psychology,* 1971, *20,* 416–422.

Hilgard, E. R., Atkinson, R. C., & Atkinson, R. L. *Introduction to psychology* (6th ed.). New York: Harcourt Brace Jovanovich, 1979.

Hinckley, R. G., & Roethlingshafer, D. Value judgments of heights of men by college students. *Journal of Psychology,* 1951, *31,* 257–262.

Hinrichsen, J. J., & Stone, L. Effects of three conditions of administration of Bem Sex Role Inventory scores. *Journal of Personality Assessment,* 1978, *42,* 512.

Hoffer, A., & Osmond, H. *The hallucinogens.* New York: Academic Press, 1967.

Hoffman, L. R., & Maier, N. R. F. Quality and acceptance of problem solutions by members of homogenous and heterogenous groups. *Journal of Abnormal and Social Psychology,* 1961, *62,* 401–407.

Hofling, C. K., Brotzman, E., Dalrymple, S., Graves, N. & Pierce, C. M. An experimental study in nurse-physician relationship. *Journal of Nervous and Mental Disease,* 1966, *143,* 171–180.

Hogan, R., & Dickstein, E. Moral judgment and perceptions of injustice. *Journal of Personality and Social Psychology,* 1972, *23,* 409–413.

Hollander, E. P. Competence and conformity in the acceptance of influence. *Journal of Abnormal and Social Psychology,* 1960, *61,* 365–370.

Hollander, S. W. Effects of forewarning factors on pre- and postcommunication attitude change. *Journal of Personality and Social Psychology,* 1974, *30,* 272–278.

Holmes, T. S., & Rahe, R. H. The social readjustment rating scale. *Journal of*

Psychosomatic Research, 1967, *11*, 213-218.

Homans, G. *Social behavior: Its elementary forms.* New York: Harcourt, Brace & World, 1961.

Horman, R. E. Alienation and drug use. *International Journal of Addictions*, 1973, *8*, 325-331.

Horner, M. S. Woman's will to fail. *Psychology Today*, 1969, *11*.

Horner, M. S. The psychological significance of success in competitive achievement situations: A threat as well as a promise. In H. I. Day, D. E. Berlyne, & D. E. Hunt (Eds.), *Intrinsic motivation: A new direction in education.* Toronto: Holt, Rinehart & Winston, 1971.

Horney, K. *New ways in psychoanalysis.* New York: Norton, 1939.

Hornstein, H. A., Fisch, E., & Holmes, M. Influence of a model's feeling about his behavior and his relevance as a comparison other on observers' behavior. *Journal of Personality and Social Psychology*, 1968, *10*, 222-226.

Horsfall, A. B., & Arensberg, C. M. Teamwork and productivity in a shoe factory. *Human Organization*, 1949, *8*, 13-25.

Hosey, K. R. The self-fulfilling prophecy among the elderly: A simulation study of age discrimination. Unpublished master's thesis, San Diego State University, 1978.

House, J. S., & Wolf, S. Effects of urban residence on interpersonal trust and helping behavior. *Journal of Personality and Social Psychology*, 1978, *36*, 1029-1043.

Houston, B. K., & Holmes, D. S. Effect of avoidant thinking and reappraisal for coping with threat involving temporal uncertainty. *Journal of Personality and Social Psychology*, 1974, *30*, 382-388.

Hovland, C. I., Campbell, E., & Brock, B. T. The effects of "commitment" on opinion change following communication. In C. I. Hovland (Ed.), *The order of presentation in persuasion.* New Haven: Yale University Press, 1957.

Hovland, C. I., Harvey, O. J., & Sherif, M. Assimilation and contrast effects in reactions to communication and attitude changes. *Journal of Abnormal and Social Psychology*, 1957, *55*, 244-252.

Hovland, C. I., & Janis, I. L. (Eds.), *Personality and persuasibility.* New Haven: Yale University Press, 1959.

Hovland, C. I., Janis, I., & Kelley, H. *Communication and persuasion.* New Haven: Yale University Press, 1953.

Hovland, C. I., Janis, I. L., & Kelley, H. H. A summary of experimental studies of Opinion change. In M. Jahoda & N. Warren (Eds.), *Attitudes.* Baltimore, Md.: Penguin Books, 1966.

Hovland, C. I., Lumsdaine, A. A., & Sheffield, F. D. *Experiments on mass communication.* Princeton, N.J.: Princeton University Press, 1949.

Hovland, C. I., & Mandell, W. An experimental comparison of conclusion-drawing by the communicator and by the audience. *Journal of Abnormal and Social Psychology*, 1952, *47*, 581-588.

Hovland, C. I., & Pritzker, H. A. Extent of opinion change as a function of amounts of change advocated. *Journal of Abnormal and Social Psychology*, 1957, *54*, 257-261.

Hovland, C. I., & Sherif, M. Judgmental phenomena and scales of attitude measurement: Item displacement in Thurstone scales. *Journal of Abnormal and Social Psychology*, 1952, *41*, 822-832.

Hovland, C. I., & Weiss, W. The influence of source credibility on communication effectiveness. *Public Opinion Quarterly.* 1951, *15*, 635-650.

Hulin, W. S., & Katz, D. The Frois-Wittman pictures of facial expression. *Journal of Experimental Psychology,* 1935, *18*, 482-498.

Hunt, M. *The world of the formerly married.* New York: McGraw-Hill, 1966.

Ickes, W., & Barnes, R. D. Boys and girls together—and alienated: On enacting stereotyped sex roles in mixed dyads. *Journal of Personality and Social Psychology,* 1978, *36*, 669-683.

Insko, C. A., & Adewole, A. The role of assumed reciprocation of sentiment and assumed similarity in the production of attraction and agreement effects in p-o-x triads. *Journal of Personality and Social Psychology,* 1979, *37*, 790-809.

Isen, A. M. Success, failure, attention, and reaction to others: The warm glow of success. *Journal of Personality and Social Psychology,* 1970, *15*, 294-300.

Isen, A. M., Clark, M., & Schwartz, M. F. Duration of good mood on helping: "Footprints on the sands of time." *Journal of Personality and Social Psychology,* 1976, *34*, 385-393.

Isen, A. M., & Levin, P. F. The effect of feeling good on helping: Cookies and kindness. *Journal of Personality and Social Psychology.* 1972, *21*, 384-388.

Jackins, H. *The human side of human beings.* Seattle: Rational Islands, 1965.

Jackson, D. N., & Paunonen, S. V. Personality structure and assessment. *Annual Review of Psychology,* 1980, *31*, 503-551.

James, W. T. A study of the expression of bodily posture. *Journal of General Psychology,* 1932, *7*, 90-94.

Jamison, P. H., Franzini, L. R., & Kaplan, R. M. Some assumed characteristics of voluntarily childfree women and men. *Psychology of Women Quarterly,* 1979, *4*, 266-273.

Janis, I. L. Personality correlates of susceptibility to persuasion. *Journal of Abnormal and Social Psychology,* 1954, *22*, 504-518.

Janis, I. L. Anxiety indices related to susceptibility to persuasion. *Journal of Abnormal and Social Psychology,* 1955, *51*, 663-667.

Janis, I. L. *Victims of Groupthink.* Boston: Houghton Mifflin, 1972.

Janis, I. L, & Feshbach, S. Effects of fear-arousing communications. *Journal of Abnormal and Social Psychology,* 1953, *48*, 78-92.

Janis, I. L., & Feshbach, S. Personality differences associated with responsiveness to fear-arousing communications. *Journal of Personality,* 1954, *23*, 154-166.

Janis, I. L., & Field, P. B. A behavioral assessment of persuasibility: Consistency of individual differences. *Sociometry,* 1967, *19*, 241-259.

Janis, I. L., & Gilmore, J. B. The influence of incentive conditions on the success of role-playing in modifying attitudes. *Journal of Personality and Social Psychology,* 1965, *1*, 17-27.

Janis, I., & Mann, L. Effectiveness of emotional role-playing in modifying smoking habits and attitudes. *Journal of Experimental Research in Personality,* 1965, *1*, 84-90.

Janis, I. L., & Terwilliger, R. F. An experimental study of psychological resistances to fear-arousing communications. *Journal of Abnormal and Social Psychology,* 1962, *65*, 403-410.

Janov, A. *The primal scream.* New York: G. P. Putnam's Sons, 1970.

Jarvick, L. F., Klodin, V., & Matsuyama, S. S. Human aggression and the extra Y chromosome: Fact or fantasy? *American Psychologist,* 1973, *28*, 674-682.

Jellison, J. M., & Mills, J. Effect of similarity and future of the other on attraction. *Journal of Personality and Social Psychology,* 1967, *5*, 459-463.

Jennings (Walstedt), J., Geis, F. L., & Brown, V. Influence of television commercials on women's self-confidence and independent judgment. *Journal of Personality and Social Psychology,* 1980, *38,* 203–210.

Jensen, A. R. *Bias in mental testing.* New York: Free Press, 1980.

Jensen, A. R. How much can we trust I.Q. and scholastic achievement? *Harvard Educational Review,* 1969, *39,* 1–23.

Jessor, R., Jessor, S. L., & Finney, J. A social psychology of marijuana use: Longitudinal studies of high school and college youth. *Journal of Personality and Social Psychology,* 1973, *26,* 1–15.

Johnson, J. E. The effects of accurate expectations about sensations on the sensory and distress components of pain. *Journal of Personality and Social Psychology,* 1973, *27,* 261–275.

Johnson, J. E., & Leventhal, H. Effects of accurate expectations and behavioral instructions on reactions during a noxious medical examination. *Journal of Personality and Social Psychology,* 1974, *29,* 710–718.

Johnson, R. N. *Aggression in man and animals.* Philadelphia: Saunders, 1972.

Jones, C., & Aronson, E. Attribution of fault to a rape victim as a function of respectability of the victim. *Journal of Personality and Social Psychology,* 1973, *26,* 415–419.

Jones, E. E. Flattery will get you somewhere: Styles and uses of ingratiation. In E. Aronson (Ed.), *Readings about the social animal.* San Francisco: W. H. Freeman, 1977.

Jones, E. E. The rocky road from acts to dispositions. *American Psychologist,* 1979, *34,* 107–117.

Jones, E. E., & Davis, X. E. From acts to dispositions: The attribution process in person perception. In L. Berkowitz (Ed.), *Advances in experimental social psychology* (Vol. 2). New York: Academic Press, 1965.

Jones, E. E., & Nisbett, R. E. (Eds.), *The actor and the observer: Divergent perceptions of the causes of behavior.* Morristown, N.J.: General Learning Press, 1972.

Jones, W. T. *A history of Western philosophy* (Vol. 1). New York: Harcourt, Brace & World, 1969.

Jonsson, A., & Hansson, L. Prolonged exposure to stressful stimulus (noise) as a cause of raised blood pressure in man. *Lancet,* 1977, *1,* 86–87.

Jospe, A. Jewish college students in the United States. *The American Jewish Yearbook* (Vol. 65). The American Jewish Committee and the Jewish Publication Society of America, 1965.

Jourard, S. M. *The transparent self.* Princeton: Van Nostrand Reinhold, 1964.

Jourard, S. M., & Friedman, R. Experimenter-subject "distance" and self-disclosure. *Journal of Personality and Social Psychology,* 1970, *15,* 278–282.

Jourard, S. M., & Lasakow, P. Some factors in self-disclosure. *Journal of Abnormal and Social Psychology,* 1958, *56,* 91–98.

Judd, C. M., & Kulik, J. A. Schematic effects of social attitudes on information processing and recall. *Journal of Personality and Social Psychology,* 1980, *38,* 569–578.

Julian, J. W., & Steiner, I. D. Perceived acceptance as a determinant in conformity behavior. *Journal of Social Psychology,* 1961, *55,* 191–198.

Jung, C. G. *Two essays on analytical psychology.* New York: World, 1956.

Kagan, J. *Changes and continuity in infancy.* New York: Wiley, 1971.

Kagan, J., & Moss, H. A. *Birth to maturity: A study in psychological development.* New York: Wiley, 1962.

Kahle, L. R., & Berman, J. J. Attitudes cause behaviors: A cross-lagged panel analysis. *Journal of Personality and Social Psychology,* 1979, *37,* 315–321.

Kahn, M. The physiology of catharsis. *Journal of Personality and Social Psychology,* 1966, *3,* 278–286.

Kahn, R. Who buys bloodshed and why. *Psychology Today,* 1972, *6,* 47–48, 82–84.

Kandel, D. B. Similarity in real-life adolescent friendship pairs. *Journal of Personality and Social Psychology,* 1978, *36,* 306–312.

Kaplan, R. M. The cathartic value of self expression: Testing catharsis, dissonance, and interference explanations. *Journal of Social Psychology,* 1975, *97,* 198–208.(a)

Kaplan, R. M. Intersex perception: The case of the Riggs-King tennis match. *Reprentative Research in Social Psychology,* 1975, *6,* 24–28.(b)

Kaplan, R. M. Some effects of attitudinal and counterattitudinal expression on anger and aggressive drive. Unpublished doctoral dissertation, University of California, Riverside, 1972.

Kaplan, R. M. Coping with stressful medical procedures. In H. Friedman & M. R. DiMatteo (Eds.), *Interpersonal relations in health care.* New York: Academic Press, 1981.

Kaplan, R. M., & Atkins, C. J. Psychological issues raised in the California Supreme Court case *People v. Collins.* Paper presented at the Western Psychological Association Convention, San Diego, California, 1979.

Kaplan, R. M., & Goldman, R. D. Interracial perception among Black, White, and Mexican American high school students. *Journal of Personality and Social Psychology,* 1973, *28,* 383–389.(a)

Kaplan, R. M., & Goldman, R. D. Stereotypes of college students toward the average man's and woman's attitudes toward women. *Journal of Counseling Psychology,* 1973, *20,* 459–462.(b)

Kaplan, R. M., & Pascoe, G. C. Humorous lectures and humorous examples: Some effects upon comprehension and retention. *Journal of Educational Psychology,* 1977, *69,* 61–65.

Kaplan, R. M., & Singer, R. D. Television violence and viewer aggression: A reexamination of the evidence. *Journal of Social Issues,* 1976, *32*(4), 35–70.

Kaplan, R. H., & Singer, R. D. Is government censorship the only answer? *Prosecutors' Brief,* 1977, *2,* 38.

Karlins, M., Coffman, T. L., & Walters, G. On the fading of social stereotypes: Studies in three generations of stereotypes. *Journal of Personality and Social Psychology,* 1969, *13,* 1–16.

Katzev, R., Edelsack, L., Steinmetz, G., Walker, T., & Wright, R. The effect of reprimanding transgressions on subsequent helping behavior. *Personality and Social Psychology Bulletin,* 1978, *4,* 326–329.

Kaufmann, H., & Feshbach, S. The influence of antiaggressive communications upon the response to provocation. *Journal of Personality,* 1963, *31,* 428–444.

Kelley, H. H. Attribution theory in social psychology. In D. Levine (Ed.), *Nebraska symposium on motivation.* Lincoln: University of Nebraska Press, 1967.

Kelley, H. H. *Causal schemata and the attribution process.* Morristown, N.J.: General Learning Press, 1972.

Kelley, H. H., & Michela, J. L. Attribution theory and research. *Annual Review of Psychology,* 1980, *31,* 457–501.

Kelly, J. A., & Worell, J. New formulations of sex roles and androgyny: A critical review. *Journal of Consulting and Clinical Psychology,* 1977, *45,* 1101–1115.

Kelman, H. C. Human use of human subjects: The problem of deception in psychological experiments. *Psychological Bulletin,* 1967, *67,* 1–11.

Kendrick, D. T., Stringfield, D. O., Wagenhals, W. L., Dahl, R. H., & Ransdell, H. J. Sex differences, androgyny, and approach responses to erotica: A new variation on the old volunteer problem. *Journal of Personality and Social Psychology,* 1980, *38,* 517–524.

Kendzierski, D. Self-schemata and scripts. *Personality and Social Psychology Bulletin,* 1980, *6,* 23–29.

Kibler, B. K., & Harari, H. Stereotypes of given names: Case studies and anecdotal evidence. Paper presented at a symposium at the American Psychological Association Convention, New Orleans, 1974.

Kiesler, C. A. *The psychology of commitment.* New York: Academic Press, 1971.(b)

Kiesler, C. A., & Kiesler, S. B. *Conformity.* New York: Addison-Wesley, 1969.

Kimmel, E. Women as job changers. *American Psychologist,* 1974, *29,* 536–539.

Kinder, D. R. Political person perception: The asymmetrical influence of sentiment and choice on perceptions of presidential candidates. *Journal of Personality and Social Psychology,* 1978, *36,* 859–871.

Kipnis, D. Does power corrupt? *Journal of Personality and Social Psychology,* 1972, *24,* 33–41.

Kipnis, D., & Vanderveer, R. Ingratiation and the use of power. *Journal of Personality and Social Psychology,* 1971, *17,* 280–286.

Kirkpatrick, C. Religion and humanitarianism: A study of institutional implications. *Psychological Monographs,* 1949, *63* (9, Whole No. 304).

Kleck, R. E. Physical stigma and task oriented interactions. *Human Relations,* 1968, *21,* 19–28.

Kleck, R. E., Ono, H., & Hastorf, A. H. The effects of physical deviance upon face-to-face interaction. *Human Relations,* 1966, *19,* 452–456.

Knight, R. C., Sheposh, J. P., & Bryson, J. College student marijuana use and societal alienation. *Journal of Health and Social Behavior,* 1974, *15,* 28–35.

Knox, D. H. *Marriage happiness: A behavioral approach to counseling.* Champaign, Ill.: Research Press, 1971.

Knox, R. E., & Inkster, J. A. Post-decision dissonance at post time. *Journal of Personality and Social Psychology,* 1968, *8,* 319–323.

Kohlberg, L. The child as a moral philosopher. *Psychology Today,* 1968, *2* (4), 24–30.

Kolata, G. B. Sex hormones and brain development. *Science,* 1979, *205,* 985–987.

Koller, P. S., & Kaplan, R. M. A two-process theory of learned helplessness. *Journal of Personality and Social Psychology,* 1978, *36,* 1177–1183.

Komaroff, A. L., Masuda, M., & Holmes, T. H. The social readjustment rating scale: A comparative study of Negro, Mexican, and white Americans. *Journal of Psychosomatic Research,* 1968, *12,* 121.

Konecni, V. J. Some effects of guilt and compliance: A field replication. *Journal of Personality and Social Psychology,* 1972, *23,* 30–32.

Konecni, V. J. Annoyance, type and duration of postannoyance activity, and aggression: The "cathartic effect." *Journal of Experimental Psychology,* 1975, *104,* 76–102.

Konecni, V. J. Experimental methodologies in aggression research. In R. M. Kaplan, V. J. Konecni, & R. W. Novaco, *Aggression in Children and Youth.* Alphem ann den Rijn, Netherlands: Sijthoff & Noordhoff, International Publishers, 1982.

Konecni, V. J., Crozier, J. B., & Doob, A. N. Effects of anger and expression of aggression on exploratory choice. Unpublished manuscript, University of Calif., San Diego, 1975.

Krantz, D. S. The social context of obesity research: Another perspective on its place in the field of social psychology. *Personality and Social Psychology Bulletin,* 1978, *4,* 177–184.

Krantzler, M., *Creative divorce.* New York: Signet, 1975.

Krasner, L. Behavior therapy. In P. H. Mussen (Ed.), *Annual review of psychology* (Vol. 22). Palo Alto, Calif.: Annual Review, 1971.

Krasner, L., & Atthowe, J. M. The token economy as a rehabilitative procedure in a mental hospital setting. In H. C. Rickard (Ed.), *Behavioral intervention in human problems.* New York: Pergamon Press, 1971.

Kraut, R. E., & Johnston, R. E. Social and emotional messages of smiling: An ethological approach. *Journal of Personality and Social Psychology,* 1979, *37,* 1539–1553.

Krebs, D., & Adinolfi, A. A. Physical attractiveness, social relations, and personality style. *Journal of Personality and Social Psychology,* 1975, *31,* 245–253.

Kremers, J. *Scientific psychology and naive psychology.* Nijmegen, Netherlands: Drukkerij Gebrakt Janssen N.V., 1960.

Kriss, M., Indenbaum, E., & Tesch, F. Message type and status of interactants as determinants of telephone helping behavior. *Journal of Personality and Social Psychology,* 1974, *30,* 856–859.

Kuhlen, R. G., & Bretsch, H. S. Sociometric status and personal problems of adolescents. *Sociometry,* 1947, *10,* 122–132.

La France, M., & Carmen, B. The nonverbal display of psychological androgyny. *Journal of Personality and Social Psychology,* 1980, *88,* 36–49.

Lambert, W. E., Hodgson, R. C., Gardner, R. C. & Fillenbaum, S. Evaluational reaction to spoken languages. *Journal of Abnormal and Social Psychology,* 1960, *60,* 44–51.

Lambert, W.W., Solomon, R.L., & Watson, P.D. Reinforcement and extinction as factors in size estimation. *Journal of Experimental Psychology,* 1949, *39,* 637–641.

Landy, D., & Sigall, H. Beauty is talent. *Journal of Personality and Social Psychology,* 1974, *29,* 299–304.

Lang, P.J. Behavior therapy with a case of nervous anorexia. Paper presented at colloquium, Temple University, May 1962.

Langer, E.J. & Abelson, R.P. The semantics of asking a favor: How to succeed in getting help without really dying. *Journal of Personality and Social Psychology,* 1972, *24,* 26–32.

Latané, B. Sex and helping: Regional differences. *Proceedings, 80th Annual Convention of the American Psychological Association,* 1972, 904.

Latané, B., & Darley, J.M. Group inhibition of bystander intervention in emergencies. *Journal of Personality and Social Psychology,* 1968, *10,* 215–221.

Latané, B., & Darley, J.M. Bystander "apathy." *American Scientist,* 1969, *57,* 224–268.

Latané, B., & Darley, J.M. *The unresponsive bystander: Why doesn't he help?* New York: Appleton-Century-Crofts, 1970.

Latané, B., & Rodin, J. A lady in distress: Inhibiting effects of friends and strangers on bystander intervention. *Journal of Experimental Social Psychology,* 1969, *5,* 189–202.

Latané, B., Williams, K., & Harkins, S. Many hands make light the work: The causes and consequences of social loafing. *Journal of Personality and Social Psychology,* 1979, *37,* 822–832.

Laughlin, P.R., Branch, L.G., & Johnson, H.H. Individual versus triadic performance on a unidimensional complementary task as a function of initial ability level.

Journal of Personality and Social Psychology, 1969, *12*, 144-150.

Lawson, E. Hair color, personality, and the observer. *Psychological Reports*, 1971, *28*, 311-322.

Lazarsfeld, P.F., Berelson, B., & Gaudet, H. *The people's choice*. New York: Meredith, 1944.

Leavitt, H.J. Some effects of certain communication patterns on group performance. *Journal of Abnormal and Social Psychology*, 1951, *46*, 38-50.

Le Compte, W., & Rosenfeld, H. Effects of minimal eye contact in the instruction period on the impressions of the experimenter. *Journal of Experimental Social Psychology*, 1971, *7*, 211-220.

Leff, D.N. Stress-triggered organic disease in this year of economic anxiety. *Medical World News*, 1975, *16*, 74-92.

Lenski, G. *The religious factor*. Garden City, N.Y.: Doubleday, 1961.

Leonard, C.V. Self-ratings of alienation in suicidal patients. *Journal of Clinical Psychology*. 1973, *29*, 423-428.

Lepper, M.R., & Greene, D. *The hidden costs of rewards*. Hillsdale, N.J.: Erlbaum, 1978.

Lepper, R.M., Greene, D., & Nisbett, R.E. Undermining children's intrinsic interest with extrinsic rewards: A test of the "overjustification hypothesis." *Journal of Personality and Social Psychology*, 1973, *28*, 129-137.

Lerner, M. J. The desire for justice and reactions to victims. In J. Macauley & L. Berkowitz (Eds.), *Altruism and helping behavior*. New York: Academic Press, 1970.

Lerner, M. J., & Miller, D. T. Just world research and the attribution process. *Psychological Bulletin*, 1978, *85*, 1030-1051.

Lerner, M. J., Miller, D. T., & Holmes, J. G. Deserving and the emergence of forms of justice. In L. Berkowitz & E. Walster (Eds.), *Advances in experimental social psychology* (Vol. 9). New York: Academic Press, 1976.

Leventhal, H. Fear communications in the acceptance of preventative health practices. *Bulletin of the New York Academy of Medicine*, 1965, *41*, (2nd series), 1144-1168.

Leventhal, H. Fear—for your health. *Psychology Today*, 1967, *1*, 54-58.

Leventhal, H. Attitudes: Their nature, growth and change. In C. Nemeth (Ed.), *Social psychology: Classic and contemporary integrations*. Chicago: Rand—McNally, 1974, 52-126.

Leventhal, H., & Niles, P. Persistence of influence for varying durations of exposure to threat stimuli. *Psychological Reports*, 1965, *16*, 223-233.

Leventhal, H., Singer, R. P., & Jones, S. Effects of fear and specificity of recommendation upon attitudes and behavior. *Journal of Personality and Social Psychology*, 1965, *2*, 20-29.

Levinger, G., & Breedlove, J. Interpersonal attraction and agreement: A study of marriage partners. *Journal of Personality and Social Psychology*, 1966, *3*, 367-372.

Lewin, K. Some social-psychological differences between the United States and Germany. In G. Lewin (Ed.), *Resolving social conflicts: Selected papers on group dynamics*. New York: Harper & Row, 1940.

Lewin, K. Studies in group decision. In D. Cartwright & A. Zander (Eds.), *Group dynamics*. Evanston, Ill.: Row & Peterson, 1953.

Lieberman, S. The effect of changes in roles on the attitudes of role occupants. *Human Relations*, 1956, *9*, 385-402.

Liebert, R. M., Neale, J. M., & Davidson, E. S. *The early window: Effects of television* on children and youth. Elmsford, N.Y.: Pergamon Press, 1973.

Life and health. Del Mar, Calif.: CRM Books, 1972.

Linder, D. E., Cooper, J., & Jones, E. E. Decision freedom as a determinant of the role of incentive magnitude in attitude change. *Journal of Personality and Social Psychology*, 1967, 6, 245-254.

Lippit, R. O. An experimental study on the effect of democratic and authoritarian group atmosphere. *University of Iowa Studies in Child Welfare*. 1940, 16, 43-195.

Litman-Adizes, T., Fontaine, G., & Raven, B. H. Consequences of social power and causal attribution for compliance as seen by powerholder and target. *Personality and Social Psychology Bulletin*, 1978, 4, 260-264.

Littlepage, G. E., & Pineault, M. A. Detection of factual statements from the body and the face. *Personality and Social Psychology Bulletin*, 1979, 5, 325-328.

Loeb, E. M. Primitive intoxicants. *Quarterly Journal of Studies on Alcohol*, 1943, 4, 387-398.

Loeb, M. Noise and performance: Do we know more? In J. V. Tobias (Ed.), *The proceedings of the Third International Congress on Noise as a Public Health Problem*. Washington, D.C.: American Speech and Hearing Association, 1979.

Leow, C. A. Acquisition of a hostile attitude and its relation to aggressive behavior. *Journal of Personality and Social Psychology*, 1967, 5, 335-341.

Loomis, C. P., & Proctor, C. The relationship between choice status and economic status in social systems. *Sociometry*, 1950, 13, 307-313.

Lord, C. G. Schemas and images as memory aids: Two modes of processing social information. *Journal of Personality and Social Psychology*, 1980, 38, 257-269.

Lord, C. G., Ross, L., & Lepper, M. R. Biased assimilation and attitude polarization: The effects of prior theories on subsequently considered evidence. *Journal of Personality and Social Psychology*, 1979, 37, 2098-2109.

Lorenz, K. *On aggression*. New York: Harcourt, Brace & World, 1966.

Lott, B. E., & Lott, A. J. The formation of positive attitudes toward group members. *Journal of Abnormal and Social Psychology*, 1960, 61, 297-300.

Lovaas, O. I., Koegel, R., Simmons, J. Q., & Long, J. Some generalization and follow-up measures on autistic children in behavior therapy. *Journal of Applied Behavior Analysis*, 1973, 6, 131-166.

Lubell, S. The "generation gap." *Public Interest*, 1968, 13, 52-60.

Luchins, A. S. Primary-recency in impression formation. In C. I. Hovland (Ed.), *The order of presentation in persuasion*. New Haven,: Yale University Press, 1957.

Luchins, A. S. Experimental attempts to minimize the impact of first impressions. In C. I. Hovland (Ed.), *The order of presentation in persuasion*. New Haven: Yale University Press, 1957.

Lundberg, G. A., Hertzler, V. B., & Dickson, L. Attraction patterns in a university. *Sociometry*, 1949, 12, 158-169.

Maccoby, E. E. Sex differences in intellectual functioning. In E. E. Maccoby (Ed.), *The development of sex differences*. Stanford, Calif.: Stanford University Press, 1966.

MacDonald, A. P., Jr. Anxiety, affiliation, and social isolation. *Developmental Psychology*, 1970, 3, 242-254.

Madsen, C. H., Madsen, C. K., & Thompson, F. Increasing rural Head Start childrens' consumption of middle-class meals. *Journal of Applied Behavior Analysis*, 1974, 7, 257-262.

Magnussen, D., & Endler, S. Interactional psychology: Present status and future prospects. In D. Magnussen & N. S. Endler (Eds.), *Personality at the crossroads: Current issues in interactional psychology*. Hillsdale, N.J.: Erlbaum, 1977.

Maitland, K. A., & Goldman, J. R. Moral judgement as a function of peer group interaction. *Journal of Personality and Social Psychology*, 1974, *5*, 699-704.

Malamuth, N. Rape fantasies as a function of exposure to violent sexual stimuli. *Archives of Sexual Behavior*, 1980.

Malamuth, N., Feshbach, S., & Jaffe, Y. Sexual arousal and aggression: Recent experiments and theoretical issues. *Journal of Social Issues*, 1977, *33*, 110-133.

Malamuth, N., Haber, S., & Feshbach, S. Testing hypotheses regarding rape: Exposure to sexual violence, sex differences, and the "normality" of rapists. *Journal of Research in Personality*, 1980, *14*, 121-137.

Malamuth, N., Heim, M., & Feshbach, S. Sexual responsiveness of college students to rape depictions: Inhibitory and disinhibitory effects. *Journal of Personality of Social Psychology*, 1980, *38*, 399-408.

Malamuth, N., & Spinner, B. A longitudinal content analysis of sexual violence in the best-selling erotica magazines. *Journal of Sex Research*, 1980.

Mallick, S. K., & McCandless, B. R. A study of catharsis of aggression. *Journal of Personality and Social Psychology*, 1966, *4*, 591-596.

Manis, M. Social interaction and the self-concept. *Journal of Abnormal and Social Psychology*, 1955, *51*, 362-370.

Mann, L., Paleg, K., & Hawkins, R. Effectiveness of staged disputes in influencing bystander crowds. *Journal of Personality and Social Psychology*, 1978, *36*, 725-732.

Manz, W., & Lueck, H. Influence of wearing glasses on personality ratings. *Perceptual and Motor Skills*, 1968, *27*, 704.

Mark, V. H. A psychosurgeon's case for psychosurgery. *Psychology Today*, 1974, *8*, 28-33.

Markus, H. Self-schemata and processing information about the self. *Journal of Personality and Social Psychology*, 1977, *35*, 63-78.

Markus, H., Hamill, R., & Smith, J. Time and the functions of the mind. *Institute for Social Research Newsletter*, Spring 1980, 3-5.

Marriot, F., Jr. Size of working group and output. *Occupational Psychology*, 1949, *23*, 47-57.

Marshall, G. D., & Zimbardo, P. G. Affective consequences of inadequately explained physiological arousal. *Journal of Personality and Social Psychology*, 1979, *37*, 970-988.

Marx, K., & Engels, F. *On religion*. New York: Schocken Books, 1964.

Maslach, C. Negative emotional biasing of unexplained arousal. *Journal of Personality and Social Psychology*, 1979, *37*, 953-969.

Maslow, A., & Mittleman, B. *Principles of abnormal psychology*. New York: Harper & Row, 1951.

Mathews, K. E., Jr., & Canon, L. K. Environmental noise level as a determinant of helping behavior. *Journal of Personality and Social Psychology*, 1975, *32*, 571-577.

Matthews, K. A., Scheier, M. F., Brunson, B. I., & Carducci, B. Attention, unpredictability, and reports of physical symptoms: Eliminating the benefits of predictability. *Journal of Personality and Social Psychology*, 1980, *38*, 525-537.

McBurney, D. H., Levine, J. M., & Cavanaugh, P. H. Psychophysical and social ratings of human body odor. *Personality and Social Psychology Bulletin*, 1977, *3*, 135-138.

McCain, G., Cox, V., & Paulus, P. The relationship between illness complaints and degree of crowding in a prison environment. *Environment and Behavior*, 1976, *8*, 283-290.

McCarthy, D. & Seagert, A. Residential density, social overload, and social withdrawal. In J. Aiello & A. Baum, *Residential crowding and design.* New York: Plenum, 1979.

McCauley, C., Stitt, C. L., & Segal, M. Stereotyping: From prejudice to prediction. *Psychological Bulletin,* 1980, *87,* 195–208.

McDavid, J. W., & Harari, H. *Social psychology: Individuals, groups, societies.* New York: Harper & Row, 1968.

McDavid, J. W., & Harari, H. Stereotyping of names and popularity in grade school children. *Child Development,* 1966, *37,* 453–459.

McDavid, J. W., & Harari, H. *Psychology and social behavior.* New York: Harper & Row, 1974.

McDavid, J. W., & Sistrunk, F. Personality correlates of two kinds of conforming behavior. *Journal of Personality,* 1964, *32,* 421–435.

McGinnies, E. Emotionality and perceptual defense. *Psychological Review,* 1949, *56,* 244–251.

McGinnis, E. *Social behavior: A functional analysis.* Boston: Houghton Mifflin, 1970.

McGinnis, J. *The selling of the president 1968.* New York: Trident, 1969.

McGrath, J. E. *A summary of small group research studies.* Arlington, Va.: Human Sciences Research, 1962.

McGuire, W. J., & Papageorgis, D. The relative efficacy of various types of prior belief-defense in producing immunization against persuasion. *Journal of Abnormal and Social Psychology,* 1961, *62,* 327–337.

McGuire, W. J., & Papageorgis, D. Effectiveness of forewarning in developing resistance to persuasion. *Public Opinion Quarterly,* 1962, *26,* 24–34.

McMillen, D. L. Transgression, self-image, and complaint behavior. *Journal of Personality and Social Psychology,* 1971, *20,* 176–179.

Mead, G. H. *Mind, self, and society.* Chicago: University of Chicago Press, 1934.

Meade, R. D. An experimental study of leadership in India. *Journal of Social Psychology,* 1967, *72,* 35–43.

Mehrabian, Albert. Inference of attitudes from posture, orientation, and distance of a communicator. *Journal of Consulting and Clinical Psychology,* 1968, *32,* 296–308.

Mehrabian, A., & Diamond, S. G. Effects of furniture arrangements, props, and personality on social interaction. *Journal of Personality and Social Psychology,* 1971, *20,* 18–30.

Meichenbaum, D., & Turk, D. The cognitive-behavioral management of anxiety, anger, and pain. In P. Davidson (Ed.), *Behavioral management of anxiety, depression, and pain.* New York: Brunner/Mazel, 1976.

Meissner, W. W. Alienation: Context and complications. *Journal of Religion and Health,* 1974, *13,* 23–39.

Messick, S. The validity and ethics of assessment. *American Psychologist,* 1980, *35,* 1012–1025.

Mikulas, W. L. *Behavior modification: An overview.* New York: Harper & Row, 1974.

Milgram, S. The experience of living in cities. *Science,* 1970, *167,* 1461–1468.

Milgram, S. *Obedience to authority.* New York: Harper & Row, 1974.

Milgram, S., Brickman, L., & Berkowitz, L. Note on the drawing power of crowds of different size. *Journal of Personality and Social Psychology.* 1969, *13,* 74–82.

Milgram, S., & Shortland, R. L. *Television and antisocial behavior: Field experiments.* New York: Academic Press, 1973.

Miller, N., & Campbell, D. Recency and primacy in persuasion as a function of the timing of speeches and measurements. *Journal of Abnormal and Social Psychology,* 1959, *59,* 1–9.

Miller, M., Maruyama, G., Beaber, R. J., & Valone, K. Speed of speech and persuasion. *Journal of Personality and Social Psychology*, 1976, *34*, 615–624.

Mills, J., & Jellison, J. M. Effect on opinion change of similarity between the communicator and the audience he addressed. *Journal of Personality and Social Psychology*, 1968, *9*, 153–156.

Mills, T. M. Power relations in three person groups. *American Sociological Review*, 1953, *18*, 351–357.

Milmoe, S., Rosenthal, R., Blane, H. T., Chafetz, M. L., & Wolf, I. The doctor's voice: Postdictor of successful referral of alcoholic patients. *Journal of Abnormal Psychology*, 1967, *72*, 78–84.

Minsky, M. A framework for representing knowledge. In P. Winston (Ed.), *The psychology of computer vision*. New York: McGraw-Hill, 1975.

Mischel, W. *Personality and assessment*. New York: Wiley, 1968.

Mischel, W. Toward a cognitive social learning reconceptualization of personality. *Psychological Review*, 1973, *80*, 252–283.

Mischel, W. On the future of personality measurement. *American Psychologist*, 1977, *32*, 246–254.

Mischel, W. On the interface of cognition and personality: Beyond the person-situation debate. *American Psychologist*, 1979, *34*, 740–754.

Mittleman, B., & Wolff, H. G. Emotions and gastroduodenal function. *Psychosomatic Medicine*, 1942, *4*, 5–61.

Mixon, D. Temporary false beliefs. *Personality and Social Psychology Bulletin*, 1977, *3*, 479–488.

Monat, A., Averill, J. R., & Lazarus, R. S. Anticipatory stress and coping reactions under various conditions of uncertainty. *Journal of Personality and Social Psychology*, 1972, *24*, 237–253.

Montapert, A. A. *Distilled wisdom*. Englewood Cliffs, N.J.: Prentice-Hall, 1964.

Moos, R. H. Conceptualizations of human environments. *American Psychologist*, 1973, *28*, 252–265.

Moriarty, T. Little murders: The victim is willing. Paper presented at the American Psychological Association Convention, New Orleans, August, 1974.

Moriarty, T. Crime, commitment, and the responsive bystander: Two field experiments. *Journal of Personality and Social Psychology*, 1975, *31*, 370–376.

Morris, C., & Small, L. Changes in conception of the good life by American students from 1950 to 1970. *Journal of Personality and Social Psychology*, 1971, *20*, 254–260.

Morris, D. *The naked ape*. New York: McGraw-Hill, 1967.

Morris, D. *Intimate behavior*. New York: Random House, 1971.

Moss, G. E. *Illness, immunity and social interaction*. New York: Wiley-Interscience, 1973.

Moss, M. K., & Page, R. A. Reinforcement and helping behavior. *Journal of Applied Social Psychology*, 1972, *2*, 360–371.

Munn, N. L. The effect of the knowledge of the situation upon judgments of emotions from facial expressions. *Journal of Abnormal and Social Psychology*. 1940, *35*, 324–338.

Mussen, P. H. Some antecedents and consequents of masculine sex-typing in adolescent boys. *Psychological Monographs*, 1961, *75*, 506.

Mussen, P. H. Long-term consequences of masculinity of interests in adolescent boys. *Journal of Consulting Psychology*, 1962, *26*, 435–440.

Naftulin, D. H., Ware, J. E., & Donnelly, F. A. The Doctor Fox lecture: A paradigm of educational seduction. *Journal of Medical Education*, 1973, *48*, 630–635.

Names can hurt. *McCall's*, February 1974.

Nemeth, C. Effects of free versus constrained behavior on attraction between people. *Journal of Personality and Social Psychology,* 1970, *15,* 302–311.

Newcomb, T. M. *The acquaintance process.* New York: Holt, Rinehart & Winston, 1961.

Nicholls, J. G. Causal attributions and other achievement related cognitions. *Journal of Personality and Social Psychology,* 1975, *31,* 379–389.

NIMH releases report on behavior modification. *APA Monitor,* 1975, *6*(3), 8.

Nisbett, R. E., & Borgida, E. Attribution and the psychology of prediction. *Journal of Personality and Social Psychology,* 1975, *32,* 932–943.

Nisbett, R. E., Caputo, C., Legant, P., & Marecek, J. Behavior as seen by the actor and as seen by the observer. *Journal of Personality and Social Psychology,* 1973, *27,* 154–164.

Nisbett, R. E., & Gordon, A. Self-esteem and susceptibility to social influence. *Journal of Personality and Social Psychology,* 1967, *5,* 268–276.

Norman, R. D. The interrelationship among acceptance-rejection, self-other identity, insight into self, and realistic perception of others. *Journal of Social Psychology,* 1953, *37,* 205–235.

Norman, W. T. Toward an adequate taxonomy of personality attributes; Replicated factor structure in peer nomination personality ratings. *Journal of Abnormal and Social Psychology,* 1963, *66,* 574–583.

Novaco, R. W. *Anger control: The development and evaluation of an experimental treatment.* Lexington, Mass.: Lexington Books, 1976.

Novaco, R. W. The cognitive regulation of anger and stress. In P. Kendall & S. Hollon (Eds.), *Cognitive-behavioral interventions: Theory, research and procedures.* New York: Academic Press, 1979.

Nunn, C. Z. Child control through a "coalition with God." *Child Development,* 1964, *35,* 417–432.

Omwake, K. T. The relations between acceptance of self and acceptance of others shown by three personality inventories. *Journal of Consulting Psychology,* 1954, *18,* 443–446.

Orden, S. R., & Bradburn, N. M. Working wives and marriage happiness. In M. E. Lasswell & T. E. Lasswell (Eds.), *Love, marriage, family.* Glenview, Ill.: Scott, Foresman, 1973.

Orne, M. T. On the social psychology of the psychological experiment: With particular reference to demand characteristics and their implications. *American Psychologist,* 1962, *17,* 776–783.

Orne, M. T. Hypnosis, motivation, and compliance. *American Journal of Psychiatry,* 1966, *122,* 721–726.

Orne, M. T. Demand characteristics and quasi-controls. In R. Rosenthal & R. L. Rosnow (Eds.), *Artifact in behavioral research.* New York: Academic Press, 1969.

Orne, M. T., & Evans, F. J. Social control in the psychological experiment. *Journal of Personality and Social Psychology,* 1965, *1,* 189–200.

Packard, V. *The hidden persuaders.* New York: McKay, 1957.

Passini, F. T., & Norman, W. T. A universal conception of personality structure? *Journal of Personality and Social Psychology,* 1966, *4,* 44–49.

Patterson, G. R., & Hops, H. Coercion, a game for two: Intervention techniques for marital conflict. In R. E. Ulrich & P. Mountjoy (Eds.), *The experimental analysis of social behavior.* New York: Appleton-Century-Crofts, 1972.

Patterson, T. L., & Petrinovich, L. New developments in sociobiology. Paper presented at the American Association for the Advancement of Science, Pacific Division, Davis, California, 1980.

Paulus, P. B., & Matthews, R. W. When density affects performance. *Personality and Social Psychology Bulletin*, 1980, *6*, 119–124.

Paulus, P. B., McCain, G., & Cox, V. Death rates, psychiatric commitments, blood pressure, and perceived crowding as a function of institutional crowding. *Environment, Psychology and Nonverbal Behavior*, 1978, *36*, 998–999.

Pederson, D. M., & Breglio, V. J. Personality correlates of actual self-disclosure. *Psychological Reports*, 1968, *22*, 495–501.

Petty, R. E., & Cacioppo, J. T. Effects of forewarning of persuasive intent and involvement on cognitive responses and persuasion. *Personality and Social Psychology Bulletin*, 1979, *5*, 173–176.

Petty, R. E., Harkins, S. G., Williams, K., & Latané, B. The effects of group size on cognitive effort and evaluation. *Personality and Social Psychology Bulletin*, 1977, *3*, 579–582.

Pfiffner, J. M. *The supervision of personnel: Human relations in the management of men.* Englewood Cliffs, N.J.: Prentice-Hall, 1951.

Pheterson, G. I. Female prejudice against men. Unpublished manuscript, Connecticut College, 1969.

Pheterson, G. I., Kiesler, S. B., & Goldberg, P. A. Evaluations of the performance of women as a function of their sex, achievement, and personal history. *Journal of Personality and Social Psychology*, 1971, *19*, 114–118.

Piacente, B. S. Women as experimenters. *American Psychologist*, 1974, *29*, 526–529.

Piaget, J. *The moral judgment of the child.* London: Routledge & Kegan Paul, 1932.

Pierce, C. H., & Risley, T. R. Improving job performance of neighborhood youth corps aides in an urban recreation program. *Journal of Applied Behavior Analysis*, 1974, *7*, 207–215.

Piliavin, I. M., Piliavin, J. A., & Rodin, J. Costs, diffusion, and the stigmatized victim. *Journal of Personality and Social Psychology*, 1975, *32*, 429–438.

Piliavin, I. M., Rodin, J., & Piliavin, J. A. Good samaritanism: An underground phenomenon? *Journal of Personality and Social Psychology*, 1969, *13*, 4, 289–299.

Polansky, N. A., & Brown, S. O. Verbal accessibility and fusion fantasy in a mountain county. *American Journal of Orthopsychiatry*, 1967, *37*, 651–660.

Postman, L. J., & Schneider, B. Personal values, visual recognition and recall. *Psychological Review*, 1951, *58*, 271–284.

Psychology Today, April, 1975, 116.

Price, R. A., & Vandenberg, S. G. Matching for physical attractiveness in married couples. *Personality and Social Psychology Bulletin*, 1979, *5*, 398–400.

Priest, R. F., & Sawyer, J. Proximity and peership: Bases of balance in interpersonal attraction. *American Journal of Sociology*, 1967, *72*, 633–649.

Pruitt, D. G. Reciprocity and credit building in a laboratory dyad. *Journal of Personality and Social Psychology*, 1968, *8*, 143–147.

Pruitt, D. G. Choice shifts in group discussion: An introduction review. *Journal of Personality and Social Psychology*, 1971, *20*, 339–360.

Pugh, W., Gunderson, E. K. E., Erikson, J. M., Rahe, R. H., & Rubin, R. T. Variations of illness incidence in the Navy population. *Military Medicine*, 1972, *137*, 224.

Pursell, S. A., & Banikiotes, P. G. Androgyny and initial interpersonal attraction. *Personality and Social Psychology Bulletin*, 1978, *4*, 235–239.

Rahe, R. H. Life crisis and health change. In P. R. A. May & J. R. Wittenborn (Eds.), *Psychotropic drug response: Advances in prediction.* Springfield, Ill.: Charles C Thomas, 1969.(a)

Rahe, R. H. Multi-cultural correlations of life change scaling: America, Japan, Denmark, and Sweden. *Journal of Psychosomatic Research*, 1969, *13*, 191.(b)

Rahe, R. H. Subjects' recent life changes and their near-future illness reports. *Annals of Clinical Research,* 1972, *4,* 250–265.

Rahe, R. H., & Arthur, R. Life change and illness studies: Past history and future directions. *Journal of Stress Research,* 1978, *4,* 3–15.

Rahe, R. H., Lundberg, V., Bennett, L., & Theorell, T. The social readjustment rating scale: A comparative study of Swedes and Americans. *Journal of Psychosomatic Research,* 1971, *15,* 241.

Rahe, R. H., Mahan, J., & Arthur, R. J. Prediction of near-future health change from subjects preceding life changes. *Journal of Psychosomatic Research,* 1970, *14,* 401–406.

Ramsy, N. R. Assortative mating and the structure of cities. *American Journal of Sociology,* 1966, *71,* 773–786.

Ransford, H. E. Isolation, powerlessness and violence. *American Journal of Sociology,* 1968, *73,* 581–591.

Raven, B. H. Social influence and power. In I. D. Steiner and M. Fishbein (Eds.), *Current studies in social psychology.* New York: Holt, Rinehart & Winston, 1965.

Razran, G. Ethnic dislikes and stereotypes. *Journal of Abnormal and Social Psychology,* 1950, *45,* 7–27.

Reese, H. W. Relationships between self-acceptance and sociometric choices. *Journal of Abnormal and Social Psychology,* 1961, *62,* 472–474.

Reid, D. H., Luyben, P. D., Rawers, R. J., & Bailey, J. S. Newspaper recycling behavior: The effects of prompting and proximity of containers. *Environment and Behavior,* 1976, *8,* 471–482.

Renne, K. S. Correlates of dissatisfaction in marriage. In M. E. Lasswell & T. E. Lasswell (Eds.), *Love, marriage, family.* Glenview, Ill.: Scott, Foresman, 1973.

Rhine, R. J., & Kaplan, R. M. The effect of incredulity upon the evaluation of the source of a communication. *Journal of Social Psychology,* 1972, *88,* 255–266.

Richardson, D. C., & Campbell, J. L. Alcohol and wife abuse. *Personality and Social Psychology Bulletin,* 1980, *6,* 51–56.

Riestra, M., & Johnson, C. Changes in attitudes of elementary school pupils toward foreign-speaking peoples resulting from the study of a foreign language. *Journal of Experimental Education,* 1964, *33,* 65–72.

Ring, K., Lipinski, C. E., & Braginski, D. The relationship of birth order to self-evaluation, anxiety-reduction, and susceptibility to emotional contagion. *Psychological Monographs,* 1965, *79* (Whole number 603), 10.

Rodin, J., & Langer, E. Long-term effects of a control-relevant intervention with the institutionalized aged. *Journal of Personality and Social Psychology,* 1977, *35,* 897–902.

Rodin, M. J. Liking and disliking: Sketch of an alternative view. *Personality and Social Psychology Bulletin,* 1978, *4,* 473–478.

Rogers, C. R. *Carl Rogers on encounter groups.* New York: Harper & Row, 1970.

Rogow, A. A., & Laswell, H. D. *Power, corruption and rectitude.* Englewood Cliffs, N.J.: Prentice-Hall, 1963.

Rokeach, M. *The open and closed mind.* New York: Basic Books, 1960.

Rokeach, M., & Mezei, L. Race and shared belief as factors in social choice. *Science,* 1966, *151,* 167–172.

Roll, S., & Verinis, J. Stereotypes of scalp and facial hair as measured by the semantic differential. *Psychological Reports,* 1971, *28,* 975–980.

Rosenbaum, M. E., & DeCharmes, R. Direct and vicarious reduction of hostility. *Journal of Abnormal and Social Psychology,* 1960, *60,* 105–111.

Rosenhan, D., & White, G. M. Observation and rehearsal as determinants of prosocial behavior. *Journal of Personality and Social Psychology,* 1967, *5,* 424–431.

Rosenman, R. H., Brand, R. J., Jenkins, C. D., Friedman, H., Strauss, R., & Wurm, H. Coronary heart disease in the Western collaborative group study: Final follow-up experience of 8½ years. *Journal of the American Medical Association,* 1975, *233,* 872–877.

Rosenthal, R. *Experimenter effects in behavioral research.* New York: Irvington, 1976.

Rosenthal, R., & Jacobson, L. *Pygmalion in the classroom: Teacher expectation and pupils' intellectual development.* New York: Holt, Rinehart & Winston, 1968.

Ross, L. The intuitive psychologist and his shortcomings. Distortions in the attribution process. In L. Berkowitz (Ed.), *Advances in experimental social psychology* (Vol. 10). New York: Academic Press, 1977.

Ross, M., & Sicoly, F. Egocentric biases in availability and attribution. *Journal of Personality and Social Psychology,* 1979, *37,* 322–336.

Rothenberg, M. B. Effect of television violence on children and youth. *Journal of the American Medical Association,* 1975, *234,* 1043–1046.

Rotter, J. B. Generalized expectancies for internal versus external control of reinforcement. *Psychological Monographs,* 1966, *80,* 1–28.

Rubin relents: Now he promotes capitalism. *Time,* August 11, 1980.

Rubin, R. T., Gunderson, E. K. E., & Arthur, R. J. Life stress and illness patterns in the U.S. Navy. II. Prior life change and illness onset in an attack carrier's crew. *Archives of Environmental Health,* 1969, *19,* 753–757.

Rubin, Z. Measurement of romantic love. *Journal of Personality and Social Psychology,* 1970, *16,* 265–273.

Rubin, Z. *Liking and loving: An invitation to social psychology.* New York: Holt, Rinehart & Winston, 1973.

Rubin, Z., & Peplau, A. Belief in a just world and to reactions to another's lot: A study of participants in the National Draft Lottery. *Journal of Social Issues,* 1973, *29,* 73–93.

Rubovits, P. C., & Maehr, M. L. Pygmalion black and white. *Journal of Personality and Social Psychology,* 1973, *25,* 210–218.

Russo, N. J., & Sommer, R. Invasion of personal space. *Social Problems,* 1966, *14,* 206–214.

Ryder, R. G. Husband-wife dyads versus married strangers. *Family Process,* 1968, *7,* 233–238.

Sabath, G. The effect of disruption and individual status on perception of group attraction. *Journal of Social Psychology,* 1964, *64,* 119–130.

Saegert, S., Swap, W., & Zajonc, R. B. Exposure context and interpersonal attraction. *Journal of Personality and Social Psychology,* 1973, *25,* 234–242.

St. Peter, S. Jack went up the hill . . . but where was Jill? *Psychology of Women Quarterly,* 1979, *4,* 256–260.

Sarason, I. G., & Hunt, T. Methodological issues in the assessment of life stress. In L. Levi (Ed.), *Parameters of emotion.* Oxford: Oxford University Press, 1974.

Sarason, I. G., Smith, R. E., & Diener, E. Personality research: Components of variance attributable to the person and the situation. *Journal of Personality and Social Psychology,* 1975, 199–204.

Sattler, J. Racial "experimenter effects" in experimentation, testing, interviewing, and psychotherapy. *Psychological Bulletin,* 1970, *73,* 137–160.

Sawrey, W. L., & Weisz, J. D. An experimental method of producing gastric ulcers: Role of psychological factors in the production of gastric ulcers in the rat.

Journal of Comparative and Physiological Psychology, 1956, *49,* 457–461.

Schaar, K. Suicide rate high among women psychologists. *APA Monitor,* 1974, *5,* 1, 10.

Schachter, S. *The psychology of affiliation: Experimental studies on the sources of gregariousness.* Stanford, Calif.: Stanford University Press, 1959.

Schachter, S., & Singer, J. E. Cognitive, social and physiological determinants of emotional state. *Psychological Review,* 1962, *69,* 379–399.

Schachter, S., & Singer, J. E. Comments on the Maslach and Marshall-Zimbardo experiments. *Journal of Personality and Social Psychology,* 1979, *37,* 989–995.

Schein, E. H. The Chinese indoctrination program for prisoners of war. *Psychiatry,* 1956, *19,* 149–172.

Scherer, D. Attribution of personality from voice. *Proceedings, 79th Annual Convention of the American Psychological Association,* 1971, 6(Pt. 1), 351–352.

Schoggen, P., & Barker, R. G. and behavioral settings: A commentary. *Journal of Personality and Social Psychology,* 1979, *37,* 2158–2160.

Schutz, W. C. What makes a group productive? *Human Relations,* 1955, *8,* 429–465.

Schwartz, S. H., & Gottlieb, A. Bystander reactions to a violent theft: Crime in Jerusalem. *Journal of Personality and Social Psychology,* 1976, *34,* 1188–1199.

Scodel, A. Heterosexual somatic preference and fantasy dependency. *Journal of Consulting Psychology,* 1957, *21,* 371–374.

Scodel, A., & Austin, H. The perception of Jewish photographs by non-Jews and Jews. *Journal of Abnormal and Social Psychology,* 1957, *54,* 278–280.

Sears, R. R. Relation of early socialization experiences to self-concepts and gender in middle childhood. *Child Development,* 1970, *41,* 267–289.

Seaver, W. B., & Patterson, A. H. Decreasing fuel-oil consumption through feedback and social commendation. *Journal of Applied Behavioral Analysis,* 1976, *9,* 147–152.

Second, P. F. Stereotyping and favorableness in the perception of Negro faces. *Journal of Abnormal and Social Psychology,* 1959, *59,* 309–315.

Seeman, M. The urban alienation: Some dubious theses from Marx to Marcuse. *Journal of Personality and Social Psychology,* 1971, *19,* 135–143.

Segal, M. W. Alphabet and attraction: An unobtrusive measure of the effect of propinquity in a field setting. *Journal of Personality and Social Psychology,* 1974, *30,* 654–657.

Seldes, G. *Encyclopedia of the great annotations.* New York: Stuart, 1966.

Seligman, C., & Darley, J. M. Feedback as a means of decreasing energy consumption. *Journal of Applied Psychology,* 1978.

Seligman, M. E. *Helplessness.* San Francisco: W. H. Freeman, 1975.

Selye, H. *The stress of life.* New York: McGraw-Hill, 1956.

Senate report blasts behavior modification. *APA Monitor,* 1975, 6(2), 9.

Serbin, L. A., Connor, J. M., & Iler, I. Sex-stereotyped and non-stereotyped introductions of new toys in the preschool classroom: An observational study of teacher behavior and its effects. *Psychology of Women Quarterly,* 1979, *4,* 261–265.

Shaver, K. G. Defensive attribution: Effects of severity and relevance on the responsibility assigned to an accident. *Journal of Personality and Social Psychology,* 1970, *14,* 101–119.

Shaw, M. E. A serial position effect in social influence on group decision. *Journal of Social Psychology,* 1961, *54,* 83–91.

Shaw, M. E. *Group dynamics: The psychology of small group behavior.* New York: McGraw-Hill, 1976.

Sherman, C. E. *How to do your own divorce in California.* Van Nuys, Calif.: Nolo Press, 1972.

Shettel-Neuber, J., Bryson, J. B., & Young, L. E. Physical attractiveness of the "other person" and jealousy. *Personality and Social Psychology Bulletin.* 1978, *4*, 612–615.

Sigall, H., & Landy, D. Radiating beauty. The effects of having a physically attractive partner on person perception. *Journal of Personality and Social Psychology*, 1973, *28*, 218–224.

Sigall, H., & Ostrove, N. Beautiful but dangerous: Effects of offender attractiveness and nature of the crime on juridic judgment. *Journal of Personality and Social Psychology*, 1975, *31*, 410–414.

Skinner, B. F. *Walden II.* New York: Macmillan, 1948.

Smedley, J. W., & Bayton, J. A. Evaluative race-class stereotypes by race and perceived class of subjects. *Journal of Personality and Social Psychology*, 1978, *36*, 530–535.

Smith, B. L., Brown, B. L., Strong, W. J., & Rencher, A. C. Effects of speech rate on personality perception. *Language and Speech*, 1975, *18*, 145–152.

Smith, G. H. *An introductory bibliography of motivation research.* New York: Advertising Research Foundation, 1953.

Smith, H. What's sexiest about men? *Cosmopolitan*, January 1975, 112–113.

Smith, M. L. Sex bias in counseling and psychotherapy. *Psychological Bulletin*, 1980, *87*, 392–407.

Snow, C. P. Either-or. *Progressive*, February 1961, 24–25.

Snyder, E. C. Attitudes: A study of homogeny in marital selectivity. In M. E. Lasswell & T. E. Lasswell (Eds.), *Love, marriage, family.* Glenview, Ill.: Scott, Foresman, 1973.

Snyder, M. Self-monitoring of expressive behavior. *Journal of Personality and Social Psychology*, 1974, *30*, 526–537.

Snyder, M., & Cunningham, M. R. To comply or not comply: Testing the self-perception explanation of the "foot-in-the-door" phenomenon. *Journal of Personality and Social Psychology*, 1975, *31*, 64–67.

Sommer, R. *Personal space.* Englewood Cliffs, N.J.: Prentice-Hall, 1969.

Sommers, A. R. Violence, television, and the health of American youth. *New England Journal of Medicine*, 1976, *294*, 811–817.

Spanos, N. P. Goal-directed phantasy and the performance of hypnotic test suggestions. *Psychiatry*, 1971, *34*, 86–96.

Spanos, N. P., & Barber, T. X. Cognitive activity during 'hypnotic' suggestibility: Goal directed fantasy and the experience of nonvolition. *Journal of Personality*, 1972, *40*, 510–524.

Spanos, N. P., & Barber, T. X. Toward a convergence in hypnosis research. *American Psychologist*, 1974, *29*, 500–511.

Spence, K. W., & Spence, J. T. Relation of eyelid conditioning to manifest anxiety, extroversion, and rigidity. *Journal of Abnormal and Social Psychology*, 1964, *68*, 144–149.

Speroff, B., & Kerr, W. Steelmill "hot strip" accidents and interpersonal desirability values. *Journal of Clinical Psychology*, 1952, *8*, 89–91.

Spielberger, C. D. Theory and research on anxiety. In C. D. Spielberger (Ed.),

Anxiety and behavior. New York: Academic Press, 1966.

Spielberger, C. D. Anxiety as an emotional state. In C. D. Spielberger (Ed.), *Anxiety: Current trends in theory and research.* New York: Academic Press, 1972.

Spielberger, C. D. Anxiety: State, trait, and process. In C. D. Spielberger and I. G. Sarason (Eds.), *Stress and anxiety in modern life,* Proceedings of the NATO Advanced Study Institute. 1976, in press.

Spielberger, C. D., Auerbach, S. M., Wadsworth, A. P., Dun, T. M., & Taulbee, E. S. Emotional reactions to surgery. *Journal of Consulting and Clinical Psychology,* 1975, *40,* 33–38.

Stake, J. E., & Levitz, E. Career goals of college women and men and perceived achievement-related encouragement. *Psychology of Women Quarterly,* 1979, *4,* 151–159.

Star, S. A. Psychoneurotic symptoms in the army. In S. Stouffer et al. (Eds.), *The American soldier* (Vol. 2): *Combat and its aftermath.* Princeton, N.J.: Princeton University Press, 1949.

Staub, E. The learning and unlearning of aggression: The role of anxiety, empathy, efficacy, and prosocial values. In J. E. Singer (Ed.), *The control of aggression and violence.* New York: Academic Press, 1971.

Staub, E., & Baer, R. S., Jr. Stimulus characteristics of a sufferer and difficulty of escape as determinants of helping. *Journal of Personality and Social Psychology,* 1974, *30,* 279–284.

Staub, E., & Kellett, D. S. Increasing pain tolerance by information about aversive stimuli. *Journal of Personality and Social Psychology,* 1972, *21,* 198–203.

Steele, C. M. Name-calling and compliance. *Journal of Personality and Social Psychology,* 1975, *31,* 361–369.

Stein, D. D., Hardyck, J. A., & Smith, M. B. Race and belief: An open and shut case. *Journal of Personality and Social Psychology,* 1965, *1,* 281–289.

Stein, R. T., & Heller, T. An empirical analysis of the correlations between leadership status and participation rates reported in the literature. *Journal of Personality and Social Psychology,* 1979, *37,* 1993–2002.

Stokols, D. A typology of crowding experiments. In A. Baum & Y. Epstein (Eds.), *Human response to crowding.* Hillsdale, N.J.: Erlbaum, 1978.(a)

Stokols, D. Environmental psychology. *Annual Review of Psychology.* 1978, *29,* 253–295.(b)

Storms, M. D. Videotape and the attribution process: Reversion actors' and observers' points of view. *Journal of Personality and Social Psychology,* 1973, *27,* 165–175.

Stouffer, S. A. *Communism, civil liberties, and conformity.* Garden City, N.Y.: Doubleday, 1955.

Strodtbeck, F. L., & Mann, D. Z. Sex role differentiation in jury deliberations. *Sociometry,* 1956, *19,* 3–11.

Stuart, R. B. Operant interpersonal treatment for marital discord. *Journal of Consulting and Clinical Psychology,* 1969, *33,* 675–682.

Struening, E. L. Antidemocratic attitudes in a Midwest university. In H. H. Remmers (Ed.), *Antidemocratic attitudes in American schools.* Evanston: Northwestern University Press, 1963.

Sullivan, J. J., & Pallak, M. S. The effect of commitment and reactance on action-taking. *Personality and Social Psychology Bulletin,* 1976, *2,* 179–182.

Suls, J., Gastorf, J., & Lawhon, J. Social comparison choices for evaluating a sex-and age-related ability. *Personality and Social Psychology Bulletin,* 1978, *4,* 102–105.

Sundstrom, E. Crowding as sequential process: Review of research on the effects of population density on humans. In A. Baum & Y. Epstein (Eds.), *Human response to crowding*. Hillsdale, N.J.: Erlbaum, 1978.

Sussman, M. B. *Sourcebook in marriage and the family*. Boston: Houghton Mifflin, 1974.

Sweet, W. H., Ervin, F., & Mark, V. H. The relationship of violent behavior to focal cerebral disease. In S. Garattini & E. Sigg (Eds.), *Aggressive behavior*. New York: Wiley, 1969.

Szasz, T. S. *The manufacture of madness*. New York: Harper & Row, 1970.

Taft, R. The ability to judge people. *Psychological Bulletin*, 1955, *52*, 1–28.

Tavris, C. Harry, are you going to go down in history as the father of the cloth mother? *Psychology Today*, 1973, *6*, 65–77.

Taylor, R. B., De Soto, C. B., & Lieb, R. Sharing secrets: Disclosure and discretion in dyads and triads. *Journal of Personality and Social Psychology*, 1979, *37*, 1196–1203.

Taylor, S. E. Hospital patient behavior: Reactance, helplessness, or control? In H. Friedman & M. R. DiMatteo (Eds.), *Interpersonal relations in Health Care*. New York: Academic Press, 1979.

Taylor, S. E., Fiske, S. T., Etcoff, N. L., & Ruderman, A. J. Categorical and contextual bases of person memory and stereotyping. *Journal of Personality and Social Psychology*, 1978, *36*, 778–793.

Tetlock, P. E. Identifying victims of groupthink from public statements of decision makers. *Journal of Personality and Social Psychology*, 1979, *37*, 1314–1324.

Thayer, S., & Schiff, W. Observer judgment of social interaction: eye contact and relationship inferences. *Journal of Personality and Social Psychology*, 1974, *20*, 110–114.

Thelen, H. Group dynamics in instruction: Principle of least group size. *School Review*, 1949, *57*, 139–148.

Thibaut, J. W., & Kelley, H. H. *The social psychology of groups*. New York: Wiley, 1959.

Thornton, G. R. The effect of wearing glasses upon judgment of personality traits of persons seen briefly. *Journal of Applied Psychology*, 1944, *28*, 203–207.

Tittle, C. R., & Rowe, A. R. Moral appeal, sanction threat, and deviance. *Social Problems*, 1973, *20*, 488–498.

Toffler, A. *Future shock*. New York: Bantam Books, 1970.

To help patient follow regimen, sign a "contract." *Medical World News*, 1974, *15*, 50.

Tompkins, V. H. Stress in aviation. In J. Hambling (Ed.), *The nature of stress & disorders*. Springfield, Ill.: Charles C Thomas, 1959.

Torrano, M. C. Tactics for restoring credibility. Unpublished master's thesis, San Diego State University, 1972.

Touhey, J. C. Comparison to two dimensions of attitude similarity on heterosexual attraction. *Journal of Personality and Social Psychology*, 1972, *23*, 8–10.

Touhey, J. C. Effects of additional women professionals on ratings of occupational prestige and desirability. *Journal of Personality and Social Psychology*, 1974, *29*, 86–89.

Tresemer, D. Fear of success: Popular, but unproven. *Psychology Today*, 1974, *7*, 82–85.

Tuddenham, R. D., & McBride, P. D. The yielding experiment from the subject's point of view. *Journal of Personality*, 1959, *27*, 259–271.

Tversky, A., & Kahneman, D. Belief in the law of small numbers. *Psychological Bulletin*, 1971, *76*, 105–110.

Tversky, A. & Kahneman, D. Causal schemas in judgments under uncertainty. In

M. Fishbein (Ed.), *Progress in social psychology*. Hillsdale, N.J.: Erlbaum, 1980.

Ullman, L. P. Who are we? In R. D. Rubin, H. Fensterheim, J. D. Henderson, & L. P. Ullman (Eds.), *Advances in behavior therapy*. New York: Academic Press, 1972.

U.S. Environmental Protection Agency. *Report to the President and Congress on noise*. Washington, D.C.: U.S. Government Printing Office, 1972.

U.S. Environmental Protection Agency. *The urban noise survey (Levels document 550-9-77-100)*. Washington, D.C.: U.S. Government Printing Office, 1977.

Valins, S. Cognitive effects of false heart-rate feedback. *Journal of Personality and Social Psychology*, 1966, *4*, 400–408.

VanGorp, G., Stempfle, J., & Olson, D. Dating attitudes, expectations, and physical attractiveness. Unpublished paper, University of Michigan, 1969.

Verinis, J., & Roll, S. Primary and secondary male characteristics. *Psychological Reports*, 1970, *26*, 123–126.

Vernon, D. T. A., & Bigelow, D. A. Effect of information about a potentially stressful situation on responses to stress impact. *Journal of Personality and Social Psychology*, 1974, *29*, 50–59.

Verplanck, W. S. The control of the content of conversation: Reinforcement of statement of opinion. *Journal of Abnormal and Social Psychology*, 1955, *51*, 668–676.

Viet vets fight back. *Newsweek*, November 12, 1979, 44–49.

Vondracek, S. T., & Vondracek, F. W. The manipulation and measurement of self-disclosure in preadolescents. *Merrill-Palmer Quarterly*, 1971, *17*, 51–58.

Vreeland, R. Is it true what they say about Harvard boys? *Psychology Today*, 1972, *5*, 65–68.

Wagner, C., & Wheeler, L. Model, need and cost effects in helping behavior. *Journal of Personality and Social Psychology*, 1969, *12*, 111–116.

Walkup, H., & Abbott, R. D. Cross-validation of item selection on the Bem Sex Role Inventory. *Applied Psychological Measurement*, 1978, *2*, 63–71.

Wallach, M. A., Kogan, N., & Bem, D. J. Group influence of individual risk taking. *Journal of Abnormal and Social Psychology*, 1962, *65*, 75–86.

Wallach, M. A., Kogan, N., & Bem, D. J. Diffusion of responsibility and level of risk-taking in groups. *Journal of Abnormal and Social Psychology*, 1964, *68*, 265–279.

Wallach, M. A., Kogan, N., & Bem, D. J. Group decision making under risk of aversive consequences. *Journal of Personality and Social Psychology*. 1965, *1*, 453–460.

Walster, E. Assignment of responsibility for an accident. *Journal of Personality and Social Psychology*, 1966, *3*, 73–79.

Walster, E., Aronson, E., & Abrahams, D. On increasing the persuasiveness of a low-prestige communicator. *Journal of Experimental Social Psychology*, 1966, *2*, 325–342.

Walster, E., Aronson, E., Abrahams, D., & Rottmann, L. Importance of physical attractiveness in dating behavior. *Journal of Personality and Social Psychology*, 1966, *4*, 508–516.

Walster, E., & Walster, G. W. Effect of expecting to be liked on choice of associates. *Journal of Abnormal and Social Psychology*, 1963, *67*, 402–404.

Walster, E., & Walster, G. W. The matching hypothesis. *Journal of Personality and Social Psychology*, 1969, *6*, 248–253.

Walster, E., Walster, G. W., & Berscheid, E. *Equity: Theory and research*, Boston: Allyn & Bacon, 1978.

Walster, E., Walster, G. W., Piliavin, J., & Schmidt, L. "Playing hard to get":

Understanding an elusive phenomenon. *Journal of Personality and Social Psychology,* 1973, *26,* 113–121.

Walster, E., Walster, G. W., & Traupman, J. Equity and premarital sex. *Journal of Personality and Social Psychology,* 1978, *36,* 82–92.

Watson, O. M., & Graves, T. Quantitative research in proxemic behavior. *American Anthropologist,* 1966, *68,* 971–985.

Webb, A. P. Sex-role preferences and adjustment in early adolescents. *Child Development,* 1963, *34,* 609–618.

Wegner, D. M., & Schaefer, D. The concentration of responsibility: An objective self-awareness analysis of group size in helping situations. *Journal of Personality and Social Psychology,* 1978, *36,* 147–155.

Weiner, B. Achievement motivation as conceptualized by an attribution theorist. In B. Weiner (Ed.), *Achievement motivation and attribution theory.* Morristown, N.J.: General Learning Press, 1974.

Weiner, B. A theory of motivation for some classroom experiences. *Journal of Educational Psychology,* 1979, *71,* 3–25.

Weiner, B., Frieze, I., Kukla, A., Reed, L., Rest, S., & Rosenbaum, R. *Perceiving the causes of success and failure.* Morristown, N.J.: General Learning Press, 1971.

Weiss, R. L., Hops, H., & Patterson, G. R. A framework for conceptualizing marital conflict, a technology for altering it, some data for evaluating it. In F. W. Clark & L. A. Hamerlynck (Eds.), *Critical issues in research and practice: Proceedings of the Fourth Banff International Conference on Behavior Modification.* Champaign, Ill.: Research Press, 1973.

Weiss, W. Opinion congruence with a negative source on one issue as a factor influencing agreement on another issue. *Journal of Abnormal and Social Psychology,* 1957, *54,* 180–186.

Weiss, W., & Steenbock, S. The influence on communication effectiveness of explicitly urging action and policy consequences. *Journal of Experimental Social Psychology,* 1965, *1,* 396–406.

Weitz, S. *Sex roles: Biological, psychological, and social foundations.* New York: Oxford University Press, 1977.

Wells, W. D., Goi, F. J., & Seader, S. A change in a product image. *Journal of Applied Psychology,* 1958, *42,* 120–121.

West, L., & Zingle, N. W. A self-disclosure inventory for adolescents. *Psychological Reports,* 1969, *24,* 439–445.

West, S. G., Whitney, G., & Schnedler, R. Helping a motorist in distress: The effects of sex. *Journal of Personality and Social Psychology,* 1975, *31,* 691–698.

White, R. K., & Lippit, R. O. *Autocracy and democracy.* New York: Harper & Row, 1960.

Whittaker, J. O. Attitude change and communication-attitude discrepancy. *Journal of Social Psychology,* 1965, *65,* 141–148.

Wicker, A. W. Attitudes versus actions: The relationship of verbal and overt behavioral responses to attitude objects. *Journal of Social Issues,* 1969, *25*(4), 41–78.

Wicker, A. W. An examination of the "other variables" explanation of attitude-behavior inconsistency. *Journal of Personality and Social Psychology,* 1971, *19,* 18–30.

Wicker, A. W. Ecological psychology: Some recent and prospective developments. *American Psychologist,* 1979, *34,* 755–765.

Wicker, A. W., & Kirmeyer, S. L. From church to laboratory to national park. In S.

Wapner, S. B. Conen, & B. Kaplan (Eds.), *Experiencing the environment.* New York: Plenum, 1976.

Wicklund, R., Cooper, T., & Linder, D. Effects of expected effort on attitude change prior to exposure. *Journal of Experimental Psychology,* 1967, *3,* 416–428.

Wiggins, J. *Personality and prediction.* Menlo Park, Calif.: Addison-Wesley, 1973.

Wiggins, J. A., Dill, F., & Schwartz, R. D. On "status-liability." *Sociometry,* 1965, *28,* 197–209.

Wiggins, J. S., Wiggins, N., & Conger, J. C. Correlates of heterosexual somatic preference. *Journal of Personality and Social Psychology,* 1968, *10,* 82–89.

Wilke, H., & Lanzetta, J. T. The obligation to help: The effects of amount of prior help on subsequent helping behavior. *Journal of Experimental Social Psychology,* 1970, *6,* 488–493.

Willis, R. H., & Hollander, E. P. An experimental study of three response modes in social influence situation. *Journal of Abnormal and Social Psychology,* 1964, *69,* 150–156.

Wilson, E. O. *Sociobiology: The new synthesis.* Cambridge, Mass.: Harvard University Press, 1975.

Wilson, P. R. Perceptual distinction of height as a function of ascribed academic status. *Journal of Social Psychology,* 1968, *74,* 97–102.

Winter, W. D., Ferreira, A. J., & Bowers, N. Decision-making in married and unrelated couples. *Family Process,* 1973, *12,* 83–94.

Wispé, L. G. & Freshley, H. B. Race, sex, and sympathetic helping behavior: The broken bag caper. *Journal of Personality and Social Psychology,* 1971, *17,* 59–65.

Wittreich, W. J. The Honi Phenomenon: A case of selective perceptual distortion. *Journal of Abnormal and Social Psychology,* 1952, *47,* 705–712.

Wolfgang, M. E. *Patterns in criminal homicide.* New York: Wiley, 1958.

Yinon, Y., & Bizman, A. Noise, success and failure as determinants of helping behavior. *Personality and Social Psychology Bulletin,* 1980, *6,* 125–130.

Zagora, S., & Harter, M. Credibility of source and recipient's attitude: Factors in the perception and retention of information on smoking behavior. *Perceptual and Motor Skills,* 1966, *23,* 155–168.

Zajonc, R. B. Attitudinal effects of mere exposure. *Journal of Personality and Social Psychology,* 1968, *9* (monogr. suppl. 2).

Zeitlin, L. R. A little larceny can do a lot for employee morale. *Psychology Today,* 1971, *5,* 22–65.

Zifferblatt, S. M., & Hendricks, C. G. Applied behavioral analysis of societal problems: Population change, a case in point. *American Psychologist,* 1974, *29,* 750–761.

Ziller, R. C., Behringer, R. D., & Goodchilds, J. D. Group creativity under conditions of success or failure and variations in group stability. *Journal of Applied Psychology,* 1962, *46,* 43–49.

Zillig, K. Einstellung und Aussage. *Zeitschrift der Psychologie,* 1928, *106,* 58-106.

Zillman, D., & Johnson, R. C. Motivated aggressiveness perpetuated by exposure to aggressive films and reduced by exposure to nonaggressive films. *Journal of Experimental Research in Personality,* 1973, *7,* 261–276.

Zillman, D., Williams, B. R., Bryant, J., Boynton, K. R., & Wolf, M. Acquisition of information from educational television programs as a function of differently paced humorous inserts. *Journal of Educational Psychology,* 1980, *72,* 170–180.

Zimbardo, P. The effect of improvisation on self-persuasion produced by role-playing. *Journal of Experimental Social Psychology,* 1965, *1,* 103–120.

Zimbardo, P. The human choice. In W. J. Arnold and D. Levine (Eds), *Nebraska symposium on motivation 1969*. Lincoln: University of Nebraska Press, 1970.

Zimbardo, P. A Pirandellian prison. *New York Times Magazine*, April 8, 1973.

Zimbardo, P., & Ebbesen, E. *Influencing attitudes and changing behavior.* New York: Addison-Wesley, 1969.

Zimbardo, P., Ebbesen, E., & Fraser, S. Emotional persuasion: Arousal state as a distractor. Unpublished manuscript. Stanford University, 1968.

Zimbardo, P. G., Ebbesen, E. B., & Maslach, C. *Influencing attitudes and changing behavior.* New York: Addison-Wesley, 1977.

Zimbardo, P. G., & Formica, R. Emotional comparison and self-esteem as determinants of affiliation. *Journal of Personality*, 1963, *31*, 141–162.

Zimbardo, P. G., Haney, C., Banks, W., & Jaffee, D. The psychology of imprisonment: Privation, power and pathology. Unpublished manuscript, Stanford University, 1972.

NAME INDEX

Abbott, R. D., 291
Abrahams, D., 66, 140
Abelson, R. P., 41, 204
Adams, N. E., 49
Adelson, J., 260
Aderman, D., 192
Adewole, A., 20
Adinolfi, A. A., 141
Adorno, T. W., 255, 256
Aiello, J. R., 311, 314
Ajzen, I., 53
Alessis, C., 66
Alioto, J. T., 181
Allen, A., 45
Allen, V., 106
Allport, G. W., 257
Altman, I., 33, 297
Amir, M., 166
Anderson, C. A., 310
Anderson, L. R., 220
Anderson, V. B., 326
Anisfeld, M., 10
Apple, W., 10
Aramoni, A., 275
Archibald, H. C., 299, 301
Arensberg, C. M., 224
Arkin, R. M., 34
Armor, D. J., 181
Aronson, E., 27, 66, 86, 126, 127, 150, 211
Aronson, V., 140
Arthur, R. J., 306
Ascani, K., 92
Asch, S. E., 64, 105
Atkins, C. J., 107
Atkinson, R. C., 94
Atkinson, R. L., 94
Auerbach, S. M., 298
Averill, J. R., 318

Bach, G., 174
Back, K., 208
Back, K. W., 131, 132
Baer, D. M., 12
Bailey, J. S., 325
Baldridge, B., 134
Bales, R. F., 217, 346
Ball, R. L., 178
Bandura, A., 47, 114, 169, 249

Banikiotes, P. G., 291
Banks, W., 215
Barber, T. X., 95
Barker, R. G., 317
Barnes, R. D., 291
Baron, R., 312
Baron, R. A., 178, 309, 310, 311
Barrett, G., 168
Bass, B. M. 213, 217
Basset, R., 91
Bauer, R. A., 64, 196
Baum, A., 312, 313, 314
Baumgartel, H., 221
Baumrind, D., 102, 333
Baune, H. B., 123
Bayton, J. A., 242
Beaber, R. J., 10
Beardslee, D. C., 14
Beattie, M. Y., 250
Becker, F. D., 315
Beckman, L. J., 267
Beets, J. L., 316
Behringer, R. D., 225
Bem, D. J., 41, 45, 46, 227, 278, 281, 284
Bem, S. L., 278, 281, 284, 290, 292, 293
Bennet, T. S., 240
Bennett, C. C., 33
Bennett, E. M., 275
Bennett, L., 306
Berelson, B., 53, 228
Berkowitz, L., 64, 163, 170, 171, 181, 191, 192, 229
Berle, A. A., 78
Berman, J. J., 76
Bernard, L. C., 290, 291
Berscheid, E., 8, 64, 123, 124, 140
Bevard, E. W., Jr., 226
Beyer, J., 47
Bickman, B., 186, 189, 191
Bickman, L., 102
Bigelow, D. A., 321
Birchler, G. R., 152
Bizman, A., 308
Black, H., 235
Blane, H. T., 11
Blau, P., 123
Blitz, R. C., 275
Block, J., 259

Blum, B., 177
Bobrow, D. G., 41
Boffey, P. M., 331
Bogo, N., 10
Bolles, R. C., 112
Bonney, M. E., 123
Borgida, E., 36
Borofsky, G. L., 198
Bossard, J. H. S., 146
Bossom, J., 235
Bowers, N., 152
Boynton, K. R., 63
Bradburn, N. M., 151
Bradley, G. W., 28
Braginski, D., 210
Bramel, D., 177
Branch, L. G., 225
Brand, R. J., 302
Braucht, G. N., 167
Bray, R. M., 255
Brechner, K., 92
Breck, S. J., 123
Breedlove, J., 151
Brehm, J. W., 86, 196
Brenner, M. H., 316
Bretsch, H. S., 123
Breuer, J., 164, 177
Briggs, S. R., 35
Brigham, J. C., 238
Broadbent, D. E., 308
Brock, B. T., 61
Brotzman, E., 76
Broverman, D. M., 286, 287
Broverman, I. K., 286, 287
Brown, B. L., 10
Brown, S. O., 33
Brown, V., 288
Brunson, B. I., 308
Bryan, J. H., 192
Bryant, J., 63
Bryson, J., 262
Bryson, J. B., 149, 150
Bugenthal, D. E., 10
Bujarski, R., 79
Burchard, W. W., 213
Buss, A. H., 35, 169
Butler, C. J., 254
Buys, C. J., 220

NAME INDEX

Byrne, D., 58, 134, 135, 291, 311

Cacioppo, J. T., 62, 64, 91
Calvin, A. D., 115
Campbell, A., 287
Campbell, D., 16
Campbell, D. E., 316
Campbell, D. T., 336
Campbell, E., 61
Campbell, J., 208
Campbell, J. L., 167
Caputo, C., 24
Carducci, B., 308
Carlsmith, J., 12
Carlsmith, J. M., 56, 86, 89, 157, 310
Carlsmith, M. M., 82
Carmen, B., 290
Carmet, D. W., 65
Carnegie, D., 126
Carson, R., 296
Cartwright, D., 78
Carver, C. S., 302, 303
Cassman, T., 9
Catalan, J., 92
Catalano, R., 316
Cavanaugh, P. H., 8
Cervin, V. B., 65
Chafetz, M. L., 11
Chaikin, A. L., 28
Cheek, J. M., 35
Chittick, E. V., 33
Christie, R., 251, 252
Cialdini, R. B., 91, 92
Clark, E. L., 242
Clark, K. B., 177
Clark, M., 195
Clark, R. D., 188
Clarkson, R. E., 286, 287
Clifford, C., 228
Clifford, M. M., 8
Cline, V. B., 167
Clore, G. L., 134
Coffman, T. L., 243, 244
Cohen, A. R., 86
Cohen, L. R., 275
Cohen, S., 308
Cohn, T. S., 228
Colamosca, J. V., 193
Cole, A. H., 196
Coleman, A. E., 302
Coleman, J. C., 297
Collins, B. E., 77, 87, 89
Cone, J. D., 326
Conger, J. C., 273
Connolley, E. S., 106
Connor, J. M., 276
Consalvi, C., 230
Cook, T. D., 66
Cooley, C. H., 31
Cooper, H. M., 108
Cooper, J., 62, 88
Cosentino, R., 289

Cowan, G., 203
Cox, D. F., 64
Cox, V., 311, 312
Cozby, P. C., 33
Creager, J. A., 288
Cressler, D. L., 323
Crockett, W. H., 20
Cronbach, L. J., 46, 143
Cross, H. A., 129
Cross, K., 260
Crozier, J. B., 308
Crutchfield, R. S., 106
Cunningham, M. R., 92, 311

Dahl, R. H., 291
Dalrymple, S., 76
Daly, M., 161
Daly, R. F., 160
Darby, B. L., 92
Darley, J. M., 28, 184, 186, 188, 190, 326
D'Atri, D., 311
Davidson, E. S., 180
Davis, G. E., 313, 314
Davis, K. E., 146, 167
Davis, X. E., 35
Davison, G. C., 303
Deabler, H. L., 289
Dean, D. G., 259
Deaux, K., 204
DeCharmes, R., 176
DeFleur, M., 58
Demerath, N. J., 251
Dermer, M., 144
Dertke, M. C., 186, 350
Deslauries, B. C., 326
De Soto, C. B., 209
Deutsch, M., 103
Dey, F. L., 308
Diamond, S. G., 316
Dichter, D., 55
Dickson, L., 130
Dickstein, E., 253
Diehl, L. A., 280
Diener, E., 44
Dill, F., 229
DiMatteo, M. R., 11
Dion, K., 8, 123, 140, 250
Dipboye, R., 8
Dittes, J., 108
DiVesta, F. J., 108
Dollard, J., 164, 318
Donnelly, F. A., 11, 65
Donnerstein, E., 168
Doob, A. N., 56, 86, 177, 308
Doob, L. W., 164
Dooley, D., 316
Dorr, D., 249
Douglas, T. J., 326
Douvan, E. A., 260
Drag, R. H., 33
Driscoll, R., 146
Dunn, T. M., 298

Dunnette, M., 208
Durkheim, E., 257
Dworkin, R. S., 16

Ebbesen, E., 55, 56, 69
Ebbesen, E. B., 133
Edelsack, L., 82
Edney, J. J., 315
Efran, M. G., 8
Ehrlich, D., 86
Ehrlich, P. R., 296, 311
Eisenberg, L., 11
Eisenberger, R., 112
Ellis, E., 213
Ellsworth, P., 12
Emswiller, T., 204
Endler, N. S., 44, 45, 108
Engles, F., 257
Enzle, M. E., 205
Epstein, Y., 311
Erikson, J. M., 306
Eron, L. D., 177, 181
Ervin, F., 160
Etcoff, N. L., 239
Ettinger, R. F., 108
Evans, F. J., 95
Evans, G. W., 308
Everett, P. B., 326
Exline, R. V., 12

Fairweather, G. W., 323
Falbo, T., 125
Feierabend, I. K., 348
Feierabend, R. L., 348
Fendrick, J. M., 53
Ferreira, A. J., 152
Feshbach, N. D., 177
Feshbach, S. 80, 157, 168, 174, 176, 181
Festinger, L., 54, 85, 86, 131, 132, 210
Fey, S., 249
Fichter, J. H., 258
Fiedler, F., 229
Field, P. B., 64
Fillenbaum, S., 11
Finney, J., 262
Firestone, I. J., 193
Fisch, E., 193
Fishbein, M., 53
Fisher, W. A., 291
Fiske, S. T., 239
Flacks, R., 259
Flanders, N. A., 226
Flay, B. R., 66
Flexner, E., 277
Foa, V. G., 211
Folmar, K., 284
Fontaine, G., 77
Formica, R., 210
Franzini, L. R., 287
Fraser, R., 299
Fraser, S., 55, 91
Frazier, E. F., 213

NAME INDEX

Freedman, J. L., 56, 86, 91, 157, 311
French, J. R. P., Jr., 77
French, R. L., 123
Frenkel-Brunswick, E., 255, 256
Freshley, H. B., 197, 201
Freud, S., 164, 177, 253
Friedan, B., 56
Friedman, H., 11, 302
Friedman, H. S., 11
Friedman, M., 302
Friedman, P., 191
Friedman, R., 33
Frieze, I. H., 23, 39
Fritz, C. E., 340
Fromkin, H., 8
Fuller, E. M., 123
Funder, D. C., 46

Gabrenya, W. K., 34
Gaertner, S. L., 201
Galbraith, J. K., 80
Gallo, P. S., 343
Gardner, R. C., 11
Gastorf, J. R. C., 13
Gaudet, H., 53
Geen, R. G., 169, 171, 180, 308
Geis, F. L., 251, 252, 288
Gelfand, D. M., 186, 250
Geller, S. H., 108
Gerard, H. B., 103, 106, 210
Gewirtz, J. L., 112
Gibb, J. R., 222
Gibbins, K., 9
Gillig, P. M., 66
Gillis, J. S., 71
Gilmore, J. B., 87
Glass, D. C., 302, 303, 307
Goffman, E., 10, 34
Goi, F. J., 61
Goldberg, L. R., 25, 278
Goldberg, P. A., 279
Goldiamond, I., 58
Goldman, J. R., 247
Goldman, M., 221
Goldman, R. D., 236, 269
Goodchilds, J. D., 225
Goranson, R. E., 191, 309, 310
Gordon, A., 64
Gordon, S. K., 13
Gottlieb, A., 197
Gorsuch, R. L., 254
Graf, R. G., 204
Graves, N., 76
Graves, T., 315
Gray, D., 12
Gray, S. W., 289
Green, J. A., 53
Green, R. B., 220
Greene, D., 117
Greenspoon, J., 115
Greenwald, A. G., 66
Griffitt, W., 126, 134, 139

Gross, A., 82
Gruder, C. L., 66, 197
Gruner, C., 63
Gunderson, E. K., 306
Gurr, T. R., 348
Guttman, I., 86

Haan, N., 245, 259
Haber, S., 168
Halamau, J., 66
Halcomb, C. G., 129
Hall, C., 314
Hall, E. T., 315
Hall, J. A., 12
Hallam, H., 168
Hallauer, D. S., 13
Hamill, R., 42
Haney, C., 215
Hanratty, M. A., 181
Hansson, L., 308
Hantover, J. P., 275
Harackiewicz, J. M., 117
Harari, H., 21, 22, 32, 36, 79, 92, 123, 186, 198, 239, 240, 243, 249, 340, 344
Harari, O., 198
Hardyck, J. A., 135, 241
Hare, A. P., 217
Harford, T. C., 289
Harkins, S. G., 223
Harlow, H. F., 270, 271
Harlow, M. K., 270, 271
Harshbarger, D., 213
Harter, M., 66
Hartman, D. P., 186, 250
Harvey, M. D., 205
Harvey, O. J., 61, 230
Hastorf, A. H., 9, 203
Hawkins, R., 62
Hawley, P., 267, 269
Hayes, S. C., 169, 326
Hayward, S. C., 326
Heider, F., 17, 35
Heilbrun, A. B., 289
Heller, M. S., 181
Heller, T., 228
Helmreich, R. L., 89
Helson, H., 16
Hendricks, C. G., 325
Henningan, K. M., 66
Henson, A., 12
Hereford, C., 65
Herjanic, M., 166
Hertzler, V. B., 130
Higbee, K. L., 80, 227
Hilgard, E. R., 94
Himmelstein, P., 33
Hinckley, R. G., 7
Hinrichsen, J. J., 291
Hodgson, R. C., 11
Hoffman, L. R., 225
Hofling, C. K., 76
Hogan, R., 253

Hollander, E. P., 107, 229
Hollis, J. F., 302
Holmes, D. S., 319
Holmes, J. G., 191
Holmes, M., 193
Holmes, T. H., 306
Holmes, T. S., 306
Holt, R. R., 298, 302
Homans, G., 123
Hops, H., 151
Horman, R. E., 262
Horner, M. S., 242, 280
Horney, K., 277
Hornstein, H. A., 193
Horsfall, A. B., 224
Hosey, K. R., 13, 36, 92
Hoskin, B., 275
Houlné, S., 79
House, J. S., 196
Houser, B. B., 267
Houston, B. K., 319
Hovland, C. I., 61, 63, 64, 65
Huesmann, L. R., 181
Hulin, W. S., 236
Hunt, J., 44
Hunt, M., 153
Hunt, T., 306

Ickes, W., 291
Iler, I., 276
Idenbaum, E., 204
Inkster, J. A., 86
Inskeep, R., 203
Insko, C. A., 20
Isen, A. M., 194, 195, 308

Jackins, H., 173
Jackson, D. N., 291
Jacobson, L., 40, 244
Jaffee, D., 215
James, W. T., 10
Jamison, P. H., 287
Janis, I. L., 63, 64, 65, 80, 87, 219, 298, 302
Janov, A., 173
Jarvick, L. F., 160
Jellison, J. M., 64
Jenkins, C. D., 302
Jennings, (Walstedt), J., 288
Jensen, A. R., 242
Jessor, R., 262
Jessor, S. L., 262
Johnson, H. H., 225
Johnson, J. E., 319, 320
Johnson, R. C., 181
Johnson, R. N., 156, 160
Johnston, R. E., 9
Jones, C., 27
Jones, E. E., 24, 35, 36, 37, 88, 126
Jones, R. A., 62
Jones, S., 81
Jones, S. A., 314
Jones, W. T., 163

NAME INDEX

Jonsson, A., 308
Jordan-Edney, N. L., 315
Jospe, A., 242
Jourard, S. M., 33
Judd, C. M., 42
Julian, J. W., 229
Jung, C. G., 253

Kagan, J., 172, 275, 298, 302
Kahle, L. R., 76
Kahn, M., 165
Kahn, R., 158
Kahneman, D., 36
Kandel, D. B., 136, 137
Kaplan, R. M., 39, 63, 65, 107, 112, 165, 174, 178, 180, 236, 266, 269, 284, 287, 321
Karlin, R., 311
Karlins, M., 243, 244
Katz, D., 236
Katzev, R., 82
Kaufmann, H., 176
Kellett, D. S., 319
Kelley, H. H., 22, 25, 35, 63, 65, 108, 211, 217
Kelley, J. A., 291
Kelman, H. C., 333
Kendrick, D. T., 291
Kendzierski, D., 42
Kerr, W., 123
Kibler, B. K., 240
Kiesler, C. A., 104
Kiesler, S. B., 104, 279
Kimmel, E., 288
Kinder, D. R., 57, 255
King, D., 309, 310
Kipnis, D., 79
Kirkpatrick, C., 257
Kirmeyer, S. L., 318
Kjos, G. L., 133
Kleck, R. E., 9
Klevansky, S., 311
Klodin, V., 160
Knight, R. C., 262
Knox, D. H., 151
Knox, R. E., 86
Kogan, N., 227
Kohlberg, L., 247
Kolata, G. B., 277
Koller, P. S., 39
Komaroff, A. L., 306
Konecni, V. J., 84, 133, 165, 166, 178, 308
Korth, B., 197
Krantz, D. S., 7, 308
Krantzler, M., 153
Krasner, L., 114
Krauss, R. M., 10
Kraut, R. E., 9
Krebs, D., 141
Kremers, J., 235
Kriss, M., 204
Kuhlen, R. G., 123

Kukla, A., 23, 39
Kulik, J. A., 42

La France, M., 290
Lambert, W. E., 10, 11
Lambert, W. W., 16
Landauer, T. K., 56, 86
Landy, D., 8, 142
Langer, E. J., 39, 204
Lanzetta, J. T., 191
Lasakow, P., 33
Laswell, H. D., 78
Latané B., 184, 186, 188, 189, 190, 197, 223
Laughlin, P. R., 225
Lawhon, J., 13
Lawson, E., 8
Lawton, S. F., 311
Lazarsfeld, P. F., 53
Lazarus, R. S., 318
Leavitt, H. J., 218
LeCompte, W., 12
Leff, D. N., 299
Lefkowitz, M. M., 181
Legant, P., 24
Lenski, G., 258
Leonard, C. V., 261
LePage, A., 171
Lepper, M. R., 62
Lepper, R. M., 117
Lerner, M. J., 27, 29, 191
Leslie, I., 299
Leventhal, H., 80, 81, 320
Levin, P. F., 194, 195
Levine, J. M., 8, 106
Levinger, G., 151
Levinson, D. J., 255, 256
Levitz, E., 267
Lewin, K., 33
Lewis, S. K., 92
Lezak, A., 308
Licktman, C. M., 193
Lieb, R., 209
Leiberman, S., 214, 340
Liebert, R. M., 180
Linder, D. E., 88, 126, 127
Lipetz, M. E., 146
Lipinski, C. E., 210
Lippit, R. O., 226
Litman-Adizes, T., 77
Littlepage, G. E., 134, 237
Loeb, M., 308
Loew, C., 169
Loomis, C. P., 123
Lord, C. G., 42, 62
Lorenz, K., 161
Lott, A. J., 125
Lott, B. E., 125
Lubell, S., 260
Luchins, A. S., 16
Lueck, H., 4
Lumsdaine, A. A., 61, 63
Lundberg, G. A., 130

Lundberg, V., 306
Lundy, R. M., 64
Luyben, P. D., 325

Macaulay, J. R., 229
Maccoby, E. E., 289
Maccoby, N., 54
MacDonald, A. P., Jr., 210
Mack, J., 220
Madsen, C. H., 326
Madsen, C. K., 326
Maehr, M. L., 245
Magnussen, D., 44, 45
Mahan, J., 306
Mahl, G. F., 298, 302
Maier, N. R. F., 225
Maitland, K. A., 247
Malamuth, N., 167, 168
Mallick, S. K., 165
Mandell, W., 61
Manis, M., 31, 236
Mann, L., 62
Manz, W., 4
Marecek, J., 24
Marino, C. J., 108
Mark, V. H., 160
Markus, H., 41, 42
Marriot, F., Jr., 221
Marshall, G. D., 138
Maruyama, G., 10
Marx, K., 257
Maslach, C., 56, 69, 138
Maslow, A. H., 235, 298
Masuda, M., 306
Matsuyama, S. S., 160
Matter, W. W., 129
Matthews, K. A., 308
Matthews, R. W., 314
Maynard, H., 323
Mayo, C., 315
McBride, P. D., 106, 108
McBurney, D. H., 8
McCain, G., 311, 312
McCandless, B. R., 165
McCarthy, D., 312
McCauley, C., 238, 241
McDavid, J. W., 108, 123, 186, 239, 240, 243, 249, 340, 344
McDonald, F. J., 249
McGinnies, E., 16
McGinnis, J., 113, 252
McGrath, J. E., 221
McGuire, W. J., 54, 69
McMillen, D. L., 194
Mead, G. H., 31
Meade, R. D., 226
Meehl, P. E., 143
Mehrabian, A., 12, 316
Meichenbaum, D., 321
Meissner, W. W., 261
Messe, L. A., 198
Messick, S., 336

NAME INDEX

Meyer, D. A., 166
Meyers, A. W., 326
Mezei, L., 135
Michela, J. L., 25
Michels, W. C., 16
Mikulas, W. L., 113
Miles, C. G., 65
Milgram, S., 96, 98, 100, 101, 102, 180, 196
Miller, D. T., 29, 191
Miller, J. A., 91
Miller, M., 10
Miller, N., 16, 318
Miller, N. E., 164
Mills, J., 64, 86, 211
Mills, T. M., 209
Milmoe, S., 11
Minsky, M., 41
Mischel, W., 35, 44
Mittleman, B., 298, 303
Mixon, D., 333, 341
Mohr, D., 92
Monat, A., 318
Montapert, A. A., 143
Moos, R. H., 44, 296
Moriarty, T., 186, 197
Morris, C., 261
Morris, D., 272
Moss, G. E., 322
Moss, H. A., 172
Moss, M. K., 194
Mowrer, O. H., 164
Mussen, P. H., 289

Naftulin, D. H., 11, 65
Natzuik, T., 108
Neale, J. M., 180
Neale, J. N., 303
Nelson, C. 252
Nelson, D., 134
Nelson, J., 134
Nemeth, C., 196
Newcomb, T. M., 133
Newsom, T. J., 326
Nicholls, J. G., 40
Niles, P., 80
Nisbett, R. E., 24, 35, 36, 64, 117
Noble, A. M., 255
Norman, D. A., 41
Norman, R. D., 235
Norman, W. T., 37
Northcraft, G. B., 203
Novaco, R. W., 166, 176
Nunn, C. Z., 80

Obitz, F. W., 92
O'Dowd, D. D., 14
Olson, D., 124
O'Neal, E. C., 181, 308
Ono, H., 9
Orden, S. R., 151
Orne, M. T., 95

Ostrove, N., 8

Packard, V., 56
Page, B., 186, 250
Page, R., 194
Paleg, K., 62
Pallak, M. S., 72
Papageorgis, D., 54, 69
Pascoe, G. C., 63
Passini, F. T., 37
Patterson, A. H., 326
Patterson, G. R., 151
Patterson, T. L., 161
Paulus, P. B., 311, 312, 314
Paunonen, S. V., 291
Penner, L. A., 186, 250
Peplau, L. A., 29, 125
Petranoff, R., 58
Petrinovich, L., 161
Petty, R. E., 62, 64, 223
Pfiffner, J. M., 224
Phelps, D., 299
Pheterson, G. I., 279
Piacente, B. S., 279, 288
Piaget, J., 246
Picciotto, S. R., 203
Pierce, C. H., 325
Pierce, C. M., 76
Pigg, R., 169
Piliavin, I. M., 197, 201
Piliavin, J. A., 148, 197, 201
Pineault, M. A., 237
Polansky, N. A., 33
Polsky, S., 181
Postman, L. J., 16
Powers, P. C., 171
Price, R. A., 140
Priest, R. F., 132
Prince, L. M., 11
Pritzker, H. A., 61, 63
Proctor, C., 123
Pruitt, D. G., 191, 227
Pugh, W., 306
Pursell, S. A., 291
Pyszczynski, T. A., 144

Rahe, R. H., 305, 306
Ramsy, N. R., 146
Ransberger, V. M., 309
Ransdell, H. J., 291
Ransford, H. E., 261
Raven, B. H., 77
Rawers, R. J., 325
Razran, G., 13
Reed, L., 23, 39
Reese, H. W., 123
Reid, D. H., 325
Rencher, A. C., 10
Renne, K. S., 151
Rest, S., 23, 39
Rhine, R. J., 65

Richardson, D. C., 167
Riddell, J., 204
Ring, K., 210
Risley, T. R., 325
Rodin, J., 39, 189, 197, 201, 312
Rodin, M. J., 135
Roethlingshafer, D., 7
Rogers, C. R., 207, 208
Rogow, A. A., 78
Rokeach, M., 135, 255, 256
Roll, S., 8
Romer, D., 197
Rosenbaum, M. E., 176
Rosenbaum, R., 23, 39
Rosenfeld, H., 12
Rosenhan, D., 192
Rosenkrantz, P. S., 286, 287
Rosenman, R. H., 302
Rosenn, M., 318
Rosenthal, R., 11, 40, 244
Ross, D., 169
Ross, L., 36, 44, 62
Ross, M., 224
Ross, M. J., 257
Ross, S. A., 169
Rothenberg, M. B., 180
Rotter, J., 37
Rottmann, L., 140
Rowe, A. R., 254
Rubin, R. T., 306
Rubin, Z., 29, 123, 138, 142, 144, 145, 147
Rubovits, P. C., 245
Ruderman, A. J., 239
Russo, N. J., 315
Ryder, R. G., 151

Sabath, G., 229
Saegert, S., 130
St. Peter, S., 275
Sanders, D. H., 323
Sanford, R. N., 255, 256
Sarason, I. G., 45, 306
Sattler, J., 236
Sawrey, W. L., 303
Sawyer, J., 132
Schaar, K., 288
Schachter, S., 131, 132, 138, 210
Schaefer, D., 197
Scheier, M. F., 308
Schein, E. H., 84
Scherer, D., 11
Schiff, W., 12
Schmidt, L., 148
Schnedler, R., 201
Schneider, B., 16
Schoggen, P., 317
Schonbach, P., 86
Schuette, D., 12
Schutz, W. C., 224
Schwartz, M. F., 195
Schwartz, R. D., 229

NAME INDEX

Schwartz, S. H., 197
Scodel, A., 236, 272
Seader, S., 61
Seagert, A., 312
Sears, D. O., 157
Sears, R. R., 165, 289
Seaver, W. B., 326
Secord, P. F., 242
Seeman, M., 259
Segal, M. W., 130, 239, 241
Seidenberg, B., 254
Seldes, G., 122, 251
Seligman, C., 326
Seligman, M. E., 38, 39
Selye, H., 322
Serbin, L. A., 276
Shaver, K. G., 28, 250
Shaw, M. E., 63
Sheffield, F. D., 61, 63
Sheposh, J. P., 262
Sherif, M., 61
Sherman, C. E., 153
Shettel-Neuber, J., 150
Shippee, G., 92
Shortland, R. L., 180
Sicoly, F., 224
Sigall, H., 8, 142
Singer, J. E., 138, 307
Singer, R. D., 112, 165, 181
Singer, R. P., 81
Sistrunk, F., 108
Small, L., 261
Smedley, J. W., 242
Smith, B. L., 10
Smith, G. H., 55
Smith, H., 274
Smith, J., 42
Smith, M. B., 135, 241, 259
Smith, M. L., 287
Smith, R. A., 254
Smith, R. E., 44
Snow, C. P., 96
Snyder, E. C., 146
Snyder, H. N., 23
Snyder, M., 33, 34, 92
Snyder, M. L., 302
Sobel, R., 221
Solomon, R. L., 16
Sommer, R., 315, 316
Sommers, A. R., 180
Spanos, N. P., 95
Speroff, B., 123
Spielberger, C. D., 298
Spinner, B., 167
Stake, J. E., 267
Stanley, J. C., 336
Star, S. A., 299
Staub, E., 176, 196, 319
Stearns, A., 191
Steele, C. M., 93
Stein, D. D., 135, 241

Stein, R. T., 228
Steiner, G. A., 228
Steiner, I. D., 229
Steinmetz, G., 82
Stempfle, J., 124
Stitt, C. L., 238, 241
Stokols, D., 295, 297, 308, 312
Stollack, E. G., 198
Stone, L., 291
Stonner, D., 169
Storms, M. D., 36
Stouffer, S. A., 257
Strauss, R., 302
Streeter, L. A., 10
Stringfield, D. O., 291
Strodtbeck, F. L., 218
Strong, W. J., 10
Struening, E. L., 257
Stuart, R. B., 151
Studer, P. G., 326
Sullivan, J. J., 72
Suls, J., 13
Sulzer, J. L., 181
Sundstrom, E., 312
Sussman, M. B., 151
Swap, W., 130
Sweet, W. H., 160
Szasz, T. S., 244

Taft, R., 235
Taranta, A., 11
Taub, B., 177
Taulbee, E. S., 298
Tavris, C., 271
Taylor, D. A., 33
Taylor, R. B., 209
Taylor, S. E., 38, 239
Terwilliger, R. F., 80
Tesch, F., 204
Test, M. A., 192
Tetlock, P. E., 220
Thayer, S., 12
Thelen, H., 222
Theorell, T., 306
Thibaut, J. W., 211
Thompson, F., 326
Thornton, G. R., 4
Tittle, C. R., 254
Toffler, A., 304
Tom, S., 56, 86
Tomplins, V. H., 299
Torrano, M. C., 68
Touhey, J. C., 134, 278
Traupman, J., 124
Tresemer, D., 282
Tuddenham, R. D., 106, 108, 299, 301
Turk, D., 321
Tversky, A., 36

Ullman, L. P., 113
Ulrich, K., 186, 250

Valins, S., 139, 312
Valone, K., 10
Vandenberg, S. G., 140
Vanderveer, R., 79
VanGorp, G., 124
Verinis, J., 8
Vernon, D. T. A., 321
Verplanck, W. S., 117
Vincent, J. P., 92, 152
Vogel, S. R., 286, 287
Vondracek, F. W., 33
Vondracek, S. T., 33
Vreeland, R., 140

Wadsworth, A. P., 298
Wagenhals, W. L., 291
Wagner, C., 192
Walder, L. O., 181
Walder, P., 186, 250
Walker, T., 82
Walkup, H., 291
Wallach, M. A., 227
Walster, E., 8, 26, 66, 123, 124, 140, 148, 211
Walster, G. W., 124, 140, 148, 211
Walters, G., 243, 244
Ware, J. E., 11, 65
Watson, O. M., 315
Watson, P. D., 16
Watson, S., 275
Webb, A. P., 289
Wegner, D. M., 197
Weiner, B., 23, 39, 40
Weiss, R. L., 151, 152
Weiss, W., 61, 63
Weisz, J. D., 303
Weitz, S., 282
Wells, W. D., 61
West, L., 33
West, S. G., 201
Wheeler, D., 92
Wheeler, L., 192
White, G. M., 192
White, R. K., 226
White, R. V., 198
Whitney, G., 201
Wiback, K., 8
Wicker, A. W., 53, 295, 317, 318
Wiggins, J., 43
Wiggins, J. A., 229
Wigins, J. S., 273
Wiggins, N., 273
Wildfogel, J., 9
Wilhelmy, R. A., 106
Wilke, H., 191
Williams, B. R., 63
Williams, K., 223
Willis, C. H., 289
Willis, R. H., 107
Willits, J. E., 204

Wilson, E. O., 161
Wilson, M., 161
Wilson, P. R., 7
Winter, W. D., 152
Wispé, L. G., 197, 201
Wittaker, 63
Wittreich, W. J., 17
Wolf, I., 11
Wolf, M., 63
Wolf, S., 196
Wolff, H. G., 303
Wolfgang, M. E., 166

Wong, T. J., 135
Word, L. E., 188
Worell, J., 291
Wright, R., 82
Wrighter, J., 123
Wullner, J., 79
Wurm, H., 302
Wyden, P., 174

Yinon, Y., 308
Young, L. E., 150

Zagora, S., 66
Zajonc, R. B., 129, 130
Zander, A., 78
Zarantonello, M., 102
Zeitlin, L. R., 253
Zifferblatt, S. M., 325
Ziller, R. C., 225
Zillig, K., 22
Zillman, D., 63, 181
Zimbardo, P., 55, 56, 65, 69, 138, 162, 210, 215, 216
Zingle, N. W., 33

SUBJECT INDEX

Abreaction, 162-165, 173-174
Adaptation level, 16
Age stereotyping, 13
Aggression:
    anger arousal and, 162-168
    biological determinants of, 158-162
    catharsis and, 162-165, 173-174
    cognitive control of, 174-176
    conditioning and imitation of, 168-171
    definition of, 156-158
    deindividuation and, 162
    empathic control of, 176-177
    hostile, 157
    humor and, 178-179
    instrumental, 157
    pornography and, 167
    prediction of, 171-173
    television and, 179-181
Alienation, 258-262
Altruism, definition of, 183
Androgyny, psychological, 288-293
Anxiety:
    group joining and, 209
    stress and, 297-299
Attitude change:
    by advocating extreme changes, 63
    by arousal and attention, 54-58
    by encouraging audience participation, 65
    by endorsing audience view, 63
    by establishing similarity with audience, 64-65
    by forewarning listeners, 62
    by gaining and maintaining credibility, 65-68
    by gauging time of argument, 63
    by gearing presentation to audience intelligence, 64-65
    by gearing presentation to audience self-esteem, 64
    by immunization against counterpropaganda, 69
    by knowing the audience, 64-65
    by letting facts speak for themselves, 62
    by presentation of arguments, 62-64

Attitude change *(continued)*
    by presenting two sides of arguments, 63-64
    by use of humor, 63
    by use of repetition, 64
Attitudes, behavior and, 52-54, 73, 75, 76
Attraction, *see* Liking
Attractiveness, physical, 8, 139-142, 250
Attribution theory, 22-25, 35-37
Audience sensitization, 54
Authoritarianism, 255-257

Balance theory, 17-22
Behavior, attitudes and, 52-54, 73, 75, 76
Behavioral settings, 317, 318-321, 322-324
Behavior modification, 108-117
Birth control, 324-325

Capricious world hypothesis, 28
Catharsis, 162-165, 173-174
Cautious shift, 227
Chauvinism, sexism and, 264, 293
Chivalry, 201
Choice shift, 227
Classical conditioning, 110-112
Climate, liking and, 139
Cognitive behavior modification, 321
Cognitive dissonance, 56, 57, 84-89, 165, 211
Cognitive science, 41
Combat neurosis, 300
Compliance:
    by concession, 91-92
    by fear, 80-82
    by force, 84-89
    by guile, 89-91
    by guilt, 82-83
    by hypnosis, 94-96
    by insult, 92-94
    by private acceptance, 103-104
    by sympathy, 83-84
Conditioned response, 110
Conditioned stimulus, 110
Conformity:
    definition of, 103
    personality factors in, 108

Conformity *(continued)*
    situational factors in, 106-108
    types of, 103
Continuous reinforcement, 112
Counterconformity, 103
Counterpropaganda immunization, 69
Counterpropaganda inoculation, 69
Credibility of persuader, 65-68

Dating, 140, 145-148
Defensive attribution, 28
Deindividuation, 162
Diads, 208
Discrimination as used in behavior modification, 113
Divorce, 152-153
Dogmatism, 255-257
Door-in-the-face technique, 91

Ecological psychology, 295 (*see also* Behavioral settings)
Emotional propaganda, 59-60
Empathy, aggression control and, 176-177
Energy crisis, 326
Environmental modification, 322-326
Environmental psychology, 295
Environments, classification of, 296-297
Equity theory, 124-125
Ethnic stereotyping, 241-245
Ethology, 161
Exchange theory, 123-124
Exposure theory, 127-130
Extinction, 111

Fear, effect of, on compliance, 80-82
Foot-in-the-door technique, 89-91, 92
Forced compliance, 87-89
Frames, 41
Frustration:
    relationship to aggression, 164
    stress and, 297
Functional analysis, environmental modification and, 324-326
Fundamental attribution error, 36, 44

Gain-loss phenomenon, 126

SUBJECT INDEX

General adaptation syndrome, 321-322
Generalization as used in behavior modification, 113
Generation gap, 259-260
Greenspoon effect, 114
Group climate, leadership style and, 225-226
Group communication, 217-219
Groups:
  dynamics of, 207-208
  effects of anxiety on joining, 209-211
Group output:
  group climate and, 225-226
  group composition and, 224-225
  group size and, 221-222
  groupthink effects and, 219-221
  risk taking and, 226-227
Groupthink, 219-221
Guilt, effect of, on compliance, 82-84

Halo effect, 237
Helping behavior:
  costs of, 193-195
  diffusion of responsibility and, 189-190
  gender and, 201-202
  imitation and, 191-193
  lifestyle and, 203-204
  location and, 195-196
  physical handicap and, 202-203
  race and, 199-201, 203
  reciprocity and, 190-191
  request style and, 204-205
  social comparison and, 187-189
  store settings and, 185-186
  temperature and, 311
Hostility, *see* Aggression
Humor, aggression and, 178-179
Hypnosis, 94-96

Idiosyncracy credit, 229-230
Impression formation, 14-16
Information-seeking conformity, 103
Ingratiation behavior, 79, 80, 126
Interpersonal attraction, *see* Liking

Jealousy, 148-150
Just world hypothesis, 27

Law of infidelity, 150
Leadership:
  contingency model of, 228-229
  idiosyncracy credit and, 229-230
  personality and, 227-228
  status and, 229-230
Leadership style, 225-226
Learned helplessness, 39
Leniency effect, 235
Liking:
  effects of climate on, 139
  effects of exposure on, 127-130
  effects of propinquity on, 130-133

Liking *(continued)*
  effects of self-perception on, 137-139
  effects of similarity on, 133-137
Liking scale, 143-145
Loafing, social, 222-224
Locus of control, 37-38
Love, 142-145
Love scale, 143-145
Low-balling technique, 91

Machiavellianism, 79, 250-253
Marriage problems, 150-152
Men's liberation, 293
Mental health settings, changing, 322-324
Moral development, stages of, 246-248
Morality:
  politics and, 254-258
  religion and, 254-258
  social development and, 253-254
Moral realism, 246
Moral relativism, 246
Motivational research, 55

Name stereotyping, 12
Nonverbal behaviors:
  bodily cues, 237
  communication, patterns of, 9
  eye contact, 12
  posture, 9
  smiling, 9
Nonzero-sum games, 342-343
Norm-seeking conformity, 103
Nutrition, 325-326

Obedience, 96-102
Operant conditioning, 112, 113
Overjustification effect, 117

Partial reinforcement, 112
Perception:
  accuracy of, 234-237
  effects of age on, 13
  effects of clothes on, 9
  effects of eye contact on, 12
  effects of hair on, 8
  effects of looks on, 8, 139-142
  effects of names on, 12
  effects of occupation on, 14
  effects of physical handicap on, 8-9
  effects of size on, 4, 7
  effects of smell on, 8
  effects of smiling on, 9
  effects of voice on, 10
  effects of weight on, 7
Personality traits, 44
Personal space, 314-316
Physical attractiveness, 8, 139-142, 250
Politics, morality and, 254-258
Pollution, 325
Popularity, 122-123
Population explosion, 324-325

Pornography, 167-168
Position, definition of, 211
Power, types of, 76-79
Power strategies, 125
Prejudice, stereotyping and, 241-245
Primacy effect, 14
Primary drive, 112
Prisoner's Dilemma game, 342-343
Propinquity, 130-133
Prosocial behavior, definition of, 183
  (*see also* Helping behavior)
Proxemics, 314-316
Psychological androgyny, 288-293

Racial stereotyping, 241-245
Rational propaganda, 58
Recency effect, 16
Religion, morality and, 254-258
Research:
  methodological, economical, and ethical issues, 331-334
  rational and empirical approaches, 328-331
Research designs:
  confounding factors, 339
  experimental and control groups, 334-335
  problem experiments, 336-338
  quasi-experiments, 338-339
  true experiments, 338
  validity and reliabilty, 335-336
Research settings:
  field experiments, 340-341
  field studies, 339
  laboratory experiments, 341-342
  natural experiments, 340
  simulation experiments, 342-343
Research statistics:
  correlational methods, 349-351
  examples of, 352-354
  parametric and nonparametric, 351
  types of data, 349
  univariate and multivariate, 352
Research techniques:
  attitude scales, 344-345
  content analysis, 346-348
  interaction analysis, 345-346
  interviews and surveys, 343-344
Risky shift, 226-227
Roles and role behavior, types of, 211-217
Romantic love, 142-145

Schemata, 41
Scripts, 41
Secondary drive, 112
Self, definition of, 30-32
Self-acceptance, 30
Self-attribution, 35-37
Self-concept, 30
Self-defense, 40
Self-denigration, 40

Self-disclosure, 32–33
Self-efficacy, 46
Self-esteem, 30
Self-image, 30
Self-insight, 30
Self-monitoring, 33–35
Self-perception, 35–37
Self-schemata, 41–43
Sex differences:
 anatomical, 267, 271–274
 hormonal, 276
Sexism, tests for, 280, 285
Sex roles:
 discrimination and, 274, 275, 278–280, 285–288
 identification with, 275, 276, 289
Sex typing, 265–267, 292
Sexual humor, aggression and, 178–179
Sexual jealousy, 148–150
Sexual prejudice, 274, 275, 278–280, 285–288
Shoplifting, 185–186, 250
Similarity, and liking, 133–137
Social comparison theory, 188, 210
Social ecology, 295
Social influence in clinical practice, 70
Social influence therapy, 71
Social loafing, 222–224
Social power, 76–79
Social reinforcement, 113–117
Social roles, 211–217
Social self, 31, 32
Sociobiology, 161

State anxiety, 298–300
Statistics, see Research statistics
Status, definition of, 212
Stereotyping:
 age and, 13
 clothes and, 9
 definition of, 248–249
 hair and, 8
 looks and, 8
 names and, 12, 239–241
 occupation and, 14
 physical handicap and, 8, 9
 prejudice and, 241–245
 size and, 6, 7
 smell and, 8
 voice and, 10
 weight and, 7
Stress:
 anxiety and, 297–299
 combat neurosis and, 299–300
 crowding and, 311–314
 economic fluctuations and, 316
 frustration and, 297
 life changes and, 304–306
 medical settings and, 318–321
 moon phases and, 316
 noise and, 306–308
 pressure and, 297
 proxemics and, 315
 temperature and, 306–311
 Type A behavior and, 302
 ulcers and, 303

Stress reduction:
 avoidant thinking and, 318–319
 cognitive behavior modification and, 321
 general adaptation syndrome and, 321–322
 information and, 319–321
 in medical settings, 318–321
Subliminal advertising, 58
Successive approximation, method of, 114
Supermale syndrome, 160
Sympathy, effects of, on compliance, 83–84

Television, effects of, on aggression, 179–181
Template matching, 45, 46
Territoriality, 315
Therapeutic communities, 323
Trait anxiety, 298–300
Triads, 208
Type A behavior, 302

Unconditioned response, 110
Unconditioned stimulus, 110

Violence, see Aggression

Women's liberation, 274, 275, 277, 293